SYSTEMS OF SOCIETY

274 5791

Howard Croft

T. Th. Soc. Sci.

Judy

SYSTEMS OF SOCIETY

An Introduction to Social Science

Manuel G. Mendoza

Vince Napoli

Sixth Edition

Miami-Dade Community College

D. C. HEATH AND COMPANY

Lexington, Massachusetts/Toronto

Dedicated To:

Danny, Manny, Tanya and Marina and
Eddie, Rich, Carlos and Lisa

Cover Photo: The Image Bank/Alberto Incrocci

Address editorial correspondence to:
D. C. Heath and Company
125 Spring Street
Lexington, MA 02173

Acquisitions Editor: Walter Cunningham
Production Editor: Celena Sun
Designer: Judith Miller
Photo Researcher: Billie Porter
Production Coordinator: Richard Tonachel
Text Permissions Editor: Margaret Roll

Published simultaneously in Canada.

Printed in the United States of America.

International Standard Book Number: 0–669–39319–3

Library of Congress Catalog Card Number: 94–71512

10 9 8 7 6 5 4 3 2 1

Preface

Systems of Society, Sixth Edition, provides a comprehensive introduction to the social sciences. By studying the findings of cultural anthropology, social psychology, sociology, economics, political science, and international relations from several perspectives, the text illustrates the interdisciplinary nature of the social sciences. For example, we view individuals and social groups as parts of an interrelated system in which each performs specific functions. We also study the conflicts that occur among individuals and social groups as they struggle for control of scarce resources. Additionally, we consider human behavior from the standpoint of social exchanges, that is, the interactions that occur between or among individuals or social groups.

☐ Focus of the Text

While the text does provide a considerable amount of factual information, its main purpose is to stimulate analytical thinking. We do not want to clutter students' minds with an enormous body of details that will quickly be forgotten once the students have finished reading the book. However, it is important to document the major points in the text. We do not focus on transient issues that will have disappeared by the time students using this text have graduated. Our primary concern is to develop conceptual frameworks that will enable students to analyze problems and issues systematically and rationally long after their formal studies have ended. This book may be used alone or with supplementary works that are problem- or issue-oriented.

☐ Organization of the Text

The book is divided into seven parts. Part I introduces the student to social science and to the various approaches used by social scientists.

The student is presented with the fundamental tools needed to understand and interpret the text's subject matter. Part II deals with the cultural system, Part III with socialization and personality, and Part IV with society and its subsystems. These four parts encompass the subject matter usually covered in the first term of a two-term social science course sequence. Part V deals with the economic system, Part VI with the political system, and Part VII with the international system. These three parts, along with the introduction, cover the subject matter usually dealt with in the second term of a two-term social science course sequence.

☐ Major Changes in This Edition

The major changes in this edition are consistent with major social, political, and economic changes throughout the world since the publication of the Fifth Edition, the most prominent of which are related to the collapse of the Soviet Union. Chapter 16, "Alternative Economic Systems," contains an overview of changes in the Soviet/Russian economy. Chapter 18, "Types of Political Systems," now includes a discussion of the collapse of the Soviet Union as well as a more detailed explanation of the political system of the United States and discussions of social contract and the U.S. Constitution. There is an expanded and updated discussion of ethnic politics in Chapter 20, "American Political Orientations and Ethnic Politics." And Chapter 25, "International Systems: The Present and the Future," has been substantially revised, including discussions of the Balance of Terror, disarmament, and changes in Eastern Europe as well as other parts of the world.

References have been updated throughout the book, and new statistical information and illustrations have been added to complement revised material. The "Selected Reading" sections at the end of each chapter have been revised and now contain brief annotations.

☐ Study Aids

The text includes several devices to facilitate understanding of the material. Each chapter ends with a glossary of important terms, a listing of selected readings, a set of multiple-choice questions, and thought and discussion questions. The end-of-chapter glossaries serve to reinforce the material presented in each chapter and provide a brief review of the major concepts. When possible, we have grouped the glossary items into meaningful units. For ease of reference we have also included, at the end of the book, an alphabetical listing of all the end-of-chapter glossary items. The selected readings provide students with a guide to important works related to each chapter. The multiple-choice sections, combined with the questions for thought and discussion, will give students an indication of their level of mastery. An answer key for the multiple-choice items is provided at the end of the book.

Numerous diagrams, charts, graphs, cartoons, and photographs, many of them new to this edition, facilitate understanding of the written material. An instructor's guide is also available.

☐ Acknowledgments

We offer thanks to the many students and teachers throughout the country who provided comments and suggestions on the Fifth Edition. We owe special thanks to Professor Marianne Bumgarner-Davis, Johnson C. Smith University; Dr. Fred Dauser, Talladega College; Professor A.P. Martinez, City College, The City University of New York; and Professor Marjorie Zamora, Morain Valley Community College. Special thanks also to our colleagues at Miami-Dade for their feedback on using *Systems of Society* through its many editions. These include Juan Clark, Jacquetta Colyer, Charles Gonzalez, Roberto Hernandez, Maria Herrera, Jeffery Lee, John McLeod, Dennis Shaw, and James Wernert. Their observations have been particularly helpful. Of course, we are totally responsible for any errors or misinterpretations.

M.G.M.
V.N.

ONE

Introduction

This part is an introduction to the subject of social science. In Chapter 1 we consider briefly the nature of social science—what it is, what it isn't, and how social scientists attempt to increase our knowledge of human behavior. We emphasize that scientific investigation is systematic rather than random, and flexible rather than rigid. Science is an attitude as well as a method, and social science differs from other sciences more in terms of content than in attitude and method. We also examine several conceptual frameworks, within which we discuss much of the material in the chapters that follow.

By reading this introductory chapter you will get the "feel" of the book and gain an understanding of some valuable tools for analyzing human behavior.

1

The Nature of Social Science

Social science is the systematic attempt to discover and explain behavior patterns of people and groups of people. It is a broad field of study that includes a variety of subject categories or disciplines such as anthropology, psychology, sociology, economics, political science, and international relations. These disciplines are all concerned with the behavior of people, but each concentrates on some separate and distinct aspect of human behavior.

Anthropology is a discipline that is partly biological and partly social. The physical anthropologist deals with questions related to the biological evolution of humans, the effects of physical environment on humans, and the anatomical differences among human races. The cultural anthropologist is concerned with the ways of life or cultures of different social groups, including the development of a culture, its current characteristics, and considerations of how it has changed and is changing. Generally, cultural anthropologists have focused their efforts on "primitive" societies, those that are relatively small, nonindustrial, and nonliterate (without a written language). By so doing, they have been able to study many cultures as wholes. Chapters 2 through 6 concern information provided primarily by anthropologists.

Psychology is a discipline that concentrates on individual rather than group behavior. Many psychologists study the behavioral, emotional, and cognitive aspects of individual functioning, including mental processes such as thought, perception, memory, learning, and intelligence. Others are more concerned with applying the knowledge of psychological principles in the form of therapeutic treatment of individuals whose patterns of behavior, emotions, and cognitions are mal-

Group Therapy
A psychologist's understanding of group dynamics allows him to help each person in this therapy group to achieve more adjustive behavior.

adaptive. Another interest of all social scientists is the field of social psychology, which is concerned with the relationship between the individual and the group and with products of that relationship such as personality development, leadership, and certain aspects of collective behavior. Chapters 7 and 8 contain information provided primarily by psychologists.

Like cultural anthropology, *sociology* concentrates on group behavior; however, unlike cultural anthropology, sociology focuses on large, modern societies. One of the major thrusts of sociology is the study of recurrent, patterned relationships among people within group settings, for example, the typical behavior of American college students

Sociologists often study patterned relationships among people within group settings.

while attending classes. Another major current in sociology is the study of social conditions. The sociologist attempts to explain, for instance, why significant numbers of American high school graduates enter college (as opposed to the psychologist who attempts to explain the motivation of a particular student). Chapters 9 through 13 are concerned primarily with sociology.

Economics is the social science discipline that concentrates on how people manage scarce resources. The economist studies supply and demand, savings and investment, and the production, distribution, and consumption of goods and services. Economists often use mathematical models to predict changes within a particular society, a geographic region, or the entire international community. This is the subject matter of chapters 14 through 16.

Political science is concerned with how people govern themselves. It includes the history, theory, organization, and administration of government. Political scientists study the distribution of power in groups, how authoritative decisions are made, and how group conflicts take shape and are resolved, as well as treating such traditional subjects as participation in political parties, analysis of voting patterns, and the structure and functioning of special interest groups. Chapters 17 through 21 are based on information provided primarily by political scientists.

International relations concentrates on the behavior of nations. Some scholars classify international relations as a branch of political science, while others see it as a separate and distinct discipline with its own body of facts and theories. Specialists in international relations deal with international political systems, diplomacy, international organizations and law, and the resolution of conflicts among nations. This is the subject matter of Chapters 22 through 25.

These social science disciplines are all broad areas of investigation, each encompassing a variety of specialties. Please note that we do not mention some disciplines (history and geography, for example) because our discussion is not meant to be exhaustive. The important point is that social science is concerned with human behavior, and if we want to better our understanding of human behavior, it makes sense to look at it from several points of view. You might also note that boundaries between the disciplines sometimes become fuzzy, and areas of investigation often overlap. For example, sociologists are often concerned with political behavior, as are economists; and social psychologists, sociologists, economists, political scientists, and international relations specialists are all concerned with the concept of culture at some time.

Having defined social science and briefly surveyed most of its disciplines, we will now consider why social science may be considered science at all: the fact that it shares with the natural sciences an attitude and a method, a general approach to problem solving. We will begin with scientific attitude.

☐ Scientific Attitude

Scientists approach their investigations with an open-minded perspective or outlook that may be referred to as **scientific attitude.** One aspect of scientific attitude is willingness to share information (*cooperation*). Ideally, at least in Western society, scientists do not keep secrets from one another. Scientific research is recorded and published in journals and anyone who is interested can make use of it. Historically, the non-

Western world has not participated in this information-sharing activity, neither within its own boundaries nor with the West. That may partially explain why, by comparison, Western scientific knowledge has forged ahead so rapidly.

The willingness to share information is supported by another aspect of scientific attitude—the courage to openly admit failure (*openness*). If you were handed a ring of 50 keys, only one of which fits a lock that you want to open, you would not expect to open the lock on the first attempt. You might try 20, 30, or even 40 keys before finding the one that fits. Under these circumstances, you would not consider yourself a failure if it takes you 20 attempts to locate the correct key, even though you would fail 19 out of 20 times. That is the nature of experimentation. The scientist expects to be wrong most of the time, and openly admits this failure whenever it occurs. Moreover, reporting failures helps others avoid the unnecessary duplication of the failing efforts.

Scientists have learned from experience that what we believe to be correct today may be disproved tomorrow when we have more information. The ancient Greeks, for example, believed that all matter in the universe could be reduced to four basic elements—earth, air, fire, and water. They were wrong. We realize that it is foolish to take the position that a particular fact or theory is absolutely correct. This realization of the *tentative* nature of our understanding of phenomena at any given time (*skepticism*) is a third side of scientific attitude.

Scientists strive for *objectivity* in their research. That is, they attempt to be impartial and rational rather than biased and emotional when carrying out their investigations. If a scientist is so bent on proving some particular point that he or she "stacks the deck" in experiments, the scientist is actually blocking the advance of scientific knowledge. But complete objectivity is probably never attained. Like most other human beings, scientists may become emotionally involved in whatever they do. They make every attempt, however, not to allow their biases to interfere with either the process or the results of their investigations.

Closely allied to the notion of objectivity is one final dimension of scientific attitude—concern with what *is* (*amorality*), as opposed to concern with what *ought to be.* One major objective of scientific investigation is to uncover cold, hard facts—the reality of life. In this sense, science is amoral. That is, it is not concerned with moral standards. Traditionally, the scientist is not concerned with what is morally right or wrong or good or evil about his or her findings. The results of experimentation are facts that increase our knowledge of the physical and/or social universe. They may be used for good or evil purposes and anyone, including scientists, may make moral judgments as to their use. Such judgments, however, are outside the realm of science.

☐ Problem Solving

Over a period of several thousand years humans have developed and used several methods for solving problems. Each of them has some usefulness, but they all have limitations. One method for **problem solving** is an *appeal to the supernatural.* By this we mean seeking guidance from some other-worldly source, either through meditation or through the revealed word of supernatural sources as recorded in sacred scriptures. Sometimes people appeal to the supernatural for another purpose—to influence the natural course of events. The Zuni Indians of the Southwestern United States, for example, when faced with a long, hard drought, perform a dance that is designed to persuade the gods to bring forth rain. Literally millions of people each day appeal to the supernatural in an attempt to solve their own personal problems. At times this method may work for them; at times it may not. They never know, however, when, or even if, their prayers will be answered.

Another problem-solving method is *appeal to human authority.* Here the problem is put to other people rather than sought from supernatural forces. When faced with a difficult problem, it certainly makes sense to get help from someone who is wise and experienced. If the problem is particularly complex, however, even a wise and experienced adviser may not be able to solve it.

Probably the most commonly used problem-solving method is *appeal to our own knowledge.* That is, we often solve problems by relying on what we already know. Our actions are based on what we have

Appeal to Human Authority
Whether on a personal or a professional basis, asking an older brother or consulting an attorney, the age-old method of seeking the advice of another person is still very widely used.

learned, both from others and from our own personal experience. Obviously, when our personal knowledge is inadequate for coping with a particular problem, we must look for help from some other source.

Perhaps we can get that help from *intuition*—a hunch, a feeling, a sudden insight that apparently sheds some light on the deep, dark problem at hand. While intuition is not a consciously derived way of dealing with problems, and therefore cannot properly be labeled a method, it is sometimes used in attempts at problem solving. The great disadvantage of intuition is that quite often it proves to be incorrect. (Ask any loser at the roulette wheel in Las Vegas.)

Logic, or systematic reasoning, is another method that has been employed to solve problems. Scientists use this tool to great advantage. By applying logic to correct assumptions, they can arrive at correct conclusions. But we have to guard against the notion that by simply applying logic to any assumption, whether correct or incorrect, we will always generate correct answers to problems. Actually, if we apply logic to an incorrect assumption, we may generate incorrect answers.

While logic has defined rules, its problem-solving sister, *common sense*, does not. Rather, we associate common sense with the thinking process of the individual person. What is common sense to one person may seem outrageous to someone else. Still, we rely on common sense to solve problems every day, and it is a good method, no doubt. In fact, if more of us applied our common sense to more of our problems more of the time, we would probably lead less frustrated lives. But, alas, common sense, too, has its drawbacks. Just think about the times your common sense has told you that one course of action was correct when, really, it was not.

We have now discussed briefly several different ways in which people solve problems. Do they actually apply in real-life situations? Judge for yourself.

The setting is a racetrack. It is five minutes before the start of the seventh race. Your problem is to figure out which horse will win the race. You have studied the racing form carefully and have determined that Dangerous Dan has better breeding, has posted faster workouts, and has performed better in past races than the other horses entered in the seventh race. You infer that a horse which has done all of those things should win the race; therefore, your logic tells you that Dangerous Dan will win. Furthermore, the last time you were at the racetrack, you bet on Dangerous Dan, and he won. Since you know he is a winner, you want to bet on him again. But suddenly you have a brilliant flash of insight, a hunch, that tells you that Rambling Ralph will be the winner. Faced with this conflict, you quickly seek out and find a friend who goes to the racetrack every day and who seems to know all there is to know about horses. He tells you that he's putting his money on Dangerous Dan. Since it is now only one minute before post time, you get in line to buy your ticket. You have decided to bet on Dangerous Dan. But as you're standing there, you notice on the tote board a dramatic change in the odds on Rambling Ralph. He drops from 10 to 1 to 5 to 1. Now, you have heard that people with "inside information" often wait until the very last minute before betting large sums of money on the horse they know will win. Your common sense tells you to bet on Rambling Ralph.

You do.

The race begins and Rambling Ralph, running free and easy, settles into a comfortable third position. As they enter the back stretch, he eases into second place. By this time you're getting very excited. At the top of the home stretch, he is challenging for the lead. You close your eyes, clasp your hands and say a short prayer. You hear a tremendous roar from the crowd; you open your eyes in time to see the horses cross the finish line; the winner—Cunning Clyde. Cunning Clyde? Damn!!

"Cunning Clyde? Damn!!"

☐ Scientific Method

We have just seen how it is possible for someone to apply six different problem-solving methods to a single problem within a span of only five minutes. While it is perhaps striking that none of them yielded the correct answer, it is more striking that they were applied in an unsystematic manner. Scientists may use some of these very same methods. However, they have learned to use them within the scope of a

Data Accumulation
The scientists pictured here are anthropologists. By uncovering the fossilized bones of extinct people and the artifacts they used, they are gathering information that may contribute to our understanding of human evolution.

general framework which has defined boundaries and working rules. We refer to this general framework as **scientific method.**

While scientific method does have defined boundaries and working rules, it also has enough flexibility to handle both the variety of approaches and the different kinds of problems posed by the economist, the sociologist, and the political scientist, as well as the biologist, chemist, and physicist. It is not a rigid, lockstep process.

One aspect of scientific method is **data accumulation.** This is the process of gathering information about the subject or area of knowledge we are going to deal with. We accomplish this through the careful observation of phenomena.

Notice that we accumulate only the data pertaining to a problem that we have recognized and defined within our subject area. We disregard any other data. It was not always this way. We can conjecture that at one time the store of data accumulated on all subjects was so small that practically any data on any subject were welcome additions to all who were concerned with gaining knowledge. As this store of data accumulated and our general knowledge increased, the information became too bulky for any individual to deal with effectively, so people began the process of dividing it into smaller units. This process of dividing and subdividing subjects has continued to the present day, so that we now have literally thousands of highly specialized subjects. Moreover, it is estimated that our general knowledge is doubling every ten to fifteen years. We can assume that fifteen years from now we will probably have some specialized subjects that do not even exist at present. It is easy to see why we must restrict data accumulation to one subject area.

Once information has been accumulated, it is labeled and placed with other similar data within some category of a particular subject. We call this process **data classification.** Classifying is necessary because it allows us to place our hands quickly and efficiently on data that is appropriate for dealing with a particular problem.

The accumulation and classification of data quite naturally leads us to another integral part of scientific method—**speculative thinking.** Here we explore possible relationships among data. **Inductive reasoning,** the process of reasoning *from* particular facts *to* a general conclusion, is a part of speculative thinking. Notice how inductive reasoning was used in the racetrack situation. Particular facts (Dangerous Dan had better breeding, faster workouts, and better performance in past races) led to the general conclusion that Dangerous Dan would win. This inquisitive probing is at the very core of all science. During this activity the brilliant flash of intuition, mentioned earlier, sometimes occurs to the scientist.

The product of speculative thinking is a **general proposition.** This is a broad statement that explains relationships among data and may further be used as a starting point for more speculative thinking. When a proposition is so general that it explains relationships among other general propositions, we call it a *theory.**

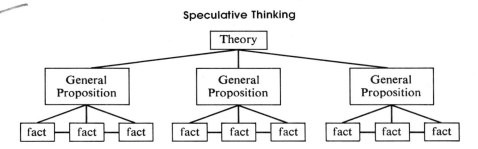

Speculative Thinking

* For a more detailed description of the term "theory" as we are using it, see George C. Homans, *The Nature of Social Science* (New York: Harcourt, Brace & World, 1967), pp. 21–27, and Peter R. Senn, *Social Science and Its Methods* (Boston: Holbrook Press, 1971), pp. 283–286. Some social scientists prefer to define theory as a working hypothesis supported by preliminary research. Actually, either definition may be acceptable, so long as: (1) the use of the term has been defined by the person using it; and (2) it includes the notion of explaining phenomena.

Once we have a general proposition to work with, we may pose a problem suggested by the general proposition. We may then formulate a working hypothesis or tentative answer to the problem. Next, we may test the working hypothesis. Suppose, for example, that we have been thinking about the process of learning. We have observed that people seem to "catch on" faster to things they can relate to easily—ideas, symbols, and processes that have meaning for them—rather than to things that do not have meaning for them. We ask the question, "Do people really tend to learn ideas that are meaningful to them faster than they learn ideas that are not?" We think the answer is yes, and we decide that a good way to determine whether or not we are correct is to conduct an experiment:

1. We read a list of ten items, spelling each one as we go, to a selected person (subject). The items are:

wax	joy
dog	tip
her	see
boy	red
set	can

(Each of these items has three letters, and each is a meaningful term to the subject.)

2. We ask the subject to repeat as many of the ten items as he can, spelling each correctly as he goes. If the subject cannot remember all the items, we reread the entire list and ask the subject to try again to remember all the items. We continue this process until the subject has correctly remembered all the items.

3. We note the number of times it takes for the subject to complete the task successfully.

4. We repeat the process in (1). This time, however, we use the following items:

wir	kum
jub	zop
lep	miz
ret	lar
wid	cik

(Each of these items has three letters, and each is *not* a meaningful term to the subject.)

5. We repeat the process in (2).

6. We repeat the process in (3).

Our working hypothesis for this experiment is stated as follows: If an individual is presented with both a list of meaningful items and a list of meaningless items to be learned, he will learn the meaningful items faster.

We test the hypothesis by conducting the experiment with several subjects. The more we test, the more reliable our results are likely to be. Also, we give half the subjects the meaningful list first and the meaningless list second. We reverse the order with the other half of our subjects. We do this to "wash out" any effects that the sequencing of events might have on our experiment. Finally, we analyze the data we have collected.

If we observe that our working hypothesis seems to be correct, we have produced evidence to support our general proposition, which is: "People tend to learn things that are meaningful to them faster than they learn things that are not meaningful to them." We may now proceed to formulate more working hypotheses which, when tested, may further support our general proposition. If we observe that our working hypothesis seems to be incorrect, we may search for another general proposition.

If you have paid close attention to what we have said so far, you will have noticed our use of **deductive reasoning.** This is another integral part of scientific method. By deductive reasoning we mean using logic to infer a *specific* statement of conditions from a *general* statement of conditions.

Explaining Phenomena

General Proposition

Problem

Working hypothesis

Repeat process using another problem

Testing of hypothesis

New general proposition needed

Positive results which support general proposition

Negative results which do not support general proposition

For example, we can make the general statement: "By studying social science, we will better understand why people behave as they do." Now, this semester you are studying social science. If our general statement is correct, we can assume that at the end of this semester you will have a better understanding of why people behave as they do than you did at the beginning of the semester. One way of determining whether or not your understanding has increased is to give you a test on principles of human behavior at the beginning and at the end of the semester. If we observe an increase in your test score, we might assume that our working hypothesis (that you have a better understanding of human behavior) is correct. This lends support to our general statement.

While the foregoing argument may seem convincing at first glance, further investigation may completely destroy it. For instance, the real reason for the increase in your score may be that you cheated on the second test, in which case we will have to find another way to determine whether or not your understanding of human behavior has actually increased. Scientists attempt to overcome this kind of snag in their problem-solving efforts by employing another aspect of scientific method—*controlled experimentation*. Here the scientist tries as much as possible to control the environment in which the experiment takes place, thus limiting the number of variables or possible influences that may alter the interpretation of findings. In our experiment concerning learning speed, for instance, we tried to limit the experimental learning situation to the two particular lists of items we used. Ideally, scientists would completely control the experimental environment.

Interpretation of Findings

A **variable** is a factor that can have more than one value. There are several types of variables. **Quantitative variables** reflect differences in numerical value: a person's income, for instance, may be $15,000 per year, or $30,000, or $1,000,000. **Qualitative variables** such as a person's sex reflect differences in category rather than number: a person may be either female or male. Variables that are thought to cause something to happen are called **independent variables;** variables thought to be affected by independent variables are called **dependent variables.** For example, we saw that the effect (dependent variable) of your scoring higher on an end-of-semester test on principles of human behavior might be caused by your studying social science (independent variable).

In this case we can say that a **correlation** exists between studying and a higher test score. A correlation is an expression of the degree or strength of the relationship between two or more variables. Correlations may be positive (when you study, your score increases) or negative (the unlikely situation that when you study, your score decreases). However, a correlation between two variables does not necessarily prove a cause-effect relationship between them. As we saw, your cheating might have been the real reason for the higher test score. Thus, some correlations reflect cause-effect relationships, while others do not.

Generally, scientists aim at discovering cause-effect relationships, but not all scientific research is explanatory in nature. Some is descriptive, and some is evaluative, and both, like explanatory research, may be used to predict future behavior. *Descriptive* studies attempt to describe reality rather than to explain it. They provide facts that increase our general knowledge and that may be used to formulate general propositions. They often reveal correlations and suggest easily recognized practical applications. For example, a descriptive study on the eating habits of midday television viewers might produce useful information for an advertising firm representing lunch food products.

Evaluation studies attempt to measure the relative success of a project or program in achieving its goals. Does an increase in the minimum legal drinking age from eighteen to twenty-one actually lead to a decrease in the number of traffic fatalities involving eighteen- to twenty-one-year-olds? Like descriptive studies, evaluation studies tend to have great practical applicability.

☐ Social Science Research

While some social science research takes the form of an **experimental design** (such as the experiment on learning meaningful symbols), most of it is observational or survey research. **Observational research** is the systematic observation of the research subject, with no attempt to alter ongoing activities. Observational research can take place in the laboratory or in a natural setting (field observation). In either case, the social scientist watches carefully but does not become directly involved in the

Observational Research

This behavioral psychologist is conducting an experiment geared to increase our understanding of how learning takes place.

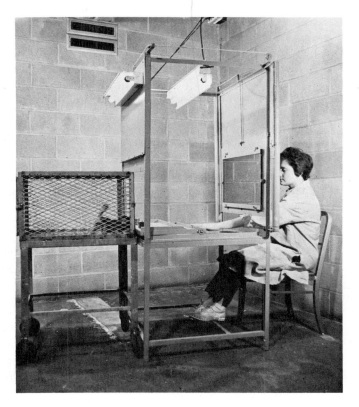

Survey Research
Data gathered from statistical samples can provide an accurate description of public opinion on any given issue.

ongoing activities. In a third type of observational research, *participant observation*, the researcher does become directly involved. Here, in an attempt to acquire deeper understanding, the social scientist interacts freely with the individual, group, or community being studied. A sociologist attempting to learn more about prison life might arrange to become a prisoner.

Survey research is the research method used most often by social scientists because surveys can provide data on identical variables from large numbers of subjects in relatively short time periods, and the data may be easily tabulated and is highly accessible for statistical analysis. The researcher asks questions of subjects to gain information from them. Survey research is used by government agencies, public opinion pollsters, and market researchers. Social scientists often rely on **statistical samples** when conducting surveys. A statistical sample is a selected number of individuals within a given population, who together represent the general characteristics of that population. A political scientist might be able to predict consistently the outcome of elections by sampling the voter preferences of only a fraction of 1 percent of the electorate if the sampling technique is adequate (that is, if the people asked do represent the voter preferences of the general population).

Generally, social science research proceeds in a series of steps with corresponding activities rooted in scientific attitude and method.

Step 1: *Identify a Problem.* The problem could range from increasing our understanding of the learning process to assessing the needs of some group within a community to helping someone get elected to public office. The important point is that the researcher identify clearly the problem at hand.

Step 2: *Review the Literature.* The researcher locates and examines relevant studies. This provides the researcher with information about the problem and how it has been studied in the past. This review may also suggest ideas that may be useful in step 3.

Step 3: *Formulate a Hypothesis.* The researcher formulates a tentative answer to the problem identified. As we have seen, the hypothesis states a relationship between two variables that can be either proved or disproved. Example: College-educated people are just as likely to obey orders as those with little formal education.

Step 4: *Choose a Research Design.* The researcher decides which research method will be used. Personal preference might determine the choice, although sometimes the nature of the hypothesis dictates the design to be followed. For example, the hypothesis in step 3 might be tested through experiment, observation, or survey. On the other hand, when testing a hypothesis dealing with the percentage of white, working-class males who are likely to vote for a particular candidate in an election, the survey method would be chosen.

Step 5: *Collect and Process the Data.* It is imperative that data be gathered accurately, carefully, and completely. This is perhaps less of a problem in experimental and observational research, where trained social scientists are collecting and processing the data directly. In survey research, however, students and other people are often employed to collect and to process the data. Inexperienced interviewers must be taught correct interviewing techniques, including how to convince respondents to cooperate and how to terminate the interview. A supervisor must call back 10 to 20 percent of respondents to verify that the interviews were conducted properly. Collected data must be classified into meaningful categories so that it may be analyzed.

Step 6: *Analyze the Data.* The researcher examines the data carefully to determine whether or not the hypothesis has been supported. If the hypothesis is unsupported, the researcher formulates new hypotheses to account for the data.

Step 7: *State Conclusions.* The researcher presents the findings and recommendations of the study either in writing, orally, or both. Scholars usually publish their findings and present them at academic conferences.

☐ Approaches in Social Science

Functionalism

This approach, alternately called "functionalism," "structural/functionalism," "systems," or the "functional-systems" approach, emphasizes that all aspects of society are interconnected and interact with each other to maintain stability. If an aspect of social life does not contribute to society's stability or survival—if it does not serve a useful function—it will be abandoned by society. If it does serve a useful function, it will survive and be handed down from generation to generation.

Functionalists do not make moral judgments. They do not say that something that is functional to the survival and stability of a system is necessarily good in a moral sense. They simply say it is *functional* or *dysfunctional* to the system. If it helps perpetuate the system (whether the system is morally good or bad), it is functional. If it creates problems for the system, it is dysfunctional. This approach assumes that society forms harmonious systems that tend to remain in balance. Talcott Parsons was a well-known functionalist scholar in the United States who supported this view.

Another functionalist scholar, Robert Merton, wrote about *manifest* and *latent* functions. Manifest functions are intended, desired, and recognized. Latent functions are unintended and, often, unrecognized. They may or may not be desired. Teaching children self-defense is intended to allow them to protect themselves. An unintended effect is that they may pick fights with other children.

Functionalists try to identify the structures that perform necessary tasks for the survival of society. They try to identify universal political, economic, religious, and other functions. Then they examine the structures that perform those functions and try to determine how the functions are performed. For example, the role of parenting is universal in all family systems, but family structures and child-rearing practices vary by society.

One criticism of the functional approach is that some patterns that do not seem to perform any useful function may persist. Another is that some patterns may be functional for some groups in society and dysfunctional for others. A liberal economist might argue that Reaganomics was functional for the rich and dysfunctional for the poor and the middle class.

In the nineteenth century Herbert Spencer distorted Charles Darwin's biological theory of evolution by applying the concept of survival of the fittest to societies. Thus, social Darwinism led Spencer to oppose programs to help the disadvantaged because he thought the programs would be dysfunctional for society. He obviously did not consider or was not concerned about the consequences for human beings who happened to be poor. Certainly, social Darwinism was dysfunctional for them.

In this book we are careful to avoid giving the impression that something that may be functional for whatever system we are examining at a given time is necessarily good for all members of the society, unless we are discussing avoiding environmental pollution, nuclear destruction, or some other calamity. We use **systems analysis** as a framework for the book because it demonstrates the interrelatedness of all aspects of social behavior. Within this framework we also use conflict theory, symbolic interaction perspective, and exchange theory.

Conflict Theory

The conflict perspective argues that social behavior is best understood in terms of conflict or tension among competing groups. Such conflict may be violent or peaceful: a violent revolution that overthrows an existing political system or a free and democratic election among competing political parties.

Karl Marx was a leading conflict theorist. He perceived history as a series of class struggles between the social class that owned the means of production and the social class that worked for them and, in Marx's view, was exploited by them. Another important conflict theorist, George Simmel, believed that conflict is inherent in society because different groups are always competing for power, scarce resources, the dominance of their value systems, and policy preferences.

C. Wright Mills believed that the tension between the strong and the weak created a breeding ground for social conflict. He and other conflict theorists have tried to identify the dominant groups in society and to understand how they achieve and maintain their power. These conflict theorists believe that social order is maintained by coercion: the more powerful members of society are able to get the less powerful members to conform, either by physical force or persuasion.

Ralf Dahrendorf believes that conflict is more a struggle for power than a class conflict over economic resources. This struggle produces instability and change in society, and, therefore, Dahrendorf argues, social scientists should focus on studying social change.

In summarizing the views of the various conflict theorists, we can say that society contains various groups that struggle with one another to acquire scarce resources such as wealth, power, or prestige. Social change occurs when these resources are redistributed among the contending interest groups. Whatever the existing arrangement may be in any time period, some groups will be dissatisfied with it and will try to change it. The result is periodic social change.

Whereas functionalism and conflict theory take a *macro* approach to social science (one that focuses on whole social systems, particularly entire societies), symbolic interaction and exchange theory use a *micro* approach (one that focuses on segments of social systems).

Exchange Theory

Exchange theorists believe that we can understand what happens in the larger society by understanding what happens between two people when they interact with one another. This approach assumes that self-interest is the universal motive that explains human behavior. People weigh potential benefits and costs in determining what they will do in any given situation.

An exchange relationship occurs whenever a person acts toward another in a way designed to generate a reward or benefit. For example, the employee works hard so that the employer will provide a pay raise. One person praises the appearance of another so that the other will give back affection. Thus, stable patterns of interaction between people are formed and maintained because the individuals involved find the interaction rewarding. George Homans and George Simmel were prominent exchange theorists.

Symbolic Interaction

People derive meaning in the world from the symbols that they learn from, and share with, other members of a group. We become social beings by learning to attach the same meanings to symbols that people already in the social group attach to them. The social unit may be a family or an entire society.

Symbolic interaction characterizes society as an intricate interweaving of subjective perceptions and the corresponding responses of the individuals who constitute the group. For example, suppose your family had taught you to perceive persons in positions of authority (teachers, police officers, employers, etc.) as potentially threatening. Your general attitude and response to your social science professor would be quite different from that of a classmate who has learned to perceive authority figures as helpful and trustworthy. In this manner symbolic interactionists attempt to understand society as it is perceived by individuals within it.

George Herbert Mead was the founder of symbolic interaction. He believed that the fundamental unit of study is the "act." He was interested in the total reaction of a person to a situation. Charles Horton Cooley focused on small groups and one-on-one interactions. He emphasized posture and nonverbal communication. Erving Goffman employed the "dramaturgical approach," in which life is conceived as a stage and people as actors who play roles and project images.

Generally, interactionists are interested in what people are thinking and feeling, as well as what they are doing. Thus motives and perceptions are considered to be as important as individual behavior.

☐ Conclusion

In this chapter we have considered the nature of social science: its definition; its subdivisions or disciplines; its similarities to the natural sciences; the methods of social science research; and four approaches in social science, including the identification of a few of the major scholars associated with each approach. Now, beginning with Chapter 2, we will explore some of the subject matter of social science from several perspectives.

GLOSSARY

Social science The systematic attempt to discover and explain the behavior patterns of people and groups of people. Social science contains several disciplines or subdivisions such as anthropology, psychology, sociology, economics, political science, and international relations. Each discipline concentrates on some aspect of human behavior that is separate and distinct from those the others concentrate on.

Problem solving The process whereby we answer questions. Examples of problem-solving methods are appeal to the supernatural, appeal to human authority, appeal to our own knowledge, intuition, logic, common sense, and scientific method.

Scientific attitude The open-minded perspective with which scientists approach their investigations. It includes cooperation, openness, skepticism, objectivity, and amorality.

Scientific method The way that scientists solve problems. It includes carefully observing events, accumulating and classifying data, inferring relationships among phenomena, formulating hypotheses and testing them in experiments, through observation, or in surveys, and analyzing the test results.

Data accumulation The process of gathering information through careful observation.

Data classification The labeling or categorization of accumulated data.

Speculative thinking The mental exploration of possible relationships among data. It is during the process of speculative thinking that scientists often have flashes of insight into the nature of phenomena.

General proposition A broad statement that explains relationships among data and may further be used as a starting point for speculative thinking. Example: People tend to repeat behavior that has been rewarded.

Inductive reasoning The use of logic to infer a general conclusion from specific facts. Example: Harry used to smoke cigarettes. (specific)

Harry died of cancer. (specific)
Therefore, cigarette smoking may cause death. (general conclusion)

Deductive reasoning	The use of logic to infer a specific statement of conditions from a general statement of conditions. Example: All men are mortal. (general) Harry is a man. (specific) Therefore, Harry is mortal. (specific)

Variable	A factor that can have more than one value. There are several types of variables, including quantitative, qualitative, independent, and dependent.
Quantitative variables	Variables that reflect differences in numerical value. Examples: yearly income; number of years of formal education.
Qualitative variables	Variables that reflect differences in category or kind rather than number. Examples: sex, religious affiliation.
Independent variables	Variables that are thought to cause something to happen. Example: Smoking (independent variable) causes lung cancer.
Dependent variables	Variables that are thought to be affected by independent variables. Example: Smoking causes lung cancer (dependent variable).
Correlation	An expression of the degree or strength of the relationship between two or more variables. Correlations may be positive or negative, but a correlation between two variables does not necessarily prove a cause-effect relationship between them.

Experimental design	The performance of controlled experiments with the aim of determining cause-effect relationships.
Observational research	The systematic observation of the research subject, with no attempt to alter ongoing activities. Observational research can take place in the laboratory, in the field, or in the form of participant observation.
Survey research	The most often used research method of social scientists. The researcher asks questions of subjects to gain information from them. Questionnaires and interviews are used in survey research.
Statistical sample	A selected number of individuals within a given population who together represent the general characteristics of that population. Statistical samples may provide pollsters, for instance, with fairly accurate descriptions of public opinion on a social issue.

Systems analysis   An approach to the study of social phenomena that focuses on the interrelatedness of all aspects of social behavior. It also emphasizes the need to examine entire social processes in order to fully understand any aspect of those processes.

SELECTED READING

Babbie, E. *The Practice of Social Research,* 5th ed. (Belmont, Calif.: Wadsworth Publishing, 1989). An overview of the theory and practice of social research.

Bernard, H. R. *Research Methods in Cultural Anthropology* (Newbury Park, Calif.: Sage Publications, 1988). A survey of how to do a field study.

Frankfort-Nachmias, C. and D. Nachmias. *Research Methods in the Social Sciences,* 4th ed. (New York: St. Martin's Press, 1992). An explanation of how social scientists do research.

Homans, G. C. *The Nature of Social Science* (New York: Harcourt, Brace & World, 1967). A short but exceptionally informative exposition of the nature of social science.

Hoover, K. R. *The Elements of Social Scientific Thinking,* 5th ed. (New York: St. Martin's Press, 1992). A presentation of fundamental concepts related to social science research.

McCain, G. and E. M. Segal. *The Game of Science,* 4th ed. (Monterey, Calif.: Brooks/Cole, 1982). An overview of how scientists do research.

Ross, D. *The Origins of American Social Science* (New York: Cambridge University Press, 1991). A survey of the development of social sciences in the United States, including discussions of how they differ from the natural sciences.

QUESTIONS

1. Dr. Jones is a social scientist who has been concentrating on the process of learning. Dr. Jones is a(n)
   a. anthropologist.
   b. economist.
   c. psychologist. .
   d. biologist.
   e. sociologist.

2. All Pontiacs are manufactured by General Motors.
   My car is a Pontiac.
   Therefore, my car was manufactured by General Motors.
   The reasoning process employed in the above syllogism is called
   a. speculative thinking.
   b. inductive reasoning. .
   c. productive reasoning.

d. intuitive thinking.

e. deductive reasoning.

3. Social science is the systematic attempt to discover and explain
   a. relationships among social phenomena.
   b. the realization of social and statistical trends.
   c. the control of particular human variables.
   d. human moral and aesthetic criteria.
   e. relationships among all phenomena.

4. Which of the following statements is true?
   a. Social scientists should not concern themselves with the process of reasoning.
   b. Inquisitive probing does not belong in scientific method.
   c. Inductive reasoning cannot be a part of speculative thinking.
   d. A theory explains relationships among general propositions.
   e. Exploring the relationships among data leads to the formation of a scientific method.

5. Which of the following is *not* an important aspect of scientific attitude?
   a. skepticism
   b. emotional involvement
   c. willingness to share information
   d. courage to admit failure
   e. objectivity

6. One of the variables in a scientific study is the yearly income of the study's subjects. This is called a(n) _____ variable.
   a. dependent
   b. qualitative
   c. factor
   d. quantitative
   e. independent

7. In a scientific study we find that as the subjects' number of years of formal education increases, their yearly income also increases. In this case the relationship between the two variables is called a(n)
   a. variable correlation.
   b. positive correlation.
   c. dependent correlation.
   d. independent correlation.
   e. negative correlation.

8. Three major types of social science research are
   a. laboratory research, survey research, and observational research.

b. experimental research, observational research, and survey research. •

c. observational research, statistical research, and survey research.

d. survey research, laboratory research, and experimental research.

e. statistical research, survey research, and experimental research.

9. Which of the following is *not* one of the typical steps in social science research?

   a. choose a research design

   b. review the literature

   c. collect and process data

   d. appeal to human authority •

   e. identify a problem

10. A working hypothesis is

   a. used to explain relationships among general propositions.

   b. used to infer a specific statement of conditions.

   c. a tentative answer to a particular problem. •

   d. a theory that has been proved.

   e. the final product of deductive reasoning.

QUESTIONS FOR THOUGHT AND DISCUSSION

1. How scientific is social science? Explain your answer.

2. Should scientists approach their work with an amoral attitude? Why?

3. Which social science discipline lends itself to the most objective investigation? Why?

Two

The Cultural System

Human beings have survived because they have created **culture**—a learned and shared social heritage that is transmitted from one generation to the next. In the following five chapters we will explore the concept of culture. We will examine its evolutionary development, its structure, and the functions it performs. Thus we will gain a knowledge of some of the external forces that help mold humans into the unique creatures that they are.

We have included Chapter 2, "The Physical Basis of Culture," because it is important to understand that culture has a physical base; that is, that human beings are physically and biologically different from other animals, and it is precisely this difference that has allowed us to develop culture.

Chapter 3 introduces several ideas essential to an understanding of culture. This chapter is perhaps most useful because of the introduction and definition of basic social science terminology. Most of the terms introduced in Chapter 3 are used intermittently throughout the rest of *Systems of Society*.

In Chapter 4 we focus on language, beliefs, and values—the cultural elements that tend to draw together people who share the same social heritage. Chapter 5 examines the concepts of race and ethnicity. Chapter 6 focuses first on culture's behavior-control elements—norms and institutions—and then moves on to the process of cultural change. The organization of the material in this chapter reflects the major idea we have attempted to put across: culture functions to control behavior within society, but culture itself is in a perpetual state of evolution.

2

The Physical Basis
of Culture

Homo sapiens is a unique animal. Faced with the problem with which all life forms must contend—the problem of survival—human beings have developed a unique means of adjusting to the environment. What are these means? How were they developed? How did humans come to be what they are? An adequate answer to these questions requires an understanding of the general theory of evolution and, more particularly, the specific capacities that human beings have developed in the battle for survival.

☐ Evolution

Generally, **evolution** refers to developmental change. In this sense, we can speak of the evolution of social customs, the automobile, or even your relationship with your best friend. Perhaps the most commonly thought of type of evolution is biological evolution, which refers to the development of all life forms, one from another, over time. Although ideas of evolution appeared earlier, it was not until the middle of the nineteenth century that a sophisticated and generally accepted theory of evolution was conceived. Prior to the modern era, most attempts to explain how we humans came to be what we are did not contain any developmental aspects. That is, these earlier explanations contained the view that all living creatures were created in the same form they are in today. By the end of the eighteenth century, however, the discovery of the fossil remains of extinct forms of animals led many scientists to formulate developmental theories about life forms.

One of these scientists was Chevalier de Lamarck (1744–1829).

Early in the nineteenth century, he proposed a theory of evolution that was based on two hypotheses: the law of use and disuse, and the law of inheritance of acquired characteristics. The **law of use and disuse** held that parts of the body that are used (that is, parts that are functional in terms of the survival of the organism) will develop and those that are not (parts that are dysfunctional) will atrophy (waste away), and possibly even disappear. The **law of inheritance of acquired characteristics** held that characteristics gained through use and disuse could be transmitted biologically from one generation to the next. Lamarck explained the evolution of groups of animals as a process in which new traits would be acquired and old ones lost over a period of many generations. Accordingly, if you were to exercise your biceps, they would develop and enlarge. The offspring you would produce from mating with another person would inherit the characteristic of well-developed biceps. If your offspring then exercised his biceps, they would develop further, and his offspring would have even better-developed biceps, and so on.

Lamarck's first hypothesis seems to be correct. Parts of the body which are exercised tend to develop and enlarge, and those which are not exercised tend to atrophy. His second hypothesis, however, seems to be incorrect. No one has been able to show that acquired characteristics can be inherited. Lamarck was on the right track when he hypothesized that a physical form can change when it interacts with the environment. He simply lacked an adequate explanation of how the interaction between the physical form and the environment takes place.

An adequate explanation later was provided by two British naturalists, A. R. Wallace and Charles Darwin, in the middle of the nineteenth century. Working independently, each of these men developed similar theories, and in 1859 they jointly submitted a paper to the Linnaean Society in London. In the same year Darwin presented their ideas to the rest of the world in his book *On the Origin of Species*. Darwin observed that the reproductive capacity of many plants and animals would cause a population explosion within a particular **species** (category of plants or animals whose structures are so similar that they can mate and produce fertile offspring) at any given time. He also observed that populations of species tended to remain relatively constant over long periods of time. He reasoned, therefore, that many young either die before reaching sexual maturity, or, if they live, are unable to reproduce. In other words, there exists a struggle for survival within species.

Moreover, Darwin observed that there was inherited variation within species (that is, not all the members of the species are exactly alike). Some variations are more favorable than others within a particular environment; and therefore those will have a better chance of survival, as will their offspring who will inherit their favorable characteristics. Darwin referred to this process of the inheritance of favorable

**Charles R. Darwin,
1809–1882**

characteristics as **natural selection.** Darwin used natural selection to explain the development of new species. The critical role in the process of natural selection is played by the environment. If the environment remains relatively constant, a species that is well adapted to it will survive, but if the environment changes, only those organisms with variations favorable (that is, adaptive) to the new conditions will survive. The survival of any given organism or species, therefore, depends upon its adaptation to environmental conditions. It is important to realize that Darwin was speaking of environmental changes that take place over long periods of time. We are accustomed to thinking of time in terms of hours or days, or perhaps even a few years; but evolutionary time may be measured in thousands and even millions of years. Darwin saw evolution as a slow, continuous process.*

Although Darwin recognized variation within species, he was not able to explain why individuals differed from one another in terms of their inherited characteristics. It was not until the early 1900s that the scientific world became aware of the basic principles of **genetics** (the scientific study of heredity), which was first discovered by Gregor

---

* Not all evolution may be slow. New ideas are challenging Darwin's notion of evolution as a slow and continuous process. For example, Niles Eldridge and Stephen Jay Gould have recently proposed the theory of "punctuated equilibrium," in which relatively short periods of sudden change alternate with long periods in which little change occurs. See their "Punctuated Equilibria: An Alternative to Phyletic Gradualism" in T. J. M. Schopf, ed., *Models in Paleobiology.* San Francisco: Freeman, Cooper and Co., pp. 82–115 and Gould's *The Flamingo's Smile.* New York: W. W. Norton & Co., 1985.

Mendel many years earlier. These principles explained how characteristics are inherited and, to an extent, why they vary from one generation to another within the same species.

Individual characteristics are products of distinct units of inheritance called **genes.** The organism inherits its genes from its parents. These genes and the characteristics they produce are fixed from the moment of conception and cannot be altered by acquiring other characteristics, such as enlarged biceps that have developed through exercising.

We refer to all of a particular organism's genetic characteristics as its **genotype.** Not all of the organism's genetic characteristics are manifested (observable) in the organism; some are latent (not observable). The reason for this is relatively simple to understand. Genes act in pairs, but both may not be equal in regard to whether or not they will be manifested in the organism. When one of the pair is *dominant* over the other, it will be manifested. The other is said to be *recessive.* The recessive gene is part of the organism's genotype, but it will not be manifested in the organism. Characteristics produced by recessive genes, however, may be manifested in some future generation when the recessive gene is not paired with a dominant gene.

We refer to all of the organism's manifested genetic characteristics as its **phenotype.** The phenotype has evolutionary significance because, in the process of natural selection, the environment acts only upon those characteristics that are manifested in the organism (the environment acts only upon the phenotype). Genotypical characteristics do not play any role in natural selection unless they are manifested in the organism (that is, unless they are also part of the phenotype).

The number of possible combinations of genes within any given individual is staggering. For example, the number of possible combinations that could be produced by the mating of two individuals each possessing 20,000 genes is 28,000,000! It is highly unlikely, therefore, that any two individuals will have the same genetic makeup. (The exception is multiple birth from the same egg, such as in identical twins or triplets in which the individuals do have exactly the same genetic makeup.)

Continuing scientific research has revealed that the organism's traits are not only due to random combinations of dominant and recessive genes. Individual traits are sometimes influenced by several genes. In fact, most of the physical characteristics of a human being are caused by the combined activity of many genes.[1] Sometimes it can be a complicated process. For example, the natural color of your skin is determined by three primary factors: the amount of a skin pigment called melanin, the distribution of the melanin in your skin, and the blood flowing through the blood vessels just below the surface of your skin. Each of these factors is influenced by the activity of several genes.

Human Variation
Human beings, like all other species, display a wide range of inherited physical characteristics.

Thus **genetic recombination,** whether in the form of random combinations of dominant and recessive genes or the combined activity of many genes, is a major source of genetic variation.

Another major source of genetic variation is **mutation.** A mutation is an abrupt, spontaneously occurring internal change in a gene. This change affects the molecular structure of **DNA** (deoxyribonucleic acid), a chemical substance that supplies coded information to the gene and that controls the heredity of all living organisms. Mutations were originally thought to be caused only by exposure to radiation or certain chemicals. After 1953, though, when James Watson and Francis Crick proposed a model for the structure and functioning of DNA, it was discovered that the majority of mutations are caused by random errors in the mating of the chemicals that constitute DNA.[2] Whatever its cause, the mutant is a genetic variant. Although some mutations may be adaptive, most are not adaptive, because a change in genetic structure threatens the balance between the organism and its environment.

Thus, genetic recombination and mutation cause variation within the species, and variation allows the process of natural selection to proceed. Organisms whose manifested characteristics allow them to adapt to the environment tend to survive; those with maladaptive characteristics do not. A new species evolves over time, as organisms with maladaptive characteristics eventually disappear completely.

Natural selection can affect the behavioral as well as the physical characteristics of a species. Two recent approaches to the evolution of behaviors are behavioral ecology and sociobiology. **Behavioral ecology** focuses on the relationship of all behaviors to the environment; **sociobiology** concentrates on social organization and social behavior. Both theories assume that natural selection accounts for the typical behaviors of a species and both involve animals primarily, although sociobiology assumes that human behavior is also partially controlled by genes. For example, an apparently genetically determined trait observable in all normal human infants within the first year of life is a fear of strangers. Sociobiologists argue that infants born with this inherent fear would be more likely to survive because they would be less susceptible to attack; the opposite would be true of infants born without the fear. So it appears that behavioral traits, such as our inherent fear of strangers, have been naturally selected and have contributed to the evolution of human beings.[3]

Sociobiologists go even further in challenging Darwin's idea of "survival of the fittest." In Darwin's original formulation, fitness meant the superiority of certain individuals within groups of competing members of the same species occupying the same territory. To the sociobiologist survival fitness means **procreative proficiency:** the ability to reproduce the most of one's own kind. The unit of survival has shifted from the individual to the genes that carry the code for reproducing similar individuals.

Such a shift provides an explanation for some otherwise perplexing behavior observed among all social creatures. For example, wasps sting attacking enemies at the cost of their own lives; birds risk death to warn other birds of an impending threat; and sterile soldier ants die to protect a reproductive queen. Such self-sacrifice does not make sense in terms of individual survival. Why then does it exist? Darwin had no answer.

Sociobiologists believe individuals act not only on the basis of individual fitness but also on the basis of **inclusive fitness,** which

Inclusive Fitness
These bees appear to have more interest in protecting their gene pool than in protecting themselves.

involves the genetic representations of individuals through their close relatives. Here, **kin selection,** rather than natural selection, becomes the key for survival. Organisms are motivated by a tendency to protect their own genes. In this view, you protect yourself so you may pass on your genes through reproduction. You also protect your relatives, because they share your **gene pool.**

Not all social scientists agree with the sociobiologists. Critics of sociobiology, such as Harvard's Sociobiology Study Group, maintain that cultural evolution, individual experience, and socialization (see Chapter 7) are far better vehicles for understanding human behavior. All of these depend on our capacity to learn. In short, we learn the roles we are to play, the rules that shape these roles, and the ways we are expected to relate to the world and to each other.

In any event, the foregoing discussion should reveal even to the casual reader that the concept of evolution itself has evolved and will, no doubt, continue to evolve. What would be most useful at this point is a consideration of some of the important factors in human physical and cultural evolution.

☐   Human Evolution

Like all other life forms, *Homo sapiens* is a product of evolution. Although all the specific facts of evolution are not known and may never be fully known, we can make some educated guesses as to how it is that human beings have evolved. It is most important, however, to note that while there is widespread agreement concerning some aspects of human evolution, there is also widespread disagreement concerning others. We have attempted to limit the following discussion to areas of widespread agreement. We believe, therefore, that most of the social scientists who are directly concerned with human evolution would agree with what is presented.

Life on this planet began at least a billion years ago, but there were no signs of human beings then. Not until 70 million years ago did the first traces of "humanness" appear—in the form of small, squirrellike, tree-dwelling prosimians (premonkeys) that lived in the tropical forest: the animals had a tendency to hold objects in their claws and a tendency to rely on their eyes rather than their noses for hunting. Both of these traits were adaptations to arboreal life (tree-living), and both were important to the survival of these small creatures. As their eyesight became more acute, they were able to manipulate more precisely the objects they held, and this led to the evolution of separate fingers. At the same time they were evolving larger parts of the brain to receive and interpret visual and tactile impressions. Information that had previously been filtered through older parts of the brain was now beginning to be filtered through the new developing brain tissue. These first primates displayed traits that have been developed and refined and are evident today in you and me.

By about 14 million years ago evolution had produced the earliest known humanlike primates, and by somewhere around 50,000 to 55,000 years ago *Homo sapiens* had evolved into the form in which we find ourselves today. It is significant to note that the gap between 50,000 and 55,000 years is both large and small. That is, 5,000 years seems like a very long time when we are used to thinking of time in terms of hours, days, weeks, months, years, and decades. (Remember that the average life expectancy for people in the United States is still considerably shorter than a century.) At the same time, 5,000 years is barely noticeable when we think in terms of a billion years. The point is that, although we are far from accurate in pinpointing some of the specific details of human evolution, we are certain that people as we know them appeared rather late in evolutionary development.

Similarities with Other Primates

We also know that human beings share certain characteristics with other members of the group of mammals to which they belong—the **primates.** Among those characteristics are: (1) limbs used for grasping; (2) great accuracy of sight; and (3) considerable development of the brain. As we have pointed out, traces of these characteristics can be found in the prosimians of 70 million years ago, and they are most fully developed thus far in human beings.

Since apes and humans are both primates, they are related. Some of the structural similarities between them are so obvious that it certainly does not take much imagination to recognize that they are more closely related to one another than each of them is to other animals in a zoo—say lions, or elephants, or alligators. In fact, apes and humans are structurally more closely related than apes and monkeys. Some people, having observed the strong similarity between apes and humans, have incorrectly applied their common sense to the general theory of evolution and have concluded that humans evolved from today's apes. Actually, humans did not evolve from today's apes or any other presently existing life form. Both probably evolved from some common ancestor which was neither human nor ape. Therefore, when you see a gorilla in the zoo, you are not looking at your evolutionary father. You are probably looking at an evolutionary cousin. A cousin-to-cousin relationship would explain the similarities between humans and gorillas.

How Humans Differ from Other Primates

True, the similarities between humans and gorillas are great, but the differences are even greater. To begin with, the normal posture of humans is upright; they stand and move about on their legs. The arms, then, are free to be used for different purposes. A gorilla may also stand and move on its hind limbs, but the general structure of its body makes this a somewhat difficult task. Generally, it is more likely to use all four limbs when moving from place to place.

Both humans and gorillas have hands, but the human hand is much more versatile than that of the large ape. The anatomical structure of the human hand, together with the considerable neuromuscular control over it, allows a human to grip objects with either great strength or with great precision. The gorilla's stubby hand can exert enormous pressure in a power grip, but the gorilla does not possess the neuromuscular control to permit it the delicate grip necessary to perform the task of shuffling a deck of cards—a relatively simple task for humans.

Both humans and gorillas have stereoscopic vision, which defines distance and depth, a characteristic they share with other apes and monkeys. But it is believed that of the three, only humans have color vision, which allows them to define objects in terms of shape, size, color, and shade better than any other animal. Humans also have a large and well-developed brain. When we consider the ratio of brain size to body mass, we find that the human brain is larger than that of any other living animal. Part of this large brain is composed of new tissue, a recent evolutionary development. Significantly, this new tissue is associated with the capacity for abstract thought and decision making. Thus, humans possess a **species-specific brain**—one that is unique among all animals in its capacity for abstract thought and decision making. In

Biological Sociology

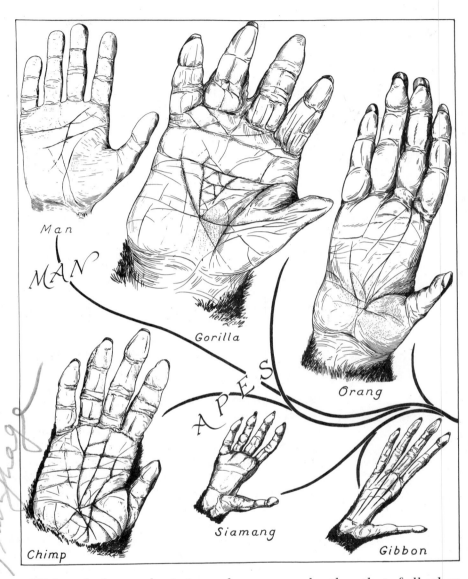

Man

MAN

Gorilla

APES

Orang

Chimp

Siamang

Gibbon

addition, the human brain is much more complex than that of all other living creatures.

Finally, we must point out that humans are the only species known to possess spoken, symbolic language. Other animals use sounds to signal one another. In fact, all mammals possess the same biological equipment that humans use to make sounds: lips, teeth, palate, tongue, nasal passage, vocal cords, and lungs. But humans assign arbitrary meanings to the sounds they make, and they use these sounds within the boundaries of arbitrary systems of their own creation. As a result, humans have a highly serviceable means of communication. Other animals, as far as we know, do not, at least under usual circumstances in the wild.*

Taken together, these characteristics—upright posture, the versatile hand, stereoscopic color vision, the large, complex, species-specific brain, and language—set humans apart from other animals, and serve as the base for their technological and intellectual achievements. Moreover, it is significant that these achievements could not have come about were it not for human society.

The social nature of humans, like their physical nature, is rooted in biology—particularly human sexuality and the helpless condition of the newborn human infant. It is sometimes thought that human sexuality is one of our more animalistic qualities. Actually, human sexuality is one of our uniquely human aspects. Unlike all other female mammals, the human female does not experience a distinct heat period (estrus) during her cycle of ovulation. From puberty to senility she is susceptible to sexual arousal and responsive to sexual stimulation. And so is the human male. He does not have to rely on odors and other signals given off by females in heat in order to become sexually aroused. The human animal, then, unlike other mammals, is a sexual creature all the time, not just during specific periods. Furthermore, it is human sexuality that serves as a basis for relatively permanent pairings of males and females. These matings allow humanity to survive; for without the atmosphere generated by such matings the helpless human infant could not survive.

The human infant is so helpless that it requires continuous attention for an extended period of time. This helplessness is the result of two factors: the relatively long time it takes for the infant to reach a physical stage in which it can survive unaided by others (an extended infancy); and its relative lack of instincts (unlearned, biologically based, complex, and repetitive behavior endemic to a species). Many newborn animals have the ability to be up and around within hours after birth, but it takes months for the human infant to learn to walk. Other animals display instinctive behavior which helps them to survive on their own. Humans, by contrast, must learn their means of survival.

The human infant requires a great deal of attention and a relatively long time to learn how to survive. Generally this occurs in the social unit of the family whose nucleus is based on the sexual attraction and mating of an adult male and female. Human sexuality, therefore,

---

* Researchers have had some success in teaching chimpanzees and gorillas to associate gestures with specific activities. For example, see Beatrice T. Gardner and R. Allen Gardner, "Two Comparative Psychologists Look at Language Acquisition." In K. E. Nelson, ed., *Children's Language.* (New York: Halsted Press, 1980), vol. 2, pp. 331–369.

provides the basis for the nucleus of a social unit in which the infant learns to be human.

During this period of "becoming human" the youngster associates with adults but does not have adult responsibilities of its own. Through a long series of concrete experiences, the brain develops the ability to think, and, eventually, to symbolize objects and ideas. The child learns a whole social heritage, a culture, which ensures not only individual survival but survival of the entire species. Upon becoming an adult, the youngster adapts what has been learned and may therefore contribute to human knowledge. Ultimately, then, "human" is defined in terms of learned and shared behavior, not biological characteristics; but without the biological characteristics they have evolved, humans could not have developed the social and cultural characteristics which permit them to survive.

Cultural Evolution

Although we cannot be sure precisely when our ancestors began to develop culture, we can be sure that certain particular events which led to the formation of culture did take place. Among the more important of such events were the beginnings of **technology,** the development of language, the discovery of how to control fire, and the beginnings of family life.

Technology

One of our ancestors' outstanding achievements was the development of crude stone tools, which laid the foundation for most subsequent technological achievements. There is evidence which indicates that humans were using pebble tools as long as 1,750,000 years ago. These pebble tools were used by people whose brain size was only one-half to two-thirds that of modern humans. We can speculate, therefore, that humans and culture evolved together. As toolmaking and the tasks performed with tools became more complex, the brain became larger and more complex. In turn, the larger, more complex brain led to the conception of more complex tasks for tools to perform and the development of more sophisticated tools. In a sense, while people were making culture, culture was making people—that is, people as we know them today.

The first tools used were, no doubt, those found in nature. A stone on the ground is nothing more than a stone until someone picks it up and throws it, whether in defense or in attack. When a natural object is used to alter the environment, even if only in a small way, it has become a tool. The first tools were natural objects which a human being realized could be used to help in some way. As the human altered the environment, control was exerted over nature.

Technology
Both apes and humans have developed technology but the difference in the respective sophistication of each makes them hardly comparable.

Humans are not the only animals that use tools; many other animals do. Sea otters, for example, use rocks to crack clam shells they have collected; some birds use thorns to extract insects from the bark of trees. In both instances the tool used is one found in nature. Other animals may even make tools. The chimpanzee picks a twig from a tree, strips its leaves, and uses it to "fish" for ants and termites in the ground. But that is the limit of chimpanzee technology. "In short, tools are used and after a fashion tools are made, but the inventory is small, the range of their usefulness limited, and their historical development absolutely zero. There is nothing to suggest that [modern] chimpanzee or ape technology has ever gone beyond the simple stripping of leaves from a branch."[4]

By contrast, human technology has advanced to a high level, and recently it has advanced so rapidly that customary ways of behaving have not been able to keep abreast of it. We can speculate that the first split-pebble tool made by a human was the result of an accident. An individual using a stone, for the purpose of pounding or mashing some other object, might have accidentally chipped the stone and discovered that the chipped stone could be used for cutting. An animal without the intelligence to do so might not recognize the utility of a chipped stone. But the human did recognize its utility and furthermore remembered it and repeated the chipping action by conscious design rather than by accident the next time. And, just as important, this first discovery was shared with others. Soon additional discoveries and inventions were made, and from this meager beginning there eventually developed a technology so sophisticated that our species was able to explore the universe.

Language

The development of language is essential to the formation of culture, because without language there could be no mature culture. Language does more than just facilitate communication. It allows us to think about the past and future as well as the present. Once our ancestors began to construct symbols, they could communicate about an object without its being present. In this manner, one person's past experiences could be communicated to another. Through symbol systems people could store such communicated experiences in their memories; this stored knowledge is the essence of culture. Language, then, facilitates the accumulation and storage of a social heritage, and the transmission of that social heritage from one generation to the next.

Fire

Undoubtedly one of the most important contributions to the formation of culture was discovering the means to control fire. We are sure that some cave dwellers used fire as long as 750,000 years ago; and we are relatively certain that humans acquired it at an even earlier date.[5] Fire extended humans' geographical boundaries by allowing them to travel into regions that were previously too cold to explore. In so doing, they could expand their knowledge as well as find new resources to exploit.

The Development of Language
This Sumer tablet bears an early map of the world, showing Babylon on the Euphrates at the center.

Before learning to control fire, humans may have slept in trees in order to avoid the attack of ground-dwelling predators. However, with a campfire to keep the predators away, they could sleep soundly and securely on the ground. This new physical arrangement for sleeping allowed group members to sleep closer to one another, encouraging interaction that contributed to the cohesion and solidarity of the group.

Fire was used for a number of purposes, from cooking to aiding in the hunting of animals. Probably the most important effect of learning to control fire, though, was the fact that the rhythm of life was changed. Before fire, the human daily cycle coincided with the rising and setting of the sun—roughly twelve hours of activity and twelve hours of rest. But fire lengthened the day. It allowed the human more time to think and talk about the day's events and to prepare strategies for coping with tomorrow. The campfire afforded the opportunity to exercise the mind in a relaxed atmosphere, away from the routine daily pressures of trying to survive. "It was around such fires, too, as man stared into the flames and took comfort in the radiating warmth, that stories became myths and world views became crystallized as philosophies."[6] Learning to control fire, then, contributed significantly to the formation of culture.

Family Life

We have pointed out that sexual attraction between an adult male and female gave impetus to the formation of the family—the most fundamental social unit found in any human society. But more than just sex was probably necessary to keep families and bands (groups of families) together. Since the group contained the learning experiences of all its members, it necessarily contained more knowledge than any one individual. And as the knowledge accumulated and stored by the group expanded, it became highly beneficial to remain a member of the group. That is, the cumulative knowledge of the group gave each group member a better chance to survive if he or she stayed with the group rather than trying to survive alone.

Another factor which contributed greatly to social cohesion was safety in numbers. A single individual might have little chance of surviving a predator's attack, but aided by the others, each group member had a much better chance of surviving such an attack.

The shift in the method of obtaining food also contributed to social solidarity. When our ancestors first came down from the trees, they relied on gathering as a method of obtaining food. They were fruit pickers, and, as such, they were constantly moving from one place to another in search of food. When they began to hunt, however, they also began to establish camps as bases of operations. Although it was necessary to establish new campsites from time to time, the camp served as a relatively permanent base of operations. This new mode of living allowed for a division of labor in which the younger men could leave the camp to hunt for game while the mothers could tend to young infants. Other men, women, and children could gather edible vegetation. The cooperation necessary to maintain such an economic system served to draw the group closer together in its struggle for survival.

But the beginning of family life had more to offer than immediate survival advantages. It afforded our ancestors a basic social unit that shared common experiences, thus carving out a social heritage that was transmitted to the young within the context of the unit itself. In a sense, families and bands provided a home for culture.

Thus the beginnings of family life along with technology, language, and fire contributed to the formation of culture—the unique means of human survival. It is this behavior expressed in learned and shared social heritage that separates human from nonhuman.

We have attempted to show that our humanness has a physical base: it is embedded in the biological being.

Nature and Humans

Nature is a life system. Within its boundaries is the air that envelops this planet, as well as all the earth's living and nonliving matter. Through the process of evolution, which performs all of the system's major functions, these elements interact with one another to maintain life.

Inputs into the system are the various forms of living matter. Conversion consists of natural selection acting upon living organisms to meet the demands of changing environmental conditions. Outputs are new forms of life which are then fed back into the system as new inputs. In this manner new life forms appear and disappear, but the cycle of life continues.

The subsystems of nature are **ecosystems.** They consist of all the relationships between living organisms and their environment in a given location. Homeostasis (balance) within ecosystems is achieved by one part of the system exploiting another. For example, shrimp exploit their environment by eating plankton, while fish exploit the same environment by eating the shrimp. Seals and porpoises eat the fish, and killer whales eat the seals and porpoises. Such "food chains" occur throughout nature, and they promote homeostasis in an interesting way. Predators (the eaters) invariably consume just enough of the prey population (the eaten) to ensure that the prey population will remain relatively constant, while they provide themselves with just enough food to keep their own species at an optimum size to survive. To some extent, this explains why Darwin observed a relative constancy in the size of populations of species.

The human is a part of nature. Unlike the other parts, however, the human has been placed in a situation in which limited physical abilities are not sufficient to ensure the survival of the species. In order to meet the demands of this situation, humans have created culture—their unique survival adaptation. But while culture serves to adapt humans to their environment, it also threatens their continued existence. Technology has allowed people to move past the level of mere adaptation to the environment. Through technology, we are consciously and perhaps unconsciously, too, altering the environment in a way that is dysfunctional not only to ourselves but to the whole life system as well. Pollution of the air, water, and soil, as well as weapons of awesome destructiveness, threaten all life on this planet. Therefore, it is important that we gain an understanding of what culture is, how it functions, and how it may be changed to ensure the survival of our life system. Chapters 3 through 6 represent our attempt to provide a starting point for such understanding.

The Impact of Human Culture
Our unique capacities have enabled us to alter the environment, but now we threaten our own survival.

REFERENCES

1. Carol R. Ember and Melvin Ember, *Anthropology*, 5th ed. (Englewood Cliffs, N.J.: Prentice Hall, 1988), p. 22.
2. G. Ledyard Stebbins, *Processes of Organic Evolution*, 3rd ed. (Englewood Cliffs, N.J.: Prentice Hall, 1977), pp. 62–63.
3. See Edward O. Wilson, *On Human Nature* (Cambridge, Mass.: Harvard University Press, 1978).
4. James F. Downs and Hermann K. Bleibtreu, *Human Variation: An Introduction to Physical Anthropology* (Beverly Hills: Glencoe, 1969), p. 102.
5. Wendell H. Oswalt, *Understanding Our Culture* (New York: Holt, Rinehart and Winston, 1970), p. 59.
6. *Ibid.*, p. 61.

GLOSSARY

Evolution	Generally, evolution refers to developmental change of any kind. One type of evolution is biological evolution, which refers to the development of life forms, one from another, over time.
Natural selection	The process by which organisms increase their chance of survival by inheriting characteristics that facilitate their adaptation to the environment. Animals such as polar bears, for example, are able to survive in their harsh natural environment because they have heavy fur.
Species	Category of plants or animals whose structures are so similar that they can mate and produce fertile offspring. Example: *Homo sapiens* (human beings).
Species-specific brain	A brain whose structure and composition is endemic to a particular species. The human species-specific brain is associated with unique language and intellectual abilities of *Homo sapiens*.
Genetics	The scientific study of heredity.
Genes	Distinct units of inheritance. Our genetic characteristics are produced by the genes we inherit from our parents.
Genotype	All of a particular organism's genetic characteristics.
Phenotype	Genetic characteristics that are observable in the organism. Example: eye color.
Gene pool	All the genes in a given population at any particular time.
Genetic recombination	A major source of genetic variation that is caused by random combinations of dominant and recessive genes or the combined activity of many genes.

Mutation	Abrupt spontaneously occurring internal changes in a gene. Mutations were originally thought to be caused only by exposure to radiation or certain chemicals. It was later discovered that most mutations are caused by random errors in the mating of the chemicals that constitute DNA.
DNA (deoxyribonucleic acid)	A chemical substance that supplies coded information to the gene and that controls the heredity of all living organisms.
Behavioral ecology	An approach to the evolution of behaviors that focuses on the relationship of all behaviors to the environment.
Sociobiology	An approach to the evolution of behaviors that concentrates on social organization and social behavior.
Procreative proficiency	The ability to produce large numbers of offspring.
Inclusive fitness	The genetic representation of the individual through surviving relatives; emphasis is on survival of the gene pool rather than the gene-bearing individual.
Kin selection	The tendency to protect the individuals with whom one shares the most genes.
Law of inheritance of acquired characteristics	Characteristics gained through use or disuse can be transmitted biologically from one generation to the next. No one has been able to demonstrate that this "law" is correct.
Law of use and disuse	Parts of the body that are used will develop and those that are not used will atrophy. This hypothesis seems to be correct.
Primates	The group of mammals to which humans belong. Primates share several characteristics, including limbs used for grasping, great accuracy of sight, and considerable brain development.
Culture	A learned and shared social heritage that is transmitted from one generation to the next.
Technology	Tools and techniques for adjusting to and changing the environment.

Ecosystem   A system that contains all the relationships between living organisms and their environment in a given location.

SELECTED READING

Campbell, B., ed. *Humankind Emerging,* 5th ed. (Glenview, Ill.: Scott, Foresman, 1988). A survey of human biological evolution.

Ciochon, R. L. and J. G. Fleagle, eds. *Primate Evolution and Human Origins* (Hawthorne, N.Y.: Aldine de Gruyter, 1987). A reader on primate evolution and human origins.

Fagan, B. M. *People of the Earth: An Introduction to World Prehistory,* 6th ed. (Glenview, Ill.: Scott, Foresman, 1989). A survey of world prehistory.

Fleagle, J. G. *Primate Adaptation & Evolution* (San Diego: Academic Press, 1988). An examination of the comparative anatomy, behavioral ecology, and paleontology of humans and primates.

Johanson, D. and M. Edey. *Lucy: The Beginnings of Humankind* (New York: Simon & Schuster, 1981). A thoroughly absorbing, behind-the-scenes look at paleoanthropology.

Leakey, R. E. *The Making of Mankind* (New York: Dutton, 1981). An overview of human biological and cultural evolution.

Pilbeam, D. "The Descent of Hominoids and Hominids." *Scientific American* (March 1984, pp. 84–96). A discussion of the divergence of the apes from Old World monkeys and the subsequent divergence of humans from the apes.

QUESTIONS

1. If Lamarck's theory of evolution were correct, parents could transmit which of the following characteristics to their children?
   a. a good suntan
   b. blue eyes
   c. brown hair
   d. thick lips
   e. type "A" blood

2. Human beings have dealt with the problem of survival by developing
   a. gene pools.
   b. phenotypes.
   c. genetics.
   d. natural selection.
   e. culture.

3. The survival of species may be best explained by which of the following?
   a. genetics
   b. technology
   c. natural selection
   d. genotypes
   e. culture

4. Most of the physical characteristics of a human being are caused by
   a. mutations that occur continuously.
   b. the person's interaction with the environment.
   c. the combined activity of many genes.
   d. the dominant genes of the person's father.
   e. random combinations of dominant and recessive genes.

5. Which of the following was *not* a significant development that led to the formation of culture?
   a. the discovery of how to control fire
   b. the practice of tree-living
   c. the development of language
   d. the beginnings of technology
   e. the beginnings of family life

6. Most mutations are caused by
   a. exposure to radioactive materials.
   b. random errors in the mating of the chemicals that constitute DNA.
   c. the genetic recombination of dominant and recessive genes.
   d. the influence of the environment on the organism.
   e. exposure to certain chemicals.

7. Sociobiologists define survival fitness in terms of
   a. procreative proficiency.
   b. kin selection.
   c. individual superiority.
   d. ecological behavior.
   e. inclusive fitness.

8. We may refer to the subsystems of nature as
   a. ecosystems.
   b. inputs.
   c. conversions.
   d. outputs.
   e. life forms.

9. Biological evolution refers to
   a. the explanation of how characteristics in life forms are inherited.
   b. the spontaneous changes that take place in life forms.

    c. an idea first proposed by Charles Darwin.
    d. the development of life forms, one from another, over time.
    e. the process of mutation.

10. One significant physical difference between humans and apes is the fact that only
    a. humans have grasping limbs.
    b. apes have great accuracy of sight.
    c. humans can stand on their hind limbs.
    d. humans have stereoscopic color vision.
    e. apes have grasping limbs.

QUESTIONS FOR THOUGHT AND DISCUSSION

1. What makes humans human?

2. How did humans come to be what they are?

3. Will there always be human races?

4. What are the prospects for human survival?

3

The Culture Concept

Several years ago an American newspaper printed the following news release from the Associated Press: "Kampala, Uganda—When President Idi Amin ordered the traditionally nude Karamojans to cover themselves, tribal conservatives forced some of those who obeyed to eat their new clothes as a penance."[1] Most Americans would react to this bit of information by shaking their heads and chuckling. Behind the head-shakes and chuckles, however, there is a great tale to be told. The storytellers are social scientists, and the tale is one of culture.

Culture is the way of life of a group of people. It is a social heritage that is learned and shared by the group. In the four remaining chapters concerning the culture system, we will examine the concept of culture and the functions that culture performs. When you finish reading these chapters, you should have a general understanding of culture, and a more specific understanding of why most Americans would react to the Kampala news release with headshakes and chuckles.

☐ The Study of Culture

A useful way to begin our discussion of the culture concept is to focus on the people who study culture and some of the methods they employ. All social scientists are concerned with culture to some degree. Those most directly concerned with it, however, are anthropologists. **Anthropology** is an extremely diverse academic discipline. It may be divided into two major divisions—physical anthropology and cultural anthropology— each containing a variety of subdivisions. Anthropologists recognize that a person is both a biological and a cultural being, and that both aspects should be studied. Therefore, regardless of their particular specialties, anthropologists strive to avoid exclusively biological or exclusively cultural explanations for human behavior.

Physical anthropology is primarily concerned with genetically transmitted characteristics. Some physical anthropologists study the origins and evolution of humans through an examination of fossil remains; others study biogenetically transmitted differences among various human groups; and still others study similarities and differences among primates. We discussed some of the findings of physical anthropologists in the preceding chapter.

Cultural anthropology is primarily concerned with socially learned traits. Among the many areas investigated by cultural anthropologists are the ways of life of extinct as well as presently existing human groups. Some cultural anthropologists specialize in the study of languages of various cultures; others concentrate on cultural stability and change.

Cultural anthropologists usually study the ways of life of small, relatively isolated groups of people. Often, these are nonliterate groups (they do not have written languages). The primary techniques used to gather data are participant observation (observation while living with the group and participating to some extent in their activities) and the use of informants (having group members tell about their way of life). Through their cross-cultural comparisons anthropologists contribute greatly to our understanding of both the similarities and differences among human groups.

A Cultural Anthropologist in the Field
We learn much about the cultures of small, relatively isolated societies through information provided by informants.

The Content of Culture

We have indicated that culture is a learned and shared way of life that is socially transmitted from one generation to the next. Although each culture varies somewhat from the others, all cultures contain a few universal characteristics. Before discussing these cultural universals, it will be useful to become familiar with two basic social science concepts—*group* and *society*. A **group** is a set of persons who interact with one another and share some joint activities. It is comprised of at least three individuals whose interactions with each other are connected by a single network of relationships. Thus, we can speak of a family or a football team as a group.

A **society** is a self-sufficient and self-perpetuating group which includes persons of both sexes and all ages. It is self-sufficient in the sense that it contains a complete set of techniques for coping with the environment, thus tending to prolong its existence indefinitely. Societies may be small (as few as 100 people, or perhaps even less) or large (millions of people). We can speak of Mundugumor society (a small New Guinea tribe), American society, or even Western society. Each is able to cope with the environment and maintain itself from one generation to the next.

Society, then, refers to a group of people; culture refers to the group's way of life. Culture can be divided into three major parts: (1) *customs*, (2) *belief systems*, and (3) *artifacts*. **Customs** are group habits. They are the ways group members actually behave. Children begin to learn customs when they are only small infants. The way to communicate, the way to keep clean, and the way to eat food are examples of customs. The fact that you use knives, spoons, and forks to eat, while a Chinese uses chopsticks, indicates cultural differences between Americans and Chinese. Americans and Chinese, however, share with all other cultures the universal of having specific customs for eating.

Belief systems are the mental components of culture, the learned and shared ideas that describe, explain, and give meaning and purpose to life. Included within the notion of belief systems are religious, magical, and normative prescriptions for conduct. Norms are standards of conduct which may or may not be religious or magical in nature. In some societies—such as the Dobuans of Melanesia—religious, magical, and other normative beliefs complement each other to such a high

Weapons of Five Different Cultures— Ancient and Modern

New Guinea spear

degree that there is a well-defined and highly consistent belief system. In other societies, such as the United States, the belief system is not nearly so well defined nor as consistent. Belief systems, however, are a part of every culture, and norms are particularly useful to the individual because they allow that person to determine in advance how his or her actions will be judged by others.

Artifacts are the objects that a society produces and uses, including the tools that are used to produce other objects. Artifacts may be developed by the society itself or borrowed from other societies. In either case, they are part of the culture of a society. Some societies, because of their relatively low level of technological development, have only a few artifacts. Other societies on a higher level of technological development have thousands upon thousands of artifacts. Americans, for instance, use a wide variety of artifacts, from safety pins to computers.

Social scientists differentiate the various elements contained within a culture by classifying them according to their degree of organizational complexity. **Cultural traits** are the simplest elements. Traits are either concrete or abstract units of meaning. They are treated by people as indivisible units, although their indivisibility is dependent upon the social context in which they are treated. An Arunta tribesman of Australia, for example, will refer to his spear as an indivisible unit when describing a hunt; however, he will refer to his spear in terms of its constituent parts (the point, the shaft, the binding, and so on) when describing how it is made. The determination, then, of whether or not a concrete or abstract unit of meaning is a trait is dependent upon how it is treated in some social context, not on some objective quality of the trait itself.

Congo dagger

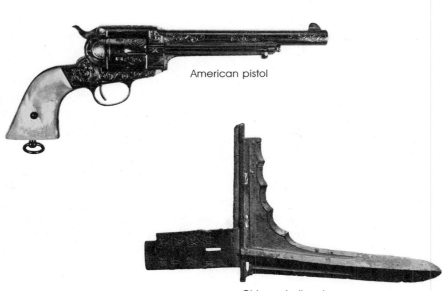

American pistol

Chinese halberd

German crossbow and stirrup

An Arunta Tribesman with His Spear
The spear's categorization as a cultural trait depends on its use in a social context rather than on any objective quality of the spear itself.

A **cultural complex** is a number of interrelated traits. Although it is sometimes difficult to determine just where a trait leaves off and a complex begins (the Arunta spear, for example), social scientists have found the term "complex" useful when describing the way of life of a particular group of people. They may speak, for instance, of the buffalo-hunting complex of the Crow Indians, which includes, among other things, the time of year to hunt buffalo, ways of locating the herd, and the kinds of weapons to be used.

A cultural complex that you might be better able to relate to is the dating complex on American college campuses. It might be interesting to see how many traits within that complex you and your classmates can identify and agree upon.

Cultural patterns represent the greatest degree of organizational complexity of cultural elements. Patterns are interrelated sets of complexes. If the hunting complex of the Crow were complemented by a religious complex, we would call the total configuration a pattern. In the same manner, the American cultural pattern of marriage and family life includes the wedding complex, the child-rearing complex, the housekeeping complex, and so forth. So we may speak of cultural traits, complexes, and patterns.

In the preceding chapter we stated that culture is the unique human means of survival. Through culture, people not only adapt to the environment, but they change the environment to suit their purposes. To accomplish its task, culture must meet certain needs which are inherent requirements for individual and group living. The needs are universal; the specific ways of meeting the needs vary from culture to culture. In *The Proper Study of Mankind*, Stuart Chase offers a list of nine universal needs.[2] Let's briefly consider them.

1. "Language—the most important of all." Group life could not function without some form of communication. And, remember, culture cannot exist without group life. Language, then, is a functional necessity for human survival.

2. "Status of the individual in the group. Who outranks whom?" In all societies there exists a system for ranking individuals and groups. Status serves the basic function of getting society's jobs done.

3. "Family and other social groups." Human beings, unlike other animals, remain relatively helpless and unable to fend for themselves for an extended period of time. The family performs the basic function of care and protection for the infant. In fact, most productive human mating takes place within the context of the family.

4. "Methods for dealing with food, shelter, clothing, and other vital materials." Here we really see human beings pitted against nature, the struggle for scarce resources.

5. "Government and law. These can be very informal but are always there." Group organization requires that there be rules and some agency to enforce them. A society without rules is like a fish out of water—it ceases to exist.

6. "Religion and ethics." Religion is a part of every society. It performs a variety of functions for both the individual and the society. Ethics refers to standards of conduct which guide human behavior.

7. "Systems for explaining natural phenomena—magic, mythology, and lately science." We credit cats with a great deal of curiosity (for example, "Curiosity killed the cat"), but no other animal has the inquisitiveness of people. Apparently, they have a need to know. They question virtually everything, and when magic, mythology, and science have failed to provide satisfactory answers, they have used religion. (Obviously, this whole book represents your authors' attempt to explain natural phenomena.)

8. "Rules regarding property, who owns what: methods for barter and trade." One of the bases for group living is cooperation. In their communal attempt to survive, people must have techniques for determining who owns what and how trade is to be conducted.

9. "Art forms—the dance, stories, songs, poems, architecture, handicrafts, and design." This, the aesthetic aspect of human behavior, also occurs in all societies. Perhaps it represents a need for people to express themselves; perhaps it represents one dimension of an inherent quest for order. In any event, we do not treat it extensively in this book as we do the others. Extensive treatment of this need is traditionally handled by our colleagues in the humanities. We are simply acknowledging the fact that it is a universal aspect of culture.

To this list we will add three more universal needs—the need for play activities, the need for a system of education, and the need for finding meaning in life. All people require some means of dealing with these needs, and they learn these from their culture. Different cultures will satisfy these needs in different ways, but all cultures will satisfy them.

Individuals, then, do not have to cope with the problem of determining how to satisfy these needs. Their social heritage provides answers for them. All that individuals have to do is to learn their social heritage. The process of learning the content of culture is called **socialization.** This is a critical process in that it ensures the survival of the culture. Through the socialization process the individual learns who and what he or she is. At birth, the human being is a mass of muscle, blood, skin, bones, reflexes, and inherent capacities. In a sense, socialization is the process of becoming human. To a great extent, the kind of person one becomes depends on how one is socialized. For example, a person socialized into Chinese culture will speak Chinese, act Chinese, even think Chinese, regardless of the biological inheritance. In *Mirror for Man*, Clyde Kluckhohn told of the son of American missionary parents who was orphaned in his infancy.[3] A Chinese family adopted him and reared him as a Chinese. Years later, upon moving to New York, he found it difficult to adjust to American life. Although he did not look Chinese (he had fair hair and blue eyes), he thought and even moved and gestured like a Chinese. His discomfort was so great that he returned to China, where he could feel comfortable living with people like himself.

The example of the orphan boy illustrates that culture serves to control behavior as well as providing a ready-made means of adapting to the environment. A necessary requirement of societal living is that behavior be controlled. This does not mean that every individual must act in only one particular way; it does mean that certain prescribed limitations on behavior are necessary. The continued welfare and sur-

The Newborn Human
This child, who at birth is a mass of muscle, blood, skin, bones, and inherent capacities, will eventually learn to be human within the context of culture and society.

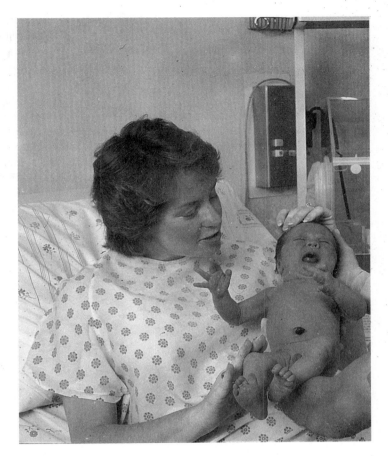

vival of the group dictate that there be such limitations. We will discuss the behavior control function of culture in depth in Chapter 6.

☐ Cultural Variation

Up to this point, we have discussed culture in terms of universals—aspects of human behavior that occur in every society. Let us now consider cultural variation. The famous anthropologist Ruth Benedict has pointed out that group life may develop in an infinite variety of directions, depending on the physical environment of the group and the imagination of its members.[4] In fact, the spectrum of possible human arrangements for living is so broad that selection is a necessity. For instance, Benedict speaks of warfare as a social theme that may or may not be used in any given culture. The Aztecs used war to obtain captives for religious sacrifices; the Spaniards treated war as a method of conquest by killing. Partly as a result of these two different conceptions of warfare, Cortez conquered Mexico in an incredibly short time in 1519. The Aztecs' notion of war prevented them from adjusting rapidly to what the Spaniards were doing. Benedict further points out that while "it is impossible for certain peoples to conceive the possibility of a state of peace ... it may be just as impossible for a people to conceive of the possibility of a state of war."[5] Eskimos, for example, understand the act of one man killing another, but they have no notion of organized mutual slaughter. The idea of one Eskimo tribe facing another in battle is as foreign to them as rubbing noses as an expression of affection is to us.

Similarly, a culture may or may not elaborate upon other social themes ranging from the specific meaning the culture attaches to adolescence to the particular restrictions it imposes upon marriage partners. It selects the themes to be elaborated. The Carrier Indians of British Columbia, for example, had a fear and horror of each girl's first menstruation. During puberty a girl was required to live in seclusion for three or four years ("the burying alive"). She was considered a threat to anyone who might even see her. The Apache Indians of the American West, on the other hand, treat girls in their first menstruation as sources of supernatural blessing—babies and old people come before the girls to have illnesses removed. In Samoa, first menstruation does not have any particular social significance.

The elaboration of cultural themes leads to the formation of **social institutions.** These are distinctive patterns that are centered around major human needs and accompanied by particular modes of social interaction. The family, for example, is a universal social institution. As previously mentioned, it helps to meet the need for the group's survival by providing care and protection for the young. All societies have institutionalized the family as a basic unit of social organization. The specific form of that organization and the kinds of relationships permitted to exist within it vary from one culture to the next, of course. A family structure consisting of one man, one woman, and their children, and in which all members contribute to some extent to the decision-making process is typical of American culture. A structure consisting of several related men, each with more than one wife, and their children, and in which the senior males of the senior generation made most of the decisions was, until recently, common among the Bathonga of southern Mozambique.

Religion and education are two more examples of universal social institutions. They, too, are distinctive patterns centered on major needs and accompanied by particular modes of social interaction. When social scientists use the term **interaction,** they are referring to the process by which communicating individuals influence each other's thoughts and actions. Some social scientists prefer to use the term "transaction" because it strongly suggests the dynamic aspect of the interaction process—the fact that the behavior of *all* interacting parties is modified by their interaction. It is because of the dynamic interaction process that we can legitimately treat social institutions as systems. Although the term "social institutions" can be used interchangeably with the term "systems" (for example, the family system, the education system, the economic system), we have chosen to use the term "systems" because we believe it communicates more effectively the concept of interaction.

Another concept that is useful in understanding cultural variation is **cultural integration.** This refers to the "fit" or "coming together" of traits, complexes, and patterns into a unified whole. All cultures are integrated. They vary, however, in the degree of integration that they possess at any given time. A highly integrated culture, such as the Zuni of the southwestern United States, has combinations of complexes and patterns that complement one another well. In fact, Ruth Benedict thought Zuni culture was so highly integrated that she characterized its configuration (its total appearance) as being organized around a single quality or **ethos**—the Apollonian quality of emphasizing emotional control and moderation in all aspects of life. Highly integrated cultures tend to produce a great sense of cohesiveness among the members of society. Since most elements are consistent with each other in highly integrated cultures, people tend to know who they are and just what their particular mission in life is. Because their elements fit together into a fairly unified whole, highly integrated cultures tend to resist change; therefore, they may not adapt well to change, particularly when it is rapid.

Cultures with a lower degree of integration, such as the American culture, have many elements that do not fit well together. This is primarily due to the existence of **subcultures,** which are distinctive variations of the larger culture shared by particular groups within the society. There are many subcultures in the United States, each having its own set of customs, belief systems, and artifacts. We can speak, for example, of nationality subcultures (Italian-Americans), religious subcultures (Jews), regional subcultures (the "Southern way of life"), and so on. Socialization for the individual in a culture with a low degree of integration is often a confusing process that produces conflict and insecurity. The son of first-generation Italian-American parents is taught to be demonstrative in showing affection for both males and females. He learns that it is proper to show affection for another male by giving him a hug. Later, upon displaying such affection to a friend at school, he is ridiculed by his classmates and becomes profoundly confused. In the long run, he will probably refrain from such behavior displays when interacting with people who are not members of his own subculture. He is likely to be confused and possibly frustrated when faced with the situation of having to determine exactly when or when not to display this trait.

An American Subculture
The Amish are a religious subculture. Although not many today keep a horse and buggy or wear the plain dress, they are bound together by their common heritage.

Sometimes the customs and belief systems of a subculture run directly counter to those of the larger culture. J. Milton Yinger introduced the term **contraculture** to identify such groups.[6] A gang of juvenile delinquents is a good example of a contraculture. Having completely rejected some of the customs and norms of the larger culture, the juvenile delinquent will probably experience severe conflict when punished for his delinquent behavior.

Even if they are not members of contracultures, most people living in a society that has a low degree of cultural integration are likely to be more insecure than their counterparts in highly integrated cultures. Finally, because their configuration is not such a unified whole, cultures with a low degree of integration tend to adapt remarkably well to rapid change.

☐ Cultures as Systems

Whether or not cultures are highly integrated, it is important that we recognize that they are not just collections of unrelated customs and norms. They are single units of linked elements, each tending to have a functional relationship with the others. In short, they are interdependent. In fact, some whole cultures are linked with one another in a *cultural pool* (for example, Western culture, which contains many variations). One way to get a grip on the notion of cultures as systems of interdependent parts is to survey studies of social change. Consider the following example.

In his classic work, *The Study of Man*, Ralph Linton describes what happened to the Tanala, a hill tribe of Madagascar, when a new technological adaptation was introduced into their culture.[7] The Tanala originally subsisted by the cultivation of dry rice. Since their land was covered with jungle growth, it had to be cleared for planting. After only a couple of crops, the cleared land had to be abandoned until it was overrun by the jungle again. In this manner, the Tanala exploited the jungle around a village until it was exhausted, and then moved the village to another place. The major organizational units within the villages were joint families (several households connected through a common head). Working as a group, each joint family owned the crops from the land they cleared, although the village as a whole owned all the land. Crops were divided among households by the heads of the joint

A Contraculture
Skinheads accept customs and belief systems that run directly counter to those of the larger culture.

families, and the variation in wealth from family to family was small. The Tanala had operated in this cooperative fashion for many years. When they began to adopt wet rice cultivation from a neighboring tribe, several drastic changes took place.

To begin with, we should point out that wet rice cultivation allows continuous use of the land. At first it was done on relatively small plots, so only single households cultivated a single plot. Thus the amount of interaction within families was restricted, and the land and rice grown in it became linked into a single trait in the minds of the people. Before long, the notion of exclusive ownership of land developed. Also, because the amount of suitable land was limited, there developed two distinct classes—landholders and landless. Wet rice cultivators refused to help dry rice cultivators in their jungle clearing efforts. Moreover, they did not want the villages to be moved. The dry rice cultivators had to move so far into the jungle that they could not return to the village at night; hence they, too, developed separate household organizations. Other changes included alteration of the marriage and kinship systems, new warfare practices, the growth of a centralized, autocratic authority, and—the introduction of slavery!

The case of the Tanala clearly reveals the systematic nature of culture. A change in one element (food technology) set off a chain reaction in which the whole social system was eventually transformed. This particular case is also an excellent example of what may happen to a highly integrated culture when change is introduced into it.

☐ Headshakes and Chuckles Revisited

At the beginning of this chapter, we suggested that Americans would react to a news release from Kampala, Uganda, with headshakes and chuckles. We also suggested that the culture concept could account for such a reaction. Will it? Let's do a little analysis and see. The article reads as follows: "When President Idi Amin ordered the traditionally nude Karamojans to cover themselves, tribal conservatives forced some of those who obeyed to eat their new clothes as a penance."

The article implies a conflict between a subculture (the Karamojans) and the larger society. In this case customs (the Karamojans traditionally go nude), norms (the Karamojans have believed in the past that it is correct or right behavior to go nude), and artifacts (clothes) are involved. The Karamojans are a highly integrated group that has elaborated the trait of nudity within their complexes and patterns. The threatened change (ordering them to wear clothes) has directly challenged part of their way of life (nudity) and has caused considerable strife within the group. The article further implies that those who were forced to eat clothes ultimately rejected the president's order in favor of retaining traditional ways. Thus the Karamojans seem to be acting as a

contraculture. The action of the tribal conservatives indicates that they are aware that change in one element of the culture may lead to change in other parts as well. It is obvious that the tribal conservatives are strongly opposed to such change, as indicated by their rather drastic action of forcing people to eat clothes.

The foregoing analysis may give you a better understanding of the culture concept, but it still does not account for headshakes and chuckles. In order to understand that reaction, we must understand something about American culture. Although it has a relatively low degree of integration, American culture has elaborated the trait of wearing clothes. A nude man walking down the street of an American city is so unusual that it invariably causes a great deal of commotion. In addition, a nude man is invariably arrested by the police, indicating a flagrant violation of the norms. Having established that Karamojan and American customs and norms regarding the wearing of clothes are directly opposed to each other, we need an understanding of one more concept, "ethnocentrism," to account for the headshake and chuckle reaction.

Ethnocentrism is the attitude of valuing one's own culture, while at the same time, devaluing others. It is a feeling of cultural superiority. To comprehend our definition of ethnocentrism better, it is necessary to define two other concepts—attitude and value. An **attitude** is a person's learned predisposition to act in a given way in a given situation. Knowing a person's attitude toward something allows us to predict how that person will act in specific circumstances. If we know, for instance, that

Clyde has a strongly suspicious attitude toward anyone who exercises authority, we can predict that he will not trust his Marine drill instructor. Attitudes are based on beliefs that ultimately rest on values.

A **value** is an idea of what is intrinsically desirable. That is, its desirability is self-evident to the person who holds it. Freedom, courage, and friendship are examples of values. One may justify one's beliefs by pointing out that they rest upon the value of freedom, but one does not have to justify freedom; it, in itself, is desirable. When we speak of ethnocentrism, then, we are speaking of a person's learned predisposition to treat his or her culture as the best, and to treat other cultures as intrinsically inferior to his or her own. This does *not* mean treating *every* aspect of one's own culture as superior to *every* aspect of other cultures. It means treating the totality of one's own culture as superior to other whole cultures.

Americans who react to the newspaper article with headshakes and chuckles are displaying ethnocentrism. Their snickers carry the implication that Karamojan culture is inferior to American culture. The fact that they merely snicker rather than display some form of outrage indicates that they do not consider the Karamojan actions a threat to American life. Whether American reactions in this case are mild or strong, they represent ethnocentrism nevertheless.

Social scientists try diligently to avoid ethnocentrism. They try to uphold the scientific attitude. They try to approach cultures with a respect for cultural differences. Such an approach is embodied in the term **cultural relativity** (some prefer to call it "cultural relativism"). This *does not* mean that all cultures or customs are equally good, or even good. Remember that culture is local, created, and changing, all of which implies a responsibility on the part of a society for the social themes it elaborates. Cultural relativity does mean judging cultures on their own terms. It means that we should "put ourselves in the other guy's shoes" before we make judgments about his behavior. Historians learned long ago that such a view is indispensable to understanding history. All of us should strive for cultural relativity in our attempt to understand human behavior.

REFERENCES

1. *Miami Herald*, July 7, 1971, p. 7B.
2. Stuart Chase, *The Proper Study of Mankind* (New York: Harper & Brothers, 1956), pp. 84–85.
3. Clyde Kluckhohn, *Mirror for Man* (New York: McGraw-Hill, 1949).
4. See Ruth Benedict, *Patterns of Culture* (Boston: Houghton Mifflin, 1934), Ch. 2.
5. *Ibid.*, p. 31.

6. J. Milton Yinger, "Contraculture and Subculture," *American Sociological Review,* 25 (October 1969), 625–635.
7. Ralph Linton, *The Study of Man* (New York: Appleton-Century-Crofts, 1936), pp. 348–355.

GLOSSARY

Culture	A way of life; a social heritage that is learned and shared by a human group.
Customs	Group habits; the usual ways of real behavior for the group. For example, it is customary in American society for people to wear clothes in public, while the opposite is true for Karamojans.
Belief systems	The mental components of culture, the learned and shared ideas that describe, explain, and give meaning and purpose to life. Included within belief systems are religious, magical, and normative or ethical prescriptions for conduct.
Artifacts	The objects that a society produces and uses, including the tools that are used to produce other objects. The ballpoint pen, for instance, is a widely used artifact in contemporary American society.
Cultural traits	The simplest elements of culture. The determination of whether or not a concrete or abstract unit of meaning is a trait is dependent upon how it is treated in a social context, not on some objective quality of the trait itself.
Cultural complex	A number of interrelated traits. A chalkboard and chalk are two of the traits that constitute the traditional classroom learning complex in American society.
Cultural pattern	Interrelated sets of complexes. Classroom learning and homework are two of the complexes that constitute the traditional pattern of public school education in American society.
Social institutions	Distinctive patterns that are centered around major human needs and accompanied by particular modes of social interaction. In this book, we treat social institutions as societal subsystems. Example: education, or the education system.
Cultural integration	The "fit" or coming together of traits, complexes, and patterns into a meaningful whole. There is great consistency in the values underlying social institutions in cultures that have a high degree of integration.

Ethos	The characteristic quality of a culture. The ethos of the Zuni, for example, includes moderation, whereas the ethos of Americans includes intense competitiveness.
Attitude	Learned predisposition of an individual to act in a given way in a given situation. If, for instance, your attitude toward learning is positive, then you will work hard to master the concepts presented in this book.
Value	An idea of what is intrinsically desirable. Example: freedom.
Ethnocentrism	The attitude of valuing one's own culture, while at the same time, devaluing others. The ethnocentric person believes his or her group is "best."
Cultural relativity	An attitude of respect for cultural differences; judging cultures on their own terms. Some social scientists prefer to use the term "cultural relativism" to describe this concept.
Group	A set of three or more persons who interact with one another and share some joint activities. A single network of relationships connects the interactions of group members. Example: a college sorority.
Interaction	The process by which communicating individuals influence each other's thoughts and actions. Some social scientists now prefer to use the term "transaction" instead of interaction.
Society	A self-sufficient and self-perpetuating group which includes persons of both sexes and all ages.
Socialization	The process of learning the content of a culture.
Anthropology	The "study of man." Anthropology is divided into two major divisions—physical and cultural—each containing several subdivisions. Physical anthropology is primarily concerned with genetically transmitted characteristics; cultural anthropology is concerned with socially learned traits.
Subculture	A distinctive culture shared by a particular group within a society. Members of subcultures participate in the way of life of both the larger society and their own subgroup. Example: Orthodox Jews.

Contraculture	A subculture with customs or belief systems that run directly counter to those of the larger culture. Example: the Mafia.

SELECTED READING

Benedict, R. *Patterns of Culture* (Boston: Houghton Mifflin, 1934). Benedict's classic comparative study of three cultures.

Hunter, J. D. *Culture Wars: The Struggle to Define America* (New York: Basic Books, 1991). An examination of the increasing conflict between moral traditionalists and cultural progressives concerning basic values in American culture.

Jankowski, M. S. *Islands in the Street: Gangs and American Urban Society* (Berkeley: University of California Press, 1991). An interesting consideration of gangs in the United States.

Kephart, W. M. *Extraordinary Groups: An Examination of Unconventional Life-Styles*, 4th ed. (New York: St. Martin's Press, 1990). A look at various subcultures in the United States.

Langness, L. L. *The Study of Culture*, rev. ed. (Novato, Calif.: Chandler and Sharp, 1987). A historical survey of theory in the study of culture.

Lipset, S. M. *Continental Divide: The Values and Institutions of the United States and Canada* (New York: Routledge, 1990). A comparison of the cultures of the United States and Canada.

Moffat, M. *Coming of Age in New Jersey: College and American Culture* (New Brunswick, N.J.: Rutgers University Press, 1989). An examination of college campus culture in the United States.

QUESTIONS

1. Which of the following is *not* a social institution?
   a. education
   b. economy
   c. society
   d. religion
   e. family

2. What do all cultural patterns have in common?
   a. They are made up of interrelated complexes.
   b. They are followed by everyone in the society.
   c. They are used by all the subcultures.

    d. They are feelings about what is good and evil.

    e. They are not followed by everyone in the society.

3. Which of the following statements is correct?
   a. All societies possess a culture.
   b. Most societies possess a culture.
   c. Only primitive societies possess a culture.
   d. Only *some* primitive societies possess a culture.
   e. Only modern societies possess a culture.

4. Socialization teaches people to understand
   a. their genetically transmitted characteristics.
   b. the objects that a society produces and uses.
   c. how to satisfy their universal needs through their social heritage.
   d. why socialism is the best way of life.
   e. how primitive tribes are able to cope with the environment.

5. What is the name of the science that studies human groups and socially learned traits?
   a. physical anthropology
   b. ethos
   c. subcultures
   d. cultural anthropology
   e. aggregate

6. The elaboration of cultural themes leads to the formation of
   a. traits.
   b. social systems.
   c. values.
   d. customs.
   e. norms.

7. Which of the following statements made by an American is an example of ethnocentrism?
   a. Americans are hard workers.
   b. I like baseball.
   c. Americans are just as good as Russians.
   d. Americans are better than Russians.
   e. I don't like Russians.

8. Society may *best* be defined as a
   a. set of persons who share something in common but do not interact with one another.
   b. set of persons who interact with one another and share some joint activities.
   c. self-sufficient and self-perpetuating group which includes persons of both sexes and all ages.

     d. group of people who regard their culture as superior to all others.

     e. group of people who live and work together.

9. The term used to describe an attitude of respect for cultural differences is

     a. ethnocentrism.

     b. cultural respect.

     c. contraculture.

     d. cultural relativity.

     e. aggregates.

10. Distinctive variations of the larger culture shared by particular groups within the society are called

     a. subcultures.

     b. patterns.

     c. minicultures.

     d. customs.

     e. aggregates.

QUESTIONS FOR THOUGHT AND DISCUSSION

1. Is culture really necessary?

2. Is there such a thing as cultural superiority?

3. What are the functional and dysfunctional aspects of subcultures in American society?

4

Language, Beliefs, and Values

All of us are involved in a collective search for meaning in life, and our culture is the medium through which this search is conducted. Culture provides a basis for common understandings and cooperation among people in society. It dictates that we and others like us who learn and share the same social heritage will have basically the same initial outlook on life, that all of us will think, feel, and act, at least initially, in a similar manner. In this chapter we will examine those cohesive aspects that constitute the core of culture, and that shed light along the path of the collective search for meaning: language, beliefs, and values.

☐ Language

Language is the most pervasive aspect of culture. It is our means of identifying objects and ideas, expressing our thoughts, and transmitting our culture. Certainly, we could learn some aspects of culture—how to drive a car, for instance—simply by observing someone driving a car. But, just as certainly, we could not transmit belief systems without the use of language. In short, without language, culture would not be possible. It's no wonder Stuart Chase refers to language as "the most important [universal need] of all."

Language may be defined as a system of symbols that have agreed-upon meanings in a given human population. To understand what language is and how it functions, we must know something about symbols. A **symbol** is something which stands for something else, and which causes us to think about the thing being symbolized. The word "computer" is a symbol; it may stand for a specific object or for the idea of a computer. Words are the most commonly thought of symbols, but objects or actions may also be symbolic: a medal might stand for an act of bravery; or the shaking of a clenched fist might stand for anger. Unless they are within the context of a system, however, symbols are not considered part of a language.

On the other hand, there could be neither language nor culture without the **symbolic process.** It is the symbolic process (the process of arbitrarily ascribing meanings) that separates man from other creatures on the earth. The noted semanticist S. I. Hayakawa says, "Animals struggle with each other for food or for leadership, but they do not, like human beings, struggle with each other for things that *stand for* food or leadership."[1]

One of the interesting and important things about symbols is that we can, by agreement, make anything stand for anything. For example, we could agree that *A* stands for pencils and *B* stands for pens; then we could change the agreement to let *A* stand for redheads and *B* stand for blonds; or let *A* stand for China and *B* stand for Russia, and so forth. The point is that we are free to assign whatever meaning we choose to our symbols. In fact, we can make symbols that stand for symbols. We could, if we so desired, let *K* stand for all the *A*'s in our example and let *L* stand for all the *B*'s. If we wanted to, we could make another symbol, *Z*, stand for *K* and *L* (a symbol of symbols of symbols). As you can see, the symbolic process operates on many different levels and is quite sophisticated.

We see the symbolic process at work all around us, and in all cultures. Servants and kings, priests and medicine men, warriors and the police all wear costumes that symbolize their occupations. Pins, buttons, ribbons, or tattoos can stand for social affiliations. Brass rings or pieces of paper can stand for wealth. Through what Thorstein Veblen called conspicuous consumption (for example, buying expensive things just to show others that one has the economic resources to buy such expensive things), the wealthy classes symbolize that they do not have to work for a living and "the not-so-wealthy, by imitating these symbols of wealth, symbolize their conviction that, even if they do work for a living, they are just as good as anybody else."[2]

Sometimes we treat symbols as though they were the things they stand for. But, as we have pointed out, there is no necessary connection between the symbol and what is symbolized. We can, by agreement, arbitrarily make anything stand for anything. When we who speak English hear the sound *horse*, we experience the image in our minds of a four-legged animal that actors ride in Western movies. The reason for this is that we have agreed that the sound *horse* stands for that animal. There is nothing about the animal that requires or even suggests that we symbolize it by the sound *horse*. We could just as well have agreed to symbolize that animal by the sound *borfo*, or *mondu*, or *spid*, or even

The Symbolic Process
Pizza Joe's hat is an unmistakable symbol of his occupation.

cow, or *railroad,* or *toe* for that matter. But we haven't agreed to call it *borfo;* we've agreed to call it *horse.* And for some of us the connection between the symbol and what is symbolized has become so strong that we can't separate the two. It sounds absurd to us, for example, to hear someone make the sound *caballo* when referring to that animal; but *caballo* is perfectly natural to a Spanish-speaking person.

Sometimes we seem to value the symbol more than what it stands for. A good example of this is the story of the man being tried for the murder of a young radical. When asked why he killed the young radical, the man replied, "It was bad enough listening to him denounce this country and everything it stands for, but when he put that match to the flag, I just couldn't take it anymore." Apparently, this man valued a symbol (the flag) more than he valued another man's life. The flag had great meaning for him. Symbols, then, help give meaning to our existence, and that is why we covet them so much in our search for meaning in life. "In one way or another, we are all like the brilliant student who cheats on his exams in order to make Phi Beta Kappa: it is so much more important to have the symbol than the thing it stands for."[3]

Kinds of Symbols

Symbols can be classified as being *referential* (concrete) or *expressive* (abstract). **Referential symbols** are those which denote or refer to real objects in the external world. The word *table* is a referential symbol: it refers to an object or a class of objects whose existence in the external world can be verified. If someone asks you what a table is, you can simply point to a table. **Expressive symbols,** on the other hand, refer to objects or events that cannot be verified in the external world. The meanings they convey are often emotional and highly personal. The word *God* is an expressive symbol. To some it may evoke feelings of love and brotherhood; to others it may evoke fear; to still others it may carry no particular emotional meaning. Some symbols, of course, are both referential and expressive. The word *father,* for example, refers to a male parent; however, to any particular person it may express authority, understanding, love, discipline, or knowledge.

Expressive symbols are particularly important to culture because they contribute to social cohesion. This is most obvious in the performance of **ritual** (a series of symbolic acts that are repeated on ceremonial occasions). Through ritual we reaffirm our group membership. Ritual activities such as singing *The Star-Spangled Banner,* repeating "The Pledge of Allegiance," or participating in religious services or in pep rallies are not designed to give us new information or to create new ways of feeling. They function to reaffirm group membership and strengthen social solidarity. If we were to observe the secret initiation rites of a college fraternity, we might hear a series of nonsense sounds that would have no referential meaning either for us or for the fraternity members. These sounds would not have any expressive meaning for us either, but they *would* have expressive meaning for the group members: they would be expressing unity and brotherhood. Thus expressive sym-

Ritual
Ritual activities such as singing the "Star-Spangled Banner" prior to the beginning of a baseball game provide confirmation of group membership and strengthen social solidarity.

bols convey emotional and highly personal meanings that contribute to social cohesion, and provide a sense of belonging for the individual.

When children are born, they have no symbols to work with. Very soon they begin to associate certain sounds with particular objects or actions. They may find that every time they squeal a certain way their mother comes to them. In this manner, they learn to communicate by means of making sounds. At this rudimentary level their symbolic action is no different from that of other higher animals. We know that many animals communicate by means of making sounds. Often such communication seems to be part of a cooperative effort to help the species survive. A baboon, for example, can express feelings of danger to other baboons by making certain sounds. In fact, there is a report of a fairly large group of wild baboons in Nairobi Park, Kenya, who, at one time, could be approached easily by car.[4] But when two of them were shot from a car, the group could not be approached by car even as late as eight months after the shooting incident. Since it is unlikely that all group members witnessed the murder, we may infer that the baboons that did see the murder learned that cars were potentially fatal, and they communicated that danger to the rest of the group.

Human beings, however, are much more sophisticated than baboons in their use of symbols. Human infants have the capacity to learn a whole system of symbols or many systems of symbols that have specific and arbitrary meanings. Their first (native) language is the one

"Spread the word. The people are coming!"

their society has chosen as its own. Language enables them not only to report events but also to report reports. That is, when a baboon shrieks, it may cause another baboon to shriek in imitation or alarm; the second shriek, as far as we know, is not about the first shriek. But when your roommate says, "I'm going to study," you can report to a third party, "My roommate says he's going to study."

Sounds, as we have seen, are indispensable to language. But not all languages contain all the sounds human beings are capable of making. "The unique quality of any language is that it includes only a small set of distinct sounds derived from the potential range of sounds."[5] A normal human infant is capable of uttering, and does in fact utter, many sounds that are not used by the adult members of his or her society. As they grow older, children learn to distinguish sounds that are appropriate to the language of their society from those that are not. They learn to make new sounds that they did not utter as infants and to forget those that are not appropriate. There is some evidence to suggest that they even lose the ability to produce some sounds.[6] This would explain the difficulty encountered by English-speaking persons when they try to pronounce correctly some words from other languages, say, French; or the difficulty of Japanese-speaking persons when they try to pronounce correctly the English words *claw, lollipop,* or *election.*

An analysis of language reveals that we select not only sounds to be included in our communication systems but also objects and actions to be symbolized. In other words, the various languages of the world are not merely systems of sounds and names that stand for the same underlying reality: they describe different views of reality. For us, war is a very real thing (just ask any combat veteran or the parents of a young man killed in battle), but for the Eskimos it does not exist. They have no notion of war; consequently, there is no word for war in the Eskimo languages. On the other hand, snow is an extremely important part of the environment in which Eskimos live; therefore, they have several words for snow, while we have only one.

The selective aspect of language, however, extends to more than just choosing sounds to stand for preexisting objects and actions. To a great extent language determines the kinds of objects and actions we experience. It restricts both the kinds of messages we can convey and the kinds we can conceive. Language does these things by structuring our process of perception.

Language and Perception

Perception refers to the awareness of aspects of the environment. Perception is always limited and selective. That is, your senses cannot possibly "take in" all that is going on out there in the external world at any given time. The most you can experience at any given time is only a fraction of what is actually happening. Your perception, therefore, is limited to what you select to be aware of. For example, right now you are sitting or standing somewhere reading this book. You are probably aware only of the idea you are presently concentrating on. If, however, we direct your attention to the weight of the book in your hands, you will temporarily lose the continuity of your thought. You will find that it is difficult, if not impossible, to concentrate at the same time on both the ideas contained in the book and the weight of the book itself. Certainly you will agree that the book always has had the quality of weight, but when you were concentrating on its ideas you were not consciously aware of the book's weight. And so it is with other aspects of your immediate environment. There are literally hundreds of events occurring around you right now that you are not perceiving. The perceptual process, then, is a selective process.

By sensitizing people to particular aspects of both the internal and the external world, language structures their perception. We can see this clearly when we compare the grammars of different languages. The Hopi Indian language, for example, emphasizes *validity* in conjugating its verbs.[7] In describing an action the Hopi must indicate whether he or she is reporting a direct experience, a belief or expectation, or a generalization about experience. The verb chosen to describe an action will communicate the nature of the evidence that is the basis for the report, but it will not specify when the action takes place. Conversely, the English language emphasizes *tense* in conjugating its verbs; the speaker always indicates whether the action is part of the past, present, or future. As you might guess, the Hopi is more conscious of validating sources of information than the English-speaking person, and the English-speaking person is more conscious of time than the Hopi.

In fact, time consciousness seems to be such a part of the English language that we treat words for time the same as we do words for material objects. This leads us to such concepts as "buying time," "saving time," or "time is money," which, in turn, lead us to emphasize speed and hurrying. In English, then, the clock *runs*, "but in Spanish *el reloj anda*, 'he walks.' This simple difference has enormous implications. If clocks run, there isn't a minute to lose! If they walk, we can take our time."[8] There is, of course, a great deal of evidence to suggest that people of different cultures conceive of time differently. For example, there seems to be no single word in the language of the Kachin people of North Burma that corresponds to the English word *time*.[9] The Kachin have several partial equivalents of *time*, each differing from the others:

The *time* by the clock is	ahkying
A long *time*	na
A short *time*	tawng
The present *time*	ten
Spring *time*	ta

The *time* has come	hkra
In the *time* of Queen Victoria	lakhtak, aprat
At any *time* of life	asak

The example above suggests that the Kachin may be even more time conscious than we are!

Our conceptions of other aspects of experience are also rooted in language. Anthropologist Edward T. Hall speaks of a learned "silent language" which structures our perceptions of space, play activities, and sexuality, as well as time.[10] He points out, for instance, that a comfortable distance for interaction in Latin America is much less than it is in the United States.[11]

Language Conveys Culture

An event described in the Cherokee language represents a different reality from the same event described in medieval Latin. Language and culture both reflect and shape each other.

[Latin Americans] cannot talk comfortably with one another unless they are very close to the distance that evokes either sexual or hostile feelings in the North American. The result is that when they move close, we withdraw and back away. As a consequence, they think we are distant or cold, withdrawn and unfriendly. We, on the other hand, are constantly accusing them of breathing down our necks, crowding us, and spraying our faces.

The reason the Latin American and the North American react differently is because each has been taught a "silent language" that structures the perception of space differently from the other.

Language, then, shapes our experience. To a great extent it determines how and what we will think. In this fashion it serves as a guide to social reality. Although he may be overstating the case somewhat, Edward Sapir seems to be striking a chord of truth when he says that human beings "are very much at the mercy of the particular language which has become the medium of expression for their society.... No two languages are ever sufficiently similar to be considered as representing the same social reality. The worlds in which different societies live are distinct worlds, not merely the same world with different labels attached."[12]

Language is the vehicle through which we know our world. As we have seen, language structures our perception of reality and gives meaning to our experiences; through it, we identify objects and ideas, and we express our thoughts. It allows us to accumulate vast stores of knowledge, and to transmit culture from one generation to the next. Language is at the very core of culture. It is the foundation upon which the cooperation necessary for human survival is based. It is one of the cohesive bonds that unite people together, hold culture together, and coordinate the efforts of people in society. And, in Hayakawa's words, "this coordination of effort necessary for the functioning of society is *of necessity achieved by language or else it is not achieved at all.*"[13]

☐   Beliefs and Values

Beliefs and values, like language, are at the core of culture. In fact, as our discussion of language has suggested, some of our most fundamental beliefs and values are intimately related to language. Talcott Parsons has emphasized this intimate relationship by pointing out that people could not possibly communicate consistently and effectively unless they had learned approximately the same sets of beliefs and values as well as symbols.[14] In order to penetrate the core of culture, then, we must gain an understanding of the nature of beliefs and values.

Beliefs are based on perception. That is, one has a belief when one perceives a relationship between two things, or between one thing and a characteristic of it. For example, you believe that this book has the quality of weight, that you are alive, that you understand the English language, that learning has some positive value, and that you are presently reading this book. You might also believe that progress is good, that rotten potatoes smell bad, and that we are in the midst of a serious environmental crisis. Collectively, your beliefs represent your understanding of yourself and your environment.

Some of your beliefs, of course, are the result of direct experience. If you ask yourself why you believe this book has the quality of weight, you will answer that you have held it in your hands, and it feels like it has the quality of weight. You would probably not feel the need to explain your belief any further. Other beliefs are more complicated, and seem to rest on more than just direct sensory experience. If you ask yourself why you believe that we are in the midst of a serious environmental crisis, for example, you might reply by citing statistics concerning the rate of air, water, and soil pollution that, taken together, logically lead to the conclusion that we are in the midst of such a crisis. If, however, you further ask yourself why you believe those statistics are correct, you might answer that you read them in books which your teacher said were reliable sources. Then you could ask yourself why you believe what your teacher said, and so on.

The point is that by asking yourself such questions you will find that all your beliefs ultimately rest upon one of two fundamental beliefs: a belief that your own sensory experience is correct; or a belief that some external authority is correct. These beliefs are so fundamental that we accept them without question. We will refer to them as **primitive beliefs.**[15]

Types of Primitive Beliefs

One type of primitive belief is a **zero-order belief.** It is a belief that is learned in childhood and continuously validated by experience throughout the person's life. Zero-order beliefs are so basic to our view of life, that we are not only unaware that *they* exist but also we are usually unaware that *alternatives* to them *could* exist. Some examples of zero-order beliefs are: a belief in the credibility of our sensory experience; a belief that objects continue to exist even when we are not looking at them; and, a belief that we are alive.

A second type of primitive belief is a **first-order belief.** It is a belief that is inferred from a zero-order belief, although we are usually unaware of the process by which it is inferred. In fact, we are usually unaware that we have made an inference. Consider the following **syllogism** (argument or form of reasoning in which two statements or premises are made and a logical conclusion is drawn from them):

Major Premise: My senses tell me that this book has weight.
Minor Premise: My senses tell me true.
    Conclusion: Therefore, this book has weight.

Earlier, when you asked yourself why you believed this book has the quality of weight, you were probably unaware of using such a syllogistic argument because you took the minor premise for granted—it is a zero-order belief. You were only conscious of the major premise (My senses tell me that this book has weight) and the conclusion (this book has weight), which, as you can see, are psychologically synonymous with each other. Although we are not usually aware of the process by which first-order beliefs are inferred, we are usually aware of our first-order beliefs, and we can easily imagine alternatives to them (the book could be weightless—if we were in space it would be). This first-order belief is based on the zero-order belief in the credibility of your senses.

Other first-order beliefs may be based on zero-order beliefs in the credibility of an external authority. For example, you might believe that the Bible is the word of God. This belief would be expressed in the conclusion of the following syllogism:

> My religion tells me that the Bible is the word of God.
> My religion tells me true.
> Therefore, the Bible is the word of God.

First-Order Belief
Faith in the efficacy of prayer is itself based on the zero-order belief in the credibility of an external authority—i.e., God.

Your belief that the Bible is the word of God would be based on your implicit belief in the credibility of your religion. Most religious beliefs are such first-order beliefs based on zero-order faith in the validity of some external authority. It might be useful for you to make a list of, say, twenty of your own first-order beliefs. By doing this, you can get a grasp on just where your most basic beliefs stem from.

We'll help you get started. If someone were to ask you when you were born, you would, no doubt, reply by stating a particular date, say May 1, 1975. After all, you do know your own birth date. But just what makes you believe that you were born on May 1, 1975? Both zero-order and first-order beliefs are primitive beliefs based on the credibility of either our own sensory experience or some external authority, and they are so basic that we take them for granted.

Effects of Experience on Beliefs

Most of our primitive beliefs are not the product of a single experience. They are usually generalizations based on a continuous stream of experiences over a period of time. Your own experiences, for instance, might lead you to believe that mathematics is difficult to understand. But many people find that mathematics is easy for them to understand. What is true for you may not be generally true for other people. We are suggesting that generalizations may sometimes be false when applied to instances which are beyond the sets of experiences upon which the generalizations are based. Is it really true that mathematics is difficult to understand (that is, that everyone has difficulty understanding mathematics)?

The process of treating generalizations as though they were universally true is called **stereotyping.** You may have a stereotyped image of athletes as being large and physically powerful individuals; or, you may have a stereotype of Swedes as having blond hair and blue eyes. Stereotyping is a useful process in that it helps us to avoid chaos by dividing our experiential world into meaningful and manageable units or categories. Stereotyping is a necessity because it is impossible to treat every person or situation as though it were unique. In fact, it is impossible to think without stereotypes. What we have to guard against are rigid stereotypes—those which are not subject to change. Rather, it makes good sense to formulate "working stereotypes," which may be altered by new experiences. If our limited contact with athletes has always been with large and powerful individuals, we will have a working stereotype of athletes as being large and powerful individuals. But if our experience brings us in contact with a jockey, we should alter our "athlete" stereotype. If we have been taught, and we believe as universally true, that all Jews are stingy, and then we come in contact with a generous Jew, we should alter our "Jewish" stereotype. (As opposed to the rigid stereotyper, who might reply, "Well, jockeys aren't *really*

athletes," or "He's probably not *all* Jewish," and so forth.) It is important to remember that stereotypes, like other generalizations, are primitive beliefs that seem to the individuals holding them to be self-evident truths, and that they are rooted in learned needs (for example, maintaining a particular self-image).

As children grow older, they learn that their senses cannot always be trusted, and that external authorities are not always correct (you may even be able to recall the first time you became aware that your parents, who "knew everything," were wrong about something). When this happens, they begin to structure **higher-order beliefs**—those in which the credibility of our senses or an authority is not taken for granted. For example,

> My doctor says that smoking can cause heart attacks.
> My doctor is a trustworthy expert.
> Therefore, smoking can cause heart attacks.

Notice that the major premise and the conclusion are not treated as being synonymous because the minor premise is not a zero-order belief. We are aware that the doctor might be wrong. The conclusion, therefore, is a higher-order belief which rests on a series of other beliefs. Some higher-order beliefs have an extensive series of other beliefs supporting them. Remember, however, that all beliefs ultimately can be shown to rest upon zero-order beliefs.

Many of our beliefs are **evaluative beliefs;** that is, they are based on our conception of the relative desirability of something. Evaluative beliefs, therefore, are ultimately based on values. Consider the following series of arguments:

> A job promotion will bring me more money.
> More money is desirable.
> Therefore, a job promotion is desirable.

But, why is more money desirable?

> More money would allow me to retire early.
> Early retirement is desirable.
> Therefore, more money is desirable.

But, why is early retirement desirable?

> Early retirement would allow me to begin painting soon.
> Painting is desirable.
> Therefore, early retirement is desirable.

But, why is painting desirable?

> Painting would help me attain self-fulfillment.
> Self-fulfillment is desirable.
> Therefore, painting is desirable.

But, why is self-fulfillment desirable? Self-fulfillment is desirable because . . . because . . . because it simply *is* desirable. At this point, no further syllogistic argument could be made because self-fulfillment is not a means to an end; it is an end in itself. Self-fulfillment is intrinsically desirable; it is a **value.**

It is possible, of course, for one person's evaluative belief to be another's value. In the first syllogism in the above series of arguments, for example, the statement "More money is desirable" is an evaluative belief which ultimately rests upon the value of self-fulfillment. However, it is possible that an individual who is asked the question "Why is money desirable?" might reply that money is desirable because it is an end in itself: that its desirability is intrinsically self-evident. As we can readily see, it would be fruitless to question this individual any further because the person's response indicates that money is one of his or her values. Thus values are always at the base of evaluative beliefs.

Like the words of a language, beliefs and values are parts of a system. That is, each culture has its own system of beliefs and values. This does not mean that all the people in a given society accept all the beliefs and values that are expressed in that society. (After all, all the people of a given society do not use all the words that are expressed in that society's language, do they?) It means that there are certain beliefs and values that are learned and shared by most members of each society. Some beliefs and values are more central to a culture's belief system than others. In highly integrated cultures, we can see that most behavior is reflective of such central beliefs and values. In Zuni culture, for example, most behavior can be explained as being reflective of the value of moderation.[16]

> The ideal man in Zuni is a person of dignity and affability who has never tried to lead, and who has never called forth comment from his neighbours. Any conflict, even though all right is on his side, is held against him. Even in contests of skill like their foot-races, if a man wins habitually he is debarred from running.

The Zuni have elaborated the value of moderation to such a great extent that it is expressed in their religious ceremonies, economic affairs, ceremonial dances, funeral rites, and domestic situations—including marriage, the disciplining of children, and even their sex lives.

Because of its large number of subcultures, American society, like others with relatively low degrees of cultural integration, expresses a great diversity of beliefs and values. Some beliefs, of course, are difficult to reconcile with others; for instance, a belief in science and a belief in witchcraft. Science is supported by most Americans, while witchcraft is not. The vast majority of Americans may tolerate a belief in witchcraft by a few individuals, but witchcraft, unlike science, is not central to the American system of beliefs and values. On the other hand, beliefs and values that are central may be given a higher or lower priority by individuals or groups within the society. For example, one study reveals that while most Americans place a relatively high value on both freedom and equality, some individuals and even groups tend to place a substantially higher priority on one than on the other.[17]

Whether expressed in a highly or loosely integrated culture, beliefs and values, like language, draw people closer together. Language, beliefs, and values are at the core of culture, and, together, they provide the base for people's common understandings of what is and what ought to be.

REFERENCES

1. S. I. Hayakawa, *Language in Thought and Action*, 2nd ed. (New York: Harcourt, Brace & World, 1963), p. 23.
2. *Ibid.*, p. 25.
3. *Ibid.*, p. 29.
4. See Wendell H. Oswalt, *Understanding Our Culture* (New York: Holt, Rinehart and Winston, 1970), p. 62.
5. *Ibid.*, p. 66.
6. See Robert B. Taylor, *Cultural Ways* (Boston: Allyn and Bacon, 1969), p. 41.
7. See Benjamin Lee Whorf, *Language, Thought and Reality* (New York: Wiley, 1956), p. 217. First published in 1940.

8. Stuart Chase, *The Proper Study of Mankind* (New York: Harper & Brothers, 1956), p. 97.

9. See E. R. Leach, *Rethinking Anthropology* (London, England: University of London, The Athlone Press, 1966), p. 124.

10. Edward T. Hall, *The Silent Language* (Garden City, N.Y.: Doubleday, 1959).

11. *Ibid.*, p. 209.

12. Edward Sapir, "The Status of Linguistics as a Science," in David G. Mandelbaum, ed., *Selected Writings of Edward Sapir* (Berkeley and Los Angeles: University of California Press, 1958), p. 162.

13. Hayakawa, p. 15.

14. See Talcott Parsons, *The Social System* (New York: The Free Press, 1951).

15. This typology of beliefs is taken from Daryl J. Bem, *Beliefs, Attitudes and Human Affairs* (Belmont, Calif.: Brooks/Cole, 1970), pp. 4–16.

16. Ruth Benedict, *Patterns of Culture* (Boston: Houghton Mifflin, 1934), p. 99.

17. See Milton Rokeach, *Beliefs, Attitudes, and Values* (San Francisco: Jossey-Bass, 1968).

GLOSSARY

Language A system of symbols that have agreed-upon meanings in a given human population.

Symbol Something that stands for something else. Symbols allow us to think about the thing symbolized.

Referential symbols Symbols that denote or refer to real objects in the external world. Example: chair.

Expressive symbols Symbols that refer to objects or events that cannot be verified in the external world. Expressive symbols often convey emotional and highly personal meanings. Example: God.

Symbolic process The process of arbitrarily ascribing meanings.

Ritual A series of symbolic acts that are repeated on ceremonial occasions. For example, traditional wedding ritual in American society includes something old, something new, something borrowed, something blue, the bride dressed in white, throwing rice at the newly married couple, etc.

Beliefs A perceived relationship between two things, or between one thing and a characteristic of it. Example: "The sky is blue."

Primitive beliefs Beliefs based directly on the credibility of either one's own sensory experience or an external authority. Primitive beliefs are so fundamental that we accept them without question.

Zero-order beliefs The most basic primitive beliefs. They are learned in childhood and continuously validated by experience throughout life. We are usually unaware not only of our zero-order beliefs, but also of the fact that alternatives to them could exist. Example: a belief that we are alive.

First-order beliefs	Primitive beliefs that are inferred from zero-order beliefs. We are usually aware of first-order beliefs, and we can easily imagine alternatives to them. Example: a belief that this book has weight.
Higher-order beliefs	Beliefs in which the credibility of our senses or an external authority is not taken for granted. Example: "We are currently in the midst of a serious environmental crisis."
Stereotyping	The process of treating generalizations as though they were universally true. Example: "All women gossip."
Value	An idea of what is intrinsically desirable. Example: justice.
Evaluative beliefs	Beliefs based on the relative desirability of something. They are ultimately based on values. Example: "A job promotion is desirable."
Syllogism	An argument in which two statements or premises are made and a logical conclusion is drawn from them. Example: My senses tell me that this book has weight. My senses tell me true. Therefore, this book has weight.

SELECTED READING

Hayakawa, S. I. *Language in Thought and Action*, 2nd ed. (New York: Harcourt, Brace & World, 1963). A witty and incisive survey of the role language plays in culture.

Klapp, O. E. *Inflation of Symbols: Loss of Values in American Culture* (New Brunswick, N.J.: Transaction, 1991). An explanation of how traditional standards become obsolete through the use of hype and other inflations of language.

Lappé, F. M. *Rediscovering America's Values* (New York: Ballantine Books, 1989). A consideration of core values in the United States.

Sapir, E. *Language: An Introduction to the Study of Speech* (New York: Harcourt Brace Jovanovich, 1949). Sapir's classic introduction to the study of human languages, originally published in 1921.

Snowdon, C. T., C. H. Brown, and M. R. Petersen, eds. *Primate Communication* (New York: Cambridge University Press, 1982). A reader on nonhuman primate communication.

Trudgill, P. *Sociolinguistics: An Introduction to Language and Society*, rev. ed. (New York: Penguin, 1983). An exploration of how one's use of language is related to factors such as sex, social class, and ethnic group.

QUESTIONS

1. One reason that language is important to culture is that language
   a. tends to ensure the survival of the most literate people.
   b. is the means by which we store and transmit knowledge.
   c. is the only element within culture that contributes to social cohesion.
   d. provides us with our most fundamental beliefs.
   e. is necessary for change to occur and without change there is no culture.

2. Which of the following statements about the symbolic process is correct?
   a. Symbols, although useful, are not necessary for language and culture.
   b. Symbols are always more important than what they stand for.
   c. Symbols always refer to real objects in the external world.
   d. Once ascribed to something, a symbol can never be ascribed to something else.
   e. We can, by agreement, arbitrarily make anything stand for anything else.

3. Which of the following is an example of stereotyping?
   a. All horses are animals.
   b. John has a vicious dog.
   c. All women gossip.
   d. I don't like black pepper.
   e. Paul Newman is a good actor.

4. A "silent language" structures our
   a. perception of space.
   b. use of symbols.
   c. basic beliefs.
   d. middle-class culture.
   e. rituals.

5. Words used to denote "concrete" things are
   a. expressive symbols.
   b. perceptive symbols.
   c. referential symbols.
   d. abstract symbols.
   e. basic symbols.

6. When a person perceives a relationship between two things or between one thing and a characteristic of it, we say that the person holds a
   a. stereotype.

   b. value.
   c. symbol.
   d. belief.
   e. language.

7. The expressive symbols used in ritual contribute to
   a. basic beliefs.
   b. syllogisms.
   c. evaluative beliefs.
   d. informative communication.
   e. social cohesion.

8. Evaluative beliefs are always rooted in
   a. language.
   b. symbols.
   c. values.
   d. cultural integration.
   e. the symbolic process.

9. The selective aspect of language deals with
   a. perception.
   b. validity.
   c. images.
   d. rituals.
   e. secondary beliefs.

10. An argument in which two statements are made and a logical conclusion is then drawn from them is
   a. a referential symbol.
   b. an expressive symbol.
   c. a syllogism.
   d. a premise.
   e. a value.

QUESTIONS FOR THOUGHT AND DISCUSSION

1. How do we know what we know?

2. Are humans the only language-bearing animals?

3. Are four-letter words really obscene?

4. What are some of the important culturally determined values in American society?

5

Race and Ethnicity

Individuals and groups differ from one another in many ways, both biologically and culturally. Racial groups are usually defined in biological terms; and ethnic groups share a common culture, among other things. The concepts of race and ethnicity are crucial to any significant understanding of the human experience. In this chapter we will examine both concepts.

☐ Race

As we saw in Chapter 2, **race** refers to a subspecies formed as the result of natural selection working on a geographically isolated population. It is a concept that is often abused as well as misunderstood. Indeed, given the manner in which it has been corrupted by both powerful tyrants and ordinary bigots, one is tempted to agree with Ashley Montagu, who believes that the term is arbitrary, unscientific, and harmful—hence, one that should not be used.[1] However, even if scholars desist from using the term, the public will continue to do so. Furthermore, to claim that races do not exist because people can be placed on a continuum from one extreme to the other for all physical traits without displaying any clear-cut "racial" boundaries is to commit the fallacy known as "the argument of the beard." Although one would be hard pressed to answer the question, "How many whiskers are needed to form a beard?" one can, nevertheless, distinguish whether or not a person is bearded.

The number of races perceived by biologists and anthropologists ranges from two to several hundred, with three, four, five, and nine being the number of categories most widely used by students of human variation. Let us examine the origins of human variation to see if any racial classification is valid.

The main reason for differences in physical appearance among our ancestors, from whom we inherited our physical appearances, is successful adaptation to local environments. Since environments differed with respect to temperature, altitude, topography, humidity, and available food supply, and in various other ways, different physical traits were conducive to survival in different locations. Conversely, other traits were nonadaptive, and people who had them died without reproducing. Given the tendency in nature toward extreme variability, something resembling the full range of genes exists in all populations. However, the frequency of traits varies according to the local environment. Formerly impenetrable barriers such as mountains, deserts, forests, and oceans isolated human populations from each other for many thousands of years, thus allowing natural selection to create racial differences.

☐ Racial Types

The most popularly used racial classification divides people into the Caucasoid, Negroid, and Mongoloid races (so-called whites, blacks, and yellows, respectively). Statistically speaking, Caucasoids have the lightest skin and eyes; the most body hair; long thin noses; light-colored, wavy hair that grays or falls out in middle age; bony features; long heads; and medium to tall, slender bodies with long limbs.

Negroids have dark skin, eyes, and hair; hair that is wooly and less likely to fall out in old age; short, wide noses; thick protruding lips; less body hair than Caucasoids; round heads; and medium to tall bodies with long limbs.

Mongoloids have yellowish-tan skin and are stocky and short-limbed. They have thick, straight, coarse, black hair on their heads; very little body hair; flat facial features; small noses; and droopy thick eyelids with folds of skin over the inner corners (epicanthic folds). They also have shovel-shaped incisors (front teeth) unlike those of the other two groups and are of medium to short height.

Caucasoids, however, are further divided into Nordic, Alpine, and Mediterranean types. Nordics are tall, slender, blue-eyed, blond, and long-headed. Alpines are of medium or short stature and are stocky in build, with darker skin, eyes, and hair than Nordics, as well as smaller noses and round heads. Mediterranean types, characterized by "Roman" noses, black, curly hair, and dark eyes, are of about the same height as Alpines but thinner, darker, and long-headed.

Mongoloids are divided into five types:

1. The Sinics, who look most typically Mongoloid but who still differ significantly among themselves, include Chinese, Japanese, Koreans, and Mongolians.

The Diversity of Race

The Caucasoid race is represented by the Norwegian girl, and the Negroid by the young Ethiopian woman (above). The young girl of the Hmong hill tribe of Laos and the Eskimo man (below) are members of the Mongoloid race.

2. The Malayans of Southeast Asia and the Philippines are smaller and darker.
3. Eskimos resemble the Sinics but have long heads and very large teeth (Sinics have small teeth).
4. Brown Micronesians are small and dark.
5. Amerinds (American Indians), who are spread throughout the Western Hemisphere, vary enormously in size, skin tone, and nose size and shape; some Amerinds look more Caucasoid than Mongoloid.

Negroids include the very tall and slender Nilotic people and, near them, the very short and lighter-skinned Pygmies of the Congo; the powerfully built Paleonegroids of western and central Africa; and the Sudanese and Ethiopian Erythriotic people, who have many Caucasoid features.

As if all this were not confusing enough, some scholars claim there are dozens of other groups that do not fit into this threefold racial classification. Furthermore, some Arabs and Indians/Pakistanis, classified as Caucasoids because of their thin lips and noses, are almost as dark as Negroids. Many other groups manifest combinations of physical characteristics that make a mockery of all existing classification systems. People simply refuse to fit into the pigeonholes. Even in Sweden, where Nordic characteristics prevail, few people have all the Nordic traits. There are tall, slender, hairy Swedes with black hair, and there are blue-eyed, blond Swedes who are also short and stocky. One study done of Swedish military personnel indicated that only 10 percent had all the physical traits attributed to the Nordic type.[2]

There are two major reasons why mixed racial types far outnumber "pure" types. First, climate and geography tend to change gradually as one travels in any direction. Consequently, the effects of natural selection on gene pools that are geographically contiguous are only moderately different. Sharp contrasts among neighboring breeding populations are rare. Second, migrations and either forced or voluntary interbreeding over the last few thousand years have practically eradicated gene pool isolation. Also, because gene frequencies result from environmental adaptation, breeding populations living in similar environments, even if they have never had contact with each other, could evolve and have evolved similar phenotypes.

If your ancestors came from tropical Africa, you probably have dark skin and wooly hair. Dark skin is caused by heavy concentrations of the brown pigment melanin, whose main function is to screen out the ultraviolet rays of the sun, which can cause skin cancer. In a sun-drenched area like tropical Africa, light-skinned people could not have survived and produced offspring; hence, they were selected out. Wooly hair provides a natural air-cooling system for the head, thereby preventing heat stroke. Hence, those who had wooly hair survived the extreme solar heat of the tropics; those who did not were selected out.

Blacks in tropical Africa usually have wide nostrils, which facilitate deep breathing in a hot and humid climate. They tend also to have more sweat glands and proportionately longer limbs than Caucasoids and Mongoloids, adaptations that enable them to release body heat and to avoid heat stroke.

If your ancestors came from Scandinavia, you probably have light skin and a long, thin nose. The long nasal passage allows cold air to be warmed before it reaches the bronchial area. Light skin enabled your ancestors to absorb enough ultraviolet rays to develop the hormone calciferol. Dark-skinned people screen out too much sunlight in cold, cloudy climates, fail to produce calciferol, and thus die of rickets as children—before mating is possible. This is how dark skin is selected out in such an environment. Retaining body heat becomes important in cold climates, so people need fewer sweat glands but more body hair to help them keep warm.

Mongoloids developed the epicanthic fold, which helps reduce the glare of the sun on the snow. Their short limbs lessen the possibility of frostbite, as do their small, flat facial features. Combined with short limbs, a short, stocky build provides a low ratio of surface to mass and helps preserve body heat, a must for survival in the cold arctic and subartic climates where Mongoloids lived for millennia before spreading out to other environments. The thick, coarse head of hair was a good insulator that contributed to body warmth, but a layer of fat instead of body hair developed to help the individual retain body heat. (In the most severely cold climates in the world inhabited by humans, body hair could get wet and freeze and thus jeopardize survival.) Mongoloids have the fewest sweat glands of the three major groups because they have had the least need to release heat. Those Mongoloids who moved to warmer climates have made other physical adjustments, which will be discussed below. Finally, Mongoloids' yellowish-brown skin is light enough to allow the necessary ultraviolet rays of the sun to penetrate but dark enough to prevent sunburns resulting from the glare of the sun reflecting off the snow.

From this discussion it seems reasonable to conclude that we are all the descendants of people who, in a Darwinian sense, were the fittest. They possessed environmentally adaptive traits that were passed on to their offspring and thus perpetuated in the gene pool.

From a biological standpoint, all races are equal. *There are no superior or inferior races.* In addition, the many migrations of the past few thousand years have substantially blurred racial distinctions in many parts of the world—a process that has been accelerated in the United States, which is literally a "nation of immigrants."[3]

☐ Independent Variance of Physical Traits

Racial distinctions are further clouded by the fact that many physical traits vary independently of others. As one moves away from the equator, body size increases. It is easier to survive in the tropics if one is small and in the arctic if one is large. The smaller person is better able to release heat because that process, as well as the process of retaining heat, is a function of the relationship of surface to mass. As organisms grow larger, their surface area is squared while their bulk is cubed. Hence, a small person produces less body heat due to small size, but loses more through his or her surface than does a large person. For the same reason, long limbs are adaptive in a hot climate, and short limbs in a cold environment. Thus, Eskimos have large bodies and short limbs, while Central American Indians, who are also Mongoloids, have small bodies and long limbs. Since adaptation to solar rays also affects skin color, it is not surprising that Central American Indians are somewhat darker than Eskimos.

Tooth and jaw sizes are correlated with diet, customs, and tool use. Australian Aborigines have the largest teeth in the world. They eat food that is hard to chew, and they use their mouths as a tool—almost like a third hand. Consequently, their teeth wear down faster over the years than do the teeth of any other known group. Given their customs, if they had small teeth, they would wear them down to the gums at a very early age, probably with dire consequences. Hence, those Aborigines with large teeth were more likely to live long enough to reproduce and leave offspring who, presumably, would also have large teeth; the others were selected out. Natural selection acts upon cultural as well as physical aspects of the environment. The Eskimos, who have softer diets than Australian Aborigines but who use their teeth as tools also (for example, to chew a leather boot to make it soft), as a group have the second largest teeth in the world.

Obviously, Australian Aborigines and Eskimos are not from the same race. Sometimes they are classified as Negroid and Mongoloid, respectively; sometimes they are classified as separate races by those who use five or more categories.

Tooth size affects jaw size. In general, the larger the teeth, the more prominent the lower half of the face. Although tooth size affects jaw size, it has no effect on other traits, such as skin color and body build. People with small faces exist in all races. Their smaller teeth are an indication that their ancestors developed sedentary agriculture and ate softer food long before the ancestors of people with big teeth and jaws. With teeth wearing down less, nature did not have to select for big teeth.

Altitude is another environmental variable that has phenotypical ramifications. Populations that have lived for thousands of years in altitudes above 10,000 feet, such as those in Tibet and the Andean mountain region of South America, have evolved huge barrel chests.

The thin air at such altitudes has less oxygen than is necessary for most human beings to survive. Any migration to these high elevations will cause some people to perish and others to adapt. The adaptation process requires an increase in red blood cells that transport oxygen or the development of an alternative oxygen-transport mechanism. Either condition requires an increase in lung capacity and a corresponding increase in chest size. Over thousands of years, natural selection favored those with the largest lungs, and any mutations in that direction became highly adaptive. Hence, today's inhabitants of the Andes or the Himalayas whose ancestors lived in either region for many generations have large barrel chests.

Peter Farb notes the difficulties inherent in classifying human variation according to observable characteristics:

> Of the numerous attempts that have been made to sort out the breeding populations of the world by noting differences in physique and in color of skin, eyes, and hair, nearly all have been largely fruitless. Skin color is altered by tanning as well as by the long-term effects of climate; brown-eyed people may nevertheless carry recessive alleles for blue eyes and thus produce blue-eyed children; body size and shape are heavily influenced by diet, health, and other environmental variables. A much more precise way to arrive at differences between populations is to compare their blood types.[4]

Of the several blood classification schemes in existence, the ABO system is the most widely used. Some people have suggested that it would be easier, more practical, and less controversial to divide humans into categories based upon relative frequencies of blood types. However, as Table 5-1 indicates, such distributions cut across other categorizations and do not themselves seem to offer much insight into human variation.[5] And so it goes.

☐ The Significance of Race

A racial typology only marks points on a continuum focusing on physical-trait clusters that are themselves arbitrarily chosen. This arbitrariness accounts for the proliferation of typologies and the lack of consensus on an appropriate one. Such a situation inevitably arises when a classification scheme is superimposed on characteristics that occur on a continuum. This brings us back to the argument of the beard.

The arrangement of hair on a face can range from a full beard on one extreme to a clean-shaven face on the other. In between, many parts of the face can be shaved or bearded. We have arbitrarily decided that certain configurations of facial hair shall be called "sideburns," "a moustache," or "a beard." Beards themselves may be subcategorized as "goatees," "full beards," and "Vandykes," among other types.

Table 5-1
Blood Type Frequencies

	O	A	B	AB
Toba Indians (Argentina)	98.5%	1.5%	0%	0%
Navajo Indians (New Mexico)	77.7%	22.3%	0%	0%
Blood Indians (Montana)	17.4%	81.2%	0%	1.4%
Aborigines (southern Australia)	42.6%	57.4%	0%	0%
Melanesians (New Guinea)	37.6%	44.4%	13.2%	4.8%
Siamese (Bangkok)	37.1%	17.8%	35.2%	9.9%
Asiatic Indians (Bengal)	32.5%	20.0%	39.4%	8.1%
Ukranians (Kharkov)	36.4%	38.4%	21.6%	3.6%
Germans (Danzig)	33.1%	41.6%	18.0%	7.3%
Germans (Berlin)	36.5%	42.5%	14.5%	6.5%
Italians (Sicily)	45.9%	33.4%	17.3%	3.4%
English (London)	47.9%	42.4%	8.3%	1.4%

Source: From *Humankind* by Peter Farb. Copyright © 1978 by Peter Farb. Reprinted by permission of Houghton Mifflin Company. All rights reserved.

The classification of beards is intrinsically no more important than the classification of races. The arbitrariness of categories is harmless as long as we draw no "sociological" conclusions from biological categories. To say that one race is better than another makes as much sense as saying that a walrus moustache is inherently better than a "Fu Manchu" or a pencil moustache. We can only say that they are different.

As Brace and Montagu point out, "In some cases what are perceived as racial differences are in fact primarily cultural differences between people whose genetically based physical characteristics are not markedly distinguishable."[6] Thus, some people speak of a "Jewish race," despite the fact that there are Mongoloid Jews in Japan, Negroid Jews in Ethiopia, and a Mexican Indian tribe of Jews, as well as Caucasoid Jews from various parts of Europe and the Middle East. In each case, the Jewish population is racially indistinguishable from the non-Jewish population in the area. And in each case, differences between Jews and other people in the geographical areas mentioned can best be explained by the concept of ethnicity.

☐ Ethnicity

Ethnicity is a sense of peoplehood—a feeling of belonging together, of being part of a group whose members have a great deal in common with each other. The term comes from the Greek word *ethnos*, meaning "race," "nation," or "people"; and also from *ethos*, meaning "custom" or "way of life." Thus, the term *ethnicity* has both biological and cultural aspects.

Ethnic group membership can be based on race (e.g., black Americans), religion (e.g., Jewish-Americans), or national origin (e.g., Mexican-

Ethiopian Jewish Boys Learning Hebrew
Jews are not a race but rather a religious ethnic group. Hence, in every part of the world where they are found, Jews tend to resemble the other local inhabitants.

Americans). An **ethnic group** is one whose members share common cultural norms, values, identities, and patterns of behavior and identify themselves and are identified by others as an ethnic group.[7] This is what Harold Isaacs calls "basic group identity." [8] The ethnic group preserves and transmits cultural traits from one generation to the next;[9] and its members tend to share similar interests, tastes, problems, backgrounds, and experiences. Consequently, they relate to and feel comfortable with each other.

Immigrants initially tend to congregate in ethnic communities, which serve as islands of familiarity in a sea of strange people and customs. In fact, Shibutani and Kwan refer to these communities as "ethnic islands."[10] By *community* we mean a combination of social systems that usually operate in a geographically delimited area and perform such major functions as socialization, material support, social control, and social participation, as well as production, consumption, and distribution.[11] Immigrants who concentrate in a given area and

Chinatown, San Francisco
Ethnic neighborhoods still exist in many American cities, even though the resident immigrant groups may have lived in the United States for generations. The Chinese have lived in California since the 1850's.

who create a more or less self-contained ethnic community are regarded as a **primary ethnic group.** This is one in which the members maintain a high level of cultural cohesiveness and within which they satisfy their basic needs and carry out their primary relationships: those that are personal, intimate, emotional, and involve the whole personality.[12]

People from any country who migrate as individuals or in small groups and who depend entirely on the host society for the satisfaction of basic needs are regarded as a **secondary ethnic group.** Usually they disperse throughout the society; but even if they remain together in one location, their small numbers prevent them from becoming a primary ethnic group. The distinction is important, because the impact of culture shock and the rate of absorption into the dominant society will vary between the two groups. We will elaborate on these topics later in the chapter.

A **minority group** is an ethnic group that is exceptionally disadvantaged, exceptionally discriminated against, or both. It is one that suffers

Gurdwara, a Sikh Temple in Queens, New York
New York City is home for a wide variety of ethnic groups.

these indignities indefinitely. Group members find it difficult to be accepted because they have physical characteristics that distinguish them from others—usually skin color. These involuntary ethnic characteristics make them easily identifiable targets of discrimination. They face considerably more formidable obstacles to success and acceptance than do members of ethnic groups whose ethnic characteristics are all, or almost all, voluntary—that is, those individuals who are not physically distinguishable from the dominant group.

In this sense, *minority* refers not to numbers but to social condition. All minorities are ethnic groups, but all ethnic groups are not minorities. Minority groups have a disproportionately small amount of political and economic power and occupy a subordinate position, as a group, vis-à-vis other groups in the society. It follows, then, that the **majority group** consists of the segment of the population that is politically and economically dominant and that may or may not be numerically larger than the subordinate groups it dominates.

One does not have to live in a segregated ethnic neighborhood to be a member of an ethnic group. However, such concentrations do serve to perpetuate the subculture and are considered to be ethnic cultural centers even by those former inhabitants who have moved to other neighborhoods. Without these neighborhoods, the ethnic group would probably dissolve into the dominant society more quickly. Its members would lose their subcultural identity and characteristics.

It is evident that ethnic communities must perform some useful functions. Otherwise, immigrants would not have flocked to them, and Little Italys, Chinatowns, Little Tokyos, Germantowns, and Spanish barrios would not have lasted for generations.

Possible Advantages of Ethnic Group Membership

The ethnic community performs the following functions:

1. *It creates an atmosphere of warmth and security beyond the family.* As Shibutani and Kwan put it, "For a great many people in ethnic minorities, these segregated communities provide a haven of refuge in what may otherwise seem an unfriendly world. Millions of men and women live their entire lives within the confines of such settlements, learning of the outside world only from hearsay. Most of these colonies are transitory and disappear after a few generations. But some ethnic groups—such as the... Jews...—have managed to retain their culture for centuries by succoring one another in such concentrations."[13]

2. *It provides the individual with knowledge of his or her roots.* It offers continuity with the past, a feeling of being "somebody" with a history and a heritage.

3. *It provides a group identity that is stronger and more personal than national identity.* Rogg says, "In American society, people are members of ethnic groups from which they derive a sense of security and identity. The need for roots, for interpersonal ties and primary group support, is increasingly important for all members of highly industrialized and urbanized societies prone to anomie."[14]

Most people would agree that modern societies, including the United States, have become very impersonal. Not only are people left alone to fend for themselves, but they become mere numbers—each one a small cog in the machine. The deterioration of the extended family serves to isolate the individual further. The need for a reference group, an extended family, a community, becomes paramount. The ethnic group rescues many people from feelings of isolation and alienation. Perhaps that is the reason why so many young members of the dominant group seek out communes, clubs, fraternities, and sororities. Perhaps that is the reason why team sports like baseball and football are so popular in America. They provide outlets for the need to belong.

4. *Ethnic groups enhance an individual's self-esteem.* "It is believed that the (ethnic) community will facilitate adjustment by providing the

immigrant with a sense of worth and by providing him with a refuge for the values and behavior patterns that he learned in his homeland."[15]

5. *It provides a pattern of groups and institutions through which a person can fulfill important needs and maintain primary group relationships.* Gordon points out, "Within the ethnic group, there develops a network of organizations and informal relationships which permits and encourages the members of the ethnic group to remain within the confines of the group for all of their primary relationships and some of their secondary relationships throughout all the stages of the life-cycle."[16]

6. *It reduces the possibility of personality disorders and culture shock by facilitating the adjustment process.* It cushions the impact of the dominant culture. The ethnic community is not an exact replica of the immigrant's homeland; it has been "watered down" by its contact with the host society. But adjustment to it is relatively much easier than adjustment to the dominant society. As the community itself becomes increasingly "Americanized," so does the immigrant. The now-secure, confident, hyphenated-American is able to cope with the dominant culture and even to adopt its traits more rapidly with a minimum of negative side effects. Gordon has equated the ethnic community with a decompression chamber in which the immigrant gradually becomes accustomed to the new pressures at hand.[17]

7. *It may lead to the development of bicultural or multicultural individuals who integrate the best of two or more cultures while feeling comfortable in each.* Adjusted biculturals not only have a dual, or hyphenated, identity, but they can emphasize whichever identity suits them best in any given situation. Thus, they acquire cultural flexibility. Such individuals can also help build bridges of understanding among ethnic groups.

Possible Disadvantages of Ethnic Group Membership

Among the possible dysfunctions of ethnicity are the following:

1. *The clannishness that usually exists in ethnic communities may create divisiveness.* Outsiders may feel excluded and become hostile. This could lead to problems between the ethnic community and the larger society, i.e., "interethnic group tension arising from lack of primary group interactions and the development of stereotyped images of other groups."[18]

2. *Excessive emphasis on the subculture by many ethnic groups could lead to societal disintegration.* If feelings of nationalism are very weak, strong

ethnic ties might tear a society apart. This is more likely to happen if some groups are continuously excluded from full participation by the majority.

Those who disagree with this criticism might point out that while nationalism binds the diverse groups together, ethnicity strengthens and legitimizes the variations within society. There is no evidence that America has been torn asunder by ethnic rivalry. Some people might consider themselves to be hyphenated-Americans, but they are no less American than others, and they share America's core culture with unhyphenated citizens.

3. *"Restriction of the individual's right to choose between cultures because of community pressures"*[19] may arise. The ethnic group leaders may become domineering and pressure members not to acculturate or assimilate.

4. *By inculcating subcultural values, attitudes, and behaviors, the ethnic group may exacerbate the cross-cultural pressures experienced by second-generation immigrants.*

5. *Segregation from the general society fosters ethnocentrism and retards the learning of English and the Americanization of the immigrant.* While this criticism may be correct in some instances, it overlooks the positive effects of individuals' knowing who they are and being proud of it. It also overlooks the fact that immigrants usually encourage their children to learn English and are very proud of them for doing so. The children often serve as interpreters for the parents whenever the latter must deal with members of the dominant society. Because language is the main transmitter of culture, the children become much more Americanized than the parents. The ensuing "culture gap" in the home often creates a great deal of friction between parents and children. To lament the fact that the child speaks the home language is to support the dubious "benefit" of the child's being unable to communicate effectively with his or her parents. It is doubtful that anyone would trade off a partially acculturated child who retains some things in common with the parents for one who is totally acculturated but who is a stranger in his or her own home.

☐ Ethnic Resurgence

Whatever one's feelings may be regarding the utility or disutility of ethnic groups, there is no doubt that America experienced an ethnic resurgence in the 1970s. The "black pride" or "black is beautiful" movement of the previous decade succeeded to some degree in improving the self-esteem of black Americans and in increasing their identification

Black Pride
Ethnicity and cultural pride are often displayed through fashion. This woman custom-designs these hats called African Crowns.

with Africa. It also helped them achieve some concrete economic and political goals. Kilson believes this "neo-ethnicity" served a rehabilitative function.[20] Other disadvantaged and some not-so-disadvantaged groups decided that it would be to their advantage to emulate the black pride movement.

Daniel Bell holds that the ethnic resurgence occurred for three reasons:

1. *The desire for primordial anchorage.* People needed to belong to smaller units and found ethnicity an easy attachment.
2. *The breakup of traditional authority structures and the decline of moral certainty.*
3. *A ready means of demanding group rights and providing defense against other groups.*[21]

It is no coincidence that the decade of the 1960s, which brought about the questioning of fundamental values and institutions in America, was the gestation period for the ethnic resurgence movement. Set adrift from traditional moorings, many Americans began to look inward to their historical roots for guidance and comfort.

The 1960s were also years of increased political rhetoric and activity and heightened political awareness. Americans were politicized in the crucible of civil rights, the Vietnam War, riots in the cities, political assassinations, landmark Supreme Court decisions, protests, and confrontations. The effectiveness of group awareness and group action was not lost on the American people. If the most oppressed ethnic group of all—black Americans—could make the country stop and listen to its grievances and act to redress some of them, certainly other ethnic groups could achieve no less. As Glazer and Moynihan pointed out in 1963, the ethnic groups in New York are also interest groups.[22] Why should it be any different elsewhere?

In general, we can say that the temper of the times brought home a fundamental truth written by Horace Kallen in 1915: "Men may change their clothes, their politics, their wives, their religions, their philosophies, to a greater or lesser extent; they cannot change their grandfathers."[23] And so we now have tee shirts and bumper stickers that read "Polish power," "I'm Latin and proud of it," and "Irishmen do it better." Our favorite is a shirt worn by a Seminole Indian that read, "America: love it or give it back."

☐ Acculturation

In analyzing the experience of America's ethnic groups, one should examine (1) the conditions in the country from which they migrated; (2) the circumstances of their departure; (3) people's attitudes regarding immigration in the receiving society; (4) the socioeconomic conditions in the receiving society; (5) the resources, both material and intellectual, brought by the immigrants; and (6) the contact situation.

The last point raises an important question: What happens when two or more ethnic groups come into contact, especially if they occupy the same territory? If the contact lasts long enough, the groups start to pick up customs from each other. The process or result of individuals or groups adopting aspects of another group's culture is called **acculturation.**

Perhaps the most authoritative definition of this phenomenon was rendered by a group of eminent anthropologists who were appointed by their colleagues to a commission charged with defining the term in 1936. "*Acculturation* comprehends those phenomena which result when groups of individuals having different cultures come into continuous first-hand contact, with subsequent changes in the original patterns of either or both groups."[24]

The degree and speed of acculturation depend on several factors, the most important of which are *age* at time of immigration and *place of settlement.* The younger the immigrant, the greater and faster the acculturation. If immigrants do not speak the language of the country to which they migrate, within a short period of time the children usually begin to act as interpreters for the parents and other adults. In addition to language, the children also acquire cultural traits of the host society very quickly. Thus, they begin to play a major role in the acculturation of their parents, depending, of course, on how receptive the parents are to the process.

If the immigrants settle in a self-contained ethnic community, the process of acculturation is considerably slowed down and the amount of acculturation is significantly reduced. On the other hand, dispersed immigrants who must mingle with members of the host society to a greater extent learn English and adopt more of the host society's beliefs, values, attitudes, and behaviors than their counterparts, and they do so more quickly.

Other factors that bear on acculturation are *education* and *occupation*. The higher the level of education at the time of immigration, the greater the acculturation. Because schools are a major socializing force, the more schooling in the adopted country, the greater the acculturation. Family, schools, peers, and the mass media play major roles in molding children into the adults they eventually become. This is the reason why it is so difficult for fully formed adults to adjust to a new society and relatively easy for youngsters. In some cases, religion also plays a significant role, although in our increasingly secularized world, its influence is diminishing.

One of the most overlooked socializing agents is occupation. The line of work chosen usually brings individuals into contact with certain kinds of people, but not with others. Furthermore, people who work together tend to form certain organizations (labor unions, business groups) and informal cliques (bowling teams, golf partners). A great deal of socialization accompanies the socializing that occurs in these settings. In the case of immigrants, if the occupation keeps them within the confines of the ethnic community, acculturation will be minimal.

First- and Second-Generation Immigrants

Eisenstadt contends that there are three measurements to determine the degree of absorption by immigrants: (1) acculturation, (2) satisfactory personal adjustment, and (3) complete dispersion of immigrants as a group within the main institutional spheres of the absorbing society.[25] In analyzing problems arising from culture contact, we are going to combine acculturation and adjustment. First, it is necessary to distinguish between first- and second-generation immigrants. The first generation (foreign-born who emigrate as adults or, in some cases, as adolescents) experience what sociologists and anthropologists refer to as **culture shock,** or the gap between expectations and reality. In any culture, growing up involves learning the statuses (positions, such as father, teacher, policeman, friend, and so forth) of one's society and the roles (the expected behavior patterns) that characterize each status. However, when one migrates to a foreign land in which people have different customs, habits, values, and beliefs, and even a different language, he or she becomes disoriented. The individual doesn't know what to expect and, in many situations, how to behave. This is culture shock.

Puerto Rican-American Family
A Puerto Rican youngster seems to be explaining American ways to his less acculturated mother—or perhaps is trying to justify his "Americanized" behavior.

The second generation (those who are born in the new country or who migrate as small children), however, faces a different problem, called **culture conflict.** Its members are pulled in two directions by equally compelling cultures. The family pulls the child in the direction of speaking the home language and maintaining the ethnic culture; at the same time, the dominant society (in this case, American society), usually through teachers and Anglo peers, pulls the child in the opposite direction, by insisting that he or she speak English and behave as an American. The child, faced with conflicting value systems promulgated by equally valid authority figures (teacher and parent), often becomes very confused. Sometimes he or she does not know what is right or wrong, what to think, or how to behave. This culture conflict often leads to an identity crisis. "Who am I?" says the child. "Am I Polish, am I American, or am I Polish-American?" The distinction between culture shock and culture conflict is important, because each problem requires a different solution.

Solutions to Acculturation Problems

The child from a non-English-speaking home faces not only culture conflict but also the inability to communicate effectively with the teacher. How this problem is handled during the initial contact with the dominant culture will very likely determine the child's success or failure in school and perhaps in life.

One approach that is sometimes used might be called "sink or swim." No special programs are devised; no special effort is made to

Bilingual Instruction
An Asian immigrant experiences bilingual education in San Francisco.

deal with the student's language problem. This course is the equivalent of teaching a group of youngsters to swim by taking them out to the middle of a lake and throwing them overboard—a few might make it to shore, but the majority will drown. This is precisely what happens to non-English-speaking students who receive no special attention.

In some American communities, there are bilingual/bicultural education programs. These seem at least to provide the special assistance needed during the transition period. Of the various programs, those most likely to reduce culture conflict combine teaching the non-English-speaking student the curriculum content in his or her native language with an intensive teaching of English. Through the application of a total bilingual, bicultural program that also teaches the student his or her native tongue and culture, culture conflict is likely to be easily overcome. The student's fluency in the home language is maintained, as is the knowledge of his or her ancestral culture. Conflict in the home is reduced and self-esteem is increased.

Quite often, the student's deteriorating ability to speak the home language becomes a great source of stress. Hence, home language maintenance programs are very helpful. As fluency in the two languages develops, the student finds that he or she can straddle two cultures, feel comfortable in both, and, moreover, enjoy an uncommonly rich situation.

Dealing with the culture shock of first-generation immigrants is more complex. Historically, such people tend to settle in "ethnic islands." Although these settings undoubtedly slow down the acculturation process, they ease the psychological impact of people's being uprooted from their homeland and transplanted to a "strange" new environment.

To ease the transition further and to speed up the acculturation process, the school system, other governmental agencies, and private, nonprofit organizations can provide useful services. English as a foreign language is usually offered, but that is not enough. The American culture must also be taught. Not only do the natives often think that immigrants have unusual customs but immigrants usually regard Americans as strange creatures as well. Cross-cultural understanding can be enhanced through classes dealing with cultural similarities and differences, attended by people from the dominant society as well as by immigrants. The immigrants should be taught practical matters, such as how our major institutions work and where they should go if they have specific problems. The courses can improve interethnic relations.

If a large immigrant population resides in any one community, all government agencies there should have some personnel who speak the immigrants' language. If there are many immigrant groups that speak different languages, a multilingual center should be maintained, where any immigrant or foreign visitor in need of assistance can call and find someone to communicate with in his or her native tongue.

Marginal Persons

There is a vast literature on second-generation immigrants, some of whom are referred to as **marginal persons.** They are considered marginal because they do not feel comfortable with either the dominant society or their own subculture. Furthermore, they are not accepted by either group. The dominant society says, "You're not one of us; you're Cuban." The first-generation immigrants say, "You speak only English, and you've given up Cuban values. You're not one of us; you're American."

The culture conflict experienced by the second generation is multidimensional. It is (1) *intrapersonal,* or within the individual, as noted above. However, it should be mentioned that many bicultural people successfully integrate both cultures by selecting what they consider to be the best of both worlds. Unfortunately, many others do not.

The conflict is also (2) *intrafamilial,* within families, because of different rates of acculturation between generations. Children learn the language and customs quickly; older folks learn the language and customs slowly, if at all.

Finally, culture conflict is usually (3) *interethnic,* or between immigrants and natives. Interethnic conflict can also exist between different immigrant groups.

It should be noted that some groups are known for making great achievements in the second generation. Jewish-Americans and Japanese-Americans are two prime examples. They have succeeded by utilizing the education system effectively. They have overcome the culture conflict.

☐ Assimilation

Although anthropologists use the term *acculturation*, sociologists prefer **assimilation.** Also, while some social scientists use these terms interchangeably, others take the position that assimilation is simply "total acculturation." If a person has acculturated to such an extent that he or she no longer has any characteristics identifying him/her with the former culture, that person has become assimilated.

Milton Gordon's Assimilation Model

In 1964 Milton Gordon attempted to bring some order to the study of immigrant absorption. In his classic work *Assimilation in American Life,* he developed a systematic classification scheme that has been adopted by most scholars in the field.

Gordon's typology includes seven types of assimilation.

1. *Cultural or behavioral assimilation.* The change in the immigrant group's cultural patterns to those of the host society. The immigrants acquire the beliefs, values, attitudes, customs, and habits of the national culture.
2. *Structural assimilation.* Large-scale entrance by immigrants into cliques, clubs, and institutions of the host society, on a primary-group level.
3. *Marital assimilation.* Large-scale intermarriage and interbreeding between natives and immigrants. In effect, this is an amalgamation of two gene pools, which eventually eliminates differences in physical characteristics.
4. *Identification assimilation.* Development of a sense of peoplehood, based exclusively on the host society. Immigrants no longer identify with the homeland or with the ethnic community.
5. *Attitude receptional assimilation.* The absence in members of the host society of prejudice against the immigrant group.
6. *Behavior receptional assimilation.* The absence of discrimination against the immigrant group.
7. *Civic assimilation.* The absence of value and power conflict between natives and immigrants. In other words, the immigrant group does not question the core culture of the host society by challenging its basic social or political orientations.[26]

While this model is presented here in absolute terms (total assimilation), Gordon emphasizes that varying degrees of assimilation can

Ethnic Tradition
Not even the rain can interrupt a 3000-year-old religious-ethnic ritual. Here a Jewish couple in Massachusetts takes the wedding vows under the canopy, a tradition in all Jewish weddings.

take place in each of the seven categories. It seems, however, that if total assimilation occurs on the first four variables, it can be assumed that it automatically has taken place in the last three. If structural assimilation has taken place, it is obvious that the dominant society is not exercising prejudice and discrimination against the immigrant group. Otherwise, that society would not have allowed immigrants into its primary groups. Likewise, if the immigrant group identifies totally with the host society, it has internalized that society's core culture and could not possibly create a culture conflict. Also, if there has been large-scale intermarriage between the two groups, there certainly would not be widespread prejudice and discrimination against the immigrants. Gordon himself points out, "Once structural assimilation has occurred, either simultaneously with or subsequent to acculturation, all of the other types of assimilation will naturally follow."[27] This is true only if *total* structural assimilation has taken place.

It is possible, however, for ethnic group members to assimilate structurally, to a high degree, but still maintain many ethnic group ties. There are, for example, Italian-Americans who do not live in ethnic neighborhoods, who belong to host-society business organizations, who hold public office, and who socialize primarily with Anglo-Americans. These same people might also attend ethnic (Italian) weddings and funerals, eat pasta at least once a week, visit "Mama" on Sundays, and go to social functions sponsored by the Sons of Italy. If asked, however, many will say they are Americans, not Italian-Americans.

Gordon also emphasizes the need to distinguish between intrinsic and extrinsic cultural traits or patterns. *Intrinsic traits,* such as those related to religion, ethical values, language, literature, and a sense of peoplehood, are more difficult to change than are *extrinsic traits*—those related to modes of dress, manners, and foreign accents. The latter are more easily changed in time by succeeding generations.[28]

Social Distance

We have all heard people say about two brothers, friends, or lovers, "They were very close" or "They weren't very close." We have also heard people refer to someone who keeps to himself or herself as "distant." Thus, the concept of social distance among individuals is commonly accepted. Social scientists began using the concept of **social distance** as early as the 1920's to explain intergroup relations.[29] They point out that people feel closer to those with whom they have a great deal in common than to those who are quite different from themselves. Hence, in most cases, social distance between two members of the same ethnic group tends to be narrower than social distance between two people from different ethnic groups. Of course, there are many exceptions.

Park defines social distance as the psychological barriers that facilitate or deter easy, spontaneous interaction.[30] People who identify with each other, who share common values and a common heritage, feel obliged to treat one another according to those shared values. However, in their dealings with someone from outside their in-group (someone from an out-group), there is not as strong a feeling to treat him or her according to the same standards. In addition, the other person's standards may be so different that he or she may be dismayed by, for example, being greeted with a hug. So we have here a case of greater social distance in interactions between two people from different ethnic groups than between two people who belong to the same ethnic group.

As we look at the variety of ethnic groups in the United States, we find differing amounts of social distance separating different paired groups. The possible pairings are many, and not enough empirical data exist to enable us to analyze all the combinations. However, attempts have been made to use *social distance from the dominant group* to measure an immigrant's chances of being accepted and assimilated by the host society.

Warner and Srole developed two scales based on racial and cultural distance to gauge an immigrant's chances of being assimilated in America.[31]

Racial Types in Order of Their Assimilative Potential
1. light Caucasoids
2. dark Caucasoids
3. Mongoloid and Caucasoid mixtures with a Mediterranean appearance
4. Mongoloids and mixed peoples with a predominantly Mongoloid appearance
5. Negroids and all Negroid mixtures

Cultural Types in Order of Their Assimilative Potential
1. English-speaking Protestants
2. Protestants who do not speak English
3. English-speaking Catholics and other non-Protestants
4. Catholics and other non-Protestants, most of whom speak allied Indo-European languages
5. English-speaking non-Christians
6. non-Christians who do not speak English

Race seems to be the single most important variable in determining social distance. Because the original host society in the United States was Caucasian, and so is the existing ruling elite, Caucasian is the standard by which people are ranked. Since Mongoloids resemble Caucasoids more than Negroids do, Mongoloids are ranked higher than Negroids on the racial stratification scale. Lighter-skinned "Nordic" Caucasians have been more accepted by the host society than have been the darker "Mediterranean" Caucasians. Scandinavians have had less difficulty assimilating than have Greeks and Spaniards.

The two cultural variables considered most important by Warner and Srole are language and religion. Obviously, if the immigrant does not speak English, he or she cannot assimilate to any significant degree. But by the second generation, almost all immigrants speak English, and the majority do so without an accent. The Irish had a leg up on other immigrants because they spoke the language dominant in America when they arrived. We can conclude, however, that language is a major factor only for the first-generation immigrant, and in many cases, only for a few years.

Religion is another matter. An insignificant number of Catholics and Jews have become Protestants since arriving in America; and probably at least as many Protestants have converted to Judaism or Catholicism. This may not be true before 1820, when conversions tended to be exclusively toward the dominant group as part of an overall assimilation process; but since then, conversions have probably been equal in both directions. More importantly, in general, religious conversions have been few.

Warner and Srole theorize that the greater the racial and cultural differences between hosts and immigrants, the greater will be the subordination of the immigrant group and the cohesion of the ethnic (immigrant) group, and the longer it will take for the immigrant group to assimilate.[32] This seems so logical that not many people will dispute it. However, there is more to culture than language and religion. Therefore, while we should recognize the importance of the two variables, it would be more accurate to take into account the full spectrum of customs, values, and beliefs in determining cultural distance. We must also consider both the dominant group's acceptance or rejection of the immigrant group, and the ethnic group's willingness to assimilate. As Gordon points out, it takes two to tango: if the other group doesn't ask you to dance, social distance will not be reduced, and assimilation will not take place; and, of course, the two groups will never sway, cheek to cheek.

Finally, we should take special notice of ethnocentrism and its effects on the relative social distance between or among groups within a society. As long as one group considers itself superior, it will always view the other group as inferior, and vice versa. This situation can lead not only to social distance but to overt antagonism between any two given groups within a multigroup society. And because overt antagonism may be dysfunctional to the society, it is important that people discard their ethnocentrism and develop cultural relativity. Otherwise, the dance itself could turn into a free-for-all.

General Theories of Assimilation

There are several general theories of assimilation that can be interpreted as either explanations of actual immigrant experiences or as ideologies stating what ought to happen to those who migrate to the United States.

Anglo conformity is one-way assimilation.[33] According to this theory Anglo-Saxons were the first to settle in large numbers, and they created the political and economic infrastructure of American society. They became the host society, and their way of life became the core culture. All subsequent arrivals shed (or should have shed) their ancestral heritage and became (or should have become) 100% Americanized (Anglicized). This theory can be diagrammed in the following manner:

Anglo/host society (A)◄─────────────────────Non-Anglo groups (B)

The **melting pot** is a blending of all the cultures and all the gene pools in the United States.[34] The core culture is a mixture of the original Anglo-Saxon traits and the cultural characteristics of all the other groups that came to America. According to this theory, each new group that arrives on our shores alters the American melting-pot culture. This theory can be diagrammed as follows:

Anglo/host society (A)   Non-Anglo groups (B)
                New Culture (C)

Cultural pluralism holds that there are many ethnic groups in the United States, some of whose members may be totally assimilated and acculturated but most of whom maintain a dual, or hyphenated, identity.[35] They participate in the economic and political mainstream, but their social lives include a majority of primary relations within their ethnic subcultures. Often, they retain the language and many of the cultural traits of their ancestral homeland. Cultural pluralism can be diagrammed as follows:

Anglo/host society (A)   Non-Anglo groups (B)
              New Culture (A + B)

Similar to cultural pluralism is the **emerging culture** theory.[36] In this case, the hyphenated identity is not like either the dominant culture or the subculture; it is a bicultural identity. An Italian-American, in this view, is different from other American groups and different from Italians in the homeland. Even Anglo-Americans are thought of as a subculture. Like the melting pot theory, emerging culture assumes that the society's core culture is altered by each new group's arrival, but the modification is slight. Emerging culture can be diagrammed in the following manner:

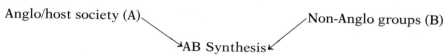

Anglo/host society (A)   Non-Anglo groups (B)
                AB Synthesis

A fifth assimilation theory is **impact-integration.**[37] It is similar to the emerging culture theory, but it places more emphasis on the process. The encounter between an immigrant group and the host society is perceived as harsh, filled with conflicts, mutual animosity, and a high degree of competitiveness.

The immigrants do not let themselves get pushed around or be placed in a subordinate position, so the eventual integration does not lead to as much homogeneity as in the emerging culture theory. Impact-integration may be diagrammed in the following manner:

Anglo/host society (A)   Non-Anglo groups (B)
                ab Integration

The great cultural diversity of American society, historically and at present, clearly indicates that neither Anglo conformity nor the melting pot theories explain the reality of the American experience. Before 1820, immigrants conformed to the Anglo-Saxon culture created by the British settlers and the Founding Fathers. Since then, we have had some type of cultural pluralism. Never have we had a melting pot as described by the originators of that concept.

In the metropolitan areas of this country either cultural pluralism, emerging culture, or impact-integration have taken or are taking place. In more homogeneous areas of the country this type of cultural integration is less apparent. It would be an interesting classroom exercise to research this issue in each community where this text is used. In Miami, Florida, where the authors live, aspects of emerging culture and impact-integration exist within the context of cultural pluralism. There certainly has been a great deal of competition, and sometimes hostility, between and among black, Haitian, Cuban, other Hispanic, Jewish, and Anglo residents. Perhaps we need a new theory to explain our reality.

REFERENCES

1. Montagu has written extensively on this subject. See especially *Man's Most Dangerous Myth: The Fallacy of Race* (Cleveland: World Publishing Co., 1965).
2. Peter Farb, *Humankind* (Boston: Houghton Mifflin Co., 1978), p. 276.
3. For example, it is estimated that 70 to 80 percent of black Americans have Caucasoid ancestors.
4. Farb, p. 267.
5. *Ibid.*
6. C. Loring Brace and Ashley Montagu, *Human Evolution: An Introduction to Biological Anthropology,* 2nd ed. (New York: Macmillan, 1977), p. 389.
7. Joan Vincent, "Brief Communications," *Human Organization* (Winter 1974), p. 375.
8. Harold R. Isaacs, "Basic Group Identity: The Idols of The Tribe," in Nathan Glazer and Daniel P. Moynihan, eds., *Ethnicity: Theory and Experience* (Cambridge, Mass.: Harvard University Press, 1975), p. 29.
9. Andrew M. Greely and William C. McCready, "The Transmission of Cultural Heritages: The Case of the Irish and the Italians," in Glazer and Moynihan, *Ethnicity*, pp. 209–230.
10. Tamotsu Shibutani and Kian M. Kwan, *Ethnic Stratification* (New York: Macmillan, 1965), p. 284.
11. Roland L. Warren, *The Community in America* (Chicago: Rand McNally, 1963), p. 9.
12. Milton Gordon, *Assimilation in American Life* (New York: Oxford University Press, 1964), p. 32.
13. Shibutani and Kwan, p. 283.
14. Eleanor Meyer Rogg, *The Assimilation of Cuban Exiles* (New York: Aberdeen Press, 1974), p. 3.

15. *Ibid.*
16. Gordon, p. 34.
17. *Ibid.,* p. 106.
18. Rogg, p. 72.
19. *Ibid.*
20. Martin Kilson, "Blacks and Neo-Ethnicity in American Political Life," in Glazer and Moynihan, *Ethnicity,* p. 237.
21. Daniel Bell, "Ethnicity and Social Change," in Glazer and Moynihan, *Ethnicity,* p. 171.
22. Nathan Glazer and Daniel P. Moynihan, *Beyond the Melting Pot* (Cambridge, Mass.: MIT Press, 1963, 1970).
23. Horace M. Kallen, "Democracy Versus the Melting Pot," *The Nation* (February 18, 1915), reprinted in his book *Culture and Democracy in the United States* (New York: Boni and Liveright, 1924), p. 60.
24. Robert Redfield, Ralph Linton, and Melville J. Herskovits, "Memorandum for the Study of Acculturation," *American Anthropologist 38,* no. 1 (January–March 1936), p. 149.
25. S. N. Eisenstadt, *The Absorption of Immigrants* (New York: Free Press, 1955), p. 11.
26. Gordon, pp. 70–71.
27. *Ibid.,* p. 81.
28. *Ibid.,* p. 79.
29. See Robert E. Park and E. W. Burgess, *Introduction to the Science of Sociology* (Chicago: University of Chicago Press, 1924).
30. Robert E. Park, *Race and Culture* (New York: Free Press of Glencoe, 1949), pp. 256–260.
31. W. Lloyd Warner and Leo Srole, *Social Systems of American Ethnic Groups* (New Haven: Yale University Press, 1945), pp. 286, 288.
32. Warner and Srole, p. 155.
33. See Madison Grant, *The Passing of the Great Race* (New York: Scribner's, 1971), and Ellwood P. Cubberly, *Changing Concepts of Education* (Boston: Houghton Mifflin, 1909).
34. The first proponent of the melting pot theory was Hector St. John de Crèvecoeur, *Letters from an American Farmer,* Originally published in 1782, (New York: Albert and Charles Boni, 1925). However, the first clear exposition of the melting pot was put forth by Ralph Waldo Emerson in 1848, *Essays and Poems of Emerson* (New York: Harcourt, Brace and Co., 1921).
35. See Horace B. Kallen, "Democracy Versus the Melting Pot," *The Nation,* February 18 and 25, 1915.
36. See Nathan Glazer and Patrick P. Moynihan, *Beyond The Melting Pot* (Cambridge, Mass.: MIT Press, 1970).
37. See Francis X. Femminella, "The Immigrant and the Melting Pot." In M. Vrofsky, ed., *Perspectives in Urban America* (New York: Doubleday, 1973).

GLOSSARY

Race	A subspecies formed as the result of natural selection working on a geographically isolated population.
Ethnicity	A sense of peoplehood; a feeling of belonging together, of being part of a group whose members have a great deal in common with each other.
Ethnic group	A subculture based on a common race, religion, or national origin.
Primary ethnic group	An immigrant group that concentrates in a given area and creates a more or less self-contained ethnic community.
Secondary ethnic group	People from any country who migrate as individuals or in small groups and who depend entirely on the host society for the satisfaction of basic needs.
Minority group	An ethnic group that is exceptionally disadvantaged, exceptionally discriminated against, or both, and whose members may have physical characteristics that distinguish them from others.
Majority group	The segment of population within a society that is politically and economically dominant and that may or may not be numerically larger than the subordinate groups it dominates.
Acculturation	The process in which individuals or groups adopt aspects of another group's culture.
Assimilation	The process of taking on a new cultural identity. Some social scientists use *assimilation* interchangeably with *acculturation*, while others treat *assimilation* as *total acculturation*.
Culture shock	A gap between expectations and reality with regard to social statuses and roles. Culture shock is experienced by first-generation immigrants.
Culture conflict	The kind of conflict experienced by second-generation immigrants as their parents teach them one cultural tradition and the dominant society teaches them another.
Marginal persons	A term used to refer to second-generation immigrants whose culture conflict may leave them feeling uncomfortable with both the dominant society and their own subculture.
Social distance	The extent to which an individual or group feels relatively close or distant from other individuals or groups.
Anglo conformity	Uni-directional assimilation in which all other American groups conform to the white Anglo-Saxon Protestant (dominant) culture.

Melting pot	A blending of all the cultures and gene pools in the United States, thus forming an "American" culture different from the original WASP culture.
Cultural pluralism	The maintenance of a dual identity and dual culture traits, both American and ethnic (subculture) by a large percentage of the U.S. population.
Emerging culture	An integrated identity not like either the dominant culture or the subculture.
Impact-integration	A process-oriented theory similar to emerging culture which emphasizes the conflict that accompanies culture contact.

SELECTED READING

Brace, C. Loring and Ashley Montagu, *Human Evolution: An Introduction to Biological Anthropology,* 2nd ed. (New York: Macmillan, 1977). This is an excellent examination of race.

Daniels, Roger, *Coming to America: A History of Immigration and Ethnicity in American Life* (New York: Harper Perennial, 1990). This is an excellent history of immigration, focusing on historical periods and individual nationalities.

Fuchs, Lawrence, *The American Kaleidoscope: Race, Ethnicity, and the Civic Culture* (Hanover and London: Wesleyan University Press, 1990). An interesting treatment of the racial and ethnic diversity in the United States and its impact on the civic culture of that society.

Glazer, Nathan and Daniel Patrick Moynihan, *Beyond the Melting Pot,* 2nd ed. (Cambridge, Mass.: The MIT Press, 1970). The classic work in American ethnicity. It focuses on the major ethnic groups in the United States: Irish, Italians, Puerto Rican, Jewish and African Americans.

———, *Ethnicity: Theory and Experience·*(Cambridge, Mass.: Harvard University Press, 1975). An outstanding book of readings. Especially good are the chapters on the Irish, Italians and Black Americans.

Gordon, Milton, *Assimilation in American Life* (New York: Oxford University Press, 1964). This is a classic work that brought order to the study of assimilation and acculturation. His classification scheme is the most widely used by scholars in the field.

Gould, Jay, *Ever Since Darwin: Reflections in Natural History* (New York: Norton, 1977). This is a fine collection of articles on evolution.

Montagu, Ashley, *Man's Most Dangerous Myth: The Fallacy of Race* (Cleveland, World, 1965). A critique of the validity of the concept of race.

Smedley, Audrey, *Race in North America* (Boulder: Westview Press, 1993). A recent treatment of the racial diversity in North America.

QUESTIONS

1. Which of the following is the most accurate statement with regard to race?
   a. Caucasoids are clearly superior to members of the other human races.
   b. Natural selection has nothing to do with racial differences.
   c. There is widespread disagreement among scholars concerning the number of human races.
   d. Race has more to do with the way people behave than with their physical traits.
   e. Mongoloids are clearly inferior to members of the other human races.

2. Ethnic group membership can be based on which of the following?
   a. race, religion, or geographical region
   b. religion, national origin, or geographical region
   c. religion, political beliefs, or race
   d. race, religion, or national origin
   e. national origin, political beliefs, or geographical region

3. Which of the following seem to be the most important factors with regard to the degree and speed of acculturation?
   a. language and values of immigrants
   b. age at time of immigration and place of settlement
   c. language of immigrants and place of settlement
   d. age at time of immigration and values of immigrants
   e. values of immigrants and place of settlement

4. Which of the following statements regarding minority groups is *false?*
   a. They are exceptionally disadvantaged, exceptionally discriminated against, or both.
   b. They find acceptance by others difficult because of their distinguishing physical characteristics.
   c. They have a disproportionately small amount of political and economic power.
   d. They are all ethnic groups, but all ethnic groups are not minority groups.
   e. They are always smaller in number than other groups within the society.

5. If your ancestors came from tropical Africa, you probably have which of the following physical characteristics?
   a. blue eyes and blond hair
   b. light skin and wooly hair
   c. dark skin and wooly hair
   d. light skin and blue eyes
   e. dark skin and blond hair

6. Which of the following phrases would *not* be associated with possible advantages of ethnic group membership?
   a. possessiveness and pressure not to acculturate
   b. a sense of security and identity
   c. refuge in a potentially unfriendly world
   d. having roots—a history and a heritage
   e. acquisition of cultural flexibility

7. The gap between expectations and reality that is often experienced by first-generation immigrants is called
   a. reality gap.
   b. culture shock.
   c. immigrant shock.
   d. culture conflict.
   e. culture gap.

8. One reason why it is difficult to make sharp racial distinctions among people is that
   a. anthropologists have not enumerated enough racial classifications.
   b. physical traits never vary independently of others.
   c. all people are really one or another type of Mongoloid.
   d. the frequency of traits is identical in all human populations.
   e. many physical traits vary independently of others.

9. Milton Gordon's assimilation typology includes "behavioral receptional assimilation," which refers to
   a. the absence of discrimination against the immigrant group.
   b. large-scale intermarriage between natives and immigrants.
   c. a change in cultural patterns to those of the host society.
   d. the absence of prejudice against the immigrant group.
   e. the absence of value and power conflict between natives and immigrants.

10. According to the scales developed by Warner and Srole, which of the following immigrants would have the worst chances of being assimilated into American society? One who was
    a. Mongoloid, Chinese-speaking, and non-Christian
    b. Negroid, English-speaking, and non-Christian

    c. Caucasoid, Spanish-speaking, and Christian
    d. Negroid, French-speaking, and non-Christian
    e. Mongoloid, Japanese-speaking, and Christian

QUESTIONS FOR THOUGHT AND DISCUSSION

1. Explain Darwin's theory of natural selection.

2. Does Warner and Srole's theory of social distance accurately describe the experience of America's ethnic groups?

3. Has migration to the United States led to Anglo-conformity, a melting-pot or cultural pluralism?

6

Behavior Control and Cultural Change

The American tourist visiting London often finds it curious and sometimes astounding that British bobbies (policemen) do not carry firearms. How, the American may ask, do the British maintain law and order within their society under these circumstances? Some have answered that the penalty for carrying firearms in England is so severe that it deters even criminals from carrying them; therefore, since criminals don't carry firearms, it is not necessary for bobbies to carry them. Although such an answer may appear to have great validity at first glance, we think the real reason for people not carrying firearms penetrates much deeper into British culture. In this chapter we will examine those aspects of culture that control, to a great extent, the behavior of people in any given society. In addition to focusing on the behavior control function, we will examine the other side of this coin—the process of cultural change.

☐ Cultural Norms

Cultural **norms** are beliefs about what constitutes proper behavior. Norms, then, are guidelines. They tell us what we ought to do and what we ought not to do. In American society it is considered proper behavior for married men and women to remain faithful to their mates and for people not to cheat on their income tax returns. However, the Kinsey reports revealed many years ago that many married people do not remain faithful to their mates, and it is common knowledge that many people do cheat slightly on their income tax returns. In these cases there

United States and England: A Difference in Cultural Norms
Two versions of the proper way to board a public conveyance.

seems to be a wide discrepancy between the ideal and real behavior patterns of the American people.

The world of what ought to be (the normative order) is different from the world of what is (the factual order), but the two are intimately related. The normative order gives direction to the factual order. In turn, the factual order influences the normative order because norms must refer to, or take into account, events or situations in the factual world. A rule requiring all Americans to face in the direction of Washington, D.C., and say a ten-minute prayer each day in order to prevent malaria might have little usefulness if such a ritual had nothing to do with preventing malaria. Similarly, Prohibition did not stop Americans from consuming alcoholic beverages, and, consequently, Prohibition was repealed. The normative order, then, is influenced by the factual order.

Sometimes the normative order and the factual order may coincide with one another. Prohibition failed not only because it was in conflict with the existing American custom of drinking but also because that custom was supported by cultural norms (that is, it was generally acceptable for adult Americans to drink). To understand the functioning of any given human society, we must understand both its normative and its factual order.

No society adheres strictly to its norms. Norms are ideals that give direction to behavior. We strive to move as far as possible in the guided direction, but we do not actually expect to achieve the ideal. Norms deal with the central problem of all human societies—preserving an acceptable balance between individual freedom and social control. In some societies, the balance may be tipped more in one direction than in the other, but in all societies, norms maintain the balance.

Norms imply obligation; that is, people *ought to* carry out some specified behavior. The culture, of course, may allow them to choose the way in which they comply. Normal behavior in American society

Punishment for Breaking Norms, Circa 1692

requires the wearing of clothes in public, but both miniskirts and maxiskirts are acceptable on the streets of any American city.

Norms don't apply equally to everyone or to all situations. What is considered proper behavior for a parent may be considered improper for his or her child; what applies to a foreman may not apply to a laborer; and the behavior we expect from a man in a given situation may not be the same as what we expect from a woman. This relative quality of norms may partially explain why we Americans expect, accept, and possibly encourage what we call "eccentric behavior" from millionaires and movie stars; but this same behavior may be considered deviant when observed in the rest of us.

The means by which we encourage people to do what they ought to do and not do what they ought not to do are called **sanctions.** There are positive sanctions (rewards) and negative sanctions (punishments). Depending upon the relative value a society places on a particular norm, rewards may vary from a smile or a pat on the back to a medal or some other valuable symbol, and punishments may vary from a frown or some unkind words to physical torture and even death.

☐ Classifying Norms

Even from this cursory discussion of norms, it would be possible to classify them along the lines of several distinctions. For example, we could categorize norms on the basis of their relative importance within a society; or we could divide them into categories based on the kinds of sanctions applied to them, the relative degree to which they approach the factual world, or the particular people to whom they apply. However, we will classify norms according to several traditional broad categories that admittedly overlap one another in terms of the particular distinctions we make. The traditional categories are **folkways, mores,** and **laws.**

Folkways

Folkways are durable, standardized, and obligatory normative patterns that are informally enforced. They are the product of an unplanned natural evolutionary process. Examples of folkways are proper use of the language, etiquette, and treating one's elders with respect. As is readily apparent, folkways are not considered vital to the survival of the society, and sanctions for them are relatively weak. We would not expect American society to fall apart at the seams if people did not say "please" when asking for something, or for a child to face a firing squad because he or she reached across the table for one of mom's biscuits. On the other hand, it is important to realize that folkways are often extremely effective in guiding behavior and that sanctions, although informal and relatively weak, may also be extremely effective. Most children who have been taught not to reach across the table usually don't do it, and if they do, a suitable signal from either mom or dad is probably sufficient to keep them from doing it again.

Scholars often distinguish special kinds of folkways, including *technicways, convention,* and *etiquette.* **Technicways** are technological folkways. They are standards for behavior connected with knowledge and techniques for using machines and tools. They demand instantaneous adjustment, and, as more of them come into being, more and more rapid adjustments will be required of people.

Folkways connected with driving a car, for example, would be classified as technicways. The behavior demanded of those who drive would include proper techniques for steering and parking, for handling the instrument panel, for changing a tire, and so forth. In fact, if the overwhelming majority of people within the society drive cars, it would be expected that generally everyone should know these basic techniques.

Convention refers to prescribed normative behavior that serves to eliminate confusion in human interaction. It is always a matter of convenience, and never a matter of morality. In other words, conventions are standardized procedures that regulate mutual activities; by convention, people act correctly or incorrectly, but their actions have nothing to do with what is morally right or wrong. The conventional greeting used by some societies consists of raising the right hand and saying "how"; in other societies a handshake and "hello" will do. In either case, the individual who fails to follow the prescribed

convention may be obstructing the free flow of interaction, but the person is not considered immoral.

Etiquette (proper manners) is also a matter of convenience in social relations, but it differs from convention in that it implies a choice of appropriate behavior for specific circumstances. Therefore, it may be used as a device for identifying an individual's standing in the social hierarchy. Certainly the manner in which children hold their forks or chopsticks may have little to do with the functional efficiency with which they eat their food. But their proper or improper use of eating utensils may determine how their social standing is judged. The fact that etiquette is a discriminating device that is a matter of social convenience is emphasized by the realization that the improper use of an eating utensil may actually be more functionally effective than the proper use. Like convention, etiquette is not concerned with morality.

Finally, we should point out that sanctions for folkways are often limited to particular groups; and, therefore, they may not be effective when applied to someone who is not a full-fledged member of the group.

Mores

Mores (pronounced *more-rays*) are norms that are considered essential for social survival. Like folkways, they are initially unplanned and their sanctions are informal. Unlike folkways, sanctions for mores are strong and usually depend on the spontaneous reactions of the group. The act of cold-blooded murder, for instance, is considered a violation of mores in many societies, and severe sanctions, such as lynching the murderer, may be applied. Mores are always concerned with morality; that is, they are morally right and their violation is morally wrong. We can readily understand, then, that the members of a society share highly favorable sentiments toward the mores. These common sentiments solidify feelings of group membership, thus providing a basis for ethnocentrism and a sense of resistance and antagonism toward groups with other mores. Mores do not need justification. Generally, they are not subject to deliberate change, and one who criticizes them will receive strong punishment. In fact, criticism of the mores may bring greater punishment than failure to live up to them. For instance, in American society advocating adultery may bring greater sanctions than actually committing adultery.

We refer to mores expressed in negative form as **taboos.** An example of a taboo that exists in every society is the rule against incest. That is, all societies place restrictions on possible mates for individuals. Proper mating relationships vary from society to society, but the incest taboo tells the members of any given society whom they may not mate with rather than whom they may mate with. Some mores, of course, may be stated both positively ("One must always tell the truth") or as a taboo ("One must not lie").

Sanctions for the violation of a mos (the singular form of mores), as we have indicated, are relatively strong. In some cases negative sanctions may be so severe that their use is obviously intended to set an example of what happens when an individual breaks the rules. It is significant that the news article concerning the Karamojans (at the beginning of Chapter 3) reported that only "some" who had worn clothes were required to eat their clothes as a penance. This sanction was no doubt strong enough to keep the rest of the society's members from wearing clothes.

Societies may also rely on the use of cautionary tales to set examples for behavior. It is possible that years from now Karamojans will be telling their young children the story of what happened to those who dared to wear clothes. In addition to supporting norms, such cautionary tales provide emotional relief for the listeners—they learn that it is possible to live through severe punishments inflicted for violating mores. Thus, mores and the sanctions that accompany them, whether experienced directly or vicariously, provide emotional relief for people, as well as aid culture tremendously in performing its behavior control function.

Informally Enforced Norms

Our discussion of folkways and mores indicates a great similarity between them. Both are planned prescriptions for behavior that have been internalized by people over time. Both have positive and negative sanctions which, although informally enforced, are effective in controlling social behavior. Both aid the individual in identifying who and what he or she is, and in providing meaning for life experiences. In fact, their similarities are so great that it makes sense to treat them as parts of the same phenomenon—**informally enforced norms.** In this manner, we can distinguish between norms which evoke stronger feelings and sanctions (mores) and those which evoke weaker feelings and sanctions (folkways). This relationship can be illustrated for American society as follows:

Informally Enforced Norms

Rape	Stealing	Drunkenness	Rudeness	Inappropriate Dress

| **MORES** (Stronger feelings and sanctions) | | | **FOLKWAYS** (Weaker feelings and sanctions) | |

Both rape and stealing are taboos in American society. They evoke strong feelings and sanctions. Rudeness and inappropriate dress are actions that are also discouraged, but they evoke much weaker feelings and sanctions than do rape or stealing. Drunkenness is difficult to classify. Generally, it evokes weaker feelings and sanctions than do rape and stealing, but stronger feelings and sanctions than rudeness and inappropriate dress. In any event, the important point is that informally enforced norms tend to control behavior.

But are they sufficient to control behavior in American society? More generally, are they sufficient to control behavior in any given society? Or, to restate the question, can a society ensure the amount of social control necessary to maintain its culture solely through informally enforced norms? The answer to this question may be yes or no, depending on the society under consideration.

If we are considering a small society (say 100 people) which is geographically isolated from other societies and which possesses a relatively high degree of cultural integration, we may find that informally enforced norms are sufficient to maintain social control. The African bushmen, the Indians of Labrador, and the Ibans of Borneo are examples of societies that at one time or another have relied entirely on these norms to control behavior. In these societies privacy is difficult to obtain: all the people know each other and each other's activities well. Moreover, the geographical isolation of these societies tends to minimize the influence of foreign cultures, thus strengthening the influence of the single cultural tradition learned and shared by the people. Under these circumstances, it is possible for informally enforced norms to exert even greater social control than in other societies which rely on additional means of control.

Conversely, in larger societies which are not isolated and which possess a lower degree of cultural integration (such as American society), more is necessary to ensure the appropriate amount of social control. These societies invariably also rely on laws.

Laws

Laws are deliberately formulated norms that are accompanied by specific, formal sanctions and enforced by some special authority. In literate societies they are always written down. In some instances laws are merely explicit representations of already existing norms; in others, they are responses to current social needs which preexisting norms have not taken into account.

Generally, laws that are explicit representations of preexisting norms, particularly mores, are the most effective laws. In American society, laws against killing tend to be more effective than laws against cheating on income tax returns. This is not only because the penalty for murder is more severe than the penalty for tax fraud but because murder is a taboo and tax fraud is not. Similarly, in England, the law against carrying firearms tends to be more effective than laws against theft because carrying firearms is a stronger taboo than stealing.

Sometimes laws are responses to current social needs. At times societies need guidance for behavior in situations which customs have not taken into account. The invention and use of the automobile, for instance, brought with it the need for a new set of "rules of the road"; pollution from internal combustion engines in automobiles has required new laws regulating their manufacture; traffic congestion and accidents involving pedestrians have dictated new laws for both drivers and pedestrians in inner-city traffic. Obviously, customs were insufficient to guide behavior in these situations.

We have pointed out that laws are accompanied by specific and formal sanctions. When the threat of punishment supports legal definitions of rights and responsibilities, law tends to communicate moral standards. In this way law performs an educational function. Law enforcement tends to "spread the word" concerning socially acceptable and unacceptable actions. Through the law and its enforcement we learn what we ought and ought not to do. This educational significance of law may explain the widespread resistance of people to changing laws that deal with moral standards. "For example, many people may question the wisdom of attempting to regulate sexual conduct through law, but they want to keep the law on the books as a public expression of what is right and proper. They fear that removal of the ban on, say, homosexual relations, would be taken as public approval."[1]

Often law confers legitimacy; that is, it specifies who has the right to exercise what kind of power in certain relationships or positions. Law

Law and the Courts
When informally enforced norms are insufficient to guide behavior. Laws provide a surer degree of social control and perform an educational function as well.

confers legitimacy when it defines landlord-tenant or employer-employee relationships; or when it defines conditions for obtaining, exercising, and holding political office. Law also serves to resolve controversies. For example, when two parties are engaged in an argument concerning property rights, they may present their arguments before a court of law. If the arguing parties believe that the legal process is fair, they will accept the outcome and a conclusive settlement will have been reached.

Like other norms, laws influence expectations. They tell us what behavior to expect in certain situations, thereby providing order and increasing predictability. On the other hand, laws may also be dysfunctional. It has been suggested that the prosecution of laws dealing with "crimes without victims" (such as loitering) drain resources that might better be used in prosecuting more serious crimes. For example, the time required for a public prosecutor to deal with a loitering case might better be used to prosecute a murder case.

Law may be classified in several ways. One way is to classify laws according to their source. Accordingly, statutory law is law that has been made by legislatures. Common law is law made by judges—either through their interpreting statutes or through their adapting legal traditions or precedents to new situations. Another way of classifying law is to distinguish between civil and criminal law. Civil law deals with disputes among private parties, and punishment is not usually connected with the settlement. Criminal law deals with offenses against society, and punishment is always a consideration in such cases. There are additional ways of classifying laws, but it is not necessary to mention them here. The point is that laws may be classified in many different ways because they tend to control behavior in many different situations. They are important norms in societies in which informally enforced norms alone are insufficient to provide the appropriate amount of social control.

Institutions

Our discussion of norms has focused upon folkways, mores, and laws and their similarities and relationships to one another. Are they related in any particular way? If so, how? The answer to the first question is yes; the answer to the second may be understood by considering social institutions.

In Chapter 3 we defined **institutions** as "distinctive patterns that are centered around major human needs and accompanied by particular modes of social interaction." We used the family as an example of a universal institution. Let's take another brief look at the family, this time concentrating on the interrelated set of norms that constitutes the family pattern.

One part of the family pattern is the marriage complex. It includes a series of folkways concerning the proper ways in which men and women may mate. In American culture these folkways include engagement, showers, a ceremony involving an exchange of vows and wedding rings, and throwing rice at the newly married couple. Mores are also included in the marriage complex; that is, keeping the vows, providing support, and so forth. In most societies (those which have laws) the marriage complex also includes laws; for example, license, right of divorce, protection against fraud, and so on.

Another part of the family pattern is the child-rearing complex. Folkways govern the relationship between parents and children in regard to authority and decision making. Mores include obligation of support and the nature of punishment. Laws define the limits of support and punishment.

We could extend this discussion to include other complexes within the family pattern, but that is not necessary: the point is simple and clear—patterns are interrelated sets of norms that form definite structures. These structures perform necessary functions for a society (in the case of the family, reproduction, child-rearing, and sexual gratification are a few). Norms, then, tend to control behavior by defining the particular ways in which a given society performs these functions.

Before we focus our attention on cultural change, it is worthwhile to consider behavior control from one final perspective, supplied by John W. M. Whiting.[2] He contends that all societies rely on at least one of the three mechanisms that are the ultimate sources of behavior control. He refers to them as sorcery, sin, and the superego.

Sorcery is an exaggerated fear of retaliation from other people. It is the basis for social control in societies that practice witchcraft. Like the other two mechanisms, it involves some form of punishment, and it is systematically instilled in the minds of young children. Sin is the dread of punishment by gods or ghosts. Like sorcery, it may serve as the primary mechanism for controlling behavior in small, isolated, and highly integrated societies. The superego is the sense of guilt and readiness to accept blame deriving from a sense of personal responsibility for one's actions. It is the primary behavior control mechanism in larger, more complex societies. All three mechanisms represent forces from which the individual cannot escape: how does one escape the power of witchcraft, or the wrath of a god, or the prodding of one's own conscience?

Whiting has supplied us with an interesting perspective on social control—one that may be pondered and debated. Whether or not these mechanisms are the ultimate sources of behavior control, they may be used to support the normative order in societies in which they are used, and to that extent it is useful to consider them when dealing with the subject of behavior control.

☐ Cultural Change

By reading what we have said about the influence of language, beliefs, and values as integrating aspects and norms as determinants of behavior, one might conclude that culture is static and unchanging. Actually, nothing could be farther from the truth. Culture is dynamic and constantly changing. In fact, language, beliefs, values, and norms, which themselves are constantly subject to change, are stabilizing elements that serve to maintain homeostasis within the dynamic cultural system.

Change comes from a variety of sources. One source of cultural change is **diffusion**—the transfer of cultural traits, complexes, and patterns from one society to another. Diffusion occurs whenever contact takes place between or among different cultures. It is considered one of the most important sources of cultural change because it accounts for a major part of it. Anthropologists have revealed that many if not most of the traits in any given culture have been borrowed from other cultures. For example, American culture, as one would expect, has borrowed heavily from other ways of life. In *The Study of Man*,[3] Ralph Linton graphically describes the "100 percent American" as one whose daily habits depend almost exclusively on traits borrowed from other cultures. The conclusion of Linton's description captures its overriding flavor. "While smoking he reads the news of the day, imprinted in characters invented by the ancient Semites upon a material invented in China by a process invented in Germany. As he absorbs the accounts of foreign troubles he will, if he is a good conservative citizen, thank a

Hebrew deity in an Indo-European language that he is 100 percent American."

One of the most dramatic examples of change resulting from diffusion was presented in Chapter 3 when we described what happened to the Tanala when they began to adopt wet rice cultivation from a neighboring tribe. This example, also supplied by Linton, revealed changes in the Tanalas' marriage and kinship systems, warfare practices, and political system as well as their method of food production.

While noting that diffusion leads to cultural change, we should also note that a culture's homeostatic elements resist the introduction of foreign traits that do not "fit" into the cultural configuration. Even traits that do fit are modified to some extent to reflect the unmistakable imprint of the recipient culture. This tendency toward consistency, supplied by a culture's homeostatic elements, tends to make even rapidly changing cultures stable and continuous.

Another great source of cultural change is **discovery-invention**—the process whereby new elements or new combinations of preexisting elements are introduced from within rather than from outside the existing culture. Discovery-invention is particularly important for cultures with advanced technologies because technological growth, like population growth, tends to advance at a geometric rate. The meaning of a geometric growth rate is illustrated dramatically by the following fact: if you were to start with a penny on June 1, double it, for a total of two cents, on June 2, and continue to redouble the amount day by day, by the end of June you would have $5,368,509.12!

If it is true that technological growth tends to advance at a geometric rate, then it is also true that a culture with a large number of artifacts will experience technological change more rapidly than a culture with fewer artifacts. As the number of discoveries-inventions increases, technological change becomes faster and faster. Alvin Toffler, who seriously questions our ability to cope with the amount of change currently being thrust upon us, provides a sobering illustration of the tremendous technological change in contemporary American culture. He points out that by dividing the last 50,000 years of our existence into lifetimes of about 62 years each, we would produce about 800 such lifetimes. Of these, "only during the last four has it been possible to measure time with any precision. Only in the last two has anyone anywhere used an electric motor. And the overwhelming majority of all the material goods we use in daily life today have been developed within the present, the 800th lifetime."[4] Certainly the pace of change is increasing in industrial societies.

Discovery-invention usually goes through a two-step process of being accepted into the culture. The first step consists of people changing their everyday behavior to accommodate the new device. The second step consists of people changing their beliefs and institutions to include the new device, and arranging means to control its effects. The time between the two steps is called **cultural lag.** The time between the introduction of the steam engine to run machines in factories and the passage of workmen's compensation laws to offset industrial accidents represents a relatively long cultural lag. The time between the invention of the automobile and the passage of laws to control its speed and direction was a relatively short one.

Change brought about by discovery-invention may reinforce, as well as alter, the already existing cultural configuration. The widespread use of television, for instance, allows literally millions of Americans to view simultaneously a speech by the President, thus exposing them to the same set of beliefs, values, and norms expressed in one language. In this manner technology reinforces the existing culture.

A third source of cultural change is planning. In many instances change is planned by organized social movements that work to make the planned change a reality. The American labor movement began to promote the idea of collective bargaining in the last half of the nineteenth century; today, collective bargaining is an accepted part of American economic life. Sometimes planned change is brought about by political revolution. The French, American, and Russian revolutions, for instance, produced changes in norms and values as well as in social structure.

Often change is planned by governments and large corporations. Governmental planning is most obvious in the passage of social legislation. The Social Security Act of 1935 and the Civil Rights Acts of 1964, 1965, and 1968 are examples of such legislation. They have fostered changes in American beliefs, values, and norms. Corporate planning for business expansion and the marketing of new products is also geared toward changing beliefs, values, and norms. Successful mass marketing techniques seem to have convinced Americans that television is an absolute necessity, when really it is merely a technological convenience. Through government and corporate planning a peasant society may jump across a cultural chasm to become an industrial society in a very short time; Russia has done so.

Today the governments of practically all industrial societies are actively planning change. With the effects of a geometric growth rate to contend with, they don't have much choice. They must anticipate and guide change in an attempt to maintain the smooth functioning of their cultural and social systems. If they do not, they are running the risk of having potentially dysfunctional elements destroy the existing systems. From the standpoint of system maintenance, then, planning is the most important source of cultural change in industrial societies.

Revolution as Cultural Change
A planned change in the mores concerning the economic, political, and social relationships of the classes was effected by the French Revolution. (Film still from D. W. Griffith's *Orphans in the Storm.* Courtesy of the Museum of Modern Art)

One final source of cultural change is change itself. The parts of a culture are interrelated so that a change in one part of the system, regardless of its source, may produce changes in other parts of the system. An excellent example of this is contained in the story of Henry Ford and his automobile. Ford's methods for producing and promoting his auto led to mass production and mass consumption becoming major components of American life. The widespread use of the automobile has produced changing American life-styles which include drive-in movies, restaurants, churches, and banks as well as summer car trips, sitting still on jammed expressways, and the expectation of thousands of people dying in traffic accidents next year. Other effects of the automobile, such as air pollution and the growth of the motel, rubber, and petroleum industries could be elaborated upon, but the point remains the same—a change in one part of the culture system may produce changes in many other parts.

Culture, therefore, is dynamic; it is vibrant and alive. Even in small, isolated societies culture changes from one generation to the next; the pace may be slow, but change occurs nonetheless. Change, then, is a fact of life. It occurs whether or not we want it or like it. The problem of each generation is to foster a positive orientation toward it, and to cope with it in a manner that is not ultimately destructive to the whole cultural system.

☐ Culture—A Brief Systemic Analysis

In this and the four preceding chapters, we have surveyed culture. We have considered its beginnings, structure, functions, and purpose. Now let's try to put it all together in a brief systemic analysis.

The culture system operates in the same fashion as other analytic systems. Inputs to the culture system are all elements that may produce change. These include ideas, objects, and behaviors obtained through diffusion, and all other traits produced through planning or technology, whether by chance or design. Conversion is the process by which raw inputs are shaped to conform with the basic orientation of the culture's integrating elements—its language, belief system, and value system. The culture's strain to consistency is most evident in the conversion process; through this process homeostasis is achieved. Outputs are the behavior control elements—norms and institutions—as well as artifacts and ideas. They, together with new change elements, are then fed back into the system as new inputs. (See diagram on p. 137.)

Culture was originally formed as a survival mechanism for human beings—a means of adapting to a changing environment. Once formed, however, systems take on needs of their own. The overriding goal of every culture is to perpetuate itself. In order to achieve this goal, the

The Culture System

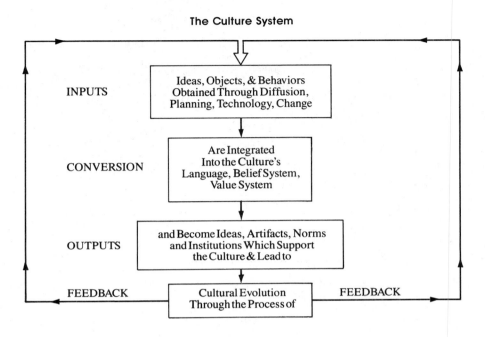

maintenance, adaptation, integration, and goal-attainment functions are performed by language, beliefs, values, norms, sanctions, and institutions in the process described in the preceding paragraph. In this manner, the social heritage is preserved.

By perpetuating themselves, however, some cultures seem to be acting as dysfunctional elements in the larger life system—nature. Remember, culture is only one of many adaptive mechanisms found in nature. Culture is functional within the total life system only to the extent that it tends to perpetuate life. But, as we pointed out at the end of Chapter 2, culture is currently threatening to upset the balance of nature in a way that may ultimately lead to the destruction of all life on this planet. Technology has put us on the horns of a dilemma in which the overriding goal of nature (to maintain life) and the overriding goal of culture (to maintain itself) are directly opposed to one another.

What will happen? Will people continue to perpetuate cultures that threaten all of nature? The answer depends on us. This means that the responsibility for people's actions is placed squarely on our own shoulders. If we want to change the direction of our culture, we can. But that will not be easy to do, for culture is a gigantic force that tends to mold people into what they, as individuals, can become. If people are to change culture, they must change themselves first, all of which impels us to focus our attention on people as individuals. In Part III we will do just that.

REFERENCES

1. Leonard Broom and Philip Selznick, *Sociology*, 4th ed. (New York: Harper & Row, 1968), p. 380.
2. John W. M. Whiting, "Sorcery, Sin, and the Superego: A Cross-Cultural Study of Some Mechanisms of Social Control." In M. R. Jones, ed., *Nebraska Symposium on Motivation* (Lincoln: University of Nebraska Press, 1959), pp. 174–195.
3. Ralph Linton, *The Study of Man* (New York: D. Appleton-Century Co., 1936), pp. 326–327.
4. Alvin Toffler, *Future Shock* (New York: Bantam Books, 1971), p. 14.

GLOSSARY

Norms	Beliefs about what constitutes proper behavior; ideal behavior patterns.
Sanctions	Means by which people are encouraged to obey norms. Positive sanctions are rewards; negative sanctions are punishments.
Folkways	Durable, standardized, and informally enforced norms that are not considered vital to a society's survival.
Technicways	Technological folkways; folkways dealing with knowledge and techniques for using machines and tools. Example: knowing how to use a pocket calculator.
Etiquette	Folkways that prescribe proper manners. Etiquette implies a choice of appropriate behavior for specific circumstances. Example: "You should chew your food with your mouth closed."
Convention	Standardized folkways that serve to eliminate confusion in human interaction by regulating mutual activities. Example: using a handshake as a standard greeting.
Mores	Standardized and informally enforced norms that are considered vital to the survival of the society. Mores are always concerned with morality, and they carry strong sanctions. (Singular: mos.)
Taboos	Mores expressed in negative form. Example: "One must not kill."

Informally enforced norms	A classification of norms that includes folkways and mores.
Laws	Deliberately formulated norms that are accompanied by specific, formal sanctions and enforced by some special authority.
Institutions	Distinctive patterns that are centered around major human needs and accompanied by particular modes of social interaction. Example: politics or the political system.
Diffusion	The transfer of cultural traits, complexes, and patterns from one society to another. Western society, for example, abandoned its own system of Roman numerals and replaced it with the more useful Eastern system of Arabic numerals.
Discovery-invention	The process whereby new elements are introduced from within rather than from outside the existing culture. Discovery refers to gaining knowledge of something previously unknown. Invention refers to applying existing knowledge in a new way.
Cultural lag	The time lapse between the change of everyday behavior of people to accommodate a new device and the change of their beliefs and institutions to include the new device and arrange means to control its effects. Example: the time between the invention of the automobile and the passage of laws to control its speed and direction.

SELECTED READING

Bernard, H. R., and P. J. Pelto, eds. *Technology and Social Change,* 2nd ed. (Prospect Heights, Ill.: Waveland, 1987). A reader dealing with the effects of Western technology on various cultures.

Chirot, D. *Social Change in the Modern Era* (New York: Harcourt Brace Jovanovich, 1986). An overview of social change throughout the world.

Johnston, W. B., and A. E. Packer. *Workforce 2000: Work and Workers for the Twenty-First Century* (Indianapolis: Hudson Institute, 1987). Projections about changes in work and workers.

Liebs, C. H. *Main Street to Miracle Mile: American Roadside Architecture* (Boston: New York Graphic Society/Little, Brown, 1985). An examination of how social change has been reflected in twentieth century changes in roadside architecture in the United States.

Reich, R. B. *The Work of Nations* (New York: Vantage, 1992). A discussion of the global economy and its implications for change in the United States.

Sumner, W. G. *Folkways* (New York: New American Library, Mentor Books, 1970). Sumner's classic discussion of norms, originally published in 1906.

QUESTIONS

1. One characteristic of mores is
   a. they are formal and are accompanied by specific sanctions.
   b. people use them to facilitate interaction.
   c. they are considered essential for social survival.
   d. people who violate them receive weak sanctions.
   e. they are guidelines for dealing with technology.

2. The time between the introduction of the automobile and the passage of laws to control its speed and direction is an example of
   a. change.
   b. cultural integration.
   c. diffusion.
   d. cultural lag.
   e. convention.

3. Cultural norms are
   a. the real behavior patterns of people.
   b. beliefs about what constitutes proper behavior.
   c. sources of great change within society.
   d. beliefs about the nature of reality.
   e. sources of diffused traits and patterns.

4. A kind of folkway that implies a choice of appropriate behavior for a specific circumstance is called
   a. technicway.
   b. etiquette.
   c. convention.
   d. taboo.
   e. mos.

5. Which of the following always carry strong sanctions?
   a. folkways
   b. technicways
   c. norms
   d. conventions
   e. mores

6. All of the following are true about folkways except one. Which one is false?
   a. They are durable.
   b. They are standardized.

    c. They are obligatory normative patterns that are informally enforced.

    d. They are the product of an unplanned, natural evolutionary process.

    e. They are considered vital to the survival of the society.

7. Diffusion refers to
    a. the transfer of cultural traits, complexes, and patterns from one society to another.
    b. the process in which existing knowledge is used in some new form.
    c. the process whereby new elements are introduced from within rather than from outside the existing culture.
    d. a source of cultural change that is always the result of planning.
    e. a means of motivating scientists to make new discoveries.

8. Laws are always accompanied by
    a. weak sanctions.
    b. strong sanctions.
    c. specific but informal sanctions.
    d. specific but formal sanctions.
    e. general but informal sanctions.

9. Mores expressed in negative form are called
    a. laws.
    b. conventions.
    c. taboos.
    d. sanctions.
    e. technicways.

10. The means by which people are encouraged to obey norms are called
    a. rewards.
    b. punishments.
    c. laws.
    d. sanctions.
    e. conventions.

QUESTIONS FOR THOUGHT AND DISCUSSION

1. Do societies really need laws?

2. Can we cope with the pace of change in contemporary American society?

3. When is culture lag really culture lag?

THREE

Socialization and Personality

Each person is a unique individual who inherits a unique set of biological characteristics and proceeds through a unique set of life experiences. In the following two chapters we concentrate on the individual.

In Chapter 7 we consider how individuals learn culture as they proceed through physiological and social development. We emphasize that both types of development follow sequential patterns that are correlated with one another. We focus on the formation and development of the self-concept, including a consideration of the social structures within which human interaction takes place. The final section of Chapter 7 concentrates on potential adjustment patterns for individuals as they deal with society's demand for conformity.

In Chapter 8 we consider the three prevailing general approaches used by social scientists to explain how each person's distinctive pattern of thoughts, feelings, and actions is formed. We also examine the theories of three particular personality theorists and discuss how each of the three general approaches may be applied. In this manner you will learn specific theories as well as general approaches to the study of personality.

7

The Socialization Process

About three hundred years ago the English philosopher John Locke likened the newborn human to a blank tablet which would be filled in by life experiences. Today we recognize that Locke's analogy contains a useful insight into human nature. Each of us inherits a unique set of genetic characteristics (our own blank tablet), and each of us proceeds through a unique set of life experiences. Differences among individuals, then, can be explained by the interaction of each person's unique biological capacities with his or her environmental experiences. A person with gross mental deficiencies will never become a genius, regardless of the environmental conditions the person experiences. Likewise, one with great intellectual capacity will never approach the limits of that capacity if the environmental conditions he or she experiences do not permit the person to do so.

Both heredity and environment, therefore, are important factors in the process of becoming human which we refer to as **socialization.** This is the process in which individuals learn the roles, rules, relationships, and culture of their society. In this chapter we will consider how the individual learns culture as he or she proceeds through physical and social cycles of development. We will briefly survey the important structures that influence socialization, the process by which people may gain the autonomy necessary to influence their own behavior, and possibly the direction their culture may take.

☐ Physical Development

Human beings are biological organisms. They possess the ability to respond to stimulation, to move, to regulate inputs and outputs of energy, and to reproduce. They proceed physically through the process of development (that is, over time, they move from simple to complex levels of organization).

In the **embryonic stage** (the first two months following conception) the organism increases in size from about 0.14 millimeters in diameter to about one and one-half inches. Cell layers that become the nervous, circulatory, skeletal, muscular, digestive, and glandular systems are formed and continue to develop. During the **fetal stage** (third month following conception until birth), the organism continues developing in such a manner that it has all of the biological equipment necessary to survive at birth. During the **neonatal stage** (roughly the first four weeks following birth), the organism "breaks in" its biological equipment. It begins to breathe, to digest, to circulate the blood, and so on. By the beginnings of **infancy** (about the first two or three years of life), the organism is well designed for sleeping, eating, and eliminating. It is during infancy that the organism truly begins to become human. The process of maturation defines the blank tablet so that experience may imprint a unique identity on it.

Maturation refers to the unfolding of the infant's biological potential. It includes the concept of **growth**—biological changes that take place over time. Such changes take place naturally (specific experience or practice is not necessary for them to occur). At the appropriate times, infants begin to see and hear, to stay awake longer, to control voluntary muscles, to sit, to stand, to crawl, to walk, to feed themselves, and to talk. Although all typical infants do not mature at the same pace, they do go through this same sequence of events during infancy. One may begin to talk at age one, while another may not talk until two; however, all normal infants see, hear, and gain control over their voluntary muscles before they begin to talk.

Growth begins at the moment of conception and continues until the individual attains biological maturity. Recent research, however, indicates that the most critical period of growth is the first 45 months (from conception until three years of age).[1] For example, brain cells grow both in number and size until about one year after birth. Afterwards, they grow only in size. If the child is undernourished both before and after birth, there can be a substantial loss of brain cells, and the brain itself may be as much as 60 percent smaller than normal! Such inadequate brain growth due to malnutrition can seriously affect the child's maturation.

As infants proceed through this growth process, they also mature cognitively. At first, their cognitive world (that is, their knowing world) is severely restricted; indeed, they seem to know nothing. But as time passes, their awareness of the environment increases, as does their ability to distinguish parts of the environment. They come to know their parents and eventually they become aware of themselves as objects. At this point they can see the world from only one perspective—their own.

Later they mature to the point where they can perceive the perspectives of other people too. Cognitive growth, then, like physical growth, proceeds in a sequential pattern as the individual moves through physiological development.

☐ Learning

As the person is developing, he or she is also learning. The two go hand-in-hand. **Learning** is modifying behavior as the result of experience. As we have previously pointed out, a human's species-specific brain is well designed for learning verbal behavior and rule making. Since it is through learning that the "blank tablet" gets filled in, it is essential that we gain an understanding of the learning process.

Learning takes place through association. In other words, the learner associates one aspect of the environment with another and modifies his or her behavior as the result of such an association. One kind of association is called **classical conditioning** or **respondent conditioning.** It is concerned with *respondent* behavior, a reflexive type of behavior that is preceded and elicited by a stimulus. For example, if someone were to place a lit match directly under your hand, you would quickly pull your hand away. Experiencing the sensation of extreme heat (the stimulus) causes the respondent behavior of pulling your hand away (the reflexive response). Early in the twentieth century, **behaviorists** discovered that such respondent behavior could be *conditioned.* Suppose, for instance, each time the lit match were placed under your hand, someone also rang a bell. Eventually, you would make such a strong association between the heat and the sound of the bell that if the bell were rung, *even without the lit match being present,* you would jerk back your hand. This process of substituting a neutral stimulus for the original and still eliciting the reflexive response is classical or respondent conditioning.

The early behaviorists made two other important discoveries. First, they found that a conditioned response would gradually diminish and eventually disappear completely if the neutral stimulus were never again paired with the original stimulus (for example, if you never again burned your hand when a bell was ringing, eventually you would stop jerking back your hand at the sound of a bell). This process is called **extinction.** Second, the early behaviorists found that the conditioned response tended to generalize to other similar but neutral stimuli (for instance, you might jerk back your hand upon hearing a buzzer or a whistle as well as a bell). This is called **stimulus generalization.**

Classical conditioning is obviously an important concept in understanding how and why we display certain learned behavior. It explains much of the learning experienced by young children. Learning a language, for instance, involves the effective substitution of words for

Operant Conditioning
Homerun Chicken has been trained to perform a certain task by rewarding it for performance, thus setting up an association between performance and reward in the mind of the bird.

things. A child hears the word *dog* while experiencing a particular animal. Later, when the child hears the word *dog*, he or she looks for that same animal.

Another type of association is known as **operant conditioning.** It is the process in which an emitted behavior produces consequences such that the probability that the behavior will be repeated under similar circumstances in the future is changed. Suppose, for example, you are visiting Las Vegas and you decide to try your luck with a slot machine. Let's assume that you have never been much of a gambler, so you decide to limit your gambling to only one dollar. You will spend this dollar by putting a quarter in the machine and pulling the handle on four successive occasions. Finally, let's say that each of the four times you play, you win a dollar. The odds are that you will play again, regardless of your previous decision to gamble only one dollar. Why? The reason is that each time you behaved in a particular way (playing the machine), you were rewarded (the machine paid off); so you anticipate that by displaying the same behavior again, you will be rewarded again. You have been operantly conditioned to play the machine because your behavior produced positive consequences.

The process by which a behavior is made more likely to occur is called **reinforcement.** Reinforcement works in two ways: one is based on the type of reinforcement, and the other on its regularity. There are two types of reinforcement that occur in operant conditioning—positive and negative. Both increase the probability that a response will be repeated. **Positive reinforcement** exists when something perceived as pleasant follows a response. Playing the slot machine in the previous example led to the accumulation of money. It is important to realize that the learner must perceive the payoff as a reward; if not, the probability that the response will be repeated is not increased. If, for example, you put a dollar in the slot machine and it paid off only a nickel, then you might conclude that the machine is not worth playing again. **Negative reinforcement** occurs when something perceived as unpleasant is removed from a situation after a response is emitted. For example, suppose that you are in the library, trying to study for an exam, and you are distracted by a couple of people nearby who are talking in loud voices. If you were to leave the room, thus getting away from the noise and regaining concentration, you would be increasing the probability that the next time you are in a similar situation, you would respond by leaving the room.

The second consideration with regard to reinforcement is its regularity. Some behaviors are **continuously reinforced**; that is, there is a payoff each time the behavior is emitted. For example, flicking up the light switch in your bedroom results consistently in the light's going on. Since you have been continuously reinforced for flicking the switch, you continue to do so. B. F. Skinner, the psychologist most often associated with operant conditioning, has found that when the usual reinforcement is not forthcoming in such situations, the result is often disturbing but sometimes humorous. Thus, if you flick the switch and the light does not come on, your initial reaction might very well be anger or laughter. Skinner has also found that continuously reinforced behaviors extinguish rapidly if reinforcement ceases. If, for instance, the light doesn't turn on when you flick the switch, it doesn't take long for you to stop flicking the switch.

Many behaviors, of course, are not continuously reinforced; their reinforcement is said to be **intermittent.** Conditioned behavior maintained by intermittent reinforcement does not generate disturbing results when reinforcement is not forthcoming, and intermittently reinforced behaviors take longer to extinguish. Suppose, for example, you know the light will turn on only sometimes when you flick the switch. In this case, you would not become disturbed if you were to flick the switch and the light didn't go on. After all, you wouldn't expect it to turn on every time, so you would keep flicking the switch for a long time before giving up on it completely. Thus, intermittent reinforcement is particularly important in a consideration of our repeated response patterns.

Although this discussion has focused on reinforcement, we must point out that it is possible to learn to behave in particular ways because we have been **punished** (penalized) rather than rewarded. According to the **law of effect,** a principle formulated by Edward Lee Thorndike, responses leading to satisfying consequences are strengthened and therefore tend to be repeated, and responses leading to unsatisfying consequences are weakened and therefore tend not to be repeated. Certainly, punishment qualifies as an unsatisfying consequence; hence, punishment as well as reinforcement can condition behavior.

Skinner recognizes two types of punishment. One occurs when unpleasant consequences follow a response (for example, being turned down upon asking someone for a date); the other occurs when a reinforcer is removed after a response (for instance, taking away a child's allowance because he or she has misbehaved). However, Skinner has severe reservations regarding the use and effectiveness of punishment. He believes that both types tend to suppress behaviors temporarily rather than to weaken the overall tendency to respond. Thus, when punishment ceases, the behavior is likely to return. In addition, punishment may produce secondary consequences that are ultimately undesirable (as, for example, when the child who is punished for "talking back" to his or her parents avoids standing up for his or her rights even when it is appropriate to do so).

A related Skinnerian concept is "aversive control," in which threats are used to encourage expected behaviors. Thus, the boss threatens to fire the worker, the parent threatens to spank the child, the teacher threatens to fail the student, and so forth. Skinner contends that aversive control, like punishment, is ultimately ineffective and/or may lead to undesirable consequences. He prefers the use of reinforcement to shape desirable, adaptive behavior.

Thus far we have identified two kinds of association: respondent and operant conditioning. A third kind is **imitation.** The learner observes the behavior of a model and then imitates that behavior. The child may learn a good portion of self-related behavior through imitation. In a traditional family, the American boy, taking his father for a model, soon learns that males are not supposed to cry, but they are supposed to go to work and provide for the family. Imitating her mother, the traditional American girl similarly learns that females cook and sew as well as tend to babies, and the daughters of more liberated mothers may learn that preparing for a professional career is of crucial importance.

Children learn many behaviors through imitation. Generally, they imitate the behavior of those who are most significant to them. Parents, movie and TV stars, athletes, astronauts, teachers, and friends may serve as behavior models for them. Much learning, then, is the result of imitation; in fact, in many languages the word for *teach* is the same as the word for *show*, and they mean literally the same thing.[2]

A fourth kind of association is **insight.** The learner "puts two and two together" and forms a new relationship between two aspects of the environment. Thus, many original learnings are products of many experiences that are put together in an instant. In his book *Learning Theory for Teachers*,[3] Morris L. Bigge tells the story of how Corporal Jones helped an army recruit gain an insight. Jones was trying to teach the recruit not to anticipate the rifle's kick by pulling back his shoulder when firing the rifle, thus spoiling his aim. The recruit was convinced that he really didn't anticipate the kick and therefore maintained that he didn't pull back until after he squeezed the trigger. When the recruit wasn't looking, Jones slipped a fired cartridge into the rifle's firing chamber. "The recruit aimed, started to squeeze [the trigger], and again jumped out of his skin. He thereby gained an insight. He was jumping before his rifle fired and thus ruining his aim. His jumping before the rifle had fired then ceased." In this manner, we learn through insight.

Learned responses tend to generalize to situations other than those in which they were learned, regardless of the kind of association that was originally made. A negative encounter with a person of a particular race or religion may produce a negative response not only to that particular person but to all people of that race or religion. Being rewarded for working hard in school may generalize to working hard in one's job, avocation, and recreational activities. Aggression learned by observing a model display aggressive behavior in a particular situation may be used in other appropriate situations. As we pointed out in Chapter 4, generalizing is necessary because it is impossible to treat all people or situations as though they were unique. When generalizations are appropriate, they may be effective when dealing with the experiential world. When they are inappropriate, they may cause undue stress or anxiety. As we experience events, we modify our generalizations. This modification of generalizations is the distinctly human process of learning concepts.

☐ Social Development

Human beings develop socially as well as physiologically; that is, they move from simple to complex statuses and roles. A **status** is a social position. Every person has several statuses. For example, the same person may have family statuses (wife, mother), an age status (thirty), a sex status (female), an occupational status (accountant), a religious status (Protestant), a nationality status (Irish-American), and so forth. Each status carries with it a **role** or roles (that is, a pattern of expected behavior). We may expect fathers to behave differently from sons, males to behave differently from females, and adults to behave differently from children.

As infants begin the process of socialization, they fill relatively simple statuses that require relatively simple role behavior. As time passes, they assume more complex statuses and roles. Generally, they move from simple statuses or roles to more complex ones: they master the simple ones and learn the basic requirements of the more complex ones. We refer to this learning in advance of future statuses and roles as **anticipatory socialization.**

Social development is correlated with physiological development so that children in all societies are not expected to fill statuses and play roles that are beyond their physical and cognitive capabilities at any given time. By the same token, it is expected that individuals will not display behavior associated with simple statuses when they are physiologically quite mature. We do not expect infants to be responsible for their own behavior, neither do we expect that adults will lie on the floor, kicking their feet and crying because they cannot get their own way in some situation.

Generally, socialization proceeds through a sequence of stages in which the individual moves from dependent to independent to interdependent statuses and roles. Although statuses and roles are defined differently from one society to the next, all societies differentiate stages of social development in roughly the same sequence: infancy-childhood, adolescence, marriage, parenthood, and grandparenthood.[4] These stages vary in duration and intensity from one society to the next. Each stage contains appropriate statuses and roles which the individual is expected to learn when he or she is in the correlated stage of physiological development.

The relationship between physiological development and social development is clearly seen in the work of the Swiss psychologist Jean Piaget.[5] In language development, for example, Piaget notes that the child's early patterns of speech are "egocentric." Young children use self-centered words such as "I," "my," "mine," and "me." They are capable of expressing their own thoughts and feelings but incapable of considering those of others. With maturation, however, they are able to take the position of others, and their speech patterns are adjusted to account for the needs and interests of others as well as their own.

Piaget has also observed that people view moral judgments in different lights, depending on their level of maturation. At first, young

Stages of Socialization
At each stage of social development, the person learns the expected behavior patterns for his/her status, then, as she/he matures physiologically, leaves them behind for a new set.

children view right and wrong in absolute terms. What is right is what has been deemed right by significant adults in their environment, and they do not have the ability to comprehend any alternatives. As they mature, they gain the ability to judge behavior in terms of its consequences so that right becomes "what I can get away with." Still later they develop the ability to view behavior from the perspective of others and to judge behavior in terms of motives or intentions. "Thus in discussing a hypothetical story, a young child may say that a boy who steals is bad; later, that a boy who is caught stealing is bad, and, at an older age, that a rich boy who steals is worse than a poor boy who steals."[6]

Frederick Elkin has pointed out that there are three preconditions necessary for the child to become socialized: an ongoing society; requisite biological inheritance (the biological capacities to develop normally); and "human nature."[7] At this point you should already have an adequate understanding of an ongoing society and requisite biological inheritance; therefore, let us direct our attention to human nature.

Elkin defines human nature in terms of two abilities. One is the ability to *empathize*, "to establish emotional relationships with others and to experience such sentiments as love, sympathy, shame, envy, pity, and pride."[8] The other is the ability to *symbolize*.

Human nature is not biologically inherited; it develops in **primary groups** (small groups such as the family, in which people have intimate and intense face-to-face contacts frequently). Since most people experience primary relationships early in life, most people have human nature. There have been some reports, however, of children who either have been raised in relative isolation[9] or who have been deprived of attention and affection as infants.[10] In both instances the children involved displayed a lack of human nature. The primary group, then, is necessary for the individual to develop human nature. Once individuals have human nature, along with an ongoing society and adequate biological inheritance, they are ready to become socialized—to become human within the context of their society.

The individual learns culture through contact with other people, but some people exert a greater influence on social development than do others. Parents, for example, are likely to have great influence on the early social development of their children. Later, particular teachers, relatives, or friends may also be especially influential in their continued social development. We refer to these more influential people as **significant others.** By serving as models, and by dispensing rewards and punishments, they teach children particular behavior patterns. Thus, significant others aid not only in the socialization process but also in the personality development of children. Along with appropriate statuses and roles, the children begin to develop unique identities as a result of interactions with significant others.

Significant Others
People who are especially influential with us serve as models in our social development.

☐ The Self-concept

Through the process of socialization the individual develops a self or **self-concept**—a conscious sense of who and what he or she is. In turn, the self, which continues to develop and change throughout life, affects the individual's socialization. Many social scientists have studied and written about the self, and we will now briefly survey what a few of them say.

George Herbert Mead speaks of the self as being fully developed when individuals have the ability to act toward themselves in the same manner that they act toward other people.[11] In other words, individuals possess a self when they can view their own thoughts, feelings, and actions as though they were the thoughts, feelings, and actions of another person; that is, when they can treat themselves as both the subject and the object of their own behavior.

In Mead's view the self develops in three continuous stages. In the initial or preparatory stage, young children imitate the actions of those

Play Stage

around them, particularly significant others. When the child's actions meet with the approval of the significant others, and positive reinforcements are given, the child is motivated to learn those actions. In this manner children begin to put themselves in the position of others. This is a critical first step in the development of the self because children must learn to take the position or role of others before they can begin to view their own behavior objectively. Recent findings support Mead's view. For example, one study reveals that one-year-olds spend more than 20 percent of their waking hours staring intently at objects in their environment.[12] This staring is a logical prerequisite to imitation.

In the play stage, children actually begin playing roles; they begin to associate particular statuses with particular behaviors. The child plays mother, father, doctor, teacher, Batman, Uncle Ralph, and so on. Such role-playing allows the child to act toward him or herself. For example, while playing doctor little Clyde may pretend that the doctor gives little Clyde an injection. By taking the roles of others, then, children first begin to direct activity toward themselves. Self development is not complete in the play stage, however, because the child does not yet possess a unified self-concept. He or she has merely learned to play a number of unrelated roles.

The self becomes complete in the game stage. As time passes, children are put into situations in which they must take several roles simultaneously (that is, they must respond to the expectations of a number of people at the same time). Mead uses the game of baseball to illustrate this situation. Throughout the game the child must visualize the intentions, expectations, and possible actions of the other players. In so doing children consider what is expected of them and the other players from the general standpoint of the team. They therefore begin to view themselves not from the position of particular individuals, but from the position of several individuals acting as a group. Mead refers to this group position as the "generalized other." It represents a set of standpoints common to the group.

Children, then, achieve a generalized standpoint from which they can judge their own behavior. They can conduct themselves in an organized and consistent manner. In addition, they use the generalized other to judge the behavior of others. Thus they have learned a framework for interaction in society. Furthermore, the generalized other allows them to behave consistently in a variety of social environments. Mead illustrates this last point by referring to the Englishman who "dresses for dinner" in the wilds of Africa.

Mead treats the self as a concept that evolves through three continuous stages as the child learns a series of roles. Once fully formed, the self continues to develop, and its development depends primarily on the reactions of others to the individual.

Charles Horton Cooley also stresses the reactions of others in self development.[13] He refers to a "looking-glass self" in which individuals view themselves from the standpoint of others who act as mirrors for their actions. In other words, individuals come to know themselves through the reactions of others to their actions. If they continually receive positive reinforcement for a particular action, they are likely to incorporate that action into their self-concept; conversely, if the reinforcement is negative, they will be likely to discard the action.

A number of social scientists have emphasized the importance of self needs in the socialization process. Generally they indicate that once the self is formed, it takes on needs of its own; and these self needs affect our perceptions and determine, to a great extent, what we will learn and what our actions will be.

Abraham Maslow has constructed a hierarchy of needs that develop from low to high.[14] This hierarchy unfolds as the lower needs are met and those of the next level emerge.

At the base of Maslow's hierarchy are the *physical* needs (air, water, and so forth). They must be met before the next set of needs emerges; indeed, they are so basic that they must be met in order to sustain life. Most social scientists refer to such needs as *primary* needs. They are unlearned, biologically based, and related to the maintenance of life itself. Once these physical needs are satisfied, *safety* needs emerge. These are learned needs that are related to physical and psychological security.

The relationship between physical and safety needs may be illustrated by considering the following situation: A hungry man is in a cave. Outside the cave there are some wild berries that can satisfy his hunger. However, outside the cave there is also a wild animal that may attack and kill him. If he stays in the cave, he will be safe from the animal's attack, but he will not be able to satisfy his hunger. If he leaves the cave, he will satisfy his hunger, but he will probably be attacked. What will he do? According to Maslow, he will satisfy his safety need until his physical need becomes unbearable. At that point he has no choice but to take his chances and try to get the berries. In effect, the safety need is nonexistent until the physical need is satisfied.

When safety needs are satisfied, *belongingness* and *love* needs arise. Maslow is referring to affectionate and satisfying relationships with other people. If the individual attains such relationships, *esteem* needs appear. The individual desires to be respected by others and to respect him or herself. Once the individual has gained respect from others and self-respect, the ultimate need appears—the need for *actualization*. The individual desires to fulfill his or her total capabilities.

Maslow portrays the person as having a developmental hierarchy of needs that affect one's perceptions, thoughts, feelings, and actions at any given time. The most basic needs are physical needs that are biologically based and unlearned. The rest of the needs, however, are self needs that have been learned or acquired through the process of socialization, and which in turn affect the individual's social development throughout life.

☐ Agencies of Socialization

Thus far, we have considered physiological development, learning, the preconditions for socialization, and the self-concept. Now let's focus our attention on the settings and groups within which human interaction takes place—the agencies of socialization.

We will briefly discuss several important agencies that perform the socializing function—the family and subculture, the neighborhood and peer group, the school, the occupation, and the mass media. Each teaches its own set of beliefs, values, and behavior patterns that are consistent with the total cultural configuration.

The Family and Subculture

The first socializing agency with which the individual has contact is the family. Its influence on the social development of young children cannot be overemphasized. The family teaches the native tongue and initial religious beliefs. It ascribes statuses and teaches appropriate sex roles. It prescribes appropriate sentiments for different occasions and sets standards for behavior. In short, it transmits the culture.

But the culture one family transmits may be quite different from the culture transmitted by another family within the same society. The difference between the two is due to the influence of different sub-cultures. We would expect the children of poor first-generation Italian Catholic parents to experience a different familial world than would the children of rich sixth-generation Irish Protestant parents. Indeed, the life-styles of these two families would probably be so different that their respective children might treat one another as foreigners. Obviously, such differences would not exist in a society in which there are no subcultures. Conversely, these differences are commonplace in a society such as ours. Each subculture has its own distinct set of beliefs, values, and behavior patterns which are transmitted through the family. In turn, each family elaborates its own unique cultural norms, which the child learns.

Much of what the child learns is connected with the expected role behavior for the statuses he or she holds within the family. Expected behavior of the eldest child may be quite different from that of the youngest; and a son may be expected to behave differently from a daughter. The child also learns future statuses and roles through obser-vation of other family members. For example, young children learn that someday they will go to work as their parents do.

As children learn such statuses and roles, they learn the content of their culture. In addition, the family provides a number of relationships for the child to experience. For example, in a family of four—mother, father, son, and daughter—there are twenty-two possible relationships for the child either to observe or to participate in directly (e.g., mother-father, mother-son, etc.). Experiencing these relationships also teaches cultural content.

The Neighborhood and Peer Group

Two more important socializing agencies are the neighborhood and peer group. Often they reinforce behavior patterns already transmitted through the subculture and the family. Some sections of large urban areas, for instance, are subcultural pockets in which practically every-one shares the same way of life. The Puerto Rican section of Manhattan is a good example. Children born and reared in that section are likely to have family behavior patterns reinforced both by their peers and by older people throughout their particular neighborhoods.

In other instances, neighborhood and peer group contacts may not reinforce behavior patterns which the child has learned at home. The peer group is particularly significant; it consists of people of roughly the same age and who share other similar statuses. The peer group begins to take on significance when the child develops a self. Once children have the ability to view their own behavior, they are likely to become more aware of their family's unique behavior patterns. At the same time they begin to act more independently. As this happens they come to identify with and rely more and more on their peers. Typically, the childhood peer group is concerned more with play activities than anything else. In adolescence it is primarily concerned with the achievement and maintenance of status. In adult life it stresses social intercourse among peers. The peer group, therefore, is an important socializing agency throughout the individual's life. From the time children develop a self until the time they die, the peer group teaches them beliefs, values, and behavior patterns.

In *The Lonely Crowd* David Riesman stresses the importance of the peer group as a socializing agency in contemporary American society.[15] In fact, he characterizes contemporary American society as being "other-directed." By this he means that today's Americans are likely to have their behavior directed by cues they receive from other people. In other words, the contemporary American depends to a great extent upon peer-group approval to indicate whether or not his or her behavior is acceptable and therefore successful. The peer group, then, is a powerful socializing structure which tempers, and may even contradict, the family's influence.

The School

Perhaps the most critical socializing agency in modern societies is the school, whose major function is to transmit the culture. Although the school is like the family in that it represents adult authority, it is unlike the family in that it has established and formalized rules. Another difference is that the school does not encourage lasting relationships between children and their potentially significant others— their teachers. They interact with a new set of teachers each year. The school also provides new sources of knowledge for the child, and the knowledge gained in school may contradict the knowledge gained at home. Exposure to this new knowledge and to a variety of new significant others allows the child the opportunity of breaking away from the influence of the family. That is why the school plays such a critical role in the socialization process in modern societies: it tends to ensure the transmission of the culture, regardless of the provincialism of the family and subculture.

In more traditional societies, education is likely to be a function of the family or religious institutions rather than of the school. In fact, many traditional societies do not have schools. The child in such societies has little opportunity to break away from family influence. Cultural transmission is ensured because of the family rather than in spite of it.

School
In modern societies it is the only socializing agency whose major function is to transmit culture.

The Occupation

Unlike the previously mentioned agencies, the occupation may not begin to socialize the individual until he or she has reached adulthood, or at least adolescence. Still, one's occupation may be responsible for the breaking down of one's older attitudes and the formation of new ones. It has been noted, for example, that workers who are promoted to management positions often display new and different attitudes toward their work situations. They begin viewing the work situation from the manager's rather than from the worker's point of view. These attitudinal differences extend into other areas of life, too. In American national politics, for instance, workers tend to support Democratic party candidates, whereas managers tend to support Republicans. Neither workers nor managers, however, tend to support the Communist party. This is so because the occupation, along with the other important socializing agencies in American society, has transmitted a political culture which includes the basic beliefs and values upon which the Democratic and Republican parties are built, but not those upon which the Communist party is built. The occupation, then, transmits parts of the larger culture, as well as its own set of beliefs, values, and behavior patterns.

The Mass Media

One final socializing agency for us to consider is the mass media—impersonal communications media that reach large, heterogeneous audiences (movies, radio, television, newspapers, magazines, and so forth). The content and themes of the mass media teach many aspects of the culture. For example, from watching television the child may learn a variety of statuses and roles, from waitress to doctor; from reading Batman comic books he or she may learn the culturally determined qualities of heroism. Although it is difficult to determine the extent of the socializing influence of the mass media, we may be sure that they have considerable effect. Like the peer group, the mass media are likely to influence one's behavior from childhood through old age.

☐ Adjustment, Anomie, and Autonomy

Society demands conformity. But how much? How far can individuals deviate from the norms before substantial pressure to conform is brought to bear upon them? This is a difficult question to answer. Certainly, the weight of tradition may tip the balance of individual freedom and social control in one direction or the other in any given society. But all societies demand a degree of conformity and have created certain mechanisms to ensure that people will do what they have to do.

Riesman speaks of three different societal types, each with its own particular mechanism for ensuring conformity.

The *tradition-directed* society is one in which the individual has little control over his or her own life circumstances. Community tradition guides behavior, and social control is maintained over the individual by the community's use of shame.

The *inner-directed* society is one in which the individual has more control over his or her destiny. There is substantially more physical mobility than existed in the tradition-directed society. Individual behavior is therefore controlled by the society's implanting a set of beliefs, values, and behavior patterns into the individual self-image. Guilt is the mechanism that maintains social control.

The *other-directed* society has a high standard of living and is consumption oriented with an emphasis on leisure and play activities. The individual receives direction from other people, and the social control mechanism is anxiety.

For each of Riesman's societal types there are three universal types of social character—**adjusted, anomic,** and **autonomous.** The adjusted character is one who has been socialized successfully. He or she conforms to the norms of society. The anomic character is one who has failed in the process of socialization. He or she is not adjusted to the norms of society. In fact, the anomic character is ruleless. He or she cannot conform without great personal suffering. The autonomous character is one who is capable of adjusting to societal norms but refuses to conform when his or her own private judgment dictates otherwise. The autonomous character, therefore, transcends culture. He or she is self-led and may contribute significantly to cultural change.

Another, although similar, treatment of autonomy is contained in Snell and Gale Putney's *The Adjusted American*.[16] They maintain that each individual has a need for an accurate and acceptable self-image, and a need to verify and expand the self through association with others and through direct action. When the individual is acting in accordance with these self needs, he or she is acting autonomously. When acting in opposition to these self needs, he or she is acting neurotically.

Sometimes the culture may value an ideal character type which is internalized into the self-image of an individual who does not actually possess the qualities of the ideal type. The submissive male who lives in a society that values male aggressiveness may see himself as an aggressive individual. He has an inaccurate self-image which has been fostered by societal norms. Thus, the Putneys speak of "normal" neurosis that exists in every society.

In previous chapters we have characterized culture as a powerful influence in shaping human behavior. In this chapter we have examined the process of socialization and the important structures contained within it. Again we have emphasized the power of culture; but we have also indicated that the individual may transcend culture. Whether we define the individual as Maslow's self-actualizing person, or Riesman's or the Putneys' autonomous person, he or she is capable of acting independently with insight and has the ability to change the direction of culture. Therefore it is possible for a person to deal effectively with the seeming dilemma between people and nature that we posed in Chapter 2.

REFERENCES

1. See Barbara Wyden, "Growth: 45 Crucial Months," *Life* (December 17, 1971), 93–95.
2. Gladys A. Reichard, "Social Life." In F. Boas, ed., *General Anthropology* (Lexington: D. C. Heath, 1938), p. 471.
3. Morris L. Bigge, *Learning Theory for Teachers* (New York: Harper & Row, 1964), p. 178.
4. James D. Thompson and Donald R. VanHouten, *The Behavioral Sciences: An Interpretation* (Reading, Mass.: Addison-Wesley, 1970), p. 41.
5. See Jean Piaget, *The Language and Thought of the Child*, 3rd ed., translated by Marjorie and Ruth Gabain (London: Routledge & Kegan Paul, 1959), and *The Moral Judgment of the Child*, translated by Marjorie Gabain (New York: Free Press, 1965).

6. Frederick Elkin, *The Child and Society* (New York: Random House, 1960), p. 23.

7. Frederick Elkin and Gerald Handel, *The Child and Society: The Process of Socialization,* 4th ed. (New York: Random House, 1984), p. 11.

8. *Ibid.*

9. See Kingsley Davis, "Final Note on a Case of Extreme Isolation," *American Journal of Sociology, 52* (1947), 432–437.

10. See René A. Spitz, "Hospitalism," *The Psychoanalytic Study of the Child* 1 (1945), 53–72.

11. George H. Mead, *Mind, Self, and Society* (Chicago: University of Chicago Press, 1934).

12. Maya Pines, "A Child's Mind Is Shaped Before Age 2," *Life* (December 17, 1971), 63–68.

13. See Cooley's *Human Nature and the Social Order* (Boston: Scribner's, 1902). Note that Cooley's work predates that of Mead.

14. Abraham Maslow, *Motivation and Personality* (New York: Harper, 1954).

15. See *The Lonely Crowd* (New Haven: Yale University Press, 1950).

16. Snell and Gale Putney, *The Adjusted American* (New York: Harper & Row, 1964).

GLOSSARY

Adjustment	The psychological state of one who has been successfully socialized and who conforms to the norms of society.
Anomie	The psychological state of one who has failed in the process of socialization. The anomic person is not adjusted to societal norms and cannot conform without great personal suffering.
Autonomy	The psychological state of one who is capable of adjusting to societal norms but who refuses to conform when his or her own private judgment dictates otherwise.
Learning	Modifying behavior as the result of experience. Learning takes place through any of the four kinds of association: classical or respondent conditioning, operant conditioning, imitation, and insight.
Behaviorist	A psychologist who focuses on observable behavior and observable conditions that may cause behavior. Behaviorists often experiment with lower animals such as rats and pigeons to identify behavioral principles that can be applied to human behavior. Sometimes they experiment with humans as well.
Classical or respondent conditioning	The association of one stimulus with another stimulus that originally was not responded to in the same fashion as the first. The association is so strong that if either stimulus is substituted for the other, the same

response will be evoked. In the process of learning a language, for example, our association between words and the objects they stand for may cause us to respond as emotionally to words as to the things they stand for.

Operant conditioning	The association of a response to a particular stimulus with a reinforcement. The reinforcement causes the response either to appear or to disappear when the stimulus is sensed. Example: John, who never before had asked a question in class for fear of appearing stupid, finally raised his hand and asked a question. His teacher smiled warmly at him, told the class that the question was an important one, and answered it. The next time John had a question to ask, he raised his hand without hesitation.
Reinforcement	The process by which a perceived reward is associated with an emitted behavior. The perceived reward is called a *reinforcer.* B. F. Skinner holds that reinforcement always increases the probability that an emitted behavior will be repeated.
Positive reinforcement	The follow-up of a response with something perceived as pleasant.
Negative reinforcement	The removal of something perceived as unpleasant from a situation after a response is emitted.
Continuous reinforcement	Reinforcement that occurs each time a particular behavior is emitted.
Intermittent reinforcement	Reinforcement that does not occur each time a particular behavior is emitted.
Law of effect	A behavioral principle that states that responses leading to satisfying consequences are strengthened and therefore tend to be repeated, and responses leading to unsatisfying consequences are weakened and therefore tend not to be repeated.
Punishment	The process by which a perceived penalty is associated with an emitted behavior. Punishment decreases the probability that an emitted behavior will be repeated.
Extinction	The gradual dying out of a conditioned response. When the conditioned behavior has completely stopped, we say that it has been extinguished.
Stimulus generalization	The repetition of a response conditioned by one stimulus in the presence of other similar but neutral stimuli.
Imitation	The kind of association that results from repeating the behavior displayed by a model.
Significant others	The most influential models imitated by a person.

Insight	Forming a previously unperceived relationship between two aspects of the environment. Insight occurs instantaneously and spontaneously.
Socialization	The process whereby individuals learn the roles, rules, relationships, and culture of their society.
Status	A social position that is accompanied by a role or several roles. Example: a medical doctor.
Role	A pattern of expected behavior that accompanies a status. Medical doctors, for example, are expected to provide physical examinations, diagnose illnesses, prescribe medicines and treatment, and so forth.
Anticipatory socialization	The "learning-in-advance" of future statuses and roles. Example: parents often prepare young children for school by teaching them some of the behavior that will be expected of them when they go to school.
Social development	The individual's movement over time from simple to complex statuses and roles.
Primary groups	Small groups in which people have frequent, intimate, and intense face-to-face contacts. Example: the family.
Self-concept	One's conscious sense of who and what one is. Interaction within primary groups is particularly important in the development of the self-concept.
Physical development	The individual's movement over time from simple to complex levels of organization. In the nine months from conception to birth, for example, the individual develops nervous, circulatory, skeletal, muscular, digestive, and glandular systems that are necessary for survival at birth.
Maturation	The unfolding of the person's biological potential. Generally, maturation proceeds through an orderly sequence of stages.
Infancy	About the first two or three years of life.
Embryonic stage	The first two months following conception.
Fetal stage	The third month following conception until birth.
Neonatal stage	Roughly the first four weeks following birth.
Growth	Biological changes within the individual that take place over time. Specific experience is not necessary for such changes to occur; that is, they occur naturally. At appropriate times, for example, the individual sees, hears, controls voluntary muscles, sits, stands, crawls, and walks.

SELECTED READING

Degler, C. N. *In Search of Human Nature: The Decline and Revival of Darwinism in American Social Thought* (New York: Oxford University Press, 1991). An examination of the biological basis of human nature and the increasing influence of biology on social science.

Elkind, D. *The Hurried Child: Growing Up Too Fast Too Soon* (Reading, Mass.: Addison-Wesley, 1981). A description of how children are being rushed through childhood in the United States.

Erikson, E. *Childhood and Society,* rev. ed. (New York: Norton, 1964). Erikson's classic exposition of identity crises that occur throughout the life cycle.

Luke, C. *Constructing the Child Viewer: A History of the American Discourse on Television and Children, 1950–1980* (New York: Greenwood, 1990). A review of research about children and television.

Meyrowitz, J. *No Sense of Place: The Importance of Electronic Media on Social Behavior* (New York: Oxford University Press, 1985). An analysis of how electronic media affect social behavior.

Robins, L. N., and M. Rutter, eds. *Straight and Devious Pathways from Childhood to Adulthood* (New York: Cambridge University Press, 1990). A collection of longitudinal studies dealing with the influence of childhood experiences on adult behavior and thinking.

QUESTIONS

1. Modifying behavior as a result of experience is called
   a. maturation.
   b. development.
   c. reinforcement.
   d. learning.
   e. growth.

2. Which of the following is a true statement?
   a. Heredity is a more important factor in the socialization process than is environment.
   b. Both heredity and environment are important factors in the socialization process.
   c. Environment is more important than heredity in the socialization process.
   d. Neither heredity nor environment is important in the socialization process.
   e. Only environment is important in the socialization process.

3. The typical sequence of social development includes movement from
   a. interdependent to independent to dependent statuses and roles.

    b. independent to dependent statuses and roles.

    c. dependent to independent to interdependent statuses and roles.

    d. dependent to independent statuses, and from independent to dependent roles.

    e. interdependent to independent statuses, and from dependent to independent roles.

4. The relationship between physiological and social development is clearly seen in the work of the Swiss psychologist

    a. George Herbert Mead.

    b. Abraham Maslow.

    c. Snell Putney.

    d. David Riesman.

    e. Jean Piaget.

5. According to George Herbert Mead, the self becomes complete

    a. in the play stage.

    b. in the game stage.

    c. when the individual becomes an adult.

    d. when the child reaches age three.

    e. in the preparatory stage.

6. The school is a critical structure in socialization in modern societies because

    a. it is the only structure that represents adult authority.

    b. the school is the first structure to socialize the child.

    c. it encourages lasting relationships between the child and his or her teachers.

    d. it tends to ensure the transmission of the culture, regardless of the provincialism of the family and subculture.

    e. the school is the last structure to socialize the individual; therefore, it has a greater and longer lasting influence on the individual.

7. According to David Riesman, the social character who is capable of adjusting to societal norms but refuses to conform when his or her private judgment dictates otherwise is

    a. autonomous.

    b. anomic.

    c. adjusted.

    d. other-directed.

    e. tradition-directed.

8. Growth begins at the moment of conception and continues until the individual

    a. reaches adolesence.

    b. attains biological maturity.

    c. ends the period of infancy.

   d. dies.
   e. enters cognitive development.

9. Learning in which behavior is conditioned by means of reinforcement is called
   a. classical conditioning.
   b. reinforcement conditioning.
   c. operant conditioning.
   d. behavior conditioning.
   e. learning conditioning.

10. Which of the following socializing agencies often does not begin to
    socialize individuals until they reach adulthood?
    a. family
    b. peer group
    c. occupation
    d. school
    e. mass media

QUESTIONS FOR THOUGHT AND DISCUSSION

1. What separates human from nonhuman?

2. What constitutes the "real" you?

3. Is there really such a thing as "individual freedom"?

8

Personality

> All the world's a stage,
> And all the men and women merely players;
> They have their exits and their entrances;
> And one man in his time plays many parts.

These lines appear in William Shakespeare's play *As You Like It.* As is so often the case with Shakespeare, these lines represent a penetrating insight into the nature of human beings. In a very real sense, each of us is an actor; and each of us plays a variety of roles. At this moment you are playing the role of "student." When you stop reading, you will begin playing another role—perhaps "friend," or "daughter," or "son," or maybe "mother" or "father."

The relationship between an actor and the role he plays is interdependent. That is, the actor gives something of himself through the process of interpreting the role (for example, Mel Gibson's Hamlet differs somewhat from Kevin Kline's); at the same time, the demands of the role influence the actor (for example, Gibson and Kline may have different interpretations of Hamlet, but when watching them perform, you have no doubt that each is playing the same particular character). The actor helps to shape the role, and, in turn, the role helps to shape the actor. And so it is in real life. Individuals give length, breadth, and depth to the roles they play, and the roles they play help to shape the individuals. This interdependent relationship is embodied in the concept of **personality.**

☐ Personality Defined

Personality may be defined as an individual's distinctive pattern of thoughts, feelings, and actions. One way to comprehend more fully the concept of personality is to look at the work of social scientists who

"One Man in His Time Plays Many Parts"
Interweaving with the words of Hamlet their own production styles, interpretations, experiences, and physical traits, Mel Gibson and Kevin Kline produce two different portrayals which are both recognizable as the melancholy Dane.

study personality. To begin with, we should point out that some social scientists who concentrate on the study of personality consider themselves psychologists, some consider themselves sociologists, others consider themselves anthropologists, and still others consider themselves social psychologists. To avoid confusion, we will use the term **personality theorist** to refer to the social scientist who studies personality.*

Generally, personality theorists study the behavior of many people, for they are interested in identifying and classifying both similarities and differences among people. They recognize the complexity and individuality of life and strive to explain the relationship between the individual and the social and biological pressures that affect behavior. They emphasize behavior characteristics that are stable: those that exist within the individual over relatively long periods of time. They concentrate more on the individual's thoughts, feelings, and actions than on biological characteristics (blood pressure, genes, and so forth). They are interested in *all* rather than just some of the individual's psychological behavior. The personality theorist "serves an integrative function with regard to knowledge of the human being. He is interested in the economic, social, and political behavior emphasized by other

* We have arbitrarily chosen the term "personality theorist." You may prefer to use Henry A. Murray's term "personologist" or some other.

social scientists. He is also interested in the processes of learning, perception, memory, development, and so forth. . . . He aims to integrate all these bits of knowledge into an overall account of the functioning of people."[1] Finally, personality theorists are primarily interested in adult human beings. They recognize that childhood experiences are an important part of the individual's development, but the purpose of their investigations of early life experiences is to find clues that explain adult functioning.

Earlier, in our consideration of the individual as an actor who plays a variety of roles, we implied a relationship between a person's innate characteristics (heredity) and characteristics or situations outside the person (environment) that influence behavior. The question of whether heredity or environment has the greater influence on a person's behavior patterns has been hotly debated over the years, and will probably continue to be debated. Let us give you an example of what we mean.

William H. Sheldon conducted an investigation that was designed to shed some light on the relationship between physique and personality.[2] By carefully studying photographs of about 4,000 male college students, he identified three primary components of physical variation. He referred to the first component as endomorphy, the characteristics of which are paramount in the fat person. He called the second component mesomorphy. The person high in mesomorphy has an athletic build. The third component was called ectomorphy, which, as you might have guessed, is characterized by the skinny person. Endomorphs, mesomorphs, and ectomorphs are somatotypes (body types) which do not usually occur in pure form. Most people are combinations of all three.

Having thus identified the primary dimensions of physique, Sheldon next identified the primary dimensions of temperament. (Sheldon prefers to refer to individual behavior as temperament rather than personality.) Sheldon rated the behavior of 33 young men over a period of one year according to a list of 50 selected behavior characteristics. He then intercorrelated the ratings to find clusters of characteristics that correlated positively (were complementary) with each other and negatively (not complementary) with other characteristic clusters. From this intercorrelation, he identified three major clusters: viscerotonia (characterized by tolerance, relaxation, gluttony, and sociability); somatotonia (vigorous activity, aggressiveness, and domination); and cerebrotonia (secretiveness, inhibition, and restraint). Finally, Sheldon found that there was a high correlation between somatotype and temperamental type (for example, the endomorphic people tended to display viscerotonia, the mesomorphic people tended to display somatotonia, and the ectomorphic people tended to display cerebrotonia).

Somatotypes
Endomorphs, mesomorphs, and ectomorphs are pictured in this photograph. Can you identify them?

But what does that mean? What accounts for this relationship between physique and personality? One might argue that heredity determines both physique and personality. Perhaps the innate characteristics cause the individual to be both endomorphic and viscerotonic. On the other hand, one might argue that environment determines both physique and personality. The nutritive balance in someone's diet, for instance, might cause that individual to be both endomorphic and viscerotonic. And so the argument continues. The important thing to understand is that most personality theorists today accept the idea that both heredity and environment contribute to personality. Some may place more emphasis on one than on the other, but there is general agreement that both should be taken into account.

☐ Personality Models

There are as many personality theories as there are theorists. Most of these theories fall into one of three basic categories—the **conflict model,** the **fulfillment model,** and the **consistency model.**[3] We will examine the general characteristics of each. In addition, we will examine three particular personality theories, one in each category. In this manner, we will gain an understanding not only of the prevailing general orientations of personality theorists, but also an understanding of the particular personality theories of three outstanding scholars in the field. In discussing each of these three particular theories, we are presenting the views of the man who constructed it. In each case the ideas are not ours, but his, and we offer them without criticism.

☐ The Conflict Model

The basic assumption of the conflict model is that the individual's personality is shaped by the interplay of two opposing forces. The *psychosocial version* of the conflict model asserts that one of the forces comes from within the individual and the other from groups or societies. The *intrapsychic version* holds that both antagonistic forces stem from within the individual. Some of the outstanding conflict theorists are Sigmund Freud, Henry A. Murray, Harry Stack Sullivan, Otto Rank, Carl Jung, and Karen Horney. Each of them, whether accepting the psychosocial or the intrapsychic version, specifies different content for the two opposing forces. In considering the conflict model, we will examine Sigmund Freud's personality theory.

Sigmund Freud (1856–1939) has probably had as great an impact on Western thought as have Charles Darwin and Karl Marx. Freud was a physician who became interested in the relationship between the physical and psychological aspects of his patients. His personality theory was developed as a result of his working closely with patients over a period of about fifty years. In developing his theory, he often changed his mind; in addition, he left several strands of thought untied. Therefore, we will concentrate on those aspects of his theory that are relatively consistent and continuing themes in his writing.

Sigmund Freud, 1856–1939
The father of psychoanalysis was also the originator of the modern conflict model of personality, which assumes tension caused by our attempt to gratify drives, while at the same time, avoiding punishment and guilt.

Freud viewed the basic thrust of living as the tendency to gratify instincts, while at the same time, avoiding punishment and guilt. In other words, we want to do what we feel like doing, but we don't want to feel guilty or be punished for doing it. In order to understand Freud's position better, we must examine his views on instincts, punishment and guilt, and the means by which the individual gratifies instincts while avoiding punishment and guilt.

Instincts

Freud believed that all people have a number of **instincts** as part of their inherent nature. (Freud *did not* use the term "instinct" to refer to unlearned, biologically based, complex and repetitive behavior endemic to a species; rather, he used instinct to mean a biologically based urge to act, or what some people commonly refer to as a "drive.") All instincts have four characteristics: a *source*, an *energy*, an *aim*, and an *object*. The source of an instinct is always a biological process within the individual. The source of the hunger instinct, for example, is the biological process of metabolism.

Energy is the tension aspect of an instinct, and this too comes from within the individual. For instance, we experience the tension of the hunger instinct as "hunger pains." The strength of the tension is determined by the relative intensity of the instinct itself—the more intense the instinct, the stronger the tension. It is important here that we understand two things: (1) instincts are signs that the individual lacks something that he or she needs; and (2) the individual always needs something, so there must always be some tension within the person. Freud says that an instinct "never operates as a force giving a momentary impact but always as a constant one. Moreover, since it impinges not from without but from within the organism, no flight can avail against it."[4]

The aim of an instinct is always to reduce the tension caused by the individual lacking something he or she needs. The object of an instinct is something that serves to reduce the tension. Although several objects may satisfy any particular instinct, they must fall within the range specified by the inherent nature of that instinct. For instance, an apple might satisfy the hunger instinct; a rock would not.

Freud saw a close connection between the body and the mind. The mental representation of the source and object of an instinct is a *wish;* the mental representation of the energy and aim is *uncomfortable emotions.* In other words, wishes and uncomfortable emotions are expressions of an individual's biological requirements.

According to Freud, there are three types of instincts—*self-preservation* instincts, the *sexual* instinct, and the *death* instinct. The self-preservation instincts—the needs for air, food, and water—are basic to survival and therefore must be satisfied. In Western societies these instincts are so easily satisfied for the great majority of people that they are not usually a source of great conflict.

The sexual instinct, on the other hand, is a source of great conflict for the individual. This is so because it matures slowly (as opposed to the self-preservation instincts which are fully developed by the time the individual is born), and because it has many aspects that can be satisfied in many ways. Since Freud devoted more attention to the sexual instinct than to the other two types, we will take a closer look at it.

The source of the sexual instinct is rooted in metabolism as it occurs in the body's erogenous zones (those parts of the body that are most sensitive to sexual stimulation, for example, the genitals, the mouth, the breasts, the anus, etc.). The energy of the sexual instinct is called **libido.** It is the tension that occurs in the body organs when sexual expression has not recently taken place. The aim, of course, is release of sexual tension through intercourse and orgasm. The most gratifying object is the genitalia of an attractive person of the opposite sex (for example, one who is attractive to the person desiring the object). Other objects, such as kissing, fondling, masturbation, and homosexual relations, are only partially gratifying.

Although Freud viewed anything less than intercourse climaxed by orgasm with an attractive person of the opposite sex as only partial sexual gratification, he recognized that such partial gratification does serve to reduce tension within the individual. He also recognized that gratification of the sexual instinct is *not* critical to the survival of the individual, as is gratification of the self-preservation instincts. Contrary to some popular opinions, a person can live a long life even though he or she receives only the slightest sexual gratification; but no one can live very long without air, food, or water.

The third type of instinct is the death instinct—the drive toward self-destruction. Freud began to theorize about the death instinct relatively late in his life, and he did not develop the notion of this instinct as completely as he did the others. Generally, he felt that the death instinct is not as strong as the others until late in life when it begins to overpower them. It could, however, become stronger during periods of life when the person may feel relatively worthless or when asleep. In addition, Freud emphasized the societal implications of the death instinct. He treated the evolution of civilization as the struggle between life and death instincts for survival of the human species.[5]

Freud referred to all three types of instincts as the **id:** the basic part of the structure of every personality. The id is the fundamental biological aspect of personality. It is represented by selfish wishes and emotions that have not been socially refined. In other words, the id is comprised of all the individual's urges to satisfy biological needs. It is a collection of raw forces that need gratification. The id is also nonrational; that is, it does not possess the knowledge of how to obtain

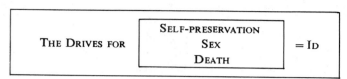

instinctual objects or the means to use this knowledge. Without some help the id would be utterly ineffective in the external world. Fortunately, it gets help from another structural element of the personality—the **ego.**

As the infant develops, a part of the mind (which at birth is comprised entirely of the wishes and emotions of the id) differentiates from the id. This differentiated part of the mind is called the ego. It develops as the infant learns to fend for itself. One aspect of the ego is rationality (the individual's cognitive, or knowing, processes of thinking, perceiving, remembering, and acting in ways that gratify instincts). One of the functions of the ego is to help gratify the instincts. When it is performing this function, it is operating according to the pleasure principle. A person unencumbered by society acts according to the pleasure principle: he or she tends to gratify his or her instincts as much as possible.

Punishment and Guilt

If all people operated solely on the pleasure principle, not only would the world be a terrible place to live in, but the fierce competition among people would invariably leave everyone unable to gratify instincts at some time or another during their lives. If, on the other hand, people withdrew from this competition and lived as hermits, they would not be able to gratify fully the sexual instinct which requires intercourse with another person. This dilemma, which Freud expressed vividly in his book *Totem and Taboo,*[6] leads people to form societies that stress cooperation and order. In this manner societies ensure a maximum of instinctual gratification for all their members. It is here, however, that Freud reveals the basic conflict of the individual in society: each person is inherently selfish and society is inherently communal. The aim of each is antagonistic to the aim of the other. But how do punishment and guilt fit into this scheme?

Punishment and guilt are rooted in society's communal requirements—its rules and regulations. Punishment comes from outside the individual; that is, when a person breaks a societal rule he or she is punished, either physically or psychologically, by other people. Such punishment increases tension in the individual. This kind of tension is experienced by the individual as **anxiety** (fear or apprehension). Freud

Superego Development
This child is learning to obey rules. When he accepts them as though they were his own, he will have what we commonly call a conscience.

referred to anxiety caused by external threats as **reality anxiety.** The person reduces reality anxiety by obeying the rules.

Guilt, on the other hand, comes from within the individual. The pattern of the punishments the individual experiences, together with verbal instruction from parents, teach the person the rules. Eventually the individual internalizes these rules; that is, he or she accepts them and treats them as though they were his or her own. When they become part of the memory, the person can feel guilt. A portion of the ego thus becomes differentiated to represent societal rules in the form of moral ideas (for example, the mind can now convey what is right or wrong, good or bad). Freud called this set of moral ideas the **superego,** which is the third structural component of the personality. When the individual does something or even thinks of doing something that is opposed to the superego, he or she experiences tension in the form of **moral anxiety** (what we commonly call a guilty conscience). The tension from guilt, like the tension from punishment, is reduced by obeying the rules.

Personality Structure

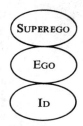

The Means to Ensure Instinctual Gratification While Avoiding Punishment and Guilt

The conflict between the id (which represents the individual's requirements) and the superego (which represents societal requirements) puts the person in a position where he or she can effectively reduce tension only by gratifying instincts, while at the same time avoiding punishment and guilt. But how does one accomplish this? There is only one way—the process of **defense.**

Defense is the mechanism whereby people reduce tension by deceiving themselves about their motives and goals. "For example, if a son's real instinctual wish is to possess his mother sexually, the defensive form of this may be the awareness of and willingness to act upon the wish to stay close to and nurture her so that no harm will befall her."[7] Note in this example that the son's real wish (to possess his mother sexually) is not consciously experienced by him. He consciously experiences only the wish to stay close to and nurture her. His ego cannot function according to the pleasure principle because his superego does not condone the idea of his having sexual relations with his mother. The only way he can reduce the tension from both the id and superego is by lying to himself. In this case, his lie is telling himself that the motive for staying close to his mother is to protect her.

Thus, defense is an unconscious function of the ego; in fact, lying to oneself cannot be effective unless the individual is unaware that he or she is lying. Or, to put it another way, a person can believe a lie only if the person doesn't know that what he or she is being told is false. The ego, therefore, has an unconscious aspect as well as a conscious one. When he deceives himself, the son in our example consciously experiences a socially acceptable wish which he carries out. The ego is now operating according to the reality principle: the son has effectively reduced his moral anxiety by putting himself in a position where he can partially gratify his sexual instinct in a socially acceptable way.

Development

Having briefly surveyed Freud's conception of the basic thrust of living and his notion of personality structure, we must examine one final aspect of his personality theory—development. Freud identified five distinct stages of personality development: *oral, anal, phallic, latency,* and *genital.* We refer to them as **psychosexual stages** because they are greatly influenced by the sexual instinct. Each stage is identified by distinctive characteristics and forms of defense. The particular experiences of individuals during each of these stages account for personality differences from one person to the next.

The first three stages are the most critical in the person's development. If experiences in these stages are satisfactory, the person will develop a mature and well-adjusted personality. Conversely, if either too frustrated or too indulged in any of these three stages, the individual will become **fixated** (will remain) at that particular stage of development. When a person becomes fixated, he or she displays in adult life the behavior patterns and characteristics as well as the defense mechanisms associated with the fixated stage. Now let's examine the psychosexual stages of development and some of the personality characteristics, and a form of defense associated with each stage.* It is important to realize that the fixated character types represent ideal, not real, people. In reality, we can think of people as being more or less one character type or another.

The oral stage lasts for approximately the first year of the person's life. During this stage the primary erogenous zone is the mouth, and the infant seeks gratification through receiving (for example, someone placing a nipple or pacifier into the mouth) and taking (a more aggressive action in which *he* or *she* places something into the mouth). The important area of conflict in the oral stage is feeding. If the infant has relatively unsatisfactory experiences during this stage, he or she will display the following characteristics in adult life: optimism-pessimism, gullibility-suspiciousness, manipulativeness-passivity, and admiration-envy. The characteristics for all character types are usually expressed in terms of two opposing extremes, such as optimism-pessimism. Freud is not clear as to whether or not any of his character types will develop just one or both of the two extremes of any given personality characteristic. Some Freudians suggest that the fixated person vacillates from one extreme to the other (first the person is optimistic, then pessimistic, and so on). One of the major defenses of the oral character is **projection**—attributing to others one's own objectionable characteristics and motives. Thus, the suspicious person might reduce

* For brevity's sake, we have limited the discussion of defense mechanisms to one for each stage. For a more detailed discussion, see Salvadore R. Maddi, *Personality Theories: A Comparative Analysis* (Homewood, Ill.: Dorsey, 1968) pp. 229–243.

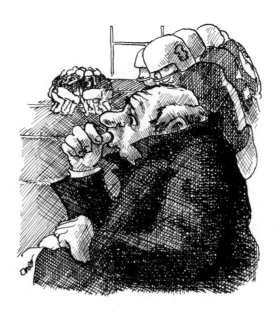

tension by projecting one of his or her own objectionable characteristics, say manipulativeness, onto another person.

The anal stage lasts for approximately the second year of life. As you might guess, the anus is the primary erogenous zone, and the child seeks gratification through giving (voluntarily voiding the bowels) and withholding (voluntarily deciding not to void the bowels). Obviously bowel training is the important area of conflict. It is the first conscious conflict between parent and child. During the infant's oral stage, the interests of the mother and child are in tune with each other; the mother wants to give and the child wants to receive or take. In the anal stage, however, the child may want to withhold when the mother wants the child to give. Anal fixation leads to the adult characteristics of stinginess-overgenerosity, stubbornness-acquiescence, orderliness-messiness, and precision-vagueness. One of the major defenses of the anal character is **reaction formation**—replacing one's true wishes and impulses with directly opposite wishes and impulses. The person using reaction formation might renounce the tendency to be messy by trying to keep meticulously clean. This kind of a "saintly" quality is typical of the anal character.

The phallic stage takes place approximately from the third through the fifth year of life. The primary erogenous zone is the genitals, and the child seeks gratification through heterosexual interaction and masturbation. The important conflict is the **Oedipus conflict,** in which the child competes with the parent of the same sex for the affection of the parent of the opposite sex. During this conflict the young boy frequently experiences **castration anxiety,** a fear that the same-sexed parent will damage his genitals; and the young girl may experience **penis envy,** a feeling of inferiority because she lacks a visible sex organ equal to a boy's. Fixation in the phallic stage produces the adult characteristics of vanity-self-hatred, pride-humility, blind courage-timidity, stylishness-plainness, and chastity-promiscuity. The major defense of the phallic character is **repression**—forcefully remaining unaware of unpleasant memories or impulses.

The latency stage spans roughly the sixth year until the beginning of puberty. During this stage the sexual instinct becomes temporarily dormant. Generally the child learns skills that are not directly related to sexuality. The relative calm of this stage is underscored by the fact that there is no character type associated with it.

The genital stage lasts from puberty to death. In contrast to the immaturity of the oral, anal, and phallic stages, the genital stage represents mature sexuality. The individual seeks gratification primarily through intercourse and orgasm; and conflicts are minimal compared to the first three stages. The genital character displays full socialization, adjustment, and potency. The major defense is **sublimation**—substituting a socially acceptable activity for an unacceptable one. Thus, a man with a strong sex drive might divert some of his sexual energy into volunteer work for charity rather than spending time with prostitutes.

In our discussion of the conflict model, we have concentrated on Sigmund Freud's theory of personality. Remember that his is only one example of the psychosocial version of the conflict model and that still other theorists prefer the intrapsychic version. If you want to know more about any of these theories, including Freud's, you can probably find many appropriate books in your campus library.

☐ The Fulfillment Model

The basic assumption of the fulfillment model is that personality is shaped by only one great force which is located within the person.* The *actualization version* sees this great force as an internal pressure to

Fulfillment Model

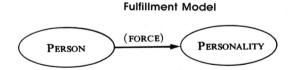

realize one's unique, genetically determined capabilities. The *perfection version* asserts that the great force within the person is an internal pressure to strive toward social ideals of perfection. A few of the outstanding fulfillment theorists are Carl Rogers, Kurt Goldstein, Abraham Maslow, Alfred Adler, Robert White, Gordon Allport, and Erich Fromm. In considering the fulfillment model, we will examine Carl Rogers' personality theory.

* A notable exception is the theory of Abraham Maslow. He speaks of two forces within the person, but they are not necessarily antagonistic to each other.

Carl Rogers, one of the outstanding contemporary personality theorists, has spent a considerable amount of time practicing psychotherapy, teaching, and writing. Like Freud, the formulation of his personality theory was greatly influenced by interaction with his patients. Rogers sees the basic thrust of living as the tendency of people to actualize their potentialities. In other words, people tend to become whatever it is in their inherent nature to be. In order to understand Rogers' position better, we must examine what he says about a person's inherent potentialities, the nature of the actualizing tendency, and the interaction between inherent potentialities and the actualizing tendency.

Inherent Potentialities

Rogers' view of the inherent nature of an individual differs considerably from Freud's. To begin with, Rogers sees all of the individual's inherent potentialities as functioning to maintain and enhance life. There is no such thing as a death instinct. Even when death is the result of a decision to kill oneself, that decision represents psychological maladjustment; it is *not* a part of one's inherent nature. Second, Rogers differs from Freud in that he *does not* see a necessary antagonism between the requirements of the individual and those of society. Maintaining and enhancing one's own life is consistent with maintaining and enhancing the lives of others in society. Thus, people should interact positively with one another. What has led Rogers to this optimistic view of the relationship between the individual and society? Is he unaware of the inhumanity that people display?

To the contrary, Rogers is well aware of people's inhumane actions. Unlike Freud, however, he is unwilling to accept these actions as being representative of a person's true nature but considers them distortions of the person's true nature. Rogers has observed that antagonism between people seems to be the result of misunderstanding and suspicion. However, when people understand one another, they may still disagree about something, but antagonism is replaced by cooperation and suspicion decreases. Furthermore, Rogers has observed that people treat others poorly when they treat themselves poorly (for example, when they feel hopeless and unworthy). Conversely, one begins to accept others only when one begins to accept oneself. For Rogers, behavior that is destructive to others is always accompanied by behavior that is destructive to oneself. The maintenance and enhancement of one's own life, then, is consistent with the maintenance and enhancement of the lives of others. Destructive behavior is expressive of maladjustment; it is not consistent with the inherent potentialities of a person.

At this point, it is reasonable to ask the question, "Just what are a person's inherent potentialities?" You may be surprised to learn that Rogers does not specify them. Actually this is not surprising when we consider that Rogers sees the basic thrust of living as the tendency to actualize one's potentialities—to become whatever it is inherent in one's nature to be. Therefore, specifying the universal content of one's potentialities would necessarily restrict the freedom of all people. Rogers sees life so much as "a changing, shifting, unfolding, unpredictable, vibrant thing, that to theorize about some set list of characteristics would amount to shackling something wild and free."[8] In other words, this "shackling" would work against the very nature of life itself.

The Nature of the Actualizing Tendency

The push to actualize inherent potentialities is a biological tendency that is rooted in all living organisms. This actualizing tendency is similar to, but encompasses more than, Freud's self-preservation instincts. It includes air, food, and water requirements; but they are only a part of the more general functional development of all living matter. The actualizing tendency encompasses the notion of growth. It includes involuntary aspects (the development of a fetus from a fertilized egg) as well as voluntary ones (going to school to acquire an education). In the first passage of one of his papers, Rogers describes the nature of the actualizing tendency. He speaks of observing some palmlike seaweed being pounded on the rocky shore of northern California by the great Pacific waves. Marveling at the ability of the seaweed to take such a beating, he says, "It seemed incredible that it was able to take this incessant pounding hour after hour, day after night, week after week, perhaps, for all I know, year after year, and all the time nourishing itself, extending its domain, reproducing itself; in short, maintaining and enhancing itself in this process which, in our shorthand, we call growth."[9]

The actualizing tendency proceeds relentlessly no matter how harsh the environment may be. Speaking of the seaweed, Rogers refers to "the tenacity of life, the forward thrust of life, the ability to push into an incredibly hostile environment and not only to hold its own, but to adapt, develop, become itself."[10] Here we can recognize another extreme difference between Rogers and Freud: the actualizing tendency aims at increasing rather than decreasing tension within the organism. Certainly tension within the organism would be increased by pushing into "an incredibly hostile environment." We should note that tension increase is a characteristic of all fulfillment models, whereas tension reduction is a characteristic of all conflict models.

Although all living organisms display the actualizing tendency, human beings display some expressions of it that do not occur in other organisms. The human being displays psychological forms of the actualizing tendency, the most important of which is the tendency toward self-actualization. By *self* Rogers means one's conscious idea of what one is. Your self, for example, is your own idea of just who and what you

The Actualizing Tendency
Olympic star Bonnie Blair strives to fulfill her potential.

are. We may also use the terms "self-concept" or "self-image" to refer to the self. The **self-actualization** tendency, then, is the push to behave and develop in accordance with one's conscious idea of what one is. But what aspects of the actualizing tendency account for the formation of a self-concept in the first place?

Rogers answers that the self-concept is formed as the result of two specialized expressions of the actualizing tendency—the need for positive regard and the need for positive self-regard. Both are learned needs. The **need for positive regard** is the person's feeling of satisfaction when he or she receives the approval of others, and the person's frustration when receiving their disapproval. The child's dependency or state of helplessness leads us to teach the need for positive regard. As the child gains the approval or disapproval of others, particularly those who are most significant to him or her, the child develops a conscious sense of who he or she is (self-concept). As the self-concept develops, the child also develops the **need for positive self-regard.** This is the degree of satisfaction or dissatisfaction felt as one perceives one's own actions. In other words, one's actions are judged by oneself as well as by others. Since the need for positive self-regard also contributes to the self-concept, the self-actualizing tendency is always in the direction of behavior and development that is consistent with the person's self-concept. The self-concept, then, plays a critical role in defining ways in which the person expresses his or her self-actualizing tendency.

The Interaction Between Inherent Potentialities and the Actualizing Tendency

Since Rogers asserts that the inherent potentialities are genetically determined, and that the self-concept is socially determined, he leaves room for conflict within the individual. It is possible for a person's self-concept to be quite different from what his or her potentialities suit the person to be. One might believe that he or she is a superior athlete, when, in fact, one's athletic potential is below average. In this case, there is a conflict between self-concept and potentialities. Rogers, however, differs from Freud; he believes that such conflict is not inevitable. When a child receives respect as a person from the significant people in the environment (for example, when behavior is generally supported and accepted), he or she experiences **unconditional positive regard.**[11] Under these circumstances, the child will develop a self-concept that is consistent with his or her inherent potentialities. Rogers calls this lack of conflict between self-concept and potentialities a state of **congruence.** The person accepts fully his or her own thoughts, feelings, and actions and develops an openness to experience (a flexibility to accept and to appreciate new experiences). The person is then fully engaged in the process of actualizing potentialities.

If, on the other hand, the person receives only partial support and acceptance from significant people in the environment, he or she experiences **conditional positive regard.** The self-concept develops only along lines of behavior that have been supported and accepted. The person learns standards that are used to judge what is valuable and not valuable about him or herself. Rogers calls these standards **conditions of worth.** Like Freud's superego, conditions of worth initially come from society, and they give the individual directions as to right and wrong and good and bad behavior.

Conditions of worth are accompanied by guilt. That is, the person feels guilt when his or her thoughts, feelings, or actions are not in

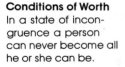

Conditions of Worth
In a state of incongruence a person can never become all he or she can be.

accordance with his or her conditions of worth. When this happens, anxiety triggers defensive behavior. Here, however, Freud and Rogers have opposing views. Freud sees defensive behavior as necessary for the individual to operate as effectively as possible; Rogers sees defense as a barrier to actualization. For Rogers, effective living means the fullest expression of potentialities. But conditions of worth and defensive behavior lead to a restriction of the individual's inherent potentialities (the condition of **incongruence.**) In a state of incongruence, a person can never become all that he or she could be. For Freud, defense produces adjustment; for Rogers, it produces maladjustment.

Development

Rogers, unlike Freud, does not specify developmental stages. He does, however, specify two personality types. One personality type is the **fully functioning person.**[12] This is the person who has received unconditional positive regard. In addition to **openness to experience,** the fully functioning person displays the following traits: **existential living** (adaptability, spontaneity, flexibility); **organismic trusting** (trusting one's own judgment); **experiential freedom** (feeling free to choose between alternative courses of action); and **creativity** (the talent to produce new and effective behavior and things). The fully functioning person has congruence between self and potentialities, but does not have conditions of worth and does not display defensive behavior. In short, the fully functioning person vigorously expresses the actualizing tendency. (Remember, this is an ideal personality type. We may speak of real people as being more or less fully functioning people.)

The second personality type is the **maladjusted person.** This person has received conditional positive regard. He or she displays traits that

Factors Leading to Maladjustment

CONDITIONAL POSITIVE REGARD
↓
CONDITIONS OF WORTH
↓
GUILT
↓
DEFENSE
↓
INCONGRUENCE
↓
MALADJUSTMENT

are exactly opposite to those displayed by the fully functioning person. He or she is in a state of incongruence, and conditions of worth lead the maladjusted person to defensive behavior. Generally, defensive functioning falls into one of two categories: repression or some form of distortion of reality. Like the fully functioning person, the maladjusted person is an ideal type. Unlike the fully functioning person, the maladjusted person does not enhance or enrich life; he or she merely maintains it.

The Consistency Model

The basic assumption of the consistency model is that personality is shaped by the individual's continuous attempt to maintain consistent feedback from the external world. In the *cognitive dissonance* version of the consistency model, consistency is determined by cognitions (thoughts, expectations, attitudes, opinions, and perceptions). In the

Consistency Model

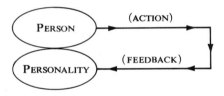

activation version, consistency is determined by customary levels of bodily tension. A few notable consistency theorists are George A. Kelly, Leon Festinger, David C. McClelland, Donald W. Fiske, and Salvatore R. Maddi. In considering the consistency model, we will examine David C. McClelland's personality theory.

David C. McClelland is a well-known contemporary personality theorist. For many years he has taught and done research in several universities. In addition, he has spent some time investigating the social applications of his personality theory in a variety of underdeveloped societies.

Universal Characteristics of Personality

McClelland follows the cognitive dissonance version. He views the basic thrust of living as the tendency to avoid large inconsistencies between what we expect to occur and what actually occurs, while at the same time encouraging small inconsistencies.[13] In other words, we tend to avoid large inconsistencies that produce anxiety, but we tend to encourage small inconsistencies that relieve boredom; or, to put it another way, we strive to predict and control the events we experience, but not to the degree that everything is predictable and controllable.

Expectancies play a major role in McClelland's theory. An **expectancy** is an idea as to the content and timing of future events. Expectancies are learned. We form them on the basis of continually experiencing similar events in similar situations. If you see the following set of numerals: 1-2-3-4-5-____ , you expect the blank to be filled in with the numeral 6. The reason you expect 6 is because in your past experience every time you have seen the numerical sequence 1-2-3-4-5 it has always been followed by 6.

Expectancies trigger reactions to experiences. Such reactions can be either pleasant or unpleasant. McClelland asserts that all individuals are born with the capacity to experience pleasant feelings **(positive affect)** and unpleasant feelings **(negative affect).** We tend to seek or approach positive affect and to avoid negative affect. Our experiences, then, lead us to approach situations that have produced positive affect in the past, and to avoid situations that have previously produced negative affect.

According to McClelland, however, not all inconsistencies produce negative affect. Only large inconsistencies do; small discrepancies between expectation and occurrence produce positive affect—they relieve boredom and stimulate the person. But how do we determine which inconsistencies are large and which are small? McClelland does not tell us. Perhaps the magnitude of the inconsistency is determined by the relative importance of the anticipated event. A person, for example, balancing a checkbook, might experience negative affect upon learning that the checkbook does not balance and that he or she is overdrawn at the bank. Another person might get a chuckle from experiencing the same event. Whatever criterion you use to determine whether an inconsistency is large or small, you should have a better understanding now of McClelland's basic thrust of living—the tendency to avoid large inconsistencies between what we expect to occur and what actually occurs, while at the same time encouraging small inconsistencies.

Thus far, we have seen that McClelland has identified three universal characteristics of personality—positive and negative affect (which are innate) and expectancy (which is learned). All people have those personality characteristics, and those characteristics can be used to explain *similarities* among people. There are three other characteristics that can be used to explain *differences* among people. They are *motives, traits,* and *schemata.*

Importance of Learning

A **motive** is a state of mind caused by a stimulus that signals the person that some pleasant or unpleasant change in the situation at hand is about to take place. If the anticipated change includes positive affect, the motive is called an *approach motive.* The person will act in such a way as to make the anticipation a reality. If the anticipated change includes negative affect, the motive is called an *avoidance motive.* The person will try to prevent the anticipation from becoming a reality. For example, if an individual who has suffered continual failure in competition faces a competitive situation, he or she will anticipate failure again, and therefore attempt to avoid the situation. Conversely, if one has experienced continual success in competition, one will anticipate success again, and therefore encourage the situation. You can easily identify such reasoning in the old saying, "Nothing succeeds like success."

In addition to giving direction to behavior, motives serve other functions. They increase the amount and intensity of behavior. When highly motivated, the individual puts out more energy to accomplish any given task. Motives also sensitize people to certain kinds of environmental cues. A person in a state of motivation seems to be more acutely aware of cues that are relevant to the particular motive directing his or her behavior. For example, a person trying to win a debate will be on the lookout for any illogical statements the opponent may make.

One additional consideration of motives is necessary—the way in which they develop. Motives are learned. Following McClelland's view of the basic thrust of living, we can understand that a person learns approach motives to situations involving small discrepancies and learns avoidance motives to situations involving large discrepancies. If a given situation holds no discrepancies, and if it is completely predictable, the person will learn to be indifferent to it. Thus the child who is given a task that is slightly beyond his or her grasp, but not beyond his or her capabilities, will learn to strive for achievement; if the task is too difficult, the child will learn an avoidance achievement motive; if the task is too easy, he or she will learn to be indifferent to achievement. McClelland, therefore, places the parents in the critical role of influencing degrees of discrepancy in situations the child faces. Although he places little emphasis on stages of development, McClelland indicates that most motives are learned in childhood. To a great extent, then, parents influence their children's personality development.

A **trait** is "the learned tendency of an individual to react as he has reacted more or less successfully in the past in similar situations when similarly motivated."[14] Traits are collections of habits. For instance, if a person has the trait of clownishness, the person will act clownish whenever a situation occurs that is similar to the ones in which he or she learned to be clownish. Although a trait is originally learned because the person has been consistently rewarded for behaving a particular way in a certain kind of situation, it does not have motivational properties. In other words, once a person has learned the trait of clownishness, the person will display that trait whenever an appropriate occasion arises because he or she is in the habit of behaving that way, not because he or she is motivated to behave that way. Traits, then, can be used to explain repeated responses.

Schemata (the singular is schema) are cognitive units that symbolize past experience. McClelland speaks of three broad classes of schemata—ideas, values, and social roles.[15] They are learned primarily by cultural transmission, as opposed to motives and traits whose learning is strongly influenced by parents and significant others. That is, schemata are often communicated by social institutions such as the church or school. The stabilizing influence of schemata on personality is clearly understood when we consider that ideas, values, and social roles tend to limit perception, memory, and thinking. For example, once a boy has internalized the role of male as being aggressive and dominant, he tends to think of all males as aggressive and dominant. He thinks it strange for a male to be passive and submissive; in fact, his expectancy of aggressive and dominant male role behavior may produce negative affect in a situation in which he encounters a passive and submissive male. Schemata, therefore, like motives and traits, are learned characteristics that help define an individual's personality.

McClelland, like all consistency theorists, is not concerned very much with a person's inherent characteristics. Personality is for the most part learned, and it is shaped more by feedback from external sources than by the person's inherent characteristics. Therefore, McClelland does not identify any personality types. Each person's personality represents his or her particular history of feedback that results from interacting with the world.

☐ **Conclusion**

In this chapter we have examined three broad personality models— conflict, fulfillment, and consistency. The discussion of the particular theories of three personality theorists was intended to accomplish two objectives: (1) to provide an examination of the theories of a few prominent thinkers in the field; and (2) to provide specific examples of each of the three broad models.

There are many other specific theories that could have been chosen to provide examples for the models. We have provided the names of outstanding personality theorists whose theories fit into each model so that you may learn more about personality. And that brings us to our final point in this chapter, which is that all three models contribute insights into the nature of individual human behavior.

REFERENCES

1. Salvatore R. Maddi, *Personality Theories: A Comparative Analysis* (Homewood, Ill.: Dorsey, 1968), p. 9.
2. See William H. Sheldon, *Varieties of Delinquent Youth: An Introduction to Constitutional Psychiatry* (New York: Harper & Row, 1949).
3. This typology is taken from Maddi; see p. 18.
4. Sigmund Freud, *Collected Papers* (London: Institute for Psychoanalysis and Hogarth Press, 1925), Vol. 4, p. 62.
5. See Sigmund Freud, *Civilization and Its Discontents* (New York: Norton, 1961, translated and edited by James Strachey), p. 69.
6. Sigmund Freud, *Totem and Taboo* (New York: Norton, 1952).
7. Maddi, p. 34.
8. Maddi, pp. 70–71.
9. See Carl R. Rogers, "Actualizing Tendency in Relation to 'Motives' and to Consciousness." In M. R. Jones, ed., *Nebraska Symposium on Motivation* (Lincoln: University of Nebraska Press, 1963).
10. *Ibid.*
11. See Carl R. Rogers, *On Becoming a Person* (Boston: Houghton Mifflin, 1961), pp. 31–48.
12. See Rogers, pp. 183–196, for a discussion of the characteristics of the fully functioning person.
13. See D. C. McClelland et al., *The Achievement Motive* (New York: Appleton-Century-Crofts, 1953).
14. D. C. McClelland, *Personality* (New York: Dryden, 1951), p. 216.
15. *Ibid*, pp. 239–282.

GLOSSARY

Personality An individual's distinctive pattern of thoughts, feelings, and actions.

Personality theorist A social scientist who studies personality.

Conflict model A personality model that assumes that personality is shaped by the interplay of two opposing forces. The psychosocial version holds that one force comes from within the individual; the other comes from groups. The intrapsychic version asserts that both antagonistic forces come from within the individual.

Fulfillment model A personality model that assumes that personality is shaped by one great force within the person. The actualization version sees the force as an internal pressure to realize genetically determined capabilities. The perfection version sees the force as an internal pressure to strive toward ideals of perfection.

Consistency model A personality model that assumes that personality is shaped by the individual's continuous attempt to maintain consistent feedback from the external world. In the cognitive dissonance version, consistency is determined by cognitions. In the activation version, consistency is determined by customary levels of bodily tension.

Instincts (Freud) The mental representation of a biologically based urge to act. All instincts have: a source (a bodily process), an energy (tension), an aim (tension reduction), and an object (that which reduces tension). The mental representation of source and object is a wish; the mental representation of energy and aim is uncomfortable emotions. Freud identified three types of instincts—self-preservation, sexual, and death.

Libido (Freud) The energy of the sexual instinct.

Id (Freud) A basic part of personality structure. It is comprised of the instincts, which are nonrational in nature.

Ego (Freud) A basic part of personality structure. It has a rational, conscious element that is represented by thinking, perceiving, remembering, and acting in ways that gratify instincts (the pleasure principle functioning). It also has an unconscious element that is represented by the function of defense (the reality principle functioning).

Superego (Freud) A basic part of personality structure. It is an internalized set of moral ideas (a conscience).

Anxiety Tension caused by fear or apprehension.

Moral anxiety (Freud) Anxiety caused by internal guilt feelings.

Reality anxiety (Freud) Anxiety caused by external threats.

Castration anxiety (Freud) A young boy's fear that the same-sexed parent will damage his genitals.

Penis envy (Freud) A young girl's feeling of inferiority because she lacks a visible sex organ equal to a boy's.

Psychosexual stages of development (Freud) Levels of personality development that are identified by distinctive personality characteristics and forms of defense. The psychosexual stages include oral, anal, phallic, latency, and genital.

Fixation (Freud)	Arrestment in a particular stage of development.
Oedipus conflict (Freud)	Conflict in which the child competes with the parent of the same sex for the affection of the parent of the opposite sex.
Defense (Freud)	The process in which individuals reduce tension by unconsciously deceiving themselves about their motives and goals. (See chapter for identification and definition of major defenses.)
Projection (Freud)	Attributing to another one's own objectionable characteristics and motives.
Reaction formation (Freud)	Replacing one's true wishes and impulses with directly opposite wishes and impulses.
Sublimation (Freud)	Substituting a socially acceptable activity for an unacceptable one.
Repression (Freud)	Forcefully remaining unaware of unpleasant memories or impulses.
Self or self-concept (Rogers)	A person's conscious idea of what he or she is.
Self-actualization (Rogers)	The drive to behave in accordance with one's self-concept.
Need for positive self-regard (Rogers)	One's satisfaction or dissatisfaction at the approval or disapproval of oneself.
Need for positive regard (Rogers)	One's feeling of satisfaction upon receiving the approval of others and the frustration upon receiving their disapproval.
Fully functioning person (Rogers)	An ideal person who does not have conditions of worth and does not display defensive behavior; has congruence and is continuously engaged in the process of actualization.
Congruence (Rogers)	The state of having a lack of conflict between one's self-concept and one's potentialities.
Creativity (Rogers)	The talent to produce new and effective behavior and things.
Existential living (Rogers)	The traits of adaptability, spontaneity, and flexibility.
Experiential freedom (Rogers)	The trait of feeling free to choose between alternative courses of action.

Openness to experience (Rogers)	A flexibility to accept and to appreciate new experiences.
Organismic trusting (Rogers)	The trait of trusting one's own judgment.
Unconditional positive regard (Rogers)	The state of receiving total support and acceptance from significant people in one's environment.
Maladjusted person (Rogers)	An individual who has conditions of worth and who displays defensive behavior; is in a state of incongruence.
Conditional positive regard (Rogers)	The state of receiving only partial support and acceptance from significant people in one's environment.
Conditions of worth (Rogers)	Standards to judge what is valuable and not valuable about oneself. Conditions of worth initially come from society, and they lead to incongruence.
Incongruence (Rogers)	The state of restricting one's potentialities.
Expectancy (McClelland)	An idea as to the content and timing of future events. We learn expectancies by continually experiencing similar events in similar situations.
Positive affect (McClelland)	Pleasant feelings.
Negative affect (McClelland)	Unpleasant feelings.
Motive (McClelland)	A state of mind caused by a stimulus that signals the person that some pleasant or unpleasant change is about to take place. If the anticipated change includes positive affect, the motive is an approach motive; if it includes negative affect, the motive is an avoidance motive.
Trait (McClelland)	The learned tendency of a person to react as he or she has reacted more or less successfully in the past in similar situations when similarly motivated. Traits are initially learned because the individual is consistently rewarded for displaying them. Once learned, however, they continue because they are habits.
Schemata (McClelland)	Culturally transmitted ideas, values, and social roles that symbolize past experience.

SELECTED READING

Feshbach, S. and Weiner, B. *Personality*, 3rd ed. (Lexington, MA: D. C. Heath, 1991). An excellent overview of personality.

Gay, P. *Freud: A Life for Our Time* (New York: Norton, 1988). An outstanding biography of Freud.

Hall, C. S., Lindzey, G., Loehlin, J. C., Manosevitz, M., and Locke, V. O. *Introduction to Theories of Personality* (New York: Wiley, 1985). A general introduction to personality theory.

Nye, R. D. *Three Psychologies: Perspectives from Freud, Skinner, and Rogers* (Monterey, Calif.: Brooks/Cole, 1986). A presentation of some of the ideas of Sigmund Freud, Carl Rogers, and B. F. Skinner.

Pervin, L. A. *Handbook of Personality* (New York: Guilford Press, 1990). A book of summaries of contemporary research and theory related to personality.

QUESTIONS

1. The term used by social scientists to refer to an individual's distinctive pattern of thoughts, feelings, and actions is
   a. trait.
   b. self.
   c. ego.
   d. personality.
   e. fixation.

2. William Sheldon's studies of the relationship between physique and personality revealed
   a. a high correlation between somatotype and temperamental type.
   b. a low correlation between somatotype and temperamental type.
   c. that mesomorphic people tended to display cerebrotonia.
   d. that ectomorphic people tended to display viscerotonia.
   e. no correlation between somatotype and temperamental type.

3. The conflict model of personality assumes that an individual's personality is shaped by
   a. two great forces that come from within the person.
   b. the interplay of two opposing forces.
   c. one great force that comes from within the person.
   d. the interplay of more than two opposing forces.
   e. the attempt of a person to maintain consistent feedback.

4. According to Freud, the deep, involuntary biological component of the personality is the
   a. id.

   b. superego.
   c. rationality.
   d. conscience.
   e. ego.

5. Rogers differs from Freud in that Rogers
   a. states that the id rather than the ego helps to resolve conflicts.
   b. does not allow for conflict within the individual.
   c. does not view conflict within the individual as inevitable.
   d. believes that inner conflict cannot be avoided.
   e. believes that inner conflicts are resolved through tension re-
      duction.

6. Which of the following are the three characteristics McClelland
   uses to explain differences among people?
   a. positive affect, negative affect, and expectancy
   b. positive affect, negative affect, and motives
   c. expectancy, traits, and motives
   d. motives, schemata, and expectancy
   e. motives, traits, and schemata

7. Freud used the term *libido* to describe
   a. the energy of the death instinct.
   b. the source of all instincts.
   c. the object of the sexual instinct.
   d. the energy of the sexual instinct.
   e. the energy of all instincts.

8. Rogers agrees with Freud that the core of personality
   a. cannot be inferred by observing phenomena.
   b. is rooted in the biological aspects of a person.
   c. is the drive toward actualization.
   d. is rooted in the mental aspects of a person.
   e. is to be understood primarily in sexual terms.

9. The fulfillment model of personality assumes that an individual's
   personality is shaped by
   a. the interplay of two opposing forces.
   b. the interplay of more than two opposing forces.
   c. one great force that comes from within the individual.
   d. two great forces that come from within the individual.
   e. the individual's attempt to maintain consistent feedback.

10. The consistency model of personality assumes that an individual's
    personality is shaped by
    a. the interplay of two opposing forces.
    b. the individual's attempt to maintain consistent feedback.
    c. one great force that comes from within the individual.

d. the interplay of more than two opposing forces.

e. two great forces that come from within the individual.

QUESTIONS FOR THOUGHT AND DISCUSSION

1. Heredity or environment—which accounts for more of the individual's behavior?

2. Freud, Rogers, or McClelland—who is more nearly correct?

3. Do we really need defensive behavior?

FOUR

Society and Its Subsystems

Humans are social animals. They live and interact with each other in society. In the following five chapters we examine society as a framework within which human interaction takes place. We discuss the nature of society, its characteristics, and four of its major subsystems and the functions they perform. In addition we briefly survey the various forms of interaction that take place on a societal level. Thus we will gain a better understanding of the relationship between people and society.

Chapter 9 establishes a two-part societal typology that may be used for comparative purposes. Chapters 10 through 13 deal with the family, stratification, religion, and education as institutional responses to basic human needs. Each chapter concentrates on the structure and functions of the societal subsystem with which it deals.

Throughout Part IV emphasis is placed on the interrelatedness of the societal subsystems and the interrelatedness of the structures contained within each of them. Continual reference is made to the societal types introduced in Chapter 9, and American society is used to exemplify one of the types—the complex society—whenever appropriate. You will gain a better understanding of the structure and functioning of American society as well as an understanding of human behavior in society generally.

9

Society and Social Interaction

Human interaction occurs on several different levels of organization. One level is the interpersonal level, in which two communicating individuals influence each other's thoughts and actions. Another is the group level, in which three or more interacting persons share joint activities. A third level is the societal level, in which interaction occurs among the members of a self-sufficient and self-perpetuating group (a society) which includes persons of both sexes and all ages. In previous chapters we have considered human interaction on the interpersonal and group levels; in this chapter we will also consider human interaction on the societal level. We will discuss the organization of the general social system as well as the various forms of interaction which take place within it. To begin with, however, we will distinguish two different types of societies.

☐ Societal Types

Societies are like sets of human fingerprints—each one is unique. Sociologists have therefore looked for similarities and differences among them so that some meaningful classifications could be constructed. The result of their investigations has been a number of two-category sets of ideal societal types. Among the most widely used of these categories are *sacred-secular, folk-modern urban, Gemeinschaft-Gesellschaft,* and *mechanical solidarity-organic solidarity.** In each of

* The writers associated with these sets are as follows: sacred-secular—Howard Becker; folk-modern urban—Robert Redfield; Gemeinschaft-Gesellschaft—Ferdinant Tönnies; and mechanical solidarity-organic solidarity—Emile Durkheim.

these four sets the two categories represent polar positions on a continuum. Moreover, the first category in each set is similar to the first categories in the other sets; likewise, the second categories share great similarities among sets. Because of these similarities, we have consolidated these four sets into one, which we will call *simple-complex*. In this manner we will limit discussion to only one set, while at the same time retaining the flavor of the original four. It is important to remember that the terms simple and complex refer to ideal societal types. They are useful when comparing or contrasting what living is like in existing societies, but it is highly unlikely that any society will fit either description completely.

Finally, bear in mind that the terms simple and complex are not necessarily meant to be descriptive of specific structures or interaction in any given society (for example, the family and the interaction that takes place within it may be more complex in a simple society than in a complex one). Rather, the terms simple and complex are meant to be descriptive of the characteristics discussed below.

Simple Societies

The simple society is relatively small and geographically isolated from other general societies. Its members are nonliterates who continuously interact with one another, but who have infrequent contact with outsiders. There is very little specialization (division of labor), and what little specialization exists is based on age and sex distinctions; therefore, practically everyone performs similar tasks. All members tend to know one another, and all learn and share the same social heritage. There are no subcultures.

Technology is simple, and relatively little economic surplus is produced. The cooperative effort necessary for the society to survive under these circumstances, together with the singular cultural tradition, tend to draw the people together into a strong, cohesive social unit. Generally there is little cultural change from one generation to the next, and traditional custom controls behavior. The culture is highly integrated, and most behavior patterns, both ideal and real, are related to sacred rather than secular beliefs and values. Religion, then, plays a large part in the lives of the people; science does not. Tradition is strong, so there is little reflection on or examination of behavior. The religious and family subsystems are the vehicles through which expectations of behavior are established; they are the primary stabilizing structures within the society.

Complex Societies

Since they are polar extremes, simple and complex societies should be opposites. They are. The complex society is neither small nor geographically isolated from other societies. Its members are literates who do not continuously interact with one another, but who do have frequent contact with outsiders. There is a high degree of specialization; therefore, people perform a wide variety of different tasks. Members do not know all other members; and, although there is a common social heritage, there are also many subcultures.

The complex society has an advanced technology which produces a large economic surplus. The cooperative effort necessary for the society to survive under these circumstances does not tend to draw the people together into a strong, cohesive social unit. Generally there is much cultural change from one generation to the next, and the response to change reflected in laws and new technicways is an important factor in controlling behavior. The culture is pluralistic rather than singular; therefore it is loosely integrated. Most behavior patterns, both ideal and real, are related to secular rather than sacred beliefs and values. Religion, then, does not play a large part in the lives of the people as a whole; science does. Since change is rapid, tradition does not have as strong a grip on individual and group behavior, and reflection and experimentation tend to be not only desirable but necessary. The education subsystem joins the family as the primary vehicles through which expectations of behavior are established; and they, together with the political and economic subsystems, are the most stabilizing structures within the complex society.

☐ Organization of Societies

Our discussion of simple and complex societal types has revealed many differences between them. At the base of these differences lies one fundamental difference upon which all the others rest—the difference in the nature of the interdependence among each society's structures. The simple society relies directly on the dependence of one person upon another to maintain its stability; the complex society relies on the interdependence of a great number of specialized tasks to maintain its stability. Let us explain.

Organization in Simple Societies

In a simple society, people work at similar tasks in similar situations. We might find, for instance, that the adult males do the hunting, while the adult females gather wild fruit and do the gardening, as well as doing the cooking and tending to the young children. The older children may assist the adult females. As one can easily see, there are not many occupations in this type of society. Although people tend to work alone or in small groups, each person is directly dependent upon the others to get the necessary work done. Relationships, therefore, are primary relationships. Daily face-to-face contacts and interpersonal and small-group interaction are the rule rather than the exception.

The people of simple societies face common problems for which they seek common solutions. This tends to standardize behavior further. To meet the demands of the seemingly unchanging environment, for example, the people know that specific, traditional roles must be performed generation after generation (for example, the role of hunter). It is therefore commonplace that most future statuses and roles for any given individual will be determined at birth. Generally, success for the individual in simple societies is defined in terms of taking the place of the same-sexed parent (that is, boys follow in their fathers' footsteps; girls in their mothers'). Each child, then, has a slot to fill in the social organization, and the socialization process will be geared for the child's learning whatever is necessary to fill his or her slot adequately.

Because of the relatively low level of technological development, the people often turn to the supernatural for solutions to problems they cannot solve empirically. The Dobuans of Melanesia, for instance, use magical words to ensure that their crops will grow. This reliance on the supernatural contributes to and reinforces the sacred cast of simple societies. Moreover, because of the relatively large amount of time devoted to daily work activities, there is a tendency to mix religious activities with work activities. The people may sing in unison or chant religiously oriented poems or stories while performing daily tasks. Such activities tend to reinforce religious and moral beliefs and values, thus integrating the culture as well as strengthening the social bond among the people.

Therefore, there is a closely knit social organization in simple societies. The people are physically, emotionally, spiritually, and culturally close to one another, and each person is dependent upon all the others for support. In a sense they blend together as parts of a single person who plays one large, multifunctional role. Large function-performing

Igorot Women and Girls Gardening in the Philippines

In a simple society with a subsistence economy, there is almost no specialization of labor, and family, economic, religious, and political structures tend to overlap.

structures in a simple society also tend to blend together; the multi-functionality of each is quite pronounced.

Since the same fundamental human needs are to be found in every society, the simple society, like all others, has structures that function to meet those needs. Most of these structures, however, are not highly differentiated (that is, separated from one another); they operate within the context of larger structures. The family and religious subsystems are the largest structures within simple societies, and the other major societal subsystems function primarily within the context of either or both of them. In other words, the needs that give rise to education, stratification, and economic and political structures are met primarily through the functioning of the family and religious subsystems within simple societies. To a great extent this is so because of the relatively small economic surplus produced in simple societies.

Since it is necessary for most of the people to work most of the time just to produce an adequate food supply and basic tools necessary to cope with the physical environment, simple societies cannot afford to support separate, highly differentiated education, stratification, and economic and political structures. The education subsystem, for example, aids in the general process of socialization and also provides specific kinds of training for people in all societies. Simple societies, however, cannot afford specialized professional educators; therefore practically all socialization and specific training takes place within the family and religious subsystems. Remember, the emphasis in simple societies is on interpersonal and small group interaction. Since the family is suitably designed for such interaction, family ties are strong and the family tends to influence the individual's behavior throughout his or her life. And where family influence diminishes, religious influence supports it or takes over.

The stratification subsystem functions to help the general society get its required work done by allocating human resources where they are needed. Generally, tasks requiring special skills and talents are highly rewarded; but since there are relatively few specialized tasks in simple societies, an elaborate stratification subsystem is not necessary. Again, the family—through its ascription of statuses and roles—and the religion—through its preachings and the rewards it may confer—ensure that people will perform the tasks necessary for the society to survive.

The economic subsystem is also relatively undifferentiated. The simple society is economically self-sufficient. It does not depend upon trade with people from other societies in order to maintain itself; rather it depends upon the functioning of a few interdependent economic roles within its own boundaries. People are socialized into these roles through the family and religious subsystems; and it is through these subsystems that the production, distribution, exchange, and consumption of goods and services are determined.

Political structures and roles are also channeled through the family and religious subsystems. In some instances a council of elders representing various families makes, enforces, and interprets the rules. In others such a council may be constituted of religious leaders. In still others the council may represent both familial and religious interests. Most councils select a leader or headman, but even he is usually only a part-time specialist who serves in his political capacity only when the occasion for doing so arises.

Thus organization in simple societies is closely knit. The mutual dependency of each person on all the others is reflected in an emphasis on interpersonal and small-group interaction and is supported by a singular culture. The lack of highly differentiated education, stratification, economic, and political structures, and the pronounced multifunctionality of the family and religious subsystems, attest to the low level of technological development and relatively small surplus produced. The structural relationship among subsystems within simple societies is illustrated in the diagram.

The Simple Society

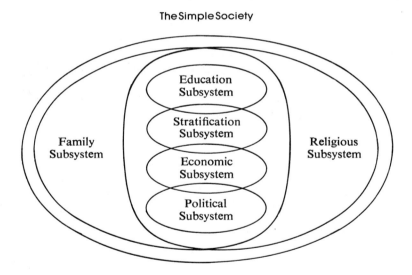

Organization in Complex Societies

In a complex society people work at a tremendous variety of specialized tasks in an equally great variety of situations. Societal interdependence is therefore based on the performance of a vast multitude of specialized tasks by a large population of people who do not know one another. In American society, which leans more toward the complex rather than the simple side of our societal continuum, we can observe this high degree of specialization. For example, the automobile you own has been created and marketed through the efforts of literally thousands of people. You may not know any of them personally, and many of them do not know each other. Raw materials were located and obtained by some specialists. Other specialists manufactured parts from those materials. These manufactured parts were marketed to auto manufacturers, who assembled them in accordance with plans designed by still

A High Degree of Specialization
In a complex society the buyer of an item such as an automobile will come in contact with only two or three of the possibly thousands whose efforts are needed to produce it.

other specialists. Once assembled, the car was transported to your local dealer, who arranged for the local advertising which enticed you to visit the showroom. There a salesperson sold you the car, several other people helped process the sale, and a couple of mechanics examined the car to see that it was in good working order. By the time you drove away from the showroom, the only people with whom you had interacted were the salesperson and the cashier. You had never met either of them prior to that day, and there is a good possibility you may never see either of them again. You really don't know anything personal about them; in fact, you may not even remember their names.

The *secondary relationships* described in the foregoing discussion are characteristic of complex societies. There are, of course, interpersonal and small-group interactions in complex societies. But much if not most interaction is societal interaction which is dominated by secondary relationships and membership in secondary groups. What holds the society together is the interplay of thousands of interdependent roles and not personal contact among people. Impersonality is the rule, and although people may complain about being identified by numbers (for example, social security numbers, credit card numbers, student numbers) rather than by their names, the precisionlike coordination of activities provides the cadence and style of life in a fashion similar to the variety of interrelated steps necessary to solve a complicated mathematical problem. Such living "by the numbers" may be impersonal, but complex societies could not function without it.

For the most part, people in complex societies are physically, emotionally, and spiritually separated from one another. The culture is loosely integrated, and subcultural ties are sometimes stronger than ties with the larger culture. People usually get emotional support from family members and close friends, and the number of close friends one has is often limited to only a few. It is commonplace in cities for people not to know their next-door neighbors; and, people who are casual friends often interact on only the most superficial levels. Generally, people are isolated from one another, and this isolation may partially explain why most people seem to guard jealously and cling tenaciously to the few primary relationships they do enjoy.

Structures are more highly differentiated in complex societies than they are in simple societies. Full-time specialists are to be found in most major societal subsystems. The education subsystem, for example, is a large, formal structure that employs the services of thousands of full-time specialists—including teachers, researchers, and administrators. As a rule, once the child enters the formal education subsystem, it, like the peer group, becomes a greater influence on his or her socialization than either the family or religion. This helps to integrate the society.

The religious and political subsystems also employ many full-time specialists. The religious specialist usually has less influence than his or

Specialization in a Complex Society
Only a few of the specialists necessary to produce a symphonic concert are visible in the photograph. Most of the others who have contributed to it (instrument makers, electricians, music educators, tailors, etc.) will probably not even hear the concert. It is typical of complex societies that the final result of their labors is often a matter of indifference to the specialists.

her counterpart in simple societies; the political specialist has more. This is particularly interesting, since religious specialists have more personal contact with the people they serve than political specialists have with their constituents. Furthermore, some religious specialists in complex societies have recently resorted to the regular use of drive-in and televised worship services in which personal contact with worshipers is an impossibility. Perhaps impersonality has become such an accepted part of the way of life that effective influence can be obtained more readily by using impersonal rather than personal means.

The economic subsystem is also large and complex. Within it a vast number of manufactured goods and available services are bought and sold. Again, impersonality is the rule. Consider, for instance, our earlier example of your buying a car. The type of transaction involved is based on the functional interdependence of many specialized economic roles being played by thousands of people, most of whom have no personal contact with one another. Most economic transactions in complex societies are based on the same kind of functional interdependence.

A large number of full-time specialists may also be found within the economic subsystem. Among the more important of these specialists are the professional managers, who coordinate the specialized roles performed within large, complex industrial and business organizations. The managers of such organizations are referred to individually as bureaucrats, and collectively as the **bureaucracy.** It is important to note that social scientists do not use the term bureaucracy to describe the nonsupervisory workers in a factory, the members of a trade union, or the top policy makers in business and industrial organizations. They use the term to describe only the hierarchy of administrative officials. Moreover, bureaucracies are not restricted only to economic organizations; they also occur in educational, religious, political, and military organizations. Max Weber identified several characteristics of bureaucracy, including impersonality, specialization, reliance on general rules, and considerable distance between upper management personnel and nonsupervisory workers.[1] Typically the paycheck a person receives in a bureaucratic organization contains the stamped signature of the organization's president—a man or woman the person may never have seen.

The tremendous number of specialized tasks in complex societies requires an elaborate stratification subsystem to allocate human resources where they are needed. As is the case in all societies, a person's initial ranking within the social hierarchy is determined by his or her

Bureaucrats

family's social position, or status, in relation to the positions of other families. But the range of possible family rankings is much greater in complex than in simple societies. This is due in large part to the fact that a family's share of the large economic surplus may be passed on from one generation to the next. A family that has accumulated great wealth tends to keep it through the institution of inheritance; and the discrepancy in wealth from the richest to the poorest family may be enormous. By contrast, simple societies produce practically no surplus to be transferred from one generation to the next.

Wealth is particularly important to family status in complex societies because it is highly correlated with political and economic power, privilege, and prestige. The members of a family that possesses great wealth tend to wield great political power and to obtain occupational privilege and prestige. The members of a poor family tend to wield relatively little political power and tend to work at low-status occupations.

But people are not completely tied to the social status they inherit from their family. They may also achieve status; thus they may move up or down the social ladder. This, of course, may also happen in a simple society, but the ladder in a simple society has fewer rungs than that of a complex society. Again, the difference may be explained by the huge range of rewards necessary to ensure that the large number of specialized tasks are performed. Stratification subsystems in complex societies, then, are large, complex, and highly differentiated structures.

The family subsystem, too, is more highly differentiated in a complex society. Initially the family in a complex society performs the same functions it does in a simple society: it provides new members for the general society; it provides a socially approved outlet for the satisfaction of people's sex drives; it ascribes initial status for the individual; it serves as the first agency of socialization; it provides an initial religious orientation for the individual; and it is the first group within which the individual experiences primary relationships. But other educational, political, and economic functions performed by the family in simple societies are not performed by it in complex societies. These other functions are performed by well-differentiated education, political, and economic subsystems in complex societies. For example, you attend school to get your formal education; you do not obtain your formal education within the context of your family. The family is therefore quite different in complex societies: it is much more highly specialized, and its enduring influence on the person's life is probably not as pervasive as in simple societies.

Even the physical organization of the family is different in the two societies. In complex societies the family tends to be small—with only parents and their children living together in the same household. In

Isolation
Often physically and emotionally separated from the larger social group, people in complex societies make heavy demands on primary groups such as the family.

simple societies the family tends to be large—with grandparents, parents, children, aunts, uncles, and cousins living together in the same household. Interestingly, the family is the only major societal structure in complex societies that tends to be smaller than its counterpart in simple societies.

Organization in complex societies reflects the high degree of specialization found within them. The interdependence of a multitude of specialized roles is what holds the society together, and secondary relationships and impersonality are to be found everywhere. People

The Complex Society

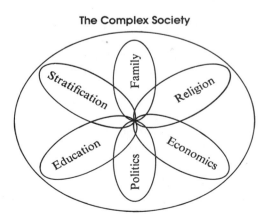

tend to be physically, emotionally, spiritually, and culturally separated from one another, and the major societal subsystems are highly differentiated structures which perform specialized functions. The structural relationships of these subsystems are illustrated diagrammatically on page 211.

As advancements in transportation and communications bring people throughout the world closer together, the scientific revolution, which began in the West several centuries ago, is spreading more rapidly. A result of this has been a trend away from simple societies toward complex ones. If this trend continues, and there is no reason to believe it won't, societies will become more and more alike. Problems and the solutions to them will be more similar from one society to the next. In fact, we can observe that the forces of industrialization have already produced similar life-styles and situations in such culturally different societies as those of the United States, Russia, Germany, and Japan. Perhaps this trend will ultimately lead to greater understanding among the nations of the world.

☐ Forms of Interaction

Societies may be viewed as webs of relationships among people; hence the changing shape of any society reflects the quality and types of social relationships occurring within it. All human interaction, whether interpersonal, group, or societal, takes place within the boundaries of the society and may be expressed in a variety of forms—the most important of which are discussed below.

Cooperation

One form of interaction is **cooperation**—the joint effort of two or more persons or groups of persons to attain a common goal. It occurs at the interpersonal level (your authors writing this book), the group level (several different organizations working together within the community to reduce water pollution), and the societal level (people doing volunteer work to help disaster victims).

Interpersonal and group cooperation are relatively easy to identify in any society; and societal cooperation is fairly obvious in societies which lean toward the simple model. But societal cooperation in a more complex society is not so obvious. When Americans pay a sales tax on items they have purchased, vote in an election, or obey traffic signals, they may be totally unaware that they are cooperating; but the American society could not continue to function effectively if they did not do these things. Cooperation, then, is necessary for societies to maintain stability.

Competition

Another form of interaction that occurs on all levels is **competition**—the mutually opposed effort of two or more persons or groups of persons to attain the same particular goal. Competition implies a set of rules that govern the conduct of the opposed parties. In all instances, fraud and physical coercion (force) are outlawed. For example, when two competing college football teams play against one another, each is striving to attain the same goal—to score more points than the other team. But points can be scored only in a limited number of legitimate ways, and the game is governed by an elaborate set of rules. Moreover, using professional players (fraud), or unnecessary roughness (physical coercion), are both unacceptable forms of behavior. "Unrestricted competition" is therefore impossible, because, by definition, all competition is restricted.

Like cooperation, competition occurs in all societies. It is possible to imagine a society in which there is no competition; but given the unlimited range of human desires and the scarcity of resources available to satisfy those desires at any particular time, it is highly improbable that a society without any competition has ever existed. Contrary to some thinking, therefore, it is incorrect to identify competition with any particular type of economic subsystem. It exists in planned as well as market economies, and is the exclusive domain of neither.

Competition may be a positive force in any society because it tends to raise levels of aspirations and thereby tends to stimulate achievement. It may be especially strong in complex societies, where rapid change is experienced continually and where rapid adjustment to change is necessary to maintain stability. But vicious competition may also be dysfunctional: it may lead to insecurity, fear, instability, and panic. Because of this, most individuals and groups do not enter into complete competition. There is a tendency to temper competition with mercy because people realize that the competitive advantage held today might be lost tomorrow; fate may "turn the tables" at any time. Tempered competition, like cooperation, is functional to the existing system. What may be dysfunctional is the opposite of cooperation—conflict.

Conflict

A form of interaction in which two or more opposing persons or groups of persons use whatever means they deem necessary to attain some particular goal is **conflict.** Conflict goes a step beyond competition—there are no prescribed rules to restrict behavior. As a result, conflict is often resolved by resorting to physical coercion, and this may lead to the injury, banishment, or destruction of one of the conflicting

Conflict

The sources of conflict in a complex society may be religious, racial, or merely the tension built up by the constant pressure to achieve. Conflict may also take nonphysical forms—often verbal—which can inflict just as heavy personal and social damage.

parties. Two conflicting individuals may fight each other to the death, or two conflicting nations may go to war.

Not all conflict, however, is of the all-out variety. There are different degrees of conflict, and most of the time it occurs in a partial rather than in an all-out manner. It is possible to get the best of an enemy without physically harming the individual. Having a person fired from his or her job, for instance, may be just as effective as having the person murdered; sharp words uttered in the presence of the right people at the right time may cut just as effectively as a sharp blade.

Such partial conflict seems to be a societal inevitability. Societies provide the basis for envy and resentment by allotting different statuses to different people, by promoting competitive ends, and by supporting and encouraging the authority of one person over another. In turn, envy and resentment lead to conflict. Since all-out conflict may be dysfunctional to the society, the society attempts to control violence. The society encourages partial conflict while attempting to control total conflict.

Accommodation and Assimilation

Two other forms of interaction are accommodation and assimilation. **Accommodation** refers to a compromise that prevents or ends conflict. A labor-management dispute over working conditions and wages could lead to conflict. Before this happens, however, labor and management may reach an agreement in which neither side obtains all of its objectives, but in which both sides obtain partial satisfaction. Conflict is avoided and work continues in a normal fashion.

Assimilation is a form of interaction in which individuals and groups come to share the same social identity. For instance, we may speak of immigrants being assimilated into a culture. Probably the most critical element in this process is the breakdown of communication barriers. For example, learning the English language would be essential to the assimilation of immigrants into American culture. Often this is a difficult task for first-generation immigrants. Assimilation does not really occur until the second or perhaps the third generation.

Collective Behavior

Cooperation, competition, conflict, accommodation, and assimilation are all forms of interaction that are guided by cultural norms. **Collective behavior** is not. Collective behavior refers to the spontaneous behavior of numbers of people in unstructured social situations. Crowd behavior, public opinion, and rumor are all examples of collective behavior. Some types of collective behavior may properly be regarded as containing interaction, while others may not. Certainly interaction takes place in a rioting crowd, but the 50 million members of the home viewing audience of a nationally televised sports event do not interact with one another. Neither do the millions of people who vote on election

Collective Behavior
In April 1993, approximately 50,000 gays, lesbians, and their supporters rallied to celebrate their right to be homosexual and to demand freedom from discrimination.

day, but election results are usually taken as a barometer of public opinion.

Collective behavior is important in a social system because it may ultimately result in the formation of new norms and values. Spontaneous and unstructured actions often lead to social movements that produce change. For example, Adolf Hitler gave impetus to the Nazi movement in Germany by delivering speeches that excited crowd behavior; in turn, the Nazis were partially responsible for the formation of new norms and values in German culture.

In this chapter we have considered the organization of societies and the forms of interaction that take place within them. Using this discussion as a framework, we may now proceed to examine in more detail the large, function-performing structures—the societal subsystems. Our examination begins in the next chapter with a consideration of the family.

REFERENCES

1. Max Weber, *From Max Weber: Essays in Sociology,* ed. and trans. by H. H. Gerth and C. Wright Mills, originally published in 1921 (New York: Oxford University Press, 1946), pp. 196–204.

GLOSSARY

Cooperation   The joint effort of two or more persons or groups of persons to attain a common goal.

Competition   The mutually opposed effort of two or more persons or groups of persons to attain the same particular goal. Competition implies a set of rules that govern the conduct of the opposed parties. Example: two football teams compete for the national championship.

Conflict   A form of interaction in which two or more opposing persons or groups of persons use whatever means they deem necessary to attain some particular goal. Unlike competition, conflict does not have rules to govern conduct. Example: two nations fight a war.

Accommodation   A compromise that prevents or ends conflict. Example: labor and management negotiate a collective bargaining contract that prevents a strike.

Assimilation   A form of interaction in which individuals and groups come to share the same social identity. Example: emigrants from several foreign countries become naturalized American citizens.

Collective behavior	The spontaneous behavior of numbers of people in unstructured social situations. Crowd behavior, public opinion, and rumor are all examples of collective behavior.

Bureaucracy	The hierarchy of administrative officials in economic, religious, political, and military organizations in complex societies. Impersonality, specialization, reliance on general rules, and considerable distance between upper management personnel and nonsupervisory workers are characteristics of bureaucratic organizations. Example: school administration.

SELECTED READING

Bellah, R., R. Madsen, W. M. Sullivan, A. Swidler, and S. M. Tipton. *The Good Society* (New York: Knopf, 1991). An analysis of American institutions and their relationship to our society.

Hall, J. R. *Gone from the Promised Land: Jonestown in American Cultural History* (New Brunswick, N.J.: Transaction, 1987). An explanation of the mass suicide of hundreds of people.

Homans, G. *The Human Group* (New York: Harcourt Brace Jovanovich, 1950). Homan's classic study of the nature of human groups.

Mumford, L. *The City in History: Its Origins, Its Transformations, and Its Prospects* (New York: Harcourt Brace Jovanovich, 1961). Mumford's classic history of the development of cities and the functions they perform for society.

Turner, R. H. and L. M. Killian. *Collective Behavior,* 3rd ed. (Englewood Cliffs, N.J.: Prentice-Hall, 1987). An overview of collective behavior.

QUESTIONS

1. The simple society
   a. has an advanced technology that produces a large economic surplus.
   b. is relatively small and geographically isolated from other societies.
   c. has a pluralistic rather than a singular culture.
   d. is one that has no complex structures.
   e. is characterized as having a high degree of specialization.

2. The term "bureaucracy" is used to describe
   a. nonsupervisory workers in a factory.
   b. members of a trade union.
   c. top policy makers in business organizations.

    d. professional managers in complex organizations.

    e. all the people who work for a large organization.

3. Stratification subsystems in complex societies are
   a. small, but highly differentiated.
   b. large, but relatively simple.
   c. large, complex, and highly differentiated.
   d. large, complex, and undifferentiated.
   e. small, simple, and undifferentiated.

4. A form of interaction in which two or more opposing persons or groups of persons use whatever means they deem necessary to attain some particular goal is called
   a. competition.
   b. cooperation.
   c. accommodation.
   d. assimilation.
   e. conflict.

5. The division of labor in simple societies is largely limited to
   a. occupational specialization.
   b. tribal specialization.
   c. age and sex specialization.
   d. political specialization.
   e. familial specialization.

6. Which of the following is characteristic of life in complex societies?
   a. primitive technology
   b. slow change
   c. little specialization
   d. secondary relationships
   e. geographical isolation

7. Which of the following statements about collective behavior is correct?
   a. It always contains a great deal of interaction.
   b. It may ultimately result in the formation of new norms and values.
   c. It is always planned and highly structured.
   d. It never contains any interaction.
   e. It never leads to social movements that produce change.

8. The most important structures within simple societies are the
   a. family and education systems.
   b. education and economic systems.
   c. family and religious systems.
   d. education and religious systems.
   e. family and economic systems.

9. One historical trend that has been observed is the
   a. trend away from simple societies toward complex ones.
   b. trend away from complex societies toward simple ones.
   c. growing number of simple societies.
   d. tendency for societies to become more different from one another.
   e. decreasing number of complex societies.

10. Cooperation is a form of interaction that occurs
    a. only on the societal level.
    b. only on the interpersonal level.
    c. only on the group level.
    d. on all levels.
    e. only on the interpersonal and group levels.

QUESTIONS FOR THOUGHT AND DISCUSSION

1. Can a society based on conflict survive?

2. Would it be easier for an outsider to adapt to life in a simple society or a complex society?

3. Is it easier or more difficult to find meaning in life in a complex society?

10

Family

Perhaps the most primary of all societal subsystems is the **family.** Relationships established within its boundaries are intimate, intense, and likely to last for a lifetime. Within the family the individual forms his or her self-concept and notions concerning the nature of society and relationships to authority. As the social unit into which the individual is born and receives initial socialization, the family is a vital link between the individual and society. Indeed, every society is only one generation removed from disaster; that is, the young must be socialized if the culture is to endure. That is why social revolutionaries almost invariably try to alter the established family pattern. The family is therefore one of the more important subsystems of any given society.

In this chapter we will deal first with the universal aspects of the family; then we will survey some differences in family structure and functions as they occur in simple and complex societies. Finally, we will make several observations in regard to the changing American family. As always we will try to show how the family is interrelated with other societal subsystems and with the society of which it is a part.

The overwhelming majority of people throughout the world have two families: the one into which they are born, and the one they help create through marriage and the bearing and rearing of children. The first is called the *family of orientation;* the second is the *family of procreation.* The link between these two families is the individual, and a consideration of the individual's relationship to each reveals the nature of the family as a universal societal structure. In the family of orientation the individual is a socially recognized product of the mating of a man and a woman. In the family of procreation, the individual is the coproducer of the socially recognized product of his or her mating with another person, and thus the coproducer of a new family. The family, therefore, is a socially recognized group of persons who are related to one another through the process of reproduction. It is a universal societal structure because it meets every society's need for continual population replacement.

Universal Functions

Producing new members for society involves more than just physical reproduction. It also involves caring and providing for the new individuals when they are young, teaching them the culture, and placing them in relation to others within the social system. We may therefore speak of four universal functions of the family that are connected with population replacement: reproduction, maintenance, socialization, and status ascription. We have already dealt with the family as a socializing structure, and the reproduction and maintenance functions are so obvious that they need no further explanation; an understanding of the status ascription function, however, requires some elaboration.

Status may be either *achieved* or *ascribed*. An **achieved status** is one that is earned. The presidency of the United States is an achieved status because the person who holds that position has done something to earn it. An **ascribed status** is one that is unearned. The monarchy of England is an ascribed status because being king or queen is a birthright which, by its very nature, is unearned. The initial statuses that an individual holds are ascribed through the family (for example, one is born either son or daughter).

The term "status" may also be used to indicate one's position within the social hierarchy. Social status may be achieved in many societies, but in all societies a person's initial social status is ascribed by the family. For example, the heir to the British throne has a higher social status at birth than does the son of a British middle-class family because the royal family holds a higher position within the British social hierarchy than does a middle-class family. One's initial social status, then, is ascribed by the family. Later, if society permits, one may achieve a higher social status.

The family performs a number of universal functions in addition to those connected with population replacement. As a societal subsystem the family must meet the individual needs of its members, providing emotional security and guidance. The family is also a socially accepted institution within which individuals may satisfy their sex drives. Although these functions may also be performed by other societal structures, they are recognized familial functions in all societies.

Structural Universals

If one understands the universal functions performed by the family, then one may easily deduce its structural nature. To begin with, the

A Nuclear Family
The two-generation (parents and children) family is typical of highly developed Western countries.

family is a biological unit that includes three fundamental relationships: **marriage** (two or more individuals sharing a socially recognized mating relationship), **parenthood** (parent–child relationships), and **siblingship** (child–child relationships). Although rooted in biology, these three basic familial relationships are also socially defined. The form of the marriage, as well as the rights and responsibilities of the marriage partners, varies considerably from society to society. And in all societies, the parent–child and sibling relationships are variously defined and continually redefined according to the relative age and the sex of those concerned. For example, in American society the nature of a parent–child relationship involving a two-year-old child is quite different from that involving a child of twenty-two. But all families are built upon a central core which consists of a father-husband, a mother-wife, and their children-siblings. We refer to this central core as the **nuclear family.***

Relationships within the nuclear family are regulated by certain universal social norms. One of these norms is the **principle of legit-**

---

* Notable exceptions are found in some groups of British Guiana where there exists an incomplete nuclear family consisting of the mother and her unmarried children. See Raymond J. Smith, *The Negro Family in British Guiana* (London: Routledge & Kegan Paul, 1956).

The Principle of Legitimacy
Almost a universal norm, the principle requires that the child have a sociological father to guide and protect him or her and to provide the child's social status.

imacy—that every child should have a sociological father to guide and protect him or her, and to represent the male link between the child and society.[1] The child's sociological father may or may not be the biological father. In the case of adoption, for example, the child acquires legitimacy through an adult male who is not his or her biological father. The relationship between father and child is strictly a socially defined relationship. None of its aspects are biological necessities, as are some aspects of the mother-child relationship. In other words, all aspects of the father-child relationship are socially regulated, and the principle of legitimacy is always one of them.

Illegitimacy is considered socially negative in almost all societies. Unless adopted, the illegitimate child has no ascribed family statuses through which to relate to other members of the society. In addition, most societies do not have institutionalized ways of caring and providing for unadopted illegitimate children. Illegitimacy is therefore almost always dysfunctional to the existing society.

There are several types of illegitimacy, the most dysfunctional of which is incestuous illegitimacy (that is, an illegitimate child produced by the mating of either father–daughter, mother–son, or sister–brother). The status of the child born of an incestuous union is particularly confusing, as is that of its parents. For instance, a child born from the union between mother and son has a father who is also its brother; its mother is married to its grandfather; its mother is also its grandmother; and its sister (half-sister) is also its aunt (i.e., the sister of its father). This confusion over statuses would completely disrupt role behavior and expectations within the family unit, thus making it difficult, if not impossible, for the family to perform its basic sociological functions.

In order to help prevent incestuous illegitimacy from occurring, all societies have elaborated taboos against incestuous intercourse (that is, sexual relations are forbidden within the nuclear family except for those between husband and wife). In some societies the incest taboo extends to other close relatives as well. **Incest taboos** serve to eliminate sexual competition within the nuclear family and to make the society more cohesive by forcing the young generation in each family to find mates outside of the nuclear unit. We use the term **exogamy** to refer to the practice of marrying outside a specific group. **Endogamy** refers to marriage within a specific group but outside the nuclear unit. **Homogamy** is marriage between people of similar social characteristics (for example, being about the same age or of the same social class) but outside their respective nuclear units. Both incest taboos and the principle of legitimacy are universal social norms which help support the structure of society as well as that of the family.

Thus far we have made observations about the universal functions and structure of the family. Before considering variation in functions and structure, we must discuss one more universal aspect of the family—**transmission** (that is, the means by which a continuity between families in successive generations is ensured).

Any given family is not a permanent group. Its existence as a separate group may be ended at any time by death or marriage. Still, we may observe a continuity between families in successive generations. The things an individual acquires in the family of orientation are carried over into the family of procreation, and many of these same things are then transmitted to his or her offspring. Since the incest taboo requires that the new family of procreation be formed by a male and a female from different families of orientation, not everything is transmitted, nor is anything transmitted unaltered. "Yet enough is transmitted to give a recognizable continuity. The transmission of the general cultural heritage and the family's own culture we call *socialization;* the transmission of membership in wider social groups, *descent;* the transmission of property, *inheritance;* and the transmission of status, *succession.*"[2]

□ Variations

While it is true that there are several universal functional and structural characteristics of the family, it is also true that considerable functional and structural variation exists in families from society to society, and within a society over time. Generally there are broad func-

The Extended Family
The extended family, which includes married children and grandchildren, is still common in the less economically developed areas of the world.

tional differences between families in simple and complex societies. For instance, one function of the family in simple societies is to provide and care for the old and disabled as well as for the young.* As societies become more and more complex, however, care for the old and disabled tends to become the function of some specialized structure such as a convalescent home. In simple societies the family acts as the prime unit of economic production. Family members work at a variety of tasks to produce the basic necessities of living. Conversely, the family in complex societies tends to act primarily as a unit of consumption. The basic necessities, as well as a great number of luxury goods and services, are produced by specialized structures. In simple societies the family performs the central educational and recreational functions; however, these too tend to be less and less a central part of family life in complex societies.

Variations in family structure are more difficult to group along simple versus complex societal lines than functional variations are. Structural variation may be great both within and between either simple or complex societies. For example, the nuclear family may be expanded to form larger household units in any given society. We may refer to these larger units as **composite families.** One type of composite family is the **extended family,** in which the married couple, and later their children, live in the same household with the parents of one of the couple. In this manner a three-generation family unit is formed. A residence rule determines with which set of parents the couple will live. In some societies the couple takes up residence with the groom's parents, forming a *patrilocal* extended family. In others the couple lives with the bride's parents, forming a *matrilocal* extended family. In still others

---

* An occasional exception is the society that exists on the barest of subsistence levels. In these circumstances older or disabled people may be killed when they can no longer provide their own means of support.

the married couple may choose which set of parents they will live with. A society with a *biolocal* residence rule may have biolocal extended families which include both sons who have brought their wives into the group and daughters who have brought their husbands. The most common form of the extended family is the patrilocal; in fact, it is found more frequently than the independent nuclear family. The residence rule for societies which employ the independent nuclear family may prescribe **neolocal** residence (the married couple living together, but separated from both sets of parents) or **duolocal** residence (husband and wife living in separate households).

A second type of composite family is the **joint** family, which is formed when brothers or cousins bring their respective nuclear families together to form a single unit. Interestingly, joint families are sometimes formed as a result of the death of the elder parents in an extended family. A joint family that forms in this fashion becomes an extended family once again when the children of the surviving parents marry and have children of their own.

A third type of composite family may be formed from the nuclear unit by one or both of the parents taking one or more additional spouses, a practice known as **polygamy.** There are three types of polygamy: one man with more than one wife (*polygyny*); one woman with more than one husband (*polyandry*); and two or more men married to two or more women (*cenogamy* or *group marriage*). By contrast to these plural matings, the form of marriage in the nuclear unit involves only

Monogamy and Polygyny

one man and one woman **(monogamy).** The prevailing form of marriage throughout the world's population is monogamy. Most of the world's population, however, lives within some form of composite family rather than within an independent nuclear family unit.

Variation from one society to the next may also be observed in regard to the locus of authority, the lines of descent, and the norms governing inheritance and succession within the family structure. For example, the decision-making process within the family may be **authoritarian** or **egalitarian.** Authoritarian families are those in which one parent dominates decision making. In a **patriarchal** family the father (or elder father in the case of an extended family) dominates; in a **matriarchal** family, the mother or grandmother dominates. Egalitarian families are those in which both parents, as well as the children in some cases, share in decision making.

The lines of descent may be reckoned through the male side (*patrilineally*), the female side (*matrilineally*), or both (*bilineally*). Generally, organized descent groupings exist throughout the world, but they are stronger in societies which tend toward the "simple" end of our societal continuum. Descent groupings transcend the immediate family in both duration and size. It is not unusual to find lineages that may be traced back ten generations, and it has been reported that some clans in China contain from 200,000 to 300,000 members.[3]

Descent groupings may perform several functions that the immediate family cannot perform as well (for example, development of economic specialization, provision of military protection from outsiders, and accumulation of large capital reserves). These functions are performed by more specialized structures in complex societies.

The norms of most societies require that property owners will their property only to members of their descent grouping, and the pattern of inheritance usually reflects the dominant pattern of family organization in the society.[4] Property inherited within a joint family system might be held in common by several family members; but property inherited within an independent nuclear family system might be held independently by each heir. Succession, or the transmission of family status, is also governed by local societal norms, and it too may reflect family organization patterns.

☐ The Changing American Family

Like all other societal subsystems, families must adapt to changing conditions in order to maintain stability. In complex societies, where the pressure of rapid change is likely to be more constant, there is likely to be a great deal of adaptation over relatively short time periods in regard to family experiences, roles, and functions. And so it is with the American family.

Let's survey some of the specific changes that have recently occurred in familial experiences, roles, and functions. Cause and effect relationships within a social system are often difficult if not impossible to define precisely. For example, a change in family structure or function may be either the cause or the effect of other changes within society; and it is sometimes difficult to determine whether a particular change is a cause or an effect of other changes. Moreover, the ultimate significance of any particular change or set of changes is always a matter of speculation. Therefore, our discussion of specific changes in the American family will focus primarily on the description of changes that have been observed. We will speculate to some degree, but we also invite you to do some speculative thinking of your own.

National Surveys

One method of determining the direction of change in society is to study the data collected through national surveys. By doing this we may note changes in the American family in regard to the divorce rate, the remarriage rate, the prevalence of single-parent families, family size, age of marriage partners, family roles, births to unmarried women, and family functions.

Increasing Divorce Rate. Throughout the twentieth century there has been a slow but steady rise in the divorce rate. In 1900 only about one in thirteen marriages ended in divorce; today about one in two marriages is projected to end in divorce. The number of separations, desertions, and annulments has also risen.

Richard H. Klemer has suggested two primary reasons for the fragility of the marriage relationship: "(1) the change in determination to stay married . . . [and] (2) the loss of satisfaction in marriage because of unrealistic marriage expectations."[5] Klemer argues that one hundred years ago the major goal of both marriage partners was marital stability; however, the major goal of both partners in today's marriage is happiness. When either partner feels that he or she has not attained happiness within the marriage relationship, he or she tends to consider seriously what has become an increasingly easy alternative—divorce. Thus the determination to stay married has been considerably weakened. When coupled with the relative loss of determination to stay married, unrealistic marriage expectations may accelerate the journey to divorce. The romantic love ideal, for example, which has become deeply ingrained in American culture, is bound to cause problems for people who have overstressed its importance. By its very nature it is unrealistic. The lady's "knight in shining armor" is not likely to act knightly much of the time because the everyday pressures of living require other kinds of role behavior most of the time. The gentleman's "lady-in-waiting" is not likely to act romantically when she is washing or ironing or putting on curlers and applying face cream before going to bed. Other marriage expectations dealing with satisfactions and role behavior may be equally unrealistic, and the determination to stay married may begin to dwindle as soon as "the honeymoon is over."

Whatever the cause of divorce, the fact remains that marriages are failing at a high rate in American society. Since divorce is almost invariably preceded and accompanied by embittered feelings, it is reasonable to assume that it has a potentially adverse affect on people. Interestingly, a marriage involving a divorced person is less likely to succeed than is a marriage involving persons who have not been divorced; and the more times a person has been divorced, the less are his or her chances for a successful marriage. Perhaps the strain of a divorce tends to have an adverse effect on the individual's ability to relate to another person in a marriage relationship. If this is the case, we might anticipate an ever-increasing divorce rate.

Divorce often affects children. Again, the assumption of a potentially adverse effect is reasonable. Certainly it would be difficult to shield children from the embittered feelings engendered by the tense situation at home. Having suffered through the dissolution of their parents' marriage, children may ultimately develop a negative orientation toward marriage. It is not unusual to find children of divorced parents expressing such a negative orientation. Conversely, it is possible that divorce could have a positive effect on children. The child of divorced parents may become determined "to avoid the mistakes my parents made." Such a view may lead to more realistic marriage expectations and a greater determination to stay married. Therefore, while divorce is always dysfunctional to a particular family, it may also be ultimately functional to a society's family subsystem. Divorce also may be functional to the divorced individual. That is, in some cases a divorce may be more desirable than continuing a bad marriage.

Increasing Remarriage Rate. Prior to 1900 the incidence of remarriage in the United States was relatively low, and most remarriages were of widowed persons. Today, three of four divorced persons remarry. This high remarriage rate seems to be signaling a shift in the cultural norm of lifelong monogamy to *serial monogamy:* the expectation of several spouses over a lifetime but only one at a time. The high remarriage rate also has led to a growing number of **blended families,** those in which at least one of the spouses has been previously married and in which there are one or more children from the previous marriage or marriages. In fact, blended families are becoming so common that it is estimated that at least 50 percent of all children will have experienced divorce and remarriage in their families.

Single-parent Families. There has been a rapid growth of single-parent families. Today, approximately 25 percent of all children live with only one parent. This figure is about twice as high as it was only a decade ago, and it is projected to continue rising. The Census Bureau has estimated that about half of all children today will spend some part of their childhood in a single-parent home.

Decrease in Size. There has been a long-term trend toward smaller families. In 1790 the average family had 5.7 members; by 1900 only 4.1 members; and by 1950 it had shrunk to only 3.5 members. The family of today is significantly smaller than that of our pioneer forefathers.

Age of Marriage Partners. For a long period of time, both males and females married at increasingly earlier ages, but this trend has been reversed in recent years. In 1890, for example, the median age of a husband at first marriage was 26.1; by 1955 it had fallen to 22.6. By 1991, however, it had risen again to 26.3. For females, the figures read age 22 in 1890, 20.2 in 1955, and 24.1 in 1991. It appears that the trend toward later first marriages will continue at least through the beginning of the twenty-first century.

Role Changes. Roles for both husband and wife have been altered within the family. Traditionally the husband brought home the paycheck and rarely participated in such mundane household chores as cooking and cleaning. The wife tended to the house and children, but she rarely brought home a paycheck. Today more married women are joining the labor force, and more men are sharing the mundane chores. For example, in 1900 only about 20 percent of women over the age of sixteen were in the labor force; however, today that figure for married women, as well as for women as a whole, is approximately 57 percent. There are also indications that the authority previously held by the husband may now be more evenly distributed among other family members. This seems to be particularly true of middle-class families.

Births to Unmarried Women. Between 1960 and 1990, the percentage of all births to unmarried women increased from 5 percent to 27 percent, a trend driven primarily by women age 20 and older. And although most unmarried childbearing is unintended, the deliberate choice to accept single parenthood has increased, particularly among professional women. For example, the incidence of single motherhood among professional women nearly tripled from 1982 to 1992, from 3.1 percent to 8.3 percent. A continuation of these trends will, no doubt, have a profound impact on the American family.

Loss of Functions. Previously significant functions of the family have been taken over by structures outside the home. Factories have taken over the production of most goods; governmental agencies have taken over the protection of lives; the school has taken over the education of children; a variety of recreational facilities and activities outside the home are absorbing people's leisure time; and religious activities are becoming the sole province of the church.

Enhancement of Functions. Some familial functions have been enhanced. The family has traditionally been a unit in which the individual may experience warm and compassionate relationships with others. Today, with secondary relationships increasing throughout other sectors of society, the affectional function of the family has taken on even greater significance. The family also has become more important in regard to economic planning. With an ever-increasing number of goods and services available to it, and a large number of wants to be satisfied, the family must plan its consumption to a greater degree than ever before.

☐ Conclusion

Our discussion of the changing American family is highly selective. Many other changes in regard to the family might have been mentioned. Our purpose, however, is not to present a complete catalog of changes that have recently occurred or that are presently occurring. Rather, we have selected several changes that appear to have some significant influence on the direction of American family life in the near future. We have also attempted to be provocative in speculating about some of the potential effects of divorce on both parents and children. We hope that this speculation will motivate you to do some creative thinking of your own.

We feel compelled to comment on two more aspects of change in the American family—homosexual marriages and nontraditional heterosexual living arrangements. Americans have long approached the subject of homosexuality with negative feelings. Traditionally the homosexual has been treated as both a social and a sexual deviant within American society. Recently, however, there have been signs of greater tolerance of homosexuality. The popular literature and the theater, movie, and television industries have been willing to treat homosexual themes in a frank manner. At the same time, many homosexuals have openly declared themselves as such; and through organized groups such as Gay Liberation and Gay Activists Alliance they are demanding equal social and legal treatment with heterosexuals. Among these demands are the rights to be legally married and to adopt children.

Homosexual "marriages" are not new. For years many homosexuals have entered into relationships that are roughly equivalent to childless heterosexual marriages. The only significant difference between these two types of marriage, other than the sexual behavior of the individuals

Homosexual Lifestyles
This child born from the woman holding her was conceived through artificial insemination. Should homosexuals be allowed to become parents?

involved and the relative secrecy of the homosexual relationship, is the fact that one is legally sanctioned and the other is not (that is, the legal definition of marriage in American society specifies a male–female relationship).

Will homosexual marriages eventually be legally accepted? If so, what about the adoption of children? What are the implications in regard to divorce? It is interesting to note that some states do allow homosexuals to become foster parents. Although this reflects a change in attitudes about parenting, the issue of adoption by homosexuals is still clearly controversial. A related issue of great controversy is the use of artificial insemination by gay females. Should homosexuals, either through adoption or artificial insemination, be allowed to become parents? A consideration of these and other related questions may provide for a lively discussion, in or out of the classroom.

Perhaps an even livelier discussion might be centered upon the subject of nontraditional heterosexual living arrangements. In American society such arrangements might include some form of plural mating. There have been reports that many Americans are experimenting with these alternative approaches to the monogamous nuclear family unit.[6] Such reports, however, are difficult to substantiate because many people who might be involved in these experiments are reluctant to make public their participation in them. Nevertheless, the reports persist, and they seem to be drawing some attention.

The prominent novelist and social critic Robert H. Rimmer indicates that alternative approaches to marriage and the family may

A Commune—An Alternative Family Style

become necessary as well as desirable for many people. He argues that as living costs continue to rise, some families may have to merge in order to survive.[7] This argument may not be as farfetched as it may appear at first glance. One may make a strong argument that the economic factor largely accounts for the formation of composite families in societies where they predominate.

Will plural matings eventually be legally accepted? If so, will they tend to strengthen or weaken the American family? Intelligent answers to these questions require the application of many of the concepts presented thus far in this book (for example, beliefs, values, norms, socialization, change, and so forth). In fact, many of the concepts yet to be presented will be useful in your consideration. Therefore we suggest that you read on before attempting to construct comprehensive answers.

REFERENCES

1. See Bronislaw Malinowski, "Marriage," *Encyclopedia Britannica* (1929), *XIV,* pp. 940–950.
2. Kingsley Davis, *Human Society* (New York: Macmillan, 1949), p. 405.
3. Ralph Linton, *The Study of Man* (New York: D. Appleton-Century, 1936), p. 201.
4. Davis, p. 409.
5. Richard H. Klemer, *Marriage and Family Relationships* (New York: Harper & Row, 1970), p. 22.

6. See "Do You Mary, and Anne, and Beverly, and Ruth, Take These Men ...,"
Psychology Today, Vol. 5, No. 8 (January 1972), 57–64, 78–82.

7. *Ibid.*, p. 62.

GLOSSARY

Family	A socially recognized group of persons who are related to one another through the process of reproduction. Most people have two families: the one into which they are born (*family of orientation*) and the one they help create through marriage and the bearing and rearing of children (*family of procreation*).
Nuclear family	A family unit consisting of a father-husband, a mother-wife, and their children-siblings.
Blended family	A family unit in which at least one of the spouses has been previously married and in which there are one or more children from the previous marriage or marriages.
Composite families	Household units that are larger than the nuclear family. Such units may be extended families, joint families, or polygamous families.
Extended family	A composite family in which the married couple and, later, their children live in the same household with the parents of one of the couple. A residence rule determines with which set of parents the couple will live. In a *patrilocal* extended family the couple lives with the groom's parents. In a *matrilocal* extended family the couple lives with the bride's family. *Biolocal* extended families include both sons who have brought their wives into the group and daughters who have brought their husbands.
Joint family	A composite family in which brothers or cousins bring their respective nuclear families together to form a single unit.
Polygamous family	A composite family in which there may be: the marriage of one man to two or more women (*polygyny*); the marriage of one woman to two or more men (*polyandry*); or the marriage of two or more men to two or more women (*cenogamy*).
Authoritarian family	Family in which one parent dominates the decision making. In the traditional Spanish family, for instance, the father makes most of the important decisions.
Matriarchal family	Family in which the mother or grandmother dominates.
Patriarchal family	Family in which the father or grandfather dominates.
Egalitarian family	Family in which both parents, and the children in some cases, share in decision making. Example: a typical middle-class American family.

Endogamy	Marriage within a specific group, but outside the nuclear unit. Example: upper class Americans tend to marry other upper class Americans.
Exogamy	Marriage outside a specific group. In some simple societies, for instance, people are forbidden to marry anyone from their own village.
Homogamy	Marriage between people of similar social characteristics but outside their respective nuclear units. Example: marriage between people of the same social class.

Marriage	Two or more individuals sharing a socially recognized mating relationship.
Monogamy	The marriage of one man to one woman.

Achieved status	A position that is earned. Example: lawyer.
Ascribed status	A position that is unearned. Example: brother.

Neolocal residence	Residence in which the married couple live together, but separated from both sets of parents.
Duolocal residence	Husband and wife living in separate households.

Incest taboo	The universal rule forbidding sexual relations within the nuclear family except for those between husband and wife.
Principle of legitimacy	The principle that every child should have a sociological father to guide and protect him or her and to represent the male link between the child and society. Illegitimacy, then, refers to the social condition of not having a father.

Siblingship	Relationships between brother–sister, brother–brother, or sister–sister.

Transmission	The means by which a continuity between families in successive generations is ensured. The family transmits culture (*socialization*); membership in wider social groups (*descent*); property (*inheritance*); and status (*succession*).

SELECTED READING

Benokraitis, N. V. *The Family* (Englewood Cliffs, N.J.: Prentice-Hall, 1993). An overview of marriage and the family.

Bernstein, A. C. *Yours, Mine, and Ours: How Families Change When Remarried Parents Have a Child Together* (New York: Charles Scribner's Sons, 1989). An examination of issues confronting blended families.

Furstenberg, F. F., Jr., and A. J. Cherlin. *Divided Families: What Happens to Children When Parents Part* (Cambridge, Mass.: Harvard University Press, 1991). A consideration of the consequences of divorce for children.

Hertz, R. *More Equal Than Others: Women and Men in Dual-Career Marriages* (Berkeley: University of California Press, 1986). A study of the ways that the earnings of women and men affect their relative power within a marriage.

Kain, E. L. *The Myth of Family Decline: Understanding Families in a World of Rapid Social Change* (Lexington, Mass.: Lexington Books, 1990). A study that argues that families in the United States are not in decline.

Millman, M. *Warm Hearts and Cold Cash: The Intimate Dynamics of Families and Money* (New York: The Free Press, 1991). An analysis of the effects of making and spending money on relationships within the family.

Murdock, G. P. *Social Structure* (New York: Macmillan, 1949). Murdock's classic cross-cultural analysis of social organization. Includes chapters on the nuclear family, composite forms of the family, regulation of sex, and incest taboos.

Wallerstein, J. S., and S. Blakeslee. *Second Chances: Men, Women, and Children a Decade After Divorce* (New York: Ticknor & Fields, 1989). A report on a study of divorced couples and their children.

QUESTIONS

1. The term *nuclear family* refers to a
   a. closely knit family.
   b. unit consisting of parents, children, and cousins.
   c. family whose central core is explosive.
   d. unit consisting of a father-husband, a mother-wife, and their children-siblings.
   e. family in which the marriage unit may include one man and two or more women.

2. Which of the following is *not* a part of family transmission?
   a. succession
   b. marriage

   c. socialization
   d. descent
   e. inheritance

3. In a patrilocal extended family, the married couple lives with
   a. the bride's parents.
   b. the groom's parents.
   c. either set of parents.
   d. neither set of parents.
   e. their next-door neighbors.

4. The marriage of one woman to two or more men is called
   a. monogamy.
   b. polygyny.
   c. cenogamy.
   d. matriogamy.
   e. polyandry.

5. Which of the following forms of marriage is more popular than each of the others?
   a. cenogamy
   b. polygyny
   c. monogamy
   d. dualogamy
   e. polyandry

6. Which of the following is *not* a universal function of the family?
   a. reproduction
   b. socialization
   c. maintenance
   d. status ascription
   e. siblingship

7. Which of the following statements about the American family is true?
   a. Some of its previously important functions have been taken over by other structures.
   b. Males are getting married younger, but females are getting married at a later age.
   c. There has been a long-term trend toward larger families.
   d. Husband and wife roles have remained unchanged.
   e. Females are getting married younger, but males are getting married at an older age.

8. The transmission of status is called
   a. descent.
   b. progression.
   c. succession.

    d. inheritance.
    e. socialization.

9. The family is a biological unit that includes three fundamental relationships. They are
    a. marriage, parenthood, and grandparenthood.
    b. parenthood, grandparenthood, and siblingship.
    c. marriage, parenthood, and blood relatives.
    d. marriage, parenthood, and siblingship.
    e. marriage, grandparenthood, and siblingship.

10. All societies have elaborated
    a. endogamy.
    b. cenogamy.
    c. incest taboos.
    d. polygamy.
    e. polygyny.

QUESTIONS FOR THOUGHT AND DISCUSSION

1. Is the family really necessary?

2. What will the American family look like in the year 2100?

3. Cohabitation—is it a viable alternative to marriage?

4. Is there really such a thing as the American family?

11

Social Stratification

All men are created unequal. And so are all women.

They are unequal not only in regard to their inherited biological characteristics, but also in regard to their inherited social situations. In fact, societies institutionalize social inequality through the systems they employ to distribute scarce values—systems of stratification. In this chapter we will examine the characteristics of stratification systems, the needs upon which they are based, the functions they perform, and the process by which they interact with other societal subsystems.

Stratification refers to the division of something into different layers or zones with each layer having its own distinctive qualities. **Social stratification** refers to the division of societies into different layers, or strata, each containing groups of people who share similar beliefs, attitudes, values, and life-styles. Social stratification also refers to the arrangement of strata on a social scale, with each stratum ranking either higher or lower than the others. Such rankings reflect the relative amounts of **power, privilege,** and **prestige** that each stratum has within a particular society. In the United States, for example, we put medical doctors on a higher occupational level than we do bus drivers, and, as a result doctors have more power, privilege, and prestige than do bus drivers. How do we account for the higher ranking of the doctors? On a much broader scale we can ask the more general question: Who gets what and why? Traditionally, two answers to this question have been presented; each seems to contain some element of truth.

☐ **Who Gets What and Why?**

Conflict Theory

One answer emphasizes the needs and desires of particular individuals and groups within society rather than the needs of society itself. Individuals and groups that have both the opportunity and the desire to seize power will do so. Having once grasped power, these people will use it not only to obtain more power but also to prevent others from getting it. In this manner, the "in" groups use power to exploit the "out" groups, and social inequality is perpetuated. Power here refers to the probability that an individual or group will be able to do what it wants to do. When it is supported by generally accepted societal norms, we call it *legitimate power,* or *authority* (as, for instance, the President of the United States having the authority to enforce antipollution laws). When it is exercised informally and is based solely on the persuasive ability of one individual or group to manipulate another, we call it *influence* (as, for example, the President's advisers having the influence to convince him to enforce antipollution laws).

Perhaps the clearest and certainly the most extensive statement of how individuals and groups use power to exploit others was presented by Karl Marx and Friedrich Engels in the nineteenth century. In *The Communist Manifesto, Capital,* and other works, they argued that the institution of private ownership of the means of production led to the division of society into social classes. Class conflict was inevitable because the owners of the means of production (the bourgeoisie) sought to enhance their power at the expense of the urban nonowners (the proletariat). By monopolizing the means of production, the bourgeoisie would monopolize and extend its power.

Other scholars have accepted the notion of *class conflict,* although many of them have denied that ownership of the means of production is the sole basis for it. C. Wright Mills and Ralf Dahrendorf are two well-known scholars who hold such a view.[1] Generally these **conflict theorists** view social inequality as the result of struggles for power by various groups in society. They stress the role of coercion in the maintenance of private property, family inheritance, and other institutions

Karl Marx, 1818–1883
Marx believed that ownership of the means of production must be transferred, by violent means if necessary, to the proletariat.

that support inequality. They tend to emphasize the role of inequality in generating conflict and to deemphasize the role of the total society in producing inequality.

Functional Theory

The second answer to the question of who gets what and why emphasizes the needs of society rather than the needs of individuals or groups. Societies need to motivate individuals to occupy important and highly valued positions that require special abilities and skills. Societies also need to motivate these individuals to play the roles associated with those positions. In order to meet these ends, societies hold out differential rewards for various positions. Generally societies will reward individuals for filling and performing the duties attached to any given position according to the functional importance of that position and the relative scarcity of qualified personnel to fill it. A position which is functionally important but which is also easily filled will not be heavily rewarded (note, for instance, teachers and garbage collectors in American society). Conversely, positions which are functionally important but not easily filled will receive heavy rewards (for example, doctors).

We refer to the proponents of this view as **functional theorists.** Talcott Parsons, Kingsley Davis, and Wilbert E. Moore are a few of the more notable functional theorists.[2] Generally they stress cooperation rather than conflict, and they view inequality as being inevitable because it is necessary for the survival of the social system.

Which of these two views is correct? Who does get what and why? Certainly we can understand that people who occupy functionally important positions that are not easily filled will receive relatively heavy rewards. But we can also understand that the institution of the family transmits status from one generation to the next, thus bestowing upon certain individuals power, privilege, and prestige whether or not they occupy functionally important positions within society. In short, "who gets what and why?" is a complex question that requires a more comprehensive answer than is provided by either of the two views mentioned so far. By drawing from both of them, however, we can assemble the more comprehensive answer we need.

An Alternative View

Gerhard Lenski has proposed just such a comprehensive answer in his book *Power and Privilege: A Theory of Social Stratification.*[3] Lenski states that there will be a struggle for rewards in every society because people are motivated by self-interest (or partisan group interest) and because many of the objects they want are scarce. Generally, people value survival, health, prestige, comfort, salvation, and affection. They also value the means by which they may attain those things: money, organizational office, and education. Society, on the other hand, tends to value maintaining the political status quo and maximizing production and the resources on which production depends. Since people must live in society to attain many of their individual goals, both cooperation and conflict are guaranteed. We might note the great similarity between Freud's view of humans in society and this one (see Chapter 8). Freud viewed humans as being inherently selfish and society as being inherently communal.

Need and power, Lenski argues, will determine the distribution of most of the products of people's labors. The need for survival and for continued productivity ensure that people will share the product of their labors to the extent required to meet those needs. In other words, goods and services necessary to keep producers alive and productive will be shared. Any surplus will be distributed according to the relative power of individuals and groups. We can see a relationship between the level of technology and the nature of the stratification system in any given society. In technologically simple societies, where little or no surplus is produced, *need* will largely determine the distribution of goods and services. As technology advances and more surplus is produced, *power* will increasingly determine the distribution. Privilege (possession or control of part of the surplus) is a product of power, and prestige (relative status value) is a product of both power and privilege, especially in societies that have large surpluses. Power, therefore, is the crucial variable in this view.

Lenski discusses five different societal types, each based on its level of technological advancement.* Before examining them, however, we need to understand two terms—class and class systems. These terms, along with individuals, represent levels of organization within stratification systems.

A **class** is an aggregate of people in a society who share similar amounts of some form of power, privilege, or prestige. For example, the unemployed in the United States constitute a class that has relatively little economic power; but professional people constitute a class that has a great deal of economic power. A **class system** is a hierarchy of classes ranked according to some particular standard. We can identify the managerial class (professional managers within organizations) as an aggregate of people who share similar amounts of prestige within the occupational class system in American society. In this case we have identified a class that is ranked relatively high within the American occupational class system. The working class ranks considerably lower because its members do not share nearly as much prestige within the

---

* Actually, Lenski acknowledges at least nine societal types. Since the characteristics of four of them are so similar to characteristics of the other five, he treats only five extensively.

Social Class
Consider the differences in values and lifestyles between the Connor family on *Roseanne* and the Banks family on *The Fresh Prince of Bel Air.*

occupational class system. We should note that not all managers share equal amounts of prestige. The president of General Motors holds substantially more prestige than the president of a small furniture manufacturing plant in Muncie, Indiana. Both presidents, however, hold more prestige than the assembly-line worker in either the Muncie or any General Motors plant.

Our definition of class is sufficiently broad to include other terms used by sociologists in describing other kinds of aggregates within stratification systems. One such term is **caste.** This is an aggregate of people who share similar inherited social positions that are quite rigid. They are rigid in the sense that there is little mobility or movement (particularly upward mobility) of individuals from one social position to another within one generation. Slaves in the American South were members of a very rigid caste. They had little chance for upward social mobility. Many sociologists have clearly distinguished caste from class on the basis of the opportunity for and the amount of upward social mobility. They characterize caste systems as social systems that lock people into certain positions on the social scale. They characterize class systems as social systems in which there may be considerable upward mobility. Actually there is some upward mobility in even the most rigid caste system (the one in India, for example), and there are some elements of caste in even the most fluid class system. Moreover, by using our definition of class, we can treat caste as a particular kind of class based primarily on social inheritance and from which it is relatively difficult to move upward. Many people believe today's black Americans constitute such a caste.

Another term used in connection with stratification systems is **estate.** An estate is an aggregate of people with distinctive, legally established rights and duties. The classic example of an estates system was the feudal system that operated in medieval Europe. In that particular system there were several strata, each linked to the others by carefully defined contracts that spelled out the prerogatives and obligations of each stratum. Obviously, the higher strata exercised more power and had greater privilege and prestige than the lower.[4] Estates systems are placed between caste and class systems in regard to relative amounts of upward social mobility. We believe that estate, like caste, should be treated as a particular kind of class—one that has distinctive, legally defined rights and duties. Aliens (noncitizens) exemplify a class that has estate overtones. For example, aliens in the United States are given the same protection under the law as are citizens, but they are legally excluded from voting or holding public office.

Status groups is a third term frequently used in regard to stratification systems.[5] A status group is a group of people who hold a common idea of what social honor is. Attorneys, Mexican-Americans, and Jews are examples of status groups in American society. Members of particular status groups often interact with one another, giving them a degree of cohesiveness not usually found in mere social aggregates. Again, in keeping with our definition of class, we treat status groups as specific kinds of classes.

A fourth and final term is **elite.** This term refers to the highest ranking segment of any given social category, whether a status group, social class, or whole society. We can speak of the elite of a given class (the president of General Motors is among the managerial elite in American society). Or we can speak of the economic or the political elite of a given society (either of which may be made up of two or more classes). An elite cannot always be treated as a particular kind of class, because sometimes it may contain more than one class.

We have seen that individuals, classes, and class systems are different levels of organization within stratification systems. The diagram (see p. 245) depicts the relationship among these three levels within a hypothetical stratification system.

There are three important sources of power within this fictional society: political activity, wealth, and work activity. As the weights in the column headings indicate, they vary in importance. Political

The Stratification System

THE POLITICAL CLASS SYSTEM (WEIGHT = 10)	THE WEALTH CLASS SYSTEM (WEIGHT = 8)	THE OCCUPATIONAL CLASS SYSTEM (WEIGHT = 7)			
Political Elite	Propertied Elite (A)	Managerial & Official Elite & Large Landowners (A)			
The Bureaucracy	Upper-middle (B)	Managers	Professionals (B)		
Active Party Members (B)		Lesser Political Officials	Merchants		
Inactive Party Members	Middle-middle	Small Farmers	Skilled Workers	Clerical Workers	Sales Personnel
	Lower-middle				
		Semi-skilled Workers			
Non-party Members Politically Indifferent (A)	The Poor	Unskilled Workers & Peasants			
Revolutionaries	The Impoverished	Unemployed, Beggars, Criminals, Etc.			

(Artists, Actors, Etc.)

activity (w = 10) is the most important source of power, with wealth (w = 8) ranking slightly ahead of work activity (w = 7). Note also that the number of classes within each class system varies (the political and wealth class systems each have six classes; the occupational class system has thirteen). Solid lines indicate well-defined boundaries between classes. Dashed lines indicate arbitrary boundaries that are not well-defined, or boundaries that are easily crossed. It would be difficult, for example, to determine precisely where the upper-middle class ends and the middle-middle class begins within the wealth class system.

The circled letters stand for people. The figure (A) represents a wealthy manager of a large corporation who is politically indifferent. Figure (B) represents an upper-middle class attorney who participates actively in one of the two major political parties. Because of his or her active political role, (B) actually may have more power than (A) in this society.

The position of the managerial elite and the amount of specialization within the occupational class system suggest that our fictional society is highly industrialized. And so it is. But what of societies that are not so highly industrialized? Could we use this same type of model to describe their stratification systems? Lenski says no. He sees a definite relationship between the level of technology and the type of stratification system a society will have. As previously mentioned, he discusses five societal types, each based on its level of technological advancement. Although some societies today exemplify each of these five types, four of the five had their beginnings thousands of years ago. Therefore, we will use the past tense to describe them. The fifth type is a relatively recent development, so we will use the present tense to describe it. Let's look at them.

☐ Societal Types

Hunting and Gathering Societies

These were the oldest human societies, and their technology was very simple. The Australian aborigines, the Pygmies and Bushmen of Africa, the Tasmanians, and some of the Eskimos were examples of hunting and gathering societies. In these societies, there was no sustained economic surplus and the economy operated on a subsistence level. That is, they consumed all they produced just in order to exist. They were small societies (an average of 50 people) that were nomadic in nature. Their reliance on hunting and gathering as methods of food production required that the group continually move from place to place in search of new game and/or natural vegetation. There was a lack of specialization in these societies. That is, there were few specialized roles, and basically everyone contributed in much the same manner in their efforts to win the struggle for survival. This lack of specialization extended even into leadership positions; headmen and shamans (medicine men) were usually only part-time specialists.

There was relative equality in the distribution of goods within hunting and gathering societies. Each person usually contributed to the best of his or her ability in the production of goods, and goods were distributed for the most part on the basis of need. There was inequality, however, in the distribution of prestige. Quite often prestige would be earned by the willingness of an individual to share what he or she had produced and the amount of actual sharing carried out. The fruits of each person's labor, therefore, were distributed throughout the society. In this manner the cultural norms provided for and encouraged the strong to help the weak.

Prestige and influence complemented each other in such a fashion that the most prestigious person, at any given time, was also likely to be the headman. Government functioned by means of persuasion rather than by coercion because any three people would have the physical capacity to oust the headman at any time. The headman had great influence but little authority. In hunting and gathering societies, the personal skills and abilities of people often determined the relative amounts of power, privilege, and prestige that they held.

Simple Horticultural Societies

These societies began to form about 10,000 years ago when primitive people enlarged their food supply by learning how to cultivate plants and by domesticating animals. The Boro of South America, the Zuni of New Mexico, and the Kiwai Papuans of New Guinea were examples of simple horticultural societies. There was some sustained economic surplus in these societies. This produced some leisure which was often taken up with ceremonial activities. The digging stick was the basic tool used in cultivation. These societies were generally larger (average size 100 to 200 people) and less nomadic than hunting and gathering societies. Economic, political, and religious organizations, including secret clubs for certain individuals, reflect the higher degree of specialization in simple horticultural societies.

Social inequalities were more pronounced and more institutionalized in simple horticultural societies. Status was a product of both personal attributes and office. An individual could obtain higher status simply by being appointed to an organizational position, regardless of his or her personal skills and abilities; but for the most part, people obtained high status because of their personal attributes. There was considerable inequality in the distribution of prestige which, as in hunting and gathering societies, was often gained by an individual giving away his or her material possessions. Political leaders held substantially more power in simple horticultural societies: so much more that, for the first time, the beginnings of tyranny could be recognized.

Advanced Horticultural Societies

These societies began to appear about 6,000 years ago. The Ngwato of Northern Bechuanaland, the Swazi of southeastern Africa, and the Maya, Inca, and Aztec civilizations that flourished in the New World were examples of advanced horticultural societies. The basic tool used in cultivation was the hoe. These people also used metal to make tools and cultivated a much wider variety of plants. They produced a much greater economic surplus and, correspondingly, they enjoyed more leisure than the simple horticultural societies. A Mayan corn farmer, for instance, could supply his family with enough corn to last them for a whole year by working only 49 days.[6]

Populations in these societies were fairly large, averaging in the thousands, with the Inca empire reaching about 4,000,000 at the time the Spaniards arrived. A significant development which occurred for the first time with advanced horticultural societies was empire building. The economic surplus in these societies was large enough to support a centralized political system which demanded large military and political structures. Rulers could exercise authority over diverse groups of people through this centralized political system. The Incas, for example, dominated many less powerful groups. The growth of the state led to more extensive trade and, with it, greater occupational specialization.

Political leaders had unprecedented power, and the gap in social inequality between the king and his chief ministers on the one hand and the slaves on the other was enormous. For the most part, status was based on one's relationship to the king and his subordinates. Three distinct social classes were formed. The first was a small minority of people who held royal favor and who lived off the surplus produced by others. The second class was an assortment of officials and specialists who served the elite and who often performed important governmental tasks. The third class was made up of the great majority of common people who supported the first two classes by producing the surplus on which they depended.

Relatively high status also could be attained in another way. In some advanced horticultural societies there developed a priestly class which was separate from the three already mentioned and which held considerable power. Although most of the economic surplus was consumed by the political elite, those who served them directly, and the priestly class, a portion of the surplus remained with its producers—the common people. By allowing the commoners to have some of the surplus, the rulers gave them an incentive to continue production and created differences of wealth among the commoners, thus reducing the probability of their uniting against the rulers.

One final development associated with advanced horticultural societies is significant: growth in the number and value of transferable resources. The transfer of power and privilege from one generation to the next was facilitated by this growth of transferable resources. Contributing greatly to this growth were the development of transferable forms of tangible assets, particularly money and cattle. In advanced horticultural societies, then, we see for the first time fairly well-defined hereditary classes.

Agrarian Societies

These societies began forming 5,000 to 6,000 years ago. By 3,500 years ago, they were established in South and East Asia, the Middle East, North Africa, and throughout Europe. In agrarian societies the plow was the basic tool used in cultivation. This technological advancement allowed a society to cross the boundary from gardening (simple and advanced horticultural societies) to farming (agrarian societies). Other significant technological advancements were the harnessing of animal power, discovery of the basic principles of metallurgy, and the inventions of the wheel and the sail. Production in agrarian societies was much greater than in advanced horticultural societies. Reflections

Agrarian Societies
Europe in the Middle Ages was an agrarian society in which agricultural methods were improved, surpluses marketed, and specialized trades developed. The majority of the population still lived in rural areas, even though the powerful ruling class resided in urban centers. [The Metropolitan Museum of Art, Harris Brisbane Dick Fund, 1926, (26.72.57)]

Martius, Aprilis, Maius, sunt tempora ueris ·   VER *Pueritiæ compar*   *Vere Venus gaudet florentibus aurea sertis ·*

of the enormous economic surplus produced in agrarian societies were their superior engineering feats (the pyramids of Egypt, the great cathedrals in medieval Europe).

The population of agrarian societies was large. Populations in the millions were the rule rather than the exception. Territories were also extremely large, with some empires controlling millions of square miles of territory. Ancient Rome and nineteenth-century Russia are good examples. The advances in military technology which were necessary to expand and control this territory contributed immeasurably to the power of the state. In twentieth-century Thailand, for example, Premier Marshall Sarit accumulated an estate estimated to be worth $140,000,000. He did this over a period of just ten years at a time when the *annual* per capita income in Thailand was less than $100.[7]

Large urban centers were characteristic of agrarian societies, but the urban population was small in comparison to the total population. Only about 5 to 10 percent of the people lived in urban centers. Still the cities dominated agrarian societies because the governing class resided in the cities. In fact, in Latin America people living closer to the center of a town had more prestige than those who lived farther away. Absentee ownership of farms was the rule rather than the exception. Generally, there was a greater division of labor in the cities than in rural areas.

Different urban centers tended to specialize in particular types of economic activities, and a basic pattern of trade emerged between the urban centers and the peasant villages. These villages supplied goods to the urban centers. In return they received services and certain desired commodities such as salt or tools which were not produced in the villages.

The increased trade and commerce that came with specialization in agrarian societies led to the inventions of money and writing, both of which contributed greatly to social control and inequality: money for capital accumulation, and writing to increase the efficiency of trade, commerce, and the administration of political systems.

Lenski distinguishes eight distinct classes in agrarian societies. The first four were privileged elements; the last four were not:

1. The Governing Class
2. The Retainer Class
3. The Merchant Class
4. The Priestly Class
5. The Peasant Class
6. The Artisan Class
7. Unclean and Degraded Classes
8. Expendables

An indication of the scope of inequality in agrarian societies is that the governing class (about 2 percent of the population), together with the ruler, received one-half to two-thirds of the national income. The retainer class, which was made up of people who served the political elite (lesser officials, professional soldiers, household servants, and so forth), performed important functions in the stratification systems of agrarian societies. They helped to integrate and maintain the systems by acting as mediators in relations between the governing class and the common people.

The relationship between the governing class and the priestly class was symbiotic (mutually beneficial). The governing class would help defend or spread the faith; and in return, the priestly class would help to legitimize the regime by recognizing and supporting its legitimacy. Also, quite often, the priestly class accumulated vast wealth through land ownership. In Latin America, for instance, wealthy people often willed much of their property to the Catholic Church, which became so rich that a powerful anti-church movement developed in some countries (most notably Mexico). When the interests of the governing class and the priestly class conflicted, a struggle for power resulted. In England, for instance, this struggle for power continued intermittently throughout the Middle Ages. The priests could challenge the governing class because they derived their powers from a source other than the ruler.

Basilica di San Vitale, Ravenna, Italy
From the time of the Egyptians and before, large agricultural surpluses have been reflected in great feats of engineering and architecture. Almost always in agrarian societies, power was divided between princely and priestly classes, occasionally combined in one priest-ruler or god-king.

The peasant class represented the majority of the population and, for the most part, was restricted to subsistence living. There was a fairly large number of "expendables" (5 to 10 percent of the population) who were forced to live by their wits or by charity. Although agrarian societies might have been able to support all their classes with a fairly decent standard of living, they did not do so. This was primarily because the privileged elements would not reduce their portion of the economic surplus.

Industrial Societies

These societies began forming about two hundred years ago. Industrial societies exist today in the United States, Russia, Japan, and in most of Europe. Technological advancements in these societies are so great that the gap in technology from agrarian to industrial societies is comparable in scope to the technological gap between hunting and gathering societies and agrarian societies. A comparison of the sources of energy used in performing "work" (pushing, pulling, lifting, cutting, and digging) reflects the enormity of this gap. In the United States in 1850, when industrialization had already begun, men and animals supplied 65 percent of the energy expended in work activities.[8] By 1950 men and animals supplied less than 1.6 percent of the work energy.[9]

New sources of energy such as petroleum, natural gas, hydroelectric power, and atomic power provide the basis for an enormous increase in production which continues to rise. Advancements in transportation and communication have facilitated the growth of market systems to such an extent that the economically self-sufficient community has all but vanished in advanced industrial societies. Practically all communities must rely on other communities for certain goods and services. With increased production has come increased consumption of resources, intensive specialization, tremendous population growth, and a shift from rural to urban living. In agrarian societies, for instance, approximately 10 percent of the population lived in urban centers, while 90 percent lived in rural areas. These figures are rapidly becoming reversed in advanced industrial societies. For example, only about 24 percent of the U.S. population is rural and only about 2 percent live on farms;[10] the exodus from the country to the city continues. This change also reflects the greater physical mobility that has come with advancements in transportation and development of both large market systems and command economies.

Generally, there is a much greater diffusion of political power in industrial societies, and the monarchical form of government so prevalent in agrarian societies has been virtually eliminated. Mass political parties have emerged, and there has been a great increase in functions performed by the state. Advancements in military technology have produced awesomely destructive weapons that have facilitated growth in the military power of governments.

Formal education is much more widespread in industrial societies and the general level of knowledge is higher than in agrarian societies. Literacy, for instance, is widespread in advanced industrial societies. In agrarian societies, by comparison, most people were illiterate.

For industrial societies Lenski distinguishes the following class systems and classes:

1. The Political Class System
2. The Property Class System
3. The Occupational Class System
   a. The Entrepreneurial Class
   b. The Class of Party Functionaries
   c. The Managerial Class
   d. The Military Class
   e. The Professional Class
   f. The Clerical Class
   g. The Sales Class
   h. The Working Class
   i. The Farming Class
   j. The Unemployed and Slave-labor Classes
4. The Educational Class System

5. Racial, Ethnic, and Religious Class Systems
6. The Class System Based on Sex
7. The Class System Based on Age

Stratification systems of industrial societies are considerably more complex than those of the first four societal types. High position within the political class system usually brings substantial rewards in all industrial societies. The value of position in the political class system in totalitarian societies, however, appears to be greater than in more democratic societies, where the distinction between party members and nonparty people is not so clear.

Property is also an important resource in industrial societies, although it seems to be losing some significance to other resources. Position within the occupational class system, on the other hand, is gaining in significance; the large number of recognizable classes within the occupational class system underscores that fact.

Another resource that is becoming more important is the amount of formal education an individual possesses. In general, there is a high

Education
As societies become more complex, formal education becomes an increasingly important resource for the individual.

correlation between the amount of education a person has and his or her particular occupation: the "better" (meaning greater amount of) the education, the "better" (meaning more prestigious) the job.

An individual's position within racial, ethnic, and religious class systems is also significant. Even in American society, which subscribes to the democratic political ideal, the color of a person's skin can be a resource that leads to advantages or a liability that leads to disadvantages.

The class systems based on sex and age are also significant, and relative position within them does have particular consequences. Generally, males have had distinct advantages over females. During the twentieth century, however, females have made some gains in the political, occupational, and educational areas.

☐ Inequality by Societal Type

The development of maturing industrial societies is significant in one final respect: They mark a reversal in the established trend toward increasing inequality. That is, when we trace the development of societal types from primitive hunting and gathering societies to agrarian societies, we see a trend of increasing inequality from the lower to higher level of technological advancement. Industrial societies, however, distribute scarce values more equitably than do agrarian societies. We notice, for instance, that in the majority of industrial societies, adult citizens enjoy the right to form and join political organizations which promote their own special interests. They also enjoy the right to vote. Thus political power is more diffused in industrial societies than in agrarian.

Relative Amounts of Inequality by Societal Types

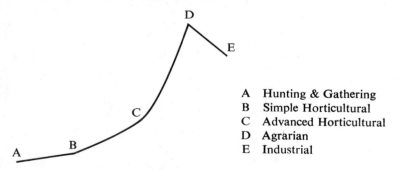

A   Hunting & Gathering
B   Simple Horticultural
C   Advanced Horticultural
D   Agrarian
E   Industrial

Furthermore, while the highest 2 percent of the population in agrarian societies usually receives at least half of the total income, the highest 2 percent of the population of democratic industrial nations only receives about 10 percent of the total personal cash income after taxes.[11]

Income may be even more equitably distributed in totalitarian industrial societies. For instance, Lenski presents evidence "that income inequality...[was] much less pronounced in the Soviet Union than in the United States."[12]

What is responsible for this turn of events? Why is inequality less pronounced in industrial societies than in agrarian? An adequate answer to these questions requires a consideration of several factors. First, technology is so complex in advanced industrial societies that it is virtually impossible for those in high organizational positions to understand completely the work of everyone below them. Because of this lack of complete knowledge, those in high positions are forced to do one of two things: (1) issue commands that are based on insufficient information; or (2) delegate to their subordinates the authority to handle certain situations. If they carry out the first alternative, they may preserve their authority, but only at the expense of efficiency and productivity. If they carry out the second alternative, they may preserve or even increase efficiency and productivity, but at the expense of their own personal authority. This dilemma invariably leads to alternating situations in which personal authority is exercised, then it is delegated, then it is exercised again, and so on. The net result is a further diffusion of power and privilege.

Second, there have been tremendously rapid and enormously large increases in productivity. Therefore, economic elites in societies in which the total value of the goods and services produced is rising rapidly find themselves on the horns of another dilemma. The only way they can maximize their total rewards is by making economic concessions to those below them. "By granting the lower classes some share in the economic surplus, they can reduce worker hostility and the accompanying loss from strikes, slowdowns and industrial sabotage."[13] In order to maximize their rewards and maintain their high position, economic elites must grant those below them a larger piece of the economic pie. Again, the net result is a reduction of inequality within the society.

Third, safe, simple, effective, and cheap means of birth control have slowed the rate of population growth in industrial societies. In the past, potential increases in per capita income (average income per person) were often consumed by expanding population. On the average, each person living in the United States between 1865 and 1914 would have had more income if the population had been expanding at a slower pace. Today, with population not expanding as rapidly, those potential increases have become real.

Fourth, in the past, a large amount of unskilled labor was necessary to get society's jobs done. Since unskilled labor was always plentiful, the majority of people were in a rather poor bargaining position. The recent knowledge explosion, however, has produced a number of occupational specialists who are in relatively short supply. These specialists can demand a higher price for their labor. As the demand for technical skills continues to rise, more and more people will receive better wages in the labor market.

Fifth, and finally, the rise and spread of democracy within the past 300 years has contributed greatly to the reduction of inequality in industrial societies. This political ideology asserts that the state belongs to the people, and wherever it has become institutionalized "a drastic new possibility has arisen: now the many can combine against the few, and even though individually the many are weaker, in combination they may be as strong or stronger."[14] Thus inequality is less pronounced in industrial societies than in agrarian societies.

Before leaving Lenski's societal types, we should note several qualifications:

1. The lines between any two societal types on this scale of technological development are not hard and fast. It is quite possible, for example, that you might study a particular society which you have difficulty classifying because it contains some elements of, say, both hunting and gathering and simple horticultural societies. Any given societal type, therefore, simply explains certain central tendencies of societies whose level of technological development is roughly the same. On the other hand, it would be relatively simple to identify gross differences between a society which fits the hunting and gathering model and one which resembles the agrarian type.

2. There may be a considerable variation among societies within each societal type. That is, not all societies within any one type order their lives in precisely the same fashion. The variation, in fact, may be so great that the lowest simple horticultural society might produce less surplus than the highest hunting and gathering society; and the highest simple horticultural society might produce more surplus than the lowest advanced horticultural society.

3. Lenski's is only one of several schemes that develop societal types based on technological advancement. It is possible to analyze the development of stratification systems using the same variable (technology), while at the same time viewing it from various perspectives.

☐ Identifying Social Classes

Lenski has divided the stratification systems of industrial societies into several class systems and a large number of classes. Other scholars, using other variables, have divided the same stratification systems in other ways. W. Lloyd Warner did a famous study of "Yankee City" in which he identified six classes:[15]

1. Upper-upper	old aristocracy with inherited wealth
2. Lower-upper	wealthy, but not accepted as equals by upper-upper class
3. Upper-middle	professionals and respected businesspersons
4. Lower-middle	semiprofessionals, small businesspersons, white-collar workers
5. Upper-lower	skilled and semiskilled workers
6. Lower-lower	unskilled workers, nonrespectables, and deviants

Similarly, Allison Davis and Burleigh and Mary Gardner identified six classes in their study of a Mississippi community.[16] In still another study, Warner identified only five classes.[17]

The number of classes that are identified is not particularly important. Carefully defining what constitutes a class in any particular study, however, is very important. Once we have clearly defined classes, we can select criteria by which to make some meaningful statements about the statistical advantages and disadvantages for people on different levels within any stratification system. For example, if we have, say, five clearly defined classes, we can then compare the incomes of a sample of people who fit into each of those five classes. [If we notice that both the range of incomes and the average income increase from the lowest (5) to the highest (1) ranking class, then we can say that members of class (2) tend to have the advantage of a greater income than members of class (4).] We should realize, however, that the boundaries between classes are always somewhat blurred. For instance, it would be extremely difficult to recognize the difference between people at the upper end of one class and those at the lower end of the next higher class. But how do we determine what constitutes a class in the first place? How do we rank people? Usually sociologists use one or more of the following three methods.

The Reputational Method

This method is based on the reputation of individuals or groups within their community, and it is most conducive to evaluating prestige levels. One way of using the **reputational method** is to select a sample of people who have lived within a particular community for a long period of time and ask them to rank other selected members of the community according to prestige on a scale that has a particular number of points, say five. Having established five different prestige strata, one could now select another sample of long-term residents to assign each of the people in the community to one of the five established strata.

The reputational method, although useful, is quite limited because: (1) all the people who are ranking others must know the people they are ranking; and (2) all the people who are ranking others must use the same criteria for ranking. In other words, the reputational method probably will work only in small, homogeneous communities. Moreover, rankings from different communities within the same society may not be comparable because the criteria for prestige may vary from one community to another.

The Subjective Method

This is a self-ranking approach. Individuals indicate their own perception of where they stand in relation to others by ranking themselves according to some predetermined criterion such as social class, prestige, or economic standing. An early attempt to use the **subjective method** asked a sample of Americans to rank themselves in one of three categories: "upper class," "middle class," or "lower class." (Eighty-eight percent responded "middle class,"[18] indicating either they didn't like calling themselves "upper class" or "lower class," or they were ignorant of class differences, or the middle class in America was unusually large!) A few years later, Richard Centers added "working class" to the previous three categories and the response indicated that the "middle class" had dwindled to only 43 percent.[19] Interestingly, 51 percent responded "working class."

Since the subjective method indicates how an individual perceives his or her own ranking in relation to others, it is important that the investigator know the reference group which the individual is using for comparison. An individual who earns $15,000 a year, who lives on the fringes of a ghetto, and who has relatively few contacts with people who earn as much or more, might rank him or herself very high. If the same individual moves to another neighborhood where there are many contacts with people who earn more than $15,000, the individual might give him or herself a lower ranking.

The weakness of the subjective method is that a person's perception of where he or she ranks might not accurately reflect the actual situation. This can present great problems, particularly if the criteria for ranking are not clear to the individual who is doing the ranking. We can see, for instance, that a person may hold a relatively high status in one class system and a relatively low status in another. Lenski points out that when such status inconsistency occurs, individuals tend to see themselves in terms of their highest status while seeing others in terms of their lowest. In American society a black doctor, when comparing him or herself to a white laborer, is likely to rank the two on the basis of standing within the occupational class system (where the doctor ranks high and the laborer ranks low). The white laborer is likely to rank the two on the basis of standing within the racial class system (where the white laborer ranks high and the black doctor ranks low).[20] While the subjective method has weaknesses, it has two advantages over the reputational method: (1) the individual doing the ranking does not have to know the others being ranked; and (2) it can be effectively used to sample a whole society, not just a small community.

The Objective Method

This method relies on certain fixed and easily recognizable criteria such as the type of occupation, the amount of education, or the amount of income, rather than the evaluative feelings and perceptions of individuals. It allows for more precise measurement than either the reputational or subjective methods and can be used to identify strata throughout a whole society. Moreover, it can be used in conjunction with community studies based on the other methods to help define social strata better and to allow us to make more meaningful statements about the distribution of scarce values within any given society. For example, if we notice that there is a strong correlation between level of education on the one hand, and the amount of prestige on the other hand, then we can say that people in society (X), who have attained (Y) level of education, are likely to have (Z) amount of prestige. If, upon further investigation, we also find a strong correlation between educational levels attained by parents and their children in society (X), then we can say that the children of parents who have attained (Y) level of education are likely to attain (Z) level of prestige within that society. In this case, we can generalize further by stating that the birth of an individual into a particular family in society (X) tends to give certain advantages or disadvantages to that individual. Note that we said "tends to." Our proposition is stated in this manner because we are identifying only a general tendency. We recognize the possibility of an individual attaining great prestige even though his or her parents' educational level is very low, and vice versa. The important point is that the objective method, particularly when it is used in conjunction with the other methods, can provide us with meaningful insights into the structure and nature of stratification systems.

☐ Who Gets What and Why?—American Style

One of the important points we mentioned earlier in this chapter and in the preceding chapter was that initial status for the individual is transmitted through the family. Individuals are born into families, and they will hold whatever rank their family holds within the stratification system—at least for the time being. But what are their ultimate chances of moving upward or downward on the social scale? What are their chances of accumulating the power, privilege, and prestige that seem to be so highly valued in contemporary industrial societies? Although we

Equality of Opportunity?
Children of an upper-middle class American family have more advantages than the backyard pool. They will go to better schools, eat better food, and probably be given greater opportunities for self-development than the children of a low-income family.

will focus on American society in attempting to shed some light on these questions, we hasten to add that the general tendencies noted seem to apply to other industrial societies as well.

Perhaps the most revered, and certainly in a sense one of the most sacred, American political documents is the Declaration of Independence. Among its several propositions is the following: "all men are created equal." Just what does that mean? Obviously it does not mean equal in a physical sense because we know that the physical structures and capabilities of individuals at birth differ, sometimes significantly. By the same token, it does not mean equal in the sense of the initial cultural advantages or disadvantages the individual will have, because these, too, differ at birth according to the particular family into which the individual is born. Many Americans believe that the "equal" refers to equality of opportunity. They would argue that we live in a society that stresses individual liberty, and that all individuals are free to develop their capabilities to their fullest extent. In other words, each of us has an equal opportunity to acquire power, privilege, and prestige. If we don't acquire all we would like to acquire, we have no one to blame but ourselves or our innate capabilities. This is an interesting argument—one that merits closer investigation. Do we really have equality of opportunity? By accumulating data through the methods we have discussed, and by carefully analyzing that data, social scientists have produced some evidence that suggests the answer to this question is an emphatic "no." Perhaps the "equal" proposition in the Declaration of Independence is as much a myth as George Washington's tree-chopping caper. Let's sample the evidence.

In 1989 the median household income in the United States was $34,213. Households with incomes of $75,000 or more represented 11.3 percent of the total, while households with incomes of less than $12,675 (below poverty level for a household of 4 persons) made up over 10.3 percent of the total.[21] These income figures begin to take on significance when we place them against occupational ratings and educational requirements for those occupations.

Recently the National Opinion Research Center conducted a survey in which a national sample of the general population rated hundreds of occupations.[22] Twenty of the highest rated occupations were:

1. Physician
2. College/university professor
3. Lawyer
4. Dentist
5. Physicist/astronomer
6. Bank officer
7. Architect
8. Aeronautical/astronautical engineer
9. Psychologist
10. Airplane pilot
11. Clergy

12. Chemist
13. Electrical engineer
14. Geologist
15. Sociologist
16. Secondary school teacher
17. Mechanical engineer
18. Registered nurse
19. Dental hygienist
20. Pharmacist

Notice that at least five of these occupations normally require advanced college degrees and no less than fifteen require at least a four-year college degree. Actually, of course, you really don't need a strict accounting of educational requirements to recognize that, overwhelmingly, people who fill most of these occupations have either four-year college degrees or at least some college education. Also, you should note that many people who fill these occupations earn over $75,000 a year and that all of them are likely to earn at least $34,213 a year, the median household income in 1989.

Twenty of the lowest rated occupations were:

1. File clerk
2. Upholsterer
3. Drill-press operator
4. Furniture finisher
5. Retail salesperson
6. Gas station attendant
7. Security guard
8. Taxi driver
9. Elevator operator
10. Bartender
11. Waiter/waitress
12. Clothing presser
13. Farm laborer
14. Household servant
15. Car washer
16. Freight handler
17. Garbage collector
18. Janitor
19. Bellhop
20. Shoe shiner

Notice that none of these occupations normally requires even a high school education, much less a college degree. Note also that only a few of these jobs are likely to have even the remotest chance of producing $75,000 a year, and that people filling several other jobs are not likely to earn the 1989 median household income of $34,213.

What do all these statistics mean? They suggest a high correlation among education, occupation, and income. People with more education tend to fill the more prestigious occupations that pay well; people with less education tend to fill the less prestigious occupations that, by comparison, do not pay well. Since education, occupation, and income are valuable resources in American society, it is clear that substantial inequality exists. But what about equality of opportunity? For example, do the children of working-class parents (manual workers in semi-skilled and skilled occupations) and middle-class parents (white-collar workers and professionals) have an equal chance to obtain a higher education, a more prestigious occupation, and more income?

In his book *Class and Conformity: A Study in Values,* Melvin Kohn cites three studies which, when correlated with one another, indicate that children of middle-class parents have greater opportunity to fill more prestigious occupations than do children of working-class parents.* He argues that occupational conditions socialize people into values, which they transmit to their children through child-rearing practices.

> Middle-class occupations characteristically deal more with the manipulation of interpersonal relations, ideas, and symbols while working-class occupations deal more with material things. Middle-class occupations are likely to be free of close supervision, while working-class occupations are more subject to standardization and direct supervision. In short, middle-class occupations demand a greater degree of self-direction; working-class occupations require that the individual conform to rules and procedures established by authority.[23]

Middle-class parents, then, tend to employ child-rearing practices which stress values that are ideally suited for middle-class occupations. Conversely, working-class parents tend to employ child-rearing practices which stress values that are ideally suited for working-class occupations. Under these circumstances, middle-class children are more likely to see the functional value of obtaining a higher education. Moreover, since the economic means to obtain such an education are more readily at their disposal, they will probably acquire that education and later fill a middle-class occupation. Working-class children are less likely to obtain a higher education and are therefore more likely to fill working-class occupations.

If you think this sounds like a vicious cycle, you should bear in mind that our contrast has been between only middle and working class— two classes that are relatively close to each other in the American

* Interestingly, one of these studies was conducted in Turin, Italy, suggesting that what is true of American society applies to Italy also. Melvin L. Kohn, *Class and Conformity* (Homewood, Ill.: Dorsey, 1969).

Institutionalized Social Inequality
Education and income, as well as occupation, are determiners of placement on the social scale.

stratification system. What could we say about equality of opportunity if we contrast two classes or aggregates of classes that are far apart on the social scale?

As you can easily understand, the chances of an individual born into the lower strata achieving the degree of education, the type of occupation, and the amount of income of an individual born into the upper strata are, statistically, anything but equal. Inequality has been institutionalized in America, as well as in all other industrial societies.

Inequality extends to other areas too. One source reveals that only 14 percent of people with low incomes reported that they were "very happy," while 38 percent of those with high incomes said they were "very happy."[24] Another source states that 30 percent of unskilled workers reported that they had no close friends, while only 10 percent of professionals, officials, and top business executives said they had no close friends.[25] Still another study reveals that low-income strata have six times as many obese women as high-income strata.[26] In short, position in the stratification system is related to almost everything about people's lives—"their political party preferences, their sexual behavior, their church membership, even their rates of ill health and death."[27]

The fact that equality of opportunity is a myth does not mean that social mobility does not exist in America. Actually, it really does exist. In fact, recent national studies on occupational mobility indicate a slight increase in intergenerational (children as compared to their parents) mobility.[28] This trend is in keeping with Lenski's observation of a decline in inequality from agrarian to industrial societies. Remember, we are dealing with tendencies or statistical trends. It is quite possible for some lower-class individuals to rise significantly within the American stratification system. It is also possible for some upper-class individuals to fall significantly. What we have tried to show is that those cases do not occur very frequently.

We alluded earlier to the "equal" proposition in the Declaration of Independence. It appears extremely difficult to accept literally that proposition as a statement of fact concerning equality of opportunity. However, if we accept it as a statement of a political ideal, we are recognizing not only established American values but also a trend in the technological development from agrarian to industrial societies.

REFERENCES

1. See C. Wright Mills, *The Power Elite* (Fair Lawn, N.J.: Oxford University Press, 1956) and Ralf Dahrendorf, *Class and Class Conflict in Industrial Society* (Stanford, Calif.: Stanford University Press, 1959).
2. See Parsons' *The Social System* (New York: Free Press, 1951) and Davis and Moore's "Some Principles of Stratification," *American Sociological Review, 10* (1945), 242–249.
3. Gerhard Lenski, *Power and Privilege: A Theory of Social Stratification* (New York: McGraw-Hill, 1966).
4. For an excellent discussion of feudalism, see Goldwin Smith, *The Heritage of Man* (New York: Charles Scribner's Sons, 1960), pp. 202–225.
5. This term was introduced by the translators of Max Weber's work. See Max Weber, *From Max Weber: Essays in Sociology*, translated by H. H. Gerth and C. Wright Mills (Fair Lawn, N.J.: Oxford University Press, 1946), pp. 186–194.
6. Sylvanus G. Morley, *The Ancient Maya* (Stanford, Calif.: Stanford University Press, 1946), pp. 154–155.
7. *New York Times*, July 10, 1964, p. 2.
8. J. Frederic Dewhurst and Associates, *America's Needs and Resources* (New York: Twentieth Century Fund, 1955), p. 116.
9. Lenski, p. 298.
10. *Statistical Abstract of the United States, 1991* (Washington, D.C.: U.S. Government Printing Office), Table 35, p. 28, and Table 1106, p. 643.

11. Lenski, p. 309.
12. *Ibid.*, p. 313.
13. *Ibid.*, p. 314.
14. *Ibid.*, p. 318.
15. W. Lloyd Warner and Paul S. Lunt, *The Social Life of a Modern Community* (New Haven: Yale University Press, 1941), p. 88.
16. Allison Davis, Burleigh B. Gardner, and Mary R. Gardner, *Deep South* (Chicago: University of Chicago Press, 1941).
17. W. Lloyd Warner *et al.*, *Democracy in Jonesville* (New York: Harper, 1949), pp. 50–51.
18. George Gallup and S. F. Rae, *The Pulse of Democracy* (New York: Simon and Schuster, 1940), p. 169.
19. Richard Centers, *The Psychology of Social Classes: A Study of Class Consciousness* (Princeton, N.J.: Princeton University Press, 1949), p. 77.
20. Lenski, p. 87.
21. *Statistical Abstract, 1991*, Table 729, p. 454.
22. *General Social Surveys, 1972–1983: Cumulative Codebook* (Chicago: National Opinion Research Center, 1983), pp. 338–349.
23. Melvin L. Kohn, *Class and Conformity* (Homewood, Ill.: Dorsey, 1969) pp. xi, x.
24. Norman M. Bradburn and David Caplovitz, *Reports on Happiness* (Chicago: Aldine, 1965), p. 9.
25. Joseph A. Kahl, *The American Class Structure* (New York: Holt, Rinehart Winston, 1957), pp. 137–138.
26. Robert G. Burnight and Parker G. Marden, "Social Correlates of Weight in an Aging Population," *The Milbank Memorial Fund Quarterly, 45* (1967), 75–92.
27. Kohn, p. 3.
28. Otis Dudley Duncan, "The Trend of Occupational Mobility in the United States," *American Sociological Review, 30* (1965), 491–498, and David L. Featherman and Robert M. Hauser, *Opportunity and Change* (New York: Academic Press, 1978).

GLOSSARY

Conflict theorists	Scholars who place great emphasis on class conflict as being responsible for the distribution of scarce values in society.
Functional theorists	Scholars who emphasize the need for certain societal functions as being responsible for the distribution of scarce values in society.
Social stratification	The division of societies into layers or strata, each containing aggregates of people who share similar beliefs, attitudes, values, and lifestyles. These strata are ranked according to the relative amounts of power, privilege, and prestige they possess.

Power	The probability that an individual or group will be able to do what it wants to do. When power is supported by generally accepted societal norms, we call it *legitimate power,* or *authority.* When power is exercised informally and is based solely on the persuasive ability of one individual or group to manipulate another, we call it *influence.*
Privilege	Possession or control of part of a society's economic surplus.
Prestige	Relative value of a status within a society. Example: accounting is a more prestigious occupation in American society than is bookkeeping.
Class	An aggregate of people in a society who share similar amounts of some form of power, privilege, or prestige.
Class system	A hierarchy of classes ranked according to some particular standard.
Caste	A kind of class that is based primarily on social inheritance and from which it is relatively difficult to move upward in the stratification system. Example: Americans born into poverty-stricken ghetto situations.
Estate	A kind of class that has legally defined rights and duties. Example: citizens.
Status group	A kind of class whose members share a common idea of what social honor is. Example: Mexican-Americans.
Elite	The highest ranking segment of any given social category. Elite may be used to describe part of a social class, a status group, a social class, part of a social class system, or part of a whole society. Example: superstars in sports and entertainment.
Objective method	The process of ranking individuals and classes in a social hierarchy on the basis of selected, fixed criteria. Occupation, education, and income are often the criteria used.
Reputational method	The process of ranking individuals in a social hierarchy on the basis of the reputation of individuals or groups within their own community.
Subjective method	The process of ranking individuals in a social hierarchy by means of self rating.

SELECTED READING

Child Poverty in America (Washington, D.C.: Children's Defense Fund, 1991). A report on child poverty as a growing social problem in the United States.

Gilbert, D. and J. A. Kahl. *The American Class Structure: A New Synthesis*, 3rd ed. (Belmont, Calif.: Wadsworth, 1987). An analysis of social stratification in the United States.

Grusky, D. B., ed. *Social Stratification: Class, Race, and Gender in Sociological Perspective* (Boulder, Col.: Westview, 1992). A reader that surveys several viewpoints on diversity and social stratification.

Katz, M. *In the Shadow of the Poorhouse: A Social History of Welfare in America* (New York: Basic Books, 1988). A history of public welfare in the United States.

Phillips, K. *The Politics of Rich and Poor: Wealth and the American Electorate in the Reagan Aftermath* (New York: Random House, 1990). An analysis of social inequality in the United States.

Rossi, P. H. *Down and Out in America: The Origins of Homelessness* (Chicago: University of Chicago Press, 1991). An examination of homelessness in the United States.

Stone, R. *The Feminization of Poverty and Older Women* (Washington, D.C.: U.S. Department of Health and Human Services, 1986). A study of poverty among older women in the United States.

QUESTIONS

1. The division of societies into different layers, or strata, each containing groups of people who share similar beliefs, attitudes, values, and life-styles, is known as
   a. socialization.
   b. social stratification.
   c. a class system.
   d. a caste system.
   e. a status system.

2. The probability that an individual or group will be able to do what it wants to do, despite resistance, is called
   a. privilege.
   b. prestige.
   c. influence.
   d. power.
   e. class.

3. The oldest known human societies are known as
   a. industrial societies.
   b. simple horticultural societies.

    c. hunting and gathering societies.
    d. advanced horticultural societies.
    e. agrarian societies.

4. A relationship exists between the level of _____ and the nature of the _____ system.
    a. technology / stratification
    b. stratification / economic
    c. economics / family
    d. labor / education
    e. education / technology

5. Functional theorists argue that
    a. societies reward individuals for filling positions for which there is a relative scarcity of qualified personnel.
    b. inequality generates conflict through institutions such as private property.
    c. class conflict is inevitable and necessary.
    d. agrarian societies are better off than industrial societies.
    e. the class system is a solution to the problems of class struggle.

6. Social stratification ranks people by their relative amounts of
    a. money.
    b. power, privilege, and prestige.
    c. prestige and mobility.
    d. conformity.
    e. influence in their jobs.

7. Melvin Kohn argues that the children of middle-class parents have greater opportunity to fill more prestigious occupations than do the children of working-class parents because
    a. child-rearing practices transmit the parents' values to the children.
    b. the middle class holds down the power of the working class.
    c. children of working-class parents drop out of school.
    d. children of working-class parents refuse to conform to rules.
    e. children of middle-class parents are more intelligent.

8. The process of ranking individuals on a social hierarchy by means of self-rating is called the
    a. reputational method.
    b. class method.
    c. subjective method.
    d. objective method.
    e. status method.

9. The highest ranking segment of any given social category is called
    a. an estate.
    b. an elite.

    c. a class.
    d. a status group.
    e. a caste.

10. The most complex stratification systems are found in
    a. agrarian societies.
    b. advanced horticultural societies.
    c. hunting and gathering societies.
    d. industrial societies.
    e. simple horticultural societies.

QUESTIONS FOR THOUGHT AND DISCUSSION

1. Is a classless society really possible?

2. Is a classless society really desirable?

3. How important is position within the American stratification system?

4. Do we really have equality of opportunity?

12

Religion

Religion has always been an integral part of human experience, and has existed in virtually every human society. Why? There have been several attempts to answer this question by explaining the origins of religion. In this chapter we will survey these proposed answers and will examine the interrelated parts of religious systems and the relationship between religious and other societal subsystems.

Our general goal is to present a scientific explanation of religious behavior. We are not concerned with specific religious beliefs and practices, except when they may serve as examples for the ideas with which we are dealing. In short, we are striving for objectivity. Viewing religion objectively is difficult for scientist and layperson alike. There are two primary reasons for this difficulty—one is emotional; the other is rational.

The emotional difficulty springs from the nature of religion itself. Religion is concerned with ultimate values. Such values are the bases upon which whole value systems are built. Therefore it is extremely difficult to view religion from a disinterested, value-free position. This emotional difficulty may easily lead to one of two positions: (1) "There is only one true religion (my own), and it is the best"; or (2) "Religion is nothing but a myth that promotes ignorance and delays progress; it serves no useful purpose." An individual holding either of these positions cannot approach the subject of religion objectively.

The rational difficulty in viewing religion objectively stems from the false assumption that people, in their religious behavior, are acting in the same logical manner as the scientist who consciously strives to overcome the emotional difficulty. In an earlier chapter we pointed out that people do not always behave rationally; sometimes they behave nonrationally. Religious behavior falls into the second category.

☐ The Origins of Religion

Exploitative and Evolutionary Theories

Early sociological and anthropological attempts to explain the origins of religion were either exploitative or evolutionary in nature. Most of them begin with some explanation for why humans created religion and proceed with a description of an evolutionary development that logically ends with the destruction of religion. Karl Marx, for instance, believed that religion had been created by the ruling class as an instrument the rulers could use to take advantage of the great mass of workers (*exploitative*). Myths could be used to justify the rulers' high positions. The rulers could use the notion of a life after death to appease the workers by claiming that people's just rewards would be given to them in the afterlife. Marx believed that religion, like the state, would wither away as society moved inexorably toward a Communist utopia.

Two evolutionary theories are **animism** and **naturism**.[1] Animism—the belief that spirits inhabit and give life to most natural objects—attributes the origins of religion to human error. In dreams one could see and talk to oneself and to people who had died. Because these dream experiences were mistaken for reality, people came to believe that everybody has another self, a soul. This soul resembles the person but "is more active, since it can cover vast distances in an instant. It is more malleable and plastic. . . . It is represented as made of matter, but of a matter much more subtle and ethereal than any we know empirically."[2] When people observed that the bodies of the dead disintegrated, they assumed that the soul of the person became a free, disembodied spirit. These spirits were believed to have the same needs, interests, and passions as living people. From time to time they would enter the bodies of the living and either cause disorders or increase vitality. The person came to believe that he or she was at the mercy of the spirits, to which were attributed all extraordinary events. Soon it was believed that inanimate objects had souls too. Thus all natural phenomena could be explained through animism.

Naturism—the belief and worship of nature gods—attributes the origins of religion to the influence of external nature on people. The impulse to religious thought and language was derived from the sensation of the infinite that people experienced when they observed and experienced nature, which they did not understand. Religion originated when prehistoric people translated natural forces such as wind and rain into personal agents—spiritual beings or gods that they then worshiped. Naturism was the first religion.

Whether they accept either naturism or animism as the correct explanation of the origins of religion, most evolutionary theorists believe that as humans continue to develop their rational capabilities, they will eventually discard religious beliefs.

Incas Worshiping the Sun
Naturism—the belief and worship of nature gods—represents the earliest religion to some evolutionary theorists.

Evolutionary religious theories are now generally unacceptable to scholars who study the sociology of religion. Indeed, most contemporary scholars do not speculate to a great extent about how religion began. Instead, they study today's societies, both simple and complex, in an attempt to understand and explain the nature of religion.

Functionalism

One of the first men who studied contemporary societies as ongoing systems was Emile Durkheim. He had closely studied the desert Arunta, an Australian aborigine society that he believed was the simplest in the world. Using their culture as a model for the earliest people, he explained the origins of religion through their religious practices. Although Durkheim's conception of the origins of religion has been discarded, his emphasis on the social significance of religion has not.

The Arunta practice a religion known as **totemism.** Arunta bands have sacred places, called totem centers, where particular species of plants or animals (totems) are found. Each band performs ceremonies to ensure the well-being of its totem. Durkheim observed that all the worship activities of the Arunta seemed to serve one basic function—the celebration of the social group itself. By participating in such celebrations, people become completely involved with a group which they need and which in turn needs them. Religious worship, Durkheim believed, was the worship of society symbolized by the totem. Religion functioned to integrate the society.

The Arunta
Their religion functions
to integrate society, as
does ours.

Durkheim's analysis of the role religion plays in meeting societal needs was at the forefront of the functionalist view in the sociology of religion.* Other scholars have since expanded and refined this view. Several functions, psychological as well as sociological, have been identified. We will discuss them. But first let's discuss the basic human need which religion satisfies and the conditions of human existence which have produced that need.

One has a need for something to explain the unknown and to justify one's existence. This can be called a need for something **supernatural,** something ultimate—something that transcends or goes beyond everyday experiences. This supernatural entity may be conceived of as a humanlike form which has humanlike qualities, or it may be understood in more abstract terms, as, for example, a life-giving energy source. However it is conceived, the supernatural is the central characteristic of religion, and a belief in the supernatural is, in part, a response to three conditions of human existence—uncertainty, powerlessness, and scarcity.

We live in a world of uncertainty. No matter how carefully we plan future events, we can never be sure that they will happen. As the saying goes, "The only things we can be sure of are death and taxes." Living in this condition of uncertainty, a person is subject to great insecurity.

* The functionalist view is paramount in the works of A. R. Radcliffe-Brown, Bronislaw Malinowski, Max Weber, Talcott Parsons, and others.

We are relatively powerless to control our life circumstances. Modern medicine, for example, has greatly improved our life chances, but can we control how long we will live or how much suffering we will endure in our lifetimes? Can we determine whether or not there will be a flood, a hurricane, or an earthquake? This powerlessness to control our life circumstances leads us to even more insecurity.

Scarcity is the third condition of human existence. We have an unlimited number of wants, but the resources available to satisfy our wants are limited. In other words, we can't always have what we want. If, for instance, ten people want a particular thing, say da Vinci's Mona Lisa, only one of them can have it. The Mona Lisa is a scarce commodity. Other things may also be scarce, and it is not unusual to find us wanting more of something than we can have. Power, for example, is a scarce commodity.

People live in society and, as we have pointed out, society requires order. Furthermore, order implies authority, and authority requires subordination. If one is to live in society, one must subordinate personal desires to some authority at times. Since authority must be exercised by someone, there will always be an unequal distribution of power in society. Some will have more of it than others, and not all of us may have as much of it as we would like to have. This condition of scarcity leads us once again to insecurity.

The conditions of uncertainty, powerlessness, and scarcity produce insecurities that worldly social conventions do not deal with effectively. These conditions raise questions to which there are no certain answers—questions which can be answered by reference to something which transcends worldly experience. For example, what is the meaning of life? Why should a human being, any human being, die of starvation in a world that produces enough food to feed everyone in it? Why should people be born with crippling birth defects that condemn them to a life of misery and pain? Why should young men die in a war?

Religion, through its supernatural reference, attempts to provide answers to these questions of ultimate meaning. By providing a reference which goes beyond empirical experience, religion presents a view of ultimate reality in which suffering, frustration, deprivation, and death may have ultimate meaning. A person might willingly suffer great hardships, perhaps even death, because he or she believes that such actions will be rewarded in some afterlife. Thus religion may facilitate one's adjustment to and acceptance of the human conditions of uncertainty, powerlessness, and scarcity.

But that does not totally explain the human need for something supernatural. There is another side to the coin. Positive as well as negative factors lead people to a belief in the supernatural. For example, how do we empirically explain the order and beauty we observe in nature, the intricacies of the human mind, the existence of joy as well as

A Question of Ultimate Meaning
The religious motivation behind self-immolation may be, like so many religious conceptions, intelligible only to the believer.

sorrow, peace as well as war, pleasure as well as pain, or the miracle of the creation itself? We don't have adequate empirical explanations for these things. Religion, then, provides answers to positive as well as negative questions of ultimate meaning.

☐ Functions

Religion performs a number of psychological functions. First, it provides security for the individual by offering stable reference points that one can use to orient oneself to new conditions in a changing world. The supernatural itself is such a reference point. Religious beliefs and values are others. The Ten Commandments, for instance, are a stable set of reference points which a person can relate to, and from which he or she can view the world.

Second, religion performs identity functions. A person verifies his or her self-concept and expands the self through association and action. As we have previously indicated, an adequate self-image is very important to each of us. By associating with others in a religious group, and by acting out rituals in accordance with the beliefs and values of that group, we come to understand better who and what we are.

Third, religion performs a supportive function. By providing emotional support in times of crisis and consolation in times of disappointment, religion helps to bring the disaffected back into the group and to maintain individual and group morale. It is significant, for example,

Identity Function
For many, religion performs both a psychological and a sociological function, helping to verify a person's self-concept and emphasizing one's sense of belonging to the group.

that in his first public statement following the assassination of John F. Kennedy, Lyndon Johnson appealed for "help" from God as well as from the American public.

Religion also performs important sociological functions. It facilitates cultural integration by **sanctifying,** or making holy, cultural norms and values. Emile Durkheim had great insight into the nature of this function. A person is more likely to live by norms when he or she sees them as being sacred. One is less likely to steal, for instance, if one's religion as well as one's society has rules against stealing. In this way, religion helps to integrate the culture. In performing this integrative function, religion helps to maintain the dominance of group goals over individual ones; thus it facilitates social control.

Finally, religion may function as an agent of change in society. This happens when religious values transcend and conflict with those of the secular world. It has been argued, for example, that Protestantism functioned as an agent of change by stressing individual freedom and thereby challenging Western societal values at the beginning of the modern era when individualism was not highly valued. Thus, religion may facilitate change.

☐ What Is Religion?

What we have done so far in this chapter is to describe religion in terms of the functions it may perform in society. In order to understand how religion operates as a societal subsystem, we will now consider its characteristics. Most of them have already been mentioned.

Perhaps the most easily recognizable characteristic of religion is a conception of the supernatural. Religions have characterized the supernatural as creatures and objects (gods, heavens), states of mind (peace), and transcendental ends (immortality). The common quality of these conceptions is their intangibility. They are truly supernatural in that they cannot be detected by the senses. They can, however, be symbolized by objects that can be known by the senses. These objects are treated as sacred, and sacred objects (the Koran, the Bible) are another characteristic of religion. People relate to sacred objects through *ritual*, which is a third characteristic of religion. Ritual, in turn, is intimately connected to beliefs, which are supported by values. Beliefs and values are also characteristics of religion. The last characteristic of religion is so obvious that it may easily be overlooked—a group of believers. When this group of believers is a large, well-established group into which members are born and later confirmed, we call it a **church** (for example, Lutherans). Churches are usually well integrated into the culture. When the believers constitute a smaller, not so well-established voluntary association which members join by conscious choice, we call it a **sect** (Jehovah's Witnesses). Sects are not usually well integrated into the culture.*

A religion, then, is a group of believers who symbolize their conception of the supernatural by sacred objects they relate to through rituals and beliefs that they value.

By treating religions as societal subsystems, we can analyze the relationships among their particular characteristics in regard to systemic stability, change, and breakdown. Furthermore, we can see how the parts of a religion relate to parts of other societal subsystems and how a religion relates to a whole society.

For example, long after Copernicus had effectively demonstrated to most of the rest of the Western world that the earth was not the center of the universe, the Roman Catholic religion persisted in officially clinging to the belief that it was. By the nineteenth century, however, many Catholics, including some high-ranking church officials, had accepted

---

* The church-sect continuum should be approached with the same caution we approach all others—with the understanding that the two opposite theoretical poles are ideal types that are not likely to exist in the real world. Many churches, then, have sect characteristics, and vice versa. See Liston Pope, *Millhands and Preachers* (New Haven: Yale University Press, 1942) and Bryan R. Wilson, *Sects and Society* (Berkeley: University of California Press, 1961).

The "Church" as a Fully Organized Religious Institution
Pope John Paul II presides at the beatification of French Marie Luise de Jesus Trichet (tapestry at top) during a ceremony in St. Peter's Basilica.

Copernicus' view (the heliocentric theory), and they no longer supported the official church position on that issue. The church subsequently changed its official position. Here is a case in which a change in one part of society (a scientific discovery) produced a strain between two parts of a religion (the believers and their beliefs) which, in turn, led to a change in the religion itself, thus promoting its stability and avoiding breakdown. (Its ability to cope with this strain is a tribute to this religious system's endurance and flexibility.) The religion was then in a position to sanctify its newly acquired belief, and thereby to sanction scientific inquiry and to integrate further the total society.

The relationship between religion and society may be more clearly understood by considering local variations of global religions. Again we can use Catholicism as an example. Catholicism is certainly a global religion. If the church were free from the influence of local cultures, then we would observe a consistency on questions of morality by true believers throughout the world. But when we examine a question such as birth control by methods other than the rhythm method or abstinence from sexual intercourse, we find an inconsistency on the part of true believers that seems to be related to local cultures. For example, American representatives to the Second Vatican Council (1962–1965) have been characterized as "liberal" on this question; whereas Italian representatives have been regarded as "conservative."* If we can accept the idea that these church officials are products of their respective cultures and that their respective cultures have elaborated different values in regard to birth control, then we can understand how American Catholics would be more likely to support one position and Italian Catholics another.

Another way of illustrating the relationship between religion and society is to consider the tendency of religious groups to create their respective gods in terms of characteristics or situations that are significant in their own cultures. We notice, for example, that societies which live in areas with long annual dry spells often have rain gods, and that animal gods are likely to have special significance in hunting societies. In different societies throughout the world where Christianity has made inroads, the Christ image is depicted in a variety of ways: In America he looks like a white Anglo-Saxon; in the Orient he looks somewhat yellow-brown and has Oriental eyes; in parts of Africa he is black. The fact that the supernatural is often conceived as having an essentially human outlook **(anthropomorphism)** emphasizes the intimate relationship between the individual and religion.

By seeing how religions relate to other societal subsystems, we can gain a better understanding of the interrelatedness of various parts of the social system. For example, when we compare religions with social stratification systems, we are immediately struck with the interrelatedness of the two. The Anglican Church in England, for instance, draws its membership from all social classes. Here we can note differences in the perception of religious services by people from different social classes within the same religion. An upper class Anglican is likely to perceive the intellectual aspects of the religious service. He or she understands the symbolism and the rhetoric that is presented. The lower class Anglican is more likely to perceive the emotional aspects. For this person, symbolism is spectacle, and a fiery sermon, which may not be comprehended intellectually, "moves" the listener nevertheless.

Another indication of the close relationship between religion and social class in societies where there are several religions can be gleaned by analyzing data on conversion from one religion to another. Americans who move up the ladder of socioeconomic success tend also to

---

* See Michael Novak, *The Open Church* (London: Darton, Longman & Todd, 1964). The conservatives advocate only rhythm method and abstinence as birth-control methods; the liberals advocate the use of a variety of birth-control methods.

convert from lower status to higher status denominations. It is not unusual to find that the bank president who comes from a working class family began his or her religious life as a Baptist, but is now an Episcopalian.

A religious system, then, is an integral part of the larger social system. Like other societal subsystems, it is influenced by society and in turn it influences society. In this sense, it affects all of us, true believers, agnostics, and atheists alike.

☐ Institutionalization and Dilemma

As religious systems develop, they become institutionalized, and with institutionalization comes an inherent set of dilemmas. In his book *The Sociology of Religion*, Thomas F. O'Dea identifies five dilemmas inherent in the process of religious institutionalization.[3] As we discuss each of these dilemmas, you might consider whether or not they seem to apply to your particular religion.

First is the dilemma of mixed motivation. Religions form around the teachings and personal magnetism of a single leader, a prophet. Christianity, for example, formed around the teachings and personal magnetism of Jesus of Nazareth. In this initial formation period, the motivation of the prophet's disciples is single-minded. That is, it focuses upon the religious values proclaimed by the prophet. The disciples are content with the personal satisfaction they receive from interacting with the prophet and from acting in accordance with his or her religious teachings. During this period, the religion is highly unstable because it focuses so strongly on one central point—the prophet. What would happen if the prophet should suddenly die?

In order for the religion to continue, it is institutionalized. That is, a structure containing a stable set of statuses and roles, privileges, obligations, and rewards is developed. An official religious hierarchy that has various levels of prestige, life opportunities, and material compensations is formed. The organizational structure functions so that the religion will continue long after the death of the prophet. Thus, institutionalization provides stability.

But it also guarantees mixed motivation. A person might be motivated now to join the clerical ranks of the organization to obtain the prestige, favor, and other rewards that accompany those statuses. In addition, since the professional clergy does obtain these rewards, it is motivated as a group to maintain the situation in which the rewards are forthcoming. It can do this because it is charged with the function of interpreting the religion's teachings. And here is the crucial point: When the religion's teachings begin to reflect the special interests of the professional clergy itself, the goals and values of the religion have been seriously transformed. And that, you may recall, is in part what the Reformation was about.

A second dilemma is the symbolic dilemma. In the early stages of a religion's development, the sacred objects and ritual have deep and fresh symbolic meaning to the group, and worship is individualized. As membership increases, however, and institutionalization takes place, worship becomes formalized, and sacred objects and ritual become routine matters. Symbolic objects and actions become usual and expected when they are used continuously. Thus they lose their original impact, and the sacred tends to become secular. The result of this process is the possible alienation of the believers. Institutionalization, then, leads to the routinization of symbols, which, in turn, leads to alienation.

Third is the dilemma of administrative order. The organizational structure which develops with institutionalization is a bureaucratic structure. Its form reflects a response to prevailing conditions as it develops. Once it takes shape, however, it tends to perpetuate itself. The administrative officials have a vested interest in maintaining their positions. They resist change (especially church reform) whenever they perceive it as personally threatening. The administrative order, there-fore, tends to be a fixed order that may be ill-equipped to handle new problems under new conditions as they arise. This whole set of circum-stances sets the clergy apart from the church's lay membership and each becomes alienated from the other.

The fourth dilemma is the dilemma of delimitation. We have noted that one of the functions of the clergy is to interpret the religion's teachings. Another is to state the original religious message in terms relevant to church members. Still another is to protect the original message against heretical interpretations. The clergy accomplishes these ends by defining the original message in terms of rules. But rules are simply specifications of behavior. They cannot adequately transmit all that was implied in the original message because they distort the original message. They substitute the letter for the spirit. Thus we have the curious situation of the church trying to avoid distortion of the faith by defining the very spirit of its teachings in the form of rules which distort the faith. In this manner it kills the dream.

The fifth dilemma is the dilemma of power. In its initial stages a religion attracts converts because they believe in its message. Gener-ally, religious converts are more fervent than people who are born into a religion. Their conversion is an act of faith in which they voluntarily accept and support the prophet's teachings. Institutionalization, however, produces an accommodation between the religion and the society and its values. When this happens, the ensuing alliance between religious and secular leaders exerts a pressure on people to join and support the religion. Thus religious membership becomes routine and

The New Future of Christianity?
The Reverend Sun Myung Moon has had great success in attracting converts to his religious movement. Pictured here is a mass wedding.

the content of faith is rendered commonplace. The religion gets power, but its followers lose their fervor and conviction.

To these five, we will add a sixth dilemma—the dilemma of property. As a religion grows and prospers, it acquires property, and with property comes property rights. This may enhance the power and prestige of the religion, thus contributing to its appeal and stability. Many of its adherents, however, may be propertyless. Therefore, the relationship between the religion and many of its adherents becomes an owner-tenant relationship rather than the free-flowing interaction between believer and religion which originally existed. As the religion acquires property, church officials acquire property, and their values tend to change from those of the propertyless church members to those of a propertied class. This difference in values may alienate some of the religion's membership.

☐ Dysfunctions

We have seen how institutionalization causes strains and conflicts both within religious systems and within whole social systems. These strains and conflicts may be functional or dysfunctional. When they facilitate change which enhances the perpetuation of the system, they are functional; when they disrupt the smooth operation of the system, they are dysfunctional.

At the beginning of this chapter we saw that religious systems provide a conception of something supernatural and, in so doing, they facilitate a person's adjustment to and acceptance of the human conditions of uncertainty, powerlessness, and scarcity. We also saw that religious systems perform psychological functions (security, identity, support) and sociological functions (integration, behavior control, change). However, in the performance of these functions the religious system may produce frustration, alienation, and conflict which are ultimately dysfunctional.

In performing the security function, the religious system may focus its adherents' attention so strongly and completely on the reference points (beliefs and values) which it provides that it helps to form provincial attitudes which inhibit scientific and social progress. This situation places religion in a direct conflict with science that may be dysfunctional for the religion as well as the whole society. The classical example of this kind of dysfunction is found in the previously mentioned situation in which the Catholic church took about 300 years to recognize the validity of Copernicus' heliocentric theory.

The identity function may help to mold the self-concept of an individual, but it may also contribute to his or her failure to develop new identities that are more appropriate to new situations as they occur. Thus religious identification may divide societies by fostering conflict among individuals and groups. Furthermore, religions sanctify identities they provide. This sanctification tends to intensify conflict because the goodness of the "ins" implies the badness of the "outs." The bitter conflict between Protestants and Catholics in Northern Ireland exemplifies this kind of dysfunction.

The ultimate consequences of the supportive function may also prove to be dysfunctional. By providing emotional support and consolation to the frustrated and deprived, religion may discourage protest which might promote change that would be beneficial to the society, especially to the less fortunate. In other words, religion may almost hypnotize people into a socially passive state.

By postponing social reform, religion may also be contributing to internal pressure which could erupt in the form of political revolution. And no one could deny that political revolution is dysfunctional to the *existing* society.

In performing the integrative and behavior-control functions, religions contribute to societal stability. But, by sanctifying societal norms and values, religions can bestow a kind of eternal significance on a society's norms and values that may not, in fact, be eternally significant for that society. Norms and values evolve in particular circumstances that may not exist under changed conditions. In this situation the old norms and values are dysfunctional to the society in that they may prevent the society from adapting appropriately to changing conditions.

Finally, we can see dysfunction as a consequence of religion's change function. The religion may provide a basis for criticism of the "establishment." This criticism, however, may be so extreme that it obscures issues and prevents more practical action from taking place. Thus, instead of facilitating conflict resolution that leads to constructive change, religion may intensify conflict, thereby creating an atmosphere in which workable solutions are more difficult to obtain.

As we have seen, religious systems, like other societal subsystems, can be either functional or dysfunctional to the larger social system. Their endurance in the face of dilemma and dysfunction over long time periods indicates the homeostatic capabilities of some religious systems.

That religion is found in all societies is testimony to the universal need for something supernatural.

REFERENCES

1. The accounts of animism and naturism are based on these works: Edward B. Tylor, *Primitive Culture* (London: Murray, 1973), Chapter 11, and Emile Durkheim, *The Elementary Forms of the Religious Life* (Glencoe, Ill.: The Free Press, 1947), Chs. 2 and 3.
2. Durkheim, pp. 50–51.
3. This discussion of institutionalization and dilemma is based primarily on Thomas F. O'Dea, *The Sociology of Religion* (Englewood Cliffs, N.J.: Prentice Hall, 1966), pp. 90–97.

GLOSSARY

Religion	A group of believers who symbolize their conception of the supernatural by sacred objects that they relate to through rituals and beliefs that they value.
Supernatural	The ultimate—that which transcends or goes beyond everyday experiences. Example: God.
Animism	The belief that spirits inhabit and give life to natural objects.
Naturism	The belief in and worship of nature gods.
Totemism	The worship of particular species of plants or animals found within the environment of the worshipers.
Sanctification	The process whereby religions make holy certain cultural norms and values. Western religions, for instance, have sanctified the Ten Commandments by treating them as God-given rules.

Anthropo-morphism	The attributing of human qualities to supernatural objects. We might, for example, attribute the qualities of love, kindness, and gentleness to our God.
Church	A well-established religious organization that consists of a large group of believers. Members are born into churches, and, later they are confirmed. Churches are usually well integrated into the culture. Example: Lutherans.
Sect	A small religious organization whose members join by voluntary, conscious choice. Sects are not usually well integrated into the culture. Example: Jehovah's Witnesses.

SELECTED READING

Durkheim, E. *The Elementary Forms of Religious Life,* translated by J. W. Swain (New York: Collier Books, 1961). Durkheim's classic treatise on the sociology of religion, originally published in 1915.

Lehmann, A. C. and J. E. Myers. *Magic, Witchcraft, and Religion: An Anthropological Study of the Supernatural* (Palo Alto, Calif.: Mayfield, 1985). A reader on topics related to the supernatural.

Malinowski, B. *Magic, Science and Religion and Other Essays* (Garden City, N.J.: Doubleday, 1954). A collection of some of Malinowski's essays dealing with topics such as religion, magic, faith, and ritual.

Robbins, T. and D. Anthony. *In Gods We Trust: New Patterns of Religious Pluralism in America* (New Brunswick, N.J.: Transaction, 1989). An overview of religion in the United States.

Roof, W. C. and W. McKinney. *American Mainline Religion: Its Changing Shape and Future* (New Brunswick, N.J.: Rutgers University Press, 1987). An examination of how traditional, organized religions in the United States are laying the foundation for religious change in the future.

Smith, H. *The Religions of Man* (New York: Harper, 1958). An excellent survey of the world's great religions.

QUESTIONS

1. Karl Marx believed that religion had been created by the ruling class as an instrument the rulers could use to take advantage of the workers. This is an example of a(n)
   a. evolutionary theory.
   b. exploitative theory.
   c. rational theory.
   d. objective theory.
   e. subjective theory.

2. The belief that spirits inhabit and give life to natural objects is called
   a. totemism.
   b. anthromorphism.
   c. naturism.
   d. sanctification.
   e. animism.

3. The psychological functions performed by religion are related to
   a. security, identity, and emotional support.
   b. a stable society that does not change.
   c. the subjective theory of religion.
   d. the number of competing religions within a society.
   e. the type of stratification system found in a society.

4. Uncertainty, powerlessness, and scarcity are
   a. the results of religion.
   b. human conditions that produce insecurities.
   c. more prevalent in simple than in complex societies.
   d. best resolved through totemism.
   e. more prevalent in the middle class.

5. Animism and naturism are theories that are considered
   a. evolutionary.
   b. exploitative.
   c. rational.
   d. objective.
   e. subjective.

6. Durkheim's functional theory of religion says that all the worship activities of the Arunta
   a. resembled animism.
   b. celebrated the social group itself.
   c. were to please their gods.
   d. were dysfunctional to the society.
   e. served to glorify the headman.

7. Religion makes cultural norms and values "holy." This process is called
   a. supernatural.
   b. supportive.
   c. dysfunctional.
   d. sanctification.
   e. social identity.

8. People relate to sacred objects through
   a. sacredism.
   b. their belief in immortality.

    c. institutionalization.
    d. the administrative order.
    e. ritual.

9. The dilemmas inherent in religion are due to
    a. a belief in the supernatural.
    b. mixed motivation.
    c. modern technology.
    d. institutionalization.
    e. uncertainty.

10. Which of the following is *not* a characteristic of religion?
    a. sacred objects
    b. rituals
    c. mixed motivation
    d. values
    e. beliefs

QUESTIONS FOR THOUGHT AND DISCUSSION

1. Will there always be religion?

2. Religion versus science—is there really a conflict?

3. What constitutes a "religious" person?

13

Education

In its broadest sense, **education** is synonymous with socialization—the process whereby the individual learns the roles, rules, relationships, and culture of his or her society. In a narrower context, however, education is the process by which individuals are systematically exposed to selected knowledge, skills, and attitudes through social structures that have been created specifically for this end. In this sense education is concerned with both teaching and learning in a structured situation.

As we saw in Chapter 7, much learning takes place incidentally within a variety of societal structures, often in unstructured situations. The individual may learn within the context of the family or job as well as that of the school. Both formal and informal learning, then, occur within the education system.

Each society has a unique education system. On the other hand, there are a few characteristics of education which occur in every society. Therefore, we will discuss both universals and variations. Our discussion of variations will be drawn along simple vs. complex societal lines, and we will allude to American education whenever it is appropriate to do so.

Our discussion begins with a consideration of the universal characteristics of education.[1]

☐ Universals

Individuals in all education systems learn through some combination of the processes of listening, watching, and doing. Although all three processes are used in every education system, a particular system may place greater emphasis on one or more of these processes. For example, the Chinese have traditionally emphasized learning by watching, while Americans have traditionally placed greater emphasis on learning by listening and doing.

A Modern Classroom
Although the instruction appears to be more individualized here than in the traditional classroom, the emphasis is still on listening and doing.

All education systems deliberately employ rewards and punishments to encourage learning and to discourage incorrect behavior. The spectrum of rewards and punishments is broad, ranging from praise and material rewards on the one side, to confinement and physical pain on the other. Within the American education system we span the whole spectrum: We praise students who learn and give them high marks, sometimes even scholarships and other prizes; we discourage incorrect behavior by scolding students and giving them low marks and, sometimes, by paddling their backsides. Other education systems may or may not employ such a wide variety of rewards and punishments, but they all consciously use rewards and punishments.

Every education system withholds certain knowledge from children. "The Chagga, for instance, maintain male superiority by informing girls that men do not defecate, whereas the Hopi tell children that the Kachina dancers are not men but gods."[2] Traditionally, sex education has not been a part of American public school education. As a result, many incorrect notions regarding sex are learned by American children and are perpetuated generation after generation. One such widespread sex myth in American society is related to the practice of masturbation. This myth has several variations: One version states that people who masturbate will get hair on the palms of their hands; another, that they will get warts on their fingers; and a third, that they will eventually go blind!

There is a tendency for the dominant group in each society to strengthen its own position by organizing the education system. For instance, in the United States, white, middle-class people direct a public school education system that has worked to their own advantage but to the disadvantage of several minority groups. It has been argued, for example, that blacks have traditionally been supplied with teachers, learning materials, and school plants that are not equal to those of whites.[3] We should also note that the socioeconomic elite in the United States has traditionally controlled private schools, tending to perpetuate elitist values and life-styles.

The education system in all societies helps to produce an emerging peer group which tends to reinforce cultural conformity. This is true in both complex and simple societies, although the adolescent peer group in complex societies may also contribute to rebellion against some of the moral standards of the parents. In simple societies there is typically no noticeable generation gap between parents and children: The child succeeds by taking the place of the parent. In complex societies, however, the child eventually competes with the parent for economic status. The education system helps prepare the child for this competition and thereby places him or her in the position of challenging some of the old values while at the same time accepting others.

Finally, education systems function to transmute as well as to transmit the culture of all societies. Through education the individual broadens his or her own perspectives. As a result, the individual may contribute to cultural change as well as becoming better prepared to cope with change.

☐ Variations

Having identified several universal characteristics of education, let us now focus our attention on variations as they occur in simple and complex societies. To begin with, we should realize that schools are not necessary for the education system to function effectively in all societies; indeed, in some simple societies there are no schools. The young child learns the specialized knowledge and skills necessary for survival by observing and imitating adults and older children. This observation and imitation usually take place informally and in unstructured situations, although often occurring within the context of the family. There are no schools because they are not needed. Youngsters learn the specialized knowledge and skills necessary for their own survival and the survival of their culture within other social structures.

While it is generally true that some simple societies do not have schools as part of their education systems, it is also true that in most simple societies adolescents do receive formal training to prepare them for ceremonies that initiate them into adult life. C. W. M. Hart points out that such initiations are "marked in the simpler societies by the utmost degree of standardization and correctness,"[4] and that the preparatory training often takes a relatively long time, sometimes as long as fifteen years.[5] It is most likely that many of the important roles, rules, and relationships, together with some crucial knowledge and skills, are learned during this intensive training period. Thus there is some formal training in simple societies, but most learning is informal and does not take place in schools.

In contrast, complex societies rely on **schools** as integral parts of their education systems. There is a vast array of specialized knowledge and skills to be mastered if the culture is to survive. Schools, then, represent the major effort of complex societies to ensure that this mastery takes place. This is not to deny that there are other structures within complex societies that teach the child (for example, the family, the peer group, the mass media, and so forth). It is merely an explanation of why there are schools in complex societies.

Margaret Mead provides another explanation. She stresses the emphasis placed on *teaching* as opposed to *learning* in more complex societies.[6] She points out that children in relatively simple societies learn what everyone agrees they should know because they must survive. They are motivated to seek knowledge from those who possess it. In more complex societies, however, the possessers of knowledge seek to transmit it to children who often cannot see its immediate value. American children, for instance, may not see any immediate value in learning history; nevertheless, they are taught history. Thus the emphasis is placed on teaching rather than on learning.

This concern with teaching in more complex societies is related to the institutionalization of religion, internal growth, and territorial expansion; and each of these in turn is related to the development of schools. As we saw in Chapter 12, with religious institutionalization comes the need to train a professional clergy, and schools are well suited to perform this task. Those who "spread the word" are taught in formal schools. Once trained, members of the clergy then create more schools. "Attention is directed toward finding neophytes . . . and adults and children become bracketed together as recipients of conscious missionary effort."[7]

Internal growth and territorial expansion reflect both technological advance and population increase, and inevitably lead to more highly differentiated societal subsystems. For example, as the political system expands, there is a need to train the growing number of civil and military administrators. Again, schools are well suited to perform this task. Moreover, as a society becomes more complex, conflicts among different factions of people tend to challenge and even threaten traditional beliefs and values. The school becomes the focal point around which the dominant group organizes the education system and thereby protects essential beliefs and values. Internal growth and territorial expansion, therefore, along with the institutionalization of religion and the need for a vehicle through which to transmit effectively a vast array of specialized knowledge and skills, all contribute to the formation of schools in complex societies.

The person in a simple society usually completes his or her educational training relatively early in life. By adolescence or even before, he or she usually has learned all that parents can teach and all that is necessary to know to ensure the perpetuation of the culture. From that point forward, he or she simply attempts to maintain proficiency in the application of the skills learned.

In a complex society people are required to learn more; therefore, their formal education takes longer to complete. Typically, young Americans do not complete their formal education until they are 17 or 18 years old; and many extend this period of formal education much longer—until they finish college. Although the period of formal education is longer in complex societies, there are prescribed time units within which the learning of particular knowledge and skills is expected to occur. As a result, much learning is incomplete. For example, all first-grade students in an American public school are expected to master certain knowledge and skills within the period of that school year. Obviously, the *D* student who passes to the second grade has not attained the same degree of mastery as has the *A* student; yet both pass to the second grade. Moreover, the pronounced lack of agreement among educators concerning just what constitutes mastery of the subject matter suggests the possibility that even the *A* student may not be achieving all that he or she could be achieving. It is significant that many American schools are experimenting with modular scheduling (that is, time blocks for certain classes and activities may vary from one another, so that not all classes and activities are conducted in the traditional 50- or 55-minute time block). It is also significant that American educators are currently attempting not only to define better what the student should master in a particular course, but also they are trying to agree on what constitutes mastery and how it should be measured. These are difficult tasks to achieve, particularly when we realize that American society is the first to attempt mass education beyond literacy. We should expect a great deal of experimentation within American education because American society is in a state of perpetual transition.

In simple societies the education system teaches values which tend to be expressed consistently throughout the society. This contributes to a high degree of cultural integration. For instance, hunting may be a way of worshiping the supernatural as well as a way of securing food.

Values taught by the education system in complex societies, however, may conflict with those taught by other socialization structures. In fact, the education system itself may teach values that are in conflict with one another. American children learn that every individual has an intrinsic worth and dignity and should be treated as such. They also learn that progress is good, and that we should always strive for improvement. Years later, the same people may find it difficult to maintain their belief in the worth and dignity of the individual when they have just been replaced in their job by a machine. Such value conflict does not contribute to a high degree of cultural integration.

☐ Education and the Teacher

One of the most striking aspects of education in simple societies is the total absence of professional teachers. Practically any given individual may teach one or more youngsters particular knowledge or skills at any given time, but no one devotes the majority of his or her working time to doing only that. Those who serve as teachers are also full participants in communal life. Hunters may occasionally teach hunting, but their primary role is to hunt, not to teach.

In contrast, complex societies employ professional teachers who are expected to devote all of their working time to specialized educational activities. Indeed, "moonlighting" by American schoolteachers is generally frowned upon by both educational administrators and the public, even though it is common knowledge that many teachers may need the money they earn from extra jobs to support their families. Furthermore, the American teacher has traditionally been discouraged from active participation in politics. He or she has been anything but a full participant in communal life.

This failure to participate fully in communal life has placed American teachers in a dilemma: on the one hand, they may be accused of being too theoretical (that is, they deal with highly abstract concepts which many see as having little or no relationship to the real world); on the other hand, they are discouraged and possibly even chastised for participating in "real-life" activities. Is the teacher too theoretical? Should he or she participate more in communal life? These questions might serve as the basis for a stimulating discussion, either in or outside the classroom.

In simple societies children learn from people who are practicing what they are teaching. They learn the basic techniques of hunting from a hunter, and they learn the basic techniques of agriculture from one who is actively engaged in farming, and so on. Such a direct relationship between what a teacher is doing and what he or she is teaching tends to ensure that knowledge and skills being taught are accurate and up-to-date.

Conversely, children in complex societies often learn from schoolteachers who are probably not practicing what they are teaching. Teachers tend to practice teaching. Since American teachers, for example, have traditionally been discouraged from active political participa-

Teaching in Simple and Complex Societies
Children in simple societies usually are taught by people who have a personal commitment to the learners. Such personal commitment is often an impossibility in complex societies.

tion, the government teacher is not likely to hold political office. Likewise the economics teacher is not likely to be a business executive, nor is it likely that he or she ever was a business executive. Since they are not actually doing what the people working within their subject area are doing, and since techniques within the field may be changing rapidly, American schoolteachers are more prone to transmit inaccurate or outdated information than are their counterparts in simple societies.

Practicing what one is teaching does not necessarily contribute to better teaching. On the contrary, it is possible that the practitioner who has extensive knowledge of his or her work may be a poor teacher. The business executive who has great knowledge and skills in management would be a useless teacher if he or she could not adequately communicate knowledge and skills to students. Furthermore, schoolteachers in complex societies must constantly extend their knowledge and skills to stay abreast of developments in their subject area. Their continual reading and thinking tend to broaden their view so that they may offer students several frames of reference on any given topic, not just one. Perhaps it is advantageous that schoolteachers in complex societies do not practice what they are teaching.

The child in a simple society learns from a teacher who has a strong personal commitment both to the learner and to the results of his or her teaching. Often children learn from their parents or other relatives who have a personal stake in seeing that they learn well. The failure of a child to learn may produce immediate negative consequences. For instance, the father who fails to teach his son to hunt properly may be jeopardizing tomorrow's family meal. The child therefore learns from a teacher who has a strong personal interest in seeing that the child learns well.

In complex societies the teacher does not necessarily have this strong sense of commitment either to the learner or to the results of his or her teaching. To begin with, the teacher and student may be strangers who will interact with one another for only a relatively short period of time. Most American schoolteachers, for example, are outsiders in the neighborhoods in which they teach. There is a good possibility that neither the teacher nor the student has ever even seen the other before

School in a Complex Society
Teachers are frequently dissociated from the results of their teaching. Their salaries probably do not depend on how well the children learn.

the first day of class. Furthermore, the teacher is likely to be dealing with a relatively large number of students at a time. It is not unusual for the American teacher to have responsibility for thirty to forty students at once. Some classes may be offered on television, and the teacher and his or her students may have scant opportunity to interact with one another. Under these circumstances it is rare that teachers can establish a personal relationship with any of their students. Typically, then, the teacher does not know his or her students personally at the beginning of the term and does not know them personally by the end of the term either. Under these circumstances the teacher-student relationship becomes a secondary relationship, and the teacher does not have a strong personal commitment to the student.

However, not all educators feel that teachers need to have a strong personal commitment to students in order to be successful. Rather, they need a dedication to their profession. In fact, some educators believe that a personal relationship between teacher and student may even be detrimental to the learning process—a teacher may be either too demanding or too lenient. It is significant that teachers whose children attend the same school in which they teach often go to great lengths to ensure that their children are not placed in their classes.

Many American educators, however, feel that a lack of close student-teacher relationships may be one reason for the failure of many students to profit from public education. They are experimenting with various kinds of classroom situations to remedy the situation.

In complex societies teachers may not be strongly committed to the results of their teaching. American teachers, for example, are unlikely to interact with any given student after the end of the term. Therefore, they have no knowledge of whether or not any given student ultimately succeeds or fails as a member of society. Even if they had such knowledge, they have no way of knowing to what extent, if any, they have contributed to their students' ultimate success or failure. Moreover, the results of their teaching generally do not affect teachers professionally. They collect their paychecks regardless of the results of their teaching. Furthermore, the amount of their paychecks is typically determined by their length of service in teaching, not by the results of their teaching: the first-year teacher earns less than the fifth-year teacher, and the fifth-year teacher earns less than the tenth-year teacher, and so on, no matter how effective his or her teaching may be. Thus there is a lack of clear incentive to teach more effectively. Often the beginning teacher soon decides that it is not worth the effort to become more proficient at teaching when becoming more proficient is not likely to bring additional professional or material rewards.

Our purpose is not to indict the teacher in complex societies. On the contrary, we believe that many teachers take a professional pride in their work. But professional pride is difficult to come by, and the reason for this difficulty may easily be understood by considering the relationship between society and education.

A complex society is increasingly dependent upon professionalism. The society functions smoothly when thousands of people successfully perform thousands of interrelated, specialized tasks. This high degree of specialization tends to produce a large number of secondary relationships. For example, a man need not know his doctor nor his lawyer personally. Similarly, the child may not need to know his or her teacher personally in order to learn. The dedicated teacher may be just as effective in dealing with students as the dedicated doctor is in dealing with patients.

But there is a fundamental difference between doctors and teachers in regard to their respective professionalism. Doctors are relatively autonomous in making professional decisions; teachers are not. The society will not permit teachers to make many educational decisions because the education system is intended to ensure the perpetuation of the larger culture. In other words, the education system is so crucial to the society that control over it cannot be entrusted only to teachers. The society itself must control the education system. For example, American society, and not its teachers, determines what will be taught, who will be taught, and how much money will be allocated to support the public education system. Conversely, doctors, and not the society, determine whom they will accept as patients, and how much they will charge for their services. Teachers have very little control over what they will be paid. Under these circumstances it is difficult to create and sustain professional pride.

☐ Education and Discontinuity

One of the most prominent differences between education in simple and complex societies is related to the way these societies treat social development. As a rule, the child in a simple society assumes increasingly complex statuses and roles as he or she develops from childhood to adolescence to adulthood in a smooth and continuous process. In complex societies, however, there is great **discontinuity** in social development. The child is expected to make an abrupt transition from childlike ways to adultlike ways during adolescence. Typically, then, adolescence is a particularly difficult and trying period for the individual in a complex society. Indeed, adolescent behavior is often trying for the adults and children as well as the adolescents themselves. The education system in a complex society contributes to and perpetuates this discontinuity.

In simple societies children are more or less free agents who mingle with just about anyone in the society. From early childhood they are free to observe the behavior patterns of adults in a variety of settings, as well as those of adolescents and other children. For the most part, they move at their own pace, learning whatever interests them from those who are willing to take the time to teach them. In a sense, they are children of the community, reared by everyone. Often, for instance, they may receive discipline from adults who are not even their relatives. Under these circumstances they glimpse a total view of life within society. Relatively soon they have a well-defined sense of who they are and where they are going. In short, they know where and how they fit into the total societal picture. They can develop gracefully into adulthood.

Children in complex societies are not free agents. For the first few years they are limited primarily to family contacts. For the most part, they are reared by their mother; she and a few of her friends, together with their father and occasionally a few other relatives are the only adults they observe. They have no notion of what their father does throughout the work week, much less of what other adults (except mother) do. Moreover, the television programs they watch are often cartoons and other equally unrealistic shows that are likely to contribute to a distorted view of life within society. They do not know how and where they fit into the total societal picture; indeed, the picture they perceive is undeveloped.

Going to school helps, but not much. Certainly their experience in school helps children to correct the sheltered and distorted view they bring on their first day of school. In effect, however, they are trading one sheltered environment for another. Throughout their childhood school experience they are completely separated from the adult world except for their interaction with teachers. If their childhood teachers are females, their concept of male roles and contributions within society is probably woefully inadequate. They are still not quite sure what their father does throughout the work week. Soon these children will be expected to act like adults, but they have not been given much preparation for adult roles and responsibility. They are about to experience the shock of adulthood.

In simple societies work and play often involve the same activity. For example, children may play at hunting while actually learning to hunt. They are therefore exposed to adult roles and responsibilities relatively early in life. In addition, they share in the performance of family tasks, thereby enhancing the learning of responsibility. Margaret Mead has reported that in Samoa, six-year-old girls often tend their younger brothers and sisters, and boys begin to learn canoeing and reef fishing at a young age.[8] These children find it easy to assume responsibility as young adults because they are gradually given more and more responsibility as they mature.

The child in complex societies does not usually play at games that are directly related to future adult roles. Typically, the American boy plays games such as baseball and football, yet relatively few boys will

An Exception
Unlike children in simple societies, most youngsters in complex societies are allowed little responsibility or opportunity to contribute economically to the family's well-being.

become professional baseball or football players. The American girl may play with dolls and play "house" from time to time, thus helping to prepare her for potential future adult roles as mother and homemaker. But these games do little to prepare her for the future adult roles she may play in a professional career or in other areas of occupational or social interaction.

Often the child in complex societies is allowed little social or economic responsibility. The American girl is not likely to begin baby-sitting until she is considerably older than her counterpart in Samoa, and the American boy may never be given responsibility equal to his sister's. Generally, adolescents cannot work full time because they spend such a large portion of their day in school which they are legally required to attend. Even part-time work may be difficult to obtain, not only because of a lack of employment opportunities but because child labor laws may prevent employers from hiring them. Children, then, are given little meaningful responsibility; yet when they reach maturity, they are expected to be responsible. It's no wonder that adulthood comes as a shock.

In simple societies the child is allowed to be fairly self-assertive. As children assume more and more responsibility, they gradually move toward assuming adult dominance. Parents do not do everything for them or monitor all their actions and attitudes. The young Samoan girl

Conflicting Signals
The child in a complex society is taught to obey adults and stifle self-assertiveness. At the same time he or she learns that the great figures of history were frequently nonconformists who flaunted the conventions of the societies in which they lived.

who tends her younger brothers and sisters is allowed great latitude in disciplining them. Thus responsibility and self-assertiveness go hand in hand as the child gradually takes on the trait of adult dominance.

Conversely, children in complex societies are not allowed a great deal of self-assertiveness. They are not allowed much responsibility and may very well be reprimanded for arbitrarily exerting dominance over younger brothers and sisters. Their parents often monitor their actions and attitudes and are likely to be overprotective as they dominate their children's lives.

Neither are children typically allowed much self-assertiveness in school. Traditionally they are taught to obey and are not permitted to dominate their peers. They are expected to be submissive toward adults, and they do not move gradually toward assuming adult dominance. Thus, "the adolescent is caught between the habit of submitting to adults and the need to be self-assertive in order to behave like an adult himself."[9] (Perhaps you have experienced such a dilemma.) Traditionally this dilemma is resolved only when children are allowed to behave like adults. When that happens, however, they are likely to experience some frustration as they are suddenly required to adjust from a submissive to a dominant psychological posture.

Recently, innovative educators have advocated a type of schooling in which the child is given a good deal of responsibility for his or her own learning very early. Such a change might well soften the wrench caused by the sudden necessity to adjust to adult norms.

Simple societies tend to permit children to release their impulses in much the same manner as do adults. The Pilagá Indians of Argentina, for example, allow children to "enjoy sexual intercourse, listen to and tell sexual stories, and smoke when tobacco is available."[10] There is not a hard and fast line between adult freedom to release impulses and childhood self-control and restraint.

In complex societies there is such a line. Unlike adults, children may not have sexual intercourse, nor may they listen to and tell sexual stories, nor may they smoke. In fact, they are often discouraged from losing their temper and even from becoming angry. In short, they are expected to be models of self-control who will be allowed to release impulses "when they get older." And, while such self-control is expected of them at home, it is demanded of them in school where the sharp separation between childhood and adulthood may be more pronounced. The adolescent may be penalized for "talking back" to the teacher but the teacher is almost never penalized or even restrained from spending a half-hour of a given class period berating his or her students for performing poorly as a group on their last test. The teacher may act like a child, but the adolescent and even the child must act like an adult.

As we have seen, the broad general differences between the education systems of simple and complex societies reflect fundamental differences in the inherent composition of those societies. As we shall see in the following chapters, there are also corresponding differences in their respective economic and political systems.

REFERENCES

1. This consideration of education universals is based on the discussion contained in George F. Kneller, *Educational Anthropology: An Introduction* (New York: Wiley, 1965), pp. 67–69.
2. *Ibid.*, p. 68.
3. An excellent discussion of the problems related to black students in the American public school education system is contained in Chapter IX of Charles E. Silberman's *Crisis in Black and White* (New York: Random House, 1964).
4. C. W. M. Hart, "Contrasts between Prepubertal and Postpubertal Education," in George D. Spindler, ed., *Education and Culture: Anthropological Approaches* (New York: Holt, Rinehart and Winston, 1963), p. 406.
5. *Ibid.*, p. 416.
6. Margaret Mead, "Our Educational Emphasis in Primitive Perspective," in Spindler, pp. 309–320.
7. *Ibid.*, p. 313.
8. See Margaret Mead, *Coming of Age in Samoa* (New York: New American Library, 1950).

9. Kneller, p. 99.
10. *Ibid.*, p. 100.

GLOSSARY

Education

Synonymous with socialization, as a rule. More specifically, education is the process by which individuals are systematically exposed to selected knowledge, skills, and attitudes through social structures that have been created specifically for this end. Since much learning takes place incidentally and in unstructured situations, the education system includes both formal and informal learning.

School

Structure in the education systems of complex societies that tends to ensure that certain specialized knowledge and skills are mastered by each generation.

Discontinuity

The interruption of the continuous process of the social development of the individual. Education systems in complex societies tend to produce discontinuity for the adolescent.

SELECTED READING

Ballantine, J. H. *The Sociology of Education*, 2nd ed. (Englewood Cliffs, N.J.: Prentice-Hall, 1989). An overview of the sociology of education.

Bloom, A. *The Closing of the American Mind: How Higher Education Has Failed Democracy and Impoverished the Souls of Today's Students* (New York: Simon & Schuster, 1987). A provocative critique of political correctness on American college campuses.

Boyer, E. L. *College: The Undergraduate Experience in America* (Prepared by the Carnegie Foundation for the Advancement of Teaching. New York: Harper & Row, 1987). A report on higher education in the United States.

Cookson, P. W. and C. H. Persell. *Preparing for Power: America's Elite Boarding Schools* (New York: Basic Books, 1985). An explanation of the ways elite boarding schools in the United States prepare students to assume positions of power within society.

The National Commission on Excellence in Education. *A Nation at Risk: The Full Account* (Cambridge, Mass.: USA Research, 1984). A comprehensive government report on the state of education in the United States.

Oakes, J. *Keeping Track: How High Schools Structure Inequality* (New Haven, Ct.: Yale University Press, 1985). An examination of the ways high schools perpetuate social inequality in the United States.

QUESTIONS

1. Which of the following statements about education in simple societies is true?
   a. Most learning is formal and takes place in schools.
   b. Most learning is informal and takes place in schools.
   c. Most learning is formal and does not take place in schools.
   d. Most learning is informal and does not take place in schools.
   e. All learning is informal and does not take place in schools.

2. Which of the following is *not* a universal characteristic of education?
   a. Education systems function to transmute as well as to transmit culture.
   b. The teacher has a strong personal commitment to the learner.
   c. There is a tendency for the dominant group in each society to organize the education system.
   d. Every education system withholds certain knowledge from children.
   e. Education systems deliberately employ rewards and punishments.

3. In her explanation of why there are schools in complex societies, Margaret Mead stresses the
   a. role of motivation in the learning process.
   b. informal nature of education in complex societies.
   c. emphasis placed on learning as opposed to teaching in complex societies.
   d. fact that schools are a natural outgrowth of the family.
   e. emphasis placed on teaching as opposed to learning in complex societies.

4. People in a simple society usually complete their educational training
   a. by the time they are eight years old.
   b. when they become parents.
   c. relatively early in life.
   d. when they reach old age.
   e. on their fifteenth birthday.

5. Schoolteachers in complex societies often
   a. are full participants in communal life.
   b. are paid relatively high salaries.
   c. do not practice what they are teaching.
   d. are accused of being too practical.
   e. have a strong personal commitment to their students.

6. Americans have traditionally emphasized learning by
   a. listening and doing.

b. listening and watching.

c. listening only.

d. watching and doing.

e. doing only.

7. One prominent difference between education in simple and complex societies is related to the
   a. use of rewards to encourage learning.
   b. basic functions of education.
   c. use of punishment to discourage incorrect behavior.
   d. means by which the dominant group organizes the education system.
   e. way these respective societies treat social development.

8. Typically, the pace of learning in simple societies is
   a. determined by the teacher who decides when the learner has learned.
   b. determined by the learner who moves at his or her own pace.
   c. governed by the school which sets learning standards.
   d. considerably faster than in complex societies.
   e. considerably slower than in complex societies.

9. Which of the following characteristics is *not* typical of the child in simple societies?
   a. responsible
   b. self-assertive
   c. secure
   d. overprotected
   e. impulsive

10. The education system in all societies helps to produce an emerging peer group which
    a. has great respect for professional teachers.
    b. tends to reinforce cultural conformity.
    c. is separated from the adult world.
    d. tends to reject established values.
    e. develops gracefully into adulthood.

QUESTIONS FOR THOUGHT AND DISCUSSION

1. American education—a purveyor of cultural lag or the hope of the future?

2. How professional is the teacher in a complex society?

3. Higher education—who needs it?

FIVE

The Economic System

Comparing different economies is a very risky business. Accurate, up-to-date information is often not available; accounting methods differ among countries; and structural differences, price-wage relationships, and differences in government policies and programs add to the confusion. In addition, no matter how objective and scientific one strives to be, we are all, alas, culture-bound to some extent. However, having mentioned these pitfalls, we shall now take the plunge.

There are many different ways to classify economic systems. Economies are sometimes divided into agricultural or industrial, highly developed or underdeveloped, command or market systems. We are going to analyze three economic systems that occupy different places on a continuum based on the degree of government control over the economy. The three countries are the United States, Sweden, and the former Soviet Union.

We chose the United States because it relies more on market mechanisms than any other highly industrialized nation in the world. We selected the Soviet Union because it had the longest history of all the centrally directed economies. The structure of Sweden's economy is similar to other social democracies, but it has some unique features and its per capita production is very high. In short, it is one of the most successful examples of democratic socialism in the world.

In Chapter 14, we introduce many important concepts in economics while developing an analytical model that we then use to study the economic systems mentioned above. Chapter 15 is an analysis of the American economy, and Chapter 16 compares alternative forms of socialism. There is also a discussion of the changes taking place in the Russian economy.

14

Economics: System, Functions, and Process

The economic system is one of the most important social systems that people have created. In fact, economic determinists claim that it has such a great impact on society that it shapes all the other social systems. Whether or not that is the case, people are usually quite concerned about economic matters.

Every society is confronted with the task of supporting itself within its environment. The main problem to be dealt with is **scarcity.** Resources are always limited relative to human wants; hence every society must economize; that is, it must decide how to allocate resources to fulfill those wants it values most, and it must create economic structures (roles and statuses) to perform these functions. In short, every society must create an **economic system** to make decisions regarding the production, distribution, and consumption of goods and services.

The type of system devised to perform these functions varies from one society to the next. Economists generally place economic systems within some classification scheme. The two major categories used are **market** and **command** systems. In order to study pure and modified forms of market and command economies we have created a model of the economic system. This systemic model can be used in studying either a single economy or several economies comparatively. (See diagram, p. 309.) Conflict is an integral part of every economic system, as individuals and groups compete for scarce resources. Thus functionalism and conflict theory provide important insights regarding the economic process.

Economic System

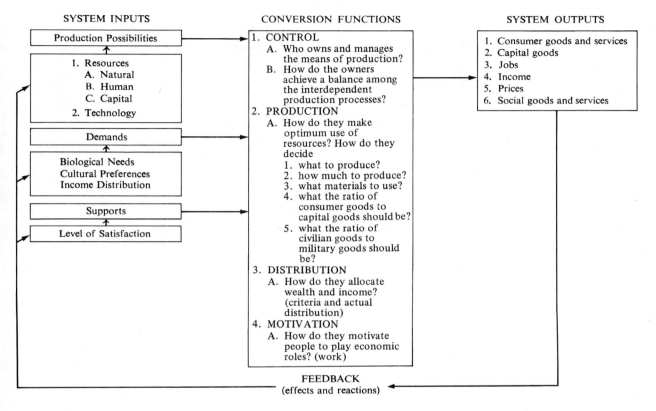

SYSTEM INPUTS

Production Possibilities

1. Resources
   A. Natural
   B. Human
   C. Capital
2. Technology

Demands

Biological Needs
Cultural Preferences
Income Distribution

Supports

Level of Satisfaction

CONVERSION FUNCTIONS

1. CONTROL
   A. Who owns and manages the means of production?
   B. How do the owners achieve a balance among the interdependent production processes?
2. PRODUCTION
   A. How do they make optimum use of resources? How do they decide
      1. what to produce?
      2. how much to produce?
      3. what materials to use?
      4. what the ratio of consumer goods to capital goods should be?
      5. what the ratio of civilian goods to military goods should be?
3. DISTRIBUTION
   A. How do they allocate wealth and income? (criteria and actual distribution)
4. MOTIVATION
   A. How do they motivate people to play economic roles? (work)

SYSTEM OUTPUTS

1. Consumer goods and services
2. Capital goods
3. Jobs
4. Income
5. Prices
6. Social goods and services

FEEDBACK
(effects and reactions)

☐ System Inputs

What is ultimately produced in any economy is a result of its production possibilities, demands, and supports. **Production possibilities** are determined by a society's natural, human, and capital resources, and by its level of technology. Economists sometimes refer to these resources as the *factors of production* (land, labor, and capital).

Natural resources[1] include the quality of the soil (Is it arable, arid, or semiarid?); the minerals and ores contained therein (Is there oil, coal, or iron ore?); the type of terrain and the resources that may be above ground (Is it mountainous or level? Is it wooded or not?); and even the weather is a natural resource (Is the climate very cold, very hot, or temperate? What is the level of rainfall? Is the area beset by hurricanes, tornadoes, or floods?). Natural resources may be used in a variety of ways to produce many different combinations of goods and services. For example, forty acres of farmland may be suitable for growing wheat or corn, or barley, or any combination of these or other goods.

Natural Resources
America is rich in natural resources but the supply can be depleted. The problems of scarcity can be seen most clearly in America's increasing dependence on foreign oil.

Human resources[2] include the size and composition of the population, its level of health and education, and the particular skills and attitudes the people have developed. These, of course, are affected by the natural resources. For example, a tropical island without coal or iron deposits is not likely to have many steelworkers; a country without very much arable land is not likely to have many farmers. A population's size and its level of health and education are important factors affecting its economic performance. For instance, a population weakened by malnutrition or widespread disease is less productive than a healthy one. A society's level and type of education has a great effect on the amount and kind of goods and services demanded and produced. A country with five million inhabitants has different production possibilities from one with five hundred million.

The composition of a population refers to the pattern of distribution of such factors as age and sex among the total population. Here is an example of the importance of a population's composition. In the 1860s Paraguay had a psychotic leader who led his country into a suicidal war against Argentina, Brazil, and Uruguay. The male population of Paraguay was decimated. After the war, the ratio of women to men over the age of twelve was 110 to 1. Besides the obvious sexual problems created by the war, the economy also suffered. Most economic roles had been played by men. Now, women, who had not been trained, had to undertake important economic responsibilities. Of course, this is an extreme case, but it illustrates the importance of the makeup of a labor force.

Human Resources
Blue-collar and white-collar workers, both men and women, are important in a modern labor force.

The rate of population growth is another crucial variable. Resources set the outside limits to the population growth within the country, other conditions being given. The rate of population growth, however, is regulated by certain components of the cultural complex: (1) The population's capacity to utilize the available resources; (2) the effectiveness of its means of contraception; and (3) the gap between the actual and the desired scales of living, together with the influence of this gap on the number of children sought per family. A population achieves economic well-being by efficiently exploiting and consuming its material environment. The level of well-being will vary directly with the abundance of the material environment (resources) and inversely with

Capital Resources
The construction of a new building, whether it is used to produce goods or services, exemplifies capital investment.

an increase in population or an increase in the rate of population growth.

Management and **entrepreneurship** are two special, related kinds of human resources. The manager's role is to make decisions regarding the daily operations of a business. An entrepreneur is an individual who initiates a business by combining the proper resources and technology. He or she is one who launches the enterprise. Both roles may be played by the same individual, but they are distinct roles. Because the entrepreneur tends to be a global thinker and the manager is someone who likes to attend to details, it is difficult to find people who can perform well in both roles.

Capital resources are manufactured goods used in the production of more goods and services. They include such items as buildings, tools, machines, and motor vehicles (buses and trucks). Capital investment creates jobs and therefore income which stimulates consumption. Increased consumption may lead to higher profits, which may be used for more capital investment.

Technology[3] is the knowledge and techniques employed in producing goods and services. The higher the level of technology the greater the amount produced with the same resources. This applies to agriculture as well as industry. Rice, for example, can be cultivated by hand as is done in most of Asia, or more modern techniques can be used. In the United States airplanes drop seeds and fertilizers on the soil, and large machines are used in harvesting the crops. In some countries with a low level of agricultural technology a large majority of the population is engaged in farming and they still may have to import food; while in the United States 2 percent of the population produces enough food to feed all Americans, and to accumulate a surplus, in spite of the fact that we pay some of our farmers not to grow food to avoid depressing prices. In the industrial sector the technological gap between rich and poor countries is also great and growing greater!

The production possibilities, then, are the various combinations of goods and services that can be produced by an economy given its resources and its level of technology. Production possibilities can be increased either by improving technology or by increasing resources or both. Regardless of how rapidly an economy is growing, it cannot catch up with people's wants. Therefore economic scarcity is always a fact of life in every economy.

☐ Demands

A distinction must be made between wants and demands. You may want to own a yacht, but you may not be able to demand it. Economists use the term **demand** to mean something that people *want and are willing and able to pay for.* If they are not able to pay for it, then no matter how badly they want it, it is not a demand in the economic sense. Demands are determined by *biological needs, cultural preferences,* and *income distribution.*

Biological needs are universal; they include such things as food, clothing, and shelter. However, the type of food and the way it is prepared, as well as the utensils used to eat it vary according to cultural preferences. Rice, for example, can be eaten with a fork or with chopsticks. It can be served with shrimp or black beans. Clothing needs are determined in part by weather conditions; but that does not explain why one society uses polyester knit suits, another uses clothing made of cotton, and a third uses animal skins. Cultural preferences are responsible for these differences. Culture also accounts for the fact that in some societies women's bodies are completely covered while in others with a similar climate they may wear grass skirts and have their bosoms exposed. People living in similar climates might live in wooden huts or in high-rise apartment buildings.

The relationship of income distribution to prices is also a significant factor affecting demand. Let us assume there is an island nation with 1,000 inhabitants. Two are extremely wealthy and 998 are extremely poor. Chances are that such an economy will not have a great demand for luxury items, since only two citizens can afford them. However, if income distribution in our hypothetical island were more equal, there would be a different mix of necessities and luxuries demanded. Hence, the combination of goods and services demanded by any population is partially determined by the distribution of income.

☐ Supports

No social system can survive indefinitely without a high level of support from society's members. If the people fail to support their economic system, it must be reformed or transformed into another type of economic system. The amount of support rendered by the people depends, in part, upon their level of satisfaction with the system's performance, particularly with its outputs. We will return to this topic in our discussion of feedback.

☐ Conversion Functions

The conversion functions are control, production, distribution, and motivation. The manner in which they are performed is determined by the type of economic system a society has. Generally economic systems are placed on a continuum which represents the extent to which the political system controls the economic system. *Bear in mind that in the real world, there are no pure market or command economies.*

Extent of Government Control over the Economy

PURE MARKET ECONOMY		PURE COMMAND ECONOMY
├──┤		
No Control		Complete Control

First, we will list the characteristics of a pure market economy; then we will see how that type of economic system performs the conversion functions.

☐ Pure Market System

A pure market economy[4] has the following characteristics:

1. There is private ownership and management of the means of production. The government owns no businesses.
2. The government follows a **laissez-faire** (hands off) policy toward the economy. There are no government regulations.
3. The profit motive and supply and demand determine prices, production, and wages.
4. People can seek employment wherever they like.

5. The branches and stages of production mesh together without conscious management, thereby balancing the interdependent production processes. This is called the **impersonal market.**
6. There are many buyers and many sellers for every product. In other words, there is plenty of competition in every part of the economic process.
7. The consumers ultimately decide what and how much is produced by voting with their money. This is called **consumer sovereignty.**
8. Businessmen have easy entry into the market for the production of every good and service. This allows them to shift production in response to consumer demands.

Let us see how a pure market system performs the conversion functions.

Control Function

In a pure market economy, the control function is performed by private citizens who own and manage the means of production. They try to operate at a maximum profit by producing as efficiently as possible the goods and services demanded by the consumers.

In order to produce X amount of automobiles, it is necessary to produce Y amount of glass, Z amount of rubber, and whatever else is needed for the production of automobiles. Balancing all the interdependent production processes for an entire economy is very difficult. The pure market system accomplishes this task without any central direction. The key to understanding how the market system functions is the **theory of supply and demand.** The following is a simplified explanation of how it works.

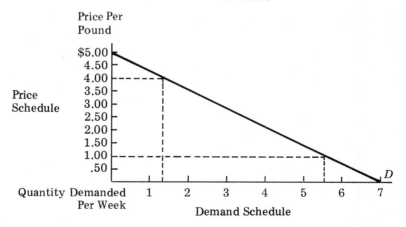

On the vertical axis we have noted a variety of prices that may be charged for steak (a price schedule), ranging from $.50 to $5.00 per pound. On the horizontal axis we have noted the quantity of steak that may be demanded. We have included in this diagram a diagonal line which represents a *demand curve*. The higher the price, the less meat people will demand; the lower the price, the greater the quantity demanded. Thus, at $4.00 per pound the families will demand only enough steak to eat about one pound a week. At $1.00 a pound families will eat five-and-a-half pounds a week.

The behavior of suppliers is also motivated by a desire for material rewards. Other things being equal, the higher the price for any good or service, the greater the profit in producing it, and the greater the inducement to supply it. Consequently, a supply curve rises as the price rises.

At $1.00 per pound producers will supply only enough steak for families to eat one pound a week. At $5.00 per pound they will supply enough for families to eat over seven pounds a week. The actual price of steak and the actual quantity produced is determined by the place at which the supply and demand curves intersect. (See diagram below.)

Steak Supply Schedule

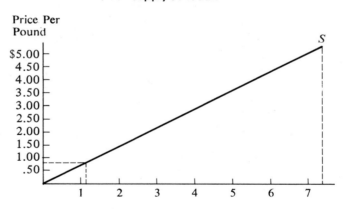

Steak Supply and Demand Schedule

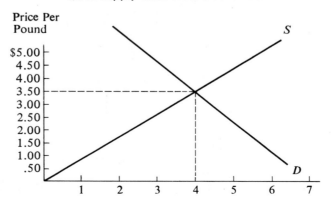

At $3.50 per pound families will buy four pounds of steak a week. At $3.50 per pound producers will supply enough steak so that families can eat four pounds a week. Thus the price and quantity of steak produced are determined by supply and demand. To put it another way: The *equilibrium price* ($3.50 in our example) is the one at which the quantity supplied equals the quantity demanded per time period (four pounds per week per family).

If there is a shortage of some item, the price will rise because the quantity demanded will be greater than the quantity supplied. Profit-motivated businesses would then begin to produce that item in greater quantities. Eventually quantity supplied would catch up with quantity demanded, and the interdependent production processes would be balanced. If perchance too much of that item is produced, the price will drop because quantity supplied will exceed quantity demanded. Businesses cannot afford to stock items that are not selling; so they will lower prices to move their inventories. Production will also drop until the quantities supplied and demanded are equal. In this way the market system achieves a balance without central direction. The supply and demand process performs this function best when all the conditions of a pure market economy are met.

Production Function

In a pure market economy production decisions are made jointly by producers and consumers. What and how much to produce, what materials to use, and other related decisions are made by the private owners of the means of production in accordance with expected consumer demands. However, if producers miscalculate consumer demand, they will lose money and perhaps go out of business. So ultimately consumers make these decisions indirectly by voting with their money. This is not necessarily a democratic process, however, because those with more money have more votes.

The higher the ratio of total production spent on capital goods, the greater the likelihood of a high growth rate, because economic growth is dependent on capital investment. Since such decisions are left to private individuals in a market system, there is no guarantee of a high economic rate of growth in such a system. If businesses are pessimistic about the economy's future, they will not invest as much. This can become a self-fulfilling prophecy. They expect business to be poor and their behavior ensures that poor business will continue. If they are optimistic about the future they will reinvest their profits, thereby increasing the chances that business will be good. However, this too can be overdone and result in an overexpansion of productive capacity. Too much production can cause business failures because the people cannot buy all the goods produced. Too much production is as bad as too little. Hence, the absence of planning or even minimal government control in a pure market economy makes it a very unstable system.

Dumping Milk as a Protest Against Low Prices
Miscalculations by buyers and producers of agricultural products have sometimes resulted in the destruction of foodstuffs to bring up the price. Such protests show the breakdown of the unregulated supply-and-demand system in which price levels may not be satisfactory to producers. Processing costs may cause the price to the customer to rise while the producer continues to be paid the old price.

Another weakness of a pure market economy is that if all economic decisions are made by private citizens, some public needs tend to be ignored because individuals are motivated by self-interest, not public interest. Also, channels to express public interests may be lacking. In such a system resources may not be used in a manner that is best for society. There may be a waste of human and natural resources, and the environment may be polluted to the detriment of all citizens (including those not yet born!). The advantages of a pure market economy are that people enjoy freedom from government controls in making economic decisions, and competition among individuals leads to maximum production efficiency.

The amount of military goods produced by an economy is primarily a government decision, even in market economies. Certain vital decisions, in areas such as welfare, education, and security are made by the government in almost all economic systems—however, not in our hypothetical model.

Distribution Function

The distribution of wealth is determined by the market mechanism. Theoretically each person is rewarded according to his or her contribution to the economy and the demand for and supply of whatever goods or services that person produces for a living. Americans found out during the Depression of the 1930s that the market may achieve equilibrium at a socially unacceptable level of unemployment. We also discovered that recovery is not automatic.

The rules of a pure market system benefit those who are able to play the game of economics well without government regulations. Such a system generally produces a very unequal distribution of wealth because some people are more successful in the market than others. It also perpetuates inequality because of property inheritance. Thus equality of opportunity does not exist. The child of a rich family has a better chance to succeed than does a child of a poor family. This situation is perpetuated generation after generation. Consequently, unregulated capitalism (a pure market system) practically guarantees inequality of opportunities as well as of incomes.

Motivation Function

In a market system, self-interest is harnessed to induce people to work. The profit motive and the desire to improve one's economic situation operate to solve the problem of motivation in most instances. The major assumption here is that people are acquisitive; therefore their behavior can be guided by economic rewards and punishments. Since people are forced to operate within a system of maximum opportunity and minimum security, they seek to accumulate material goods.

A theoretical model is not a perfect mirror of reality; it is instead a simplification that helps us to understand reality. Although there are no pure market systems in existence, we can learn a great deal about the various modified market systems that we will examine in the following chapters by first understanding the pure model. The same holds true for command systems. Let us now turn to a pure command model which stands at the opposite extreme from a market system.

☐ Pure Command System

A pure command economy[5] has the following characteristics:

1. It has a comprehensive central production plan that covers all economic activity for the entire economy.
2. A small group of political leaders determines the aims of the central plan. All command economies exist in conjunction with political dictatorships.
3. The government controls all the means of production.
4. Labor is allocated by command. The government determines where people work.
5. The government determines prices and wages (rather than having this determined by supply and demand).
6. Production is managed by government officials who fulfill predetermined production quotas.
7. Consumption is determined through rationing.

Let us see how a pure command system performs the conversion functions.

Control Function

In a pure command economy the government has complete control of all the economic processes. Everyone works for the government, including managers of economic enterprises whose job it is to meet production quotas in order to fulfill a portion of the central plan.

The interdependent production processes are balanced by the people who construct the central production plan for the whole economy—a group of central planners. This is an incredibly difficult job, especially in a large country. Any mistake made by the planners will have a snowballing effect. If, for example, they underestimate the need for steel, all products requiring steel (such as tools and machinery) will not be produced in sufficient quantity. The products that are manufactured with those tools and machines will also not be produced in sufficient quantity. This snowballing effect is difficult to stop in a command economy. In a market system the situation would rectify itself eventually because the shortage would lead to increased prices for the products in short supply, and profit-motivated businesses would increase the supply. However, in a market system there is always a time lag. In a command economy the problem must be detected in time to rectify it. It may not be identified until it is too late to do anything about it. Perhaps those responsible for the error will try to cover it up. It seems extremely difficult for the central planners to know all the information required to make all the decisions for the entire economy. Because there are so many variables to consider, mistakes are inevitable when planning involves all the fine details of the economic process. Obviously, mistakes are also made in a private enterprise economy. The resulting absence of profits, however, leads to a quick attempt to rectify the errors. No business wants to experience a sustained loss.

Production Function

Production decisions are made by the central planners. These people have a great influence on the standard of living and on the economic growth rate because they determine the ratio of consumer goods to capital goods. If their goal is a high growth rate, they can reduce the production of consumer goods. If their goal is to maximize the current standard of living, they can increase the ratio of consumer goods.

A command economy is in a better position to utilize its resources more fully, though not necessarily more efficiently, than is a market system. The government can eliminate unemployment; it can also ensure that all production facilities are being utilized to capacity. One of its strengths is that the planners can make decisions on the basis of what is best for the entire economy as they see it; whereas in a market

The Textile Industry in China
Chinese textile workers and their managers implement production decisions made by central planners.

system the individual owners of the means of production do not have an incentive to do so; they are pursuing individual goals which may be contrary to the general society's interests (for example, fighting costly antipollution measures).

Distribution Function

The government decides income distribution according to its leaders' values. Leaders may be motivated by egalitarian or elitist ideals. Distribution may be highly differentiated or very equal. Whatever criteria are used, a pure command economy does not leave the results to chance.

Motivation Function

Workers can be motivated by coercion, by material incentives, or by moral exhortations. Of the three, the last seems to be the least effective. Sometimes, as in Castro's Cuba, moral exhortations may be accompanied by the threat of force. In a command system, motivation depends upon the values of the government leaders. Equalization of income may cause difficulties in filling certain jobs or in encouraging people to work hard. A wage differential seems more effective in motivating workers, but then equalization of income is thwarted. This is a great dilemma if equalization of income is a goal.

☐ System Outputs

The outputs of the economic system in either the market or command models are as follows:

1. **Consumer Goods and Services.** Any good or service not used in the production of other goods or services falls into this category. Consumer goods include such diverse items as apples, automobiles (for personal use), and refrigerators. Services may include services at a restaurant, barber shop, or massage parlor, and even the use of a motel room.

2. **Capital Goods.** These are goods made for use in the production of other goods and services. They include such items as taxis, factories, hand and power tools, and a psychiatrist's couch.

3. *Jobs.* An economy's level of technology and the amount of goods and services it produces are related to the number and types of jobs available. This is an important system output because it affects the level of employment, the income of those who work (and of those who don't have a job), and it also affects aggregate demand (the combined demand of all the people).

4. *Income.* Most income is job-related (wages). However, in a market system, income is also derived from interest, rents, dividends, and profits. Two important variables to look for here are: (1) income distribution and (2) the relationship of income to prices.

5. *Prices.* If prices rise faster than income, the standard of living declines. Prices may be set by the market or by a planning agency. Rising prices in some sectors of a market economy indicate a need to reallocate resources to those sectors to satisfy consumer demand. If higher prices reflect a shortage of goods and not an increase in cost, profit-motivated businesses will enter the market and increase production. In a pure command economy the price mechanism cannot be used to allocate resources efficiently, because prices are planned and may not reflect market conditions.

6. **Social Goods and Services.** Every economy may produce revenue for the government through government taxation, and sometimes through profits of government-owned businesses. Part of this revenue is used to provide roads, schools, hospitals, welfare, parks, recreation areas, and other social goods and services. This is an important output in every system, and in some countries it may be a very large percentage of total output.

☐ Feedback

Feedback is the people's reactions to the system's outputs communicated as new inputs. Negative feedback may take the form of boycotts, sabotage, work slowdowns, a declining level of support for the leaders as reflected in elections or public opinion polls. Positive feedback may also be reflected in polls and elections, or in a rise in the stock market. The outputs may affect the production possibilities, for example, by increasing capital resources; they may alter demands by raising or lowering income, or by redistributing income. The outputs may cause a profound change in the people's level of satisfaction with the system's performance, causing a corresponding change in the level of support. A drastic decline in support may lead to a radical change in the economic decision-making process, either by a change in policies, a change in leaders, or even a change to a different type of economic system.

Thus we see that the economic process involves a circular flow. The feedback loop allows the system to correct its course if the outputs are not the desired ones and corrective measures are available. For instance, the American economic system's outputs from 1929 to 1933 created feedback that led to important systemic changes. Primarily it led to a different role for the government in the economic system. This brings us to a discussion of the major dysfunctions that may afflict an economic system.

☐ Major Dysfunctions

1. **Depression.** A depression is a severe decline in economic activity, usually characterized by high unemployment, diminishing profits, decreasing productivity, and many business failures. A minor economic decline is usually referred to as a **recession.** The Great Depression of the 1930s left an indelible mark on the United States. In its wake, it left a drastically revised economic system with a greatly expanded governmental role in the economy; and it also scarred a generation of Americans, who, having grown up in an era of great scarcity were, perhaps, more conscious of financial security and more materialistic than either the preceding or succeeding generations. Many Americans who grew up in the 1930s maintained a psychology of scarcity even if they later became very wealthy.

The generation of Americans who grew up in the 1960s enjoyed an era of financial security. Their major concerns revolved around civil rights, peace, and individual freedom to choose one's life-style. Thus we can partially explain the so-called "generation gap" by the fact that one generation experienced a severe depression of long duration and the succeeding one did not. In the 1980s there was a return to more materialism and less concern for eliminating social and economic injustice.

2. **Inflation.** Inflation refers to a reduction in the purchasing power of money which is generally reflected by rising prices. It usually results when demand increases more rapidly than production. The increased demand could arise from an overexpansion of the money supply. Inflation hurts everyone because it erodes everyone's purchasing power, but some people are hurt more than others. Those with high incomes or incomes that rise faster than the rate of inflation are not hurt as badly as those with low incomes or incomes that increase more slowly than the rate of inflation. The people affected most drastically are those on fixed incomes, because they suffer a declining standard of living in direct proportion to the rate of inflation. Unfortunately, these are usually people who are already poor and who can least afford a decline in purchasing power.

A high level of inflation can be disastrous. One of the worst cases of inflation in modern times occurred in Germany in the 1920s. In 1923 the German mark was a stable currency. The exchange rate was sixty-two marks to the American dollar. Eighteen months later, the exchange rate was one dollar for four trillion, three-hundred-billion marks! German money was being printed in extremely large denominations not formerly used. Nevertheless, people had to take money in wheelbarrows in order to buy food for one day's consumption. Prices and wages rose by the hour. Workers were paid twice a day so they could spend their morning pay at lunchtime before prices would rise again.

Many Germans who had spent a lifetime saving a fortune, or at least a nest egg, for their old age watched it all vanish. They could take their life savings and buy a loaf of bread with it. This economic catastrophe

Inflation in Europe
In 1922–23 the currencies of Germany, Austria, and Poland became so worthless that groceries had to be purchased with wheelbarrows full of bills, and some people even used money to paper their walls.

had serious political repercussions. Although this hyperinflation was one of the worst economic crises in modern history, and nothing today approximates it, there are many countries that currently suffer a high rate of inflation.

Argentina, Peru, Uruguay, and Brazil are four Latin American countries that have often seen prices more than double within a year's time. Brazil suffered from psychologically induced inflation. Businesses expected their costs to rise, so they automatically increased prices periodically. Predictably, because everyone else did the same, costs would rise. Workers also expected the cost of living to rise and consequently asked for increased wages frequently in order to compensate for the inflation. And of course prices would always rise.

Whether you believe in a **wage-push theory of inflation** (increased labor costs cause higher prices) or in a **price-pull theory** (higher prices charged by businesses cause workers to demand more pay just to stay even), the fact remains that an inflation psychology becomes a self-fulfilling prophecy. People expect the cost of living to increase and they act in such a manner that the cost of living inevitably rises. Breaking this cycle usually requires a change in government policy.

3. **High Unemployment.** A high level of unemployment is wasteful. It is economically inefficient because human resources lie idle. But the social and psychological cost may be even greater. In many societies masculinity is defined, in part, as the ability to support a family. Certainly this is true in American society. Thus the Great Depression of the 1930s, in which unemployment reached 25 percent nationally, made many men feel emasculated.

Unemployment
The economy of a nation with a high unemployment rate is not healthy, but the problems resulting are not only economic ones.

Poor People's March on Washington, 1968
The Reverend Ralph Abernathy (center) leads his supporters from Resurrection City on a protest march of the poor against the agricultural department and Congress.

Sometimes an economic system has a built-in unemployment problem. One type of *structural unemployment* afflicts agricultural economies. Very often, agricultural work is of a seasonal nature. Therefore, during part of the year, there is near full employment; and during the rest of the year there is a great deal of unemployment. Another type of unemployment, called *technological unemployment,* afflicts industrial societies primarily. Technological advances may make many industrial jobs obsolete. Unless displaced workers are retrained for other jobs that may be created by new technology, they become unemployable. Agricultural economies may also face a technologically-based unemployment problem.

4. **Extreme Inequality of Income.** A highly unequal distribution of wealth is economically dysfunctional because it leads to underconsumption, which keeps demand low. A low level of demand is not good for business. It may also be politically dysfunctional if a large majority of citizens perceive that they have nothing to lose by overthrowing the existing system. Most people would also judge extreme economic inequality to be highly undesirable for moral reasons.

Some income inequality exists in all economies, but we are referring here to a situation in which there is widespread poverty. If everyone lives above the poverty level, income inequality may be easier to tolerate. What is important is that people believe they are receiving a fair deal. People will act to preserve a system if they feel they have a stake in it.

☐ Performance Criteria for Evaluating Economic Systems

There are many ways to measure an economy's performance. Some of the following are commonly used by economists.

1. **Gross National Product (GNP).** Gross national product is the total value of all final goods and services produced by an economy within a specified time period, usually a year. It can be computed by adding up all consumption, investment, and government spending. However, it is a rough measurement at best. **Net national product (NNP)** is derived by subtracting depreciation from GNP. Tools and machinery used in production become obsolete and are subject to wear and tear. This is what accounts for depreciation. **National income** is the total income earned by individuals and corporations for producing the GNP. It is derived by subtracting indirect taxes from NNP. **Disposable income** is what is left after subtracting **direct taxes** and adding welfare payments. Disposable income is the income that people have to save or spend. GNP is one of the most widely used performance criteria.

2. **Per Capita Income.** Per capita income is another widely used measurement for comparing economic systems. It is derived by dividing total national income by total population. A country with a population of 100 and a national income of $100,000 has a per capita income of $1,000. The significance of per capita income depends upon the distribution of wealth. Consider the following hypothetical example:

The island of Elita has 1,000 inhabitants: 500 people who each have an income of $1,000,000 per year and 500 gardeners who work for them at an average salary of $25,000 per year. Elita's per capita income is over $500,000. But knowing that does not tell us much about its residents' standard of living. Per capita income is a more useful yardstick if income is normally distributed; that is, if most people have an income near the average, and the number of people diminishes as you move away from the average in either direction. Our hypothetical island of Elita has a bimodal distribution curve. (See diagrams that follow.)

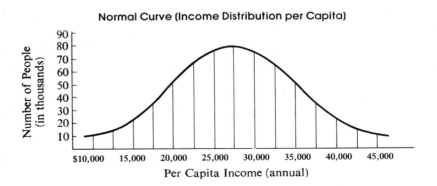

Normal Curve (Income Distribution per Capita)

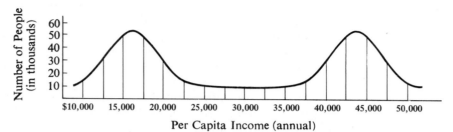

Bimodal Curve (Income Distribution per Capita)

Per Capita Income (annual)

3. **Rate of Economic Growth.** Rate of economic growth is another criterion for measuring an economic system's performance. In order to gauge real economic growth, it is necessary to subtract the amount of increase in GNP which is due to inflated prices. If, for example, GNP increases 10 percent from one year to the next, but prices rise by 7 percent during the same period, the real rate of economic growth is only 3 percent. If, on top of that, population has increased by 3 percent, GNP per capita remains the same as the previous year. Many underdeveloped countries often find themselves in just such a predicament. A low economic growth rate can have a disastrous effect on a country whose people have high expectations of experiencing a higher standard of living.

The three criteria discussed thus far—GNP, per capita income, and economic growth rate—are the ones used most frequently to measure an economy's performance. The following three are also important measuring tools.

4. **Degree of Price Stability.** Rapid or extreme price fluctuations indicate an unhealthy economy. All economic systems try to avoid this problem, usually through government actions. We will see in a later chapter how most modified market and command systems have overcome this problem to a large degree. Every economy strives to attain at least relative price stability.

5. **Level of Unemployment.** This is a critical social factor as well as an economic one. Besides the obvious economic waste, high unemployment also reaps great social ills. To anyone who is self-supporting and to those with a family to support, unemployment is a personal tragedy. If such individual situations are not too widespread, government assistance and private charity might ameliorate the problem significantly. However, if the problem is a general one, it can be very difficult to cope with. Unemployment leads to economic waste because of the value of goods and services not produced. Unemployment rates show the percentage of employable people seeking a job who cannot find one.

Unemployment is not a problem that only the poor must face. It can strike almost anyone, and with disastrous results. There was the case a few years ago of a foreign service officer in his mid-forties who was discharged because he had not been promoted for a certain period of time. After unsuccessfully seeking a job for over a year, he committed suicide in hopes that his family could collect on his life insurance, and they would not have to endure economic sacrifices any longer.

6. **Distribution of Wealth.** This is yet another important consideration in evaluating an economic system's performance. Not only is the actual distribution important but so is the possibility of advancement for those at or near the bottom. The wealthy maintain high income levels because their accumulated wealth provides part or all of that income. In short, money makes money. Those with little wealth, on the other hand, receive their income primarily or exclusively from wages. Hence, their jobs are their only source of income, and they are susceptible to forces over which they have little control. The tax structure is also significant because it may be used to redress economic inequities, or it may be used to perpetuate them.

The last four criteria we will mention are much more difficult to measure than the first six. Nevertheless they are important.

7. **Technological Progress.** Progress is the degree to which production techniques improve over time. The higher the level of technology, the greater the level of production (given the same amount of resources).

8. **Consumer Satisfaction.** This is very difficult to measure, but it should be an important consideration in evaluating an economic system. In a pure command economy, consumer satisfaction depends upon the leaders' values. Usually it is not even an input since the central planners make decisions based on goals set by the political leaders and tend to disregard consumer interests. In a market system the private owners of the means of production try to anticipate consumer demand in making production decisions.

9. **Subjective Evaluation of Rationality.** This is an important criterion for evaluating an economy. What is considered rational by one person may appear irrational to another. In this case one must rely on intersubjective truth. When an overwhelming majority of experts on a subject agree on something that cannot be empirically proved right or wrong, their collective judgment is called **intersubjective truth.** For example, the judgment that we must score the American economy low on rationality is widely held by experts who score it high on other standards. The amount of money we spend on alcohol, tobacco, and violent video games, they say, could be better spent on health, education, and welfare. The continued production of inefficient automobiles in an age

of rapidly diminishing oil reserves and the resultant need to import ever larger amounts of oil and foreign automobiles may be considered highly irrational. Some economists claim that judgments with respect to rationality of ends (goods and services produced) cannot be made. They claim that rationality is a matter of whether the best means known are used to achieve the ends. But an end cannot be judged as being rational or irrational. This is a legitimate position, but we disagree with it.

10. **Ecological Effects.** These must also be taken into account when evaluating an economic system.[6] Ecology did not become a major issue until 1970, but henceforth, in making economic decisions, we must consider such factors as environmental pollution and resource depletion. Unfortunately, market economies (even the modified ones) will find it very difficult to cope with this problem. As long as production decisions are made exclusively by profit-motivated private owners and managers of the means of production, ecological effects will be given minimal consideration; and the entire society will pay the social costs. Although it seems logical to assume that command economies could handle ecological problems well because of their centralized decision-making process, their record is no better on ecology than that of market systems. Most economic problems, like the ecological ones, require an interdisciplinary approach to solve them. Nowhere is this more apparent than in the problems related to economic development, to which we now turn.

A Temperature Inversion over Los Angeles Natural conditions and pollutants combine to produce smog. In Tokyo, London, Hong Kong, and New York, manufacturers have given little thought to the environment. Now the entire society will bear the costs of correcting the situation.

☐ Economic Development

Although every country is concerned with economic development,[7] in this final section we will focus on the problems faced by under-developed* countries. In these countries, most of which are in Asia, Africa, and Latin America, the people are caught in a vicious circle of poverty. (See diagram.)

Circle of Poverty

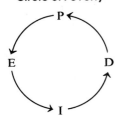

Low income (I) causes a low level of demand (D), which, in turn, leads to a low level of production. This causes employment to be low (E), which is the reason for low income. There are many problems involved in breaking out of this vicious circle of poverty. The first problem confronting the government of an underdeveloped country is the creation of an economic infrastructure. The infrastructure consists of transportation, power, and communications systems, and of banking and credit facilities. Without a developed infrastructure an economy cannot effectively utilize its natural, human, and capital resources.

Capital is generally in short supply because a low production level exists. When consumption needs are not adequately satisfied, it is very difficult to produce large quantities of machines and other capital goods. Outside capital is sorely needed. An underdeveloped country may or may not have large quantities of natural resources, but it usually lacks the technological know-how and the skilled labor to develop whatever it does have. Foreign aid programs for underdeveloped countries generally stress capital resources. It is difficult for underdeveloped countries to generate a substantial increase in their own capital resources because they would require a large surplus of production over and above their consumption demands. An increase in capital to stimulate economic growth can be self-generated only if a country reduces its production of consumer goods and services. And it is very difficult in an underdeveloped country in which the majority of people are poor to convince them that they have to reduce consumption to help the country's economic growth. Hence such countries have a great need for foreign investment in capital goods. This investment may take the form of grants or loans from other countries or from international lending agencies, or it may take the form of direct investment by foreign individuals and corporations.

Entrepreneurship is in short supply because in such countries there usually are not many people who have capital to invest. And if they do,

---

* The term "underdeveloped" is in disrepute. In order to avoid offending poor countries, economists use terms such as "developing," "less developed," and "emerging" nations. None of these is suitable. The highly developed countries are also "developing"; Britain, a highly developed country, is "less developed" than the United States; and, although many of the underdeveloped countries in Africa and Asia recently "emerged" from colonialism, most of the underdeveloped countries in Latin America "emerged" 180 years ago. Consequently, we will use the terms "underdeveloped" and "highly developed."

they may not be business-oriented. Managerial skill also tends to be scarce because the education system in such countries generally does not offer business courses, and the opportunities for on-the-job training are not very great.

Most underdeveloped countries are also saddled with one-crop economies. The majority of citizens are farmers who produce a single crop—such as coffee, sugar, cocoa, or bananas. The one crop tends to be the country's main export and consequently the main source of foreign exchange. Foreign exchange is needed to modernize the industrial and the agricultural sectors of the economy.

Because prices for agricultural commodities tend to fluctuate in the world market, these one-crop economies have low stability. And because the developed countries have failed to guarantee the underdeveloped ones a reasonable price for their commodities, the latter need to diversify and modernize their agricultural production. Crop diversification offers the same insurance as having a large portfolio of stocks and bonds. If one suffers losses on one stock, there is a chance that it will be made up by gains in another. Mechanization of agriculture increases production efficiency and quantity. And it releases workers to participate in the industrialization process, if industrialization is economically feasible for that country at that particular time.

In most underdeveloped countries there is a revolution of rising expectations caused by an increased awareness brought about by modern communications and transportation. People in these countries know that it is possible to enjoy a much higher standard of living than they have. They not only want improvements, but they want them quickly. Hence it is necessary in such countries for the government to play an important role in the development process. We shall now examine the political variables involved.

An efficient and honest leadership is greatly needed. The leaders must be thoroughly committed to economic development and know how to go about achieving it. They must be honest because capital is in scarce supply and every bit of it must be used properly. Because the government is going to play a large role in the economy, there must also be a well-trained and honest civil service. Unfortunately, many underdeveloped countries have emerged from colonialism recently and are led by men who were very adept at uniting the people to remove the colonial power, but who know little or nothing about economics or public administration. Most of these countries also lack an effective civil service because the colonial powers who ruled them in the past did not train the natives to hold important government posts. In other areas, such as Latin America in which most countries have been independent for over 170 years, a tradition of graft and corruption is so deeply embedded in the political culture that government jobs are usually treated as opportunities to make money and nothing more.

Political stability is also necessary for economic development. Foreign capital will not be attracted to an unstable country because of the great risk involved. Yet foreign capital, and the production techniques that usually accompany it, may be vital ingredients in the mix needed for economic development. Indeed, political instability may even lead to a flight of domestic capital to foreign countries where investment is less risky.

Economic and political development go hand in hand. The primary unit of government in the world today is the nation-state. A state is comprised of a population occupying a territory with more or less clearly defined boundaries. It is governed by a political system that is sovereign within those boundaries (that is, it has final jurisdiction over the legitimate use of force). A nation is a group of people who may share certain characteristics (language, race, tradition, religion), and who feel a sense of belonging to this group (nationalism). It is this bond, this sense of belonging, the feeling of "us" and "them" that characterizes a nation. For example, there was a Jewish nation long before the Jewish state of Israel was created in 1948. Now it is a nation-state. Most people in the world live in nation-states. At this writing there are about 175 of them.

Many underdeveloped countries in Asia and Africa emerged from colonialism in the 1960s, and the problems they face are compounded because they have to work on economic and political development simultaneously. Politically they are faced with the problems of *state building, nation building,* and *participation.* **State building** refers to the creation of the political structures necessary to govern a country, for example, political parties, legislatures, courts, and so forth. **Nation building** refers to developing a feeling of patriotism and nationalism among the people. Most of the countries that acquired independence recently have boundaries that correspond to the administrative boundaries established by the colonial powers. Consequently, diverse and sometimes antagonistic groups are included within these boundaries, and in some cases groups have been divided by such boundaries. This makes it very difficult for national leaders to receive the degree of loyalty which the people feel for their tribal and village leaders. In the case of Nigeria the differences among its citizens led to a bloody civil war in the 1960s. The persecution of the Ibos (the best educated and cultured group in the country—sometimes referred to as the "Jews of Africa") and the subsequent secession of Biafra led to the massacre of millions of people.

Participation is a third political development problem. Leaders of newly independent countries seek to increase the people's participation in the political system. They are not necessarily seeking active participants, but they do seek the passive allegiance, the loyalty of the people. They want the people to consider the national government to be the

Poverty in Ethiopia
The vicious circle of poverty and hunger has cost this mother the life of her child.

legitimate leadership of the country. Legitimacy (the belief by the people that the leaders have the right to rule, and that their decisions are binding on the people) is sought by all political leaders. In established countries, legitimacy is usually inherited by each new set of leaders if they follow the accepted procedure for acquiring political power. In a newly emerging country the leaders must somehow create this sense of legitimacy.

All of these political development problems are tied in with economic development. Since the government must play a central role in economic development in these countries, it must have legitimacy. In addition to the economic growth problems we discussed earlier, the government must also deal with the distribution of wealth. Since economic power is related to political power, political democracy requires a relatively equitable distribution of wealth. Values aside, political expediency requires economic equity in order to develop a sense of loyalty toward the new government.

There are also important cultural variables involved in economic development. Secularization is important. If the religious system is the primary concern of the people, and they have no desire to improve "this life," economic development will not take place. What usually happens in such societies is that some citizens become secularized, some maintain an "other-worldly" orientation, and the majority are in a transition stage.

In order for rapid economic development to take place, society must be increasingly secular, and the people must exhibit some degree of acquisitiveness. That is, they must want to improve their material circumstances; they must want to increase their standard of living. Otherwise they will lack the motivation necessary to achieve economic development. It also helps if a "work ethic" is one of their cultural traits. The belief that work is good and not something to be avoided contributes significantly to economic growth.

Finally, the education system plays an important role in economic development. There is a positive correlation between a country's level of education and its standard of living. The first step is to eliminate illiteracy. Free primary education should be available to everyone. Second, vocational and secondary schools should be created to teach the skills needed in a developing economy. Third, higher education is needed to train leaders in all walks of life: political, economic, social, and artistic.

The task of developing an economically underdeveloped country is extremely difficult. The probability of success varies greatly from one country to another. In fact, statistics indicate that the gap between rich and poor nations is increasing. The requirements for success touch on every aspect of a society's culture, not just the economic.

REFERENCES

1. A good source is Marion Clawson, ed., *Natural Resources and International Development* (Baltimore, Md.: The Johns Hopkins Press, 1964).
2. For an excellent analysis of human resources see Eli Ginzberg, *Manpower for Development: Perspectives on Five Continents* (New York: Praeger, 1971).
3. The importance of technology is explored in Michael Shanks, *The Innovators: The Economics of Technology* (New York: Penguin, 1941).
4. Any good principles of economics textbook contains an explanation of a pure market system.
5. George Halm analyzes a pure command system in *Economic Systems: A Comparative Analysis*, 3rd ed. (New York: Holt, Rinehart and Winston, 1968), pp. 235–254.
6. Marshall Goldman, *Ecology and Economics: Controlling Pollution in the 70's* (Englewood Cliffs, N.J.: Prentice Hall, 1972) evaluates environmental deterioration in several countries.
7. See Robert L. Heilbroner, *The Great Ascent* (New York: Harper & Row, 1963).

GLOSSARY

Entrepreneurship	A specialized form of labor which functions to initiate a business by combining the proper resources and technology.
Management	A specialized form of labor which functions to make decisions regarding the day-to-day operations of a business.
Production possibilities	Goods and services which may be produced within a society. Production possibilities are limited by the society's natural, human, and capital resources, and by its level of technology. Economists often refer to natural resources as *land,* and to human resources as *labor.* Land, labor, and capital are often referred to as the *factors of production.*
Capital	Manufactured goods used in the production of more goods and services.
Demand	The desire for a particular good or service, together with the willingness and ability to pay for it.
Scarcity	The existence of insufficient means to fulfill relatively unlimited wants.
Consumer goods and services	Any goods or services not used in the production of other goods and services.
Social goods and services	Goods and services designed to be used jointly rather than individually by the members of a society. Examples: roads, schools, hospitals, welfare services and facilities.
Economic determinism	The idea that social evolution is caused by economic forces.
Economic system	The social system consisting of structures and roles that function to make decisions regarding the production, distribution, and consumption of goods and services.
Pure command economy	An economic system in which the government exercises complete control over the economy. (See chapter for other characteristics.)
Pure market economy	An economic system in which the government exercises no control over the economy. (See chapter for other characteristics.)
Laissez-faire	The policy of noninterference in economic matters by the government.
Consumer sovereignty	The power of the consumer to determine what and how much is produced, through consumer demand.
Impersonal market	An economy in which the branches and stages of production mesh together without conscious management.

Theory of supply and demand	The higher the price for any given good or service, the greater the profit in producing it; therefore, the higher the price, the greater the amount supplied. The higher the price for any given good or service, the less likely is a buyer to buy some of it; therefore, the higher the price, the less the amount demanded. The actual price of a given good or service and the actual quantity produced are determined at the point at which quantity supplied equals quantity demanded.
Nation building	The development of a feeling of patriotism and nationalism among the people of a state.
State building	The creation of the political structures necessary to govern a country. Examples: political parties, legislatures, courts.
Depression	A severe decline in economic activity, usually characterized by high unemployment, diminishing profits, and many business failures.
Inflation	A reduction in the purchasing power of money which usually results when demand increases more rapidly than supply and which is generally reflected by rising prices.
Price-pull theory of inflation	Higher prices charged by businesses cause workers to demand more pay just to maintain the present level of their purchasing power.
Recession	A minor economic decline.
Wage-push theory of inflation	Increased labor costs cause higher prices.
Disposable income	National income less direct taxes, plus welfare payments.
Gross national product (GNP)	The total value of all final goods and services produced by an economy within a specified time period, usually a year.
Intersubjective truth	The collective judgment of an overwhelming majority of experts when they agree on something that cannot be empirically proved right or wrong.
Net national product (NNP)	Gross national product less depreciation costs.
National income	Net national product less indirect taxes.
Per capita income	National income divided by the total population.

SELECTED READING

Students can benefit by reading the latest edition of any of the many macro-economics textbooks available.

Greenwald, Douglas and Associates, *The McGraw-Hill Dictionary of Modern Economics,* 3rd edition (New York: McGraw-Hill, 1983).

Heilbroner, Robert, *The Making of Economic Society* (Englewood Cliffs, N.J.: Prentice-Hall, 1970). The author's writing is very clear, concise and entertaining, yet scholarly. This is a good paperback introduction to economics.

Heilbroner, Robert L. and Lester C. Thurow, *Economics Explained* (New York: Simon and Schuster, 1982). This is an excellent introduction for the beginning student.

QUESTIONS

1. What is ultimately produced in any economy is a result of all of the following except
   a. production possibilities.
   b. demands.
   c. supports.
   d. services.

2. Which of the following does *not* determine an economy's production possibilities?
   a. natural resources
   b. technology
   c. human resources
   d. demand
   e. capital resources

3. The role of management entails
   a. initiating an enterprise by combining the proper resources and technology.
   b. overseeing the day-to-day operations of a business.
   c. being an entrepreneur.
   d. chairing a board of directors' meeting.

4. Supports are determined by
   a. level of satisfaction.
   b. biological needs.
   c. cultural preferences.
   d. income distribution.
   e. none of the above.

5. Which of the following is a characteristic of a pure command system?
   a. There is private ownership and management of the means of production.
   b. People choose their places of employment.
   c. There are many buyers and many sellers for every product.
   d. There is central planning.
   e. Production is determined by consumer sovereignty.

6. Which of the following is a characteristic of a pure market economy?
   a. It has a comprehensive central production plan.
   b. Labor is allocated by command.
   c. The profit motive and supply and demand determine prices, production, and wages.
   d. Consumption is determined through rationing.
   e. The government controls all the means of production.

7. According to the theory of supply and demand, the equilibrium price is the one at which
   a. the quantity supplied equals the quantity demanded per time period.
   b. the number of buyers equals the number of sellers.
   c. labor and management both receive a fair income.
   d. the government and private enterprise agree both the consumer and the producer are being treated fairly.

8. Unfortunately, measures designed to reduce unemployment often cause
   a. inflation.
   b. depression.
   c. extreme inequality of income.
   d. all of the above.

9. Which of the following systems is *not* a part of the economic infrastructure?
   a. transportation
   b. power
   c. natural resources
   d. communications
   e. banking and credit

10. *Laissez-faire* in an economic system essentially means that
    a. production is determined by consumer sovereignty.
    b. labor is allocated by command.
    c. governmental interference in economic affairs is opposed.

d. more governmental control in managing economic affairs is desired.

e. none of the above.

QUESTIONS FOR THOUGHT AND DISCUSSION

1. What are the strengths and weaknesses of market and command economies?

2. Explain the major dysfunctions that may afflict an economy, how they are related to each other, and what can be done about them.

3. Describe the circle of poverty.

15

The United States: Regulated Capitalism

The American economy is a modified market system. It is perhaps best called **regulated capitalism** because, although the means of production are almost entirely privately owned, there is a high degree of government regulation, decision making by large corporate enterprises and to a lesser extent by large labor unions. All of these things are departures from *laissez-faire* capitalism. We will begin by examining the *production possibilities*.

☐ Natural Resources

The production possibilities of the American economy are enormous.[1] The United States is 3,615,211 square miles in area. Nearly half the continent was covered with virgin timber when the first European settlers arrived. Wood was used in building houses, tools, furniture, and many other products; it was also used for fuel for cooking and heating. Unfortunately, the early settlers cut down trees and burned forests indiscriminately to a point that 900 million acres of forest were significantly reduced. If our present wood-use patterns continue, we will soon be consuming more than can be grown on the remaining land. In addition, the world's ecology is being seriously affected as forest land is diminishing throughout the world, causing environmental deterioration. In 1986 the United States cut 30 percent more timber than in 1980. If this rate of increase continues, it can only lead to disaster.

America was also endowed with large tracts of fertile farmland, and weather conditions have generally been propitious for farming. In fact, before 1837 the United States had primarily an agricultural economy.

Coal Mining in the United States
The United States has almost one-third of the world's coal reserves.

During the nineteenth century a series of Homestead Acts enabled Americans to obtain tracts of land from the federal government which became theirs to keep or to sell. The only stipulation was that they must cultivate the land for five consecutive years. In the twentieth century, small private farms have been replaced, for the most part, by large commercial agricultural enterprises and medium-sized family farms.

Nowhere in the world is there an industrial center without easy access to coal. Of all the minerals on earth, coal has played the most important role in the industrialization process. It has been estimated that the United States has 32 percent of the world's known reserves and 19 percent of the world's annual production. Coal is used in heating and in producing steel and many synthetic products. The United States may be returning to an emphasis on coal, as petroleum becomes increasingly expensive and scarce, although by 1985 the polluting effects of coal had slowed down the transition.

The United States also has some reserves of petroleum and natural gas. With half the automobiles in the world, it consumes 40 percent of the world's petroleum output, with ever-increasing amounts being imported from Venezuela, Mexico, Saudi Arabia, Kuwait, and elsewhere. The possibilities are good that new reserves will be discovered, many of them under the oceans. America's dependence on imported oil, however, is expected to continue. Major oil-producing countries have formed a cartel to control prices and production. The Organization of

Petroleum Exporting Countries (OPEC) has become one of the most powerful multinational groups in the world. The United States, fearful of its escalating dependence on imported oil, has initiated conservation programs and put into effect other measures to reduce that dependence. However, that policy is endangered whenever a pro-development administration rather than a pro-environment administration occupies the White House. Natural gas has been discovered primarily by people drilling for oil. Both oil and gas are cleaner than coal, and petroleum has the added advantage of being easy to store and to transport. The United States has 38.2 percent of the world's known natural gas reserves and 24.0 percent of the world's production.

Iron ore deposits are not only greater in the United States than elsewhere, but these deposits are located close to coking coal and often near transportation facilities such as waterways. This combination of factors permitted the United States to produce 12 percent of the world's steel in 1989, making it the leader in that field; and steel is the most important building material in the world. Without steel, industrial development could not have reached its current heights.

The United States is the world's leading producer of the following metals: copper (17 percent), which is primarily used as a conductor of electricity; aluminum (23 percent), which is used extensively in aircraft manufacture; and zinc (4 percent), which is used in galvanizing and in alloys. The United States also ranks high in the production of magnesium (44 percent), lead (22 percent), limestone (17 percent), and gypsum (15 percent).

There are important chemical minerals that the United States also has in great abundance. The fertilizer industry has flourished because the United States is a world leader in the production of nitrogen (13 percent), phosphate (32 percent), and potash (5 percent). High fertilizer production has increased crop yields and reduced water contamination by recovering nitrogen in sewage treatment plants.

With 29 percent of the world's known salt deposits and 20 percent of the world's sulphur output, the United States has an abundance of minerals used to produce basic industrial acids and alkalis. Acid is used in products such as storage batteries, and alkali is used to produce items such as soap and bleach.

America's most abundant natural resource, however, is water. Most of the water used in the United States is used to generate hydroelectric power. The United States generates 22.5 percent of all the hydroelectric power in the world. This water is returned to our streams without any loss in quality. The rest of it, unfortunately, is not. Industrial, agricultural, and human waste is rapidly polluting rivers, lakes, and streams. Even where there are sewage treatment plants they are usually inadequate. Besides using water for drinking, bathing, shaving, and swimming, we use it for making steel, cooling cars, generating power, fishing, and for a multitude of other purposes. It has been said that "of all our resources, it is perhaps water that we have mismanaged the most. We change rivers into sewers, lakes into cesspools. We heap abuse on it till it would appear we didn't care whether we shared the same globe with it. Yet all life depends on water. Even man's."[2]

The water supply in the United States is adequate for current needs, but the demand for clean water is increasing every day. In the more densely populated areas shortages are already occurring, and the problem is compounded by pollution. The eastern half of the United States has adequate rainfall, but much of the western half does not. Therefore, dry farming and irrigation are two methods used where rainfall is sparse.

Overall, the United States is very rich in natural resources. In fact, it is more richly endowed in this respect than any other country in the world. Furthermore, this natural wealth is multiplied by a very high level of production technology. Not only is current technology highly advanced, but current business and government expenditures on research and development are sufficient to keep the United States at the forefront of most future developments.

☐ Human Resources

In 1990 America's population of 250 million increased at an annual rate of 1 percent; this represents 6 percent of the world's population. Life expectancy at birth was about 76, higher than most countries in the world but lower than some Western European nations. The United States is tied with seven other countries in eleventh place. For Caucasians the figures are about 1 percent higher than the average, and for non-Caucasians, about 5 percent lower. The average infant mortality rate in 1990 was 9.0 per 1,000 live births (with sixteen nations having a lower rate) (see Tables 15-1 and 15-2).

Table 15-1
Infant Mortality (per 1,000 live births), 1990

Country		Country	
Japan	5	Spain	8
Finland	6	Australia	8
Sweden	6	Belgium	8
Switzerland	7	Austria	8
Netherlands	7	*United States*	9
France	7	Italy	9
Canada	7	New Zealand	10
Ireland	7	Israel	10
Germany	7	Greece	11
Denmark	8	Czechoslovakia	12
Norway	8	Bulgaria	12
Great Britain	8	Poland	16

Source: World Development Report, 1992, p. 273.

Table 15-2
Life Expectancy at Birth,
1990

Country	Total	Female	Male
Japan	79	82	76
Switzerland	78	81	74
Sweden	78	80	75
Australia	77	80	73
Norway	77	81	74
Netherlands	77	81	74
France	77	81	73
Italy	77	80	73
Canada	77	81	74
Greece	77	80	74
Spain	76	80	74
United States	76	79	72
Israel	76	78	74
United Kingdom	76	79	73
Germany	76	79	72
Belgium	76	80	73
Austria	76	79	72
Finland	76	79	72
New Zealand	75	78	72
Denmark	75	78	72
Ireland	74	77	71
Bulgaria	73	75	70
Czechoslovakia	72	75	68

Source: World Development Report, 1992, p. 219; 1991, p. 267.

Females not only outlive males in the United States: they also outnumber them 51.3 percent to 48.7 percent.

According to figures released by UNICEF in September, 1993, the homicide rate for young people in the United States, aged 15–24, is by far the highest in the industrialized world—five times that of Canada, the country in second place. Nine out of ten young people murdered in industrialized countries are killed in the United States. In fact, the total number of homicides far exceeds that of the twelve European Common Market countries combined. The U.S. culture of violence undoubtedly contributes to the country's low ranking in life expectancy among industrialized countries.

Education is another crucial variable in a labor force's composition. The United States has universal free education through primary and secondary school. Although this record is equaled by some other advanced nations, the United States and Canada are the only countries in the world to offer mass higher education. It ranges from very expensive to no charge, depending upon the school and the student's ability to pay. The recent phenomenal growth of two-year and four-year community colleges has put an inexpensive college education within commuting distance of many Americans. The government has played an important role in the expansion of higher educational opportunities, especially with the GI bills after World War II. But even in the nineteenth century the government encouraged higher education through its land-grant college program. It provided land for building many of the state universities that exist to this day. Most of these were agricultural and mechanical colleges.

One of the current problems, however, is that in the 1980s the cost of higher education increased enormously. The federal government also drastically cut every government student loan program and simultaneously discontinued government grants to students from low-income families. Unless this is reversed, the United States may lose its lead in mass higher education, and we may see a downward trend in the percentage of 18- to 24-year-olds attending college in the United States.

Managerial skill and entrepreneurship can be found in great abundance in the United States. America is a business-oriented society and its whole system reflects this fact. In addition to specialized business schools and business programs offered at most colleges and universities, many private companies provide on-the-job training in management and other business fields. The relatively large number of entrepreneurs is a result of the economy's general prosperity, and its essentially private-enterprise orientation. In 1966, only 14 percent of college students majored in business. In 1986, however, 26 percent were business majors. By 1991, that figure had dropped to 18 percent.

The early settlers were generally a hardy breed—many of whom had to survive a perilous journey to the New World and sometimes a struggle in the wilderness. These vigorous pioneers believed in hard work, individual initiative, and the profit motive. Many of them were Calvinists who believed in the "Protestant ethic." They not only believed that work was good for its own sake ("idle hands do the devil's work"), they believed the accumulation of material wealth on earth was an indication that one would go to heaven. Material success was deemed to be an indication of "God's will." Only a chosen few, they thought, were destined to go to heaven, so everyone was motivated to work hard to demonstrate that he or she was one of the chosen few.

The government's open immigration policy in the nineteenth century ensured an abundant labor force for America's industrial revolution. The absence of a hereditary aristocracy or a rigid social stratification system encouraged people to work hard to move up the socioeconomic ladder. An added benefit of the open immigration policy was the fact that many immigrants came from more technologically advanced countries and consequently brought valuable knowledge and skills to America. However, since the end of World War I, the United

States has passed a series of acts restricting the number and types of immigrants it will welcome. In order to reflect reality more accurately, the inscription on the Statue of Liberty which reads "give me your tired, your poor . . ." should be changed to "give me your M.D.s, your nuclear physicists, and your North Western Europeans!"

America's human resources are large, varied, generally healthy, educated, and technologically skilled. Except for a relatively large percentage of dependent children and aged (in relation to other highly developed nations), the United States ranks very high in human resources.

☐ Capital Resources

Capital resources may be either self-generated or provided by foreign investors.[3] When the United States launched its industrial revolution, about 1840, it benefited from a large influx of foreign capital, especially from British investors. Much of the investment was in railroad building. The government made this type of investment very attractive by donating the land for the rights of way. The period from 1840 to 1860 accelerated America's transition from an agricultural to an industrial economy. It spawned financial institutions which provided a great deal of domestic credit to American entrepreneurs to supplement foreign investment. Such credit was needed because of new business ventures which required enormous capital investments, such as railroad building.

The twenty years following the Civil War witnessed the expansion of a new form of business enterprise—the corporation. Now, not only could capital be acquired through profits and domestic lending agencies, a good deal of capital could also be obtained by selling corporate stocks and bonds. During the period 1865–1885 capital goods accounted for 22 percent of GNP. From 1870 to 1900 GNP tripled. Government policies were aimed at promoting industry, contributing to business growth.

Capital investment increased at the turn of the century because of several important developments: the discovery and exploitation of large oil deposits; the invention of the internal combustion engine; the harnessing of electricity and the subsequent construction of electric power plants; the building of roads and highways; and the invention of the telephone and the building of telephone systems. In short, within the space of a few years, the United States had a revolution in transportation, communication, and power systems.

This country has been at the forefront of technological innovation ever since. Thus, given its wealth of natural, human, and capital resources, combined with its high level of production technology and its value system, the production possibilities of the American economy are the greatest in the world.

☐ Demands

Despite a very unequal distribution of wealth, the American economy provides for the biological needs of the vast majority of its citizens, but such provision is certainly not commensurate with the economy's capabilities or people's expectations. In the 1980s the poorest 20 percent of the population suffered an 11.5 percent decrease in their share of total U.S. income. In fact, the 60 percent of the population with the lowest income suffered a 7.5 percent decrease. The next 35 percent stayed even, and the richest 5 percent increased its share of total U.S. income by 11 percent. Hence, the 1980s saw a transfer of income from the poor and the middle class to the richest 5 percent of the population.[4]

Whatever their income, Americans have a high propensity to consume. Thorstein Veblen, a famous American economist, wrote in 1899 that the leisure class advertised its economic success by engaging in **conspicuous consumption**:[5] spending money as a status symbol, usually in order to "keep up with the Joneses." This is probably true of most Americans, regardless of socioeconomic class. A very large advertising industry creates a strong desire on the part of consumers to purchase; and planned obsolescence (making things so they break down or wear out quickly or go out of style frequently) also adds to the propensity of Americans to consume. Easy availability of credit is another contributing factor. Since you don't need advertising to sell scarce goods, the large advertising industry is a result of America's abundance. Americans, then, demand a constantly increasing standard of living and a high production of consumer goods.

☐ Supports

Americans usually give strong support to their economic system. However, they tend to blame the government for any dysfunction that may occur in the economy, such as inflation, depression, recession, or high unemployment. The political party in power may suffer at the polls if Americans are forced to endure economic hardships. But support for the system remains generally high. In 1848 Karl Marx predicted that highly industrialized capitalist nations would make living conditions impossible for the working class, causing it to overthrow the government and replace the capitalist economic system with communism. This has not happened. Americans believe in private property, the profit motive, and the value of hard work; they have no ethical reservations regarding the acquisition of material goods. Veblen rightly pointed out that American workers do not want to overthrow the system; they want to increase their standard of living within the system. Even the poor seek reform, not revolution.

Government economic policies since the 1930s have been designed largely to cushion the fluctuations of the market system and to avoid major economic dysfunctions. The relative success of such policies has increased general satisfaction with the economy's performance.

☐ Characteristics and History of the American Economy

The American economy is certainly not a pure market system, but, of the four economic systems covered in this chapter and the next, it has the least government control over the economy. Some of the characteristics that either modify or add to those of a pure market system are:

1. *Practically All the Means of Production Are Privately Owned.* Even utility companies, a type of business that many other countries have nationalized because they are natural monopolies, are predominantly privately owned in the United States. A major exception is the Tennessee Valley Authority (TVA), which provides wholesale electric power to several states in the Appalachian region. Other exceptions are municipal enterprises.

2. *The Government Regulates Many Business Activities.* After the Civil War several great fortunes were amassed during the remainder of the nineteenth century—almost all of them by the most unscrupulous behavior imaginable. This was the era of the "robber barons."[6] Railroads charged exorbitant rates where they had a monopoly and gave secret rebates to customers where competition existed. John D. Rockefeller invented the **trust**—a scheme which eliminated competition by having major stockholders in competing companies cooperate to set industry-wide prices (as high as the market would bear). J. P. Morgan invented the **holding company** which produced nothing but which owned controlling shares of stock in many other companies. Many schemes were concocted to swindle a gullible public that was all too eager to invest with well-known "captains of industry." Thus the public was often induced to buy worthless or watered stocks. An example of

John Pierpont Morgan, 1837–1913
This American banker and financier, who invented the "holding company," has been referred to as one of the "robber barons" of the turn of the century.

unscrupulous profit making was the fact that, along with their regular products, meat-packing houses processed filth, rats, roaches, and even parts of human beings who were unfortunate enough to fall into a vat while meat was being processed.

At the turn of the century the United States had the greatest inequality in the distribution of wealth in its entire history. More than half the nation's wealth was concentrated in the hands of a few "enterprising" families. Quite often, when workers tried to organize a labor union, their employers would hire gangsters to beat them up. At times even the army was used against organized workers. Then the organizers were fired and "blacklisted" so they could not find another job. Most government officials condoned such activities or looked the other way, many of them receiving payoffs. Commodore Vanderbilt once said that he did not have any trouble buying off state legislators, "and they don't cost much."

America became aware of many of these unscrupulous and unhealthy business practices through the writings of a group of people known as the **muckrakers.** Frank Norris exposed the railroads in *The Octopus;* Ida M. Tarbell wrote *The History of the Standard Oil Trust;* Upton Sinclair wrote a brilliant exposé of the Chicago meat-packing houses in *The Jungle;* and there were other muckrakers who attacked the status quo. A series of legislative acts ensued, which included railroad legislation in the 1880s, antitrust legislation in 1890, and the Pure Food and Drug Act in 1906; but it was many years before some of these were strictly enforced. For a long time the Sherman Antitrust Act was only used to prevent the formation of labor unions. An important step was taken in 1914 when the **Federal Reserve System** was created to help regulate the money and banking system.

However, it was not until the 1930s that the government began large-scale regulation of the economy. Franklin Roosevelt's **New Deal** included the creation of many regulatory agencies, such as the Securities and Exchange Commission (SEC), the Federal Communications Commission (FCC), and many others. More recently, all levels of government have become ecology conscious, and have begun to impose regulations on business in order to protect the environment. America's modified market system may accurately be referred to as "regulated capitalism." It should be noted, however, that the regulators are often controlled by the firms they are supposed to be regulating. This, of course, is detrimental to consumers.

3. *Government Policies Have a Great Impact on the Economy's Performance Because the Government Is the Largest Spender in the Economy.* A reduction in government spending depresses the economy, and an increase inflates it. Therefore the government cannot simply consider the merits of its spending programs but also the overall economic

impact of continuing, increasing, reducing, or eliminating such programs.

4. *Labor Unions Permit Workers to Bargain Collectively, So Wages Often Are Not Determined Exclusively by Supply and Demand.* Approximately one-eighth of the labor force is organized. Most organized workers belong to small, relatively weak unions. Even though they enjoy greater security than nonorganized workers, their pay is probably not significantly higher than it would be if they were not organized. However, members of the Teamsters, the United Auto Workers, some of the construction workers unions, and others enjoy a significantly higher income than they would if they had to bargain individually with large corporations for their wages.

5. *Consumers Have Only Limited Sovereignty Because They Are Induced to Buy Many Products Through Advertising.* The advertising industry is designed to increase sales for its clients. Sometimes it fails (the Edsel was a flop); but more often it achieves some measure of success (for example, the Mustang). Advertising's defenders claim that increasing demand is good for the economy, and that the industry provides consumers with valuable information. Advertising's detractors argue that the industry convinces people to buy things they don't need with money they don't have. They claim it takes advantage of people's insecurities by doing such things as intimating that a particular brand of toothpaste or deodorant will enhance one's appeal to the opposite sex more than another brand will. Usually such claims are invalid. Detractors also claim that increasing demand is only good during a recession when the economy needs to be stimulated; otherwise it can be inflationary. Its primary effect is to influence the consumers' choice of products. Advertising probably has both positive and negative consequences. For better or for worse it is a permanent part of the American economic system, and it seems to be quite effective.

6. *Most Natural Monopolies Are Privately Owned.* A **monopoly** exists when one firm dominates an industry, either nationally or locally. Public utilities are called **natural monopolies** because it is economically not feasible to have more than one telephone, natural gas, or electric company in one city. Such firms can operate profitably only if they can enjoy economies of scale; that is, if they have a very large number of customers. Then they may reduce the cost per unit of the services they supply. Because they are natural monopolies they are usually owned and operated by the government in most countries. But not in the United States. As mentioned before, the Tennessee Valley Authority (TVA) is the main exception. Instead the government regulates the rates these private companies may charge. Sometimes the members of such regulatory agencies are friendly to the utility com-

panies they are supposed to regulate in the public interest. The results in such cases are not favorable to consumers. Those who advocate government control of public utilities argue that a capitalist market system functions properly only if there is competition. The absence of competition in the public utility field places it outside of a free market system; therefore profits generated by such enterprises should accrue to the general public either through reduced rates or through government services. Obviously, privately owned utility companies disagree.

7. *Only a Handful of Companies Dominate Almost Every Major Industry.* They do not compete with each other in terms of pricing; they compete in terms of packaging and advertising. They are called **oligopolies.** At one time there were eighty-seven companies in the United States that produced automobiles. Now there are three: General Motors (with sales that exceed the GNP of over 90 percent of the countries in the world), Ford and Chrysler. Three companies dominate the steel industry: U.S.X., Bethlehem, and National Steel. Three companies dominate the aluminum industry: Kaiser, Reynolds, and Alcoa. Just a handful of companies control the petroleum industry, led by Exxon. The same is true in several other major industries, such as business machines: IBM, Xerox, and Unisys.

In all of these industries comparable products have similar or identical prices, regardless of which firm produces them. Some people believe that illegal price fixing takes place. Others claim that collusion is not necessary; each industry has a **price leader** (GM, U.S.X., Exxon, IBM, and so on), and every time the price leader increases prices, the

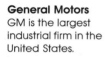

General Motors
GM is the largest industrial firm in the United States.

others follow suit. Thus in most major industries in the United States there is oligopolistic competition which leads to less price competition. This is certainly a radical departure from a pure market system.

In the defense industry, companies receive lucrative contracts that guarantee profits through a cost-plus arrangement. One company, Lockheed Aircraft, received financial assistance from Congress when it was in deep financial trouble in 1972. The Chrysler Corporation was also bailed out in 1979 by the government. In 1988 hundreds of savings and loan institutions were failing and the U.S. government was expected to come to the rescue. Oil companies enjoy a depletion allowance of 23 percent, and many businesses have received tax breaks for reinvesting their profits. Such tax breaks are rationalized by saying that they help create jobs for workers. But there is no such guarantee. It is possible that reinvestment may take the form of labor-saving machinery, which might result in some workers losing their jobs. These facts might lead one to believe that there is capitalism for the poor and the middle class, and socialism for the rich.

The concentration of industry in the United States is far greater than most citizens imagine. In 1992, the top ten industrial companies in sales were General Motors ($132,775 billion), Exxon ($103,447 billion), Ford ($100,786 billion), IBM ($65,096 billion), General Electric ($62,202 billion), Mobil ($57,389 billion), Philip Morris ($50,157 billion), DuPont ($37,643 billion), Chevron ($37,464 billion), and Texaco ($37,130 billion).

8. *The Government Tries to Cushion Business Cycles Through Fiscal and Monetary Policies.* Prior to the Depression of the 1930s, the widely accepted feeling was that the government should not interfere in the economy. Rugged individualism was extolled. In fact, around the turn of the century, the prevalent economic philosophy combined the economic ideas of Adam Smith with the biological ideas of Charles Darwin and his followers.

Adam Smith, a British economist, is considered the father of modern economics. His book *The Wealth of Nations*, published in 1776, is a classic. He lived in an age in which most scholars believed that all human activity was governed by natural laws. Smith believed that he had discovered such laws which governed economic activity, and thus he provided the world with the first scientific explanation of the capitalist economic system that emerged from the Industrial Revolution.

The economy, said Smith, is ruled by the "laws of the market." These laws are *self-interest* and *competition*. Everyone (including those in business) is motivated by self-interest. According to Smith each person's self-interest turns out to benefit the general society because of what Smith called "the invisible hand." Business people invest their money to make profits for themselves; they are not motivated by philanthropic considerations. Nevertheless they inadvertently benefit society by producing goods, services, and jobs that would not otherwise be available to the general public. This invisible hand works, however, only as long as there is plenty of competition in every part of the economic process; there must be many buyers and sellers for every product and no large concentrations of industry that might impede free competition.

For about two-and-a-half centuries prior to the publication of *The Wealth of Nations*, several governments had interfered with the market system. The effect had been to reduce competition, an effect that Smith deplored. He advocated a *laissez-faire* (government hands-off) policy. If large corporations which interfered with free competition had existed in his day, as they do now, Smith would have vigorously objected to this state of affairs as well. Free competition, said Smith, ensured that consumers would vote with their money for those goods and services they desired by purchasing them, and against those they rejected by not buying them. The free market, thought Smith, makes the consumer king. However, whenever free competition is eliminated, whether by government or oligopolistic business practices, the consumers lose their sovereignty. That is why we conclude that today Adam Smith would favor government participation to restore price competition.

Smith's theory, accepted in the United States since the inception of the Republic, was combined in the 1880s with a philosophy called **social Darwinism.** In 1859 Charles Darwin explained the theory of evolution in a book called *The Origin of Species*. He explained that life is a struggle for survival in which organisms that adapt best to a changing environment survive and others do not. This process of "natural selection" is based on the notion of "survival of the fittest" (see Chapter 2).

Although Darwin was only referring to biological selection, several scholars began applying his theory to human societies. In every society, they said, some people rise to the top and some sink to the bottom through natural selection. Those who are poor and sick suffer because they are unfit to survive and should not be helped by the government because such actions would interfere with the improvement of the human race. If allowed to survive, these disadvantaged people would transmit their inferior minds and bodies to their offspring. Therefore the government should not assist these people in any way. Many businessmen embraced this philosophy that offered scientific sanction for exploitation of workers.

This philosophy prevailed in the United States and parts of Europe for about three decades beginning around 1880. Its major exponents were Herbert Spencer and William Graham Sumner.[7] It was reinforced by the Horatio Alger "rags to riches" stories. In each of these works of fiction, the hero begins life in abject poverty, and through hard work, thrift, and luck he eventually becomes wealthy—hence respectable— thereby realizing the American dream.

Relative stability prevailed in the United States until 1929, when a severe depression began which lasted for over a decade. The Great Depression of the 1930s took a heavy toll. Unemployment reached 25

The American Dream and the Great Depression
Untold millions of Americans read and believed in Horatio Alger's classic "rags-to-riches" version of the American dream. Consequently, they were shocked when unemployment rates reached 25 percent during the period following 1929. For many able-bodied men it was wait in line for bread and soup or starve.

percent; those fully employed worked long hours for wages that were 60 percent lower than they had been in the twenties; from 1929 to 1933 GNP dropped 50 percent, while investment dropped 94 percent. Thirty-three percent of the banks and other businesses failed; and 15 percent of the population was on welfare.

The causes of the Depression are not entirely agreed upon by economists. Some blame overproduction and underconsumption which resulted primarily from a maldistribution of wealth. Money was concentrated in the hands of a few, so that many lacked sufficient buying power necessary to maintain a vigorous economy. Other economists claim that contraction of the money supply was to blame. Perhaps, it was a combination of these and other factors.

Whatever the causes, the effects were dramatic. People who grew up in the 1930s developed a psychology of scarcity, as opposed to those who grew up in the 1980s and who developed a psychology of affluence. This accounts in part for the so-called generation gap. Much of the older generation feels economically insecure; this includes many who are now financially well off. They tend to be very concerned about security and materialism. The younger generation has not undergone a long period of economic deprivation; hence they are not as security-conscious or materially-oriented. To many senior citizens, the Great Depression was the most traumatic experience they have ever undergone. Many may never get over its effects.

During the Depression young people had to quit school to help support their families and were often frustrated by the lack of jobs. Some of them roamed the countryside looking for work, sometimes stealing in order to eat. Formerly successful business executives slept on park benches and sold apples on street-corners. Some of them committed suicide. Hobo jungles existed outside of all major cities, and tramps could be seen everywhere begging for food and other necessities. Even farmers, who generally constitute a conservative element in every society, were marching with pitchforks and preaching revolution. Radical alternatives were very popular, and many Americans began to look to Communist and Fascist solutions. This is the psychological environment that existed when Franklin Roosevelt became President in 1933. His solution was neither to maintain the status quo nor to opt for any revolutionary solutions; instead he chose to preserve the system by reforming it. Roosevelt's answer to the Great Depression was the New Deal.

The New Deal

The New Deal created many public works projects in order to provide jobs. The government put people to work on projects such as building schools, hospitals, auditoriums, post offices, dams, housing projects, and beautifying parks. These projects were not designed to compete with private enterprise. The government provided people a measure of security by establishing minimum wages, unemployment insurance, and social security. Farmers were given price supports and emergency mortgage loans. Workers were encouraged to organize labor unions so they could bargain collectively with their employers. New regulations were established for banking and credit. The Federal Deposit Insurance Corporation (FDIC) was created to protect bank accounts; and the Securities and Exchange Commission (SEC) was created to oversee stock market operations. Jobs were created for young people through two programs: the Civilian Conservation Corps (CCC) provided full-time jobs on conservation projects; and the National Youth Administration (NYA) provided part-time jobs for students who stayed in school. In order to stimulate the economy the government engaged in heavy deficit spending.

A certain amount of recovery occurred, but it was not until World War II that the United States fully emerged from the Depression. In fact, Roosevelt's attempts to balance the budget, combined with a tight monetary policy, caused the economy to contract in 1937. Roosevelt, therefore, had no blueprint for recovery. However, he surrounded himself with brilliant men and took their advice. There were two reasons why Roosevelt developed the New Deal programs: he believed that the government is ultimately responsible for maintaining the country's prosperity; and he had an experimental, pragmatic nature which enabled him to try a number of solutions in an attempt to get America out of the Depression. Some of his policies were similar to the ideas of the British economist John Maynard Keynes. Keynesian economic theo-

New Deal Programs
A wide variety of jobs was provided by the WPA, the CCC, and other government programs after 1932. Here young CCC workers are digging an irrigation ditch on Forest Service lands in Montana.

ries influenced the American government's economic policies, until Ronald Reagan became president in 1981.

Keynesian Economics

Keynes believed that a nation's prosperity could be maintained by government policies. Until 1981 the American government had accepted a major role in maintaining the economy on an even keel, trying to avoid depression, inflation, and high unemployment. It tried to flatten out the ups and downs of the economy by pursuing counter-cyclical policies. Many of these fiscal and monetary policies were first suggested by Keynes. We are only going to use one simple equation to explain Keynesian economics. To simplify our model, we are excluding the roles played by imports and exports.

$$GNP = C + I + G$$

Gross national product is equal to consumption plus investment plus government spending. Think about economic activity as being like the amount of air in a bicycle tire. If there is too much air, the tire develops a bulge and eventually there is a blowout. If it has too little air, it develops a flat. In either case the bicycle does not function properly. The same is true of the economy. Too much demand may overheat the economy, thereby causing inflation. Too little demand leads to unemployment, lower profits, and possibly to a depression. Although a bicycle tire only has one valve through which air passes in or out, the economy has three valves: consumption, investment, and government spending. If an increase or decrease in consumption or investment is not accompanied by an opposite reaction by the government it can lead to a blowout or a flat tire in the economy. Measures by the government to counteract those developments come under two headings: fiscal policies and monetary policies.

Fiscal Policies

Fiscal policies have to do primarily with government spending and taxation. If the economy is experiencing a decline, the government may, among other things: (1) lower taxes in order to leave more disposable income in the hands of investors and consumers in the hopes that they will spend it, thereby stimulating the economy; or (2) increase government spending, thereby directly stimulating the economy.

If, however, the economy is suffering from the opposite malady, inflation, the government can take measures to depress the economy. It might (1) increase taxes, thereby reducing disposable income which could be used for investment or consumption; or (2) reduce government spending, thereby reducing demand for goods and services (an action that usually leads to a reduction in prices). What is important about fiscal policy is that it helps keep aggregate demand high enough to achieve full employment of resources, but no higher because that would cause inflation. Aggregate demand is the combined demands of all the people.

Monetary Policies

Monetary policies are administered by the Federal Reserve System. This is a central banking system consisting of twelve regional banks. It is run by the Federal Reserve Board, headed by a chairman who has great power and staffed by members chosen by the government, big banks, and small banks. The board exercises two types of direct controls over the commercial banks (these are the ones that you and I do business with) that are members of the Federal Reserve System. The Board controls (1) the reserve requirement and (2) the discount rate. The **reserve requirement** is the percentage of deposits that a bank must keep on hand in case its depositors wish to withdraw part or all of their deposits. If it is 20 percent, this means that member banks must retain one out of every five dollars deposited. The **discount rate** is the interest rate that the Federal Reserve banks charge the commercial banks for loans. Commercial banks do not derive all of their reserves from depositors. Some of their reserves are borrowed from the Federal Reserve banks which have the power to print money. If the discount rate is 9 percent, the interest charged by commercial banks will be slightly higher.

In order to depress the economy, the Federal Reserve Board may either raise the reserve requirement or the discount rate or both. In order to stimulate the economy, it would do the opposite. Lowering the

The Federal Reserve Bank of New York
Monetary policies are administered by the Federal Reserve System, and this bank is a primary agent for managing inflation and recession by expanding and reducing the money supply.

reserve requirement releases money which can be borrowed for investment or consumption. This is called a loose money policy. Raising it is called a tight money policy. Raising the discount rate will cause a rise in interest rates and a corresponding drop in money borrowed. If you want to buy a house this year and the interest rates go up, it will cost you a lot of money on a long-term mortgage. Conversely, if you plan on buying a house next year, but the interest rates drop this year, you might be encouraged to spend your money now, thereby stimulating the economy.

Open bond market operations, however, are by far the most important monetary tool available for stimulating or depressing the economy. This refers to the buying and selling of government securities by the Federal Reserve Bank of New York (as an agent for the Federal Open Market Committee and/or the United States Treasury Department). These transactions directly affect the country's money supply. When the "Fed" buys securities in the open market, it increases the amount of money in circulation by putting it back in the hands of investors. When it sells these securities back to the public, it takes money out of circulation.

These fiscal and monetary policies enable the government to manage the economy to a point where it might avoid a severe depression or inflation. However, periods of recession and inflation can still occur.

Supply-Side Economics

Whereas Keynesian economics emphasizes the demand side of supply and demand—stimulating or depressing demand to fight inflation or recession—supply-side economics proposes to manipulate the supply side of the equation. Both Democratic and Republican Presidents from Franklin Roosevelt to Jimmy Carter used fiscal policies: increasing or decreasing taxes and government spending, and encouraged the Federal Reserve Board to increase or decrease the money supply (monetary policy) to flatten the ups and downs of the business cycles. This counter-cyclical approach worked fairly well until the late 1970s when recession and inflation (a situation called stagflation) proved difficult to combat. The increased importation of petroleum, while prices increased tenfold in eight years, caused double-digit inflation even during a recession.

Ronald Reagan came to power in 1981 supporting a supply-side approach. Instead of depressing demand to fight inflation, he proposed to increase supply by cutting taxes, primarily to businesses and to the wealthy. The President assumed that the increased disposable income would be invested, create jobs, increase the production of goods and services, and, consequently, increase government revenues despite the tax cut because higher profits and income would create a larger tax base.

This did not occur. The federal government experienced $200 billion plus annual deficits. Hence, the government was borrowing over $200 billion yearly to pay its debts. Foreign investors have been providing half the money needed, so that inflationary pressure on interest rates has been only half as much as it would be without foreigners buying U.S. government bonds. On the other hand, the United States is becoming indebted to foreigners to such an extent that it has gone from being the world's greatest creditor nation in 1980 to being the world's greatest debtor nation by 1987, a situation that still exists in 1993.

According to David Stockman, Director of the Office of Management and Budget in the first Reagan administration, the 25 percent tax cut was supposed to be accompanied by a 25 percent cut in spending. Since this would have caused great suffering for millions of Americans, Congress would not go along. Hence, the tax cuts should have been abandoned. They were not, and the national debt tripled under Reagan. In 1980 we paid $50 billion in interest on the national debt, and in 1988 we paid $150 billion, which is about half of what we spent on national defense. By 1993 that figure had increased to almost $300 billion, because by the end of President Bush's term in January 1993, the national debt had quadrupled since 1980.

It is ironic that President Reagan is blamed for the 1981–1982 recession, the worst since the Great Depression of the 1930s, and he is given credit for lowering both inflation and interest rates, when his policies had nothing to do with these circumstances.

The Federal Reserve Board, which is independent of the presidency and which sometimes does the opposite of what the president and Congress are doing, increased interest rates and tightened the money supply enormously in President Carter's last years in office because the inflation rate rose above 12 percent. That is why interest rates soared to 21 percent in 1980.

The theory of monetary policy holds that higher interest rates will convince some consumers and investors to postpone consuming and investing until interest rates decline to an acceptable level, thus reducing demand. However, if people assume that interest rates will continue to climb, they will borrow anyway. Hence, in the short term, monetary policy actually fuels the inflation. Eventually, the people get the message, and demand drops and so does inflation.

The problem with using monetary policy to fight inflation is that it can cause a recession and that it can take one to three years to work. This is what happened in the Carter/Reagan transition years. The turning point occurred in 1981. The precipitous drop in demand that year caused the horrendous 1981–1982 recession. It also broke the inflationary spiral. As inflation dropped and the economy took a nosedive, the Fed began to reduce interest rates until eventually they were low enough to invite borrowing once again by investors and consumers. Consequently, the economy began to recover in 1983.

The Fed, not Jimmy Carter, was responsible for the high interest rates in 1980, and was partially responsible for double-digit inflation because, in the short term, higher interest rates are inflationary. The Fed, not Ronald Reagan, was responsible for the 1981–1982 recession caused by those very high interest rates. The Fed, not Ronald Reagan, was responsible for bringing down inflation and interest rates. Reagan's 25 percent income tax cut, combined with other business tax cuts in 1981–1983, if not countered by the Fed's monetary policy, would have increased both inflation and interest rates significantly.

Reagan's huge annual deficits would have increased interest rates, because the price of money, like any other commodity, is related to the demand for and the supply of that commodity. With the Federal government competing with private investors and consumers for loans to the tune of $200 billion annually for a limited money supply, interest rates would have risen enormously. Unfortunately, both the electronic and print media have perpetuated the myth that Reagan caused the recession, and that his policies reduced both inflation and interest rates.

It seems that Presidents Carter and Reagan had less to do with the ups and downs of the U.S. economy during the 1977–1988 period than did the Federal Reserve Board. This is especially true during the Reagan years when the President was stimulating the economy while the Fed was deflating it.

If the combined stimulating effect of the Fed's loosening monetary policy and the Bush administration's huge deficit spending had caused an increase in the inflation rate, the Fed would have tightened the money supply and increased interest rates. The economy grew at a healthy rate during Clinton's first year as president. Nevertheless, the Fed increased interest rates in February, 1994 to stem any possible inflation.

To summarize, in the 1980s Keynesian economics was still alive with respect to monetary policy but not with respect to fiscal policy. Supply-side economics did not work the way its proponents expected but was continued by George Bush. If fiscal policy is used once again in a countercyclical manner by Bill Clinton, the role of monetary policy may not be as prominent as it has been in recent years.

Critics of supply-side economics claim that it is a thinly disguised version of the old trickle-down theory. David Stockman gave credence to this assertion in an interview with a national monthly publication.

According to the trickle-down approach, if there is a recession, high unemployment, increasing poverty, the government should not help the people affected directly. Rather, it should reduce taxes to the rich and to large businesses, and these people will invest their money, create jobs, and stimulate the economy.

Unfortunately, the tax cut has no strings attached. The rich can, if they like, take the money and put it in a Swiss bank account, or buy a yacht and tour the Mediterranean. The American economy and the bulk of the American people do not necessarily benefit from trickle-down/ supply-side economics. In fact, a later section on poverty will demonstrate that a transfer of income from the poor and the middle class to the rich has occurred.

Conversion Functions

Control. In the United States private citizens and corporations own and manage the means of production within the framework of government regulations. A balance is achieved among the interdependent production processes through the interaction of market forces and corporate planning.

Agriculture. There was a time in America when over 90 percent of the population was engaged in farming. In 1988 only 2 percent of the labor force worked on the land; and it not only produced sufficient food and fibers for the entire American population but also a surplus.

Mechanization, improved fertilizers, breeding of improved varieties of plants and animals, the control of plant and animal diseases, improved methods of soil conservation and increased knowledge of soil chemistry, and widespread use of insecticides have all contributed to

Market Gardening in the United States
Giant-size farms such as this one in California make up only 29 percent of the total number of farms but turn out 90 percent of the produce sold.

the modernization and high production efficiency of American agriculture. The shift from subsistence to commercial farming has been dramatic. Table 15-3 illustrates the distribution of ownership and the percentage of total production of different sizes and types of farms.

Twenty-nine percent of the farms produce over $40,000 per year each; however, these large farms account for 90 percent of sales. At the other extreme, 59 percent of farms earn less than $20,000 annually; they only have 5 percent of total farm sales. The concentration of wealth in agriculture parallels that of industry.

Table 15-3
Breakdown of U.S. farms by sales, 1990

Economic Class	Percent of Farms	Percent of Sales
Less than $20,000	59	5
$20,000–$39,999	12	5
$40,000–$99,999	14	13
$100,000–$249,999	10	21
$250,000–$499,999	3	14
$500,000–$999,999	1	11
$1 million and over	1	31

Source: U.S. Bureau of the Census, *Statistical Abstract of the United States: 1992* (Washington, D.C., 1992), p. 648.

Industry. The three types of business organizations are **individual proprietorships, partnerships,** and **corporations.** In modern America, the importance of the first two types has diminished greatly. Both are characterized by unlimited liability. If the business fails, its creditors have a claim on the personal holdings of individual proprietors and partners. A corporation, on the other hand, is considered a separate entity from its owners. It has limited liability, that is, shareholders are liable only for the amount they have invested in the business. If the corporation goes bankrupt, its creditors cannot collect one penny from the stockholders' other personal assets.

Corporations account for 75 percent of total production in the United States. Those who argue that ownership is widely dispersed point to the fact that there are over 25 million stockholders in the United States. Conversely one writer argues that stockholdings are really highly concentrated: he points out that "among the 200 largest nonfinancial corporations, the top 1 percent of the stockholdings include approximately 60 percent of the common stock of these corporations."[8] He says that "*investment ownership* is widely diffused whereas *control ownership* is highly concentrated."[9] One study claims that the top 1 percent owns 76 percent of all corporate stock.[10]

Adam Smith's free market system, populated by small, competitive enterprises, no longer exists. It has been replaced by oligopolies in 391 industries, according to a Senate investigating committee in 1957. Today there are close to 500 oligopolistic industries.

Management Decision Making

Production. What and how much to produce, and what materials to use are management decisions made by private businesses based on anticipated consumer demand, availability of resources, and profitability. In agriculture, the government also plays a role. The government pays farmers not to grow certain products because otherwise there would be a surplus of those goods. Such a surplus would depress prices and create an agricultural crisis. This program also enhances the soil conservation program. Subsidies are used as an inducement to set land aside for conservation purposes. In addition, the government guarantees prices to farmers through its price **parity** program. Parity prices provide farmers the same buying power that they had in whatever year is used as a base. If, for example, the base year is 1929, and the price farmers received for 50 bushels of wheat that year enabled them to buy a month's groceries, then the price they receive for 50 bushels of wheat this year must also enable them to buy a month's groceries. Actually, farmers are given a percentage (usually 70 to 80 percent) of parity, not full parity. The government's farm program consists of price supports to achieve parity and subsidies to encourage soil conservation and discourage overproduction which would lead to depressed prices. Nevertheless, in 1985 farmers suffered a severe depression, and farm mortgage foreclosures were at the highest level since the Depression. At the same time, the president was trying to reduce federal assistance to farmers in an attempt to return to a more pure market system.

In industry, extremely large corporations make decisions that have an enormous impact on the entire economy. A relatively small number of individuals and groups have a controlling interest in these corporations through "interlocking directorates, intercorporate stockholdings, concentrated stock ownership by individuals or groups in several corporations, common servicing by financial organizations, investment blocs, trade and business associations, . . . and informal or tacit agreements and understandings."[11]

Is it private enterprise? *si!* Free enterprise? no!

Four economists had this to say about production in the American economy:

> Corporate management decides on the character of the product, its quality, its price. It decides how much is to be spent on research, on production, on the promotion of sales. It decides which part of earnings is to be reinvested and in what field, where plants are to be built, and where other plants are to be closed down. In making these decisions, corporate management cannot ignore the signals of the market. On the other hand, neither is it compelled to behave in exact accordance with the dictates of the market. In this important sense, corporate management partially supplants the pricing mechanism in the determination of the allocation of resources in the United States.[12]

Many production decisions are also made by government. In 1980 military spending alone accounted for about 5.4 percent of GNP. Defense contractors receive orders from the government and their production is geared to that demand. However, those corporations also have friends who are involved in government decision making and they have lobbyists who influence other decision makers. This is what is generally called the "military-industrial (and governmental) complex." By 1990 military spending accounted for 22.6 percent of total government expenditure.

Distribution. Income is distributed according to market factors, union contracts, taxation, welfare, pensions, business decisions, and the distribution of wealth. It also depends to some extent on the state of the economy's health at any given time. The actual distribution will be discussed below during the evaluation of the system's performance.

Motivation. Material incentives are used primarily to motivate people to work. For business executives this may include expense accounts, stock options, and other benefits in addition to salaries. For white-collar workers, only fringe benefits such as health insurance and perhaps pension plans are usually added to their wages or salaries. Those on the lower end of the income scale are more difficult to motivate because there may not be a significant difference between the low wages they earn if they work and the welfare benefits they receive if they do not. If welfare or supplementary income is reduced in direct proportion to people's earnings, there is no material incentive to work.

Generally speaking, differentiated income levels are determined by the relative scarcity of workers in different occupations. Great scarcity leads to higher income, and vice versa. The higher pay offered the occupants of under-supplied work categories should serve as an inducement to others to enter such occupations. However, unequal opportunities at birth and afterward interfere with this market process. It seems, then, that the problem of low motivation among some groups and individuals can best be solved by equalizing opportunities.

☐ Evaluation of the American Economy

The American economy's outputs can best be analyzed by using the performance criteria discussed in the previous chapter: gross national product (GNP), per capita income (or per capita GNP), rate of economic growth, degree of price stability, level of employment, the distribution of wealth, technological progress, consumer satisfaction, subjective evaluation of rationality, and ecological effects.

GNP, GNP Per Capita, and Economic Growth Rate

In 1990 the United States' per capita GNP was the eighth highest in the world, behind Switzerland, Finland, Japan, Sweden, Norway, Germany, and Denmark (see Table 15-4).

The American economy, however, does not grow as rapidly as many other economies (see Table 15-5).

From 1960 to 1965 the American economy experienced its highest level of real growth since World War II. The preceding five-year period was the worst since the Great Depression. The recession of 1957–1958 was responsible for the low annual rate of growth (0.4 percent per capita). From 1965 to 1971 the growth rate declined, but it began to increase again in 1972. In 1974 it began to decline once more, but then moved upward again in 1976 and continued until 1980. In 1981–1982 the U.S. suffered the worst recession since the 1930s. The economy recovered in 1983 and continued to improve through 1988, although the stock market crashed on October 19, 1987. From 1965 to 1990 the average annual growth rate was 1.7 percent.

Price Stability

By inflation we mean a rise of price levels in general. We emphasize "in general" because some prices rise and some fall as a result of changes in the relative supply and demand for particular products. The main

Table 15-4
GNP Per Capita 1990

Country	1990 GNP Per Capita (U.S. Dollars)
Switzerland	32,680
Finland	26,040
Japan	25,430
Sweden	23,660
Norway	23,120
Germany	22,320
Denmark	22,080
United States	21,790
Canada	20,470
France	19,490
Austria	19,060
Netherlands	17,320
Australia	17,000
Italy	16,830
United Kingdom	16,100
Belgium	15,540
New Zealand	12,680
Spain	11,020
Ireland	9,550
Greece	5,990

Source: World Development Report, 1992, published for the World Bank by the Oxford University Press, 1992, p. 219.

Table 15-5
Average Annual Increase in GNP 1965–1990 (Percentages)

Country	GNP Per Capita	Country	GNP Per Capita
Japan	4.1	Spain	2.4
Norway	3.4	West Germany	2.4
Finland	3.2	Denmark	2.1
Italy	3.0	Great Britain	2.0
Ireland	3.0	Australia	1.9
Austria	2.9	Sweden	1.9
Greece	2.8	Netherlands	1.8
Canada	2.7	*United States*	1.7
Belgium	2.6	Switzerland	1.4
France	2.4	New Zealand	1.1

Source: World Development Report, 1992, published for the World Bank by the Oxford University Press, 1992, p. 219.

reason why America has suffered periodically from high inflation is war and its aftermath. Government expenditures increase significantly during wartime, thereby increasing demand for goods and services. This higher demand (in excess of increased production) causes demand-pull inflation, unless the government maintains price and wage controls.

If a war causes people to postpone consumption because of scarcity or rationing, the end of the war unleashes the bottled-up demand and usually causes high inflationary pressures. World War II caused such problems. The Vietnam War, however, caused inflation for another reason. From 1955 to 1965 price increases averaged 1.7 percent.[13] This was not bad because almost everyone's income increased at a higher rate during that period, especially after 1960. However, the escalation of the Vietnam War in 1965 brought on increased aggregate demand and this was not accompanied by tax increases, rationing, or price controls. In 1969 prices rose by 5.6 percent and in 1970 by 6.5 percent. This high rate of inflation, coupled with the American public's reaction to it, prompted President Nixon to institute a new economic policy in August 1971, which began with a freeze on wages, prices, and rents. Slowly the American economy began to respond. Phase Two, initiated ninety days later, removed the freeze, but imposed controls to be administered by newly constituted wage and price control boards.

Monetary policies had failed to curb the inflation in the short run. Higher interest rates did not deter investors from borrowing; they merely passed on the increased operating costs to the consumers in the form of higher prices. Consumers continued to buy despite higher interest rates. Consequently anti-inflation monetary policies actually added to the inflation. Monetarists claim that such policies do work, but that a time lag of eighteen months to 3 years is required for monetary policies to take effect. However, they failed to work at all during the Johnson administration. Fiscal policies were not used effectively either. It is impossible to reduce government expenditures during wartime, especially when many domestic government programs are already inadequately funded. As Arthur Okun says: "When Vietnam expenditures were piled on a budget that was appropriately expansionary, fiscal policy became an overexpansionary engine of inflation."[14] The ideal economic solution was to increase taxes. But, with a presidential election coming up, President Nixon did not consider such a move to be politically desirable. Hence, since the problem needed attention, he decided to impose direct controls. During the Nixon-Ford administration (1973–1977) inflation rose to over 11 percent annually and then declined. This was precipitated by a quadrupling of the price of crude petroleum by the OPEC nations (Organization of Oil Exporting Countries). Most other industrialized countries suffered even higher inflation (see Table 15-6). During Carter's fourth year in the presidency (1980), inflation rose above the 12 percent mark, due primarily to a better than

400 percent increase in oil prices charged by OPEC nations. By 1984, due primarily to the Fed's monetary policy, inflation dropped to 4 percent.

Table 15-6
Inflation 1965–1990

Country	Average Annual Percent Change (1965–1990)	1980–1990
Japan	7.8	1.5
Netherlands	7.6	1.9
West Germany	5.2	2.7
Austria	5.8	3.6
Switzerland	5.3	3.7
United States	6.4	3.7
Canada	7.2	4.4
Belgium	6.6	4.4
Norway	7.7	5.5
Denmark	9.2	5.6
United Kingdom	11.2	5.8
France	8.0	6.1
Sweden	8.3	7.4
Italy	11.2	9.9

Source: World Development Report, 1992, p. 243.

Employment Level

Full employment, as far as the general public is concerned, means that everyone who wants a job can find one. But there are many people seeking jobs who are not capable of holding one for either psychological or physiological reasons, or because of a structural or temporary unemployment situation. Therefore, most economists agree that an unemployment rate of 3 to 4 percent is to be considered "full employment."

Before the Great Depression, it was generally assumed that unemployment was not a problem to be dealt with by the government. High unemployment, if it did occur, was presumed to be a temporary problem that would be automatically rectified by the market system. A ten-year depression, which saw the unemployment rate fluctuate between 14 percent and 25 percent, changed a lot of people's minds. A Democratic president, convinced that the government is responsible for the public welfare, was elected in 1932. He took the position that general prosperity and full employment must be achieved. In 1946 a Republican-dominated Congress agreed. It passed the Employment Act of 1946, which charged the government with pursuing full-employment policies. Thus full employment is a bipartisan goal in the United States, although it has rarely been achieved.

When we talk about unemployment we are talking primarily about those at the bottom of the economic ladder. Those at the top and in the middle are scarcely affected. Thus, a general unemployment rate of 6 percent can be disastrous for the poor, the black, the unskilled, the poorly educated, the very young, and the very old. It can mean an unemployment rate of 40 percent for people in some of these categories. In some cities the rate of unemployment may be as high as 50 percent for the black, poor, unskilled, uneducated, and the very young or very old. Doctors, dentists, and bank presidents are not affected very much by an increase of 1 percent in unemployment; one million poor people are.

The great dilemma we face is this: Policies aimed at reducing unemployment usually fuel the fires of inflation, and policies designed to fight inflation tend to increase unemployment. The Democratic party is usually more concerned with solving the unemployment problem, and the Republican party is more concerned with inflation. The Nixon administration, faced with both problems simultaneously (high unemployment and high inflation), chose to fight the latter. Consequently the American economy suffered a recession in 1969–1970. When the measures taken did not suffice, the President instituted direct controls.

Table 15-7
Unemployment, 1965–1990 (in percentages)

Country	1965	1970	1975	1980	1990
Sweden	1.2	1.5	1.6	2.0	1.5
Japan	1.2	1.2	1.9	2.0	2.1
Germany	0.3	0.6	3.6	2.9	5.2
United States	4.5	4.9	8.5	7.1	5.5
Australia	1.3	1.4	4.9	6.1	6.9
Great Britain	2.1	3.1	4.1	7.0	6.9
Italy	4.0	3.5	3.2	3.9	7.0
Canada	3.9	5.9	6.9	7.5	8.1
France	3.9	5.9	6.9	7.5	9.2

Sources: Statistical Abstract of the United States, 1976, p. 850; 1980, p. 902; 1992, p. 838.

Table 15-7 compares unemployment in the United States with other industrialized economies. In the decade from 1955 to 1965, unemployment averaged 5.4 percent, ranging from a high of over 7 percent from 1958 to 1960, to a low of less than 4 percent from 1965 to 1968. In the period 1970–1971, it hovered at the 6 percent mark. In the decade from 1955 to 1965, inflation averaged 1.7 percent per annum. In the period 1969–1970 it averaged 6 percent. From 1971 to 1975, the unemployment rate averaged 6.1 percent, and from 1976 to 1980, it rose to 6.8 percent. By 1991 the U.S. unemployment rate was 6.7 percent. Some people, however, have been more seriously affected than others. While in 1991 non-Hispanic white Americans had a 6.0 percent unemployment rate, Hispanic unemployment was 9.8 percent, and black unemployment was 12.4 percent. Teenage unemployment stood at 19.8 for males and 17.4 for females. However, the white teenage unemployment rate was 16.3 percent, while black teenagers suffered an astronomical 36.3 percent unemployment rate. Education is still the best insurance against unemployment; in 1991 only 2.8 percent of college graduates were jobless. However, 5.9 percent of high school graduates and 11.0 percent of dropouts were unemployed.

The Distribution of Wealth

The distribution of wealth in America, as in most countries, is very unequal and became more unequal in the 1980s.

In 1980, the top 40 percent received 65.9 percent of all income, but in 1990 they received 68.1 percent. Conversely, in 1980, the bottom 40 percent received 16.7 percent of total U.S. income, but in 1990 they received only 15.4 percent (see Table 15-8). The top 5 percent received

Table 15-8
Percent Distribution of Aggregate Income, 1960–1990 (Families)

Year	Lowest Fifth	Second Fifth	Middle Fifth	Fourth Fifth	Highest Fifth	Top 5%	President
1960	4.8	12.2	17.8	24.0	41.3	15.9	Eisenhower
1968	5.6	12.4	17.7	23.7	40.5	15.6	Kennedy, Johnson
1976	5.4	11.8	17.6	24.1	41.1	15.6	Nixon, Ford
1980	5.1	11.6	17.5	24.3	41.6	15.3	Carter
1986	4.6	10.8	16.8	24.5	43.7	17.0	Reagan
1990	4.6	10.8	16.6	23.8	44.3	17.4	Bush

Source: Current Population Reports: Money Income of Households, Families, and Persons in the United States, 1986, p. 13; 1990, p. 202.

more income than the bottom 40 percent! In fact, in the 1980s the rich got richer, and the poor got poorer. The middle-class suffered a 5.8 percent decrease in its share of total income, while the top 5 percent of society increased its share by 13.7 percent between 1980 and 1990. And the 20 percent of the population with the lowest income suffered an 11.5 percent decrease in its share of total national income. This trend was accelerated in the Bush administration. There was an even greater maldistribution among the two largest U.S. minorities. Black Americans had 41.3 percent of the lowest quintile, and Hispanic Americans 35.8 percent. At the other extreme, only 8.5 percent of African Americans and 8.7 percent of Hispanics were in the highest quintile. Tragically, 51.9 percent of young people (15–24 years old) were in the lowest quintile. From 1991 to 1992, the poorest fifth saw their incomes decline by $154, while income for the richest fifth increased by $3,572 (they had 46.9 percent of total income).

Between 1960 and 1968, there was a redistribution of income from the top 40 percent to the bottom 40 percent. This occurred primarily as a result of the Great Society's war on poverty. For the first time, working poor joined nonworking poor in receiving government assistance, and in-kind programs, such as food stamps, Medicaid, and new public housing were added to the government's arsenal to fight poverty.

Although part of the cash redistribution was reversed by 1980, the in-kind benefits were substantially increased. Table 15-9 indicates that when the latter benefits are included, the percentage of the population living in poverty had declined.

Table 15-9
Percent Living in Poverty
1950–1991

Type of Poverty	1950	1965	1968	1980	1991
Official Poverty[a]	30%	18%	13%	13%	13.5%
Net Poverty[b]	27%	11%	8%	6%	11.0%

[a] Based on total cash income including government assistance.
[b] Based on adding in-kind government benefits to cash transfers.
Sources: Adapted from Charles Murray, "The War on Poverty, 1965–1980," *The Wilson Quarterly,* Autumn, 1984, pp. 104–105. *Statistical Abstract of the United States,* 1992, p. 460.

By 1991, however, the official poverty figure increased to 13.5 percent, and the in-kind programs were drastically cut. A conservative estimate is that net poverty increased from 6 percent in 1980 to 11 percent in 1991. Blacks continue to suffer triple the poverty rate of whites. In 1990, the official poverty rate was 9.4 percent for whites, 25.2 percent for Hispanics, and 29.7 percent for blacks. In 1992, the poverty rate increased to 14.5 percent, increasing in 33 states. The number of people without health insurance coverage increased by two million in the U.S. that year, and the number of people on food stamps rose by 1.7 million.

Table 15-10 shows family incomes in 1990 by region of the country.

Table 15-10
Median Family Income
by Region, 1990

Region	Median Family Income
Northeast	$41,092
West	36,837
Midwest	37,370
South	34,242

Source: Current Population Reports: Money Income of Households, Families, and Persons in the United States, 1991.

Table 15.11 shows the median family income for families divided by race. Female income was approximately 65 percent of male income for all ages and levels of education.

Table 15-11
Median Family Income
for Blacks, Hispanics,
and non-Hispanic
Whites, 1990

	Dollars
All	35,353
White	36,915
Black	21,423
Hispanic	23,431

Source: U.S. Bureau of the Census, Current Population Reports, Series P-60, no. 174.

The best chance minority groups have of increasing their income is through education. Table 15-12 clearly demonstrates how education and income are correlated.

Table 15-12
Median Family Income
by Education of Head
of Household (25 years
or older), 1990

Education	Median Family Income
Elementary	
8 years or less	$13,523
High School	
1–3 years	18,191
4 years	28,744
College	
1–3 years	35,724
4 years	47,083
5 years or more	54,636

Source: Current Population Reports: Money Income of Households, Families, and Persons in the United States, 1990, p. 18.

It is widely believed that America's progressive federal income tax structure redistributes incomes to effect transfer payments from the rich to the poor. This belief contains a grain of truth, but not much more. The 25 percent across-the-board income tax cut (1981–1983) benefited the rich more than the poor, as did lowering the top tax bracket. A person who would have paid $100,000 in taxes per year received a $25,000 annual reduction, while someone who would have paid $1,000 received a $250 reduction. Since low-income people generally suffered a concomitant loss of benefits because these were drastically reduced in the early 1980s by the federal government, low-income people suffered a decline in their standard of living during this period. Those with high incomes enjoyed a substantial increase. Hence, the net effect of the tax cuts and the government program cuts was to transfer income from the poor to the rich.

Federal taxes are progressive, but state and local taxes are regressive. Poor people pay a higher percentage of their income in state and local taxes than do people with higher income. For example, if someone who earns $15,000 yearly pays a 4 percent sales tax on a $6,000 automobile, the $240 tax is twice the percentage of their income paid by someone with a $30,000 annual income who buys an identical auto. In addition, people don't actually pay the stated rates on their gross incomes. There are deductions that reduce taxable income, and there are many more of these for people in higher income brackets than for those with lower incomes. As the Governor of Florida, Reubin Askew, pointed out in his keynote address to the 1972 Democratic National Convention, "a businessman's lunch of steak and three martinis is tax deductible, while a workingman's lunch of cheese and salami is not!" That is one reason why the personal wealth of those at the top was not diminished by our tax system until 1976 (see Table 15-13). The 1981 business tax cuts benefited primarily the wealthy, so that this redistribution process has been reversed. A study on corporate taxes released in December, 1983, indicated that the business share of federal tax revenues declined by more than 20 percent in 1983. The General Accounting Office study also stated that the burden was shifted to individuals.[15] Another study, conducted in 1985 by the Brookings Institute, indicated that a portion of taxes formerly paid by the rich was shifted to the poor in the period 1966–1985.[16] Categories that contain a disproportionate number of poor are blacks, Hispanics, American Indians, the young, the old, agricultural workers, the ill, the poorly educated, and female-headed households.

Table 15-13
Personal Wealth—Value of Assets Held by All Persons, Top One-Half Percent, and Top One Percent: 1962–1976

Year	Top ½%	Top 1%
1962	21.2	26.8
1969	20.4	25.8
1972	20.5	26.0
1976	13.8	18.3

Source: Statistical Abstract of the United States, 1984, p. 481.

Progress in reducing poverty was very slow in the 1970s as compared with the 1960s, when America was waging a war on poverty. In the six-year period from 1963 to 1969, poverty in families with a male head dropped from 15.4 percent to 8.0 percent (a 7.4 percent decline), while in the six-year period from 1972 to 1978, it dropped only 0.8 percent, from 7.4 percent to 6.6 percent. The trend was the same in female-headed households for the same six-year periods—a 10 percent decline in the 60's and a 4.6 percent drop in the 70's. In the 1980s poverty in male-headed households almost doubled, from 6.6 percent to 11.9 percent. During the same period, poverty in female-headed households increased by a third, from 32.3 percent to 42.4 percent. The Bush administration continued the trend of transferring income from the poor to the rich.

The probability that a family will live in poverty diminishes as the educational level of the head of household increases. The poverty rate in 1990 for families in which the head of household (twenty-five years or older) had some elementary school education is 25.5 percent; some high school education, 18.5 percent; and some college education, 4.0 percent.

The percentage of children under sixteen years of age living in poverty in 1990 was 21.1. That includes 16.3 percent of white, 45.6 percent of African-American, and 39.2 percent of Hispanic children. Poverty levels for children under eighteen years of age increased significantly from 1979 to 1990: from 11.4 to 15.1 for whites, from 40.8 to 44.2 for blacks, and from 27.7 to 39.7 for Hispanic youngsters.

A 1993 study by UNICEF found that the U.S. poverty rate for children was more than double that of any other major industrialized nation. The study also found that in the previous twenty years poverty among children increased only in the United States and Great Britain, while other industrialized nations reduced poverty among children.

Realistically, many U.S. families with incomes higher than the government-established poverty level are actually living in poverty.

Table 15-14
Budget for a Four-Person Urban U.S. Family, 1967–1981

Year	Low Standard of Living	Intermediate Standard of Living	High Standard of Living
1967	$ 5,915	$ 9,076	$13,050
1970	6,960	10,664	15,511
1972	7,386	11,446	16,558
1974	9,198	14,333	20,777
1976	10,041	16,236	23,759
1978	11,546	18,622	27,420
1979	12,585	20,517	30,317
1980	14,044	23,134	34,409
1981 [1]	15,323	25,407	38,060

[1] The Reagan administration stopped compiling these statistics in 1981. The reason stated was budget reduction.
Sources: Statistical Abstract of the United States, 1980, p. 487; Bureau of Labor Statistics News, 1981.

Budgets for an urban family of four for low, intermediate, and high standards of living were computed annually by the Bureau of Labor Statistics (see Table 15-14). The low standard is probably a more realistic estimate of the poverty level, and it is twice as high as the government's poverty standard.

There are many government programs designed to help the poor, but there are also many government subsidies that benefit the rich. Fifty-five percent of the subsidies to farmers are paid to the 11 percent in the top income brackets. Business tax credits, oil depletion allowances, deductible business expenses, and some other government policies are subsidies for the rich which reduce or are paid out of tax revenues. Middle-income Americans pay the most taxes and receive the fewest benefits for their tax dollars.

Technological Progress

The United States uses the most advanced technology in both industrial and agricultural production. This includes *mechanization,* the use of inanimate sources of *power* for activating the machines, and *techniques,* or methods, for transforming resources into goods and services. Commercial inventions are either of the labor-saving variety or the material-saving type. The emphasis in the United States has recently shifted from the former to the latter.

Subsidies to Business: A Controversial Issue
Government contracts, guaranteed loans, tax credits, depletion allowances, and deductible business expenses can all be seen as welfare payments to the wealthy. However, they may also have the effect of maintaining high employment in key areas of the economy. Seen here is the 767 assembly line at the Boeing Company, Everett, Washington.

In recent times the trend everywhere seems to be toward those inventions which will (1) give greater flexibility to the location of industry and hence to a greater utilization of resources, such as the motor vehicle, electric power, and air transportation; (2) give greater production per man-hour, such as the farm tractor, moving belt assembly, and other forms of automation; and (3) provide a greater utilization of raw materials or the substitution of what is abundant in nature for what is becoming rare.[17]

We are now in the midst of a *cybernetics* revolution. There are machines that operate other machines. These computers are self-corrective—if there is a mistake in the output, a feedback mechanism communicates this information to the computer, which then makes the necessary adjustments.

The United States will remain at the forefront of production technology in the foreseeable future because it spends vast sums of money on research and development (known in the field as R & D). Government and industry share the expense, with the government paying the larger share. Bell Telephone, General Electric, Eastman Kodak, and DuPont are among the most active private companies engaged in research. Most of the research is in the military and space industries. However, much of the knowledge acquired in these areas can be transferred to other fields. Most of the government expenditures on R & D are utilized by private firms, and the rest of it is used by government agencies and universities. In some specific fields, Japan, West Germany, and other countries have surpassed U.S. technology.

R & D in Industry
Research is vital to the improvement of production technology. Computers play an increasingly important role in many aspects of modern research and development.

Consumer Satisfaction and Rationality

Consumer satisfaction and rationality are the most difficult to measure of all the performance criteria for evaluating an economic system. Despite the distortions created by oligopolistic decision making and by advertising, the American economy quantitatively must be ranked high in consumer satisfaction because Americans do vote yes or no with their dollars, and their votes are effective. American businesses generally take a value-free position regarding the goods and services they produce—whether they be peace medals or Polaris missiles. However, qualitatively many American consumers are dissatisfied and are turning increasingly to imported products.

Rationality is another matter. In the private sector there is prosperity; but in the public sector there is poverty. Americans have waged and won the battle for abundant consumer goods; but housing, health care, and Headstart programs are not adequately funded. Our prisons and mental hospitals are a disgrace. There is a great need for efficient mass transit systems. We need to increase expenditures on education. Instead of encouraging people to increase their consumption of material goods, we should provide them with more parks, concert halls, art galleries, public libraries, theaters, sports arenas, vocational training and adult education centers and other artistic, educational, and recreational facilities. We need to emphasize the *quantity* of life less, and the *quality* of life more. We need to stop considering all public spending a waste and recognize that more of it, well spent, can substantially improve the lives of all Americans. We need to stop considering planned obsolescence in the private sector something that is "good for the economy" and recognize it for the waste that it is. And we need to take a careful look at our economy's effects on the environment.

Ecological Effects

As the world's greatest producers, Americans are also the world's greatest polluters. In addition to production-related polluting, environmental deterioration is also caused by population growth and urbanization. Society must choose between continuing to produce traditional goods and services at current levels despite the accompanying harm to the environment, or reducing traditional production in order to improve the environment. This is called the production-environment trade-off. The three main ecological trade-offs are described in Table 15-15.

We need **zero population growth,** more resources devoted to environmental protection and less to traditional goods and services; and we need smaller, less densely populated cities. To the extent that Americans are willing to make these trade-offs, environmental deterioration can be reduced. However, such a move would require a reversal of historical trends and strongly held values. The right to bear children—as many as one desires—is a cherished right that few Americans seem willing to

Table 15-15
Ecological Trade-offs

Category of Trade-off	Losses	Gains
Population-Environment	Curtailment of "right" to unrestrained child-bearing.	Improves prospects for a better environment for the living. Takes some of the pressure off natural resources. Helps avoid an eventual ecological catastrophe.
Production-Environment	Some traditionally measured GNP.	Better environmental protection. Higher effective levels of living through less pollution (cleaner air, cleaner water, quieter surroundings). More resources devoted to wise land-use planning, resulting in a more pleasing environment and more aesthetic surroundings.
Urbanization-Environment	Some of the scale advantages of the mega-cities	Some advantages of a sense of community or of neighborhood resulting from lower population densities.

Source: Phillips W. Foster, *Introduction to Environmental Science* (Homewood, Ill.: Richard Irwin, 1972), p. 121.

relinquish. Voluntary restraints are considered acceptable, even desirable; but legal ones are not.

An ever-increasing standard of living, measured in quantifiable terms, is almost synonymous with "the American way of life." It would be difficult indeed to convince Americans, especially those near the bottom of the economic ladder, to give up this goal. A reversal of urbanization may not be so difficult to achieve. For the first half of the twentieth century, Americans moved from rural to urban areas. Since the end of World War II they have been moving out of the central cities and into the suburbs. The tranquility, safety, and cleanliness of the countryside are now luring many people out of the suburbs and into such areas. Some are even migrating to countries such as Australia and New Zealand which offer the beauty of unspoiled nature. It remains to be seen if Americans are willing to make the trade-offs necessary to protect the environment at home, or if they are just going to leave. The federal government created a $1.6 billion superfund in 1980 to clean up the 546 most dangerous toxic waste sites in the country, out of an estimated 22,000. By the end of 1984, only six had been cleaned up

The Production-Environment Trade-off
Zero population growth, fewer goods and services, smaller cities, and commitment of extensive funds for ecology could be traded for an improved environment. Are enough Americans willing to make the trade?

totally. Congress allocated more billions, but as of the end of 1988, the Reagan Administration was still dragging its feet. The early appointment of people like James Watt, Ann Gorsuch, and Rita Lavelle, who used to work for polluting industries, did not augur well for the cleaning up of the environment. The situation did not improve in the Bush administration. Clinton, however, appointed strong environmentalists to top positions and has started to revamp the superfund program.

REFERENCES

1. Statistics on natural resources were compiled from the following sources: *Statistical Abstract of the United States: 1980;* Shepard D. Clough and Theodore F. Marburg, *The Economic Basis of American Civilization* (New York: Thomas Y. Crowell, 1968), pp. 17–34; *The Times Atlas of the World,* comprehensive edition (Boston: Houghton Mifflin, 1967), p. xxiv; *The Odyssey World Atlas* (New York: Golden Press, 1967), pp. 28–31.
2. Phillips W. Foster, *Introduction to Environmental Science* (Homewood, Ill.: Richard D. Irwin, 1972), p. 32.

3. Two excellent sources on this subject are Bert G. Hickman, *Investment Demand and U.S. Economic Growth* (Washington D.C.: Brookings Institution, 1965) and Raymond G. Goldsmith, *Capital Market Analysis and the Financial Accounts of the Nation* (Morristown, N.J.: General Learning Press, 1972).

4. United States Bureau of the Census, *Current Population Reports,* Series P-60, no. 157, 1986.

5. Thorstein Veblen, *The Theory of the Leisure Class* (New York: Modern Library, 1934).

6. The essence of the era is captured by Matthew Josephson in *The Robber Barons* (New York: Harcourt, 1934).

7. See Herbert Spencer, *Social Statics* (New York: Appleton and Co., 1880) and William Graham Sumner, *Essays of William Graham Sumner,* ed. by A. G. Keller and M. R. Davie, Vol. 2 (New Haven: Yale University Press, 1934).

8. Robin M. Williams, "Major Structural Characteristics of the Present American Economy," in *Understanding American Society,* ed. by Robert C. Atchley (Belmont, Calif.: Wadsworth, 1971), p. 76.

9. *Ibid.*

10. Robert J. Lampman, cited by Donald W. Calhoun, *Social Science in an Age of Change* (New York: Harper, 1971), p. 366.

11. Williams, p. 74. See also Thomas Dye, *Who's Running America,* 4th ed. (Englewood Cliffs, N.J.: Prentice Hall, 1986).

12. Clair Wilcox, Willis Weatherford, Jr., Holland Hunter, and Morton Baratz, *Economies of the World Today* (New York: Harcourt Brace Jovanovich, 1966), p. 150.

13. Wilcox, p. 166.

14. Arthur M. Okun, *The Battle Against Unemployment,* rev. ed. (New York: W. W. Norton, 1972), p. xvii.

15. Reported in the *Miami Herald,* December 1, 1984, p. 5A.

16. Reported in the *Washington Post,* February 15, 1985.

17. Clough and Marburg, p. 43.

GLOSSARY

Corporation   A form of business organization in which ownership of the enterprise is divided into equal shares, any of which may be owned by one or more individuals. Corporations are considered separate entities from their owners, and the shareholders are liable only for the amount of money they have invested in the enterprise.

Holding company   A corporation that holds enough of the stock of another corporation to permit it to direct the latter's affairs.

Individual proprietorship   A form of business organization in which one individual owns and manages, assumes all the risks of, and derives all the profits from, an enterprise.

Partnership	A form of business organization created through a contractual arrangement between two or more individuals, each of whom assumes full personal liability for the debts of the joint enterprise.
Trust	A scheme designed to eliminate competition. The voting rights of the majority of the voting stock of two or more corporations are assigned to a number of trustees who then direct the affairs of the corporations to the mutual benefit of all the stockholders. Recently "trust" has been used to designate any large corporation or combinations of corporations exercising monopolistic control over the production or distribution of a particular good or service.

Federal Reserve System	The central banking system of the United States, consisting of twelve regional banks and run by the Federal Reserve Board, which is staffed by members chosen by the government, big banks, and small banks.
Fiscal policies	Approaches to government spending and taxation, designed either to stimulate or depress the economy.
Keynesian economics	Derived from the theories of the twentieth-century British economist John Maynard Keynes, who held that government could and should maintain equilibrium within the economic system by controlling the level of consumption and investment through its fiscal and monetary policies.
Monetary policies	Approaches to the control of the money flow within an economic system by means of a central banking system.
New Deal	A variety of measures initiated by President Franklin D. Roosevelt to promote social security and economic recovery from the Depression in the United States during the 1930s. The various measures dealt with industrial recovery, control of public utility holding companies, farm relief, direct unemployment relief, old-age pensions, and unemployment insurance, among others.
Parity	The condition of being equivalent. The term is often used in regard to the government's policy of guaranteeing prices to farmers for agricultural products by providing farmers with the same buying power they had in whatever year is used as a base.
Discount rate	The interest rate charged by Federal Reserve banks to commercial banks for loans.
Regulated capitalism	A modified market system in which the means of production are almost entirely privately owned, but in which there is also a high degree of government regulation and decision making by large corporate enterprises and to a lesser extent by large labor unions. Example: the American economy.

Reserve requirement	The percentage of deposits that a commercial bank must keep on hand to meet the demands of its depositors. The reserve requirement is determined by the Federal Reserve Board.
Monopoly	The condition of having control over the supply of a product, thus permitting the release of the supply at a rate which yields the most profitable price.
Natural monopoly	A monopoly due either to natural conditions (for example, a monopoly over the oil in the Middle East and the United States) or to characteristics inherent in a particular business (for example, a monopoly over the electricity in a geographical region).
Oligopoly	A market situation in which only a handful of companies dominate an industry. These companies compete in terms of packaging and advertising rather than in terms of price.
Price leadership	The practice in some industries of the largest producer (the price leader) setting prices and the other producers accepting the prices thus set.
Adam Smith	An eighteenth-century British economist who is considered the father of modern economics. Smith believed that a free market in which businessmen were motivated by self-interest and in which competition existed throughout the economic process would produce desired goods and services of the best quality, at the most favorable price for the consumer, and in the optimal quantity.
Conspicuous consumption	Spending money for luxury items for the purpose of demonstrating that one has the means to make such purchases rather than for the satisfaction of a normal consumer demand.
Muckrakers	A group of American writers who exposed unscrupulous and unhealthy business practices in the United States in the late nineteenth and early twentieth centuries.
Social Darwinism	A social philosophy prevalent in the latter part of the nineteenth and early part of the twentieth century. Social Darwinists believed that people who were fit to survive would rise to the top of a society and those who were unfit to survive would sink to the bottom. Social Darwinism, then, offered scientific sanction for the exploitation of workers by the "captains of industry."
Zero population growth	The condition that exists when population size remains constant because the number of births and deaths are equal to one another.

SELECTED READING

Fortune, April issue.

> Every April, Fortune Magazine publishes lists of the top U.S. companies in sales, profits, and other statistics.

Hornbeck, David W. and Lester M. Salamon, Ed., Human Capital and America's Future (Baltimore: Johns Hopkins University Press, 1991).

Income, Poverty, and Wealth in the United States: A Chart Book, U.S. Bureau of the Census, Current Population Reports, Series P-60, No. 179, U.S. Government Printing Office, 1992.

> Annual statistical analysis of a variety of economic indicators.

Keynes, John Maynard, *The General Theory of Employment, Interest, and Money* (New York: Harcourt Brace Jovanovich, 1964).

> This classic work on Keynsian economics was originally published in 1936.

Malkin, Lawrence, *The National Debt* (New York: Mentor, 1988).

> The author explains how America became the world's largest debtor nation, what it means, and what steps need to be taken to turn the situation around.

Reich, Robert, *The Next American Frontier* (New York: Times Books, 1983).

> Outstanding analysis by our current Secretary of Labor of the problems in the U.S. economy, and suggestions for reversing the downturn that began around 1970.

Skinner, Andrew, ed., *Adam Smith: The Wealth of Nations* (New York: Penguin).

> The first scholarly interpretation of Capitalism was Adam Smith's 1776 publication.

Statistical Abstract of the United States, issued annually.

> Annual statistics of a variety of economic, political, health, social and other indicators in the United States.

UNICEF study on children and poverty, September, 1993.

> This is the foremost publication on worldwide poverty among children.

World Development Report, 1992.

> Annual economic and other indicators for almost all the countries in the world. An excellent source for comparing relative changes on a global scale.

QUESTIONS

1. Before 1837, the American economy was primarily
   a. agricultural.
   b. industrial.

    c. growing at a rapid pace.

    d. balanced between industry and agriculture.

    e. dependent on international trade.

2. The ethnic group with the highest poverty rate in America is:
   a. Hispanic Americans
   b. Black Americans
   c. Anglo Americans
   d. Jewish Americans

3. Capital investment in the United States increased at the turn of the century for a number of reasons. Which of the following was *not* one of them?
   a. the invention of the cotton gin and the subsequent revolution in clothing manufacture
   b. the invention of the telephone and the building of telephone systems
   c. the harnessing of electricity and the subsequent construction of electric power plants
   d. the invention of the internal combustion engine and the subsequent building of roads and highways
   e. the discovery and exploitation of large oil deposits

4. Since 1980, the income structure of the United States has
   a. been altered in favor of the poor.
   b. been altered in favor of the rich.
   c. been altered in favor of the middle class.
   d. remained basically unchanged.
   e. remained the same for the middle class, while the poor have improved relative to the rich.

5. The American economy generally emphasizes
   a. consumer goods.
   b. capital goods.
   c. a high propensity to save.
   d. rapid economic growth.
   e. laissez-faire economic policies.

6. Which of the following characteristics does *not* apply to the American economy?
   a. Practically all the means of production are privately owned.
   b. The government pursues laissez-faire economic policies.
   c. Government policies have a great impact on the economy's performance because the government is the largest spender in the economy.
   d. Most natural monopolies are privately owned.

7. The term which best characterizes American industry is
   a. monopoly.

b. perfect competition.
c. oligopoly.
d. price competition.

8. According to Adam Smith, in a capitalist market economy production decisions are ultimately made by
   a. consumers.
   b. managers.
   c. stockholders.
   d. government.

9. The government's attempt to cope with the Great Depression was called
   a. the Fair Deal.
   b. the New Deal.
   c. the Square Deal.
   d. the Great Society.
   e. the New Frontier.

10. The United States is number one in the world in which of the following categories?
   a. per capita GNP (highest)
   b. life expectancy (highest)
   c. infant mortality (lowest)
   d. illiteracy (lowest)
   e. none of the above

QUESTIONS FOR THOUGHT AND DISCUSSION

1. How does the United States compare with other industrialized countries in life expectancy, infant mortality, higher education, unemployment, inflation, economic growth, and per capita GNP?

2. Compare the economic theories of Adam Smith, Karl Marx, and John Maynard Keynes.

3. Explain supply-side economics, and its impact on the U.S. economy.

4. How has income been distributed in the United States under different presidents?

16

Alternative Economic Systems

Nothing in modern history has had a greater impact on people throughout the world than the *Industrial Revolution*. Beginning in England around 1750, it spread to other European states and then across the Atlantic Ocean to the Western Hemisphere. Its effects were felt even in remote areas as a search for new markets and raw materials developed. The Industrial Revolution held out the promise of a new day: a day in which an advanced production technology would eliminate poverty from the face of the earth. But, to the wage-slave in a nineteenth-century sweatshop, it must have seemed an empty promise, a hoax, an evil curse. The factories and the mines bent, twisted, and maimed the minds and bodies of men, women, and even of little children. British Parliamentary investigating committees uncovered the worst abuses still raging in the 1830s and 1840s. The following is taken from the transcripts of two such investigations:

> What age are you?—Twenty-three.
> Where do you live?—At Leeds.
> What time did you begin to work at a factory?—When I was six years old. . . .
> What kind of mill is it?—Flax mill.
> What was your business in that mill?—I was a little doffer.
> What were your hours of labor in that mill?—From five in the morning till nine at night, when they were thronged.
> For how long a time together have you worked that excessive length of time?—For about half a year.
> What were your usual hours of labor when you were not so thronged?—From six in the morning till seven at night.

What time was allowed for your meals?—Forty minutes at noon.

Had you any time to get your breakfast or drinking?—No, we got it as we could....

Your labor is very excessive?—Yes; you have not time for any thing.

Suppose you flagged a little, or were too late, what would they do?—Strap us....

Girls as well as boys?—Yes.

Have you ever been strapped?—Yes.

Severely?—Yes....

Supposing you had not been in time enough in the morning at these mills, what would have been the consequences?...If we were a quarter of an hour too late, they would take off half an hour; we only got a penny an hour, and they would take a halfpenny more.[1]

My father has been dead about a year; my mother is living and has ten children, five lads and five lasses; the oldest is about thirty, the youngest is four; three lasses go to mill; all the lads are colliers, two getters and three hurriers; one lives at home and does nothing; mother does nought but look after home.

All my sisters have been hurriers, but three went to the mill. Alice went because her legs swelled from hurrying in cold water when she was hot. I never went to day-school; I go to Sunday-school, but I cannot read or write; I go to pit at five o'clock in the morning and come out at five in the evening; I get my breakfast of porridge and milk first; I take my dinner with me, a cake, and eat it as I go; I do not stop or rest any time for the purpose; I get nothing else until I get home, and then have potatoes and meat, not every day meat. I hurry in the clothes I have now got on, trousers and ragged jacket; the bald place upon my head is made by thrusting the corves; my legs have never swelled, but sisters' did when they went to mill; I hurry the corves a mile and more under ground and back; they weigh 300 cwt.; I hurry eleven a day; I wear a belt and chain at the workings to get the corves out; the getters that I work for are naked except their caps; they pull off all their clothes; I see them at work when I go up; sometimes they beat me, if I am not quick enough, with their hands; they strike me upon my back; the boys take liberties with me; sometimes they pull me about; I am the only girl in the pit; there are about 20 boys and 15 men; all the men are naked; I would rather work in mill than in coal-pit.[2]

The British experience was duplicated in varying degrees in other countries. The inhumanity that accompanied the early period of industrialization led many people to believe that there was some inherent evil in the capitalist economic system. Their proposed solutions varied, but almost all sought to restructure the economy along socialist lines. They can generally be grouped into three categories: Utopian socialists, Fabian socialists, and Marxists. The Utopians withdrew from society and formed their own communities; the Fabians managed to restructure the economy peacefully by working within the system; and the Marxists sought change by overthrowing capitalism and substituting a

Exploitation of Child Labor
These young boys worked as mine helpers in West Virginia circa 1900.

collectively owned, centrally directed economy. We will now analyze each of these varieties of socialism and examine examples of each.

Utopian Socialism

There have been three types of utopian thinkers.[3] One type is primarily a philosopher, one who is interested in pointing out what is wrong with existing societies and in developing the characteristics of an ideal community. A second type creates such ideal communities in works of fiction, either with the hope that the dream will be realized someday, or as a literary exercise that will stimulate thought. A third type is the activist—an organizer. This type initiates or at least participates in the formation of an ideal community. Of course it is possible for one person to play all three roles; and many utopian thinkers have done so.

The appeal of an ideal social arrangement is irresistible to many people. The thought of creating a perfect society, free of all the social ills that plague humankind, one that will bring forth people's good qualities, can be an exhilarating experience. Of course one person's utopia may be another one's dystopia. There is no universal consensus on what constitutes an ideal life or an ideal society. There may be widespread agreement on a few basic features, such as adequate food, clothing, and shelter; but once one goes beyond the basic necessities disagreement increases.

In every case utopian thinking has been linked to social goals. Utopians ask the question, "What should be the goals of an ideal social order?" The answers have more often been provided in literary utopias than in systematically reasoned philosophical dissertations. People generally seem to be more interested if such arguments are presented within the framework of a novel. Thus, Edward Bellamy (*Looking Backward*), H. G. Wells (*A Modern Utopia*), and B. F. Skinner (*Walden Two*) were far more successful with their novels than with their books, articles, and essays. Even that great defender of capitalism, Ayn Rand, reached her largest audiences in such novels as *Atlas Shrugged* and *The Fountainhead*. Sometimes utopian novels are written as a warning of some dangerous future possibility—dystopia—such as George Orwell's *1984*. Aldous Huxley wrote both of dystopia (*Brave New World*) and his version of utopia (*Island*). In every case these and other utopian writers were disseminating their social philosophies using a literary form.

Let us turn now to those who created utopian communities, those who built upon their dreams. These are the people who heeded the advice of Henry David Thoreau: "If you have built castles in the air, your work need not be lost; that is where they should be. Now put the foundations under them."

Robert Owen

Robert Owen was perhaps the most influential utopian of all. At twenty-nine years of age he was the manager of the industrial town of New Lanark, Scotland. There he implemented his philosophy, whose central thesis was that people are infinitely malleable. Individuals, he said, are conditioned by their surroundings and are capable of leading happy and productive lives given the proper environment. Owen was an early believer in behavioral (or social) engineering. Given the proper incentives, said Owen, an individual's best potentialities can be realized. He practiced what he preached.

At New Lanark workers were provided with decent housing, good working conditions, adequate pay, education for their children (who were not allowed to work), and aesthetic surroundings at home and at work. The mills at New Lanark were immensely profitable, and young Owen amassed a fortune. He became the most popular man in Europe. But he was still not satisfied. Although his employees were far better off than their contemporaries who worked for other industrialists, Owen felt that they should enjoy the full fruits of their labor, including the vast profits they produced for their employers.

Consequently, he expanded his theories of social organization to include the concept of "villages of unity and cooperation." These villages were to be self-contained units of about a thousand inhabitants. The people would own the means of production collectively and share equally in the benefits derived therefrom. All would live and work together in a great spirit of cooperation. After failing to convince Parliament of the necessity of publicly financing such ideal communities,

Owen decided to sell his financial interests in New Lanark and personally found such an experiment in America.

This man, who had fought for years and finally persuaded Parliament to pass the first law limiting the working hours of women and children (in 1812), bought a complete village in southwest Indiana in 1825. It consisted of 30,000 acres bought from the Rappites, a religious colony of Germans who had founded their own utopia called Harmonie. Owen renamed the village "New Harmony." His reputation was such that he was invited to explain his plans to the President of the United States and to the House of Representatives. The rules and regulations he established for New Harmony included the abolition of private property, religion, and marriage.

Owen's first and fatal mistake was to entrust others to operate the community for the first year, while he returned to England. A certain disharmony also prevailed because he did not screen the 900 residents carefully. Although there were many intelligent and hard-working New Harmonites, there were also many less industrious types who came to enjoy Mr. Owen's hospitality.

Business did not flourish. Medicine and "the necessities" were provided to the inhabitants free of charge. Food and clothing were provided as well as free education for the children. Dances and concerts were held once a week, and five military companies were maintained. All this apparently was at Mr. Owen's expense. The venture failed to pay its way, and its generous founder lost 80 percent of his wealth on this social experiment. The experiment, however, was not an unqualified

New Harmony
Robert Owen's experimental village failed through neglect and poor management.

failure. Many of its creative inhabitants succeeded in effecting social reforms throughout the Midwest. New Harmony's educational innovations—its nursery school, kindergarten, and trade school, and especially its free public school system—had a lasting effect on the United States.

Meanwhile, back in England, the Consumer Cooperative movement began as a result of Owen's writings. When he returned to England, he founded the world's first labor federation, the Grand National. Its initial success was a measure of his popularity. However, after reaching a membership of approximately one-half million, the federation declined rapidly.

Although Owen undoubtedly had a great impact on subsequent history, it was not due to his utopian experiments. Rather he is known as the "father of British socialism" because of the important role he played in the cooperative and labor movements. These groups became the rank and file of the British Labour party founded in 1908.

John Humphrey Noyes

New Harmony was a secular utopia; many others had a religious orientation. One of the more interesting examples of a religious utopia was the Oneida Community in New York State, founded in 1847 by John Humphrey Noyes.[4] This utopia combined Biblical communism and free love. He called his philosophy "perfectionism." He found in the Bible justification for common ownership of property. What distinguished Noyes from other Christian socialists was that he included people in his definition of property. Owning people was considered the same as owning property! He defined ownership as "exclusiveness with regard to women and children." This led to his plan of "multiple marriage." One should not love one another in pairs, but as a group. Each person was married to all. This would give free rein to everyone's "amative" or love impulses; it would certainly reduce adultery; and young people would be able to satisfy their sexual desires without waiting until they become of conventional marriage age.

Noyes did not view this arrangement as sinful in any way. He did not consider it to be "free love" since everyone was in permanent union with everyone else and everyone provided for the support of any children that might result from such unions. Noyes explained it thus: "Free love with us does *not* mean freedom to love today and leave tomorrow; nor freedom to take a woman's person and keep our property to ourselves; nor freedom to freight a woman with her offspring and send her downstream without care or help; nor to regret children and leave them to the street and the poorhouse. Our community are *families*, as distinctly bounded and separated from promiscuous society as ordinary households."[5] The elders controlled the propagation of children and sug-

Women Bookkeepers at the Oneida Community
The Community combined radical ideas of sexual equality and property with a strong Biblical strain and earnest hard work.

gested that the young of one sex should be paired off with the aged of the other sex.

In order to accomplish "perfectionism" Noyes insisted that "the sin system, the marriage system, the work system, and the death system, were all one, and must be abolished together."[6] In this way, he said, "holiness, free-love, association in labor, and immortality constituted the chain of redemption and must come together in their true order."[7]

According to those who visited the Oneida Community, it flourished for over thirty years primarily because of good management and hard work. If it had not been for the negative view taken by its neighbors, particularly regarding the sexual arrangements, the community might have continued longer in its existing state. Instead, in 1881 it was transformed into a joint stock company, Oneida Community, Ltd., which still functions prosperously as a manufacturer of silverware.

While it lasted it lived by three principles postulated by Noyes: moral continence, multiple marriage, and mutual criticism. Free sexual intercourse between any consenting partners was encouraged; but haphazard procreation was discouraged. Thus, moral continence, the practice of "self-control," was used as a form of birth control. Mutual criticism was a practice whereby people would criticize each other in order to correct each other's faults. Noyes believed this would lead to moral improvement and fellowship. Multiple marriage and moral continence provided women with sexual equality and control of their reproductive functions. Thus women's liberation and sensitivity training flourished at Oneida.

The community contained factories, farms, orchards, and cattle. It produced a variety of goods with great care which gained for the community a reputation for skilled workmanship. Its membership included professionals, as well as farmers and mechanics. Artistic endeavors were encouraged, and the people enjoyed a library with 5,000 volumes, and many newspapers and periodicals. A printing press was extensively used to disseminate all kinds of messages, most of which emanated from the prolific pen of the charismatic leader, John Noyes.

Impact of Utopian Socialism

In the United States there were over 170 utopian experiments in the nineteenth century. Some survived for many years; others collapsed within a few months. Some were religious, and some were secular. Some practiced celibacy, and others engaged in free love. It was a century of social experiments in America, and, although none of the utopian experiments survived in their original forms, many of them introduced new ideas which continue to influence American thought and behavior to the present time. The utopians were quite different from each other and they varied in their impact on society. However, they also shared some important characteristics: They believed that people are basically good, their characters infinitely malleable and susceptible to environmental conditioning; they saw injustice and sought to banish it by restructuring society according to socialist principles, emphasizing collective ownership of property and of the means of production, and equal distribution of wealth; they sought radical but peaceful changes (none preached violence); they withdrew from the general society to conduct their social experiments; and they believed that reforming the economic system would improve the overall quality of life.

The emergence of communal experiments in the last third of the twentieth century indicates that the idea of utopia is still alive and well, even though the "castles in the air" still seem to have shaky foundations.

☐ Marxism–Leninism

A different reaction to the dehumanizing effects of the Industrial Revolution is embodied in the philosophy of Karl Marx, an angry man who saw in capitalism a system of degrading exploitation of the working class. Marx developed a theory of historical development which indicated that historical evolution would culminate in a final stage in which pure communism would prevail.[8]

Marx was influenced by many of the intellectual trends of his time. It was an age in which intellectuals believed that every aspect of life is governed by laws of nature; and that humans, through the exercise of their reason, could discover and understand these natural laws. It was an era in which people placed science and reason on a pedestal, and

Karl Marx and Friedrich Engels
This proved to be one of the most significant partnerships in history.

Karl Marx was a devout worshiper—a true believer. He synthesized the ideas of the British classical economists, French political theorists, and German philosophical idealists. He was even influenced by St. Simon, the French utopian socialist, although it was Marx who first used the term "utopian" in a derogatory manner to distinguish his own "scientific socialism" from previous theories. But it was the deep and widespread suffering of the men, women, and children who toiled in the mines and factories that fueled his passions.

When Marx attended the University of Berlin in 1836, he came under the influence of Hegelian philosophy. George W. F. Hegel had developed a philosophy of change, with ideas as the causative factors for that change. By ideas he meant what is currently referred to as ideologies or belief systems. Each period in history has an ideology which explains and justifies the existing social system. Each society also produces a group of dissidents who are unhappy with the system and who reject the ideology. Hegel referred to these opposing forces as *thesis* and *antithesis*. In the ensuing struggle the two merge into a *synthesis* which contains the best features of both. A new social system is then created based upon the new belief system. This represents a higher stage in human development.

Historical development is a continuous process; therefore the synthesis now becomes a new thesis which causes its antithesis as a reaction to it, and they eventually merge into a synthesis. Each synthesis transforms society and represents a higher stage of historical development. Hegel referred to this pattern—thesis-antithesis-synthesis—as a dialectical pattern. Since he considered great ideas to be the generating force for historical change, he called his philosophy of history *dialectical idealism*. This process is shown in the diagram below.

Dialectical Idealism

Thesis ⟶ Antithesis
Syn(thesis) ⟶ Antithesis
Synthesis ⟶ etc.

At first Marx was totally convinced by Hegel's philosophy, but he later modified it extensively. In fact, he completely reversed the cause and effect relationship of ideas and material factors. After reading St. Simon's writings, Marx became convinced that economic factors, not ideas, are responsible for historical change. Marx's economic interpretation of history is called **dialectical materialism.**

Dialectical Materialism

Marx borrowed the dialectical pattern from Hegel, but in place of ideas he substituted economic factors as the dynamic force in history. Economic circumstances determine everything else, including ideas. Marx's followers claim that he found Hegel standing on his head, and he turned him right side up. History, said Marx, is a series of class struggles. Every society, regardless of its level of technology, has two main social classes: the owners of the means of production (the exploiters) and those who work for them (the exploited).

The relationship between owners and workers varies according to the level and type of production technology. The relationships are different, for example, between an agricultural and an industrial economy. Even within these categories there are significant differences. A small farmer with one or two employees treats his workers differently than does a large landowner with many employees. The relationship between workers and owners is different in a small machine shop than it is in General Motors. Marx referred to this as the **social relations of production.** He considered it to be coequal in importance with the mode of production; that is, the technology of production. These two factors are the most important aspects of any economic system, and they are closely interrelated.

The mode of production and the social relations of production determine the characteristics of the class struggle. The owning class is the thesis; by exploiting those who work for them it creates its antithesis. Periodically technological advancements create a new mode of production, thereby rendering the existing social relations of production obsolete. Quite often a new class rises to power if the owners of the old means of production do not acquire the new means of production. The new group then overthrows the old group and transforms society (synthesis).

Marx assumed that government is an inherently evil institution created by the dominant class (the owners), which it uses to keep the subservient class in line. The dominant class uses the government to impose its values on the general society and to change the entire culture for its own benefit. Economic power leads to political power which is then used to perpetuate economic privilege. Thus, whenever there are new owners of the means of production, there must be a change in government.

Marx claimed that the economic system is the substructure, or foundation, which shapes the social, political, and ideological "superstructure" at each stage in history. Just as the foundation determines the shape of a house (one cannot build a rectangular house on a square foundation), so the economic system gives form and meaning to the culture and civilization of those who live within that society.

Historical Materialism

Historical materialism is an explanation of the past, the present, and the future using the theoretical model described above (dialectical materialism). According to Marx, the first stage in human history was *primitive communism*. The principle of private property did not yet exist, because everyone lived in communal groups. Everything was owned collectively and shared according to need. The weakness of the system was that it operated at a poverty level. The people were hunters and gatherers who lived in nomadic tribes. Since there was no surplus that anyone could accumulate, survival depended upon a high degree of cooperation. Competitiveness under these material circumstances would have spelled the end of human existence.

Eventually, some of the groups began a primitive type of horticulture and agriculture. Wars led to the taking of prisoners who were made into slaves. Thus, class conflict began. Under *slavery* the two antagonistic classes were slaves and slaveowners. Not only was the concept of private property introduced, but it also included human beings under that definition.

Advancing agricultural technology made the system of slavery obsolete. It ushered in the feudal system comprised of feudal nobles and their vassals or serfs. Large agricultural landholdings became the dominant means of production, and those who held these estates became the exploiting class.

Spreading Propaganda
Communist party members are shown here distributing literature in February of 1917, paving the way for the revolution in Russia that took place in November.

The emergence of the Industrial Revolution made feudalism obsolete. The new ruling class of capitalists then restructured society to suit their purposes. Marx explained that the French Revolution (1789) removed the landed aristocracy from political power, and substituted in its place the newly rising class of capitalists who owned the factories and the mines. Thus, capitalism replaced feudalism. Marx said that the two antagonistic classes now were the **bourgeoisie** (capitalists) and the **proletariat** (workers).

That is how Marx explained historical development up to his time. He also believed that his theory could help him predict the future. He held that fluctuations in the business cycle, which seem to be endemic to capitalism, would lead to a greater concentration of wealth. Each decline in the business cycle would cause some of the marginal members of the bourgeoisie to lose their property and to become members of the proletariat. Thus they would have nothing left to sell but their labor.

Whenever the economy recovered and prospered once again, the new proletarians could not return to their former status because they lacked the capital to reenter the market as businessmen. Consequently each contraction of the economy allowed the larger businesses to absorb the smaller ones. The result was that periodically the bourgeoisie would get smaller and richer, while the proletariat would become larger and poorer. Eventually the proletariat would realize that their poverty and suffering could only be ended by changing the economic system. Hence they would develop class consciousness, unite, overthrow the government, and institute a *dictatorship of the proletariat.*

In this historical stage, the means of production would be collectively owned by the workers. The operating principle of the system would be "from each according to his ability, to each according to his *work.*" This antithesis to capitalism was to be a temporary stage which eventually would transform itself into the final stage in history—*pure communism.*

The operating principle of pure communism is "from each according to his ability, to each according to his *need.*" Its main characteristics would be great material abundance, a classless society, the withering away of government, and a population shorn of selfishness and imbued with generosity. Getting from the dictatorship of the proletariat to pure communism is not clearly explained by Marx, but this is what we have been able to deduce from his writings.

When the proletariat takes over, the bourgeoisie is eliminated. Thus a classless society replaces class struggle. Since Marx believed the only governmental function was the exploitation of the class that does not own the means of production by the class that does, the government would now wither away. It would disappear because now only one class would remain, and that class would collectively own the means of production. There would be no one left to exploit. The government withers away when the classless society emerges; "the government of persons is replaced by the administration of things, and by the conduct of processes of production."

Hegel had said that the dialectic never ends. Marx claimed that the dialectical process ends because there is no antithesis to pure communism. No class is being exploited or subordinated in any way. No one would be motivated to attack a system that is good for all. One might suppose that to question Marx on this would be like asking Adam if he was being unfaithful to Eve. His reply would be "with whom?"

Marxian Economics

Marx meticulously spelled out in detail how capitalism would inevitably collapse because it contained the seeds of its own destruction (the proletariat). But he was very vague on what would follow. *The Communist Manifesto,* which he coauthored in 1848 with Friedrich Engels, expounded his philosophy in general terms. It was basically an emotional call to action. His most scholarly work, in which he explained "scientifically" the downfall of capitalism, was *Das Kapital,* published in three volumes between 1867 and 1895. The last two volumes were put together by Engels after Marx's death in 1883 and published posthumously.

In *Das Kapital*, Marx explained the demise of capitalism employing the following theories:

1. **The Labor Theory of Value.** The value of a product is the amount of human labor required to produce it, including the labor it took to produce any machines involved in production.

2. **The Subsistence Theory of Wages.** The value of labor in the market is the socially necessary labor it takes to keep the laborer alive. No matter how many hours worked, only subsistence wages will be received.

3. **The Theory of Surplus Value.** This is value created by the workers that they do not receive. Workers are forced to work more hours than their own subsistence demands, but they are only paid enough to subsist. If they need to work only six hours to provide for their subsistence, but they work twelve hours, the employer pays them a subsistence wage and keeps the rest as profit. This is a form of exploitation, Marx said.

4. **The Gravedigger Theory of Capitalism.** According to Marx the collapse of capitalism will occur in the following manner: In order to expand output at the expense of their competitors, some capitalists will increase wages to attract more labor. Other businessmen then introduce labor-saving machinery in their plants to compensate for lost workers and to keep wages down. This creates unemployment, and the competition from unemployed workers reduces wages back to a subsistence level. However, the businessman is simultaneously substituting nonprofitable means of production for profitable ones. The businessman, it is assumed, paid full value for the machine, but it is only from living labor that he can realize a profit through the mechanism of surplus value. Therefore, as he reduces the number of his workers his profit rate declines. Yet each capitalist, to get a step ahead of his competitors, increases his effort to place labor-saving machinery in his factory. The result is that the profit rate continues to decline.

Then the recurring business cycles increase in severity. Profits are cut to the point at which production is no longer profitable. Workers cannot buy back the products they produce. Production, on the other hand, is constantly increasing due to the increased amount of machinery. Goods are then sold below value and bankruptcy results. Workers accept wages below subsistence and machinery is sold below value. Eventually recovery occurs. There is an increasing concentration of industry.

During crises bigger firms absorb the smaller ones. The middle class begins to disappear due to the disappearance of small businesses during each successive crisis and due to the increased cost of starting a new business since much machinery is required. Eventually the working class, which is increasing in number, becomes disciplined, united, and dissatisfied enough to overthrow capitalism.

Analysis of Marxism

Critics of Marxism are plentiful. Marx gave us a great deal to work with. One has to struggle mightily to make 7,000 years of recorded human history fit neatly into a dialectical pattern which is supposedly generated by economic determinism and class struggle. Economic factors are very important, as Marx rightly pointed out, but the idea that the variety of life-styles, social structures, ethical systems, artistic tastes, and so forth, that exist among and within societies is a result of the economic substructure is not supported by the facts. Economics is very important, yes; economics is everything, no!

Class struggles have existed and do exist in many countries, but not in all. It is not a universal principle of human history. Democratic socialists and liberal capitalists have brought about major reforms and sometimes a complete restructuring of the economic system with the acquiescence, if not always the consent, of the owners of the means of production.

Nor is Marx very clear on the dialectics of change. Except for the French Revolution which seems to bear out his contention that capitalists replaced a landed aristocracy as a ruling class, there is not much historical evidence to support the rest of the theory. Marx's conclusion is as utopian as the schemes concocted by the utopian socialists that he criticized so vehemently. His prognostication of a future utopia, based upon an alleged law of history, does not appear on the horizon.

Communist countries, led by elites, seem less likely to create a classless society than do Western democracies with welfare economies; and the latter are not likely to experience a withering away of the government either, since the elevation of the less privileged citizens seems to require an expansion of governmental power.

Government is necessary because people's preferences frequently come into conflict. Unless a government exists to mediate these differences and to make decisions on issues in which unanimity is lacking, society will be governed by the law of the jungle. Hence government can never wither away unless everyone agrees on everything—a circumstance not likely to occur among human beings.

In pluralistic democracies the government is not the instrument of any single group. There are many special interest groups that exercise varying degrees of influence over government policy, and usually only in limited areas; no single group runs it.

The misery of the proletariat has not increased in Western democracies, largely due to enlightened government legislation and the growth and power of free labor unions. In some democracies socialist parties have brought about major changes in the economy after gaining power by "ballots" instead of "bullets."

An analysis of Marxian economics must begin with his basic premises. The cornerstone of Marx's analysis is the labor theory of value, which no noncommunist economist accepts today. This primitive economic assumption omits the value of technological know-how, managerial ability, capital formation, natural resources, and the law of supply and demand. Modern economists claim that in many situations the value of a product is its opportunity cost: what one has to give up to acquire it.

A worker's wage level is determined in part by the level of economic development in that country. In advanced, industrialized societies workers receive much more than a subsistence wage, while in underdeveloped countries wages are lower. The type of economic system is of secondary importance, unless it is a command economy in which a small group of leaders may decide to keep wages low in order to increase capital formation. Yet Marx predicted this would occur in capitalist countries.

The theory of surplus value assumes that only those who work with their hands produce value; even most Communist countries today reject this assumption.

It is obvious that Marx had little knowledge of microeconomics. No businessman will purchase a machine for which he has to pay full value, as defined by Marx. He expects to make a profit from the machine. Greater mechanization does not necessarily lead to reduced profits but to greater efficiency; Marx assumed a static labor demand, yet mechanization has actually created more jobs and reduced the human effort involved in the production of goods. Finally, the mentality of businessmen dictates that they will not continue to produce in ever-increasing quantities even though demand for their products decreases.

The reaction against democracy and religion for allowing the conditions of early capitalism to prevail was justified. Marx saw great human suffering all around him during the early stages of industrialization and believed the cause to be some intrinsic evil in the capitalist economic system. He borrowed ideas from anyone whose writings served to support his position. By 1845 he had reached his conclusions and his later writings were attempts to justify them. This process can hardly be called "scientific." But in order to create an effective system Marx had to appeal to the reverence for science and natural laws that prevailed. It was highly significant that Marx emphasized that the dialectic was inevitable, thereby rendering any opposition to it pointless.[9]

Perhaps the most distressing consequence of this dependency on science as the ultimate justification for values was the opportunity it allowed the Marxists to escape the burden of responsibility for their actions. According to them they are merely carrying out the demands of the historical situation and are in no way personally to blame for the unpleasantness required by history. The effects of this historical justification were even worse in Marxism than they were in other similar credos because of the dialectic which not only tolerated evil and distress, but actually expected them and in fact depended on them for the historical dynamics that must in time bring victory.

Marx obviously underestimated the ability of people living under capitalism to control social processes; in short, he was too deterministic. Yet the process had barely begun when Marx died and he was largely justified in his pessimism. We must give him credit for accurately predicting that booms would be followed by depressions. One can hardly blame him for underestimating the tremendous economic growth that occurred after his death and which raised the standard of living to an unprecedented high level. But he can be criticized for not realizing the power of the people in a democracy. He should have noticed the growth in power of common people as the suffrage was extended in England in 1832 and again in 1867 as well as in America. He did mention in a speech in Holland in 1881 that perhaps a revolution was unnecessary in America and England.

Marx's interpretation of history left out the possibility of compromise. He believed the ruling classes always defend their position to the bitter end. If he had only looked around him during his thirty-four years in Britain, he would have seen the Tories making important concessions, instead of rigidly clinging to their power.

What makes Marxism so dangerous is its appeal:

> But in Marxism, the socially conscious intellectual finds more than scientific sanction for his ethically motivated sympathies. He finds as well, because of the particular character of Marx's "scientific" theories, absolute certainty that his ideals will be realized. It was this feature of inevitability that made Marxism then, and continues to make it now, so appealing to young idealists willing enough to run risks in the name of social justice, but eager for assurance that the risks, deprivations, and sacrifices will not be made in vain.[10]

Marx the Man

It is difficult to come to grips with Marx the man. Intellectually he was a child of the enlightenment, particularly the humanist and scientific trends. He was also influenced by British classical economics, French political theory, and German idealism. Basically, Marx was a humanitarian with a great social conscience, yet imbued with an unremitting hatred for those he considered responsible for the misery and suffering he witnessed and experienced throughout much of his lifetime. Paradoxically his own philosophy stated that being members of the economic elite they really could not help acting as they did, because people are all conditioned by their economic circumstances.

Congress of the Communist International, 1935
The Russian Communist pantheon at that time consisted of Marx, Engels, Lenin, and Stalin.

Even if he did overemphasize the role of economic factors in history, he made us aware of the fundamental importance of economics. Although he himself was a primitive economist by modern standards, he provided the world with many insights into capitalism's weaknesses.

Marx was primarily a preacher. However, the age in which he lived made it necessary that his preaching take the garb of science. Nearly one-third of the world adopted his ideas, as modified by Lenin, as its official creed. His impact on history has been enormous.

Lenin

Marx's theories were expanded and modified by Vladimir Lenin, the architect of the first Communist revolution. These are the major changes he made, based upon his evaluation of Marx's writings and his personal experiences as a Marxist revolutionary.[11]

1. *Party as Vanguard.* Marx had stated that the proletariat would develop class consciousness, unite, and overthrow the bourgeois government, and institute a dictatorship of the proletariat. Lenin said this was not true. He said that left to their own devices the proletariat does not develop class consciousness—it only develops trade unions. Therefore it is necessary to create a political party (the Communist party) to act as the vanguard, or leadership, of the proletariat. This is a significant departure from Marxism because it has had very important consequences. Every country that has experienced a violent Communist revolution has a *dictatorship of the party over the proletariat,* instead of a dictatorship of the proletariat.

This is ironic because Marx, who was born in Prussia, the most politically oppressive state in Europe, hated dictatorship. He thought in terms of social classes, not political parties, and would not be happy to see that in so-called communist countries a single political party rules and allows no political freedom. He would say that the proletariat exchanged one group of exploiters for another. It would not be too farfetched to say that if Marx were alive today he would be an anticommunist!

2. *Composition of Party.* The party was to be comprised of a small, highly-disciplined, tightly-knit group of professional revolutionaries. A professional revolutionary is one who devotes his or her entire life to the cause of revolution. He or she subordinates family, regular sources of income, and everything else to the revolutionary cause. Lenin reasoned that a small group of such individuals could wield great power, overthrow the bourgeoisie, and lead the proletariat through the difficult period which would culminate in pure communism. Having a small group would also minimize the possibility of being infiltrated by the Tsar's secret police.

3. *Democratic Centralism.* Party policies could be openly debated before the leaders reach a final decision. However, once the party leaders adopt an official position on any issue all debate is to cease. There can be no revision of the party line and no deviation from it.

4. *One Party State.* Only one party is to be allowed—the Communist party. The proletariat would lead the state; the party would lead the proletariat; and the party would be ruled by the principle of democratic centralism. Since only one social class would be allowed to exist—the proletariat—and since the Communist party is supposed to represent that class, there is no need for any other political party.

5. *The Theory of Imperialistic Wars.* Marx had stated that capitalist countries would collapse because of overproduction of goods which the public could not purchase. Consequently increased mechanization would be counterproductive and would cause the demise of capitalism. However, by 1916 Lenin was in the uncomfortable position of having to explain why capitalism was still thriving long after Marx had made his prediction. As a result, he developed the **theory of imperialistic wars.** In formulating this theory he relied heavily on a book written in 1911 by an English economist named John Hobson. According to Lenin capitalist countries had temporarily averted the calamity predicted by Marx by engaging in imperialism. Through imperialism and colonialism they were able to dump their surplus goods on the underdeveloped nations they conquered. Thus they resolved the immediate pressure of overproduction. They were even able to increase the stan-

dard of living of the proletariat in the advanced industrialized nations. Thus the underdeveloped countries of the world became the proletariat, and everyone in the advanced nations was to be considered part of the world bourgeoisie. Since all capitalist nations would find themselves in the same situation, imperialistic wars would occur among them because there are only a limited number of countries that could be colonized.

6. *War Is Inevitable.* Lenin believed that war between communist and capitalist nations is inevitable. He did not think the two could coexist. Being a pragmatist, however, were he alive today in the nuclear age, he would probably accept the policy of peaceful coexistence.

7. *Tactical Retreats.* Lenin instituted the policy of using tactical retreats when faced with an insuperable obstacle. The important thing, he said, is for the Communist party to survive. If this involves taking one step backward in order to take two steps forward at a later date, then one must retreat. His New Economic Policy in 1921, which was a retreat to capitalism, was a good example of this principle in operation.

8. *The Weakest-Link Theory.* Lenin said that the first communist revolution took place in Russia because the bourgeoisie was weaker in that country, relative to the proletariat, than in any other country. In the chain of capitalist countries Russia was the weakest link. This contrasted with Marxist theory which predicted that the revolution would take place in the most advanced capitalist countries.

☐ The Soviet Union: State Socialism

Marx was basically a utopian even though he would have denied it; Lenin was a skillful organizer and political activist. Marx formed the First Workers International in 1864, which was dissolved in 1876. Lenin took over a faction of the Social Democratic Party (a group of Marxist Russian exiles) in 1903, and he forged a revolution that changed the world. Clearly Lenin's impact on history has been greater than Marx's.

Let us now trace the development of the Soviet economic system from its inception in November 1917 to its demise in 1991. We shall begin by examining the production possibilities.

Natural Resources

Russia occupies approximately one-seventh of the earth's land mass, 8.6 million square miles. Much of it, however, is unfit for human habitation. It is about one-half forest (almost 2.5 billion acres), one-fourth arable land, and one-fourth wasteland. It suffers from harsh weather conditions: a very cold climate and little rainfall. Table 16-1

Table 16-1
Primary Energy
Production, 1987
(percent of world total)

Country/Region	Total Primary Energy	Coal and Lignite	Crude Petroleum	Natural Gas	Hydro and Nuclear Electricity
United States and Canada	23.0%	22.7%	19.1%	29.6%	29.6%
Asia	25.0%	29.8%	30.7%	09.9%	16.6%
Soviet Union	23.3%	17.1%	21.2%	37.9%	10.8%
Europe	14.2%	20.8%	07.4%	13.9%	31.7%

Source: U.S. Bureau of the Census, *Statistical Abstract of the United States: 1990*, p. 853.

shows how in 1987 the Soviet Union compared with the United States and Canada combined and with Europe and Asia, with respect to the production of energy. Tables 16-2 and 16-3 compare several countries with respect to both the production and consumption of energy. The United States and the former Soviet Union rank first and second respectively in both categories. Between them in 1988 they produced 40 percent of the world's energy and consumed over 40 percent. The collapse of the Soviet Union and the Soviet empire and the reunification of Germany between 1989 and 1991 have made it impossible to find accurate statistics for the post-1988 period for Russia and a united Germany.

Table 16-2
Energy Consumption by
Country, 1988 (coal
equivalents)

Country	Total and Percent (million metric tons)	Per Capita (kilograms)
World	10,013.2	1,959
United States	2,057.9 (20.6%)	10,015
Soviet Union	1,953.8 (19.5%)	6,888
China (mainland)	820.1 (8.2%)	756
Japan	480.0 (4.8%)	3,921
West Germany	339.6 (3.4%)	5,594
United Kingdom	282.0 (2.8%)	4,948
Canada	275.0 (2.7%)	10,540
East Germany	129.2 (1.3%)	7,764

Source: U.S. Bureau of the Census, *Statistical Abstract of the United States: 1991*, pp. 854–855.

Human Resources

In 1988, Russia's 283 million inhabitants constituted 7 percent of the world's population. The population is growing at an annual rate of 0.9 percent, the same as the United States. The labor force totals over 130 million. Although population density is low (10 persons per square kilometer), 48 percent of the population lives on 6 percent of the former Soviet Union's territory. The distribution of the labor force forms an interesting contrast with the United States.

Table 16-3
Energy Production by
Country, 1988

Country	Electric Energy Production (billion kwh)	Crude Petroleum Production (million metric tons)	Coal Production (million metric tons)
World	11,026	2,919	3,450
United States	2,857	410.1	783.5
Soviet Union	1,698.4	624.0	599.0
Japan	753.7	0.6	11.2
Canada	504.3	79.2	38.6
China (mainland)	537.8	136.8	346.4
West Germany	428.9	5.6	79.3
United Kingdom	308.2	109.4	101.8
East Germany	118.3	—	—

Source: U.S. Bureau of the Census, *Statistical Abstract of the United States: 1991*, pp. 854–855.

In 1988, the USSR had 14.2 percent of the work force in agriculture, 45 percent in industry, and 41 percent in services. That same year, the United States had only 2 percent of its work force in agriculture, 32 percent in industry, and a whopping 66 percent in services.

In just twenty seven years, the Soviet Union reduced its percentage of the work force engaged in agriculture from 42 to 14. Most of the shift (18 percent) was to industry, and 7 percent was to services. Industrialization, then, is not the only measure of economic advancement. Few people in agriculture and many in services are other measuring devices. The USSR was advancing in all three categories.

Women played a very large role in the Soviet economy. In the Soviet Union women comprise 53.7 percent of the labor force, including 29 percent of construction workers. The comparable figures in the United States are 44 percent of the work force and 3.7 percent in construction.

By world standards the work force is healthy and well educated. People are encouraged to lead productive lives. Thus Russia's human resources are vast, for the most part well-prepared, and highly motivated. The transformation to a market economy, starting in 1991, has had limited success by 1993. The dissolution of the U.S.S.R. has caused turmoil in the 15 former republics. It remains to be seen if Russia can make a successful transition to democracy and a market economy.

Capital Resources

Before 1991, government control had been used to ensure heavy investment in capital goods. Sometimes over 30 percent of production was designated for capital (producer) goods. Part of it replaced worn out or obsolete machinery, and the rest was used to increase national productive capacity. Thus, most of the time, the Soviet Union was able to achieve a high rate of economic growth.

Women in the Soviet Economy
In all areas of the Russian economy, professional as well as technical, women play a significant role.

Technology

Russia joined the Industrial Revolution long after most European countries did. This meant, however, that Russia could take advantage of existing technology. When England began the Industrial Revolution, the machines used were small, requiring the light touch of women and children. Usually, these machines were employed in weaving cloth. By the time Russia got into the act heavy industry had come into being. Thus, contrary to the British, the Russians began with heavy industry; and consequently they developed a small but strong proletariat. Since heavy industry requires large investments, in Russia these came primarily from a few members of the nobility and from foreign investors. Thus Russia did not develop much of a bourgeoisie. This made it easier in 1917 to overthrow a bourgeois government.

Under Stalin, the Soviet Union had industrial spies in all the advanced Western countries, stealing blueprints. The Russians never observed patent rights. More recently, since they have made such dramatic technological advances, they have conducted their own research projects. Since the transition to a market economy, Russia has been plagued with different economic problems than it had under communism. This has caused great discontent as production has declined, unemployment has risen, and expectations of a higher standard of living have been frustrated. The demand for more consumer goods than were available under communism continues after the dissolution of the communist system.

Characteristics and History of the Soviet Economy

The Soviet economy[12] was not a pure command system, but it had more government control over the economy than any of the other economic systems we are studying. Here are some of its main characteristics:

1. *Practically All the Means of Production Are Government Owned.* After the revolution, Lenin moved quickly to implement the spirit of the ideas put forth by Marx. He nationalized large-scale industry; centralized the administration of industry and banking; established workers' councils in all factories to protect proletarian interests; let farmers take over large farms and make collectives out of them; established state control over trade and transportation; and initiated a policy of equalizing wages.

1917–1921—War Communism. The initial period after the revolution was chaotic. Many Russians had not accepted Communist party rule, and Russia suffered a bloody civil war. Admiral Kolchak's White Army was fighting against the Red Army led by Leon Trotsky. In addition, the Allied Powers in World War I sent expeditionary troops into Russia after Lenin pulled Russia out of the war. The Allied intent was to aid the White Army in the hopes of getting Russia back into the war against Germany. Otherwise Germany could concentrate all its troops on the Western front. The Allies left Russia in 1920. By the spring of 1921 the Soviet economy was a shambles.

The war, the allied intervention, poor administration, and a drought caused the Soviet economy to decline drastically. By 1921 industrial production had dropped 85 percent and agricultural production 33 percent below the 1914 level. The Communist party was on very shaky ground. So Lenin decided to institute a tactical retreat in order to save communism. He reintroduced a measure of capitalism.

1921–1928—New Economic Policy (NEP). Trade and transportation were placed in private hands. The government abandoned its efforts to collectivize agriculture. By 1926 the economy had reached the 1914 production level once more. Lenin was incapacitated by a stroke in 1922, and he died in 1924. A struggle for power ensued in which Joseph Stalin and Leon Trotsky were pitted against each other. Among the issues disputed was the method of achieving rapid industrialization—a goal that all Soviet leaders had accepted. Two positions developed. The *rightist position* was that the NEP should be continued indefinitely, because the party was not strong enough to coerce the people into a regimented society. The *leftist position* was that it had been very difficult for Russia merely to regain its 1914 production level; if Russia was to become a top economic power in the world, it would require even greater sacrifices by the people—and the people would not make these sacrifices willingly. Hence, the NEP must be replaced by strict regimentation and great sacrifice. Ironically, Stalin, who held the rightist position, defeated Trotsky and then adopted the leftist position on this issue. By 1928 Stalin was in complete control of the Soviet Union.

1928–1940—First Five-Year Plan and Collectivization of Agriculture. Stalin began the drive toward industrialization by formulating a very ambitious five-year plan. It exceeded its goals and set the stage for a series of five-year plans used by the government ever since. Forced collectivization of agriculture met with great resistance. Stalin then employed police terror tactics and succeeded in collectivizing agriculture by 1933. By his own admission between 5 and 10 million peasants were killed in the process. The peasants resisted collectivization by slaughtering their livestock, burning their grain, and destroying their buildings. As a result, Soviet agricultural production did not reach the 1928 level again until 1958.

Stalin achieved a growth in GNP which averaged 7 percent a year from 1928 to 1940. He achieved this by controlling the terms of trade between industry and agriculture; that is, he starved the agricultural sector of the economy in order to reap a large surplus which was then invested in heavy industry. He controlled the real wages (buying power) of workers by raising prices more rapidly than wages. Thus the workers' standard of living declined as capital goods production increased. And Stalin limited social overhead drastically in order to use that money for heavy industry. Social overhead capital is money spent by governments for roads, education, hospitals, and so forth. Stalin also borrowed heavily from Western technology.

Soviet Agriculture. In the Soviet period 97 percent of the land under cultivation was comprised of collective and state farms. On collective farms each family derived a share of production commensurate with its contribution. Thus some families had higher incomes than others. On state farms workers received wages. The Soviet government preferred the latter arrangement, but the collective farm workers were reluctant to switch. About 18 percent of all agricultural production came from the 3 percent of the land that workers tilled on their own time. They often raised chickens or livestock or grew vegetables. In 1988, then-First Secretary Gorbachev announced plans to lease land to farmers.

2. *There Was Central Control and Planning.* The government directed all production. Planning was conducted by **Gosplan,** the central planning agency. The overall production decisions were made by the leaders of the party. Gosplan then implemented the goals according to a system of priorities, which were (1) defense, (2) heavy industry, (3) light industry, (4) agriculture, and (5) consumer goods.

Plans were made for a period of five years and supplemented by annual plans which showed where the economy was supposed to be at the end of each year. Each factory manager was then given a production quota. The manager was encouraged to reach or exceed his or her quota by a bonus system which could double his or her income. Consequently managers would do practically anything to reach their quotas. After receiving the quota they had to submit requisitions for workers, money, and material required to reach the quota. There was an understandable tendency to exaggerate. That is why 29,000 of the 30,000 Gosplan employees were out in the field (the others were in Moscow)—in order to check on the requisitions to determine if they were reasonable. Managers tended to resist technological innovations because they upset the system devised by the managers to earn their bonuses. The quota was usually increased when new machines were introduced.

There is much waste when central planning is as detailed as it was in the Soviet Union. If a mistake is made it tends to have a snowballing effect. A shortage in steel, for example, means that all the other production processes that require steel won't be able to reach their quotas. And everyone they furnish with processed materials won't be able to meet their quotas, and so on. Since production quotas are usually given in terms of quantity, quality and style are usually ignored. For example, the manager of a shoe firm may produce a lot of small-sized shoes and not enough large sizes because this mix requires less leather. This actually happened in the Soviet Union. There was nearly a riot in one part of the country because shoes were falling apart on people's feet. Needless to say, style was largely ignored in their system.

3. *After 1965 the Soviet Leaders Changed in Part to a Profit and Loss System.* In order to earn their bonuses managers had to show a profit in addition to reaching a quantitative quota. The managers were not guaranteed that the state would purchase their products; they had to send salespeople to the retail outlets to convince other managers to buy their products. Consequently more attention was then paid to quality and style. Workers were also given material incentives for productivity

High Quality Machinery for Energy Industry
Senior foreman at the turbogenerator's workshop and a team leader of assemblers work at the "Electrotyazhmash" works in the Ukraine.

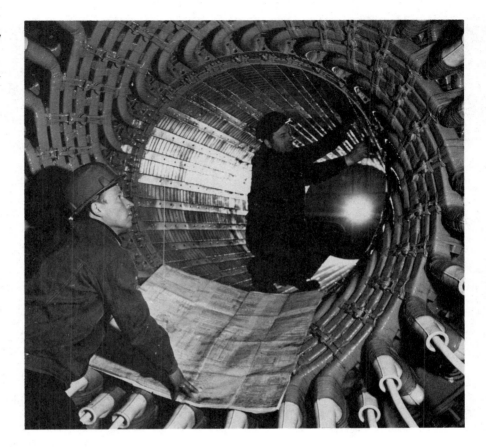

instead of hero medals. The profit and loss system was used primarily in consumer goods production. Until 1960 the Soviet economy was growing at a 6 to 7 percent annual rate. Since then it has slowed down. In 1988 Gorbachev announced that he wanted to start selling stock in businesses to workers. Since 1991, when Gorbachev lost power and was replaced by Boris Yeltsin, the Soviet Union has collapsed into fifteen different republics, with Yeltsin as president of Russia, the largest, with a population of 150 million.

Yeltsin was totally committed to a complete market economy, without any of the security measures provided by the previous Communist regime. He instituted a "shock therapy" strategy which Western advisors and Russian economists had strongly recommended. He ended the central allocation of resources, Gosplan, price and interest rate controls, as well as controls over the *ruble* exchange rate. He privatized state enterprises and eliminated subsidies for those enterprises. He instituted a free trade policy, a monetarist tight money policy, and a balanced budget. Finally, he abandoned comprehensive social entitlement programs.

The results were disastrous. Price controls were eliminated at the beginning of 1992, causing terrible inflation (over 20% per month). The collapse of the Soviet empire in 1989 also led to the 1992 breakup of COMECON, the East European trade policy organization run by the Soviets (which also included Cuba and North Korea). Industrial production plummeted because the new private enterprises could not get credit to pay for supplies and wages. An estimated 85% of the population sank below the poverty level. In 1991, GNP dropped by 11% and in 1992, by 22%. In addition, consumer spending sank 38% and investment 48%, while prices increased 2500% in 1992.

The social price for this rapid transition to capitalism has been very great. Many children are begging in the streets, and crime, including organized crime, has become a very serious problem. Russia has become a third world country. A very wealthy new elite has arisen, as former Communist Party bigwigs work the system as efficiently as any robber barons did in the United States at the beginning of the twentieth century. One result of the suffering and the disappointment with this "shock therapy" is that many Russians are beginning to believe that maybe the Communists were right to say that capitalism leads to social and economic devastation. But most do not want to return to the old system.

Some of Yeltsin's opponents, including those who feel that a market economy must be the ultimate goal for Russia, believe that he moved too quickly; the price of "shock therapy" is too great. The great debate is over means, not goals. However politically oppressive the communists were, people were accustomed to full employment, low inflation, low-cost housing and food, and free higher education and medical care. Given Russian history and culture, it seems that Democratic Socialism, as practiced in most European democracies, is more likely to succeed than laissez-faire capitalism. The Russian people like their political democracy and do not want to give it up. However, it becomes progressively difficult for them to suffer increasing economic deprivation. Within the leadership ranks, there are those who support a military takeover with an accompanying Nazi-like system, and those who favor the return of communism. Yeltsin and his successors must tread this tightrope very carefully to prevent the resurgence of totalitarianism.

☐ Evaluation of the Soviet Economy: Pre–1991

In the 1980s the Soviet economy seemed to be doing poorly compared to the past. The policy of perestroika involved a reorganization of the economy to make it more efficient.

GNP, GNP per Capita, and Economic Growth Rate

It is difficult to compare the old Soviet Union with the United States because accounting methods differ somewhat; but Soviet GNP seemed to be approximately 55 percent of U.S. GNP. Per capita GNP, however, was only about 47 percent of the U.S. figure. In total GNP it ranked third behind the United States and Japan in 1989. However, in per capita GNP it trailed behind almost all other industrialized countries. In the period 1955–1960, the Soviet economy grew at the gross rate of 6.3 percent and a per capita rate of 4.6 percent. In the period 1960–1980, gross production increased at an annual per capita rate of 4 percent. This exceeded U.S. growth during that period. Table 16-4 shows real production increase in selected countries.

The relative success of the Soviet economy in the past was due to the following reasons:

1. *Forced Savings.* People were forced to keep consumption low because their incomes were controlled and because the production of consumer goods was low. The surplus was invested in capital goods.

2. *Borrowed Technology.* Under Stalin industrial spies stole blueprints from more advanced industrialized countries. By getting into the industrializing game late they didn't have to wait for inventions as did other countries which industrialized a century or so earlier.

Table 16-4
Average Annual Rates of Growth of GNP per Capita (in percentages), 1980–1990

Country	GNP per Capita
Japan	4.1
USSR*	4.0
Canada	3.4
United States	3.4
Spain	3.1
United Kingdom	3.1
Norway	2.9
Denmark	2.4
Italy	2.4
France	2.2
Sweden	2.2
Austria	2.1
Germany	2.1
Netherlands	1.9

*1960–1980
Source: World Development Report, The World Bank, 1992, p. 221.

3. *Factories Operated 24 Hours a Day.* Factories worked three shifts, thus utilizing production facilities fully.

4. *Everyone Works.* The motto was "no work, no food." There was no unemployment insurance in the Soviet Union. If you were able-bodied and did not work you were not paid anything. Almost all women worked. In fact most street cleaners and garbage collectors in the Soviet Union were women. Of course, if you were disabled or of retirement age you were eligible for a pension.

5. *Material Incentives.* Material incentives began to play a major role in the Soviet economy after 1965.

Price Stability and Unemployment

Russian planners had been able to keep inflation under control in recent years. Since 1947, consumer prices generally remained stable. However, before that the rate of inflation was very high. Although consumer goods prices increased more rapidly than wages did from 1928 to 1947, until recently real wages increased significantly.

Unemployment was not a major problem in the Soviet Union. Everyone was supposed to be guaranteed a job. In fact not working could get one into trouble. There was a category of crime in the Soviet Union that does not exist in democratic societies—economic crimes. These included absenteeism, work slowdowns, profit making, hiring employees, and many others. Although being unemployed was not necessarily considered a crime, an unemployed, able-bodied person was considered a parasite and could have been imprisoned.

There was in the Soviet Union a certain amount of disguised unemployment. That is, many enterprises employed more workers than they needed. Since everyone was guaranteed a job, one had to be provided even if a person was not needed by the enterprise. This was a form of inefficiency, and there is no way to determine the extent to which this occurred in the Soviet Union. Although disguised unemployment is economically inefficient, it may be socially beneficial. Perhaps because of this policy, the Soviet Union was spared the worldwide depression of the 1930s.

Summary

The Soviet economic system had most of the features of a command economy: There was central planning and government control of the means of production; Communist party leaders determined the aims of the central plan; and the government determined prices and wages. However, there was not much rationing; workers had considerable freedom to choose their places of employment; and many firms were put on a profit and loss basis, which meant that market forces were

Table 16-5
Durable Consumer
Goods in Use in the
Soviet Union and
Selected Other
Countries (per 1,000
population), 1988

Country	Telephones*	Radio Receivers	Television Receivers
Soviet Union	113	319	686
United States	760	2,120	812
Australia	550	1,273	484
Canada	780	960	586
Czechoslovakia	246	274	395
Denmark	864	452	526
France	608	895	399
East Germany	233	669	759
West Germany	650	956	379
Greece	413	415	175
Italy	488	790	419
Japan	555	863	589
Norway	622	795	350
Spain	396	302	380
Sweden	890	875	395
Switzerland	856	401	408
United Kingdom	524	1,146	435
Finland	617	997	486
Iceland	525	620	306
Luxembourg	412	625	250
Netherlands	639	912	478
New Zealand	697	917	372

*1987

Source: U.S. Bureau of the Census, *Statistical Abstract of the United States: 1991*, p. 845.

involved to some extent. Finally, there was a small private sector in agriculture, which expanded considerably under Gorbachev. Nevertheless, although the Soviet Union did not have a pure command system, it was basically a state-controlled economy. In between the USSR's state socialism and the United States' regulated capitalism lie several varieties of democratic socialism. Unlike utopian socialism which withdrew from society and Marxist socialism which preached the violent overthrow of society, this movement sought to construct a socialist economy by peaceful evolutionary means, through ballots instead of bullets. Those who preached this gradualist approach were the members of the Fabian Society.

☐ Fabian Socialism

The Fabian Society was established in 1883 by a group of British intellectuals. The name is derived from the Roman general Quintus Fabius Cuncator, whose patient, cautious tactics wore down Hannibal's forces. *A Manifesto*, written by George Bernard Shaw, contains the major principles of the Fabians. These include the following:[13]

That it is the duty of each member of the State to provide for his or her wants by his or her own Labor.

That a life interest in the Land and Capital of the nation is the birthright of every individual born within its confines and that access to this birthright should not depend upon the will of any private person other than the person seeking it.

That the most striking result of our present system of farming out the national Land and Capital to private persons has been the division of Society into hostile classes, with large appetites and no dinners at one extreme and large dinners and no appetites at the other.

That the practice of entrusting the Land of the nation to private persons in the hope that they will make the best of it has been discredited by the consistency with which they have made the worst of it; and that Nationalization of the Land in some form is a public duty.

That the pretensions of Capitalism to encourage Invention and to distribute its benefits in the fairest way attainable, have been discredited by the experience of the nineteenth century.

That Men no longer need special political privileges to protect them against Women and that the sexes should henceforth enjoy equal political rights.

That no individual should enjoy any Privilege in consideration of services rendered to the state by his or her parents or other relation.

That the State should secure a liberal education and an equal share in the National Industry to each of its units.

That the established government has no more right to call itself the state than the smoke of London has to call itself the weather.

That we had rather face a Civil War than another century of suffering as the present one has been.

The Fabians appealed to the social conscience of the nation, even those whose power they sought to diminish. They believed that in a society which could be changed from within by legislation, there was no justification for a violent revolution. The *Basis* of the Fabian Society was hammered out in 1887.[14]

The Fabian Society consists of socialists.

It therefore aims at the reorganization of society by the emancipation of land and industrial capital from individual and class ownership, and the vesting of them in the community for the general benefit. In this way only can the natural and acquired advantages of the country be equitably shared by the whole people.

The Society, further, works for the transfer to the community of the administration of such industrial capital as can be conveniently managed socially. For, owing to the monopoly of the means of production in the past, industrial inventions and the transformation of surplus income into capital have mainly enriched the proprietary class, the worker being now dependent upon that class for means to earn a living.

If these measures be carried out, without compensation (though not without such relief to expropriated individuals as may seem fit to the community), rent and interest will be added to the reward of labor, the idle class now living on the labor of others will necessarily disappear, and practical equality of opportunity will be maintained by the spontaneous action of economic forces with much less interference with personal liberty than the present system entails.

For the attainment of these ends the Fabian Society looks to the spread of socialist opinions, and the social and political changes consequent thereon, "including the establishment of equal citizenship for men and women." It seeks to achieve these ends by the general dissemination of knowledge as to the relation between the individual and society in its economic, ethical and political aspects.

These principles have been somewhat modified since. Democratic socialists today do not insist that the chief means of production be nationalized; some would leave them primarily in private hands, but they would tax profits and income heavily and progressively. Others would socialize the means of production by forming cooperatives to own and manage these holdings. What has not changed is the basic goal of economic democracy; and the only means that democratic socialists are willing to employ are gradual, peaceful, within-the-system reforms. Sidney Webb, one of the Fabian Society's leaders, said it best:[15]

> Advocates of social reconstruction have learned the lesson of democracy, and know that it is through the slow and gradual turning of the popular mind to new principles that social reorganization, bit by bit, comes. All students of society who are abreast of their time, socialists as well as individualists, realize that important organic changes can only be (1) democratic, and thus acceptable to a majority of the people, and prepared for in the minds of all; (2) gradual, and thus causing no dislocation, however rapid may be the rate of progress; (3) not regarded as immoral by the mass of the people, and thus not subjectively demoralizing to them; and (4) in this country at any rate, constitutional and peaceful.... There is every day a wider consensus that the inevitable outcome of democracy is the control by the people themselves, not only of their own political organization, but, through that also, of the main instruments of wealth production; the gradual substitution of organized co-operation for the anarchy of the competitive struggle; and the consequent recovery, in the only possible way, of what John Stuart Mill calls the enormous share which the possessors of the instruments of industry are able to take from the produce. The economic side of the democratic ideal is, in fact, socialism itself.

Wherever democratic socialism has taken hold, it has been shaped by the unique history and culture of the people. The Scandinavian socialist democracies are different from the British type, and even different from each other. We are going to examine the economic system of Sweden, because it is one of the most successful examples of democratic socialism by almost every standard.

☐ Sweden: Democratic Socialism

Natural Resources

In 1990 Sweden had the fourth highest per capita production in the world. The United States now ranks eighth. The land covers 173,350 square miles, making it larger than Germany, Japan, Italy, and Great Britain. Only 12 percent of the population lives in the northern half of the country, because of the extremely cold weather in that region. Sweden has extensive forest resources which it uses to very good advantage; for example, it leads the world in the production and export of wood pulp. Forests cover more than half the country. Although most of the land is not suitable for farming, 9 percent is cultivated, making Sweden almost self-sufficient in foodstuffs. Perhaps its most vital resource is iron ore. Not only is it plentiful, but it is also of very high quality. As a result, Sweden has a prosperous iron and steel industry. However, it has very little coal, and what it does have is poor in quality. Sweden is one of the very few industrialized countries in the world that developed without the benefit of large coal deposits. The country also has rich copper, silver, and gold deposits. Its enormous hydroelectric power plants are equal in importance to its timber and iron ore. Waterfalls, rapids, and dams provide most of the nation's electricity.

Human Resources

Sweden's population of 8.6 million people is increasing at a low 0.4 percent per annum. Life expectancy is one of the highest in the world (78 years in 1990, 75 for males and 80 for females), and the infant mortality rate is the lowest (6 per 1,000 live births in 1990). Sweden also has the lowest percentage of dependent children (fourteen years and under) of any country in the world. But this does not necessarily mean that their work force is proportionately the largest, because a high percentage of the population is over sixty-four. Sweden ranks twelfth in economically active population in the world. The excellent education system has reduced illiteracy to less than 1 percent of the population over fourteen years of age.

The shift in emphasis from agriculture to industry has changed the composition of the work force. Since only 9 percent of the land is suitable for farming, Sweden's mechanized farm system has enabled many workers to shift to industry.

Its population is very homogeneous. It has no racial, ethnic, or other divisions that have caused difficulties in other countries. Women comprise 47.8 percent of the labor force. Of the population aged twenty to twenty-four, 38 percent are enrolled in higher education. This figure is exceeded only by the United States (63 percent) and Canada (66 percent). Thus, we can see that Sweden's human resources are highly developed. The people are well educated, quite healthy, and very pro-

Lumbering in Sweden
More than half of the land area of the country is covered with forests, utilized here more efficiently than anywhere else in the world.

ductive. The distribution of the labor force is 4.2 percent in agriculture, 34 percent in industry, and 61 percent in services.

Capital Resources

Sweden's meteoric production increases in the 1950s and 1960s were due largely to a very high rate of capital investment. In the late 1960s and throughout the 1970s, investment decreased. The average annual increase in gross domestic investment was higher in the 1980–1989 period (1.8 percent), than it was in the 1965–1980 period (0.9 percent).

Technology

Sweden's production technology is very advanced. For example, it makes much better use of its timberland than either the United States or the Soviet Union, both of which also have an abundance of timber. The high degree of efficiency employed by the Swedes in the lumber and related industries is also employed in iron and steel production. Its development of hydroelectric power is another example of high efficiency. Undoubtedly their high investment in education has paid handsome dividends. Sweden has been able to increase its production possibilities by applying advanced technology to a rich store of resources.

Conversion Functions

There are many routes to socialism. Sweden has avoided excessive direct ownership of the means of production. Although the government plays a significant role in the economy, only 14 percent of the labor force is employed by the central government and only 6 percent by state-run companies. The broadcasting, telephone, and postal services are state controlled. The government owns about half the transportation system: most of the railway system, half the buslines, and 20 percent of the airlines. The third largest commercial banking system in Sweden is a state enterprise. The government also operates a chain of restaurants, and shares ownership with private companies in a few special credit-granting agencies. In addition, the state monopolizes trade in liquor and tobacco.

Most of the government's industrial interests are in mining, metalworking, and forestry. In 1957 it assumed sole operation of the largest iron mine in the country. Previously, it had shared ownership with a private company since 1907. Government enterprises have been formed primarily to create jobs, not because of socialist philosophies. The government has been following similar policies since the turn of the century, long before the Social Democratic party assumed the reins of power.

The cooperative movement also plays an important role in the economy.

Local consumer cooperatives account for about 15 percent of all retail sales, and 25 percent in food alone. The cooperative movement also owns impor-

Harnessing Sweden's "White Coal"

Sweden has many hydroelectric plants that are clean and economical sources of power.

Iron Mines
Kiruna in Sweden's Lapland is famous for its high-yielding iron ore mines.

tant manufacturing interests, especially in the production of consumer goods. Local producer cooperatives predominate in the supply of prepared meats and dairy products. The largest cooperative enterprise, KF, owns some 30 plants which manufacture margarine, vegetable oils and other food products, wearing apparel, and products of wood and metals.[16]

Half the Swedish population belongs to either consumer or producer co-ops; but only 5 percent of the labor force is employed by these organizations. Private industry employs 66 percent of the working population. The co-ops operate about 5,000 stores, 100 department stores, and a few discount houses. Seventy percent of the retail food business is conducted by 9,000 self-service stores, one-fourth of which are owned by co-ops.

There is a growing trend toward oligopolies in a few industries, but Sweden is still primarily a nation of small businesses. Sixty percent of the total number of manufacturing plants have five or fewer employees. Seventy-five percent of the manufacturing plants have less than ten employees. Only 0.5 percent of all manufacturing firms employ over 500 people. But these large firms employ one-third of all manual workers.

Wholesaling and retailing is dominated by large chain stores. Almost all new stores built in the past twenty years emphasize self-service. Independent store owners are a rapidly diminishing breed. However, large private enterprises have decentralized their productive activities to a great extent. In this way they can take advantage of cheaper labor in areas of higher than average unemployment. In agriculture, family farms predominate. About one-third of the holdings are of less than twelve acres. Another one-third is comprised of holdings between twelve and twenty-five acres. The farmers who belong to this

Cooperative Store
Cooperatives abound in Sweden, including this supermarket.

two-thirds own only 20 percent of the total acreage under cultivation. On the other hand, 1 percent of farmers own 10 percent of the acreage. The smaller holdings are probably less efficient, because they cannot employ costly mechanization to the extent that the larger ones can.

☐ Evaluation of the Swedish Economy

Overall, the economy seems to be highly successful in meeting the needs of its people. Let us now apply the same evaluative tools to Sweden that we used to analyze the United States and the Soviet Union.

GNP, GNP per Capita, Economic Growth Rate

Sweden's per capita gross national product is the fourth highest in the world. In the period 1960–1970, total GNP increased at an average annual rate of 4.4 percent and per capita GNP at 3.5 percent. From 1973 to 1978, the comparable figures were 1.3 percent and 0.8 percent. However, the economy began to recover from this slump as shown by the annual percent changes from 1977 to 1978, which were 2.3 for the total GNP and 1.9 for per capita GNP. Table 16-6 shows Sweden's economic growth over a thirty-five year period.

Table 16-7 shows how Sweden compared with other highly industrialized countries in the period 1965–1990. Mining and manufacturing account for 35 percent of the gross national product. These are the pillars of Swedish industry. In the service sector, trade is the most important item (see Table 16-8).

Table 16-6
Sweden's Growth in
GNP

Sweden's Economic Growth			
1955–1960 Total	1960–1970 Total	1970–1980 Total	1980–1990 Total
3.4	4.4	2.4	2.2

Source: Economic Survey of Europe, "Structural Trends and Prospects in the European Economy," Part I (New York: United Nations, 1970), p. 58, *World Development Report,* The World Bank, 1984, p. 219; 1992, p. 221.

Table 16-7
Per Capita GNP (1990)
and Average Annual
Growth Rate, Selected
Countries (1965–1990)

Country	*Per Capita National Product in 1990 (U.S. dollars)*	*Average Annual Growth Rate 1965–1990 (%)*
Japan	25,450	4.1
Norway	23,120	3.4
Canada	20,470	2.7
Sweden	23,660	1.9
United States	21,790	1.7
United Kingdom	16,100	2.0

Source: World Development Report, The World Bank, 1992, p. 219.

Table 16-8
Distribution of Gross
Domestic Product
(percent) in the Swedish
Economy

	Gross Domestic Product		
	1960	1982	1990
Agriculture	7%	3%	3%
Industry	40	31	35
(Manufacturing)[a]	(27)	(21)	(24)
Services	53	66	62

[a]Manufacturing is a part of the industrial sector.
Source: World Development Report, The World Bank, 1984, pp. 223, 259; 1992, p. 223.

Major areas of production are iron and steel, lumber and other forest industries, and metalworking, which is made possible by the availability of high-grade steel and cheap electric power. Sweden also ranks very high in shipbuilding. Its foreign trade is high and very diversified in both goods and markets. In the agricultural field, 80 percent of income is derived from raising livestock. Milk and meat, in that order, are the most important commodities in this area.

Three recent trends in the Swedish economy are mechanization, concentration, and internationalization. Industry, agriculture, and even forestry are sectors that have experienced increased mechanization in recent years. A movement toward concentration of industry is also beginning to develop. Sweden's low tariff policy lets foreign businesses compete freely with domestic producers. Only the most efficient domestic producers survive. This is leading to an oligopolistic concentration in some areas. Internationalization is a direct result of business concentration. These large firms are now expanding into foreign countries in a big way.

Price Stability and Employment Level

Labor is a scarce commodity in Sweden, in part, because the government pursues a full employment policy with great vigor. Since World War II the unemployment rate has averaged 1.75 percent and has not exceeded 3.1 percent. In 1990 Sweden had the lowest unemployment of all industrialized countries (1.5 percent). Government-sponsored retraining courses enroll about 1 percent of the labor force each year. This policy has caused trade unions to support advancing production technology rather than opposing it as is the case with unions in most countries. Workers in Sweden know that the government will commit all its resources to find jobs for displaced workers and to retrain them. Consequently, although Sweden has the highest percentage of unionized workers in the world, strikes almost never occur.

Unfortunately, full employment puts great pressure on prices because it requires keeping aggregate demand high. The result is that Sweden has a fairly high rate of inflation. Before oil prices increased tenfold in the 1970s, Sweden had a 4.3 percent rate of inflation. Since then it has been about 8.3 percent. But as long as wage increases exceed price increases the economy will continue to flourish. Sweden was one of the few countries not greatly affected by the worldwide depression of the 1930s. It suffered a decline in 1933, but by 1935 the economy was healthy once again.

Distribution of Wealth

Sweden is thoroughly committed to the principle of setting a minimum standard of living that guarantees everyone a decent living. However, taxes are quite high in order to support this minimum standard. It is very difficult to become rich in Sweden, but it is also next to impossible to live in poverty. Table 16-9 compares taxes in several highly developed countries. It shows that Swedish taxes are the highest among the countries listed, although Denmark is a close second.

Table 16-9
Taxes as a Percentage of Gross Domestic Product and Expenditure, Selected Countries, 1989

Country	National and Local Taxes and Social Security Contributions
Sweden	56.1
Denmark	49.9
Netherlands	46.0
Norway	45.5
France	43.8
West Germany	38.1
United Kingdom	36.5
United States	30.1

Source: Statistical Abstract of the United States: 1992, p. 836.

These tax revenues are used by Sweden to support the most comprehensive social welfare program in the world. It ranges from completely free medical care to annual paid vacations for housewives. It includes low-cost building loans to encourage home ownership and a host of other benefits such as social security, unemployment insurance, and job retraining programs. Sweden has security "from the womb to the tomb." It has succeeded in leveling living standards to a great extent, at a fairly high level, and it has done so within a framework of political freedom. Sweden has also equalized the distribution of income to a greater extent than have most industrialized countries (see Table 16-10).

Table 16-10
Percentage Share of Household Income, by Percentile Groups of Households

Country	Year	Lowest 20%	Second Quintile	Third Quintile	Fourth Quintile	Highest 20%	Highest 10%
Japan	1979	8.7	13.2	17.9	23.7	36.3	23.0
Sweden	1981	8.0	13.2	17.4	24.5	36.9	28.8
Netherlands	1983	6.9	13.2	17.9	23.7	36.3	23.0
Italy	1986	6.8	12.0	16.7	23.5	41.0	25.3
West Germany	1984	6.8	12.7	17.8	24.1	38.7	23.4
Finland	1981	6.3	12.1	18.4	25.5	37.6	21.7
United Kingdom	1979	5.8	11.5	18.2	25.0	39.5	23.3
Canada	1987	5.7	11.8	17.7	24.6	40.2	24.1
Denmark	1981	5.4	12.0	18.4	25.6	38.6	22.3
United States	1985	4.7	11.0	17.4	25.0	41.9	25.0

Source: World Development Report, The World Bank, 1992, p. 277.

A Suburban "Village" in Sweden
Sweden has begun to tackle her problem of low supply of certain commodities such as housing. Shown here is a new suburban center with a shopping district (no automobiles allowed) surrounded by an apartment complex, located thirty minutes from Stockholm by subway.

Downtown Stockholm
Stockholm is a typical, modern European city.

Consumer Satisfaction and Rationality

The Swedes claim they have eliminated poverty in their country. There are no slums; and free education, medical care, and social amenities are available to all. Consumers, however, are not entirely satisfied. Full employment, when coupled with high per capita GNP, leads to high aggregate demand which may exceed the economy's ability to supply the amount of consumer goods demanded. Housing is a good example. A young couple that wishes to live in an apartment may have to wait several years to find a vacancy in the larger cities. Rent controls aggravate the situation because they discourage apartment building.

Sweden's ability to exclude itself from the two world wars in the twentieth century spared the country the kind of destruction suffered by others. Its policy of neutrality has paid handsome economic dividends over the years. Military expenditures in 1990 accounted for only 6.3 percent of total expenditure. Table 16-11 shows the breakdown of GNP in terms of consumption, investment, and government spending for selected countries in 1990. The figures seem to indicate that the United States, Italy, Great Britain, and France are currently concentrating on immediate consumption; Japan is emphasizing economic growth; and Sweden and Denmark are using the public sector more to equalize the distribution of income and to solve socioeconomic problems.

Table 16-11
Percentage Allocation
of Gross National
Product to Various Types
of Expenditure, Selected
Countries, 1990

Country	Private Consumption	Public Consumption	Gross Domestic Investment
United States	67	18	16
United Kingdom	63	20	19
France	60	18	22
Italy	62	17	21
Japan	57	9	33
Canada	59	20	21
West Germany	54	18	22
Denmark	52	25	17
Norway	50	21	21
Sweden	52	27	21

Source: World Development Report, The World Bank, 1992, p. 235.

Summary

The Swedish economy has been enormously successful. It ranks at or near the top no matter what social or economic indicator is used to analyze its performance. It has managed to overcome most of the worst features of regulated capitalism and state socialism. The Swedes have capitalism without poverty, and socialism without coercion. And they have managed to maintain political democracy and diplomatic neutrality through two world wars and a number of limited wars. Sweden is clearly a shining example of democratic socialism—a "middle way" between the American and Soviet systems.

☐ Conclusion

We have traveled a long way in this chapter. We began by explaining how the excesses of the Industrial Revolution during its early stages alienated many people. It operated within a system of raw, unregulated capitalism which left the many at the mercy of the few. The reactions were varied, but usually they involved a revulsion against individualistic, competitive, private enterprise. Many of those who sought to change the economic system wanted to replace it with a collectively-owned, cooperatively-managed economy. These men and women called themselves socialists. No matter how different their solutions were, they were united in their opposition to a capitalist market economy. This common feeling tended, most of the time, to blur their differences.

Today, however, the situation has changed. The democratic socialist countries are much closer to the United States, the epitome of modern capitalism, than they are to countries that have state socialism and political dictatorship. The social democracies have not only achieved many economic changes without sacrificing political democracy, but they have even maintained a large private sector in their economies. Their ties with the United States and other largely capitalist states are based primarily on a compatibility of political ideals and realities.

The authors have traveled extensively and frequently throughout Western Europe. The social democracies have been very impressive. Political freedom exists on a par with the United States. At the same time, economic disparities are less noticeable; slums are less prevalent; poverty, harder to find; lifestyles, more easygoing (it is not uncommon for working-class people to spend the entire month of August at the beach). A standard of living comparable to the United States is achieved in many Western European social democracies, without the stress of a rat race. (For example, many people enjoy two- or three-hour lunches.) Seven of the ten countries with the highest standard of living are social democracies.

Contrary to what Karl Marx said, it is possible for countries with different economic systems to have similar political systems. And political bonds quite often seem to be so strong that they transcend economic differences. In the next part we will keep this in mind as we focus our attention on the political system.

REFERENCES

1. Evidence given before the Sadler Committee by Elizabeth Bentley, from *Parliamentary Papers, 1831–1832*, London, 1832, xv, quoted in Eugen Weber, ed., *The Western Tradition* (Lexington: D. C. Heath, 1959), pp. 565–566.
2. Evidence given before Lord Ashley's Mines Commission of 1842 by Patience Kershaw, from *Parliamentary Papers*, London, 1842, xv–xvii, appendix 1; appendix 2, quoted in Weber, pp. 569–570.
3. An excellent general survey is Peyton E. Richter, ed., *Utopias: Social Ideals and Communal Experiments* (Boston: Holbrook, 1971).
4. See Maren Lockwood Carden, *Oneida: Utopian Community to Modern Corporation* (Baltimore: The Johns Hopkins Press, 1969).
5. John Humphrey Noyes, *History of American Socialisms* (Philadelphia: J. B. Lippincott, 1870), p. 639.
6. *Ibid.*, p. 630.
7. *Ibid.*, pp. 630–631.
8. See Robert C. Tucker, *The Marx-Engels Reader* (New York: W. W. Norton, 1972).
9. Arthur P. Mendel, ed., *Essential Works of Marxism* (New York: Bantam, 1961), pp. 9–10.
10. *Ibid.*, p. 3.
11. See Henry M. Christman, ed., *Essential Works of Lenin* (New York: Bantam, 1966).

12. For a good brief historical analysis of the Soviet economy, see Chapter 2 in Clair Wilcox *et al., Economies of the World Today,* 2nd ed. (New York: Harcourt, 1966), pp. 25–48. See also *The Soviet Union in the 1980's,* Erik P. Hoffman, ed., (New York: Academy of Political Science, 1984).

13. From G. B. Shaw, *A Manifesto,* Fabian Tract No. 2, London, 1884, in Eugen Weber, ed., *The Western Tradition* (Lexington: D. C. Heath, 1959), pp. 661–662.

14. In Harry W. Laidler, *History of Socialism* (New York: Thomas Y. Crowell, 1961), p. 189.

15. *Fabian Essays* (Boston: The Ball Publishing Co., 1908), pp. 30–31.

16. Bengt Rydén, "The Swedish Economy," in Ingemar Wizelius, ed., *Sweden in the 60's* (Stockholm: Almquist & Wiksell, 1967), p. 116. See also *Growth to Limits: The Western European Welfare States Since WWII,* Peter Flora, ed., (New York: Walter de Gruyter, 1988) vol. 1, pp. 1–116.

GLOSSARY

Bourgeoisie Marx's name for the capitalist class.

Democratic centralism (Lenin) Party policies could be openly debated before the leaders reach a final decision. However, once the party leaders adopt an official position on any issue all debate ceases. There can be no revision of the party line, and no deviation from it.

Dialectical materialism (Marx) Karl Marx's theory of social change which holds that a class struggle exists between the owners of the means of production (the exploiters) and those who work for them (the exploited). Periodically technological advancements create a new mode of production, thereby rendering the existing social relations of production obsolete. Often a new class rises to power if the owners of the old means of production do not acquire the new means of production. The new group then overthrows the old group and transforms society. The process then repeats itself as the new owners exploit the workers.

Fabian socialism A nineteenth-century social philosophical movement whose adherents sought gradual and peaceful reforms within the system. Fabian socialists favored the nationalization of the chief means of production and heavy, progressive taxes on both profits and income. Democratic socialism is the outgrowth of Fabianism.

Gosplan The central planning agency of the Soviet Union.

Gravedigger theory of capitalism (Marx) Competition among capitalists leads to the introduction of labor-saving machinery. In effect, the capitalist cuts into profit by substituting nonprofitable means of production (machinery) for profitable ones (human labor). At a certain point production becomes unprofitable. Some capitalists are therefore forced out of business. Eventually recovery occurs, but the number of capitalists has been reduced, and there has been a corresponding increase in the number of workers. The cycle then repeats itself, increasing in severity each time. Eventually the large working class becomes disciplined, united, and dissatisfied enough to overthrow capitalism. Thus capitalism digs its own grave.

Historical materialism (Marx)

Karl Marx's explanation of the past, present, and future. A series of class struggles based on dialectical materialism eventually lead to pure communism, a future utopia characterized by great material abundance, a classless society, the withering away of government, and a population shorn of selfishness and imbued with generosity. Pure communism is the ultimate historical stage.

Industrial Revolution

The conditions that existed during the latter part of the eighteenth and the early part of the nineteenth centuries when changes in production techniques caused the factory system to replace the domestic system.

Labor theory of value (Marx)

The value of a product is the amount of human labor required to produce it, including the labor required to produce any machines involved in production.

Leninism

The social-political-economic philosophy of Vladimir Lenin, the architect of the first Communist revolution. Lenin expanded and modified Marx's theories to include the following ideas: a political party (the Communist party), comprised of a small, highly-disciplined, tightly-knit group of professional revolutionaries, would act as the vanguard, or leadership, of the proletariat; democratic centralism; a one-party state; the theory of imperialistic wars; the inevitability of wars between Communist and capitalist nations; the use of tactical retreats; and the weakest-link theory.

Marxism

The social-political-economic philosophy of Karl Marx. The principle notions contained in Marx's philosophy include: dialectical and historical materialism, the labor theory of value, the subsistence theory of wages, the theory of surplus value, and the gravedigger theory of capitalism.

Mode of production (Marx)

The technology of production.

New Economic Policy (NEP), 1921–1928

A tactical retreat by Lenin which was designed to save communism in Russia. Trade and transportation were placed in private hands, and the government abandoned its efforts to collectivize agriculture. Joseph Stalin supported the NEP until 1928, when he began to pursue the collectivization of agriculture and industrialization through strict regimentation and great sacrifice of the population.

Proletariat

Marx's name for the working class.

Robert Owen	British utopian socialist who invested heavily in utopian experiments. He is known as the "father of British socialism" because of the important role he played in the cooperative and labor movements.
Social relations of production (Marx)	The relationship between owners and workers, which varies according to the level and type of production technology.
Subsistence theory of wages (Marx)	The value of labor in the market is the socially necessary labor it takes to keep the laborer alive. Workers, then, receive only subsistence wages, regardless of the number of hours they work.
Theory of imperialistic wars (Lenin)	Capitalist countries had temporarily averted collapse by engaging in imperialism. Through imperialism and colonialism they would create markets for their surplus goods, thus resolving the immediate pressure of overproduction. In this view the underdeveloped countries became the proletariat, and the capitalist imperialist countries became the world bourgeoisie. Because all capitalist countries are driven by this continually growing need for markets, they go to war against each other to compete for areas to colonize.
Theory of surplus value (Marx)	Workers are forced to work more hours than their own subsistence demands, but they are paid only enough to subsist. The value of the "extra" labor (the labor not required to subsist) is called surplus value. It is pocketed by the employer as profit. Marx labeled this return on investment "exploration".
Turnover tax	A tax added to every item sold in the former Soviet Union. It varies from 3 percent to 100 percent.
Utopian socialism	Nineteenth-century social philosophical movement whose adherents sought to avoid the evils of capitalism by restructuring society according to socialist principles. They sought radical but peaceful changes, emphasizing collective ownership of property and of the means of production, and equal distribution of wealth.
Weakest-link theory (Lenin)	The first Communist revolution took place in Russia because the bourgeoisie was weaker there, relative to the proletariat, than in any other country. In the chain of capitalist countries, Russia was the weakest link.

SELECTED READING

Erikson, Robert, Erik Jorgen Hansen, Stein Ringen, and Hannu Uusitalo, ed., *The Scandinavian Model: Welfare States and Welfare Research* (Armonk, New York: M. E. Sharpe, Inc., 1987).

The articles cover the social democracies in Scandinavia: Norway, Sweden, Denmark and Finland.

Gorbachev, Mikhail, *Perestroika* (New York: Harper and Row, 1987).
The former Soviet leader explains the changes he believes are necessary for his country to survive and flourish.

Hovals, Matyas Janos, and Marton Tardos, ed., *Reform and Transformation in Eastern Europe: Soviet-type Economics on the Threshold of Change* (New York: Routledge, Chapman and Hall, 1992).
This is an analysis of the changes taking place in the post-Communist era in Eastern Europe at a time when the transition was changing constantly.

McIntosh, Mary E. and Martha Abele Mac Iver, "Building Democracy and Capitalism in Central and East Europe: The Micro-Level Linkages." Paper presented at the Annual Meeting of the American Sociological Association, Miami Beach, Fl, August 13–17, 1993.
The authors, who both work for the U.S. Information Agency, discuss the linkage between capitalism and democracy.

World Development Report, 1992.
The best annual comparison using economic indicators of over 100 countries.

QUESTIONS

1. The Utopian socialists were
   a. violent revolutionaries.
   b. economic reformers.
   c. defenders of the status quo.
   d. searchers for a lost past.

2. Karl Marx was influenced by
   a. the age of reason.
   b. the scientific revolution.
   c. St. Simon's economic theories.
   d. George Hegel's philosophy of history.
   e. all of the above.

3. According to Karl Marx, the dynamic force in history is
   a. economic.
   b. ideological.
   c. political.
   d. sociological.
   e. psychological.

4. The theory of surplus value states that
   a. the value of a product is the amount of human labor required to produce it.

  b. the value of labor in the market is the socially necessary labor it takes to keep the laborer alive.

  c. workers are forced to work more hours than their own subsistence demands, but they are only paid enough to subsist.

  d. capitalist countries will collapse because they produce more goods than the public can buy.

5. According to the theory of imperialistic wars, the following sequence of events will occur in capitalist countries.

  a. overproduction, imperialism, war

  b. overproduction, war, imperialism

  c. imperialism, war, overproduction

  d. war, overproduction, imperialism

  e. imperialism, overproduction, war

6. The cooperative movement is important in which of the following economies?

  a. the Soviet Union and the United States

  b. Sweden and utopian socialist economies

  c. Sweden and the Soviet Union

  d. utopian socialist communities and the Soviet Union

7. Post-cold-war Russia in 1993 was moving towards what kind of economy?

  a. Democratic socialism

  b. Utopian socialism

  c. Democratic capitalism

  d. Totalitarian capitalism

8. The Fabian socialists advocated

  a. armed revolution.

  b. utopian experiments.

  c. peaceful evolution.

  d. nationalization of the chief means of production.

  e. both (c) and (d).

9. The Swedish economy does well in all but which one of the following?

  a. inflation

  b. telephones per capita

  c. per capita GNP

  d. equality of income

  e. unemployment

10. Which of the following does not characterize pure communism according to Marx?

  a. decrease in material abundance after dictatorship of the proletariat

    b. classless society
    c. gradual withering away of government
    d. unselfish population
    e. one class owning means of production

QUESTIONS FOR THOUGHT AND DISCUSSION

1. Why did socialist ideology begin in the nineteenth century?

2. Compare Marxism–Leninism with democratic socialism in both theory and practice.

3. What are the similarities and differences between the Swedish and former Soviet economic systems?

4. How has the Russian economy evolved after the collapse of communism?

Six

The Political System

This section offers the student a variety of approaches to the study of politics, including systemic, traditional, behavioral, philosophical, and comparative. Because these are not mutually exclusive, they sometimes overlap.

The study of governments has been replaced by the study of political systems. The units that compose a political system are not all included within the official governmental framework. Therefore, in order to gain a broad understanding of politics, we examine all forms of human behavior that shed light on the subject.

In Chapter 17 we approach this task within a systemic framework devised by the founder of the systems approach in political science. We then deal with a variation of it that concentrates on the structures and functions of political systems.

Chapter 18 takes a more traditional approach, as it deals with different types of political systems and structures as well as various typologies used to classify them. We have added short sections on social contract theory, the basics of the U.S. political system, and the collapse of the Soviet Union. In Chapter 19 we take a critical, detailed look at American political culture, citing many empirical studies to justify this interpretation.

Chapter 20 delves into American political orientations—liberal, conservative, radical, and reactionary. It also strongly criticizes the left-right spectrum approach and the attempt to apply it to the American political process. It concludes with an examination of American ethnic political subcultures. The final chapter in this section, Chapter 21, compares the political cultures of Latin America, Great Britain, and Russia. It explains the Almond and Verba political culture classification scheme and closes with a discussion of cultural integration.

17

Politics: System and Functions

"Everything is political," commented a character in *Fiddler on the Roof*. If that were true, there would be no point in using the term **"politics."** We need a definition that helps to distinguish between those activities which are political and those which are not.

☐ What Is Politics?

One political scientist defines politics as "who gets what, when, and how."[1] Another says that politics has to do with the "distribution of advantages and disadvantages."[2] These definitions make valid points; however, the economic and social stratification systems also help to determine the distribution of advantages and disadvantages; they too deal with the question of who gets what, when, and how. We need a more exclusive definition.

Two sociologists have written that politics is "the struggle for power to name the personnel and decide the policies of government."[3] This definition establishes a clear-cut boundary between the political and the nonpolitical. However, it does not serve us if we want to study nongovernmental politics, for example, the politics of a college, a corporation, a labor union, or a family. Nor does it permit us to study the politics of consensus. Politics does not always involve struggle; at times it involves cooperation. In fact, no political system can function without a great deal of cooperation.

Although the following definition is not the one we are going to use, it is broad enough to include all types of political activity and narrow enough to distinguish the political from the nonpolitical; it also excludes the notion that all politics involves struggle: *Politics is the process through which any group selects its leaders, determines its policies, and distributes advantages and disadvantages.* The Lions Club, for example, is involved in helping people with eyesight problems. This civic organization also holds dances, picnics, and other social affairs. However, whenever the members get together to pick the club's leaders or to determine its policies, they are involved in political activity. All groups, therefore, from the family to the international system, sometimes engage in politics.

There is, as you can see, no universally accepted definition of politics. Several are acceptable. But it is important that a definition correspond to one's scope of interest. It must also include the idea that politics is a *process* in which some people exercise *power* over others and in which some people's *preferences* prevail over others. Perhaps the definition that best defines the scope of this study and that fits the other requirements stated above is the following: *Politics is the process through which the authoritative allocation of values takes place.*[4]

In any community there are issues that affect the general population: where to build a road, whether to use property for a school or theater, whether or not the United States should intervene in the Middle East. Invariably, people will disagree on the course of action to be taken on such public issues. The group must find a way to decide which policy to pursue on a given issue. Consequently, every community must either live by the Darwinist concept of "survival of the fittest,"* or it must create some authority that people consider to be legitimate and that is given the power to make binding decisions for the community. The decisions made in this manner are "authoritative" because they are considered binding by the community; and such decisions "allocate values" because they distribute advantages and disadvantages by determining whose values shall prevail, whose preferences become public policy. Thus, the seemingly universal desire to maintain some semblance of order and stability involves creating a **political system.** Such a system is then used not only to make public decisions peacefully and rationally but also to solve problems collectively which cannot be solved individually. Thus, our focus is on the "political system." We have already distinguished the "political" realm of human activity and we have previously explained what a system is.

---

* In 1859 Charles Darwin explained the theory of evolution in a book called *The Origin of Species.* He explained that life is a struggle for survival in which organisms that adapt best to a changing environment survive, and others do not. The process of "natural selection" is based on the notion of "survival of the fittest." Herbert Spencer and others then applied Darwin's theory to human societies; thus creating the philosophy known as "Social Darwinism."

Robert Dahl says that "a political system is any persistent pattern of human relationships that involve, to any significant extent, power, rule or authority."[5] According to David Easton, the political system is "that system of interactions in any society through which binding or authoritative allocations are made and implemented."[6] The political system is one of many types of social systems. A social system is *a cluster of interrelated roles and objects that revolve around a certain type of activity*.

Those activities that we call political have to do with power and influence. **Power** is the ability to make authoritative decisions which allocate values to society, that is, the ability to make binding decisions for a group. **Influence** is the ability to help determine decisions made by those who have power. The lobbyist has influence; the decision maker who is influenced has power.

Let us now review the function of the political system. People's values differ regarding both the principles they believe in and the public policies they prefer. Whose preferences shall prevail and whose shall be ignored? Whose shall be partially satisfied? In many cases, promoting one value necessarily excludes others. These questions are decided through the political process. In the absence of a political system, there is anarchy; the decision-making process becomes chaotic—it's "every man for himself." There would be no freedom and no security. Even the strongest may be overthrown if the weak gang up on them. Consequently, throughout history and in every part of the world, people living in groups tend to organize a political system in which some of their society's members are entrusted with the power to make binding decisions for the group. This is what the political process is all about; that is why a political system is created.

When the people obey the rules made by the authorities they do so because they consider the process by which the rules came into being to be legitimate; they generally consider the rules themselves to be fair and necessary; and they believe that the people who made the rules have the legitimate right to do so. No government has the power to police all its citizens twenty-four hours a day to exact compliance with the laws. A vast majority of citizens must voluntarily comply with the laws if the political system is to survive. If there are rules that the people do not accept, they are usually changed. The use of liquor was outlawed by the eighteenth amendment to the Constitution (prohibition). The people did not accept it; they drank anyway. Eventually the rule was changed. The twenty-first amendment was enacted to rescind the eighteenth amendment. No government can enforce a law that the people reject. Such laws also encourage lawlessness in general. The public's acceptance of laws is absolutely necessary. Thus, every society creates a political system for the purpose of authoritatively allocating values. That, indeed, is the political system's function, its reason for being.

☐ A Systemic Model

David Easton introduced the systems approach to the study of politics.[7] Easton's model of the political system focuses on *inputs, outputs, feedback, supports, demands,* and *stress.* His main concerns are to determine how political systems function, and how and why they endure. He is particularly concerned about the effect of **stress** on the political system. Why do some systems survive no matter how much stress is placed on them, while others collapse very easily? In order to answer this question, Easton created the following political model:

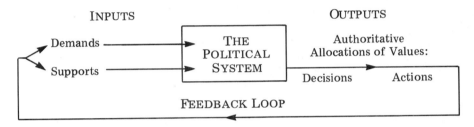

INPUTS   OUTPUTS

Demands ——————→   THE   Authoritative
                 POLITICAL   Allocations of Values:
Supports ——————→ SYSTEM
                                 Decisions   Actions

FEEDBACK LOOP

How Political Systems Function

People who are governed by a political system place **demands** on it regarding a variety of issues. For example, some people may want to escalate or withdraw from a war; they may want the government to control or not to control prices and wages. The greater the demands, the greater the stress on the system because more resources must be used to satisfy them. The level of support given by the people to the political

Stress
Vietnam protest, a case in which the government's allocation of values was not accepted as binding by large numbers of people.

system may range from very high to very low, depending upon how satisfied they are with the system's performance. A high level of support reduces stress, and a low level increases it. If the stress becomes too great, the political system may collapse. If a system suffers great stress and still survives, it ranks high in stability; if it collapses, it may be transformed into another type of system.

The American political system has survived a bloody civil war, two world wars and five other major military conflicts; it has survived a major depression and several recessions in the twentieth century; and it has survived major scandals in the White House in the administrations of Ulysses Grant, Warren Harding, and Richard Nixon. The American system ranks high in stability. On the other hand, between 1945 and 1958 French governments collapsed frequently. The system was so unstable that practically any dysfunctional occurrence would cause a systemic collapse.

Anything that disturbs the smooth functioning of a system is said to be *dysfunctional;* anything that facilitates the smooth functioning of a system is said to be *functional.*[8] We must always be careful to state functional for what and to whom. A policy may be functional for the perpetuation of a political system in its existing form, but dysfunctional for many individuals within the system. For example, an absolute monarchy may be functional for the king and his associates, but not for the

Functionalism in Society
People obey rules primarily because they believe them to be just and necessary.

bulk of his subjects. Obviously, a great deal of stress is dysfunctional to a political system. Consequently, political leaders strive to keep stress to a minimum, although some stress is necessary to justify a system's existence.

The outputs are the decisions and actions of the government. They include such things as taxation, military conscription, welfare payments, and many other policies.

Feedback consists of people's reactions to the outputs, as they are relayed back to the decision makers in the form of new inputs. These positive and negative messages encourage the political leaders to continue some policies and to change others. They may or may not respond favorably to the public's demands; but the feedback loop lets them know how the public feels about governmental policies.

Importance of Support

Easton identifies certain aspects of the political system which he refers to as the basic political objects: the *political community*, the *regime*, and the *authorities*. A **political community** is any group for which authoritative allocations of values are made. The United States, a municipality, and even a classroom can be thought of as political communities. Your teacher allocates values in the classroom by distributing *A, B, C, D*, and *F* grades (or whatever grading system is used at your college or university). The college itself is a political community in which administrators allocate values by distributing promotions, leaves, pay, and working conditions for the faculty; and for the students they decide what courses are going to be offered, at what times, what the class sizes will be, what kinds of services will be available at the bookstore, the cafeteria, and the library. This is similar to the different levels of government in which authoritative allocations of values are made for a political community (national, state, or local).

Regime refers to "type of government" (e.g., monarchy, democracy). And the type of government of any group consists of the rules by which they play the game of politics. The regime of Great Britain is a parliamentary democracy (or a constitutional monarchy); in the United States it is a democratic republic (or a presidential democracy). The **authorities** are the people who occupy positions which enable them to make binding decisions for a political community. They are the legitimate officeholders.

In order for a political system to have **legitimacy** (that is, widespread acceptance of the leaders' right to rule), the people who are governed by it must consider themselves to be a political community; this means that they consider themselves to be a cohesive unit comprised of people who "belong together" (on a nation-state level, this is referred to as nationalism); they must support the regime, that is, believe in the rules governing their political system. And they must

The Authorities
The 103rd United States Congress.

support the authorities (they must believe that the authorities have the legitimate right to rule).[9] These attitudes are necessary to integrate the political system. This type of support enables a system to withstand a great deal of stress. It is the glue that holds the society together. What happens, however, if a significant portion of the population fails to support the political community?

In 1861 the United States was torn apart when "the South" seceded from the Union. Lack of support for the political community on the part of Southerners led to secession and civil war. The same thing happened a century later in Nigeria when members of the Ibo tribe formed the secessionist state of Biafra. When a group of people feel that they are no longer a part of a larger political unit, they might attempt to secede from the larger group if it is feasible; for example, if the disillusioned group is geographically concentrated. This usually leads to a revolt against the central authority. A more recent example is Bangladesh seceding from Pakistan. The Biafrans failed because the major powers did not support them. The East Pakistanis succeeded in creating the independent state of Bangladesh because the United States, the USSR, and India supported them.

If the people of a country generally support the political community but fail to support the regime, it will probably lead to **revolution** (a radical transformation of the political, economic, and other social structures). What we are referring to is not just a change of leaders, but a drastic change throughout the entire social system. If there is a high level of support for the political community and for the regime, but a low level of support for the authorities, neither secession nor revolution is likely; what is likely is a change of authorities. This may occur either through an election, an impeachment, or a **coup d'etat** (a nondemo-

Pakistani Soldiers
Pakistan, divided and
unstable, failed to
maintain a unified
political structure.

cratic change in leadership, without a corresponding change in the
political and other social structures).

In the United States many people do not distinguish among these
political objects. If someone strongly supports the political community
(the United States) and the regime (a democratic republic) but opposes
the president in power, some people will accuse that person of being
"disloyal," "unpatriotic," or "unAmerican." These different orientations
exist because some people think of the political system as fused whereas
others perceive it as composed of separate aspects. Differences also exist
because there are two distinct kinds of support.

Support may be either *specific* or *diffuse.* Specific support is directed at an individual because of something he or she has done. For
example, people who believe the government should not be involved in
social welfare programs would increase their support for a president
who drastically reduces federal expenditures on such programs. Diffuse
support is directed at the office rather than the individual. If someone
says, "I did not vote for the man and I do not like his policies, but I

support him because he is the president," that is an example of diffuse support. It does not result from what the president does but rather from his status. This attitude is the result of **political socialization** which is carried out from a very early age in the home and the school, and which is usually reinforced by peer and work groups and by the mass media.

In some political communities (and the societies of which they are a part) respect for authority is deeply ingrained in the culture. In others, with a more egalitarian outlook, freedom to criticize authority figures is allowed and even encouraged. As one scans the 160 or so nation–states that span the globe, it is clear that the two dozen remaining democracies emphasize freedom of dissent; and the dictatorships emphasize respect for authorities. In other words, democracies emphasize specific support (the authorities have to earn it), and the dictatorships stress diffuse support (the authorities demand it).

Hitler was able to commit atrocities without much opposition because German political culture was authoritarian. The society resembled a hierarchically structured military apparatus. One's superiors were to be obeyed without question, and one could expect the same response from subordinates. Such a political culture is not conducive to the development of democratic political structures. An overemphasis on respect for authority—whether it be for political leaders, teachers, or parents—undermines the very foundation of democracy, which is that the leaders must be held accountable by the people rather than vice versa.

Since the family is the primary socializing structure, the political socialization process that children receive at home helps determine whether they are attracted to and vote for authoritarian or democratic candidates later in life, when given a choice. If they are allowed to voice an opinion at home, and if they receive explanations when rules and decisions are imposed on them by their parents, as adults they will expect similar consideration from their political leaders. If instead they are not asked their opinion, if they are not given explanations, they will probably feel more comfortable as adults with political leaders who are "tough" rather than considerate, and who tell them rather than ask them what to do. Such people will not tolerate those who criticize and dissent from the political authorities. They will want the government to repress the critics and dissenters. Thus, diffuse support, an overemphasis on respect for authority figures, and a failure to distinguish among political objects leads some people to develop an antidemocratic political orientation. Chapter 19 will examine empirical data to determine the extent to which such attitudes exist in the United States.

Easton's model identifies important aspects of the political process; it shows how they are interrelated, and it demonstrates the circular flow of political activity. His concept of feedback is perhaps his greatest conceptual contribution because it shows how leaders can correct their course as they guide the ship of state. His model, however, treats outputs rather lightly and omits the *conversion process* (the translation of individual and group demands into governmental policies). It is as if the decision-making process takes place inside a closed box. One can see what goes in and what comes out, but not what happens in between. This, of course, is where power and influence are exercised. It is where the authoritative decisions are made.

Gabriel Almond and Bingham Powell have constructed a model of the political system that incorporates many of Easton's ideas[10] (see diagram). They concentrate primarily on the functions that must be performed by every political system no matter how it is structured. These universal political functions represent the major aspects of the political process. You can see below how this model differs from Easton's.

The Political System

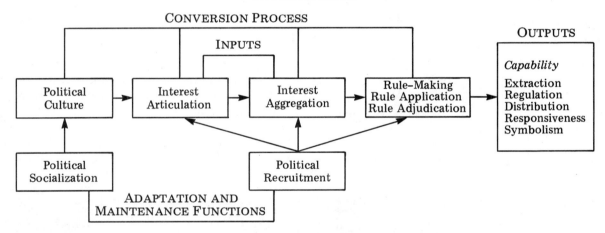

□ A Structural-Functional Model

Political culture refers to people's orientations toward the general political system and its subsystems.* It consists of people's values, beliefs, attitudes, and habits as they affect political behavior. A society's political culture is a subsystem of the general culture, that is, the total pattern of learned and shared behavior of that society.[11]

The political system operates within such a framework. The political culture is one of the settings within which the political process takes

---

* An interesting source on this subject is Gabriel Almond and Sidney Verba, *Civic Culture* (Boston: Little, Brown, 1965). They develop a typology of political cultures based on people's orientations toward the general political system, the inputs, the outputs, and the self (as a political role player).

place. It may also be thought of as the sociopsychological environment that conditions political behavior. The political culture limits the kinds of demands that people will make on the political system. By defining acceptable and unacceptable behavior, it also determines the manner in which political conflicts can be resolved. For example, political differences among the authorities in the United States are usually resolved within the democratic framework of the Constitution.

☐ Inputs

Interest articulation is the process of communicating demands to the political decision makers. It corresponds to Easton's "making demands for authoritative allocations of value." **Interest aggregation** refers to the process of sorting out which interests will be pushed and which will be discarded. It involves narrowing down and combining the demands made upon the authorities to a manageable number of reasonable policy alternatives. We shall consider these two functions separately.

Interest Articulation

First, we will examine the structures that perform the interest articulation function. Interests may be articulated by individuals or groups. Powerful individuals may find it useful to articulate their interests on an individual basis, but usually individuals are not as effective as groups. Generally, the term "interest group" is used to denote people who are linked by occupation, education, socioeconomic class, or some other bond, and who are aware of these ties. Almond and Powell discuss four types of interest groups that engage in interest articulation.

Interest Articulation
First Lady Hillary Rodham Clinton testifies at a Congressional hearing on health care.

Types of Interest Groups. *Anomic interest groups* are spontaneous, informal, unstructured interest articulators. Their activities may range from peaceful (unplanned) demonstrations to violent riots or even assassinations. Sometimes these activities also are planned by established groups. If they are, they do not truly represent anomic interest articulation. In some countries such activity is rare; in others it is commonplace. This type of interest articulation became a factor to contend with in American politics in the 1960s. Prior to that time it was relatively insignificant.

Nonassociational interest groups are based on class, ethnic, racial, regional, or other such ties. They have no formal, ongoing structure or established procedures for articulation. They operate intermittently. Since they lack effective leadership and organization, they are not very successful interest articulators. Examples would be the working class, Mexican-Americans, African-Americans, and "the South." Members of these categories may have certain interests in common by virtue of membership, but they are too loosely organized to be effective. Of course they also have many differences which may overshadow their similarities.

Institutional interest groups are formal organizations whose primary functions are something other than interest articulation. These may include organizations such as churches, the military, bureaucracies, and political parties. Factions or cliques within these organizations, rather than the entire body, usually act as interest groups. In the American political system the Pentagon and other government agencies often function in this capacity.

Associational interest groups are structures created especially for interest articulation. They are characterized by permanent organization, and staffed by full-time professionals who follow established procedures. Their primary function is interest articulation; and they perform this function very effectively. Some of the most successful American associational interest groups are the National Rifle Association (NRA), the American Medical Association (AMA), the National Association of Manufacturers (NAM), and the American Bar Association (ABA). Effectiveness is usually a product of wealth, organization, cohesiveness, and purpose. These organizations rank high in all four categories.

Interest Aggregation

Interest articulation provides the "raw" demands of the people, and interest aggregation refines, prepares, and serves these demands to the authorities. Alternative demands often become issues that are "thrashed out" within interest aggregation structures. The flow of policy then travels to the output structures which then must do their own "thrashing out."

Associational Interest Groups
Organized specifically to serve as interest articulators and often professionally run, such groups are the most effective among the pressure groups.

Interest aggregation is a crucial link in the conversion process. A failure to perform this function properly can cause a political system to break down. In France, for example, there is a multiparty system comprised of narrowly-based, uncompromising, ideologically oriented political parties. Rather than aggregating demands they perform the interest articulation function. They merely add their voices to those of other groups that contribute raw, unprocessed inputs. This is very difficult for the authorities to cope with. Extreme demands are not filtered out; the number of demands is not narrowed down. At times the stress on the political system has become so great that governments have collapsed.

We have discussed the aggregative role of political parties. Other interest aggregating structures may be administrative agencies in the executive branch of government, the mass media, universities, and political conventions. In the United States the major political parties hold national conventions every four years to determine who shall be the party nominee for President. In this case, however, instead of presenting alternative policies for government leaders to choose from, the conventions present alternative presidential and vice presidential candidates and party platforms for the people to choose from. Thus, two functions are performed at once—interest aggregation and political recruitment. Interest aggregation is involved in weighing the demands made by different factions within the party in constructing the party platform (which is a statement of policies regarding the major issues of the day).

Civil Rights Movement
Interest articulation is exemplified by this anti-pornography demonstration.

Interest Aggregation
This scene from the 1992 Democratic Convention showing Bill Clinton and Al Gore demonstrates the compromise of interests that led to the selection of two moderate candidates for President and Vice President.

Political parties seem to be the main aggregators in modern political systems. Two-party systems (which are coalitions of diverse groups) perform this function within the party structure. Multiparty systems often have coalition governments because no party commands a majority of voters. Hence the aggregation function generally takes place at the coalition level after elections have been held. Political parties in a multiparty system tend to articulate narrow interests rather than aggregate diverse ones. Actually, in both cases, aggregation takes place among a coalition of groups; but in a two-party system the groups coalesce within party structures, rather than each group forming its own party as is the case in the multiparty systems. In a two-party system, the voters choose among the compromise candidates presented by each party. In a multiparty system, voters might initially find their choice more satisfying; however, they have no say in the subsequent coalition government that usually must rule because no party can win a majority of votes.

Interest Aggregation Styles. The manner in which a structure performs a function is called style. Almond and Powell have distinguished three styles of interest aggregation: pragmatic bargaining, absolute-value oriented, and traditionalistic.

A *pragmatic bargaining* style involves a willingness to compromise and a search for accommodation. The give and take of pragmatic bargaining minimizes emotional intensity, and practically guarantees that extreme demands will be weeded out. Two-party systems tend to employ a pragmatic bargaining style. Such parties are called *brokerage parties* because they represent a coalition of diverse groups. In order to

Political Recruitment
Presidential candidate
Bill Clinton campaigns
in 1992.

keep such a party together, a good deal of compromise and accommodation are necessary.

Multiparty systems, which tend to have *doctrinaire* (ideologically based) *parties*, generally use an *absolute-value oriented* style of aggregation. This involves a refusal to compromise for the sake of accommodation. Such rigidity, usually accompanied by a great sense of self-righteousness, makes aggregation difficult if not impossible. This type of orientation is also typical of totalitarian one-party systems (Communist and Fascist). Catholic, Communist, and Socialist parties in France and Italy are examples of this aggregative style. However, an important distinction needs to be made here. In totalitarian systems all structures tend to be absolute-value oriented, while in countries such as France and Italy some bargaining takes place within other (nonparty) political structures.

A *traditionalistic* style of interest aggregation relies on the past to determine future policies. It is prevalent in premodern political systems where the political structures are undifferentiated and political orientations are diffuse. In such countries other social systems (religious, kinship, and so forth) tend to play more important roles than the political system, and the political authorities may have a lower status than other elites.

There is one more point we should make about interest aggregation before we move on to the governmental functions and structures. We have already noted that a failure to aggregate interests properly may increase systemic stress by presenting too many unprocessed demands to the authorities. This results from a failure to narrow down policy alternatives. But systemic stress may reach a highly dysfunctional level even if demands are narrowed down. This may occur even if only two or three policy alternatives are presented to the government—if these alternatives are far apart, mutually exclusive, and presented in an uncompromising manner. This problem is called "fragmentation in aggregation patterns." This is most likely to occur, of course, in political systems characterized by an absolute-value oriented style of interest aggregation.

The Rule-Making Function. Every society lives by a set of rules—written or unwritten. We may examine the *source* of these rules (deities, charismatic leaders, elected officials), their *nature* (religious or secular), their *degree of flexibility* (are they considered traditional and unchanging, or tentative and subject to change?), the *type of structures* that perform the rule making function and *how they relate* to each other, and the *relationship between rule making and other functions*.

Modern political systems are characterized by permanent structures that make rules covering a wide range of issues; such rules are subject to change. The types of structures engaged in these activities are primarily legislatures and executives at all levels of government. At the national level Americans may tend to think of Congress as the main rule-making structure. It certainly does play a significant role in this capacity, but most major legislation is initiated by the President. In foreign affairs the President has few checks on his rule-making power.

The Rule-Making Function
The Texas House of Representatives exercising its rule-making responsibilities.

The balance of power between legislative and executive structures may vary at different times between levels of government, types of political systems, and within the same political system.

Whenever courts establish precedents by deciding issues on which the law is vague or nonexistent, they too are making rules. Such rule making by judicial precedent is called "common law." On occasion bureaucratic agencies may also engage in rule making, although this is not their primary function. Their primary function is rule application, to which we now turn.

The Rule-Application Function. In traditional societies large rule-application structures with broad-ranging powers are unnecessary because the people fully accept their traditional rules; consequently transgressions are few. In modern societies the opposite is true. The transitory and secular nature of rules reduces both commitment to and compliance with those rules. That is why modern societies have highly differentiated rule-application structures. Such differentiated structures also enable modern political systems to cope with complex problems.

In most political systems bureaucratic structures are charged with primary responsibility for implementing rules. This is a crucial function: having laws on the books means nothing without enforcement.

The Rule-Adjudication Function. Rules are made and enforced; however, sometimes they are broken. Who decides whether or not a rule has been broken? And, if it has, what should be done about it? To answer these questions one must consider the rule-adjudication function. In modern societies this function is performed mainly by courts of law. However, other structures also make adjudicative decisions. A police officer who shoots a fleeing suspect may already have judged the suspect guilty. All bureaucratic agencies must interpret the rules they are charged with implementing.

The multifunctional nature of political structures sometimes causes people to become confused. For example, in the United States most people assume that the "separation of powers" principle developed by the founding fathers means that there are clear-cut functional boundaries in the American political system. Therefore, if the people disagree with a Supreme Court decision which establishes a new precedent (rule making), they claim the Court is going beyond its true function (rule adjudication).

Rule adjudication, like all other political functions, takes place within a cultural context. As a political culture changes its values, beliefs, and behavior patterns, it is normal to expect those who perform the rule-adjudication function to take those changes into account. The various authoritative functions are interrelated. In a democracy, if

Rule Making, Rule Application, Rule Adjudication

A state legislature in session, a policeman making an arrest, and a court in session.

citizens are dissatisfied with a rule application, they may appeal to an adjudicative structure. If they are dissatisfied with the adjudicative decision, they may appeal to a higher level adjudicative structure or they may appeal to the rule makers to change the rules.

To maintain support for the political system, it is important that people believe the adjudication function is performed in an impartial manner. This belief is enhanced when the adjudicative structures are autonomous.

☐ Outputs

Outputs may be thought of in several ways: as the result of a rational processing of demands, as a method whereby those in power seek to perpetuate themselves in their position, or as a method whereby a political system adjusts and adapts to its environment. For David Easton it is primarily the latter. For Almond and Powell it is a combination, with emphasis on the former. They use the term "capability" in referring to the behavior of the system as a unit. Systemic outputs can be classified in terms of capabilities.

Capabilities

Almond and Powell rightly point out that substantive policy outputs cannot be classified according to type of political system. A totalitarian Communist state may be peaceful or aggressive in its foreign policy outputs. A democratic political system may do a great deal to help the poverty-stricken, or do nothing at all. The data for any specific political system at any given time can only be ascertained through empirical research. Capability analysis deals with various types of system performance. It gauges a political system's level of performance in five categories: extraction, regulation, distribution, symbolism, and responsiveness. These categories are based on the political system's relationship with its domestic and international environments.

Extractive Capability. Extractive capability is the political system's ability to utilize the nation's natural and human resources to achieve societal goals. It involves things such as a willingness on the part of the people to pay taxes, to serve in the armed forces, and in general to provide whatever resources the government asks for.

Regulative Capability. Regulative capability is the distinctive capability of political systems: it involves control, especially the ability to back up enforcement of rules with coercive measures. An important question is: What areas of life are affected by regulations? In democratic systems there are relatively few political regulations that limit freedom to dissent. This enables citizens to use the political system to redress grievances and rectify injustices emanating from other social systems. In totalitarian states the individual is at the mercy of the system. Since by definition totalitarian states seek "total" control over every aspect of life, individuals cannot use the political system to redress grievances. The only recourse left to citizens in such systems is to engage in unlawful acts such as sabotage and work slowdowns. If an economic system is highly regulated but the political system is not, then the people can rectify economic injustices through political action. Indeed, they can even change the economic system itself. Hence the amount and type of political regulation in a society determines the extent to which citizens may use the system to effect change.

Distributive Capability. Distribution refers to the allocation of values such as wealth, power, prestige, and opportunity by the political system to individuals and groups in society. Lasswell's definition of politics applies primarily to the distributive capability: "Who gets what, when, and how." That is the most important question to ask about distribution. Another is, "How effectively does the system meet people's needs?" You might also be interested in the amount of distribution, or the range of people receiving benefits. A list of government expenditures should yield such information.

Symbolic Capability. Symbolic capability is the ability of the political system to gain support from the population by manipulating symbols such as nationalism and patriotism. This involves the use of the flag, the national anthem, the pledge of allegiance, military ceremonies, and even explicit calls for national unity. When the president of the United States says to the people, "I know that in spite of any differences we may

Symbolic Capability
The bright, articulate young people of the sixties saw JFK as one of themselves, a leader who, for the first time in many years, reflected their interests and attitudes toward government and society.

have as individuals, you are for America," he is using symbolism to increase diffuse support for his administration.

Responsive Capability. Responsiveness involves the relationship between inputs and outputs. It is the degree to which outputs reflect the demands made by the people. We want to know to whom the system is responsive, to what degree, and in what policy areas. In order to find the answers, we must trace the entire flow of policy from interest articulation to outputs.

There are several ways in which a political system may respond to demands. These are: *repression* (stifle the demand); *indifference* (ignore it); *substitution* (for example, give the people a war when they are demanding welfare); and *accommodation* (satisfy the demand). We measure responsive capability primarily in terms of the latter. High responsive capability reflects a great deal of accommodation to demands. Responsiveness to a particular category of demands may become institutionalized. That is, the response to a specific demand may go beyond satisfying that immediate need. It may involve setting up machinery to deal with that type of demand on a permanent basis. Once the response is institutionalized in this manner, that type of demand need not be articulated any longer in order to elicit the desired response from the political system. Although President Johnson's "war on poverty" program was not a total success, it was an attempt to institutionalize a response to specific demands made by those living in poverty and their spokespersons.

Responsive Capability
In September 1974 a Boston police escort accompanied school buses carrying children to schools outside their neighborhoods. The local government was responding to the public right to desegregated schools and using its regulative capability to guarantee this right.

Summary of Capability Analysis. All of the concepts we have used in examining the domestic capabilities of national political systems can also be used in analyzing their international capabilities. In fact, the two are related although high capability in one does not ensure high capability in the other. Germany's domestic capabilities are much higher than its international capabilities. Being on the losing side of two world wars in the twentieth century has severely restricted its international capability. Yet, in political and economic development it is one of the most advanced countries in the world.

The adaptation and maintenance functions are *political socialization* and *political recruitment.** Just as an automobile requires lubrication and an oil change periodically, and antifreeze when the weather gets cold, a political system requires socialization and recruitment to keep it operating smoothly.

Political socialization is the process through which people learn about and adjust to their political culture. They internalize cultural values, beliefs, attitudes, and habits that orient their political behavior. **Political recruitment** is the process of selecting leaders for the political system in each of its structures.

Political communication is another important function in the Almond and Powell model. It is represented in the diagram by the arrows. The flow of communication within and among political structures is a crucial component of the political process. No political system can be effective if the political communication function is not properly performed.

The two political models discussed in this chapter can be used to analyze any political system, because they are not geared to any particular type of system. This makes them excellent instruments for comparative analyses. In the following chapter we will examine several classification schemes used to categorize political systems.

REFERENCES

1. Harold D. Lasswell, *Politics: Who Gets What, When, How* (Cleveland: The World Publishing Company, 1958).
2. Lewis A. Froman, Jr., *People and Politics: An Analysis of the American Political System* (Englewood Cliffs, N.J.: Prentice Hall, 1962), p. 3.
3. John and Mavis Biesanz, *Modern Society*, 3rd ed. (Englewood Cliffs, N.J.: Prentice Hall, 1964), p. 453.
4. David Easton, *A Systems Analysis of Political Life* (New York: Wiley, 1965), p. 21.

* These functions help a system to maintain itself and to adapt to any changes in its environment.

5. Robert A. Dahl, *Modern Political Analysis,* 2nd ed. (Englewood Cliffs, N.J.: Prentice Hall, 1970), p. 6.
6. Easton, p. 50.
7. David Easton, *The Political System* (New York: Alfred A. Knopf, 1953).
8. For an extensive discussion of functionalism, see Robert K. Merton, *Social Theory and Social Structure,* rev. ed. (Glencoe, Ill.: The Free Press, 1957).
9. See Max Weber, *Max Weber: Essays in Sociology,* ed. by Hans K. Gerth and C. Wright Mills (New York: Oxford University Press, 1958). Weber wrote about the different bases of legitimacy: traditional, rational-legal, and charismatic.
10. Gabriel Almond and Bingham Powell, *Comparative Politics: A Developmental Approach* (Boston: Little, Brown, 1966).
11. See Ruth Benedict, *Patterns of Culture* (Boston: Houghton Mifflin, 1934).

GLOSSARY

Authorities	People who occupy positions that enable them to allocate values authoritatively for a political community.
Demand	An expression of opinion that an action should or should not be carried out. Demands are inputs into the political system.
Political community	Any group for which authoritative allocations of values are made.
Regime	A type of government.
Stress	Pressure caused by demands which are difficult for the political system.

Capability	The behavior of the political system as a unit.
Extractive capability	The political system's ability to utilize the nation's natural and human resources to achieve societal goals.
Regulative capability	The political system's ability to enforce rules with coercive measures.
Distributive capability	The political system's ability to allocate values to individuals and groups in society.
Symbolic capability	The political system's ability to gain support from the population by manipulating symbols.
Responsive capability	The political system's ability to produce outputs which reflect demands.
Interest aggregation	The process of narrowing down and combining the demands made upon authorities to a manageable number of reasonable policy alternatives.

Interest articulation	The process of communicating demands to political decision makers.
Political culture	The total pattern of ideas, behavior, and orientations toward the political objects of a society.
Political recruitment	The process of filling political roles.
Political socialization	The process through which people learn about and adjust to their political culture.
Political communication	The transmission of information (through words or actions) which enables a political system to function.
Political development	The progression through various political stages that are ranked hierarchically according to criteria established by the person(s) doing the ranking; an increase in the capacity of a political system to generate outputs which affect the other social systems. Important aspects of political development are: *state-building* (creating political structures), *nation-building* (developing a sense of nationalism), *participation* (increasing the number of people who are politically involved), and *distribution* (the redistribution of wealth or income by the political system). *See also* structural autonomy.
Rule adjudication	Determining if a rule has been broken, and, if so, what will be done about it.
Rule application	Enforcing and administering societal rules.
Rule making	Establishing the rules by which a society will function.
Structural autonomy	The ability of a structure to perform its function(s) independently.

Coup d'etat	A nondemocratic change in leadership, without a corresponding change in the political and other social structures.
Influence	The ability to help determine decisions made by those who have power.
Legitimacy	A characteristic possessed by a political system when the members of the political community believe that the authorities have the right to rule, and that their decisions are binding on the people.
Political system	The social unit comprised of interdependent roles and structures which interact to authoritatively allocate values for a society.
Politics	The process through which the authoritative allocation of values takes place; the process through which any group selects its leaders, determines its policies, and distributes advantages and disadvantages to its members.

Power   The ability to make authoritative decisions which allocate values to society.

Revolution   A radical transformation of the political, economic, and other social structures.

SELECTED READING

Almond, Gabriel and Bingham Powell, *Comparative Politics: A Developmental Approach* (Boston: Little, Brown, 1966).
This core volume was used by Almond and his associates as a model for studying various political systems in their country studies series, and in their analytical studies series.

Almond, Gabriel, Samuel P. Huntington and Myron Weiner, *Understanding Political Development: An Analytic Study* (Boston: Little, Brown, 1987).
An analytical updating of the previous work.

Dahl, Robert, *Modern Political Analysis* (Englewood Cliffs, New Jersey: Prentice Hall, 1970).
The author follows up his classic work on pluralist America, WHO GOVERNS?

Dawson, Richard E., Kenneth Prewitt and Karen S. Dawson, *Political Socialization*, 2nd ed. (Boston: Little, Brown, 1977).
This is part of Almond and associates' analytical studies series.

Easton, David, *A Systems Analysis of Political Life* (New York: Wiley, 1965).
The classic work applying the systems approach to political analysis.

Easton, David, *The Analysis of Political Structure* (New York: Routledge, 1990).
A followup of the author's 1965 book.

Easton, David, John G. Gunnel and Luigi Graziano, *The Development of Political Science* (New York: Routledge, 1991).
The book deals with the evolution of the discipline.

QUESTIONS

1. Demands cause stress, according to Easton's theory, for all but one of the following reasons. The one that does not apply is:
   a. There is lack of public support.
   b. The political system may not have the resources to fulfill them.
   c. They may be incompatible with other demands.
   d. There may be too many demands to process.

2. Which of the following would be an example of specific support?
   a. a citizen writing a letter to the editor of a newspaper supporting a congressman who did him a favor
   b. an ecological interest group working out an agreement with a major company on pollution control
   c. a minority group demonstration in support of civil rights legislation
   d. an expression of patriotism

3. Increased stress on the political system tends to
   a. increase support.
   b. decrease demands.
   c. increase support and decrease demands.
   d. decrease support and increase demands.
   e. decrease both support and demands.

4. The psychological environment within which the political process takes place is
   a. political socialization.
   b. political culture.
   c. interest articulation.
   d. interest aggregation.

5. An anomic interest group could best be described as
   a. a group based on loose ties.
   b. a group whose primary function is something other than interest articulation.
   c. a group that is composed of spontaneous, informal, unstructured interest articulators.
   d. a group whose structure was created especially for interest articulation.

6. A politician who waves the flag instead of dealing with specific problems is using
   a. extractive capability
   b. regulative capability
   c. distributive capability
   d. symbolic capability

7. In the American political system, political parties, administrative groups, and the mass media
   a. act as interest articulators.
   b. act as interest aggregators.
   c. form the basis of the political culture.
   d. act as political socialization agents.

8. In which of the following political systems does interest aggregation play the most important role?
   a. a totalitarian system
   b. an authoritarian system
   c. a democratic system
   d. an absolute monarchy

9. Strong support for the political community and the regime, and weak support for the authorities could lead to a
   a. revolution
   b. secession
   c. civil war
   d. coup d'etat

10. Extractive capability refers to the political system's ability to
    a. allocate values to individuals and groups in society.
    b. utilize the nation's natural and human resources to achieve societal goals.
    c. enforce rules with coercive measures.
    d. produce outputs that reflect demands.

QUESTIONS FOR THOUGHT AND DISCUSSION

1. How can David Easton's systemic model help to explain Mikhail Gorbachev's policies of "glasnost" and "perestroika," and the collapse of Soviet Communism?

2. How do functionalists and conflict theorists differ in explaining the political process?

3. Explain Almond and Powell's authoritative decision-making functions.

18

Types of Political Systems

Ever since scholars began studying politics they have created classification schemes. Twenty-three centuries ago Aristotle spoke of government by the one, the few, or the many. Rule by one for the benefit of all is **kingship;** if for the benefit of that single person it's called **tyranny. Oligarchy** is government by the few in the interest of the well-to-do; and for the good of all it's known as **aristocracy.** In Aristotle's terms democracy is government by the many for the benefit of the poorer classes only (the meaning of democracy has changed for us). A modern classification scheme along these lines would distinguish between democracy and dictatorship. The following characteristics are typical of the two types.

	Aristotle's Classification	
Rule by	*For the good of all*	*For personal interest*
one	kingship	tyranny
few	aristocracy	oligarchy
many	polity	democracy

In a **democracy** the majority has ultimate power, which is exercised primarily through free and periodic elections of the leaders. Thus, the leaders rule by consent of the governed and are held accountable by the people for their actions. The power of the leaders is limited, usually by a constitution. In order to have real competition for political office, opposition parties must have free access to the mass media so that they can reach the people with their messages. In a democracy those in power must allow criticism and dissent; they must protect civil liberties and respect minority rights; and they must consider those opposed to their rule as opponents, not enemies. Three main assumptions of democracy are that (1) people are capable of self-government, (2) they are rational, and (3) they desire liberty.

In a **dictatorship** there is rule by one or by a few, and no free elections are held. Sometimes rigged elections take place; at other times they are dispensed with altogether. The leaders rule without the consent of the governed, and the people are held accountable for their actions by the leaders, instead of the other way around. There are no constitutional limits on the power of the leaders. No opposition to the leadership by other political groups is permitted. Criticism by individuals and groups or by the mass media is suppressed. Civil liberties and the rights of minorities are ignored; and anyone opposed to those in power is considered an enemy. Three assumptions made by proponents

Table 18-1
Comparison of Democracy and Dictatorship

Democracy	Dictatorship
1. Rule by majority	Rule by one or few
2. Free and periodic elections	No free elections
3. Leaders rule by consent of the governed	Leaders rule without consent of the governed
4. Leaders are held accountable by the people for their actions	People are held accountable by the leaders for their actions
5. Leaders are limited in their power either by a written or unwritten constitution	No constitutional limits on power of leaders
6. Opposition has free access to the mass media so that they can reach the people	No opposition permitted and mass media is usually controlled
7. Allows criticism and dissent	Suppresses criticism and dissent
8. Protects civil liberties	Suppresses civil liberties
9. Respects minority rights	Ignores rights of minorities
10. Those opposed to group in power considered opponents	Those opposed to group in power considered enemies
Assumes that people are	
1. Capable of self-government	Incapable of self-government
2. Rational	Irrational
3. Desirous of liberty	Desirous of order

of dictatorships are that (1) people are incapable of self-government, (2) they are irrational, and (3) they prefer order to liberty.

Table 18-1 shows a side-by-side comparison of the characteristics and assumptions mentioned above.

☐ Democracies

Democracy can be either direct or representative. In a **direct democracy** the people vote on every political decision. A town meeting in which all adults can vote periodically on local government decisions is an example of direct democracy. This is not feasible in modern societies with large populations, large geographical areas, complex problems, and a large number of decisions to be made in a short time span. Thus, **representative democracy** is used in modern societies. Elected representatives, who periodically stand for reelection, govern on behalf of the people.

The United States and Great Britain are the two oldest continuing democracies in the world. Although they share all of the characteristics of democracy listed above, their political systems differ significantly. The British system is a parliamentary democracy. In a parliamentary system the people do not elect the prime minister or any other member of the executive branch (the cabinet) to those positions. The people elect the members of the House of Commons (MP's), who hold all real political power. The House of Lords, a hereditary group, is mostly an advisory body. Whichever political party wins a majority in "Commons" becomes the executive party. Its leader becomes the prime minister, and

Direct Democracy
A town meeting is an occurrence in which all adults can vote on community issues.

he or she selects other elected MP's to form the cabinet (the executive branch). Therefore, the prime minister's party is usually a majority in Parliament, although it is possible that no major party acquires a majority. When that occurs the party with a plurality forms a coalition with the third party to produce a majority. The absence of a separation of powers reduces the possibility of gridlock.

By contrast, in the United States the executive (president) is elected separately from the legislative branch. The terms of office do not coincide: the president is elected for four years, senators for six, and representatives for two. The voters participate directly in the presidential elections. Thus, it is common for campaign promises not to be realized because the Congress and the president can, and often do, disagree. A majority of Congress might even be, and often is, from a different political party than the president. This tends to reduce accountability, because each can blame the other for not solving problems. The absence of party unity, and the U.S. emphasis on individualism, can lead to gridlock even when one political party controls both Congress and the presidency.

Contrary to the British system which has a hereditary chamber (House of Lords) and concentration of power in the other chamber of Parliament (House of Commons), the American bicameral (two-house) legislature has no hereditary organization; instead the Senate and House of Representatives share legislative power. The Senate has pri-

Parliamentary Democracy
Political power in the oldest continuing democracy in the world is wielded by the British House of Commons shown here.

Constitutional Monarchy
In the British system the prime minister is head of government (political leader) and the Queen is head of state (ceremonial leader).

ority in foreign policy, whereas the House initiates all appropriations bills.

The British cabinet, which is chosen by the prime minister from elected members of Parliament (MP's), reports to Parliament. The American cabinet, which is selected by the president with the approval of the Senate, reports to the president. In both systems, cabinet members head the most significant executive agencies.

There are very important differences between a British prime minister and an American president. The president is constitutionally limited to two terms of office and cannot dissolve Congress. The prime minister, on the other hand, can serve an unlimited number of terms and can dissolve Parliament and call for a new election. This might occur because a prime minister believes his party can win an election at that time, or because Parliament voted "no confidence" in the prime minister and called for a new government. In the United States, Congress can impeach a president (which only happens under severe circumstances), but this act is not followed by an election in which all Congressional seats are at stake.

Because the United States has no royal family, the president is both **head of government** and **head of state.** The latter position involves being the ceremonial leader of the country. As such, the president cuts the ribbon at new buildings, buys the first box of Girl Scout cookies each year, and throws out the first baseball to start each new season, among other ceremonial duties. In Britain the prime minister is head of government, but the Queen is head of state. She symbolizes the unity and tradition of the British people; and she and other family members attend to ceremonial duties, thus freeing the prime minister for political and governmental affairs.

The most significant judicial difference between the two systems is that the U.S. Supreme Court has the power of **judicial review.** That means that it can declare an act of Congress or of the president to be unconstitutional. The Supreme Court interprets the U.S. Constitution. In Great Britain no such power resides in the judiciary for the simple reason that Britain has no single constitutional document that serves as a governmental guide. Instead its "unwritten constitution" consists of all the laws ever passed by Parliament (statutory law), all the judicial precedents handed down through British history (common law), and all the customs and traditions of British politics. That is the British constitution; therefore, no government act or decree can be ruled unconstitutional, because it automatically becomes a part of the constitution.

Thus we see that in the American system there is a **separation of powers** among the three branches of government and a system of **checks and balances.** The president appoints Supreme Court justices and the Senate approves or disapproves. The Supreme Court can declare an act of Congress or of the president to be unconstitutional; and Congress can impeach a president or a Supreme Court justice. Furthermore, the president can veto an act of Congress; but Congress can override his veto if it can muster a two-thirds majority in both houses.

In the British system, however, the powers are **fused,** and the only check on government that is not self-imposed (e.g., customs and traditions) is the people's power at the ballot box and the opposition party. In Great Britain, the major political party out of power is referred to as the "loyal opposition," and is paid a salary by the government. The party leaders form a "shadow cabinet" that is a counterpart to the one in power. Thus, the party in power must remain alert, and if an election causes a sudden change of leadership, the new party in power is able to effect a smooth transition in taking over the government. Their election campaigns last only three weeks.

Britain's two-party system consists of the Labour and Conservative parties. The Liberal party, which used to be a major party before it was replaced at the turn of the century by the Labourites, received only about 5 percent of the vote before the 1980s. Since then it has joined with the Social Democratic Party and become a strong contender for power. Because the British have a **unitary system** of government (i.e., all power resides at the national level), their political parties are also centralized and are highly disciplined. Any party member who fails to follow the party platform and votes against the party is removed.

In the American two-party system neither the Democrats nor the Republicans are paid for being in the opposition party. The United

States has a **federal system** in which power is divided between the national government and the states. Therefore, the national political parties are nothing more than loose coalitions of state parties which more or less coalesce every four years to try to elect a president. Even the state parties are loose coalitions of diverse individuals and groups. With few exceptions there is little or no party discipline, and members are not drummed out of the party for voting against their leaders, the majority, or the platform. It is a much more individualistic arrangement. In general, American political parties are undisciplined, fragmented, and loosely organized.

There are some significant electoral differences between the British and American political systems. Compared to the British three-week campaigns, American elections are marathons. They tend to last many months, and some candidates have been known to campaign for years.

The British electorate is basically homogeneous. Most people come from the same religious and ethnic background. They have the same history and culture. The American electorate, on the other hand, is socially, ethnically, and culturally heterogeneous. This diversity tends to heighten political distinctions.

Electoral rules differ also. Whereas American candidates can only run for public office in the district or state in which they live, British candidates can represent a district regardless of where they live. This is due to a difference in the theory of government. A British MP represents

President Clinton's Cabinet
The American cabinet reports to the President (the executive) unlike the British cabinet, which is responsible to Parliament (the legislature).

Table 18-2
Differences between
the British and
American Political
Systems

British	American
1. Parliamentary system: majority party in legislature selects the executive branch	Presidential system: executive elected separately from legislative branch
2. Prime minister's party is usually a majority (at least a plurality) of Parliament	President may or may not have a majority in Congress
3. Hereditary House of Lords	No hereditary chamber
4. Legislative power concentrated in House of Commons	Legislative power shared by Senate and House of Representatives
5. Cabinet responsible to Parliament	Cabinet responsible to the president
6. Prime minister can serve unlimited number of terms	President limited to two terms of office
7. Prime minister can dissolve Parliament and call for new elections	President cannot dissolve Congress
8. Prime minister is head of government; Queen is head of state	President is both head of government and head of state
9. Parliament can vote "no confidence" in the prime minister and call for new government	Congress can impeach the president (not likely)
10. No judicial review	Judicial review
11. Unwritten constitution	Written constitution
12. Fused power	Separation of power
13. The people and the opposition party check the government, not other branches	Branches of government check and balance each other
14. Paid opposition party	Unpaid opposition party
15. Unitary system	Federal system
16. Highly disciplined, centralized political parties	Undisciplined, decentralized political parties (loose coalitions)
17. Short election campaigns	Long election campaigns
18. Homogeneous electorate	Heterogeneous electorate
19. Candidates can represent a district regardless of where they live	Candidates can only run for office in the district or state in which they live
20. Officials are supposed to govern	Officials are supposed to represent
21. Periodic elections at flexible intervals not to exceed five years	Periodic elections at specified intervals

the nation; a member of the U.S. Congress represents a district. In Britain officials believe they are elected to *govern* for the good of all, as determined by the elected officials. In the United States officials believe they are elected to *represent* their constituency. They are therefore to be guided not by their own judgment but by the desires of their constituency. In practice, American officials do not religiously follow the representative theory of government. Most achieve some sort of balance. Their British counterparts are more likely to pursue the notion that they were elected to govern, not represent; of course, they cannot completely neglect the electorate's wishes.

In the United States periodic elections are held at specific intervals. Presidential elections, for instance, take place every four years. In Great Britain, periodic elections are held at flexible intervals not to exceed five years. A prime minister might dissolve Parliament and call for new elections anytime after six months have passed since the previous elections. He might do so because he believes that "going to the people" will increase his majority or (if he leads a coalition government) his plurality; or he might call for new elections because a "no confidence" vote against his government has taken place in Parliament. In any case, he cannot wait more than five years. In wartime, however, the British have exceeded the five-year maximum, determining that they could not afford the divisiveness of a national election until after the war ended. In the British system there seems to be a high level of accountability.

The parliamentary system seems to work best in countries with two major parties, because it minimizes the possibilities of coalition governments. It is least stable in multiparty countries like Italy, because it is almost impossible for any party in such a system to win a majority of votes; and it is difficult to form a lasting, stable coalition of several parties.

The American political system was founded by people who were very concerned about the dangers of a dictatorship. Because of this concern, they created a system with separation of powers, federalism, and checks and balances. Some people believe the Founding Fathers were too cautious. Because of all the checks and balances, critics say that the American political system is an exercise in frustration. They find the system too slow in responding to the need for change, because it is so easy to block change within the governmental structures. These critics point to the speed and facility with which needed reforms such as national health-care programs have been enacted by the parliamentary democracies of Europe decades ago. Meanwhile, in the United States debates continued for twenty-five years before the passage of a weak medicare bill that only covers those sixty-five years of age and over.

Those who defend the checks and balances claim that it is a good thing that change comes about slowly because "haste makes waste."

Those who oppose social and economic reforms are pleased that the system has an inherent conservative bias that favors keeping things as they are.

☐ Dictatorships

Dictatorships are generally divided into two categories: *authoritarian* and *totalitarian.* An *authoritarian dictator* is primarily interested in perpetuating himself in political power. He is not interested in imposing any particular ideology on the people. He does not care about their private lives. As long as one does not pose a threat to the political power of an authoritarian leader, one can live one's life without political interference. However, if a person does pose a threat to the political power of an authoritarian leader, he or she will be arrested and either jailed, exiled, or executed. There is no political freedom in an authoritarian dictatorship, but there is freedom in other spheres of life.

Characteristics of Totalitarianism

A *totalitarian dictator,* as the root *total* implies, seeks complete control over every aspect of life—political, economic, religious, educational, recreational, social. He wants to control all the organizations to which people belong, such as women's, youth, and labor groups. This is accompanied by government control over the mass media and the education system for the purpose of mass indoctrination.

The indoctrination is considered necessary because there is a comprehensive ideology (such as **communism** or **fascism**) that the totalitarian leader uses to justify his control and which he wants everyone to accept. This legitimizes his absolute rule. The ideology is comprehen-

Authoritarian and Totalitarian Dictators
Saddam Hussein of Iraq is a typical authoritarian leader. Deng Xiaoping of China heads the most powerful totalitarian dictatorship in the world.

sive in that it purports to answer all the great philosophical questions of the ages, and it claims to explain all past, present, and future history in terms of one all-encompassing idea. This might be a class struggle, a master race, or some other simplistic explanation of history.

Totalitarian dictators cannot tolerate opposition or criticism. Hence, they invariably establish a one-party system. No other political party is allowed to exist. The official party is said to represent the best interests of all the people, but only an elite can belong to it. It consists of those who have an elevated "revolutionary consciousness."

A terroristic police is usually an integral part of totalitarianism. **Terror** is the unpredictable use of force. All political systems use a certain amount of force to maintain order, but its use is usually predictable. If someone commits a crime, it is defined by law, and punishment is prescribed for violators. However, when terror is used one never knows beforehand if a certain act will be construed by the leaders to be a crime. In the dispensing of "revolutionary justice" arbitrary decisions are often made.

The effect of terror is twofold: (1) Some people become so paralyzed with fear that they do nothing. Since one cannot predict whether or not a given act will be construed as "counterrevolutionary" by the authorities, to act is to risk offending those in power. (2) Others react by going overboard to please the new revolutionary leaders, to let them know they are in step with the revolution. In either case, the revolution-

Terror
The Nazis used terror (arbitrary and unpredictable acts) on the Jewish population of Warsaw.

ary leaders benefit. To make terror effective, totalitarians create a secret police to enforce their control.

Extensive use of propaganda is another totalitarian tool. No system can survive indefinitely solely on the basis of coercion. Eventually, the people must support the system if it is to endure. Consequently, totalitarian leaders utilize the mass media and the education system to indoctrinate as many people as possible, in order to acquire mass support. Because of their greater vulnerability, emphasis is placed on the youth. The young are more idealistic and less experienced. Hence, they are more susceptible to propaganda appeals.

In order to distract the people from the harsh life they lead under totalitarian rule, the leaders incessantly harp on real or imagined enemies. This is done to instill a feeling of permanent crisis which is supposed to make sacrifices necessary. They seek scapegoats so the people will not blame the leader or the system for their misery. Stalin evoked the specter of "capitalist encirclement." Hitler blamed all problems on the Jews. Castro rails against "Yankee Imperialists."

People who are frustrated by economic or political problems because they either cannot identify the source of their problems or cannot retaliate against the source tend to seek some vulnerable substitute upon which to vent their hostility. For example, a man who is angry at his boss may take it out on his wife; or the wife may vent her anger on the kids. At a societal level, blacks in the South and elsewhere were victimized more frequently when the economy was depressed than when it prospered. Hitler succeeded in turning the German people on the Jews. Such substitute objects of hostility are usually powerless and easily identifiable by skin color or some other obvious characteristic.

Charismatic Leader
Fidel Castro consolidated his totalitarian rule because of his charismatic personality.

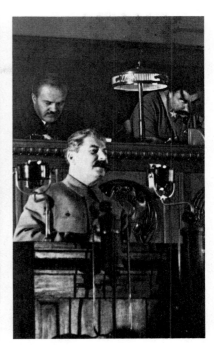

Varieties of Totalitarianism

Nazi Germany, Fascist Italy, and Communist Russia represent three types of totalitarianism that emerged in the twentieth century.

Totalitarian movements are usually led initially by charismatic leaders who are able to mobilize the masses. These are usually succeeded by managerial types who then consolidate the revolution. Charisma is an overused, misused term that is often confused with popularity. A charismatic leader is one who has a strong personal magnetism. The people who follow him often think of him as a superhuman being with mystical powers. He seems able to accomplish the impossible. He also seems to be a true believer who is totally dedicated to the cause. His lieutenants give unwavering loyalty and allegiance to their leader, and are often chosen primarily for their loyalty instead of their skills.

The charismatic leader is able to mesmerize the masses, who believe he can accomplish anything. Such leaders often lead spartan lives and seem not to care about the material things that drive other people. They seem, instead, to be driven by a simple purpose—the great cause which they espouse. Therein lies their strength.

Perhaps the best example of a modern charismatic leader is Fidel Castro, especially in the early days of the Cuban revolution. Like a modern Moses, the bearded leader appeared to have come down from the Sierra Maestra mountains to lead his people to the promised land. With his Christlike image and his great oratorical skills he mesmerized the vast majority of the Cuban people with his televised marathon speeches. He thus destroyed many critics and dissenters who often fled the country after being victims of one of his televised tirades. Hitler and, perhaps to a lesser degree, Lenin were also charismatic leaders who created totalitarian dictatorships.

Totalitarian systems usually have command economies. The leaders wish to control the economy totally in order to marshal all the country's resources to achieve the aims of the revolution. Freedom of choice in production, distribution, and consumption would dilute the leader's power to achieve his goals. Therefore, freedom of choice is not permitted.

It is important to note that in a totalitarian state all social systems are geared to the best interests of the state, rather than of the individuals who comprise it. The welfare and the rights of the individual, whether political, economic, social, or psychological, are completely subordinated to the goal of the state as defined by the leaders.

Totalitarianism also tends to be imperialistic. Of course, some democracies have also been imperial powers. Soviet communism, German nazism, and Italian fascism all followed an expansionistic foreign policy. Mussolini marched into Ethiopia in 1936, Hitler took Poland and Czechoslovakia in 1939, and the Soviet Union took control of six East European countries after World War II. Castro has not succeeded in taking over or subverting Latin American countries only because the United States will not allow him.

Differences between Soviet and Nazi Totalitarianism

Although the German Nazis and Russian Communists shared the characteristics mentioned above, they also had significant differences. The Russian system is revolutionary, whereas the Nazis were counter-revolutionary in a socioeconomic sense. The Russians claimed to benefit the working class at the expense of those who were economically better off. On the other hand, the German and Italian Fascists received the support of the middle and upper classes in whose name they conducted the revolution. Furthermore, the Nazis achieved power constitutionally (they were voted in), whereas the Russian Communists achieved power through revolution.

Despite Marxist ideology, Communist revolutions have taken place in pre-democratic and pre-industrial societies. Communism seems to be the solution sought by underdeveloped countries with a history of dictatorship. Conversely, post-democratic and post-industrial societies in crisis are much more susceptible to fascism.

Both ideologies are comprehensive but differ as to content. Nazi ideology stresses nationalism, racism, imperialism, inequality, the superiority of Aryans, and sexism (the superiority of men over women). Communist ideology stresses internationalism, egalitarianism, and a classless society without government controls. Needless to say, there is sometimes a significant gap between the ideology and the reality.

Communism appeals to peasants and workers, whereas nazism (or fascism) appeals to the middle class and the industrialists. The reason for this is that the Communists have the government take over the means of production and claim their policies will benefit lower income people by redistributing the wealth. The Nazis controlled the economic structures in conjunction with the industrialists. They permitted the continuation of large private enterprise; they did not nationalize industries. As you can see, the Communists partially abolish private property, but the Nazis did not.

One big weakness of the Nazi regime was that the economy was strictly geared for war. Without war it could not survive. On the other hand, the Soviets emphasized heavy industry. Their system could survive in peacetime as well as in wartime. Consequently, the Nazis used only military means to try to expand their power, whereas the Russians were willing to use various means, including subtle ones to accomplish the same end.

When the Nazis first reached power they had mass support; otherwise they could not have been elected. The Russian situation was different. Lenin's view had prevailed within the Communist party, keeping the membership small. Consequently, when the Communist takeover occurred in November 1917 there was very little mass support.

The final point to be made regarding the differences between the two systems perhaps explains why one succeeded and the other failed. When the Communists took over, they turned society upside down. They completely eliminated preexisting elites. When the Nazis took over, they kept the same military and industrial leaders and shared power with them (see Table 18-3). Thus, they never fully established total-

Table 18-3
Differences between
Nazi Germany and
Soviet Russia

German Nazis	Russian Communists
1. Counterrevolutionary	Revolutionary
2. Achieved power constitution-ally	Achieved power through revolution
3. Post-democratic and post-industrial societies are susceptible	Pre-democratic and pre-industrial societies are susceptible
4. Ideology stresses nationalism, racism, imperialism, inequality, superiority of Aryans and men	Ideology stresses internationalism, egalitarianism, and a classless society without government control
5. Appeals to middle class and industrialists	Appeals to peasants and workers
6. Economic structure controlled but not owned by government	Means of production owned by the state
7. Private property remains	Private property is partially abolished
8. Economy geared for war	Economy stresses heavy industry
9. Used military means to expand their power	Willing to use various means, including subtle ones, to expand their power
10. More mass support at first	Less mass support at first
11. Must resort to force perpetually because former elites not abolished	Can eventually use more subtle means to maintain totalitarian control because former elites are replaced

itarian control. They could not effectively carry out the Nazi indoctrination program because they did not control all the centers of power. Therefore, although the Soviets could eventually let up on the use of force because they had no powerful internal opponent, the Nazis had to continue to use brute force indefinitely to maintain their power. Such a system is doomed to failure.

As a political economy, Soviet communism may be labeled totalitarian socialism. Because the Nazis preserved private enterprise their system might be referred to as totalitarian capitalism; or, since they never achieved the total control reached by the Communists, perhaps we should call it authoritarian capitalism. Utilizing the same evaluative criteria, the United States can be said to have democratic capitalism, and the British, democratic socialism.

As politicoeconomic systems the two that are least clearly differentiated by most Americans are democratic socialism and totalitarian socialism. We dealt with the economic differences in Chapter 16. In this chapter we compared democracies and dictatorships. Table 18-4 shows the differences between the democratic and totalitarian versions of socialism, and demonstrates that the former is a modified market system with political democracy, and the latter is a modified command system with political dictatorship.

Ideology

Every political or other social system has an underlying ideology that both explains and justifies the system. It also condemns other systems. Leaders can use an ideology to justify their power, to give legitimacy to their positions. The ideology itself may or may not limit their behavior in certain ways.

A comprehensive ideology is a belief system—a set of ideas, values, and attitudes; it is also a perception of the world regarding reality, truth, and morality in a number of contexts: political, economic, social, and cultural. It explains the past, the present, and the future, gives meaning to life, and shapes thought and action. It may, indeed, be a call to action.

Communism and Fascism are comprehensive ideologies. Their proponents explain everything, seek solutions to concrete problems, and derive the meaning of life, society, the world, and history through their ideologies. Being, of necessity, a simplified version of reality, a model stripped of life's inconsistencies and variations, an ideology cannot accurately depict the real world with all of its complexities. Yet true believers try to make sense of the world within an ideological framework (in contrast to those who merely use ideology to justify what they want to do, or have done).

Less comprehensive ideologies, like democracy, are based on a general agreement of broad concepts, such as freedom, equality, justice, due

Table 18-4
Differences between
Democratic Socialism
and Totalitarian
Socialism
(continued on p. 482)

Democratic Socialism	Totalitarian Socialism
Economic Differences	
1. Only partial control of means of production (government guides)	Total control of means of production
2. Gradual takeover of production	Sudden takeover of production
3. Payment for nationalization	No payment for expropriation

Table 18-4
(continued from p. 481)

Democratic Socialism	Totalitarian Socialism
4. Mixed welfare market economy	Command economy
5. Consumer sovereignty and balance between consumer and capital goods	Consumer goods at bottom of list of priorities
6. Maintenance of capitalism	Elimination of capitalism
7. Extension of democracy from the political to the economic sphere	Extension of dictatorial practices from the political to the economic sphere
8. No quota or priority system	Quota and priority system used
9. Progressive taxation	Turnover taxation

Political Differences	
1. Genuine elections are held	Elections are a farce (no opposition), or are not held
2. Leaders elected for a stipulated period of time	Leaders attain power by revolution
3. Freedom of speech encouraged	Speech must coincide with dominant myth
4. Emphasis on individual welfare	Emphasis on need of the state
5. Practice due process of law	Use terror and coercion
6. Develops in countries with a great deal of democratic experience	Develops in countries with authoritarian histories
7. Ideology stresses parliamentary majorities	Ideology stresses class struggle
8. Government held accountable by the people	People held accountable by the government
9. National movement	International movement
10. More than one political party	One-party system
11. Pluralistic society (many centers of power)	Monistic society (one center of power)
12. Aim to please all classes	Aim to please only working class

process, and the right to dissent. These general guidelines, however, are ideals to strive for, and are not necessarily approximated in all instances by all people. In fact, there is often a wide gap between the real and the ideal. Furthermore, because they are general guidelines, they are subject to diverse interpretations. Wide disagreements persist regarding specific applications. That is why the U.S. Supreme Court is constantly having to interpret and reinterpret constitutional issues.

Within countries with less comprehensive ideologies there are sub-groups that agree with each other on general principles, but that believe in different variations of the common theme. These variations might be called political orientations. For example, within the ideological framework of American democracy, there are liberal, conservative, radical, and reactionary orientations. The different beliefs, values, and perceptions of these groups will be addressed in a subsequent chapter.

☐ Social Contract

Social contract theory holds that there is a reciprocally binding social contract between governments and their citizens. John Hobbes, John Locke, and Jean-Jacques Rousseau, three 17th- and 18th-century political philosophers, wrote extensively on the subject. A strong belief in natural laws existed among intellectuals during this historical period, and the founding fathers of the United States created the new Republic based on some of those notions.

In a state of nature man is born free. He gives up certain decision-making powers to a government in exchange for protection, and respect for individual rights. As the U.S. Declaration of Independence stated in 1776, whenever a government does not honor its part of the contract, the people have a right to unite, overthrow the government, and institute a new one that will. In 1690 Locke mentioned life, liberty, and property as the most important natural rights. In the U.S. Declaration of Independence written by Thomas Jefferson in 1776, he changed it to life, liberty, and the pursuit of happiness. In the French Declaration of the Rights of Man in 1789, it was changed to liberty, equality, and fraternity. In both cases it is clearly stated that governments must respect the people's "natural rights."

☐ The United States Political System

The major features of the American government are a separation of powers, checks and balances, and federalism. The executive, legislative, and judicial branches of government have separate, but overlapping responsibilities. Congress passes the laws, but the president usually presents a comprehensive list of proposals that are acted upon by Congress. If the president does not agree with any laws passed by Congress, he or she can exercise a veto power. However, Congress can override a presidential veto if both the House of Representatives and the Senate can muster a two-thirds majority.

The Supreme Court has jurisdiction over the constitutionality of any laws passed by Congress, or any acts of the President. If such a law or act is ruled unconstitutional, it is null and void. Congress can impeach and remove a sitting president if he or she has committed certain illegal acts. It can also impeach a Supreme Court justice. This separation of powers and checks and balances were instituted by the founding fathers to prevent a dictatorship. To prevent a military takeover, the writers of the Constitution made the president the Commander in Chief of the Armed Forces. Their fear and mistrust of a permanent, professional military led them to pass the Second Amendment to the Constitution giving citizens the right to bear arms for the purpose of forming a militia to defend the country from foreign enemies. With the advent of standing armies in the twentieth century, the right to bear arms is no longer an absolute right, despite claims to the contrary by the National Rifle Association, which is funded primarily by weapons manufacturers.

The first ten amendments to the Constitution are known as the Bill of Rights. They focus primarily on freedom of speech, press, and religion, and the right to assemble peaceably to petition the government for a redress of grievances (First Amendment). The Fourth through Eighth Amendments guarantee citizens the right to due process of law.

Federalism refers to a division of power between the national government and state governments (who then delegate some authority to local governments). The twentieth century has seen an increase in the power of the national government as many problems have become too complex for state and local governments to handle.

The United States has two major political parties (Democrats and Republicans), and periodic third parties that have not won any elections, but have sometimes determined which of the two major party Presidential candidates wins an election. Running for public office has become extremely costly as electronic campaigning has become necessary, and print advertising has become more expensive. A wide array of media specialists and polling services add considerably to campaign expenses. Telephone banks, literature, signs, speechwriters, advance men and women, speakers, research (focus groups and opposition research, as well as the polling mentioned above) are deemed necessary to win a campaign and they cost money. Very often the winning candidates are the ones who can raise the most money.

Interest groups also play a significant role in American politics. There are many thousands, but only a few hundred have a great deal of influence over major politicians, and probably only a few dozen have a significant impact at the national level. These include the National Rifle Association, the American Medical Association, the American Farm Bureau, the National Association of Manufacturers, the American Federation of Labor-Congress of Industrial Organizations, and others affiliated with the military-industrial complex, the elderly, foreign policy, and many other issues. Some of these are so influential that they have blocked significant legislation not to their liking for decades. Politics has been called the art of the possible. Interest groups play a major role in determining what is possible and what is not. It is not too farfetched to say that Thomas Jefferson and his cohorts would not recognize the American political system today.

☐ The Collapse of the Soviet System

The emergence of Mikhail Gorbachev in 1985 brought to power the first Soviet leader born after the 1917 Communist revolution. Gorbachev was considered a reformer who would humanize communism through glasnost (openness—the right of the people to criticize the government, the leaders, and their policies), and perestroika (economic and political restructuring). He also decided to end the cold war with the West, and give up the Soviet empire. The East European countries, which comprised the empire, gave up communism, and East Germany reunited with West Germany—all with Gorbachev's blessing. He also sought mutual disarmament with the United States, at a much faster pace than the U.S. wanted. He viewed himself as a great visionary who would bring peace and prosperity to his people. What Gorbachev did took great courage. On one side he had conservatives who wanted to return to communism; keep a centralized economy, a strong military, and the Soviet empire. On the other side he had people like Boris Yeltsin who wanted a laissez-faire market system and the abolition of communism, to be replaced by some sort of democracy.

Pulled by both sides, Gorbachev saw himself as a middle-of-the-road liberal reformer who would humanize Soviet society while keeping the Communist party in power (perhaps with two or more communists running for each public office). Friedrich Engels, Karl Marx's collaborator in almost all of Marx's writings, once said that people who make a revolution sometimes wake up the next day to discover that the revolution they made is not at all like the one they had envisioned. Gorbachev unleashed a series of social forces that he could not control. As far as the Russian people were concerned, he did not go far enough fast enough. The fourteen non-Russian Republics seceded from the Soviet Union, led by the Baltic states—Latvia, Estonia and Lithuania. He even lost control of the Russian Republic to Yeltsin, the former Communist party leader of Moscow, who had been given that post by Gorbachev.

Yeltsin, for his part, seemed to be moving too far too fast in changing the economy to a laissez-faire market system, while ignoring the people's economic needs. Simultaneously, in September, 1993, he seemed to be dealing with his political opponents in a not-too-democratic manner. It is too early to know the outcome of that power struggle in such a fluid political setting. However, the fact that Russia has had a dictatorial political culture for a thousand years does not portend well for the future.

GLOSSARY

Aristocracy (Aristotle)	Government by the few for the good of all.
Oligarchy (Aristotle)	Government by the few for their personal interests.
Kingship (Aristotle)	Rule by one for the good of all.
Tyranny (Aristotle)	Rule by one for personal interest.
Democracy	Rule by a majority, with respect for minorities, free elections, limits on the power of leadership, and respect for civil liberties. In a *direct democracy* individuals decide public policies at community meetings. In a *representative democracy* elected representatives govern on behalf of the people.
Dictatorship	Rule by one or a few, with no free elections, no limits on the leaders' power, and no respect for the rights of minorities or for civil liberties. An *authoritarian dictator* seeks only political control. A *totalitarian dictator* seeks total control over every aspect of life.
Communism	A totalitarian dictatorship whose ideology stresses equality, internationalism, a classless society, and no government control. This system has developed in pre-democratic and pre-industrial societies with an authoritarian tradition. It is revolutionary, nationalizes the economy, and in some countries (e.g., the USSR) is imperialistic. Preexisting elites are eliminated.
Fascism	A totalitarian dictatorship whose German variety (nazism) stressed nationalism, racism, imperialism, inequality, sexism, and the superiority of Aryans (the master race concept). This system in slightly different form developed in Italy as well. Post-democratic and post-industrial societies in crisis seem to be most susceptible to this type of dictatorship. Power was gained constitutionally and there was cooperation with preexisting elites.
Monism	There is one center of power in society. Dictatorships are monistic.
Pluralism	There are many centers of power. Democracies are pluralistic.

Unitary system	All government power resides at the national level. Lower levels of government owe their existence and continuation to the national government. Such systems may be either democratic or dictatorial. Great Britain is an example of a democratic unitary state.
Federal system (federalism)	Power is divided between the national government and smaller geographical units (states, provinces, cantons). The United States, Canada, and Switzerland are examples.
Fused powers	Executive and legislative branches of government are merged, as in Great Britain.
Separation of powers	The executive, legislative, and judicial branches of government are separate, as in the U.S. system of government.
Checks and balances	Each branch of government can limit the power of the others. For example, in the United States, the President can veto legislation; the Supreme Court can rule on the constitutionality of executive or legislative actions; Congress can impeach a President or a Supreme Court justice.

Head of state	Ceremonial leader of country.
Head of government	Political leader of country.
Judicial review	The power of the Supreme Court to decide if an act of Congress or of the President is constitutional.
Terror	The arbitrary and unpredictable use of force.

SELECTED READING

Brand, Jack, *British Parliamentary Parties: Policy and Power* (New York: Oxford University Press, 1992).
An important discussion of the mother of modern parliamentary democracies.

Clawson, Dan, Allen Neustadt and Denise Scott, *Money Talks: Corporate PACS and Political Influence* (New York: Basic Books, 1992).
An important book that analyzes how money influences elections and the political process in general.

Craig, Thomas, *There to Here: Ideas of Political Society: John Locke and his Influence in 300 Years of Political Theory* (New York: Harper Perennial, 1991).
Shows how Locke's two treatises on government influenced many

subsequent theorists. The U.S. Declaration of Independence draws heavily from his writings.

Curtis, Michael, ed., *The Great Political Theories* (New York: Avon Books, vol. 1, 1961; vol. 2, 1962).
An introduction to the writings of the great political thinkers.

Dahl, Robert, *Democracy, Liberty and Equality* (Oslo: Norwegian University Press, 1986).
Another important contribution to our understanding of the democratic process by the father of modern pluralist theory.

Duch, Raymond M., "Tolerating Economic Reform: Popular Support For Transition To A Free Market In The Former Soviet Union," *American Political Science Review*, September, 1993, pp. 590–608.
The author reports on a series of surveys conducted in the Soviet Union shortly before its collapse.

Gorbachev, Mikhail, *Perestroika: New Thinking for Our Country and the World* (New York: Harper & Row, 1988).
Provides an insight into Gorbachev's gradualist approach to evolve away from a totalitarian political system and a centralized economy in the Soviet Union.

Gwertzman, Bernard and Michael T. Kaufman, ed., *The Collapse of Communism* (New York: The New York Times, 1990).
A chronicle of the early period in the demise of communism in Eastern Europe.

Lloyd, S. A., *Ideals as Interests in Hobbes' Leviathan: The Power of Mind Over Matter* (New York: Cambridge University Press, 1992).
The author analyzes the thinking of one of the three giants of social contract theory.

Mayhew, David R., *Divided We Govern: Party Control, Lawmaking and Investigations 1946–1990* (New Haven: Yale University Press, 1991).
An interesting historical treatment of the American political process.

McIntosh, Mary E. and Martha Abele MakIver, *Building Democracy and Capitalism in Central and East Europe: The Micro-Level Linkages*, Paper Presented at the Annual Meeting of the American Sociological Association, Miami Beach, Fl, August 13–17, 1993.
The authors, both from the U.S. Information Agency, discuss the difficulty in establishing both democracy and capitalism in countries with little or no historical experience in either. This is not a government document.

Rozman, Gilbert, ed., *Dismantling Communism: Common Causes and Regional Variations* (Baltimore: Johns Hopkins University Press, 1992).
An interesting treatment of a major modern political phenomenon.

Simmons, John, *The Lockean Theory of Rights* (Princeton, N.J.: Princeton University Press, 1992).

Another treatment of Locke's contribution to social contract theory and individual liberties.

Soe, Christian, ed., *Comparative Politics: 92/93 Tenth Annual Edition* (Guilford, Conn: The Dushkin Publishing Group, 1992).
An annual compilation of significant articles.

QUESTIONS

1. Of the following assumptions, the one that does not pertain to *democracy* is:
   a. Men and women are capable of self-government.
   b. People are rational.
   c. People prefer order to liberty.
   d. People desire liberty.
   e. Each person is an individual (the liberal perspective).

2. Which of the following is a characteristic of the British parliamentary democracy?
   a. People do not elect head of government or any other member of executive branch to their positions.
   b. There is no hereditary group that acts as an advisory body.
   c. The head of the government's party is rarely in the majority party of the legislative body.
   d. There is *no* concentration of power in either chamber of the legislative branch.
   e. The executive is elected separately from the legislative branch.

3. A similarity found in both the British parliamentary system and American representative democracy is:
   a. In both systems, cabinet members report directly to the executive head (the prime minister in Britain and the president in America).
   b. In both systems, cabinet members head the most significant executive agencies.
   c. There exists an equal concentration of power in both legislative houses—House of Lords/House of Commons and Senate/House of Representatives.
   d. People participate directly in the elections of officials for the executive branch.
   e. In both systems, terms of office for both executive and legislative branch members coincide.

4. A significant difference between the president and the prime minister is:
   a. The president, in addition to being political leader, is also the ceremonial head of the country.

b. The prime minister is in charge of all political affairs as well as ceremonial duties.

c. The American president will never be found cutting ribbons at new buildings whereas the prime minister may specifically be asked to do so.

d. none of the above.

5. The U.S. judicial system is different from the British judicial system in that
   a. the U.S. Supreme Court cannot declare an act of Congress to be unconstitutional, but in Britain the high courts can make such declarations against Parliament.
   b. the U.S. judicial system has an "unwritten Constitution" that consists of all the laws passed by Congress; therefore any government act automatically becomes a part of the Constitution.
   c. the U.S. Supreme Court has the power of judicial review, whereas in Great Britain no such power resides in the judiciary.
   d. there is no significant judicial difference between the two systems.

6. A significant difference between an authoritarian dictator and a totalitarian dictator is that an authoritarian dictator
   a. seeks overwhelming control over the political, economic, religious, educational, social, and even recreational aspects of life.
   b. places great emphasis on use of mass indoctrination.
   c. justifies control through a comprehensive ideology.
   d. will not pose problems to those individuals who aren't political threats.
   e. tries to get more involved in people's private lives.

7. In writing the U.S. Declaration of Independence in 1776, Thomas Jefferson borrowed heavily from the philosophy of
   a. Voltaire.
   b. Rousseau.
   c. Locke.
   d. Hobbes.

8. A system that stresses nationalism, inequality, and racial superiority is
   a. communism.
   b. capitalism.
   c. socialism.
   d. anarchism.
   e. fascism.

9. The First Amendment to the U.S. Constitution focuses on
   a. freedom of speech.
   b. freedom of the press.
   c. freedom of religion.
   d. the right to assemble peaceably.
   e. All of the above

10. Mikhail Gorbachev's glasnost policy referred to
    a. Political restructuring.
    b. Economic restructuring.
    c. Openness.
    d. Ending the cold war.
    e. All of the above

QUESTIONS FOR THOUGHT AND DISCUSSION

1. In what ways are democracy and dictatorship opposite forms of government?

2. What are the advantages and disadvantages of the British and U.S. forms of government?

3. Explain social contract theory.

19

American Political Culture: A Critical Analysis

Culture is a society's total pattern of learned and shared values, beliefs, attitudes, and behavior. This cultural heritage is transmitted, usually with some modification, from one generation to the next. Cultural change is generally a very slow process. Hence, it is possible to define and to analyze a society's culture, and thereby gain important insights into its social processes.

Political culture refers specifically to beliefs, values, attitudes, habits, and behavior regarding political matters. Because each of society's members internalizes such cultural characteristics, political culture can also be considered the psychological context which conditions each person's political orientation.

One may speak of the **general political culture,** which consists of the core values and the predominant behavior patterns accepted by most people; of **elite political culture,** which only includes the orientations of politically significant (that is, powerful or influential) individuals and groups; or one may focus on societal divisions or factions by emphasizing political subcultures. In this chapter we will examine the general and elite political cultures; and in the following chapter we will focus on the subcultures.

☐ Characteristics of America's General Political Culture

In the United States people generally tend to stress their private affairs, and express little concern for public issues. Americans are more concerned about the size of their homes, television sets, and automobiles than they are about corruption in government, a clean and safe environment, and adequate medical care at a reasonable cost. They become interested in public policies only if they are directly and significantly hurt by a particular situation, such as unemployment, inflation, or war.

Private Orientation

America's private orientation accounts in part for the high degree of political apathy and the dearth of accurate political information among its citizens. The political apathy manifests itself in a variety of ways. Many Americans do not take advantage of the right to choose their leaders in free elections, a right that people have fought and died for. The simple act of voting in presidential elections is forsaken by many citizens, as indicated in Table 19-1. Indeed, almost all other democracies have a higher voter turnout. Since 1968, voter turnout for presidential elections in the United States has dropped from 60.9 percent that year to 55.2 percent in 1972, 53.5 percent in 1976, 52.6 percent in 1980, 53.1 percent in 1984, 50.1 percent in 1988, and increased to 55 percent in 1992.

Level of education is related to voter turnout. In 1988 36.7 percent of elementary, 54.2 percent of high school, and 77.6 percent of college graduates reported voting for president.

In many state and local elections the turnout figures are as low as 15 to 25 percent. Thus, there is apathy with respect to voting. When the U.S. voter turnout is measured as a percentage of voter registration, the ranking increases from 23rd to 11th.

Table 19-1
Voter Turnout Percentages in Democratic Nations (Most Recent Major National Elections as of 1983)

Country	Percentage	Country	Percentage
Belgium	95	Denmark	83
Australia	94	Norway	82
Austria	92	Greece	79
Sweden	91	Israel	78
Italy	90	United Kingdom	76
Iceland	89	Japan	74
New Zealand	89	Canada	69
Luxembourg	89	Spain	68
West Germany	87	Finland	64
Netherlands	87	Ireland	62
France	86	*United States*	*53*
Portugal	84	Switzerland	48

Turnout for the United States is based on the voting-age population; for other countries, it is based on registered voters. Apart from the United States, registration is more or less universal, so these comparisons are roughly correct. Low voting in Swiss federal elections, it should be noted, is a unique case. The federal government there plays a minor role compared with the cantons, and there is little political competition at the national level.

Source: Harvard/ABC News Symposium (1984:7).

Table 19-2
Voter Turnout in Democratic Nations as a Percentage of Registered Voters (Most Recent Major National Elections as of 1983)

Country	Percentage	Country	Percentage
Belgium	95	Portugal	84
Australia	94	Denmark	83
Austria	92	Norway	82
Sweden	91	Greece	79
Italy	90	Israel	78
Iceland	89	United Kingdom	76
New Zealand	89	Japan	74
Luxembourg	89	Canada	69
West Germany	87	Spain	68
Netherlands	87	Finland	64
United States	*87*	Ireland	62
France	86	Switzerland	48

Source: Harvard/ABC News Symposium (1984:7).

The percentage of the voting-age population that is registered to vote has declined in recent years. In 1984 it was 73 percent. It dropped to 71 percent in 1988, and to 67 percent in 1990. As Tables 19-3 and 19-4 indicate, age, education, and ethnicity are significant variables that show variations in registering and voting.

Table 19-3
Voting-Age Population, Percent Registering and Voting in Presidential Election Years, 1976-1988

Characteristics	1976		1980		1984		1988	
	Reg.	Vote	Reg.	Vote	Reg.	Vote	Reg.	Vote
TOTAL	66.7	59.2	66.9	59.2	68.3	59.9	66.6	57.4
Age								
18-20 years old	47.1	38.0	44.7	35.7	47.0	36.7	44.9	33.2
21-24 years old	54.8	45.6	52.7	43.1	54.3	43.5	50.6	38.3
25-34 years old	62.3	55.4	62.0	54.6	63.3	54.5	57.8	48.0
35-44 years old	69.8	63.3	70.6	64.4	70.9	63.5	69.3	61.3
45-64 years old	75.5	68.7	75.8	69.3	76.6	69.8	75.5	67.9
65 years old and older	71.4	62.2	74.6	65.1	76.9	67.7	78.4	68.8
Ethnicity								
White	68.3	60.9	68.4	60.9	69.6	61.4	67.9	59.1
Black	58.5	48.7	60.0	50.5	66.3	55.8	64.5	51.5
Hispanic	37.8	31.8	36.3	29.9	40.1	32.6	35.5	28.8
School years completed								
8 years or less	54.4	44.1	53.0	42.6	53.4	42.9	47.5	36.7
Some high school (1-3 years)	55.6	47.2	54.6	45.6	54.9	44.4	52.8	41.3
High school completed	66.9	59.4	66.4	58.9	67.3	58.7	64.6	54.7
Some college (1-3 years)	75.2	68.1	74.4	67.2	75.7	67.5	73.5	64.5
College (4 or more years)	83.7	79.8	84.3	79.9	83.8	79.1	83.1	77.6

Source: Data compiled from U.S. Bureau of the Census, Current Population Reports, *series p-20, No. 453, and earlier reports.*

"FRANKLY, I DON'T CARE ONE WAY OR THE OTHER ABOUT VOTER APATHY"

There are various reasons for this political apathy. Lack of knowledge is one important consideration. Polls indicate that only 55 percent of the adult population know how many U.S. senators each state has, and less than 20 percent can name the three branches of the federal government.[5] Before 1970, less than 50 percent knew their congressman's name.[6] A national study of seventeen-year-olds in 1987

Table 19-4
Voting-Age Population, Percent Registering and Voting in Congressional Election Years, 1978-1990

Characteristics	1978 Reg.	1978 Vote	1982 Reg.	1982 Vote	1986 Reg.	1986 Vote	1990 Reg.	1990 Vote
TOTAL	62.6	45.9	64.1	48.5	64.3	46.0	62.2	45.0
Age								
18-20 years old	34.7	20.1	35.0	19.8	35.4	18.6	35.4	18.4
21-24 years old	45.1	26.2	47.8	28.4	46.6	24.2	43.3	22.0
25-34 years old	55.5	38.0	57.1	40.4	55.8	35.1	52.0	33.8
35-44 years old	66.7	50.1	67.5	52.2	67.9	49.3	65.5	48.4
45-64 years old	74.3	58.5	75.6	62.2	74.8	58.7	71.4	55.8
65 years old and older	72.8	55.9	75.2	59.9	76.9	60.9	76.5	60.3
Ethnicity								
White	63.8	47.3	65.6	49.9	65.3	47.0	63.8	46.7
Black	57.1	37.2	59.1	43.0	64.0	43.2	58.8	39.2
Hispanic	32.9	23.5	35.3	25.3	35.9	24.2	32.3	21.0
School years completed								
8 years or less	53.2	34.6	52.3	35.7	50.5	32.7	44.0	27.7
Some high school (1-3 years)	52.9	35.1	53.3	37.7	52.4	33.8	47.9	30.9
High school completed	62.0	45.3	62.9	47.1	62.9	44.1	60.0	42.2
Some college (1-3 years)	68.7	51.5	70.0	53.3	70.0	49.9	68.7	50.0
College (4 or more years)	76.9	63.9	79.4	66.5	77.8	62.5	77.3	62.5

Source: Data compiled from U.S. Bureau of the Census, Current Population Reports, *series p-20, No. 453, and earlier reports.*

determined that 32 percent did not know what the Declaration of Independence was for and 68 percent did not know when the Civil War took place.[7]

Americans generally believe that government is too complicated for them to understand, and unfortunately the percentage of the population that feels that way is increasing.[8]

Some people say politics and government are so complicated that the average man cannot really understand what is going on.						
	1952	*1956*	*1960*	*1964*	*1968*	*1987*
Agree	69%	62%	56%	66%	71%	69%
Disagree	29%	35%	39%	31%	19%	—
Other	2%	3%	5%	3%	10%	—

These are important statistics, because American democracy is based upon the assumption that the average person understands the system and makes rational political decisions as a result. Instead, we have a highly confused electorate. Just prior to the 1976 Florida presidential primary, a Miami newspaper interviewed a thirty-two-year-old male who voted for McGovern in 1972 and was voting for Wallace in 1976. A student of one of the authors also said he was voting for Wallace. His reason was that his first choice, Ralph Nader, was not in the race. Neither man said his vote was a protest. They simply failed to see any inconsistency in their voting patterns.

Many Americans even report feelings of restriction in discussing political affairs. Very few feel free to discuss politics with anyone.[9]

	U.S.
Don't feel free to discuss politics with anyone	18%
Don't feel free to discuss it with many people	19%
Feel free to discuss it with a few	34%
Feel free to discuss it with anyone	29%

One of the reasons for not discussing politics is not having enough information to carry on an intelligent conversation. The lack of political knowledge stems from various sources. First, most Americans are relatively satisfied with their political system, and therefore are content to let others play the active roles. As a result, however, whenever they do participate their comments and actions tend to be based on opinions and emotions rather than on accurate information and rational analysis. Second, it takes time and effort to be well-informed. Citizens find themselves caught up in time-consuming necessary endeavors related to earning a living, taking care of a family, and enjoying a few leisure-time activities. Third, the American political system is difficult to understand because of its complexity. It is comprised of various levels and types of government—over eighty thousand—ranging from a local school board to the national government. It contains two major political parties which lack clear-cut, easy-to-understand philosophies, and which contain members with widely divergent views on all issues, public or private. These things can cause voter confusion.

In addition, when the average American citizen enters the voting booth he or she is likely to face a long ballot containing the names of forty or fifty individuals—most of whom are unknown to the voter—who are running for ten or twenty public offices, some of which the voter cannot describe. There may also be perhaps five or ten bond issues or constitutional amendments, none of which the voter understands, because they are written in legalese, not English.

Beyond the information problem, Americans are politically apathetic for other reasons as well. Many citizens do not express their political convictions publicly because of the controversial nature of politics. The following quote gives some of the considerations of citizens in making public their political convictions and concludes with the foreseeable result.[10]

> The democratic right of freedom of speech does not insure that people will feel free to express their political convictions publicly at all times. Threats of governmental action will deter some. Others will be blocked from talking or acting in behalf of their political beliefs out of fear of losing friends, alienating neighbors and endangering marriages, jeopardizing their positions in groups, losing business, jeopardizing their jobs, endangering production in their plants, facing community pressures, or exposing their feelings of self-esteem to threat. These are consequences which many people are unwilling to face and, to avoid these consequences, they impose a self-censorship on their political expression, participation, and even emotional involvement. . . . In a democratic society, politics are controversial, and controversiality, while it may encourage interest, also has potential interpersonal consequences which may foster political inactivity.
>
> One general factor contributing to political apathy is the feeling that activity is futile. The individual feels that even if he were active, the political results he desires would probably not come to pass. There is consequently no point in doing anything.

This political apathy exists because people are poorly informed; the political system is, in fact, as people say, terribly complex; people generally are too busy to devote much time to political matters; and

they feel their efforts would not change anything, so why bother? They do not even want to discuss politics because they risk having their egos bruised because they don't know what they're talking about; and they also avoid such discussions because they want to be well-liked, and political discussions often cause hard feelings. For all these reasons, political competence in the United States is very low.

By contrast, in Britain, where the political parties have clear-cut philosophies and platforms, and where strict party discipline is the rule among leaders, it is easy to be an intelligent voter. One only has to examine a few party platforms, select the one most acceptable, and only vote for members of that party. Thus, the British electorate has a high level of political competence.

There are other types of political participation besides voting. In 1972, Sydney Verba and Norman Nie conducted a national survey that found that 22 percent of adult Americans were "political inactives," 15 percent were "voters only," and 4 percent were "parochials" [people who did not vote or even discuss politics, but who would contact a person in government if they had a personal problem in which (usually local) government might help.] "Communitarians" (20 percent) were people who participated in civic, but not campaigning activities; "Campaigners" (who did not participate in civic activities) were 21 percent; and 11 percent were "complete activists" (those who voted, contacted government officials for personal reasons, campaigned, and were involved in civic affairs).

In 1993, Verba, Schlozman, Brady and Nie published a study of political participation focusing primarily on activists. They broke down their sample by variables such as socioeconomic status (advantaged/disadvantaged), attitudes (conservative/liberal), and type of benefits received, if any (non-means tested/means tested). Means tested benefits include Medicaid, food stamps, housing subsidies and Aid to Families with Dependent Children (AFDC). Non-means tested benefits include social security, Medicare, veterans benefits and educational loans. The study focused on seven types of political activities: voting, contacting government officials, protesting, involvement in community activities, membership in public boards, working in a campaign, and making financial contributions.

Not surprisingly, they found that people who were economically advantaged were two to fifteen times as likely to be politically active than those who were disadvantaged. Conservatives were slightly more likely to vote and to contribute money to campaigns. Liberals were slightly more likely to be campaign workers, and much more likely to engage in protests (46% to 28%).

Table 19-5
Proportion of Votes, Campaign Money, Contacts, and Protests from Various Population Groups

Political Activities	Socio-Economic Status		Attitudes		Benefits	
	Advantaged	Disadvantaged	Conservative	Liberal	Non-Means-Tested	Means-Tested
Percentage of sample	17	19	38	30	29	9
Votes						
Activists	26	13	38	34	30	9
Activity	26	13	38	34	30	9
Campaign work						
Activists	36	6	36	40	27	7
Activity	31	7	33	43	30	10
Contributions						
Activists	40	4	40	36	27	4
Activity	65	1	42	35	25	2
Contacts						
Activists	30	7	38	36	28	7
Activity	34	6	38	36	27	6
Protests						
Activists	30	2	28	46	20	7
Activity	31	2	25	52	22	6

Source: Sydney Verba, et al., "Citizen Activity: Who Participates? What Do They Say?" *American Political Science Review,* June 1993, p. 309.

Socioeconomic level and whether one receives means-tested benefits are more significant than political attitudes in identifying important public issues. The following two tables show that recipients of means-tested benefits are by far the most concerned about basic human needs, and somewhat more interested in educational issues. These are the content areas of activities that they are most likely to participate in, although this group has the lowest overall political participation rate.

The disadvantaged are significantly more interested in issues and more likely to participate in activities that have to do with basic human

Table 19-6
Respondents
Mentioning Particular
Issues as the Subject of
Their Activity

Issues	All	Population Groups (Percentage)		
		Disadvan-taged	Advan-taged	Receives Means-Tested Benefit
Basic human needs	10	21	8	32
Economic issues	10	5	12	9
Social issues	10	6	12	9
Education	12	10	15	18
Environment	9	2	8	2
Crime or drugs	9	10	6	8
Foreign policy	3	0	3	0

Source: Data compiled from U.S. Bureau of the Census, Current Population Reports, *series p-20, No. 453, and earlier reports.*

needs. There is not much difference between disadvantaged liberals and conservatives on this issue. The biggest difference between advantaged liberals and conservatives is in their focus on economic issues. Conservatives are two-and-a-half times as likely to focus on economic issues.

Table 19-7
Liberal and
Conservatives
Mentioning Particular
Issues as the Subject of
Their Activity

Issues	Disadvantaged		Advantaged	
	Liberals	Conserva-tives	Liberals	Conserva-tives
Basic human needs	21	17	10	8
Economic issues	7	7	7	17

Source: Data compiled from U.S. Bureau of the Census, Current Population Reports, *series p-20, No. 453, and earlier reports.*

Political communication differs, not only regarding contacts with government, but frequency as well. The economically advantaged are much more likely to be activists, and much more likely to communicate their concerns frequently than other groups. Those who receive means-tested benefits score the lowest on both counts, followed by the economically disadvantaged.

We can conclude that economic circumstances are a much more significant indicator of political participation, especially effective participation, than is political orientation (liberal/conservative). Most importantly, those in power are most likely to listen to citizens, even activists, who articulate their concerns, demands, and policy preferences frequently. Thus, the economically advantaged also tend to be politically advantaged. The economically disadvantaged who are most dependent on government assistance are the least likely to be heard by

Table 19.8
Mean Activity Score by Demographic Characteristics, Attitudes, Needs, and Receipt of Benefits

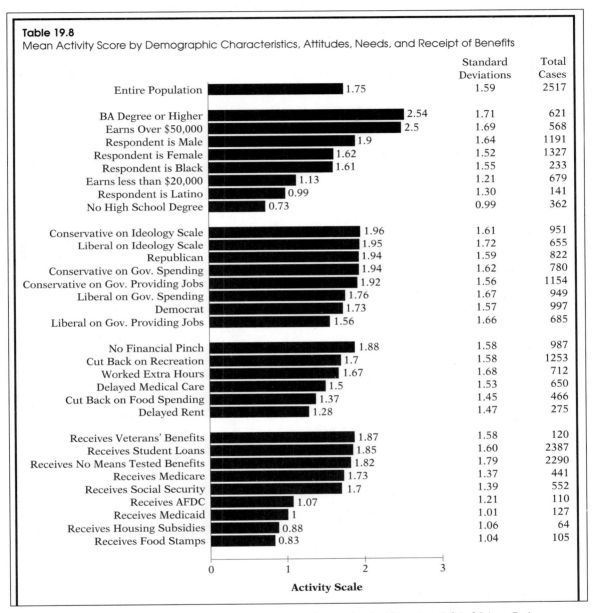

	Activity Scale	Standard Deviations	Total Cases
Entire Population	1.75	1.59	2517
BA Degree or Higher	2.54	1.71	621
Earns Over $50,000	2.5	1.69	568
Respondent is Male	1.9	1.64	1191
Respondent is Female	1.62	1.52	1327
Respondent is Black	1.61	1.55	233
Earns less than $20,000	1.13	1.21	679
Respondent is Latino	0.99	1.30	141
No High School Degree	0.73	0.99	362
Conservative on Ideology Scale	1.96	1.61	951
Liberal on Ideology Scale	1.95	1.72	655
Republican	1.94	1.59	822
Conservative on Gov. Spending	1.94	1.62	780
Conservative on Gov. Providing Jobs	1.92	1.56	1154
Liberal on Gov. Spending	1.76	1.67	949
Democrat	1.73	1.57	997
Liberal on Gov. Providing Jobs	1.56	1.66	685
No Financial Pinch	1.88	1.58	987
Cut Back on Recreation	1.7	1.58	1253
Worked Extra Hours	1.67	1.68	712
Delayed Medical Care	1.5	1.53	650
Cut Back on Food Spending	1.37	1.45	466
Delayed Rent	1.28	1.47	275
Receives Veterans' Benefits	1.87	1.58	120
Receives Student Loans	1.85	1.60	2387
Receives No Means Tested Benefits	1.82	1.79	2290
Receives Medicare	1.73	1.37	441
Receives Social Security	1.7	1.39	552
Receives AFDC	1.07	1.21	110
Receives Medicaid	1	1.01	127
Receives Housing Subsidies	0.88	1.06	64
Receives Food Stamps	0.83	1.04	105

Activity Scale

Source: Sydney Verba, et al. "Citizen Activity: Who Participates? What Do They Say?" *American Political Science Review,* June 1993, p. 306.

those whose decisions affect the quality of their lives. And the worse their economic circumstances, the less likely they are to voice their needs.

Table 19.9
Representation of Various Levels of Need: Logged Representations Scores by Type of Activists

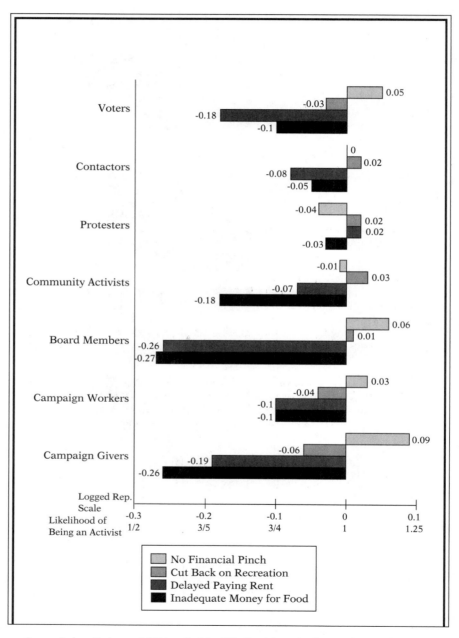

Source: Sydney Verba, et al. "Citizen Activity: Who Participates? What Do They Say?" *American Political Science Review,* June 1993, p. 308.

Individualism

Individualism and extreme competitiveness are two other important characteristics of American political culture. A sociologist, Philip Slater, described America's emphasis on individualism: "We seek a private house, a private means of transportation, a private garden, a private laundry, self-service stores, and do-it-yourself skills of every kind. . . . Even within the family Americans are unique in their feelings

---

The individual owes his first duty to the State and only secondarily to his personal welfare.

	U.S.
Agree	25%
Disagree	68%

---

that each member should have a separate room, and even a separate telephone, television and car, when economically possible."[11] He could have added, "a separate bathroom." Almond and Verba also found that individualism supersedes duty to the state in the minds of most Americans.[12]

Extreme Competitiveness

All their lives Americans are encouraged to compete, to win, to be the best. It starts in school with kindergarten and on the athletic field with the Little Leagues. If you have spent any time at all watching Little League games, you have probably seen a manager or coach who thinks he's another Vince Lombardi. It doesn't matter to him that these are kids, and not the Green Bay Packers. He plays the first team practically all the time, and lets the other kids suffer. He screams when they make a mistake; and, in general, acts like a Marine drill sergeant in boot camp. Never mind teaching the kids sportsmanship; never mind letting all of them have fun. The only thing that matters to this fellow is winning. Thus, we reinforce good athletes, and perhaps scar others for life with a feeling of inferiority. What they do learn is that they must compete.

After finishing or dropping out of school, young people are forced to compete for jobs, and then for promotions and pay increases. The work ethic that emphasizes individual effort, self-reliance, and competition is drummed into the American mind consistently. The reality of the competitive struggle to earn a living in the marketplace reinforces that teaching. Consequently, Americans who are working are generally reluctant to support social and economic reforms to elevate those at or near the bottom of the economic ladder. There is a widespread lack of compassion for the underprivileged, who are termed "losers." Many myths are perpetuated to justify not helping these people.

The myth persists among the general population that the majority of people on welfare are able-bodied men who drive Cadillacs, when the statistics indicate that the overwhelming majority are single or divorced mothers with dependent children. The myth persists that most welfare recipients are black, when the statistics clearly indicate that the majority are Caucasian. The myths persist because a society that is socialized to believe that anyone who is willing to work can find a job, and anyone who works can get ahead, cannot accept the fact that some people are willing to work but cannot find a job, and some work very hard and still remain poverty-stricken. One writer concludes: "Most Americans continue to profess a strong confidence in the possibilities of personal achievement in the American milieu. A great many continue to believe that personal success is attainable by hard work and skill."[13]

As previously mentioned, this attitude has its roots in the Protestant work ethic, and has been subsequently reinforced first by Social Darwinism, and then by the Horatio Alger stories. Some people might think that only older Americans think this way. However, even American youth accept this popular belief, as indicated by these responses from a 1972 survey.[14]

Any able-bodied person can secure a job if he tries hard enough.

Percent Agreeing

College students	Non-school youth	High school students
54	82	82

It is ironic that the less educated and less privileged are not as sympathetic to the problems of the underprivileged as are the more educated. However, even among college students a majority accept the dominant view. When grade-point average is introduced as a variable, some interesting results occur. A majority of *A* students reject the assumption; and college students with a *C* average are shown to be no different on this attitude from non-college educated youth.[15]

It was generally acknowledged in the 1972 presidential elections

---

Any able-bodied person can secure a job if he tries hard enough.

Percent Agreeing

College students				High school students			
A	B	C+	C	A	B	C+	C
45	52	61	78	77	79	86	87

that the more liberal candidates, McGovern and Humphrey, were much more likely to support programs to help the underprivileged than were the more conservative candidates, Nixon and Wallace. It would seem logical, then, for lower income individuals to support either McGovern or Humphrey, but as Table 19-10 shows, this was not the case. The rugged individualism and self-reliance preached by Nixon and Wallace apparently appealed to many young people who lacked a college education.

Table 19-10
Preconvention Choice
of Youth, Summer 1972

	College Students	Non-school Youth	High School Students
McGovern or Humphrey	60%	41%	42%
Wallace or Nixon	25%	47%	47%

Source: Adapted from *Saturday Review*, October 14, 1972, p. 70. Copyright © 1972 by *Saturday Review*. All rights reserved. Reprinted with permission.

Impersonalism

Lack of compassion for the disadvantaged is also due to the impersonalism that characterizes American society. People are taught to "mind your own business if you want to stay out of trouble." We have cases of people being beaten, stabbed, and even killed before dozens of witnesses and no one even bothering to call the police. The Kitty Genovese case in 1965, in which thirty-seven people reported they had seen a man stabbing a woman off and on over an extended period of time but not one bothered to call the police, is an example of this phenomenon. A similar case occurred in 1976 when an elderly man bled to death on a busy sidewalk while people actually stepped over him. We also have thousands of sick old people committed to institutions that are not fit for human habitation. In many cases they were committed to such "nursing homes" by their own children. How can anyone expect people who are so impersonal with their own parents to exhibit compassion for millions of underprivileged people whom they do not even know?

Materialism

At the root of the callousness is another important cultural characteristic—materialism. Success in the United States is usually measured in monetary terms. People are judged more often than not by the amount of money they make. Young people are discouraged from entering interesting or humanitarian occupations if they do not pay much.

Apparently, they've been paying attention. College freshmen have been polled since 1966, and the changes in their attitudes are startling. When asked in 1970 what their essential or important objectives were, 39 percent said "being very well off financially." In 1986, 73 percent made that statement. Whereas 69 percent stated "help others who are in difficulty" in 1966, this figure dropped to 57 percent in 1986. Finally, those who said they "wanted to get involved in cleaning up the environment" dwindled from 43 percent in 1970 to 16 percent in 1986.[16]

As an illustration of the materialism that pervades American society, we can turn to one of the government agencies that has been created for the welfare of the citizens, the Food and Drug Administration (FDA). It is alarmingly understaffed, its safety standards are sometimes frightening, and the director who was appointed in 1969, Dr. Charles Edwards, seemed to be more concerned with prices and profits than he was with safety. Dr. Edwards was asked in a Senate hearing why there could be up to 150 insect fragments or rodent hairs in a half-pound of chocolate candy. Dr. Edwards replied that to improve the standards would increase the price of candy.

It was then pointed out that the FDA was permitting food processors to include additives, preservatives, and coloring to food which added nothing to the nutritional value but which either had produced cancer in laboratory animals or had not been properly tested to determine if they were harmful. Dr. Edwards replied:

> You get the Naders on one side, who say, "really you shouldn't have to take *any* risk," and you get industry on the other side, who say you should be willing to take perhaps a greater risk than you or I feel we should. Somewhere in the middle probably lies the real answer. Just how much protection does the consumer want? Because we're going to eventually begin to talk about big dough, I mean big dough. And we're beginning to step on the toes of the free enterprise system. We've already begun it. Jesus, we already have.[17]

In other words, he is saying to the American people, "How much money are you willing to spend for food to avoid getting cancer?" And he assumes the answer is, "Not very much." In 1976 red dye #2, the most widely used food coloring, was shown to be a cancer-causing agent in animals. The FDA (with a new director) decided to outlaw this product, but a court injunction allowed it to be sold while further investigations were conducted. Instead of placing the burden of proof on the producer, it was placed on the state to prove that red dye #2 was harmful. When it was finally outlawed, red dye #40 was allowed to replace it. This was also shown to be carcinogenic.

A similar attitude prevails at the Bureau of Narcotics and Dangerous Drugs (BNDD). Both the FDA and the BNDD are reluctant to step on the toes of the drug manufacturing companies. These companies

"Don't you remember me? I'm the guy who inspected your place last time—seven years ago."

manufacture millions of pills and other drugs that find their way into the illicit drug traffic. Nothing is done to stop them.

America's materialism was caused by two historical factors: (1) the great economic opportunity presented by a vast land rich in natural resources and (2) the absence of a hereditary aristocracy. If one was not doing well financially, it was possible to simply "move west." The lack of a privileged class enabled Americans to climb up the social ladder simply by accumulating wealth. Thus, materialism became the way to "get ahead." Some of the wealthiest and most highly respected families in America accumulated their fortunes through unscrupulous means. But the means proved to be no obstacle in climbing the social ladder.

These five characteristics explain why in the entire history of the United States we have had only two brief periods in which Congress passed a great deal of reform legislation: Franklin D. Roosevelt's first term of office (the New Deal) and Lyndon Johnson's first two years in the presidency (the Great Society). The first occurred because of a depression of such length and severity that traditional values had to be discarded; and the second took place because John Kennedy had been assassinated, and the American people and the Congress tried to compensate somehow for his tragic death by passing legislation he had sought to pass as President. However, in the absence of an extreme crisis, these five characteristics (the private orientation, individualism, extreme competitiveness, impersonalism, and materialism) of the

American people tend to favor the status quo and to discourage social change. In contrast, other societies have political cultures that stress more collectivism and cooperation (Israel, Great Britain, and the Scandinavian countries in particular), and are more personalistic (Latin American countries).

Racism

Racism is another striking American cultural characteristic. **Racism** is a belief in the inferiority of one race in relation to another. This belief is usually accompanied by prejudice (an attitude) and discrimination (an act). Black people were brought to this country as slaves, and although slavery was abolished in 1862, just a few years later African Americans were again sold out in the political compromise of 1876. Despite constitutional amendments and court rulings designed to protect the rights of blacks, they still do not enjoy equal treatment; many Caucasian Americans still consider blacks to be inferior. A Harris poll in 1968 showed that 44 percent of whites interviewed admitted they believed that most white people have more native intelligence than African Americans. The same poll showed that 34 percent of whites believed that whites care more for their families than do blacks. Not only did this poll indicate that many Caucasians believe their race is intellectually and morally superior to blacks, but the percentage who held these views was higher than it was five years earlier (39% and 31%).[18] A University of Chicago study published in 1987 showed that "41% of Americans believe a person who claims blacks are genetically inferior should be allowed to teach at a university." The same study found that "53% of Americans think African Americans shouldn't push themselves where they're not wanted."[19]

American racism can be attributed primarily to two historical developments: America's westward expansion and its unique system of slavery.[20] In one case nonwhite people were exploited because they were an obstacle to continental expansion. More than half of the American Indians were killed, an act that was justified by defining American Indians as inferiors and uncivilized savages. The danger in defining groups of people as inferior is that one no longer feels morally obligated to treat them as human beings.

Although American Indians are still discriminated against today, they comprise less than 1 percent of the population. Consequently, they have been neglected even by most social reformers until very recently (notable exceptions are Jane Fonda and Marlon Brando). The American Indian Movement (AIM) seems to be the staunchest defender of American Indian rights.

In Latin America natives were also killed, but not slaughtered in comparable proportions. When the Spanish conquistadores came to the western hemisphere, they brought no women with them. Because they were in a situation in which they could only satisfy their sexual desires with Indian women, intermarriage became common, and, therefore, Indians were not considered to be uncivilized subhumans. On the other hand, the British, French, and Dutch who settled in North America brought their families with them. Their primary contact with the American Indians involved fighting against those who resisted the white settlers' encroachment on their land.

A similar contrast existed with respect to slavery. In Latin America slaves were considered to be unfortunate human beings who temporarily found themselves in a difficult situation. They were never considered subhuman property to be treated as objects. Families were not divided. Many slaves were able to buy their freedom with work or money (manumission).

Conversely, in the United States there existed one of the most inhumane forms of slavery in history. Slaves were considered property no different from livestock, to be bought and sold without regard for family ties. The women were frequently sexually assaulted, and the men thoroughly emasculated. In order to train them for slavery, every effort was made to systematically destroy the language, awareness of history, religion, culture, customs, and family structure of these African people. It was also illegal to teach them to read.

These differences account for the much higher degree of racism, prejudice, and discrimination prevalent in the United States. Gunnar Myrdal amply documented racial prejudice in this country in *An American Dilemma*, in the 1940s. Some progress has been made since then. A 1966 study showed that 52 percent of Caucasian Americans would be upset if African Americans moved into the neighborhood. In a 1990 study, 5 percent of Americans said they would not like blacks as neighbors. However, if large numbers of blacks were to move into their neighborhoods, 26 percent of whites would move. In 1978, it was 51 percent, and in 1963, it was 78 percent.

Table 19-11
Attitudes toward
Housing Integration

Question: Would you move if a black family moved next door?		
	1963	*1978*	*1990*
Yes	45 percent	13 percent	5 percent

Source: The Gallup Poll Monthly, June 1990, p. 24.

A Gallup poll in 1967 indicated that 48 percent of Caucasian Americans would support laws prohibiting interracial marriages; in 1987 that figure dropped to 24 percent. Nevertheless, 87 percent of Americans expect special problems with marriages between blacks and whites.[22] In 1986, 48% of American teenage girls would consider marrying a man of a different race if they loved him.[23]

There are some indications that the situation is improving, but not very rapidly. When it comes to voting, however, the reduction in prejudice is substantial, as documented in Table 19-12. Yet 11 percent of Americans think blacks have too much power in America in 1987.[24]

Table 19-12
Political Equality for
Minorities

Question: If your party nominated a generally well-qualified man for president, and he happened to be a (Jew) (Atheist) (Black) would you vote for him? How about a woman?				
Would Vote for:	*1958*	*1978*	*1983*	*1987*
Woman	52%	76%	80%	82%
Jew	62%	82%	88%	89%
Black	38%	77%	77%	79%
Atheist	18%	40%	42%	44%

Source: Index to International Public Opinion, 1987–1988, pg. 466.

Undoubtedly, the degree of racial prejudice varies according to the activity. But in every case there seems to be a loss of support for general principles when they are applied to blacks. Myrdal's thesis of American racism was tested, as shown in Table 19-13.

There are other indications that prejudice is difficult to eradicate in the United States. In 1987 *Public Opinion* reported that 50 percent of Americans think quotas to increase the number of minority students in colleges should be illegal.

Also in 1987, the University of Chicago published a survey showing that 58 percent of Americans think blacks have worse jobs, income, and housing than whites because they just don't have the motivation or will power to pull themselves up out of poverty. The same study showed that thirty-four years after the Supreme Court school desegregation decision, 10 percent of Americans still thought that black and white students should go to separate schools. A 1990 Gallup poll indicated that the more blacks attend integrated schools, the greater the objection of the white parents.

Blacks and Indians have not been the only ones to suffer for their pigmentation. Japanese-Americans were herded into concentration camps during World War II, but not German-Americans. The Louisiana territory was purchased from the French, and Alaska from the Russians; but we took California, Arizona, New Mexico, and Texas from the dark-skinned Mexicans.

Among young people higher education is significantly reducing prejudice toward minority groups. Several studies indicate that college students are less than half as likely to be prejudiced about minorities than high school and nonschool youth.[25]

Given the facts documented above, and assuming that racism and prejudice are undesirable characteristics, the greatest hope for America is to expand its higher education to as many people as possible.

Table 19-13
The Effect of Prejudice Stimuli upon Traditional Values (in percent)

Tradition Value Support		*Value under Stress*		*Loss of Support from Stress*
1. I believe in the principle of brotherhood among men.		1. I would be willing to invite Negroes to a dinner party in my home.		
Agree	94	Agree	29	65
Undecided	5	Undecided	4	
Disagree	1	Disagree	67	
2. Public facilities should be equally available to everyone.		2. I would be willing to stay at a hotel that accommodated Negroes as well as whites.		
Agree	83	Agree	61	22
Undecided	4	Undecided	4	
Disagree	14	Disagree	35	
3. Under our democratic system people should be allowed to live where they please if they can afford it.		3. I would be willing to have a Negro family live next door to me.		
Agree	60	Agree	35	25
Undecided	6	Undecided	2	
Disagree	34	Disagree	63	
4. I believe that all public recreational facilities should be available to all people at all times.		4. I don't think I would mind if Negro children were to swim in the same pool as my children.		
Agree	63	Agree	38	25
Undecided	6	Undecided	8	
Disagree	31	Disagree	54	

Source: Frank R. Westie, "The American Dilemma: An Empirical Test," *American Sociological Review*, Vol. 30 (August 1965), p. 532. Reprinted by permission.

Table 19-14
Integrated Schools, 1990

Question: Would you have any objection to sending your children to a school where a few, half, or more than half the children are black?			
	Few	*Half*	*More than half*
Yes	1%	10%	31%
No	99%	87%	63%

Source: The Gallup Poll Monthly, June, 1990, p. 26.

Table 19-15
Attitudes of Youth
Toward Minorities

Minority groups would improve their situation faster if they did not agitate as much as they do.							
Percent Agreeing							
College Students			Non-school Youth		High School Students		
27			60		62		
College Students					High School Students		
A	B	C+	C		A	B	C+	C
19	28	29	38		56	62	61	64

Despite the fact that the United States is a nation of immigrants, ignorance of immigrant contributions is widespread. A 1987 poll found that 44 percent of Americans cannot name a significant contribution made to America by immigrants.[26] Another study found that 78 percent of Americans think that refugees entering the country are an important threat to America. The same 1984 study found that 37 percent of Americans think a man from England who wants to start a new life for himself here should not be admitted to America.[27] A certain amount of antisemitism is demonstrated by the fact that 34 percent of American gentiles said they wouldn't want their children marrying Jews.[28]

Anti-intellectualism

Anti-intellectualism is another important aspect of American political culture. Americans pride themselves on their pragmatism. Being practical is held in the highest esteem. And although most intellectuals are also practical, the image of the absent-minded professor or of the mad scientist are popular myths, Benjamin Franklin and Thomas Jefferson notwithstanding.

Most Americans believe that intellectuals make useful contributions only if they invent an electric light bulb or construct the theory of relativity. This can have serious socioeconomic ramifications because the people "have an antipathy to formal thinking which has caused them to shy away from programs of long-range social change. Thus American thought is tentative, fragmented, directed at the immediate object, and open to change at both ends."[29]

Often the attitude against intellectuals is simply that they are "impractical idealists." At other times they are labeled as "subversives." The reason for such harsh judgment is based upon a critical difference in educational backgrounds. Most Americans have been socialized in their homes and schools to believe that in America we have a near perfect society. Or at least that if we do have faults, they are minimal and

White Racism
In a confrontation over school busing in South Boston, 1976, a black attorney is attacked with a flagpole while Old Glory waves in the land of the free and home of the brave.

we are still far superior to other societies. The corollary is that if one does not agree with that assessment, one should move elsewhere ("America, love it or leave it!").

Intellectuals, on the other hand, are more difficult to satisfy. They have higher standards. They believe in the pursuit of truth as the highest goal, no matter where it leads them. They have studied other cultures, societies, systems, and perhaps, have traveled widely. They have a better basis for comparison, and they are usually not reluctant to point out our weaknesses. Many intellectuals perceive a need to be social (or economic or political) critics. To improve society, it is necessary to first identify what is wrong with it. What good does it do to pat ourselves on the back and say how great we are? That attitude is not going to eliminate poverty, racism, or any of the other ills that beset us. The result is that intellectuals tend to emphasize the negative in the hope of improving the quality of life.

The majority of the American people, however, perceive this critical attitude as being subversive. Intellectuals make them feel uncomfortable by questioning deeply held values and beliefs as well as revered institutions. To criticize America is thought to be unAmerican. The general reaction is, "If you criticize this country, it must be because you don't like it."

The arrogance of many intellectuals in their personal dealings with others does not help their cause. Sometimes they are condescending or impatient with those who disagree with them—particularly if such people are less educated. The normal reaction to such assaults on one's ego is to retaliate; to put one's psychological defense mechanisms into gear, and to attack the person who questioned one's intelligence and made one feel intellectually inferior, if not downright stupid. Thus, arrogant intellectuals contribute to anti-intellectualism.

Seymour Martin Lipset, a well-known political sociologist, believes that attacks on specific segments of the academic community have been aimed, not at intellectuals, but at the opinions of the group. He points out:[30]

> Until recently, we did not have any conservative intellectuals. The dominant coloration of the social science academicians, of the most significant literary figures, of the intellectual journals of opinion, has always been on the left of the political spectrum. Thus, anti-intellectualism has been a natural weapon of the conservatives.

In support of his reasoning, we may point to the epithet "egghead" used against Adlai Stevenson when he ran for president in 1952 and 1956; and applause received by Governor George Wallace in his presidential campaigns when he railed against "pointy-headed professors" and "pseudointellectuals." In both cases it was primarily the liberalism of the targets that evoked the venom.

Intellectuals are often considered "different." They are interested in ideas and "highfalutin" activities like reading books and attending plays. They do not conform to the patterns of thinking and behaving that characterize the general populace. A conservative intellectual has written about the typical American: "He makes an ideology of normality; he asks not 'What am I?' but 'What is it customary and proper to be around here?' "[31]

In 1835 Alexis de Tocqueville wrote in *Democracy in America,* "I know of no country in which there is so little true independence of mind and freedom of discussion as in America." He was not referring to legal restraints but to voluntary ones. One wonders what he would have said had he been around in the early 1950s when Senator Joseph McCarthy launched a witch-hunt against many intellectuals.

The political effect of this attitude is that, although intellectuals rule in most countries of Europe and elsewhere, they play mainly an advisory role in America. Their advice is judged by lawyers and those in business who do rule. Furthermore:

> Unlike Europeans, the Americans have had no "grand political theory"; they rarely talk of the "state" or even of "government," but rather of "the government" and "the administration." It is almost as if there were a fear of principles because they might lead to commitments from which it would be difficult to extricate oneself.[32]

There are certain contradictory political beliefs held by many Americans who believe in some abstract ideal but not in its practice. Interestingly, as maligned as our politicians are, they generally come closer to the ideals of freedom, democracy, equality, and justice than do members of the general population. In the following section we will explore some of the generally held contradictory beliefs of the public and compare them with some aspects of the elite political culture.

☐ Contradictory Beliefs toward Government

The public strongly believes that America has the best form of government in the world; yet there is widespread cynicism and mistrust of politicians and politics. One political analyst, Robert Dahl, writes that it is really impossible to find an American opposed to the principle of democracy; that even those who are critical of specific aspects of the system generally support the broad elements of it; and that whenever change is deemed necessary, the means advocated are legal, within-the-system processes. Dahl concludes: "Thus Americans tend to express satisfaction rather than discontent with their lot. Most Americans claim that life in the United States is the best they could attain anywhere in the world; almost no one wants to emigrate."[33]

However, when asked, "How much of the time do you think you can trust the government in Washington?" Americans displayed a lack of trust in their national government, as the data in Table 19-16 indicate.

Herbert McClosky has done considerable research on the political attitudes of political influentials and the electorate. He defines "influentials" as "those people who occupy themselves with public affairs to an unusual degree, such as government officials, elected office holders, active party members, publicists, officers of voluntary associations, and opinion leaders."[34] These people make up the political elite.

He makes it clear that this is not a cohesive group but rather scattered individuals throughout the nation who share certain attitudes and concerns. His findings show that there is much more cynicism

Table 19-16
How Much Americans Trust Their National Government (in percent)

	1968	1966	1964	1958
Always	7	17	14	15
Most of the time	54	48	62	56
Some of the time	36	28	22	23
None of the time	0	3	0	0
Don't know, no answer	3	4	2	6

Source: Inter-University Consortium for Social Research (ICPR).

and distrust of politicians among the general voting public than among the influentials (Table 19-17). By 1986, the situation had not improved. That year, *Public Opinion* reported that 76 percent of Americans think congressional candidates make promises they have no intention of fulfilling.[35]

Table 19-17
Political Influentials vs. the Electorate: Responses to Items Expressing Cynicism toward Government and Politics

Items	Political Influentials (N = 3020)	General Electorate (N = 1484)
	% Agree	
Most politicians are looking out for themselves above all else.	36.3	54.3
Both major parties in this country are controlled by the wealthy and are run for their benefit.	7.9	32.1
Many politicians are bought off by some private interest.	43.0	65.3
The laws of this country are supposed to benefit all of us equally, but the fact is that they're almost all "rich-man's laws."	8.4	33.3
There is practically no connection between what a politician says and what he will do once he gets elected.	21.4	54.0
All politics is controlled by political bosses.	15.6	45.9

Source: Herbert McClosky, "Consensus and Ideology in American Politics," *American Political Science Review,* Vol. 58 (June 1964), p. 368. Tables 19-16 and 19-19 through 19-22 are reprinted by permission.

In February 1976 the *Wall Street Journal* reported the results of several studies that demonstrated the continuing lack of confidence of Americans in their political process:[36]

> "There is a belief that the process is so unresponsive and dishonest that it cannot be used by voters for their purposes," says Patrick Caddell, a pollster for many Democrats. His Cambridge Survey Research surveys show that "fully 4 out of 10 respondents say it doesn't make any difference who wins elections."
>
> A grim array of polling evidence indicates that alienation and cynicism toward politics and government have become pervasive after a confidence-shattering decade stretching from Vietnam through Watergate and a deep recession.

The article then goes on to list the following items:[37]

By a margin of almost two to one, a Caddell poll finds that people "believe most politicians don't really care about me." [In 1987, 55% felt that way.]

58% believe that "people with power are out to take advantage of me," according to a Louis Harris survey. [A 1987 Harris poll found that 66% of Americans felt this way, an increase from 1976.]

49% believe that "quite a few of the people running the government are a little crooked," according to Market Opinion Research, Inc.

68% feel that "over the last 10 years, this country's leaders have consistently lied to the American people," a Caddell study finds.

57% believe that "both the Democratic and Republican parties are in favor of big business rather than the average worker," according to a survey by Peter Hart, a pollster for many Democrats.

These studies reveal the contradiction in American political culture that the people believe they have the best political system in the world, but they do not trust the process or the authorities who rule. Compounding the contradiction is the fact that the electorate also feels a sense of political incompetence and futility (see Table 19-18).

Despite the seeming alienation from the political system, Americans have more pride in their political system than in any other aspect of American life, or than people from the United Kingdom, Germany, Italy, or Mexico (Table 19-19). More recent studies indicate that there is still mistrust of, and lack of confidence in, the national government. In 1987, *Public Opinion* reported that 40% of Americans believe that, generally speaking, government is the problem.[38] Another 1987 study showed that 76% of Americans think the government wastes money.[39] The following month, *Public Opinion* reported that 70% of Americans think the government does not know how to eliminate poverty even if it were willing to spend whatever necessary.[40]

The notion that "all men are created equal" is written into the Declaration of Independence, and is a well-known tenet of American

Table 19-18
Political Efficacy, 1952-1988

Statement: "People like me don't have any say about what government does."						
	1952	*1960*	*1968*	*1976*	*1984*	*1988*
Agree	31%	27%	41%	41%	33%	41%
Disagree	68	72	58	56	66	58
Don't know, not ascertained	1	1	1	3	1	1
Total	100%	100%	100%	100%	100%	100%
(*N*)	(1,799)	(1,954)	(1,337)	(2,403)	(1,978)	(1,775)

Source: Survey Research Center; Center for Political Studies National Election Studies. Data provided by the Inter-university Consortium for Political and Social Research.

Table 19-19

Aspects of Nation in
which Respondents
Report Pride; by Nation

Percentage who say they are proud of	U.S.	U.K.	Germany	Italy	Mexico
Governmental, political institutions	**85**	46	7	3	30
Social legislation	13	18	6	1	2
Position in international affairs	5	11	5	2	3
Economic system	23	10	33	3	24
Characteristics of people	7	18	36	11	15
Spiritual virtues and religion	3	1	3	6	8
Contributions to the arts	1	6	11	16	9
Contributions to science	3	7	12	3	1
Physical attributes of country	5	10	17	25	22
Nothing or don't know	4	10	15	27	16
Other	9	11	3	21	14
Total % of responses*	158	148	148	118	144
Total % of respondents	100	100	100	100	100
Total number of cases	970	963	955	995	1,007

*Percentages exceed one hundred because of multiple responses.

Source: Gabriel A. Almond and Sidney Verba, *Civic Culture: Political Attitudes and Democracy in Five Nations*, p. 64. Copyright © 1963 by Princeton University Press. Reprinted by permission of Princeton University Press. A 1986 Gallup poll of public opinion determined that 89% of Americans are very proud of being American. This shows a slight increase in national pride in twenty-six years.

ideology. It is, perhaps, the least supported by the people, either as a fact or as a value. On equality even the influentials are not very supportive (see Table 19-20 below). Thus, we see that the elite are stronger supporters of political equality, the electorate of economic equality, and they are about even on social equality, but neither is highly supportive of the general concept.

When these results are combined with the prevalence of racism as demonstrated earlier, it becomes clear that belief in equality should not be included as a characteristic of American political culture.

Freedom, Democracy, and Justice

In the United States people widely accept and strongly support abstract concepts such as freedom, democracy, and justice. In actual practice the support is not so strong. This is especially true in regard to tolerance of critics and dissenters. Americans indicate a high level of support for freedom of speech, press and religion, but if asked if an atheist should be allowed to criticize Christianity on television, there is a substantial drop off in support for these First Amendment rights. The due process amendments are not highly supported either.

Table 19-20

Political Influentials vs. the Electorate: Responses to Items Expressing Belief in Equality

Items	Political Influentials (N = 3020)	General Electorate (N = 1484)
	% Agree	
Political Equality		
The main trouble with democracy is that most people don't really know what's best for them.	40.8	58.0
"Issues" and "arguments" are beyond the understanding of most voters.	37.5	62.3
Most people don't have enough sense to pick their own leaders wisely.	28.0	47.8
Social and Ethnic Equality		
We have to teach children that all men are created equal, but almost everyone knows that some are better than others.	54.7	58.3
Regardless of what some people say, there are certain races in the world that just won't mix with Americans.	37.2	50.4
When it comes to the things that count most, all races are certainly not equal.	45.3	49.0
Economic Equality		
Labor does not get its fair share of what it produces.	20.8	44.8
I think the government should give a person work if he can't find another job.	23.5	47.3
The government ought to make sure that everyone has a good standard of living.	34.4	55.9
There will always be poverty, so people might as well get used to the idea.	40.4	59.4

Source: Herbert McClosky, "Consensus and Ideology in American Politics," *American Political Science Review*, Vol. 58 (June 1964), p. 366.

CBS conducted a survey[41] to determine the degree of support for the rights embodied in the Bill of Rights. Three questions dealt with the first amendment, which reads as follows:

Article I. "Congress shall make no law respecting an establishment of religion, or prohibiting the free exercise thereof; or abridging the freedom of speech or of the press; of the right of the people peaceably to assemble and to petition the government for a redress of grievances."

Table 19-21
Political Influentials vs. the Electorate: Responses to Items Expressing Support for *General Statements* of Free Speech and Opinions

Items	Political Influentials (N = 3020)	General Electorate (N = 1484)
	% Agree	
No matter what a person's political beliefs are, he is entitled to the same legal rights and protections as anyone else.	96.4	94.3
I believe in free speech for all, no matter what their views might be.	89.4	88.9
Nobody has a right to tell another person what he should and should not read.	81.4	80.7
You can't really be sure whether an opinion is true or not unless people are free to argue against it.	94.9	90.8
Unless there is freedom for many points of view to be presented, there is little chance that the truth can ever be known.	90.6	85.2
Freedom of conscience should mean freedom to be an atheist as well as freedom to worship in the church of one's choice.	87.8	77.0

Source: Herbert McClosky, "Consensus and Ideology in American Politics," *American Political Science Review,* Vol. 58 (June 1964), p. 363.

Table 19-22
Political Influentials vs. the Electorate: Responses to Items Expressing Support for *Specific Applications* of Free Speech and Procedural Rights

Items	Political Influentials (N = 3020)	General Electorate (N = 1484)
	% Agree	
Freedom does not give anyone the right to teach foreign ideas in our schools.	45.5	50.7
A man oughtn't be allowed to speak if he doesn't know what he's talking about.	17.3	30.7
A book that contains wrong political views cannot be a good book and does not deserve to be published.	17.9	50.3
When the country is in great danger we may have to force people to testify against themselves even if it violates their rights.	28.5	30.3

Items	*Influentials*	*Electorate*
	% Agree	
If someone is suspected of treason or other serious crimes, he shouldn't be entitled to be let out on bail.	33.3	68.9
Any person who hides behind the laws when he is questioned about his activities doesn't deserve much consideration.	55.9	75.7
In dealing with dangerous enemies like the Communists, we can't afford to depend on the courts, the laws, and their slow and unreliable methods.	7.4	25.5

Source: Herbert McClosky, "Consensus and Ideology in American Politics," *American Political Science Review,* Vol. 58 (June 1964), p. 364.

The first question in the CBS survey dealt with peaceful assembly:

Question. As long as there appears to be no clear danger of violence, do you think any group, no matter how extreme, should be allowed to organize protests against the government?

Results

	Percent of People
Yes	21
No	76
Sometimes	—
No response	3

Least supportive of the right to assemble peacefully are women, older people, the less educated, those with low incomes, Catholics and Protestants (as opposed to Jews, secularists and others), Caucasians, and Southerners. The University of Chicago study published in 1987 found that 31 percent of Americans think organizing protest marches and demonstrations against the government should not be allowed.[42]

The second question in the CBS survey dealt with a free press:

> *Question.* Except in time of war, do you think newspapers, radio, and television should have the right to report any story, even if the government feels it's harmful to our national interest?
>
> *Results*
>
> | | Percent of People |
> |---|---|
> | Yes | 42 |
> | No | 55 |
> | Sometimes | 1 |
> | No response | 2 |

Least supportive of press freedom are the same groups as above, except that race ceases to be a factor. A majority of both whites and nonwhites oppose this freedom. In 1987, the University of Chicago also found that 30 percent of Americans think publishing pamphlets to protest against the government should not be allowed. The same study discovered that 37 percent of Americans favored removing from public libraries books opposing churches and religion. Freedom of religion took a beating in another question in that survey. A majority of Americans (54 percent) said they think a person who speaks out against churches and religion should not be allowed to teach in a university.

The third question in the CBS study dealt with free speech:

> *Question.* Do you think everyone should have the right to criticize the government, even if the criticism is damaging to our national interest?
>
> *Results*
>
> | | Percent of People |
> |---|---|
> | Yes | 42 |
> | No | 54 |
> | Sometimes | 1 |
> | No response | 3 |

Nonsupporters of free speech are similar to nonsupporters of a free press, except that race and region of the country are not determining factors, and on this issue, men are less supportive than women.

One of the "due process" amendments of the Constitution is Article VI. It prohibits preventive detention, among other things. It reads as follows:

Article VI. In all criminal prosecutions, the accused shall enjoy the right to a speedy and public trial, by an impartial jury of the State and district wherein the crime shall have been committed, which districts shall have been previously ascertained by law, and to be informed of the nature and cause of the accusation; to be confronted with the witnesses against him; to have compulsory process for obtaining witnesses in his favor, and to have the assistance of counsel for his defense.

The survey question dealt with preventive detention:

Question. If a person is suspected of a serious crime, do you think the police should be allowed to hold him in jail, until they can get enough evidence to officially charge him?

Results

	Percent of People
Yes	58
No	38
Sometimes	1
No response	2

The same groups who oppose a free press favor preventive detention; however, a much higher percentage of Midwesterners than people from other parts of the country agree to hold suspected criminals without formal charges. Another survey discovered that 50 percent of Americans believe the accused are guilty until proven innocent.[43] This is the exact opposite of the foundation upon which the American system of justice is built.

The major aspects of democracy were discussed in the previous chapter. The degree of support among Americans for such principles is shown in Table 19-23.

The scientific studies from the 1960s to the 1990s cited in this chapter tend to indicate that the American electorate is politically ignorant, apathetic, confused, and incompetent. The people are cynical and mistrustful of politics and politicians and also nonsupportive, in practice, of major aspects of American ideology, such as democracy,

Table 19-23
Political Influentials vs. the Electorate: Responses to Items Expressing "Rules of the Game"

Items	Political Influentials (N = 3020)	General Electorate (N = 1484)
	% Agree	
There are times when it almost seems better for the people to take the law into their own hands rather than wait for the machinery of government to act.	13.3	26.9
The majority has the right to abolish minorities if it wants to.	6.8	28.4
We might as well make up our minds that in order to make the world better a lot of innocent people will have to suffer.	27.2	41.6
If congressional committees stuck strictly to the rules and gave every witness his rights, they would never succeed in exposing the many dangerous subversives they have turned up.	24.7	47.4
Almost any unfairness or brutality may have to be justified when some great purpose is being carried out.	13.3	32.8
Politicians have to cut a few corners if they are going to get anywhere.	29.4	43.2
People ought to be allowed to vote even if they can't do so intelligently.	65.6	47.6
To bring about great changes for the benefit of mankind often requires cruelty and even ruthlessness.	19.4	31.3
The true American way of life is disappearing so fast that we may have to use force to save it.	12.8	34.6

Source: Herbert McClosky, "Consensus and Ideology in American Politics," *American Political Science Review*, Vol. 58 (June 1964), p. 362.

freedom, equality, and due process. The people possess these characteristics: a private orientation, individualism, extreme competitiveness, impersonalism, materialism, racism, and anti-intellectualism. From what we saw in the chapter, it is safe to conclude that the American people would not adopt the Bill of Rights today.

Given these facts, the burning question becomes, "How has American democracy survived so long?" There are two major reasons. First, although most Americans do not render specific support for American ideals, they do manifest a high degree of diffuse support. While they are highly critical of the actual political process, they are highly supportive of the general system (Remember, 89 percent said they are very proud to be Americans). Although they oppose specific applications of liberal democracy, they support the broad concepts.

Second, and most important, American democracy survives because "it is only necessary for the politically active citizens to believe in and practice democratic ideals in order for democracy to work."[44]

As the McClosky data indicate, the political elite is more democratic and libertarian than the general public; it is less cynical than the electorate; and it has a greater sense of political competence. The political elite is also more realistic in its expectations and more patient in pursuing its goals.

Table 19-24 shows the contrast between the political elite and the general electorate on a number of characteristics. As a result of the general political culture characteristics of America, political candidates shy away from reasoned arguments and specific issue positions. Instead, they make broad "symbolic" appeals to the people through slogans such as "We must keep America strong," "Our goals are peace and prosperity," or "We must reduce the power in Washington and return it to the people." In no instance is a specific issue addressed by these broad slogans. No American wants a weak America; no one favors war and poverty; and Washington was given power because individuals and lower-level governments could not solve many problems.

An aspect of politics that confuses most Americans is political labels. In one study[45] people were asked either to agree or disagree with

"I'm a conservative, and I'm sick and tired of these wild-spending liberals. What this country needs is another FDR to push for solutions to help the people."

Table 19-24
Political Influentials vs.
the Electorate:
Percentage Scoring
High & Low on
Democratic and Anti-
democratic Attitude
Scales[a]

Scale	Political Influentials (N = 3020)	General Electorate (N = 1484)
	(%s down)	
Faith in Democracy		
% High	40.1	18.5
% Low	14.4	29.7
Procedural Rights		
% High	58.1	24.1
% Low	12.3	31.3
Tolerance		
% High	61.3	43.1
% Low	16.4	33.2
Faith in Freedom		
% High	63.0	48.4
% Low	17.1	28.4
Ethnocentrism		
% High	27.5	36.5
% Low	46.9	36.3
Elitism		
% High	22.8	38.7
% Low	41.0	22.4
Totalitarianism		
% High	9.7	33.8
% Low	60.1	28.4
Right Wing		
% High	17.5	33.1
% Low	45.3	28.9
Left Wing		
% High	6.7	27.8
% Low	68.7	39.3
California F-Scale		
% High	14.7	33.5
% Low	48.0	23.5

[a]Differences between the influentials and the electorate on all the scales in this table are by Kolmorov-Smirnov and Chi-Square tests, statistically significant at or beyond .01 percent level of significance. All scales were divided into thirds. Percentages shown indicate those who scored in the highest or lowest third.

Source: Herbert McClosky, "Consensus and Ideology in American Politics," *American Political Science Review*, Vol. 58 (June 1964), p. 365.

propositions couched in ideological terms, such as "the federal government is interfering too much in state and local matters" or "we should rely more on individual initiative and ability and not so much on government welfare programs."[46] The same people were then asked whether they approved of specific federal programs. Depending upon the replies, the respondents were then placed on a liberal-conservative scale on each set of questions. Table 19-25 below shows the remarkable results. It appears that 65 percent of the public is liberal, but only 16 percent know it; and only 14 percent of the people are conservative, but half think they are.

Table 19-25
Liberalism—
Conservatism on
Ideological and
Programmatic Levels

	Ideological	*Specific Programs*
Completely liberal	4% }16%	44% }65%
Predominantly liberal	12%	21%
Middle-of-the-road	34%	21%
Predominantly conservative	20% }50%	7% }14%
Completely conservative	30%	7%

Source: Polls: Their Use and Misuse in Politics by Charles W. Roll, Jr., and Albert H. Cantril, p. 123. Copyright © 1972 by Basic Books, Inc., New York. Reprinted by permission.

The feeling that government has a responsibility to look out for the economic welfare of the public is a liberal position. Yet, despite the fact that many more people consider themselves conservative than liberal, a high percentage exhibited liberal positions on such issues. Many Americans also held the belief that business needs to be more closely regulated by the federal government, another liberal position. According to the journal *Public Opinion,* in 1987 an astounding 89 percent of American women thought that there should be a federal law guaranteeing maternity leave.[47] Yet 50 percent of women voted for the conservative George Bush for president in 1988 and only 49 percent for the liberal Michael Dukakis who was more likely to support such legislation. The Clinton administration passed such a law in 1993.

In another study cited by *Public Opinion* in 1987, 88 percent of Americans thought that the government must keep a sharp eye on business to get it to clean up its own air and water pollution,[48] but Dukakis, who was endorsed by every environmental group in the country, only received 46 percent of the 1988 presidential vote, while Bush, who was not endorsed by any environmental group, received 54 percent of the vote. A 1986 study by Opinion Research Corporation showed that 43 percent of Americans think that the government should limit the profits companies make,[49] and another study they conducted in 1987 indicated that Americans think business as a whole is making too much profit.[50] Reinforcing these findings is a 1987 University of Chicago study indicating that 37 percent of Americans think the government should control prices.

The role the government should play in the economy is usually considered one on which liberals and conservatives strongly disagree. One would expect that with liberalism on the decline as a general philosophy in the late 1980s, not many people would support strong government participation in the economy. Yet, several studies show otherwise. The University of Chicago found that 68 percent of Americans favor government financing of projects to create new jobs. In fact, 43 percent went so far as to say that the government must see to it that everyone has a job and that prices are stable, even if it means restricting the rights of businessmen. They also discovered that 56 percent of Americans think it is the responsibility of government to meet everyone's needs, even in case of sickness, poverty, unemployment, and old age. A third said that all Americans should be given an income large enough to provide a decent life for their family, no matter their work, and 29 percent think the government should reduce the difference in income between people with high and low incomes.[51] In a *Business Week*/Harris poll conducted in July 1987 a majority (54 percent) of the respondents said they thought that as a result of federal deregulation, job safety, environmental quality, and product safety have all declined.[52]

The smart politician campaigning for public office should then call him or herself a conservative, but take a liberal stance on the issues. Such inconsistency will place a candidate in the middle of the American mainstream and should win a lot of votes.

The smart politician should also deal with issues emotionally, not rationally; otherwise a positive response will not be forthcoming. Why are emotional appeals made?

> As an issue arises, each candidate jockeys for primacy in the opinion-formation process in an effort to see that the mass media reflect his own position. This cannot be achieved through rational appeals and so it must be achieved emotionally. The method is to stigmatize as fearful, dangerous, and alien the position one opposes; to give emotional patriotic coloration to the opinion one supports; and to do everything possible to see that the mass media express this bias.
>
> The responsible candidate who wishes to present the issue rationally is faced with a cruel choice. He must choose between his personal integrity as a responsible democratic leader interested in enhancing the rationality of the political process, and his conviction that the interests of the people can be served only if he emotionalizes the positions he believes to be sound, inducing them to follow the course of reason by manipulative appeals to the irrational. To be a successful democratic leader he must, like his opponents, become a demagogue.[53]

After examining the massive amount of evidence and the scholarly analyses of same, after witnessing and participating in the American political process for many years, one can only reach one logical conclusion with respect to American democracy: the political elite holds it together; and in spite of a politically illiterate and somewhat authoritarian electorate, we somehow muddle through.

REFERENCES

1. Gabriel A. Almond and Sidney Verba, *Civic Culture: Political Attitudes and Democracy in Five Nations*. Copyright © 1963 by Princeton University Press. Reprinted by permission of Princeton University Press. Quoted material is from pp. 89, 263, and 120.
2. Donald J. Devine, *The Political Culture of the United States* (Boston: Little, Brown, 1972), p. 168. This passage and others quoted from Devine in this chapter are copyright © 1972 by Little, Brown and Company, Inc., and are reprinted by permission.
3. *Public Opinion*, November/December 1986.
4. Cited by Lewis Lipsitz, ed., *The Confused Eagle* (Boston: Allyn and Bacon, 1973), p. 13.
5. Devine, p. 38.
6. *Ibid.*
7. Diane Ravitch and Chester Finn, *What Do Our 17-Year-Olds Know?* (New York: Harper & Row, 1987).
8. *Ibid.*, p. 39, *Public Opinion*, May/June 1987.
9. Almond and Verba, p. 83.
10. Morris Rosenberg, "Some Determinants of Political Apathy," in L. Earl Shaw and John C. Pierce, eds., *Readings on the American Political System* (Lexington, Mass.: D. C. Heath, 1970), p. 251.
11. Philip E. Slater, *The Pursuit of Loneliness: American Culture at the Breaking Point* (Boston: Beacon Press, 1970), p. 10.
12. As cited in Devine, p. 193.
13. Robert Dahl, ed., *Political Oppositions in Western Democracies* (New Haven: Yale University Press, 1966), p. 41.
14. *Saturday Review*, October 14, 1972, p. 69.
15. *Ibid.*
16. U.S. Dept. of Commerce, Census Bureau, *Statistical Abstract of the United States: 1988*, p. 142.
17. *Life*, October 20, 1972.
18. Frank Joyce, "Racism in the United States," in Lipsitz, *op. cit.*, p. 143.
19. *General Social Surveys 1972–1987*, conducted for the National Data Program for the Social Sciences at National Opinion Research Center, University of Chicago.
20. Joyce, "Racism in the United States," in Lipsitz, *op. cit.*, p. 138.
21. *Public Opinion*, July/August 1987.
22. General Social Surveys 1972–1987.
23. Simmons Teenage Research Studies, "Opinions on Current Issues, Female Teens 12–19," *Seventeen*, 1986.
24. *Public Opinion*, July/August 1987.
25. *Saturday Review*, October 14, 1972, p. 69.
26. Louis Harris, *Inside America* (New York: Vintage, 1987).
27. Kane, Parsons & Associates, "A Survey of Public Attitudes Toward Refugees and Immigrants," 1984).
28. *Public Opinion*, July/August 1987).
29. Max Lerner, *America as a Civilization* (New York: Simon & Schuster, 1957), p. 718.
30. Seymour Martin Lipset, "The Fuss about Eggheads," in Francis X. Davy and

Robert E. Burkhart, eds., *Perspectives on Our Time* (Boston: Houghton Mifflin, 1970), p. 139.

31. Richard Hofstadter, "Democracy and Anti-Intellectualism in America," in Davy and Burkhart, *op. cit.*, pp. 142–143.
32. Lerner, p. 359.
33. Dahl, *op. cit.*, p. 40.
34. Herbert McClosky, "Consensus and Ideology in American Politics," *American Political Science Review*, Vol. 58 (June 1964), p. 363.
35. *Public Opinion*, November/December 1986.
36. *Wall Street Journal* (February 2, 1976), p. 1.
37. *Wall Street Journal* (February 2, 1976), p. 1.
38. *Public Opinion*, November/December 1987.
39. *Public Opinion*, March/April 1987.
40. *Public Opinion*, May/June 1987.
41. Robert Chandler, *Public Opinion* (New York: R. R. Bowker, 1972). © 1972, CBS Inc. Reprinted by permission.
42. *General Social Surveys 1972–1987.*
43. Lewis Lapham, Michael Pollan, and Eric Etheridge, *The Harper's Index* (New York: Henry Holt, 1987).
44. V. O. Key, "Public Opinion and the Decay of Democracy," *Virginia Quarterly Review*, XXXVII (Autumn 1961), p. 493.
45. Charles W. Roll, Jr., and Albert H. Cantril, *Polls: Their Use and Misuse in Politics* (New York: Basic Books, 1972).
46. *Ibid.*, p. 123.
47. *Public Opinion*, March/April 1987.
48. *Ibid.*
49. *ORC Issue Watch*, Opinion Research Corporation, June 1986.
50. *ORC Issue Watch*, Opinion Research Corporation, November, 1987.
51. *General Social Surveys, 1972–1987.* Conducted for the National Data Program for the Social Sciences at National Opinion Research Center, University of Chicago.
52. *Business Week*/Harris Poll, July 20, 1987.
53. Harvey Wheeler, *The Rise and Fall of Liberal Democracy* (Santa Barbara, Calif.: Center for the Study of Democratic Institutions, 1966), p. 13.

GLOSSARY

Political culture — A society's beliefs, values, attitudes, habits, and behavior regarding political matters.

General political culture — The core political values accepted by most people and the predominant political behavior patterns of a society.

Elite political culture — The orientations of politically powerful or influential individuals and groups within a society.

Private orientation	The tendency to stress private affairs as opposed to concern for public issues.
Individualism	A concern with one's own personal welfare as opposed to a concern with the public welfare.
Competitiveness	An emphasis on winning, irrespective of the consequences.
Impersonalism	A relative lack of concern for others.
Materialism	The doctrine that success is measured in terms of the acquisition of money and the objects it can buy.
Racism	The belief in the inferiority of one race in relation to another.
Anti-intellectualism	A distrust of intellectuals who are thought to be impractical and subversive.

SELECTED READING

Aram, John D., *Presumed Superior: Individualism and American Business* (Englewood Cliffs, N.J.: Prentice-Hall, 1993).
> The author demonstrates the prevalence of individualism in American society and its role in the business community.

"Intimidation and Violence: Racial and Religious Bigotry in America," *United States Commission on Civil Rights* (Wash., D.C.: The Commission, 1990).
> This publication documents the continuation and forms of religious and racial bigotry that still exist in the United States.

Levine, Myron A., *Presidential Campaigns and Elections: issues, images and partisanship* (Itasca, Il.: F. E. Peacock Publishers, Inc., 1992).
> This is an excellent analysis of the various aspects of political campaigning.

Powell, Thomas F., *The Persistence of Racism in America* (Lanham: University Press of America, 1992).
> The author demonstrates that racism persists in our society.

Rose, Douglas, ed., *The Emergence of David Duke and the Policy of Race* (Chapel Hill: University of North Carolina Press, 1992).
> This book shows how an important member of the racist, reactionary wing of American politics attracted many voters in his political campaign.

Survey Research Center; Center for Political Studies, National Election Studies. This University of Michigan research center has a sterling record for conducting studies and disseminating data on a wide variety of social indicators. Their national election studies deal with part of the subject of this chapter.

U.S. Department of Commerce, Census Bureau, Statistical Abstract of the United States (Wash., D.C.: Government Printing Office, Annual). Provides statistics in a variety of areas annually. The data on politics is extremely valuable.

Verba, Sidney, Kay Lehman Schlozman, Henry Brady and Norman H. Nie, "Citizen Activity: Who Participates? What Do They Say?," *American Political Science Review,* June 1993, pp. 303–318.

This article is an expansion and an updating of the classic 1972 study on political participation by Verba and Nie.

The Gallup Poll Monthly, See especially June 1990.

One of the premier polling organizations in the world reports many of its findings in this monthly journal.

QUESTIONS

1. Americans generally tend to be
   a. interested in public policies only when indirectly affected by a particular situation.
   b. public-oriented.
   c. greatly involved in political affairs.
   d. politically apathetic.
   e. exercising more and more their right to vote.

2. Which of the following is not a reason for the political apathy in the U.S.?
   a. widespread dissatisfaction with the existing political system.
   b. lack of knowledge
   c. belief that government is too complicated
   d. absence of the feeling of freedom to discuss politics with others
   e. belief that political activity is futile

3. Which group is most sympathetic to the problems of the under-privileged?
   a. college-educated citizens
   b. less-educated and less-privileged citizens
   c. high-school students
   d. blue-collar workers
   e. white-collar workers

4. A 1993 political participation study by Verba and others found that:
   a. The economically advantaged were several times more likely to be politically active than those who were disadvantaged.

   b. Liberals were more likely to contribute money and vote than conservatives.

   c. Conservatives were more likely to be campaign workers and engage in protests than liberals.

   d. People's political attitudes were more significant than socioeconomic levels in identifying important public issues.

5. The country that stresses collectivism and cooperation in its political culture least is
   a. the U.S.
   b. Israel.
   c. Great Britain.
   d. Norway.
   e. Sweden.

6. A belief in the inferiority of one race in relation to another is best known as
   a. prejudice.
   b. discrimination.
   c. racism.
   d. class struggle.
   e. racial pride.

7. A federal law guaranteeing maternity leave was passed by the U.S. Congress in the administration of President:
   a. Jimmy Carter
   b. Ronald Reagan
   c. George Bush
   d. Bill Clinton

8. Intellectuals have been criticized for many things in America. Which of the following is not true of intellectuals?
   a. They tend to be social critics.
   b. They question deeply held values and beliefs.
   c. Arrogance hurts their cause at times.
   d. They tend to emphasize the negative to improve the quality of life.
   e. They have no better basis for comparison of social systems than any average citizen.

9. Success in the United States is generally measured in what terms?
   a. aesthetic
   b. religious
   c. economic
   d. service to mankind
   e. educational

10. According to a 1970 CBS survey, which of the following rights guaranteed by the First Amendment to the Constitution is supported by a majority of Americans?
    a. peaceful assembly
    b. freedom of speech
    c. freedom of the press
    d. all of the above
    e. none of the above

QUESTIONS FOR THOUGHT AND DISCUSSION

1. What does the Verba, et al. 1993 study of political participation tell us about U.S. political culture?

2. Why does the United States have a lower voter turnout than other industrialized democracies?

3. Has racism increased, decreased, or stayed the same in the United States?

20

American Political Orientations and Ethnic Politics

American political culture is fragmented into various political orientations or subcultures. The political labels that Americans use in classifying themselves and others is our theme in this chapter.

Political orientations develop from attitudes that are made up of values and beliefs. The following example shows how they are related.

Belief—All rappers are violent
+
Value—Violence is bad
Attitude—Dislike for rappers

Generally, attitudes result from clusters of beliefs and values, rather than from a single set as shown above. All of one's attitudes regarding politics combine to form one's political orientation.

Beliefs + Values = Attitude
+
Beliefs + Values = Attitude
+
Beliefs + Values = Attitude
Political orientation

Why is it important to study political orientations? Because many scientific studies conducted over the last four decades indicate that the general population has little interest in politics and little accurate information regarding political issues. This is understandable since most people are relatively satisfied with the political system and they are faced with more pressing, time-consuming problems in their daily lives. This means, however, that whenever people do talk about politics they stress opinions and evaluations, not information. Therefore, whenever they engage in political activities such as voting, they do so primarily on the basis of their political orientations—their political attitudes and inclinations. That is why we have devoted a chapter to American political orientations. We will begin by discussing some of the classification schemes commonly used in the United States, and then we will suggest an alternative conceptual framework.

The manner in which political labels are often used by the mass media and, to a lesser degree, by members of the academic community is often confusing. If the purpose of using words is to convey thoughts and feelings as accurately as possible, our overused political labels need to be revised and defined more precisely. It is not uncommon to pick up a newspaper and read: "Leftist Students Riot in Mexico" or "Right-Wing Elements Gain at Polls in Germany." Such headlines scream messages at the American public, who are not quite sure of their meanings, but who often experience a deep emotional reaction to the terms "left" and "right."

Unfortunately, scholars are sometimes just as guilty of using political terms imprecisely, and perhaps as an epithet against those with whom they disagree, as are the pundits of radio, television, and the print media. Use of the terms "left" and "right" originated during the French Revolution, and resulted from a seating arrangement in the

"Chinese Students Demonstrate for the Democratization of the Regime"
This April 17, 1989 photo had this caption: "Thousands of students demonstrate in Beijing on the occasion of the death of Hu Yaobang, the former head of the Communist Party whose exaggerated liberalism earned him the nickname 'the Democrat' and resulted in his dismissal from office." The imprecise use of political labels contributes to the average person's confusion over politics.

legislature. Obviously, this use has no relevance to American politics today and results in a serious oversimplification of a complex situation. Although political labels can serve as a useful shortcut in the reasoning process, improper use can lead to misunderstandings, confusion, and hence to erroneous judgments.

Usually people are assigned political labels as a result of their philosophical orientations or group memberships. The term "socialist" implies a certain economic and philosophical orientation (although there are several varieties). "Radical" refers to someone who seeks a drastic change in the status quo and/or is willing to employ drastic means to attain his or her goals. "Democrat" refers to membership in a particular political party.

These and other labels are then arranged on a spectrum from "extreme left" to "extreme right" in some manner, depending on who is doing it. If students are asked to do this, with the categories listed here, they usually place them on the spectrum as shown in the diagram.

Categories

Communist	Democrat	Moderate
Fascist	Republican	
Socialist	Liberal	
Capitalist	Conservative	
Reactionary	Radical	

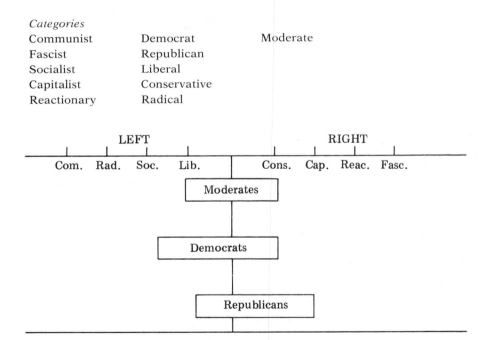

This arbitrary scheme, which may vary somewhat according to who sets it up (which is a tribute to its precision), begins on the extreme left with Communists and ends at the extreme right with Fascists—probably the two terms misused most frequently. In between, on the left, we find radicals, socialists, liberals, moderates, Democrats and Repub-

Radical? Reactionary? Conservative? Liberal? Although within both major political parties in the United States we find a wide range of political ideologies, the Republican party is clearly dominated by conservatives. Here we see Ronald Reagan, the most conservative President since Herbert Hoover, renominated for the presidency at the 1984 Republican Convention, accompanied by then Vice-President George Bush.

licans. On the right we have reactionaries, capitalists, conservatives, moderates, Democrats, and Republicans as well. Needless to say these categories sometimes overlap.

If you are confused at this point or disagree with the arrangement of categories, it is understandable. There are, of course, capitalists who are liberal (whatever that is); socialists who are moderate; Democrats and Republicans who are capitalists or socialists. Sometimes terms are combined, and people are labeled radical liberals. Perhaps the zenith of ambiguity was reached by the New Jersey politician who described himself as a moderately liberal conservative.

Given this political Tower of Babel we can ask ourselves, Is it any wonder that people shy away from political discussions? And if they do indulge, is it surprising to find that they usually deteriorate into heated arguments? Or that out of a failure to communicate effectively people become confused and frustrated? The answers are obvious and the reason is clear: Few people understand very precisely what anybody else is saying. The terms used are ambiguous and confusing, and few bother to define them.

Let's take another look at the headlines mentioned earlier: "Leftist Students Riot in Mexico." It is not unreasonable for a rational human being to ask, "What the hell is a leftist?" According to the diagram, a leftist might be a Communist, radical, socialist, liberal, moderate, Democrat, or Republican. "Right-Wing Elements Gain at the Polls in Germany." What in heaven's name is a right-winger? Such a person might be anything from a moderate to a member of the American Nazi party, or even a right-handed pitcher for the New York Mets!

Besides being vague and confusing, these categories, as they are usually positioned politically, are also misleading in other ways. The left-right syndrome implies that Communists and Fascists are ideologically and behaviorally far apart, at opposite extremes of the spectrum, when actually they are very much alike. Both try to influence or control every aspect of life, use violence, employ terror tactics (the *arbitrary* use of force), make extensive use of propaganda, destroy or take over all existing institutions and associations, monopolize the educational system and the means of communication, employ a secret police, embrace a comprehensive ideology which purportedly guides their activities and justifies their monopoly of power, and so on, *ad nauseam*.

This weakness of categories can be resolved by using a circular diagram in which Communists and Fascists meet in the back, thereby demonstrating how similar they are.

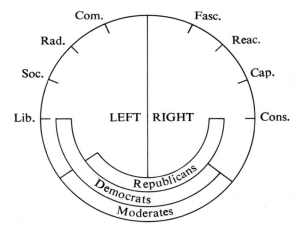

This scheme, nevertheless, contains all the other weaknesses inherent in the first framework and furthermore implies:

1. That liberals are closer to Communists than they are to conservatives.
2. That conservatives are closer to Fascists than they are to liberals.
3. That liberals and conservatives are at opposite extremes of the circular spectrum, when in reality they have more in common with each other than either has with Communists or Fascists.
4. That liberalism may be a step in the direction of communism, which appears to be an extension of liberalism.
5. That conservatism may be a step in the direction of fascism, which appears to be an extension of conservatism.

In short, changing the shape of the spectrum will not eliminate these weaknesses. What is needed is a new conceptual framework which excludes the terms "left" and "right" and the concept of a spectrum. The diagram below shows an alternative scheme used and modified by one of the authors in classroom teaching over a number of years.

Attitude Toward Social Change

Optimistic	Pessimistic	
LIBERALS	**CONSERVATIVES**	*Willingness to work within existing political system*
Will work only within system		
Willing to work outside of system		
RADICALS	**REACTIONARIES**	

The vertical axis separates those who are optimistic toward social change from those who feel that any change will probably make matters worse. This difference stems from their respective views of society's proper role in the life of individuals, the proper goals that should be pursued, and their interpretations of present-day realities. Liberals and radicals believe American society contains inequities and injustices and, since they value equality and justice, they seek social change. Conservatives and reactionaries perceive reality differently—they don't see much inequality and injustice. Indeed, reactionaries tend to believe there is too much equality. Consequently both groups tend to resist social change. The horizontal axis separates those who pursue their goals only by working within the existing political system from those who will use any means to attain their goals—even if it means working outside the system. This difference, we think, is far more significant than differences in attitudes toward social change which roughly correspond to the left-right division examined earlier. In other words the horizontal axis separates those who adhere strictly to the democratic process from those who will abandon it if the results are not to their liking.

Let us now examine more closely the political orientations of liberals and conservatives, beginning with their similarities and then turning to their differences.

☐ Similarities between Liberals and Conservatives

1. *They are not ideologically oriented.* They examine society's problems and take a stand on an issue-by-issue basis. There is no comprehensive

A Liberal Candidate
Edward M. Kennedy exemplifies the nonideological, pragmatic approach to working within the system for change. To liberals, the use of the federal government to solve economic and social problems is justified by their definition of liberty as ''the ability to choose among alternatives.''

ideology that dictates to them a general position to be taken on all matters.

2. *They are pragmatic.* Their expectations are realistic. They don't want to waste their time pursuing unattainable goals. Radicals and reactionaries, on the other hand, often tend to be unrealistic in determining what is possible.

3. *They are willing to compromise.* No matter how strongly they feel on any given issue, they recognize that the democratic process involves give and take and seldom does anyone fully attain all of his or her goals. Hence they are willing to settle for less than the ideal.

4. *They are patient.* One criticism often leveled at liberals by radicals who share their concern for social and economic justice is that liberals are "willing to wait forever" to attain their goals. Conservatives and liberals tend to accept defeat as a temporary setback.

5. *They seek their goals only within the constitutional framework.* A willingness to abide by the results of the democratic process and an unswerving allegiance to the process characterize both liberals and conservatives.

There are, of course, also significant differences between these two philosophical orientations that comprise the mainstream of American ideology.

☐ Differences between Liberals and Conservatives

1. *Liberals favor change; conservatives support the status quo.* As they examine the issues, liberals, who are optimistic about social change, are more likely than are conservatives to reach the conclusion that some kind of change is needed. Conservatives don't see much wrong with society. They are afraid that tampering with a basically good system will probably make matters worse.

2. *Liberals see government as a friend; conservatives as a necessary evil.* Their views of the proper role of government provide an interesting contrast and are, in fact, a reversal of their positions during the eighteenth century. Conservatives view government as a "necessary evil." Since they value order and stability highly, they recognize the necessity for government but cling to the belief that "the government that governs least governs best." Any power given to government should be given reluctantly and, if possible, temporarily—to be taken back at the first opportunity. Conservatives view any increase in government power as a decrease in individual freedom. This might be called the "see-saw" theory. Furthermore, they believe the government that is geographically closest to the people more closely represents their interests. Hence state government is more representative than the national government and local government is best of all. The liberal view of government is just the opposite. Liberals see government as a friend, a positive instrument that the people can and should use to help solve problems and improve lives. They do not view government participation in social and economic matters as a threat to individual freedom. Rather, they believe an increase in governmental power has often led to an increase in freedom for large segments of the population.

The freedom of black Americans has been increased substantially (although not nearly enough) by federal intervention to protect civil rights.* A large expansion of governmental power in the economic sphere, beginning in the 1930s, has increased the freedom of many former victims of economic deprivation.** This conclusion stems from the following definition of freedom to which many liberals subscribe:

---

* The writings, speeches, and actions of black liberals such as Martin Luther King and Jesse Jackson generally have supported an increase in government power to protect civil rights.
** Many government programs, beginning with Franklin Roosevelt's New Deal, have been aimed at alleviating poverty.

Freedom is the ability to choose among alternatives. If people are poor or discriminated against, their freedom is curtailed. It is limited because they have few alternatives from which to choose. If government action increases the number of choices available to them, then a growth in governmental power has increased their freedom.

Since most racial discrimination was institutionalized by state governments, and since these unjust laws were struck down by the national government, liberals have more faith in the latter than in the former. Also, in this age of Keynesian economics the national government also fights inflation, depression, and poverty, although not with sufficient vigor to satisfy liberals. State and local governments do very little in these areas. Hence liberals reject the conservatives' attitude of mistrust of big government.

In the eighteenth century the views were reversed. Liberals wanted a weak central government and conservatives wanted a strong one. At that time only the well-to-do had political power, and the government reflected their views and interests exclusively; since they had a large stake in preserving the status quo, they quite naturally wanted a strong central government to do their bidding. Conversely, liberals such as Thomas Jefferson wanted the government to have as little power as possible since it did not then represent the interests of the common man.

Conflict theorists point out an element of class struggle, because conservative politicians tend to defend the interests of the people with higher incomes, and liberal politicians seem to be more concerned with the problems faced by those with lower incomes. In 1987, Republicans in Congress (who are mostly conservative) voted for pro-business bills 76 percent of the time but voted pro-labor only 23 percent of the time. Conversely, congressional Democrats (most of whom are liberal) voted in favor of pro-business bills 36 percent and pro-labor bills 80 percent of the time.

All conservatives, of course, are not wealthy; but they share with affluent conservatives the view that government is inherently oppressive and that people should help themselves and not look to government for solutions to their problems. They are also confident of eventual personal success without government assistance. It should be noted that by the mid-1970s many liberals began to agree with the conservative position that local government should play a larger role in formulating and implementing social and economic programs. However, they still looked to the national government if dissatisfied with the results of local efforts.

3. *Liberals are primarily concerned with political freedom; conservatives, with economic freedom.* Both liberals and conservatives place freedom first among priorities, but their definitions differ. This can best be illustrated by looking at certain American developments in the 1930s

and in the early 1950s. In the period between the world wars the greatest threat to freedom was fascism. In the United States Fascist-oriented groups were formed. Neither liberals nor conservatives became terribly concerned over this development. As long as these groups did not actively try to overthrow the government they were not breaking the law.

After World War II the greatest threat to freedom emanated from the Communists. Liberals generally took the position that Communists had the right of free speech and the right to assemble peaceably. Only if they broke the law should they be prosecuted. Conservatives, on the other hand, became very disturbed about communism and participated in or supported the witch-hunting activities of Republican Senator Joe McCarthy in the early 1950s.

McCarthy's undemocratic tactics succeeded in harassing many liberals but uncovered practically no Communists plotting the overthrow of our government (which was ostensibly his goal). Two questions arise: First, why did most conservatives at least tacitly accept McCarthy's undemocratic behavior? Second, why did conservatives and liberals react in the same manner toward domestic Fascists but differently toward domestic Communists? The answer is simple: Communists nationalize business holdings and eliminate capitalism; Fascists are just as dictatorial in the political and other spheres as are Communists—BUT—they leave the private enterprise system alone for the most part and do not confiscate businesses and property. The difference, then, is that liberals are primarily concerned with *political* freedom (they don't want to interfere with free speech or the right to assemble peaceably—even if they disagree with a group's philosophy) and conservatives are primarily concerned with *economic* freedom and therefore consider communism to be a far greater threat than fascism, because the former eliminates the private enterprise system.

Many of the disagreements between liberals and conservatives stem from this basic difference. Conservatives often claim that liberals are "soft on communism" because they don't want to persecute domestic Communists. Liberals answer that they just want everyone in their democratic society to enjoy political freedom—even those whose philosophical orientation they find abhorrent. Furthermore liberals claim that all countries that have had violent Communist revolutions had conservative governments and that liberalism is a more effective anti-Communist philosophy because its adherents are committed to rectifying the injustices and inequities that Communists claim they will eliminate, and liberals strive to do it without sacrificing political freedom, and thus reduce the attraction communism has for the underprivileged. With the recent downfall of communism in Eastern Europe, this argument has become somewhat muted.

One of the purposes in writing this chapter was to emphasize the

similarities between liberals and conservatives, yet much more space
was devoted to a discussion of their differences. This was done because
this is largely what mainstream American politics is about. The differences deal mainly with the substance of public policy; the similarities deal with the process. What is democracy if not an agreement
on procedures?

Part of our thesis is that radicals and reactionaries also have greater
similarities than differences. What do they have in common?

☐ Similarities between Radicals and Reactionaries

1. *Both are dissatisfied with the existing political system.* Both are willing
to work outside of the constitutional framework to achieve their goals,
and they often resort to violence.

2. *They are ideologically oriented.* They embrace a comprehensive ideology which purports to answer all the great philosophical questions
and which provides a ready-made answer to all issues. They do not
examine issues on an individual basis.

3. *They are unwilling to compromise.* Politics to them is an all-or-nothing
proposition. Compromise is considered "selling out" or "watering

down" their goals. Since compromise is a basic ingredient of the American political system, radicals and reactionaries often exclude themselves from the normal political process. Radicals claim that the system is so rotten to the core that it cannot be reformed. Hence it must be overthrown. Reactionaries believe we have departed so far from the intent of the founding fathers (probably because of Communist infiltration) that the system no longer works.

4. *They are idealists.* Both are dreamers who have a vision of a utopian society that must be established.

5. *Both believe in a conspiracy theory.*[1] Reactionaries claim that the 1954 Supreme Court desegregation decision was a Communist plot hatched in Moscow to create racial warfare in this country. They say that fluoridation of the water is a Communist plot to poison the American people. They claim that sex education in the schools is a Communist scheme designed to weaken the moral fiber of our youth. Some even claim that diet soft drinks are part of a Communist plot to lower our blood sugar level, so the Communists can take us over while we are weak. John Birch Society literature frequently espouses a belief in the conspiracy theory; so does much of the radical literature.

Radicals who usually laugh at these reactionary claims have their own conspiracy theory. Everything they don't like is blamed on the "establishment," or the "ruling elite," or the "military-industrial complex." Most liberals and conservatives, on the other hand, believe we have a pluralistic society in which many groups vie for power and influence, although some also believe in the ruling elite theory.

☐ Differences between Radicals and Reactionaries

If radicals and reactionaries have all these characteristics in common what is it that distinguishes a radical from a reactionary? Radicals are oriented toward the future—they reject the past and hate the present; the utopian society they hope to create has never before existed except perhaps in the minds of a few individuals. They are optimistic about social change and new ideas. They claim to be concerned primarily about social and economic justice. Usually they say they favor equality; quite often, however, they are elitist and pay only lip service to egalitarianism.

Reactionaries are oriented toward the past—they want to return to the "good old days." They have idealized some period in the past all out of proportion to reality (the Revolutionary period, the McKinley era, the Wild West, or some other period); and they want to return to what they imagine things were then. Somehow our society has "lost its way" and we must get back on the "right track." They are pessimistic about

The Ku Klux Klan in Connecticut, 1992
Probably the preeminent expression of reactionary opinion in America is the Klan, whose goal has been to thwart the progress of social equality. Active in the South in the twenties and thirties, the KKK experienced a rebirth in the sixties and has widened its power base to dissociated groups in the North in the seventies, eighties, and nineties.

social change and new ideas and they want to perpetuate privilege and inequality. Actually what reactionaries are probably seeking is a lost youth. Their complaints probably are not caused by society but rather by age (one rarely sees a seventeen-year-old reactionary!).

☐ Other Differences

The main argument between liberals and radicals has to do with procedure. The latter accuse the former of being so "hung up" on democratic process, and of being so patient in their quest for democratic goals, that they will probably wait forever while injustice reigns supreme. Liberals reply that radicals are "throwing out the baby with the bath water." Discarding democracy will only lead to more injustice. The answer is reform, not revolution.

Conservatives and liberals have a different argument. Conservatives claim they too are interested in social and economic justice; but they want to proceed with great caution and slow deliberation. They don't want to tamper with the system very much because they feel it is the best of all existing systems and are afraid to make things worse. Besides, their concept of justice includes a highly stratified society.

Liberals answer that the conservatives' fear of tampering with the system perpetuates injustice and sets the stage for revolution. The choice is between peaceful and violent change—not between change and maintaining the status quo. Change is inevitable! No matter what reform is involved, liberals say we are progressing too slowly, and conservatives say we are moving too quickly.

Conservatives and radicals are so far apart that they have trouble communicating. Usually their conversations consist largely of threats and insults. Reactionaries do not participate in this dialogue because either they don't speak to nonreactionaries or, if they do, they simply accuse them of being Communists, or dupes. There is a tendency on their part to oversimplify political distinctions to a greater degree than do members of the other three categories.

☐ Summary and Conclusions

The following conclusions appear to be evident:

1. Similarities between liberals and conservatives are more significant than their differences.
2. Similarities between radicals and reactionaries are also greater than their differences.
3. The greatest cleavage exists between liberals and conservatives on one hand and radicals and reactionaries on the other.
4. The meanings of these terms are precise.

   (a) Liberals are pragmatic, examine the issues, are not predisposed by allegiance to a comprehensive ideology, are willing to compromise on their policy preferences, consider it only a temporary setback when their policies are defeated, are patient in pursuing their goals, will seek to attain their goals only within the limits of the Constitution, are optimistic about social change, have faith in the government (especially at the national level), seek social and economic justice through government action if necessary, give top priority to political freedom for all, and will not sanction any exceptions to this rule.

   (b) Conservatives are pragmatic, examine the issues, are not predisposed by allegiance to a comprehensive ideology, are willing to compromise on their policy preferences, consider it only a temporary setback when their policies are defeated, will seek to attain their goals only within the limits of the Constitution, are pessimistic about social change, have little or no faith in govern-

The Radical Movement

In the seventies, radicalism was the domain of the young and minorities in America. Unwilling to wait while liberals gradually introduce reforms, radical groups demand immediate change.

ment (especially at the national level), believe the status quo is just and want to maintain it, and give top priority to economic freedom.

(c) Radicals are dissatisfied with the existing political system and are willing to work outside the limits set by the Constitution, often resort to violence, are not interested in specific issues so much as they are in establishing the dominance of their particular ideology, are unwilling to compromise, believe that things are wrong in America because of a conspiracy, are dreamers who want to create a perfect society, are oriented toward the future (their utopia has never before existed), and their main goal is establishing social and economic justice, but are willing to sacrifice political and economic freedom.

(d) Reactionaries are dissatisfied with the existing political system and are willing to work outside the limits set by the Constitution, often resort to violence, are not interested in specific issues so much as they are in establishing the dominance of their particular ideology, are unwilling to compromise, believe that things are wrong in America because of a conspiracy, are dreamers who want to create a perfect society, are oriented toward the past (want to return to the "good old days"), want to put us back on the "right track," and want to perpetuate privilege and inequality.

5. Each of the other labels mentioned at the beginning fits into one of these four categories.

Attitude Toward Social Change

	Optimistic	Pessimistic	
	LIBERALS Socialists	**CONSERVATIVES** Capitalists	*Willingness to work within existing political system*
	Will work only within system		
	Willing to work outside of system		
	RADICALS Communists	**REACTIONARIES** Fascists	

The term "moderate" is not included because it is a relative term—an authoritarian dictator is moderate compared to a Nazi. Democratic socialists are liberal; capitalists (captains of industry) are usually conservative; Communists are radical, and Fascists are reactionary.

Admittedly these categories are subjective, but at least they are defined precisely. Hopefully they constitute an improvement over the left/right approach. Many readers may disagree with these definitions—some may not like the schematic arrangement at all. We are not completely satisfied with it either. However, if it touches off a dialogue that leads to a more standardized, precise, and relevant terminology, it will have served its purpose. According to the 1988 statistical abstract of the United States, in 1986 22 percent of first-year college students said they were liberal, while 19 percent said they were conservative. That is 2 percent higher for both political orientations than in 1980. However, it is a drop of 12 percent for liberalism since 1970.[2]

Obviously this chapter has dealt with more than political labels; it has also attempted to explain certain aspects of the four major political orientations competing for dominance in present-day America. The politics of today consist largely of the interplay of these political ideals. The outcome is uncertain, but the results will determine the course of American politics in the foreseeable future. It will be interesting to see if the two mainstream philosophies will be seriously challenged in the twenty-first century, as they were in the 1960s.

It should be noted that people may be conservative politically and liberal on some other subject (for example, sex). The categories used here pertain exclusively to the political domain, although there is an inevitable overlap with the economic sphere. Also, people cannot be pigeonholed. In reality, people may be liberal on some issues and conservative on others.

Finally, we deem it necessary to make a distinction between active and passive members of these classifications. Some people speak liberalese but behave very conservatively. Others use the rhetoric of radicalism but act in a liberal manner. It is probably best to use the active rather than the passive dimension in employing this classification scheme. Hopefully the descriptive aspect of our analysis is objective; however, any semblance of objectivity noted in the evaluation of these political orientations is purely accidental.

If the preceding analysis is correct, American society may be compared to an automobile that lurches forward in spurts, as liberals try to step on the gas while conservatives try to step on the brakes. The process is further complicated by the fact that reactionaries are trying to shift into reverse gear and radicals want to steer the car into a wall—in the hope that they will survive the crash and wind up with a new and better car.

No wonder American society seems to be weaving down the path to the future as if some drunk were doing the driving. For those who insist on smooth riding, American society must seem to be in need of major repairs, or at least a minor tuneup.

☐ Ethnic Political Subcultures

Despite the myth that America is a melting pot, the fact remains that perhaps as many as 50 percent of Americans are influenced by their ethnicity—that is, their ancestral nationality or their racial or religious orientations—in forming their political attitudes, party affiliations, voting behavior, and political activism. Hence, ethnic groups constitute important political subcultures in the United States; and in many local, state, and national elections, they can decide the winner. Total political

assimilation has not occurred, and anyone running for public office in multiethnic communities or states, or for the presidency, has to take the ethnic factor into consideration in planning campaign strategy.

Political Participation

Before looking at other aspects of political behavior, let us first examine the degree of political participation in a wide variety of ethnic groups. Political scientists Sidney Verba and Norman Nie have developed a political participation scale composed of four types of behavior: voting, political activism, communal participation, and particularized contact. Political activism refers to contributing money, campaigning for candidates, and so on; communal participation refers to membership in civic organizations; and particularized contact refers to personally contacting political leaders by mail or telephone, or in person.

Table 20-1 on p. 553 summarizes the degree to which each of the ethnic groups listed deviated either positively or negatively from the U.S. average on each factor and overall.

Irish Catholics and Scandinavian Protestants have the highest level of overall public participation. These groups have the highest percentage who engage in all four categories of participation. Blacks, Italians, Hispanics, and Irish Protestants have the lowest proportion of what might be called "complete political participation."

Slavic and Polish Catholics have the highest voter turnout, and Hispanics and blacks have the lowest. Irish Catholics are by far the most involved in campaigning and similar activities, while French Catholics are the least involved. When it comes to joining civic organizations, Scandinavian Protestants and Irish Catholics rank highest by far. On the other hand, Italians and Hispanics are the least involved in such activities. Finally, we note that French Catholics are by far the group most likely to personally contact a political figure in order to solve a problem or communicate on issue positions, while blacks are the least likely to take such an approach.

What emerges from the data is that American ethnic groups manifest a wide range of political styles and degrees of participation. Italian-Americans will vote in large numbers but will not join civic organizations. Thus, a politician seeking the Italian vote would waste his time addressing such organizations, although he would probably benefit from speaking at a Sons of Italy gathering. If you are planning to run for political office and are looking for campaigners, Irish Catholics would probably respond more favorably than any other ethnic group, but you won't recruit many French Catholics. If you have the support of black voters, spend a lot of time and energy on a get-out-the-vote drive, because African Americans have a much lower than average voter turnout. In the 1980 presidential race 50.5 percent of blacks and 29.9

Table 20-1
Ethnic Group Political
Participation

Group[a]	Voting Scale	Political Campaigning Scale	Communal Participation Scale	Particularized Contact Scale	Overall Participation Score[b]
Protestants					
British	+6.2	+6.8	+13.6	+0.5	+10.4
Scandinavian	+31.2	+19.2	+23.3[c]	+19.1	+32.0
German	+10.1	+2.3	+11.5	+2.2	+9.0
Irish	−6.3	−11.7	−15.4	−10.3	−18.0
Catholics					
Irish	+30.7	+42.4[c]	+22.3	+15.7	+41.0[c]
German	+29.3	+5.1	+0.7	+7.7	+10.7
French	+14.2	−25.8	−7.8	+33.4[c]	−6.6
Italian	+17.6	−15.4	−32.5	+14.0	−14.3
Slavic	+35.6	+4.1	−14.6	+17.5	+11.2
Polish	+37.5[c]	−3.7	−9.0	+4.7	+6.2
Jews	+22.9	+16.3	+12.0	+0.5	+19.0
Blacks	−24.9	−6.4	−11.4	−15.0	−19.9
Spanish	−0.9	−0.9	−24.7	−10.9	−13.3

[a]Refers to race, religion, national origin, or a combination of these variables.
[b]Represents participation in all four categories and not an average of the four.
[c]Represents the highest percentage of participation in each category.
Source: Compiled from Andrew M. Greeley, "How Conservative Are American Catholics?" Reprinted with permission from the *Political Science Quarterly* 92 (Summer 1977): 199–218.

percent of Hispanics voted, compared to 60.9 percent of non-Hispanic whites. When only citizens are counted as eligible, the Hispanic vote increases to 44.1 percent but is still very low. In 1988, the figures dropped slightly for Hispanics (28.8), and non-Hispanic whites (59.1), and increased slightly for black voters (51.5).

Party Affiliation and Voting

Traditionally, Jews are heavily Democratic, Catholics are mostly Democratic, and Protestants are mainly Republican. In the past, it was believed that as group incomes rose and group members became more educated, they would move to the suburbs and switch their political affiliations from Democrat to Republican. This consequence of upward socioeconomic mobility has not materialized, except among German Catholics. Jews, who have the highest median family income in the United States, are still heavily Democratic. As Catholics increased their standard of living substantially from the 1950s to the 1970s, the ratio of

Democrats to Republicans has not changed much. What has occurred is that a large proportion of young people have rejected both parties and registered as Independents. 1972 was the first time that Catholics voted Republican in a presidential campaign. In 1976, they returned to the Democratic party. However, in 1984, 56 percent voted for Reagan, and in 1988, 52 percent voted for Bush. In 1992, they gave Clinton a plurality over the other two candidates.

Voter identification with the Republican party in the post-World War II era has fluctuated from a high of 40 percent in 1946, to a low of 22 percent in 1975, after Watergate. Two-term Presidents are usually most popular the year they are re-elected: Roosevelt in 1936, Eisenhower in 1956, and Nixon in 1972. Each time, the percentage of the electorate identifying with the President's party increased. The same occurred in 1984. Reagan won in a landslide, and the Republican party picked up followers.

Table 20-2
Political Party Affiliation, 1984 (By Percent)

	Republican	*Democrat*	*Independent*
Total	28	42	30
Blacks	5	81	14
Whites	32	36	32
Hispanics	24	49	27
Protestants	33	40	27
Catholics	24	44	32
Jews	15	57	28

Source: Gallup Poll conducted in June and July, 1984. N = 6,093

Some people spoke of a voter realignment. That has not occurred since FDR was elected during the Depression. Nixon's 1972 landslide and Reagan's 1984 landslide were both accompanied by 28 percent of the voters identifying with the Republican party. Hardly a remarkable statistic when one considers that 42 percent of the voters identified with the Democrats and that 30 percent called themselves Independents.

There have been more Independents than Republicans since the mid-1960s. This has not, however, been catastrophic for Republican presidential candidates, who have actually won five of the last seven presidential campaigns. Thus party identification, which had not varied much as of October, 1993, is not a perfect indicator of voting behavior in presidential races. Issues such as war and peace, poverty and prosperity, as well as ideology and ethnicity motivate voters.

Johnson was the last Democrat to receive a majority of Protestant votes as shown in Table 20-3. This occurred because Goldwater was perceived by the electorate as an ultra-conservative. Catholics voted

Table 20-3
Racial and Religious
Vote, 1964–1976,
(By Percent)

	1964		1968			1972		1976	
	Johnson	Goldwater	Nixon	Humphrey	Wallace	McGovern	Nixon	Carter	Ford
Black	97	3	5	94	1	87	13	83	17
White	59	41	47	38	15	30	70	48	52
Protestant	55	45	49	35	16	31	69	46	54
Catholic	75	25	33	59	8	40	60	55	45
Jewish	90	10	15	83	2	63	37	68	32

Source: Adapted from Gerald Pomper, ed., *The Election of 1976* (New York: David McKay, 1976), p. 61; Mark R. Levy and Michael S. Kramer, *The Ethnic Factor: How America's Minorities Decide Elections* (New York: Simon & Schuster, 1972), statistical index; and The American Institute of Public Opinion (the Gallup Poll). As found in Reid Luhman and Stuart Gilman, *Race and Ethnic Relations: The Social and Political Experience of Minority Groups* (Belmont, Calif.: Wadsworth Publishing Co., 1980), p. 257.

Republican in 1972 for the first time; the reason for this exception was that McGovern was perceived as an ultra-liberal. Some Catholics and Protestants will cross traditional party lines if they perceive their party's candidate as an extremist. Otherwise, they will vote as they have traditionally. In 1992, Ross Perot siphoned off 21 percent of the Protestant vote, most of which would have gone to George Bush. In 1988, Bush received 81 percent of the white born-again Christian vote, and that figure dropped to 61 percent in 1992. Perot got 15 percent of that vote. There was a similar dropoff for Bush with the Catholic vote, while Perot picked up 20 percent.

Although Jews, blacks, and Mexican-Americans vote solidly Democratic, Jews are susceptible to liberal, third-party candidates, and blacks and Mexican-Americans have very poor turnouts on election day. Nevertheless, votes that come in blocs can make a difference in close elections. In 1960, John Kennedy won Texas and New Mexico and, consequently, the election, because of the Chicano vote (85 percent nationally). Lyndon Johnson received 90 percent of the Chicano vote in 1964. Hubert Humphrey lost in 1968, but he won in Texas because of the Chicano vote (87 percent nationally). Had Reagan not won in a landslide in 1980, Chicanos could have made a difference in California, where Hispanics (mostly Chicano) account for 20 percent of the population. Table 20-4 on p. 556 shows the breakdown for the 1980, 1984, 1988, and 1992 presidential elections.

Hispanics comprise 33.1 percent of the voters in New Mexico, 17.7 percent in Texas, 16.1 percent in California, 13.3 percent in Arizona, and 9.8 percent in Colorado. The vast majority of these Southwest Hispanics

Table 20-4
Racial and Religious
Vote, 1980–1992
(By Percent)

	1980			1984		1988		1992		
	Carter	Reagan	Anderson	Mondale	Reagan	Bush	Dukakis	Bush	Clinton	Perot
Black	86	10	2	90	10	12	86	11	82	7
White	36	56	7	37	63	59	40	41	39	20
Hispanic	56	35	8	61	37	30	69	25	62	14
Protestant	39	54	6	34	66	66	33	46	33	21
Catholic	46	47	6	44	56	52	47	36	44	20
Jewish	45	39	14	69	31	35	64	12	78	10

Sources: 1980 data: Gallup Poll, Press Release, Dec. 21, 1980 and *New York Times* Poll, Nov. 4, 1980. 1984 data: composite of *Time*, Nov. 19, 1984, and *U.S. News and World Report*, Basic Data; ABC-TV Exit Polls, reported in *U.S. News and World Report*, Nov. 19, 1984, p. 27. The 1988 data is from the *New York Times/CBS News* poll, *New York Times*, Nov. 10, 1988, p. 18. *N.Y. Times*, Nov. 5, 1992, p. 3B.

are Mexican-Americans. In the Northeast, Hispanics are predominantly Puerto Rican. In New York state, 8.3 percent of the voters are Hispanic; much more in the greater New York City area. Although 8.5 percent of Florida voters are Hispanic (mostly Cuban), they are concentrated in Dade County (Miami), where they comprise 50 percent of the nearly 2 million people in the county. In 1988, Hispanics nationally voted for the Democratic presidential candidate 69 percent to 30 percent for the Republican. This was a higher Democratic edge than the 61 to 37 percent vote in 1984, and 56 to 35 percent in 1980, when 8 percent voted for Anderson. The trend continued in 1992.

African-American voters can make a difference in many states, especially in those where they account for over 20 percent of the population: Mississippi (36.8 percent), South Carolina (30.5 percent), Louisiana (29.9 percent), Alabama (26.4 percent), Georgia (25.9 percent), and North Carolina (22.4 percent). There are also at least fifteen cities in which over 40 percent of the population is black—among them, Washington, D.C.; Newark, New Jersey; and Gary, Indiana.

Blacks, Jews, Italians, and Slavs tend to vote very heavily for political candidates of their own ethnic group regardless of party affiliation. However, such candidates tend to be overwhelmingly Democratic, and most of the others are Independents. Only a few are Republicans. However, blacks in Massachusetts voted overwhelmingly for a Republican senatorial candidate, Edward Brooke, and helped to elect him, despite a large black Democratic registration margin over Republicans. The Irish tend to be the ethnic group least likely to vote for someone just because he is of the same ethnic background, and Chicanos also seem to be looking at candidates more from an issue than an ethnic orientation.

We keep emphasizing the role of ethnic voters in the Democratic party because they have been the backbone of the coalition of interests that compose that party. The backbone of the Republican party had been white Protestants from the Midwest and elsewhere, and, lately, from the South. It is a far more homogeneous and unified group than the Democrats, especially after Goldwater's very poor showing in 1964 which followed a bitter fight for the nomination and a deep party split. Republicans have avoided such divisiveness ever since.

Democrats cannot win national elections without the ethnic vote, and Republicans have been making some inroads. German and Italian Catholics have reduced their affinity for the Democrats slowly, and even Slavic and Irish support has slipped. The loss of Italian votes can be fatal for the Democrats, because the Italian vote is substantial in Illinois, New Jersey, New York, and Pennsylvania, all of which have many electoral votes. The Irish vote is concentrated in New York, Massachusetts, Connecticut, and Rhode Island, and the Slavic vote is substantial in Michigan, Illinois, New Jersey, New York, and Pennsylvania. The Jewish vote is most important in New York, where Jews constitute a higher percentage of the electorate by far than anywhere else.

Table 20-5 shows how different ethnic groups voted in the 1980 and 1984 Presidential elections.

One group we have not mentioned yet is Puerto Ricans. They are overwhelmingly Democratic, but their impact has been small for two reasons. They are primarily concentrated in the Northeast in some of the most populous states, which dilutes their strength; and they have a very poor voter turnout, which further reduces their impact. In 1960, they gave Kennedy 76 percent of their vote; in 1964, they voted 86 percent for Johnson; and in 1968, 83 percent voted for Humphrey.

Although there were very few blacks and Hispanics in Congress in the 1980s, both groups have tried to increase their strength by forming ethnically based interest groups in Congress. In 1993 the Hispanic Congressional Caucus is composed of only seventeen members, all in the House of Representatives, and its impact has been negligible. The Black Caucus, which has thirty-eight, has made some marginal impact, but not a great deal.

Some ethnic groups are as concerned with foreign affairs as they are with domestic issues. Eastern European and Cuban refugees, who fled from Communist-dominated countries, are very anti-Communist and

Table 20-5
Ethnic Group Vote for President Reagan, 1980, 1984 (By Percent)

Ethnic Group	1980	1984
English/Scotch/Welsh	59	70
German/Austrian	57	67
Irish Protestant	54	62
Scandinavian	53	62
Italian	50	58
Irish Catholic	49	56
Polish/Slavic	39	51
Hispanic	35	37

therefore very concerned with U.S. policy toward their former homelands and toward Communist countries in general. Hungarians, Poles, and Czechs who fled from Communist revolutions are very sensitive on this point. Whether they are Catholic, Protestant, or Jewish, they tend to vote Democratic, although the 1980 elections did not fit the historical pattern. Jews, of course, are very pro-Israel and, despite their liberalism, will not vote for a candidate whose Middle East policies are detrimental to Israel.

Anyone who believes that the United States is a melting pot in which immigrants and their descendants no longer maintain ethnic identities and are not politically influenced by ethnic considerations does not understand American society or the American political process. Although overt ethnicity declined somewhat in the 1980s, ethnic voting patterns remain a potent force in U.S. politics.

☐ Miami/Dade County Ethnic Politics: A Case Study

Miami is a great case study in ethnic politics. The greater Miami area has undergone a major ethnic transformation since 1960, as Table 20.6 indicates:

Table 20-6
Dade County
Demographics: 1960–
1990

	1960	1970	1980	1990	Population Change 1960–1990
Anglo	80%	62%	48%	32%	− 172,000
Hispanic	5%	24%	36%	49%	+ 903,000
Black	15%	15%	17%	21%	+ 258,000

Source: 1990 U.S. Census.

Non-Hispanic white flight began in 1970. More than 172,000 moved out, but some Anglos were born in Dade County during that period. Jews are included in this category (12-15% of total population). Many blacks in Miami are foreign-born, including many Haitians, Bahamians, Jamaicans, and Trinidadians, and account for most of the increase from 1970 to 1990. The local black leadership is largely of West Indian descent.

The big change, however, is the Latinization of Dade County. Cubans are the largest Hispanic group, and the one with the greatest political, economic, and educational resources. In 1990, 70 percent of Dade County Cubans were foreign born, 30 percent U.S. born.

Originally, when the first wave of post-Castro Cubans came to the United States (1959–1962), they were dispersed throughout the country. However, for a variety of reasons, including the weather, retirement age, and the growing Cuban political, economic and cultural power structure in Dade County, they began to migrate back to Miami, which eventually became the Cuban-American Mecca in the United States, as New York has been for Jewish-Americans, and San Francisco for Chinese-Americans.

Table 20-7
Percent of Cubans in U.S. who live in Dade County

1960	1970	1980	1990
23.6%	36.8%	50.5%	54.0%

Source: 1990 U.S. Census.

The table above shows the increasing concentration in Miami of formerly dispersed Cuban refugees. These large numbers, combined with the high level of human resources that the first wave brought to South Florida, enabled them to create a self-contained ethnic community. One could literally fulfill all of one's needs in Spanish, within the ethnic enclave, through the stages of one's life. Of course, only the oldest members of the community do that, as the overwhelming majority of Cubans are bilingual, many English-dominant. These Cubans have been joined by many other Hispanics fleeing from political turmoil or economic hardships in their Latin-American homelands. The following two tables demonstrate the dwindling percentage of Dade's Hispanic population that is Cuban-American.

Table 20-8
Cubans as percent of Dade County Hispanic Population

1970	1980	1990
83%	70%	59%

Source: 1990 U.S. Census.

Table 20-9
Hispanic Population of Dade County, 1990

Ethnicity	Population	Ethnicity	Population
Cubans	562,000	Peruvians	16,000
Nicaraguans	74,000	Guatemalans	8,000
Puerto Ricans	69,000	Ecuadorans	8,000
Colombians	54,000	Salvadorans	7,000
Dominicans	23,000	Panamanians	7,000
Mexicans	23,000	Others	80,000
Hondurans	18,000		

Source: 1990 U.S. Census.

The second wave of 270,000 Cuban refugees (1965–1973) brought a much higher percentage of lower-middle and working class migrants. The 1980 Mariel Boatlift, which brought 125,000 more Cubans in four months (the third wave), consisted of at least 90 percent working class people. Whereas the first two waves were 96 percent white, the third wave was 30 percent black. Thus, there were racial and class differences among the ethnically similar Cuban population in the United States.

The true test of the importance of ethnic politics in Miami is the voting and other political behavior of Cuban Americans, irrespective of race and social class. The political solidarity is such that Ronald Reagan received 92 percent of the Cuban-American vote for president in 1984, although he cut a number of social programs that benefited low income refugees (e.g., the meals program at senior citizens centers). When asked what they thought of these cuts, the affected elderly Cubans replied, "If the President cut those programs it must be because he needed the money for something more important."

The primacy of foreign policy among refugees from communist revolutions leads them to dismiss the domestic policies of presidents who are perceived to be very anti-communist. When Fidel Castro's regime collapses and is replaced by a non-communist government, the generally liberal social and economic position on domestic issues held by most Cuban Americans will probably lead to support for the Democratic Party, similar to the position of Puerto Rican and Mexican Americans who together comprise 75 percent of U.S. Hispanics.

In the Florida State Legislature, according to the third FIU (Florida International University) Cuba Poll in 1993, the Cuban-American legislators, all Republicans, voted about 90 percent pro-labor, a higher percentage than did the Democratic legislators. Other social issues yielded similar results.

All Dade County cities with large Hispanic populations have Cuban mayors (Miami, Hialeah, Coral Gables, West Miami, Sweetwater and Hialeah Gardens), and, except for Coral Gables, a majority of city commissioners as well. Six of the thirteen county commissioners are Cuban, as are the county manager, the city manager of Miami, and the Dade County school superintendent. Blacks have four of the Dade County Commission seats, and one of the five City of Miami commission seats, as well as several seats in the State Legislature. There are also two Cuban and two black Congresspersons from South Florida (one male and one female of each). In every case, each ethnic group voted for its own candidates. This is no different from New York, or any of the other multicultural communities in the United States.*

---

* Miami's Cuban-American Mayor, Xavier Suarez, did not run for re-election in 1993. A non-Hispanic white, who had been mayor of Dade County for two decades before the position was abolished, defeated Miriam Alonso, a Cuban-American who ran a very divisive ethnic campaign for mayor of Miami. Interestingly, her strong ethnic appeals fell on deaf ears with younger Cuban-Americans, most of whom voted for Steve Clark. It seems that blatant political ethnocentrism has received a serious setback in Miami's Cuban-American community.   *(continued)*

REFERENCES

1. See William P. Geberding, "Liberals and Radicals: A Conflict of Ideologies," *The Reporter,* Feb. 8, 1968, 14–17.
2. *Statistical Abstract of the United States: 1988*, p. 142.

SELECTED READING

Almond, Gabriel A. and Sidney Verba, *Civic Culture* (Boston: Little Brown, 1965).

This is the classic work that developed a typology of political cultures: participant, subject, parochial and civic.

Ashmore, Harry S., "Where Have All the Liberals Gone?" *The Center Magazine,* Vol. 2, No. 4 (July 1969).

A strong defense of liberalism.

Bronner, Stephen Eric, *Moments of Decision: Political History and the Crises of Radicalism* (New York: Routledge, 1992).

An historical analysis of radicalism.

Buckley, William F., ed., *Did You Ever See a Dream Walking?* (Indianapolis: Bobbs-Merrill, 1970).

In this reader, the authors explain the varieties of conservatism.

Davidson, Chandler, *Race and Class in Texas Politics* (Princeton, N.J.: Princeton University Press, 1990).

The author presents the role ethnic and social class play in Texas politics.

Geberding, William P., "Liberals and Radicals: A Conflict of Ideologies?" *The Reporter* (February 8, 1968): pp. 14–17.

A liberal defends his cause and attacks radicalism.

Grenier, Guillermo J., and Alex Stepick, ed., *Miami Now: Immigration, Ethnicity, and Social Change* (Gainesville, Fl.: University of Florida Press, 1992).

An outstanding book of readings written by social scientists from various disciplines and ethnic backgrounds. They describe the inter-ethnic competition for political and economic power, as well as the bilingual and anti-bilingual forces that began in Miami, and then became national struggles.

Alonso turned off the non-Cuban Hispanics, as well as the black and white non-Hispanics. It should be noted that the Cuban-American community gave up its three out of five majority on the city commission, as well as the mayoralty (the mayor is one of five commission members). This does not mean that there is a decline in ethnic politics, so much as it means a decline in the effectiveness of divisive ethnic appeals. It also reflects a growing political maturity that transcends purely ethnic appeals in Miami's Cuban-American community.

Grenier, Guillermo, Hugh Gladwin and Douglas McLaughen, *The 1993 FIU Cuba Poll* (Miami: Florida International University, July 1, 1993).

This is the third poll of Cuban Americans conducted in as many years. Although most of the questions dealt with Cuban American attitudes toward Cuba, some have to do with local matters. The poll verifies a popular joke in the area. This is the only U.S. city in which it is necessary to have a foreign policy in order to run for local public office.

Levy, Mark E. and Michael Kramer, *The Ethnic Factor: How American Minorities Decide Elections* (New York: Simon & Schuster, 1972).

The first comprehensive analysis of ethnic politics.

New York Times, Nov. 5, 1992, Section B, Elections.

This section contains a complete breakdown of the 1992 Presidential vote, by ethnicity, income, age, gender, Political Party affiliation, and many other variables.

Portes, Alejandro and Alex Stepick, *City on the Edge: The Transformation of Miami* (Berkeley: University of California Press, 1993).

The authors describe the Latinization of Miami, the creation of parallel power structures, the plight of the Haitians, and the frustration of native American blacks. Miami is a city with no mainstream. They describe the complex social dynamics and ethnic tensions of this "city on the edge."

QUESTIONS

1. The American ethnic group that scores the highest on the overall political participation scale is
   a. Irish Catholics.
   b. Scandinavian Protestants.
   c. Jewish Americans.
   d. British Protestants.

2. According to popular usage, the term *leftist* refers to
   a. Communists.
   b. Socialists.
   c. liberals.
   d. radicals.
   e. all of the above.

3. According to popular usage, the term *right-winger* refers to
   a. reactionaries.
   b. conservatives.
   c. Fascists.

    d. laissez-faire capitalists.
    e. all of the above.

4. Which of the following groups tends to resist social change?
    a. liberals
    b. conservatives
    c. radicals
    d. reactionaries
    e. both (b) and (d)

5. Which of the following groups of voters is least interested in foreign policy?
    a. Jewish Americans
    b. Black Americans
    c. Polish Americans
    d. Cuban Americans
    e. Slavic Americans

6. Which of the following Hispanic groups gave 92 percent of its vote to Ronald Reagan in the 1984 presidential election?
    a. Puerto Ricans
    b. Mexican Americans
    c. Cuban Americans
    d. Dominican Americans

7. Conservatives believe that the level of government that best represents the people is the
    a. national, because it balances the needs of all the people.
    b. state, because it combines the advantages of both the national and the local levels.
    c. local, because it is geographically closest to the people.
    d. world, if one could be established, because it would eliminate the barriers that separate us now.

8. In South Florida politics, African Americans have all of the following *except*
    a. Four out of thirteen Dade County Commissioners.
    b. Two members of the U.S. House of Representatives.
    c. Several members in the State Legislature.
    d. Two City of Miami Commission seats.

9. Which groups are willing to abide by the results of the democratic process regardless of the outcome?
    a. liberals and radicals
    b. conservatives and reactionaries
    c. liberals and conservatives
    d. radicals and reactionaries
    e. conservatives and radicals

10. On which point do liberals and conservatives differ?
    a. their definition of freedom
    b. their patience in pursuing political ideals
    c. their way of seeking goals within the constitutional framework
    d. their pragmatism
    e. their ideological orientation

QUESTIONS FOR THOUGHT AND DISCUSSION

1. Discuss the similarities and differences among liberals, conservatives, radicals, and reactionaries.

2. Explain why the left–right political spectrum concept does or does not make sense in the United States today.

3. What role has ethnicity played in participation and voting preference in the United States?

4. Compare and contrast ethnic politics in Miami with other metropolitan areas in the United States.

21

Comparative Political Cultures

In this chapter we will examine several dimensions of **political culture** by focusing on aspects of political life in a number of countries. In addition we will briefly survey a typology of political cultures.

The following conversation actually took place between one of the authors and a student, and exemplifies one aspect of Latin American political culture.

> "Tell me, Pedro, why did you leave Cuba?"
> "I left my country because Fidel is a Communist."
> "You don't like communism?"
> "Are you kidding? I hate it. Fidel took away our freedom."
> "In your opinion, Pedro, if the Castro regime were overthrown tomorrow what do you think Cuba needs to replace Fidelismo?"
> "A strong man!"

Pedro's remarks are typical, not only of Cuban refugees but of Latin Americans in general. It is perfectly natural to most Latin Americans to preach freedom and also to advocate the leadership of a strong man. It is part of their political culture.

☐ Latin American Political Culture

Latin American political culture differs in many ways from that of the United States. When reading the following discussion, you should bear in mind that the generalizations we make about Latin American political culture do not hold true for every country in the region. Still, these generalizations are useful because they depict the general approach of most Latin Americans. Understanding these generalizations will enable you to understand the subconscious assumptions underlying Pedro's response in the opening dialogue.

Machismo is an important part of the general culture in Latin America. It manifests itself in political activity as in everything else. Literally translated it means masculinity; but it means much more than that. The ideal macho (male) has many sexual conquests to his credit and has never backed down to another man in any situation. He has an exaggerated sense of pride, honor, dignity, and passion, and a tendency toward violence. This cultural ideal has significant political consequences. In order for any man to achieve high public office (and to maintain his position), he must approximate this ideal. Inevitably, this leads to a succession of political leaders who are very macho. Since democracy necessitates compromise, and machismo precludes it, democracy in Latin America is on shaky ground.

In 1993, all the Latin American countries were (technically) democracies except for Cuba; however, this may be a temporary situation. In the 1950s there was also a wave of democracies, most of which returned to dictatorships in the 1960s. Even now, the same political party has ruled Mexico since 1929. In Venezuela, a two-party democracy since 1958, there was an attempted military coup in 1992. In Nicaragua, Violeta Chamorro defeated the Sandinista dictator, Daniel Ortega, in free elections. But the Sandinistas continue to control the military and the interior ministry (police). Other so-called democracies in the region are also on shaky ground.

Machismo also leads to a Latin American political tradition of **caudillismo** (kow-dee-yees-mo). A caudillo is a strongman, usually a military leader, who rules his country with an iron fist. Consequently, *authoritarianism* is the rule, rather than the exception, in Latin America. In most Latin American countries opposition parties generally are not allowed to criticize the party in power too vigorously (if, indeed, opposition parties are permitted to exist). Quite often, being very critical of the government is considered treason. The consequences often can be very severe. That is why so many political leaders out of power live in exile. In keeping with the tradition of rewarding caudillismo and machismo, however, former leaders (especially military men) quite often are given pensions while they live in exile. These pensions, of course, may be discontinued if the leader in exile is too critical of the regime in power. Some new governments, those that radically transform society, are rebelling against the system. Therefore, they play politics by different rules. They may try to extradite the exile leaders to bring them to trial and to punish them for alleged crimes against the people. In some cases, they might even attempt to assassinate the exiled leader on foreign soil.

Caudillismo
The Latin American version of a dictator is usually a military figure who rules his country with an iron fist. General Augusto Pinochet of Chile typified this tradition for many years.

Military governments abound in Latin America. *Militarismo* is a result of Latin American history. Almost all their historical heroes are military men. The conquistadores such as Pizarro, Cortez, and Cabeza de Vaca were exceptionally brave military leaders who conquered a continent with just a small band of men. Independence leaders such as Simon Bolivar and Bernardo O'Higgins were military leaders who could have been presidents for life because of their great popularity. Even Latin American countries with civilian leaders are susceptible to military takeovers most of the time. The military in most Latin American countries considers itself the defender of the constitution. Any time it is unhappy with its civilian leadership it may topple the government, claiming the president acted in an unconstitutional manner.

Militarism is even considered a good thing by some civilian leaders. Once, while working as a tourist guide in Washington, D.C., one of the authors drove two members of the Argentine House of Representatives and their wives from Washington to New York. The conversation was very enlightening. The two men discussed many political issues and personalities. Every time they were critical of some political figure they said he "lacked a military mind"! An American politician, especially if he is a Republican, would probably criticize someone because he doesn't act in a "businesslike" manner. Not all Latin American countries are as militaristic as Argentina (which is currently enjoying a period of democracy), but many are quite so.

One exception is Costa Rica. When Pepe Figueres became President of Costa Rica in the 1950s he abolished the armed forces, and used the money allotted in the budget for military expenditures to hire teachers. A former teacher of one of the authors had been an ambassador to Latin America. He told of one trip he made to several Central American countries, visiting Nicaragua first and Costa Rica second. The political cultures of these neighboring countries are surprisingly dissimilar. When he landed in Nicaragua he was met by then President Somoza, who was dressed in full military regalia and accompanied by a large group of soldiers. After inspecting the troops they rode in a limousine to the presidential palace where they conducted their business in a very serious and formal manner.

The next day the ambassador flew to Costa Rica, where he was met by President Figueres. The President wore a short-sleeved shirt and a pair of slacks and was driving an old Ford. He was not accompanied by soldiers. As they drove to town they came upon a Costa Rican citizen whose car had stalled. The President stopped the car and inquired about the man's problem. The man apparently was not at all surprised to see the President. His reaction was, "Oh, Don Pepe, I think the trouble is with the carburetor"; whereupon they both craned their necks over the open hood and began tinkering with the engine.

This story tells us a great deal about the political cultures of both countries and helps to explain why one was a dictatorship and the other a democracy. The Costa Rican case, especially, points out two other characteristics of Latin American political culture: **paternalism** and **personalismo.**

Latin Americans, even those who live in democratic countries, tend to view their leaders in a paternalistic manner. The government, which is personified by the leader, is supposed to "take care" of the people, as a parent takes care of a child. This is an extension of the Feudal Agricultural system in which the *patron* of the *hacienda* had power over all the *peones,* who worked and lived on his land. He even granted permission for marriages to take place. When the national independence movements created nation-states, the leader usually became the equivalent of a *patron* for the country. Many Americans may be fond of their president, but they usually don't consider him a father image. American culture is not paternalistic because it is not personalistic; and paternalism is a natural outgrowth of personalism.

If you ride a public bus to school or work every day in the United States, you probably know the bus driver only casually, if at all. You don't know his family, his aspirations, or his philosophy of life. In fact there is probably a sign in the bus that says, "Do not speak to the driver." If you rode the same bus every day in Latin America you probably would know all of these things and more about the driver and everyone else who rides the bus. Talking goes on constantly, personal information is shared, and the driver participates in the exchange. In Latin America people quite often know everyone they deal with on a very personal basis. For example, they would not buy an insurance policy from someone they did not know. Letting your fingers do the walking through the yellow pages is no substitute for calling your Uncle Tito to find out whom to call.

In the United States we buy our groceries in a supermarket where we push a little cart around, load it up, and then pay a cashier, who totals up the bill on a machine and then may hand us some trading stamps along with the change. The entire operation is very impersonal. We generally do not discuss our personal lives with the cashier or any other employee. Latin Americans, on the other hand, shop in small grocery stores whose owners and employees are their personal friends. A visit to the store becomes, in part, a social visit. The butcher might ask when your sister's boy friend is going to marry her, how your kids are doing in school, or when your widowed aunt is going to visit the store. Even Latin Americans who migrate to the United States retain much of their personalismo. The self-contained Spanish-speaking subcultures that exist in several U.S. cities manifest this personalistic behavior.

Personalismo is such a strong Latin American trait that political parties in Latin America are often referred to by their leaders' names; for example, there have been Fidelista, Vargista, and Peronista parties in Latin America. When the leader is no longer active, his party usually collapses. Latin Americans place their faith in men rather than in laws or in a type of political party. If the man does not live up to their expectations, they merely seek another man; they do not question the efficacy of placing their faith in men rather than in laws or in a type of political system. Doing so would cause them to question one of the cornerstones of their entire culture. In a time of crisis in the United States and in Great Britain the people place their faith in an individual (Roosevelt and Churchill are examples), but after the crisis has subsided they revert back to a nonpersonalistic orientation.

Individualism is another important characteristic of Latin American political culture. This is related to machismo. Even though a Latin American man may perceive his president as the father of his country, he does not always obey his political father. Instead he reserves the right to decide whether or not to obey a particular law. He considers himself just as macho as the men who enact and administer the laws; hence if he considers a law unjust he probably will not obey it. This is especially true if he has a personal friend who can keep him out of trouble. After all, he is as good as any other man. It is as if he were saying, "The president is no better than I am; he puts his pants on the same way I do—one leg at a time." This attitude toward law is not conducive to political stability.

Lack of compliance with the law has its roots in the colonial period. The "Laws of the Indies" was a set of rules that governed the New World.

However, enforcement was impossible because of the great distance from the mother country (Spain), the vastness of the New World, and the primitive transportation system available at the time. Thus settlers quite often had the option of obeying or disobeying laws; and many of their descendants still exercise this option. This attitude should not be confused with the principle of a "higher law." Rather than appealing to a higher law, a Latin American who disobeys the law is simply rejecting the president's law.

Individualism is carried so far that new leaders quite often write a new constitution after they assume power. "I'm not going to rule with somebody else's constitution!" That is why Bolivia, Venezuela, the Dominican Republic, Peru, Ecuador, Haiti, El Salvador, and Honduras have each had over twenty constitutions. It is a way of announcing that the country is "under new management." It also results from two other important cultural characteristics—**continuismo** and a fondness for **legalism.** Sometimes, if a president is prevented from succeeding himself by the constitution, he merely writes a new one. In that way he perpetuates himself in office (continuismo) and it is all done legally (legalism). The United States, which achieved its independence before any Latin American state did, has struggled along with only one Constitution.

Another significant contrast between the United States and Latin America relates to the definition of democracy. In the United States we refer to democracy as a *process*. As long as we have free elections at periodic intervals we feel we have a democratic system. If our elected officials do not live up to our expectations we vote them out of office at the next election.

Latin Americans define democracy as a *result*. They are more concerned about their leaders' *performance in office* than in the process by which they attained their positions. If the man is performing well, very often the people will permit him to dispense with the election process. On the other hand, Americans put up with incompetents and connivers as long as they are freely elected. Americans place a higher value on legitimacy than on performance. The British, we think, have overcome the weaknesses of both the American and Latin American methods. The British observe the democratic process but retain the right to vote politicians out of office without waiting a specified period before holding elections. We will return to British political culture later on.

Most Latin Americans feel powerless to control their destinies, and this leads to two interesting cultural characteristics. It leads, first of all, to a strong *belief in fate* (*que sera, sera*—whatever will be, will be). This feeling of powerlessness goes beyond political considerations. The majestic Andes mountains and the many natural disasters that Latin Americans suffer (earthquakes, floods, hurricanes) make them feel humble and powerless before nature. Since humans are considered to be at

The Power of Speech
Powerlessness sometimes leads Latin American politicians to substitute words for actions. This television picture was picked up in Florida as Fidel Castro broadcast one of his marathon speeches, which sometimes lasted for hours. Fidel's actions in Latin America are somewhat curtailed by the overwhelming military power of the United States, especially since the collapse of the Soviet Union in December, 1991.

the mercy of fate, Latin Americans do not take failure personally. "Well, I tried but luck was not with me." On the other hand, Americans believe they are the masters of their fate. Hence if they fail in some endeavor, they blame themselves. "Where did I go wrong?" Thus a disappointment that may cause a North American to land on a psychiatrist's couch may merely lead to a shrug of the shoulders in Latin America (*Fue el destino,* "It was fate").

The sense of powerlessness that most Latin Americans feel often leads them to *substitute words for actions*. It might be said that they substitute symbolic rewards for material rewards. Since they are powerless to gain the latter, style replaces substance. Latins take great pride in writing and speaking ability. Americans often appoint businessmen as ambassadors to other countries; Latins appoint poets and other literary figures. Fidel Castro's well-known oral marathons, some of which lasted all night, would have turned off the "Yanquis," but in the early years they entranced the Cubans. This love for rhetoric even affects their legal system.

Latin Americans are more concerned about having good laws on the books than they are about applying them. They seem to feel that writing a law or a constitution solves problems, whether or not the laws are obeyed. Unlike the American Constitution which is vague and procedural, Latin American constitutions are very specific and deal with substantive matters. They spell out in great detail how social and economic affairs should be handled. The Mexican constitution limits the amount of land an individual can own, and the size varies according to the degree of the land's fertility. The Cuban constitution of 1940 stipulated that employers must give pregnant employees time off with pay beginning three months before the baby is due until three months after it is born. Then the mother must be given two hours off daily so she can nurse the baby. Such detailed constitutions are not always enforced, but Latin Americans can point to their constitutions with pride and say, "This is truly a clear indication that we are democratic."

Graft and corruption exist in most political systems to some extent. But in Latin America they are an accepted part of the political culture. In order to explain this attitude it is necessary to go back to the colonial period. The Spanish monarchs did not appoint officials in the New World on the basis of merit. Public offices were sold to the highest bidder. Naturally, if people pay for a public office they are likely to treat it as an investment on which they expect to make a profit. And that is precisely what happened in colonial Latin America. The people expected and still expect their government officials to make a lot of money while in office. Hence graft and corruption are an integral part of Latin American political culture. Actually some government officials are very honest, but a great many are not. In fact, in some countries a public official who does not increase his wealth while in office is considered stupid. This is sometimes referred to as a concessionary view of public office. One, of course, acquires a concession in order to make money. This attitude hinders the development of a professional administrative class. Such a professional bureaucracy is necessary to attain rapid economic growth, which is a primary goal of most Latin American countries.

Anti-Americanism is also very prevalent in Latin America. It is a result of their political culture and their subservient relations with the United States. In the past the United States has intervened in the internal affairs of many Latin American countries, economically, politically, and militarily. Although Latin Americans do not like being dominated by the United States, many Latin countries are economically dependent on American trade, aid, and investments. Sometimes they also depend on the United States for military defense. This is a blow to their egos, but they often find themselves boxed into a corner because of their dependence. This leads inevitably to anti-Americanism. Consequently, whenever possible, they take an independent stance on foreign policy. Some Latin American nations have even nationalized American business holdings in their countries. This is a way of exerting both anti-Americanism and nationalism.

Anti-American sentiment in Latin America should not be confused with pro-communism. It results rather from machismo and other cultural characteristics. In international relations the primary concern of Latin American nations is nonintervention in the internal affairs of any state by any other state. (Read that: "Yanqui, stay home!") Americans who have not studied the history of American foreign relations with Latin America very carefully tend to equate anti-Americanism with communism. But, as we have indicated, this anti-Americanism is really expressive of nationalist, not Communist, sentiment. Thus studying Latin American political culture sheds light not only on their internal politics but also on their foreign policies. The interplay of their culture and American economic and military penetration in their lives explains a great deal about Latin American politics.

In 1993, the Clinton administration convinced Congress to approve the North American Free Trade Association (NAFTA) treaty, uniting the U.S. with Canada and Mexico to abolish tariff barriers. The Caribbean wants to be included immediately. The rest of Latin America will probably join eventually. Such economic interdependence would probably reduce anti-American sentiment significantly.

We have examined the general political culture of Latin America. As we turn our attention to Great Britain, we will focus on the elite as well as the general political culture. British culture is more akin to the American than is the Latin, but there are some very interesting differences as well.

British Political Culture

The rights of Britons to speak, assemble, publish, travel, worship, and so forth are very closely guarded. *Liberty* is a very strong cultural belief in Great Britain. It has evolved over a period of many centuries as a part of the British democratic ideal and is one of the most cherished aspects of British culture. For example, Britain has not had a period in its recent history in which civil rights were compromised as they were in the United States in the early 1950s. The British wouldn't stand for a witch-hunt in the name of anti-communism or anything else. Consequently there is no British Civil Liberties Union because there is no need for one.

However, *inequality* is also deeply ingrained in British culture. Upward mobility is much more prevalent in the United States than it is in Great Britain. The American belief in equality has its roots in the Jacksonian tradition and, however compromised in practice, it remains an important cultural characteristic. Although the British have a welfare system that has equalized the standard of living to a great extent, they maintain a more rigid social stratification system than does the United States. Moreover, the working class does not resent it. The British believe each class has certain things it can do best, including ruling the country. Working-class members are proud of their status. They remain content as long as their interests are represented by some members of the ruling class. The Labour party was founded in 1908 by the Fabian Society, whose leadership was comprised of upper class intellectuals. These intellectuals invited political and business leaders into their homes and talked to them about the need for reforms. In this manner they were able to improve the lot of British workers to some degree. These workers, who comprise the backbone of the Labour party, are content to let their "betters" represent their interests in the political arena.

Since the British believe that some people are meant to rule because they are better educated and wiser, there is a great *deference to political authority* in Great Britain. This orientation to political authority is certainly different from the American. In the United States many people look down upon politicians. In England it is an honor to be called a professional politician. British subjects display a *sense of trust* toward their politicians that Americans do not. This leads the general public in both countries to view the roles of their elected officials differently.

In the United States elected officials are considered *representatives* of the popular will. They are not supposed to make independent decisions but rather to represent the will of their constituents. In Great Britain elected officials are *governors*. The people elect them on the basis of party and platform. Once elected, however, they are supposed to govern for the public good, based upon their own individual judgments and not those of their constituents. In 1971 Parliament voted to have Great Britain join the European Common Market despite the fact that the vast majority of the people expressed a desire to stay out of it. This sense of trust in politicians enables public officials to make public policy in privacy. Such privacy in the United States would be frowned upon by the electorate. In fact, in late 1975 the U.S. Senate passed a "Government in the Sunshine" law designed to reduce significantly the number of Senate hearings conducted behind closed doors.

Tradition plays an important role in British politics. The *Crown* (the royal family) symbolizes the unity and continuity of the British system. Although the royal family no longer exercises any real power, its leader acts as head of state—welcoming foreign visitors, dedicating new buildings, and performing other ceremonial duties. The public follows the royal family's activities as avidly as young Americans keep up with their idols in the athletic and entertainment fields. However, concern for tradition does not signify an aversion to change. Quite the contrary. The British have altered their economic system, for example, to a much greater degree than have the Americans.

Change, however, must be *evolutionary*, it must come only after careful deliberation. It is interesting to note that the Fabian Society had a turtle as its symbol. This *gradualist approach to social change* has permitted England to enjoy a high degree of stability at all times. Revolutionary parties are free to compete in the political marketplace without harassment, but they gain few adherents because they run counter to the general political culture.

Another value on which there is high consensus is *welfare*. This is not a new idea. Belief that the government should provide the basic necessities of welfare can be traced back to medieval times in England. This belief has been expanded considerably by the Labour party, but other parties differ on this issue only on the extent, and not on the need for government responsibility.

An interesting contrast between British and American priorities regards higher education and medical care. Americans insist on making higher education available to all at little or no cost, but fail to push strongly for a national health insurance program. In Britain it is the opposite. "The contrasting English and American attitudes toward free higher education and free medical care reflect the extent to which values in England are related to efforts to insure against hardship, whereas in America greater emphasis is placed upon opportunities for advancement."[1]

Collectivist attitudes are another important aspect of British political culture that can be traced back to medieval times. In fact, the British political system can properly be called "government by committee." Committees are established to deal with every problem. All interested parties are represented on these committees. This is called *collective consultation*. In the United States it is called participatory democracy. Whatever name it goes by, it means that all individuals and groups should participate in making decisions which affect them. It is interesting to note that the British political elite, which has no formal check on its power except the electorate, does not abuse its power. Indeed, it dilutes its own power by appointing representatives of all interest groups to assist in policy making. By political elite we mean those who play a significant role in the political system.

In examining the British elite political culture one trait stands out: a *strong sense of responsibility to the people;* a strong commitment to duty. A reverence for tradition and custom causes the elite to behave as ladies and gentlemen, to exercise their power cautiously and moderately, and to trust all other members of the elite, even if they are members of different political parties. Elite political culture is characterized by a certain amount of personalism, and a feeling of separateness from nonelites. School ties are especially important in the higher echelons of British government. Political leaders of different parties probably have more in common with each other than any party leaders have with their rank-and-file members. However, since British politicians generally conduct themselves as befits their role, they retain the high esteem of the general public.

Differences in structure between British parliamentary democracy and American presidential democracy account for some of the cultural differences between the two societies. The American political system was designed primarily to prevent anyone from becoming a dictator. The founding fathers were afraid of tyrants. Hence they built into the Constitution so many checks and balances and separation of powers that the American political system, as we said in an earlier chapter, is often an exercise in frustration. Consequently it is very difficult to effect change. Americans may elect a president who promises to bring about needed reforms. However, after he is elected, he may be confronted with a recalcitrant Congress, Supreme Court, or bureaucracy that refuses to go along with the reforms. The result is that the American people conclude that: "You can't trust a politician. He'll promise you anything in order to get elected, but he will not deliver on his promises." Undoubtedly there are American politicians who make empty promises in order to get elected. But there are also many others who fully intend to deliver on their promises but who find themselves frustrated by all the checks and balances on their power. Thus it is no great surprise to discover that most Americans distrust politicians.

British politicians are not necessarily more honest than are American politicians, but the British system permits politicians to deliver on their promises. In the first place, there is no separation of powers between the executive and legislative branches of government. They hold national elections in which every seat in Parliament (in the House of Commons) is at stake. The major parties nominate candidates for all the seats. Generally, there is a high degree of party unity for the program which each party has carefully outlined for the people. This makes intelligent voting very simple for the British. All the people have to know about the candidates running for office from their districts is their party affiliation. The people vote for the party, not for the person.

Whichever party gains a majority in the House of Commons controls the executive branch of government. As we stated earlier, the leader of that political party becomes prime minister, and he can appoint up to 100 members of his party to the cabinet (which is the executive branch). Thus cabinet members are also members of the legislature; there is no complete separation of powers. The program that the majority party has promised to enact is then enacted. Problems generally do not arise in fulfilling these promises because the executive automatically has a majority in the legislature. Thus the British trust their politicians because under the British parliamentary system the leaders are able to deliver on their promises. And the leaders know that the people will hold them directly accountable for doing so. Thus differences in governmental structure account for some of the differences between British and American political culture.

In a parliamentary system sometimes no party has a majority and a coalition government must be formed. In Britain, this has been a rare occurrence, because there were only two major parties. In the 1980s, however, a strong third party evolved thereby increasing the possibility of a coalition government in the near future. If that happens, the parties in coalition must then compromise on their programs.

☐ Russian Political Culture

Let us now turn our attention to the Russian general and elite political culture. In Russia, as in Great Britain, an important cultural belief is that some people are better suited to rule than others. Contrary to the British, however, Russian political culture for centuries has not stipulated that the leaders be democratically elected. The gradual democratization and liberalization which characterized the political evolution of the Western democracies did not occur in Russia. The Mongol invasions interrupted the development of democracy in Russia in the late Middle Ages. It also implanted a predilection for what historians used to refer to as Oriental despotism. This type of dictatorship is extremely cruel and arbitrary because the power of the leaders is unchecked. This is the cultural heritage the Russians had at the time of the Communist revolution in November 1917. Consequently it was not difficult for the Russian people to accept the arbitrary and absolute power of the Communist party. It fit in perfectly with the political culture. Thus **autocracy** is and has been the dominant cultural characteristic of Russian politics for centuries. In many ways the Communist system was a continuation of the old tsarist system. The Tsars had a secret police, exile to Siberia, no free elections, and other characteristics that often are attributed to the Communists. Thus, contrary to common belief in the United States, most of the dictatorial actions of the former Soviet leaders can be attributed primarily to Russian history, and not to Communist ideology. In fact, with *perestroika*, free elections of a limited nature were held in 1989 and Boris Yeltsin was subsequently elected president of Russia, a position he still held in early 1994. It remains to be seen if this is a short-term aberration or a permanent change.

Collectivism is another important aspect of Russian political culture. The Communist party of the Soviet Union (CPSU) provided collective leadership for the nation; its Central Committee provided collective leadership for the party; and the Presidium (Politburo) and the Secretariat provided collective leadership for the Central Committee.

It is significant that Khrushchev's denunciation of Stalin in 1956 focused on his one-man rule and his mistreatment of Communist party officials. Stalin was criticized primarily because he did not observe the collective leadership principle, not because of his mistreatment of the general population. No mention was made of Stalin's murder of five million peasants (Stalin's figures) between 1928 and 1933.

Khrushchev was deposed because he had become too independent and made decisions without consulting other party leaders. More

Collectivism

Soviet Russia's collectivist approach is shown here by a collective farm and by the joint meeting of the Communist Party Central Committee, the USSR Supreme Soviet, and the RSFSR Supreme Soviet.

recent Soviet leaders were very careful in observing a collectivist approach. Thus collectivism is an important part of the elite as well as the general political culture of Russia. Economic collectivism also has its roots in the tsarist past. Collectivized agriculture is as old as Russia. Collective farming was merely expanded, not invented, by Stalin.

Utopianism, industrialism, and *totalitarianism* were three other important Soviet cultural characteristics. The first came from their Marxist-Leninist ideology. Karl Marx predicted in 1848 (in the *Communist Manifesto*) that all societies would eventually evolve into Communist utopias, (he did not use the term but that is what he described), characterized by great abundance, the absence of a government, a classless society, and a population untainted by selfish interests. This would come about, said Marx, because of an inexorable historical process that he called dialectical materialism. Although Soviet leaders did not claim to have developed such a utopian society yet, they insisted that this was the ultimate goal of their rule.

Lenin and his successors emphasized rapid industrialization as a necessary prerequisite toward the attainment of this goal. Stalin, especially, concentrated on industrialization practically to the exclusion of all other goals. Totalitarianism was instituted supposedly to marshal all resources to attain rapid economic growth through industrialization. Totalitarianism means controlling every aspect of all citizens' lives to the fullest extent possible. Thus the Communist party not only monopolized political power but also the economic system, the education system, communications, transportation, recreation, the arts, and everything else it was capable of controlling. According to Marx, Communist revolutions were supposed to occur in advanced industrialized societies in which great abundance would permit a high standard of living for everyone once the distribution system was changed. However, the first Communist revolution (and all others since) occurred in a feudalistic agrarian society that had barely begun its industrial revolution. Hence Soviet leaders claimed it was necessary to institute totalitarianism until such time as great abundance would be achieved. Then and only then could the state wither away as the classless Communist utopia became a reality.

Mikhail Gorbachev, Russia's leader from 1985 to 1991, instituted the policies of *glasnost* and *perestroika:* openness and restructuring of the Soviet political and economic systems. He also softened Soviet foreign policy. He tried to humanize Communism, and failed. Instead, he unleashed social forces that he could not control, so he lost power. It remains to be seen if Boris Yeltsin and his successors can overcome a thousand year authoritarian political culture. Several political polls in 1991 and 1992 indicated strong attitudinal support for democracy. The mass opposition to the attempted military coup in August 1991 indicates behavioral support for democracy.*

---

* See Gibson, James L. "Mass opposition to the Soviet putsch of August, 1991. Democratic participation in the (former) Soviet Union." Paper presented at the 1993 annual meeting of the American Sociological Association, Miami Beach, August 13–17, 1993.

☐ A Typology of Political Cultures

The preceding analysis of Latin American, British, and Russian political cultures (with passing references to the United States) was not meant to be exhaustive. We merely wanted to give you a taste of the flavor of politics in these areas by discussing certain aspects of their political cultures. We have not attempted to develop a typology of political cultures. Other scholars have. The most prominent writer in this area is Gabriel A. Almond. He and his associates at Stanford University and elsewhere have developed an interesting typology which we will now discuss. It is based on orientations toward political objects.

Almond and Verba[2] concerned themselves with three types of orientation: affective (how people feel about politics), cognitive (what they know about politics), and evaluative (what political judgments they make).

Types of Orientations

Affective—feelings, emotions
Cognitive—knowledge, information
Evaluative—value judgments

They also selected political objects which they considered most important: the general political system, the inputs, the outputs, and the self as a political actor.

Political Objects

System
Inputs
Outputs
Self

Almond says that every political system is embedded in a particular pattern of orientations to political action (a political culture). Although every system is a mixture, Almond identifies three pure types: parochial, subject, and participant. In a *parochial-political culture* the people may be dimly aware of a central political authority but they know very little about it. The cognitive (knowledge) level is low. Neither do they identify with the input and output structures and functions. They never get to articulate their interests, and they are not affected very much by the political system's outputs. Obviously, then, the people lack any orientation to the self as a role player in the system. The people believe, feel, and judge themselves to have no power to bring about change through the political system, or to be affected by it.

In a *subject-political culture* the people are passively loyal. They know about and have some feelings toward the general political system, and they are aware of how the system's outputs (decisions and actions) affect them. But the people do not know what role they themselves can play as political actors or how they can affect the input structures by making demands on the system. Consequently their relationships to political objects, as we stated earlier, are passive. However, they do feel an allegiance to the government.

In a *participant-political culture* individuals play an active part in every facet of political activity. They need not feel positively toward the political system, but they need to feel something. Their knowledge level is high, and they participate personally in political activity of some sort at some time.

Cultural Patterns		**Political Objects**		
	system	*inputs*	*outputs*	*self*
Parochial	0	0	0	0
Subject	1	0	1	0
Participant	1	1	1	1

Since there are no pure types of political culture in the real world Almond and Verba have made their models more useful by discussing certain combinations. In a *parochial-subject culture* the majority of people still have parochial orientations, but a significant number have developed an allegiance to the general political system and are aware of the consequences of its actions. Mexico in the 1930s was a good example of this type of political culture. President Lazaro Cardenas (1934–1940) was a social and economic reformer who captured the imagination and loyalty of many Mexicans. Although his reforms caused a large minority to become loyal to the national government, for many years the majority of his countrymen continued to feel a greater allegiance to their towns and villages.

Most modern societies have a *subject-participant culture.* Very few pure parochials remain, but the number of participants usually is still a minority. Thus the majority of citizens fall into the subject category. The Soviet Union today is a prime example of a subject-participant culture, as is the United States, although the number of participants in Russia is probably the smaller of the two. Neither system has many parochials.

Most emerging nations have a *parochial-participant culture.* These nations tend to have a highly active but small group of participants who are trying to politicize the large majority of citizens who are still parochials. The majority of people in such countries united to throw out the colonial power that had ruled over them in many cases but then returned to their tribal, ethnic, racial, or regional groupings. They seldom emerged from the fight for independence with strong feelings of nationalism. The major problem confronting national leaders in these nations is not in increasing the number of participants (they may not want any more) but in developing a large subject culture that will be loyal to the new system and help it to achieve its goals.

The ideal mixed political culture, according to Almond and Verba, is the *civic culture.* They claim that the British come closest to this ideal. The civic culture is a mixture of traditional and modern orientations and of participant, subject, and parochial subcultures. Indeed, each citizen is a composite of these orientations and subcultures. Concern for tradition guarantees that time-tested values and procedures will not be discarded; and a commitment to modernization permits the adoption of new and more useful values and procedures. The participant aspect ensures the continuation of democratic processes; the subject aspect maintains a high level of acceptance and support for the system; and the parochial aspect ensures that commitment to political activities is mild most of the time for most people, so that a high level of intense participation is avoided. High intensity tends to magnify differences and minimize similarities of interest. A highly politicized culture could conceivably lead to a great deal of instability. Thus the ideal is not a totally participant culture but rather a moderate mixture of all three types.

☐ Cultural Integration

In comparing different political cultures it is useful to examine the degree to which they are integrated or fragmented. A highly integrated political culture leads to political stability and a poorly integrated one causes political instability. Nigeria provides a good example of a fragmented political culture. The civil war that led to the secession of Biafra resulted because Nigerian citizens felt a greater allegiance to a subculture than to the general culture.

When Nigeria gained its independence from England, its boundaries were established according to the former colonial administrative boundaries. It did not take into account regional, tribal, ethnic, racial, and religious differences. Sometimes the boundaries divided tribes, and at other times groups who were quite different from each other were thrown together. The new national government had great difficulty integrating these diverse subcultures.

At the other end of the spectrum is England whose highly integrated political culture provides the setting for a very stable political system. As Lord Simon put it: "Our parliamentary system will work as long as the responsible people in different parties accept the view that it is better that the other side should win than that the constitution should be broken."[3] The high consensus in Britain is due largely to the racial, religious, and ethnic homogeneity that characterizes its population, and also to the fact that it is a mature, affluent country that can live with temporary failure.

Somewhere between England and Nigeria on this spectrum is France. Not only are there many French political parties, but they generally have a narrow base, and in many respects can be called political subcultures. However, nationalism is also very strong. French citizens, therefore, are pulled in two directions at once: toward national unity and toward political fragmentation. Hence, although France lacks the degree of consensus that the British manifest, its political culture is much more integrated than is Nigeria's.

☐ Summary

To summarize, the political culture of a state or region is the psychological environment within which political activity takes place. In this chapter we discussed certain aspects of general and elite political cultures, and of subcultures as well. We examined Almond and Verba's pure and mixed types of political culture. And we pointed out that the degree of cultural integration affects the degree of political stability of a political system. In explaining these concepts we delved into the politics of Latin America, Great Britain, the United States, and the Soviet Union (with brief references to France and Nigeria).

REFERENCES

1. Richard Rose, *Politics in England* (Boston: Little, Brown, 1964), pp. 46–47.
2. Gabriel Almond and Sydney Verba, *Civic Culture* (Boston: Little, Brown, 1965).
3. Lord Simon, quoted by L. S. Amery, "The Nature of British Parliamentary Government," in *Parliament: A Survey*, ed. by E. Campion (London: Allen & Unwin, 1952), p. 40.

GLOSSARY

Autocracy	Absolute and arbitrary dictatorship. Dictators are answerable to no one but themselves.
Caudillismo	The Latin American practice of having strong, dictatorial leaders, usually military men.
Continuismo	Self-perpetuation in office.
Individualism	Reserving the right to decide whether or not to obey a particular law.
Legalism	Performing within the letter of the law, especially within the framework of a self-written constitution.

Machismo   A cultural trait of the ideal male in Latin America. It includes extreme masculinity, hard living (in both work and play), bravery, pride, honor, dignity, and sexual prowess.

Paternalism   A political relationship between leaders and followers which resembles the relationship between parents and children.

Personalism(o)   Emphasis on primary relationships. Personal connections prevail in the political process.

Political culture The beliefs, values, attitudes, and habits of a group that affect its members' political behavior.

SELECTED READING

Barghoorn, Fredrick C., *Politics in the USSR* (Boston: Little, Brown, 1966).
This is an excellent application of the Almond and Powell model to the USSR.

Gibson, James L., Mass Opposition to the Soviet putsch of August 1991: Democratic participation in the (former) Soviet Union, Paper delivered at the 1993 Annual Meeting of the American Sociological Association, Fontainebleau Hilton, Miami Beach, Fl, August 13-17, 1993.
This paper describes the evolution of Russian political culture as exemplified by the people's opposition to the attempted military coup of 1991.

Gomez, R. A., *Government and Politics in Latin America* (New York: Random House, 1963).
This small paperback is an excellent introduction to Latin American political culture.

Nicholson, Peter P., *The Political Philosophy of the British Idealists: Selected Studies* (New York: Cambridge University Press, 1990).
This book presents the ideas of some of Britain's great political thinkers.

Rose, Richard, *Politics in England* (Boston: Little, Brown, 1964).
An excellent analysis based on Almond and Powell's comparative politics model.

QUESTIONS

1. The political culture of a country is reflected most strongly by
   a. the laws as written in the constitution.
   b. the formal structure of the political system.

    c. the political beliefs and habits of the general public.

    d. the laws passed by the congress and the state legislatures.

2. A Latin American would most likely agree that a necessary component of good government is

    a. a strong leader with a military mind.

    b. a constitution that focuses on procedures.

    c. a businesslike presidential figure.

    d. a system of checks on presidential power by the judicial and legislative branches.

3. Anti-American sentiment in Latin America is largely the result of

    a. a pro-Communist attitude on the part of the people.

    b. the people's subservient relationship with the United States. (It is a blow to their egos to be so dependent economically and militarily on the U.S.)

    c. heavy tourism and the air of superiority exhibited by most American tourists.

    d. the United States government's policy of isolationism, which deprives Latin American countries of badly needed tourism, private investment, and government aid.

4. In Great Britain the public attitude toward politicians is one of

    a. trust. (Politicians govern for the good of the country as determined by their personal judgments, not those of the constituencies that elected them.)

    b. disgust. (Most politicians are corrupt and will sacrifice the needs of the people for their own political or financial gain.)

    c. awe. (Britons look upon their leaders as godlike with infinite wisdom.)

    d. equality. (Britons feel equal to the politicians and therefore expect them to act according to the decisions of the majority of the people.)

5. Change in Great Britain is usually

    a. revolutionary. (The people feel strongly that their archaic system must be changed by any means necessary, including violence.)

    b. voted on by the people in a national plebescite and acted upon immediately.

    c. a slow deliberate process, in order to maintain a high level of stability within the government.

    d. impossible, because the British are trapped by tradition. (This causes a general aversion to change for fear that cherished traditions will be lost.)

6. The dominant characteristic of Russian politics for centuries is best described by which of the following?

    a. socialistic—rule by white-collar workers

    b. autocratic—absolute power by a single political group or person

    c. anarchy—Because Russia is so large, the laws really never have had an effect on the average person.

    d. representation on government committees by interest groups chosen by the people

7. Which was not a Soviet Russian cultural characteristic?
    a. Utopianism
    b. Totalitarianism
    c. Industrialism
    d. Individualism
    e. Collectivism

8. Gabriel Almond and Sidney Verba concerned themselves with three types of orientation toward political objects: cognitive, affective, and evaluative. Which of the following definitions is correct?
    a. cognitive: knowledge; affective: value judgments; evaluative: feelings.
    b. cognitive: knowledge; affective: feelings; evaluative: value judgments.
    c. cognitive: feelings; affective: knowledge; evaluative: value judgments.
    d. cognitive: value judgments; affective: feelings; evaluative: knowledge.

9. Which series of statements accurately describes a subject political culture?
    a. The people are passively loyal. They have some knowledge of the political system and how its decisions and actions affect them. However, they do not know what roles they themselves can play in the political system.
    b. The people play an active part in every facet of the political system. Although they may not agree with all aspects of the system, they are knowledgeable and will participate in some sort of political activity at some time.
    c. Although the knowledge level is low, the people try to play some role in political decision making. They feel a strong allegiance to the government and will try to affect the input structures by making demands on the system.
    d. The people have a dim awareness of a central political authority. Their knowledge level is low, and they feel powerless to bring about change through the political system because the effects of the political outputs on them personally are minimal.

10. According to Almond and Verba, the ideal political culture would be
    a. a participant culture, because of the high intellectual level.

b. a subject culture that is extremely loyal and not likely to cause political instability.

c. a parochial-participant culture. (This blend is perfect because one group is knowledgeable and active in government, while the other is passive and uninterested in politics, thereby providing a balanced and stable society.)

d. a civic culture that combines parochial, subject, and participant cultures.

QUESTIONS FOR THOUGHT AND DISCUSSION

1. Compare the British, American, Russian, and Latin American political cultures.

2. What are the differences among parochial, subject, participant, style and civic cultures?

3. Explain the concept of cultural integration.

SEVEN

The International System

Students of international affairs face a level-of-analysis problem—deciding what level of analysis will yield the greatest insights. Should the focus be on individuals, nation-states, or the global political system? Perhaps it would be more fruitful to concentrate on the types of interactions that occur between the units that compose the international system. In this section we have tried to do all these things. Chapter 22 deals with the basic assumptions held by national foreign-policy decision makers and with the role of nation-states and multinational organizations in world affairs. Chapter 23 includes various types of international interactions, such as diplomacy, war, and economic relations. Chapters 24 and 25 focus on the international system; the former covers the past, and the latter deals with the present and the future.

22

The Actors

Whatever area of the social sciences one studies, it is best to begin by examining the basic assumptions held by the leading scholars and by the most important decision makers in the field: the theorists and the practitioners. This is especially true in the field of **international politics,** because the leading scholars in this field are often among the top government advisers on foreign policy matters. A community of scholars who specialize in international affairs exists in most of the world's leading capitals, where national leaders frequently seek their knowledge and advice. U.S. foreign policy advisers have their counterparts in all major countries.

In this chapter we will deal with the units (actors) of the international system and will attempt to characterize their behavior. We will examine both **national** and **international actors.** If we want to understand current and future foreign policy decisions, it will help to know how those who will make these decisions reach their conclusions. It is important to begin by examining fundamental assumptions because different assumptions lead to different conclusions and hence to different policies.

Before World War II America was essentially an isolationist nation. It was primarily concerned with its internal affairs and avoided an active role in international politics. Consequently, it lacked the centuries of experience in international relations that many other countries had acquired. When the war ended, it was apparent to most people that America's "splendid isolation" was over. Technological advancements in transportation, communications, and weaponry had abolished the significance of distance and of national desires to remain aloof from foreign entanglements. The world had become a mass of interdependent peoples, and a policy of isolationism was no longer feasible.

A new breed of international relations specialists was born. Before World War II diplomatic historians and international lawyers dominated the field. Their explanations and postulations were now deemed by many people to be naive and irrelevant. In the United States a scholarly debate raged around the following issue: What course should American foreign policy take now that isolationism was no longer feasible? As a result there developed two diametrically opposed approaches to the study and practice of international politics. One approach, called **political realism,** placed primary emphasis on national interests defined as power. The other, called **political idealism,** emphasized morality and legal structures.

☐ Realism and Idealism

It should come as no surprise that realists and idealists perceive their own and each other's positions differently. The most celebrated realist in the post-war period, Hans Morgenthau, was a very active participant in this post-war debate. This is how he defined his position.[1]

> The realist school believes that the world, imperfect as it is from the rational point of view, is the result of forces inherent in human nature. To improve the world one must work with those forces, not against them. This being inherently a world of opposing interests and of conflict among them, moral principles can never be fully realized, but must at best be approximated through the ever temporary balancing of interests and the ever precarious settlement of conflicts. This school, then, sees in a system of checks and balances a universal principle for all pluralist societies. It appeals to historic precedent rather than to abstract principles, and aims at the realization of the lesser evil rather than the absolute good.

Political realism, by striving for the "lesser evil" rather than the "absolute good," places a political analyst in the decision maker's shoes rather than on Mount Olympus. Given a specific set of circumstances, what rational alternatives are available, and what would be the probable consequences of pursuing each course? This is the question scholars should ask. According to this view we should not develop an abstract ideal world in which there are no moral or ethical lapses, because most human beings just don't fit this model. Some individuals may approximate it, but nation-states never do. Thus, the realists view the world according to a "conflict" model and the idealists perceive it as conforming to a "fulfillment" model. Perhaps, as in personality theory, both models are too simplistic.

The key concept for realists is *interest defined as power.* Every country pursues its **national interests,** not some abstract moral ideal; and to

Lyndon Johnson
He was unable to convince the public that the Vietnam War was in America's national interests.

further those interests it is necessary to acquire power. Realists claim this is a universal principle of international politics; indeed it is the central factor. This concept does not, of course, tell us specifically how any given state will act at any particular time; however, its proponents claim it will provide clues that will enable us to calculate how a given nation may act (if it acts rationally) under particular circumstances, by putting ourselves in the decision maker's position.

Morgenthau also claims that *national interests are arranged in hierarchical order.* First, there are those which must be pursued at all costs, because their attainment is indispensable for the national, or individual, existence and welfare. Second, there are those which might be pursued under favorable circumstances. Third, there are those which, however desirable in themselves, can never be pursued because they are beyond the reach of available strength.[2]

This hierarchical ranking of interests seems to make a lot of sense. However, individuals may reach different conclusions regarding what is essential and what is desirable but unattainable. For instance, Lyndon Johnson (a realist) pursued a policy toward Vietnam which Hans Morgenthau (The Realist) disagreed with. President Johnson assigned a number one or two ranking to a policy that Morgenthau placed in the third rank of interests. Hence we need more rigorous theorizing than that provided by "political realism" in order to understand international politics. We will offer some suggestions later in the chapter.

Prudence is another key concept of the realist school. Morgenthau says:[3]

There can be no political morality without prudence; that is without consideration of the political consequences of seemingly moral action. Realism, then, considers prudence—the weighing of the consequences of alternative political actions—to be the supreme virtue in politics. Ethics in the abstract judges action by its conformity with the moral law; political ethics judges action by its political consequences.

This position, at the state level, may be compared to an individual's pursuance of situational ethics. The point is that individuals may choose to sacrifice their lives for a moral cause, but nation-states cannot. After all, what virtue is there in moral purity if the price of achieving it is the political impotence or destruction of a nation?

Idealists, of course, hold an opposing view. Bear in mind that we are presenting polar positions of what is essentially a continuum. The major assumption of idealists is that *nations should conduct their foreign relations using morality as their guideline, not selfish national interest.* Woodrow Wilson's foreign policy pronouncements clearly place him in the idealist school. For example, he refused to recognize the Mexican government after it achieved power through revolution. He said that henceforth the United States would offer diplomatic recognition only to those governments that attained power through constitutional means. "All others are immoral!"

Of course if nations had pursued such a policy in the late eighteenth century the United States would have had no diplomatic ties whatsoever. Wilson, at least during his early years in the presidency, was an extreme idealist.

Morgenthau describes the idealist position in the following manner:[4]

> Political idealism believes that a rational and moral political order, derived from universally valid abstract principles can be achieved here and now. It assumes the essential goodness and infinite malleability of human nature and blames the failure of the social order to measure up to the rational standards on lack of knowledge and understanding, obsolescent social institutions, or the depravity of certain isolated individuals or groups.

It may seem strange to the reader that we let the father of political realism present the idealist position. However, idealists generally present their conclusions without stating the basic assumptions about the nature of people, conflict, and social institutions that led to those conclusions. Hence it is necessary to trace their reasoning processes back to their unstated assumptions. Since Morgenthau has done this better than anyone else has, we cite his description of the idealist position. Let us address ourselves to these points. First of all, there is no universal morality. Every society has its own set of values and beliefs, and although they may be similar to each other in many cases, in others they are not; and even when societal values are similar in a general sense, they often conflict in specific circumstances. Furthermore, the abstract nature of most moral norms allows leaders great latitude in implementing them.

Conflicting views of morality are inevitable as long as there is no world culture. At best, culture is transnational in certain historically linked parts of the world; for instance, in Western civilization. There are, indeed, certain values that are generally accepted by several countries. But certainly the Latin American branch of Western civilization differs significantly from the Western European. And even within each region specific states have developed unique cultures which often embrace distinct views of morality. Besides, even when states seemingly differ little in their value orientations they sometimes war against each other. In the absence of any universal moral precepts it is useless to indict national governments for not adhering to moral principles in conducting their foreign relations. In fact, they do adhere to such principles; those which are dominant societal values. National leaders, as members of a society, have internalized their society's principal values.

Lenin wrote that anything which furthers the cause of communism is moral and ethical, including theft and murder. (And from a Communist point of view it is!) Woodrow Wilson said, "Let's make the world safe for democracy." (He meant eliminate all dictatorships.) Objectively speaking, neither man was immoral; each was true to his own sense of morality.

Such idealism, however, if not tempered by prudence can lead to more, not fewer, wars. It can lead to more international conflict simply because one does not compromise one's moral principles. If carried to its logical conclusion, such moralistic foreign policy making makes it impossible for any state ever to reach a compromise with another state whose moral principles differ from its own. On the other hand, a state may indeed compromise on some of its national interests. The United States morally disapproves of any totalitarian system, but prudence dictated that we compromise with the Soviet Union. In this case unyielding and uncompromising anticommunism in the name of morality would probably have led to the most devastating war in the history of humankind. When nations equate their national interests with "God's will" or "dialectical materialism," or some other moral or historical force, they are more likely to wage war.

Even to invoke morality in conducting discussions of foreign policy is fruitless. Each side believes it is morally right; consequently nobody thinks their position is immoral. We're all good guys! Therefore if one means to engage in fruitful discussions regarding foreign policy, it is best to shun "moral" arguments. It is far better to discuss what a state's national interests are and why a particular policy furthers or retards those interests. It's not that morality doesn't matter, but national leaders must operate under particular circumstances at a particular point

V. I. Lenin
His belief that anything which furthered the cause of communism was ethical and moral is based on the belief that the ends justify the means. Like Wilson, he was not willing to compromise his moral principles.

in time. Under such conditions the range of rational alternatives is limited. That is why Morgenthau asserts that states must seek the "lesser evil" rather than the "absolute good." The morally ideal course of action is rarely if ever available or even agreed upon.

National leaders are primarily responsible for the general public's confusion on such matters. They invariably invoke moral principles in support of national policies, when actually they select policies that they believe will further their nation's own interests. An example is President Johnson telling the American people that we were fighting in Vietnam to preserve freedom and democracy; whereas, in fact, there never has been freedom or democracy in either half of Vietnam. He might have explained why he believed it was in our national interest to remain in Vietnam, but unfortunately he chose to speak in vague, moralistic terms, as do virtually all national leaders.

Another significant contrast between realists and idealists involves the conflict resolution function. Realists claim that nation-states are the primary actors in international affairs and that therefore international conflicts must be resolved in terms of power relations. Idealists counter that the nation-state system is inherently conflict-ridden and that the use of power is immoral. They claim that lasting world peace can be achieved only by creating a world government, which would adjudicate conflicts among its component parts (nation-states). Some idealists want to eradicate national boundaries altogether.

Here we have a conflict between political and legal approaches. Realists contend that political processes, because of their adjusting and accommodating nature, can best serve to settle international disputes. If a nation's interests are severely violated by a legal ruling it would be impractical for that nation to risk such a ruling. In fact it will not do so. Therefore one should not expect states to abdicate their responsibilities by submitting all disputes to an international body which may not take their national interests into consideration. This does not rule out voluntary decisions to submit disputes to adjudication or arbitration procedures. Actually realists believe a variety of diplomatic techniques, some of which involve third parties, often can be employed by states to reconcile their differences, but only at their own discretion.

Idealists take a legalistic approach because bilateral diplomatic techniques often fail and sometimes result in war. Not all idealists are pacifists; some recognize the necessity of "just" wars, but a significant number renounce war under any circumstances.[5] Realists tend to consider the latter simply naive and the former extremely dangerous because they are likely to engage in moralistic crusades (similar to the religious wars of the sixteenth and seventeenth centuries, or Iran's more recent behavior under the Ayatollah Khomeni).

According to realists power is amoral. In terms of the subject at hand it should be considered an instrument of foreign policy, devoid of any inherent moral content. Power may be used in a moral as well as in an immoral manner. But it cannot be judged except in relation to its use. Furthermore, in the absence of a world government and because one is unlikely to be formed in the foreseeable future, we must deal with current realities, which means maximizing national power to deal with any contingency.

Realists admit that the nation-state system resulted from dynamic historical forces which may someday replace it with other institutional forms of government. But historical forces on a worldwide scale evolve very slowly. Those of us living today are not likely to witness the formation of a world government. Leaving language and other cultural differences aside, political considerations make it unlikely. For example, in Dade County (Miami), Florida there is a weak metropolitan government comprised of 27 municipalities and a large unincorporated area. Power within this system is highly decentralized. All efforts to consolidate these governments have failed. Hence in Dade County there are 27 fire departments, 27 police departments, and so on, *ad nauseam*. Global differences are even greater. This being the case, what are the chances of establishing a world government? Not very great. Hence it is a waste of time and brainpower to dwell upon the need for world government in searching for solutions to current problems. It is far more useful to take into account the real alternatives and to try to make rational decisions on world affairs on that basis.

One last point needs airing before we drop the realist-idealist dialogue. Implicit in Woodrow Wilson's statement, "Let's make the world safe for democracy," is the assumption that a nation's internal political system determines its foreign policy. It implies that a world composed exclusively of democratic states would foster peace. Ob-

Woodrow Wilson (right) at Paris, 1918
Wilson's Fourteen Points embodied the idealist position that nations should conduct their foreign relations according to the dictates of morality, not selfish national interests.

viously internal factors do affect foreign policy decisions. But the *type* of political system a nation has cannot help us predict the content of its foreign policies. Democratic countries have been imperialistic and isolationist, warlike and peaceful; the same is true of dictatorial states.

The distinguishing characteristic of international politics is that it takes place in the absence of a supreme political authority. Because of this, nation-states must assume total responsibility for national survival and national security. Indeed, realists claim that this is every state's primary goal, regardless of its ideology or form of government. Consequently the dynamics of the international political system differ significantly from those of nation-states. The latter operate within a governmental framework, and this makes all the difference in the world. That is why we should refrain from automatically trying to apply concepts that are true of other types of political activity to international politics—in most cases they just don't apply.

It is possible, of course, to incorporate some idealistic aspects into a realistic foreign policy. For example, former President Jimmy Carter exerted pressure on countries that needed the United States more than the United States needed them if they were violating human rights. Jacobo Timerman, who was exiled from Argentina while that country's military dictatorship was "disappearing" people they suspected of opposing the government, says that Carter's human rights policy saved thousands of lives in Argentina. However, if a country with an oppressive government played an important role in U.S. national defense, e.g., Iran under the Shah, we did not pressure them.

In summarizing these two approaches we would like to point out that although we have been much more critical of the legalistic-moralistic (idealist) approach, the power and interest (realist) school also has severe limitations. However, the realists seem to contribute much more than do the idealists to an understanding of this subject.

It is necessary to utilize other analytical tools also to better understand foreign policy and international politics. However, as we stated in the beginning of this chapter: If we understand the basic assumptions on which foreign-policy decisions are made, we can better understand past, present, and future international relations. Since all national leaders seem to follow the precepts of the realist school, a study of these precepts, whether you agree with them or not, will help you gain that understanding.

☐ Scope, Intentions, and Capabilities

In examining a nation's foreign policy, we might gain insights by determining its **scope of interest.** It may be *globalist, regionalist,* or *isolationist.* A state has a globalist foreign policy if it believes that its range of interests encompass the entire world. American presidents since Harry Truman have taken this position. However, for the major period of our history, beginning with George Washington's term of office, our leaders were isolationists. They believed we should focus on our internal affairs and avoid "entangling alliances." Some Americans still hold this view. Others take a regionalist position.

American regionalists generally adhere to a "sphere of interest" philosophy. They usually consider the Western Hemisphere and Western Europe to be our sphere of interest. Beyond that, whatever happens in Eastern Europe, Asia, or Africa should not concern us. Therefore, in assessing a state's foreign policy it is useful to determine its scope of interest.

The **intentions** of a nation-state are also indicative of the direction of its foreign policy. States may be divided into *status quo* and *revisionist* powers. A status quo state is one that is satisfied with its geographical boundaries and with its power and influence. A revisionist state obviously is one that is not satisfied and that also seeks to change the status quo.

Another distinction that may be useful in analyzing nation-states is relative capability. **Capability** is defined as the military, political, economic, and psychological resources of a nation which may be employed to influence the behavior of other states to further its own national interests. It is possible to quantify capability and to rate nations accordingly. The three major categories used are *superpowers* (the United States and the former Soviet Union), *great powers* (England, France, China, and West Germany; Japan also is potentially a great power), and *lesser powers* (all other states). In the latter category there are great differences in military might, for example, between Costa Rica and Italy.

In analyzing **foreign policy outputs** we can assess a particular state's chances of success in pursuing a given policy by examining that state's scope, intentions, and capability relative to that of other interested parties. In analyzing that state's entire range of foreign policies, we can then apply Morgenthau's hierarchical ranking of national interests: (1) those which must be pursued at all costs, (2) those which may be pursued under certain favorable circumstances, and (3) those which may be desirable but which cannot be pursued because of insufficient capability. We then may be able to predict both what the state may try to accomplish and the degree of success it is likely to achieve.

International Actors

Thus far we have discussed the primary actors in international relations—nation-states. Ninety years ago this might have been sufficient, but not today. There are many **international actors,** some of which play important roles in the current international system. These are organizations that contain members of two or more nation-states.

The growth of multinational organizations in the twentieth century has been phenomenal, especially in the post-World War II period. Some are universal, others regional; some are multipurpose, others serve only one function (military, economic, political, cultural, or humanitarian). Some are public and others are private, but perhaps the most interesting distinction is between **international** and **supranational** organizations. The distinction involves the degree of independent decision making reserved by the member states and the degree to which member governments have delegated power to the new multinational institutions. International means among nations; and supranational means above nations.

Table 22-1 lists criteria for distinguishing between these two ideal types. Bear in mind that in practice international actors often exhibit characteristics of both types.

If we apply this distinction to the United Nations, it is clearly more international than supranational. Decisions of the Security Council (which has primary responsibility for peace-keeping operations) are subject to the veto power of its five permanent members: the United States, Russia, China, France, and England. Although the General Assembly has a majoritarian decision-making structure, its decisions are not binding on nation-states. The same is true of its specialized agencies (World Health Organization, Food and Agriculture Organization, and so forth). Furthermore, decision makers are almost always guided by their national governments.

The Secretariat is a permanent executive structure which conducts

Table 22-1
Characteristics of
Multinational
Organizations

Supranational Organizations	International Organizations
1. Decisions made by majority vote	Every state has a veto
2. Decisions are binding on all members (including those who voted against them)	Decisions are merely recommendations
3. The organization has an executive with authority to carry out decisions	Executive branches of member governments carry out decisions
4. Human and legal persons (like corporations) are directly subject to its authority	Only states are subjects, not persons
5. Decision makers vote according to their own judgments, not on instructions from their national governments	Decision makers are almost always instructed by their national governments
6. The institution itself may expand its powers in response to new conditions and demands	Only member governments may expand the organization's power
7. Withdrawal from membership is difficult and often fatal to the organization because of the high degree of integration involved	Members may easily withdraw, often without too much negative impact on the organization

the ongoing business of the organization. It is headed by the Secretary-General, who is himself an important force for world peace. However, his effectiveness is severely limited by the global divisions that are reflected in the United Nations. Under existing conditions, the UN serves the following peace-keeping functions:

1. It is a world forum in which international disputes may be aired, thereby allowing nations to blow off steam and sometimes to save face while avoiding armed conflict.
2. It provides peace-keeping machinery that states may use to resolve international disputes peacefully.
3. It serves to mobilize world opinion against acts of armed aggression.
4. It strengthens the tendency to seek peaceful solutions to international problems.

There are many regional organizations that also play an important role in the international system. With few exceptions these also are international. The most notable exception is a system comprised of

United Nations General Assembly

The distinguishing characteristic of international politics is that it takes place in the absence of a supreme political authority. The United Nations is a "talking shop," where international tensions may be aired, thus sometimes avoiding or delaying armed conflict.

political, economic, and social structures created in Western Europe. It is in this part of the world that the highest degree of supranationalization has developed. This applies primarily to the organizations within the European Community (EC). Since their members often act as a bloc in world affairs, these organizations are important international actors. In 1993 they were on the verge of becoming essentially one superstate in the economic sphere.

Multinational corporations also play an important role in international affairs. This is significant because such organizations are not contained by national allegiance to any country; rather they are motivated by profit and growth. They can help or hurt a nation's economy greatly, but are difficult to hold accountable. Many of these organizations are conglomerates (involved in diverse industries). The publicity involving IT&T and its alleged activities in Chilean politics has caused fear in many underdeveloped countries that do business with these corporate giants. The enormous wealth of the oil companies, the rising oil prices, and the energy crisis all combine to make a world highly dependent on oil as an energy source very concerned about these organizations. Four of the ten largest corporations in the world are oil companies. The inability of nation-states to control such multinational corporations, or even to know what they are doing, has made the governments of some countries wary of letting them do business in their countries. Because of the increasing dependency on imported oil by both industrialized and underdeveloped countries, the oil cartel known as OPEC (Organization of Petroleum Exporting Countries) has probably become the single most important international actor in the world today. OPEC's quadrupling of oil prices in 1973 and 1979 created a wave of inflation throughout the world.

Military alliances, such as the North Atlantic Treaty Organization (NATO) and the former Warsaw Pact, also played a major role in global politics. Indeed, large numbers and diverse types of international actors exist, ranging from the International Postal Union to the International Red Cross. They all serve important functions and are an integral part of the current international system. But, at least for the time being, nation-states continue to make the primary decisions in international relations.

☐ Conclusion

We have pointed out in this chapter that nation-states (national actors) play the leading role in international affairs, while some international actors play strong supporting roles. There has been a great deal written in recent years about the decline of nation-states and about their increased permeability (national systems have become increasingly open to external influences). Consequently, it is said that supranational regional and universal actors are going to replace nation-states as primary units in world affairs.

It is true, of course, that national systems are becoming more open. But it does not necessarily follow that they are becoming less integrated. Indeed, the internal cohesion of nation-states seems to be increasing. Nor does there seem to be a great supranationalizing trend, except perhaps in Europe. The twelve member countries of the European Economic Community have created several supranational organizations. For example, the European Common Market has unified and integrated the member states' economies to a great extent. Furthermore, the European Parliament makes decisions of a binding nature, albeit on a limited number of issues. This portends, perhaps, a reduction of nationalism in the future, as regionalism plays an ever-increasing role in this area.

Migration, in comparison to the nineteenth and early twentieth centuries, has slowed to a trickle. And the total expenditures of all multinational organizations combined is less than one-thirtieth of that spent by national governments. The flow of communication and travel is much more dense within than among nation-states.[6]

People's feelings are also important to consider. There is a much higher degree of voluntary compliance with national laws than there is with international laws. Furthermore, if there is an earthquake in Bolivia or Turkey, the American people may feel sorry for those who suffer and offer some assistance, probably in the form of food and clothing; but they are not likely to send enormous sums of money to alleviate conditions. However, if we suffer a natural disaster within our country, the President is likely to declare a state of emergency. He would probably declare a county or state a disaster area and earmark a large sum of tax revenues to help the disaster victims. The American people (from all 50 states) who have paid these tax revenues would not complain about such expenditures, and may even give from their own pockets to alleviate the situation.

This is a far cry from the day when our philosophy was "every man for himself." However, it is also a far cry from 1921, when the American government helped to feed 11 million Russians who were starving. These facts seem to indicate that there is a higher degree of integration within nation-states and a lower degree in the international system, although it is increasing somewhat in Western Europe. Thus nationalism remains the strongest force in world politics, and it is gaining strength in most countries.

One more point should be added to this argument. Tax revenues are often used by national governments to redistribute the wealth among its regional units. In America the per capita income in our richest state is only three times as great as it is in our poorest state. Among the 186 countries that span the globe the ratio of per capita income is 30 to 1. Can you imagine what the response of the American people would be if our government tried to redistribute our wealth on a worldwide basis to achieve the same 3 to 1 ratio that we have within our own country? The president would probably be impeached! All of this indicates that nationalism is the strongest ideology in the world, and that nation-states will probably continue to be the primary actors in world affairs in the foreseeable future.

You may have noticed that we focused on nation-states in this chapter but spoke of the basic assumptions made by national leaders. While we can speak of such social units (nation-states) as being the primary actors in international affairs, we must be careful not to reify them. People, not states, make decisions. Therefore, it is necessary to focus on the decision makers who act on behalf of these states.

Table 22-2 is a summary of the basic assumptions held by realists and idealists. Most of these assumptions were discussed in this chapter; the others will be dealt with in the following one.

Table 22-2
Comparison of Realism and Idealism

Realist Theory	Idealist Theory
1. All nations act in such a manner as to achieve their national goals and further their national interests. They do not act from altruistic motives.	Nations should conduct their foreign relations using morality as their guideline, not selfish national interest.

Table 22-2
Comparison of Realism
and Idealism

Realist Theory	Idealist Theory
2. Conflicts arise because the respective national interests of states are often incompatible. Conflicts do not arise because of misunderstandings or because national leaders or ideologies are evil.	Conflicts arise in the world because either states are led by evil leaders or motivated by evil ideologies, or because there is some misunderstanding between nations that can be settled by improved communications and increased contacts between the peoples of the world.
3. These conflicts will be settled in terms of power relations, not through ideology, morality, or legal structures. Of course, nations can and do avail themselves of the good services of third-party mediators, but only at their own discretion.	International organizations can and should solve major world conflicts.
4. All nations strive to maximize their power since in the final analysis this is the means through which international conflicts are resolved.	Power is immoral. Therefore states should strive to reduce their military might and refrain from using it.
5. The ultimate goal of all nations is national security or national survival.	The ultimate goal of nations should be the maintenance of peace and renunciation of all wars.
6. All of these assumptions are true of all states regardless of their ideology or form of government.	International politics is an extension of national politics. Therefore democratic countries will have a different foreign policy than authoritarian states.
7. The primary actors in international politics are nation-states, not international organizations, supranational organizations, subnational groups, or individuals.	Lasting world peace can be achieved only by creating a supranational (world) government. The reorganization of governmental structures will lead to a change in behavior, and a shift of loyalty.
8. Diplomacy should be conducted in secret, but the results should be made public.	Diplomacy should be conducted in public where everyone can see what is going on.
9. Foreign policy decisions should be made by leaders who have access to all information available and who have advisers trained in international relations.	Foreign policy should conform to public opinion.

REFERENCES

1. Hans J. Morgenthau, *Politics Among Nations*, 6th ed. (New York: Knopf, 1978), p. 3.
2. Morgenthau, "National Interest and Moral Principles in Foreign Policy," *The American Scholar, 18* (Winter 1948–1949), p. 210.
3. Morgenthau, *Politics*, p. 10.
4. *Ibid.*, p. 3.
5. *Speak Truth to Power: A Quaker Search for an Alternative to Violence*, American Friends Service Committee, 1955.
6. Karl W. Deutsch, "The Impact of Communications upon International Relations Theory," Abdul A. Said, ed., *Theory of International Relations* (Englewood Cliffs, N.J.: Prentice Hall, 1968), pp. 74–92.

GLOSSARY

International actors	Organizations that contain members from two or more nation-states and that play a role in international relations.
International organization	A multinational institution whose members (nation-states) retain independent decision-making power.
National actors	Nation-states that play a role in the international system.
Supranational organization	An organization that can make decisions which are binding on all members (nation-states), including those that did not vote for that decision.
Capability	The military, political, economic, and psychological resources of a nation, which may be employed to influence the behavior of other states in order to further its own national interests.
Intentions	The desire of a state either to maintain its existing geographical boundaries and its power and influence (*status quo* intentions), or to change one or both factors (*revisionist* intentions).
Foreign policy outputs	Decisions and actions of nation-states that affect other states.
Scope of interest	The size of the geographical area with which a state is concerned in its political activities. It may be *globalist* (encompassing the whole world), *regionalist* (encompassing a limited geographical area—usually including states in close proximity to it), or *isolationist* (concerned only with domestic affairs).
National interests	The enduring objectives pursued by nation-states—such as self-preservation (of its people, its territory, and its way of life); control over

decision making which affects the above; and economic advantages, international prestige, and so on.

Political idealism	An approach to the study and practice of international relations which stresses morality and legalism.
Political realism	An approach to the study and practice of international relations which stresses power and interests.

International politics	(We use this term interchangeably with international relations, international affairs, world politics, and global politics.) Relations between people or groups that cut across national boundaries, with special emphasis on the political, military, and economic aspects.

SELECTED READING

Billington, James H., "Realism and Vision in American Foreign Policy." *Foreign Affairs,* Vol. 65, No. 3, Council on Foreign Relations, 1987.
An interesting analysis of realism in American foreign policy by the Director of the Library of Congress.

Ferguson, Yale H. and Richard W. Mansbach, *The State, Conceptual Chaos, and the Future of International Relations Theory* (Boulder: L. Rienner Publishers, 1989).
An analysis of international relations theory.

Knutsen, Torbjorn L, *The History of International Relations Theory* (New York: Manchester University Press, 1992).
A good historical treatment of international relations theory.

Morgenthau, Hans J., *Politics Among Nations*, 6th ed. (New York: Knopf, 1978).
This is the classic international relations text that provides a comprehensive analysis of political realism and idealism.

QUESTIONS

1. Idealists claim that
   a. the emergence of multinational organizations has increased the degree of conflict inherent in the nation-state system.

b. the use of power is immoral; nevertheless, international conflicts must be resolved through the use of power because there is no alternative.

c. nation-states are the primary actors in international affairs, and international conflicts must be resolved in terms of power relations.

d. the nation-state system is inherently conflict-ridden, and the use of power itself is immoral.

2. Realists claim that every state's primary goal, regardless of its ideology or form of government, is
   a. to create some type of world government to achieve world peace.
   b. to preserve the nation-state system in which each state assumes primary responsibility for its national survival and national security.
   c. to achieve a conflict-free environment without the use of power.
   d. to entrust regional organizations with primary responsibility for the survival of the nation-states and their national security.

3. A distinction that is useful in analyzing nation-states is relative capability. This term refers to
   a. the tangible aspects of military power, such as weapons and troops.
   b. the military, political, economic, and psychological resources of a nation that may be used to influence the behavior of other states in order to further its own national interests.
   c. the ability of a nation-state to exercise control over its own people within its national boundaries.
   d. the intangible aspects of power, such as the unity of the people, the degree to which they support their leaders, and the prestige the state enjoys throughout the world.

4. Which of the following is Morgenthau's hierarchical ranking of national interests?
   (1) those that may be pursued under certain favorable circumstances
   (2) those that may be desirable, but that cannot be pursued because of insufficient capability
   (3) those that must be pursued at all costs
   a. 1-2-3
   b. 3-2-1
   c. 2-1-3
   d. 3-1-2

5. Which of the following is *not* a characteristic of a supranational organization?
   a. Withdrawal from membership is difficult and often fatal to the organization because of the high degree of integration involved.

     b. Decision makers are almost always instructed by their national governments.

     c. Human and legal persons (like corporations) are directly subject to its authority.

     d. Decisions are binding on all members (including those who voted against them).

6. According to the authors, the strongest political ideology in the world today is
     a. globalism.
     b. isolationism.
     c. capitalism.
     d. nationalism.
     e. communism.

7. The major distinction between international and supranational organizations is
     a. the degree of decision-making power reserved by the member states and the degree delegated to the multinational organization.
     b. the degree of cultural homogeneity that exists among the members of the organization.
     c. the number of nation-states involved in the organization.
     d. the degree of mobility within the multinational organization.

8. When using the term *international actors,* the authors are referring to
     a. nation-states that play a role in the international system.
     b. nation-states that interact within the context of a multinational organization.
     c. those government officials involved in foreign policy decision making.
     d. organizations that contain members from two or more nation-states and that play a role in international relations.

9. Political realists claim that one of the most important principles in international politics is *prudence,* which is defined as
     a. taking the political consequences of one's actions into consideration.
     b. taking into account the legal consequences of one's actions.
     c. being cognizant of the moral consequences of one's actions.
     d. reflecting upon the social consequences of one's actions.

10. Which of the following statements is *not* true?
     a. There is no universal morality.
     b. Societal values may be similar in a general sense but often conflict in specific circumstances.

    c. Conflicting views of morality are inevitable as long as there is no world culture.

    d. The abstract nature of most moral norms leaves leaders with less latitude in implementing them.

    e. It is possible for states that seemingly differ little in their value orientations to war against each other.

QUESTIONS FOR THOUGHT AND DISCUSSION

1. Discuss the pros and cons of the realist and idealist approaches to international relations.

2. Identify several American foreign policies in different parts of the world, and analyze them using Morgenthau's hierarchical ranking system.

3. Choose a current major international conflict, and recommend a foreign policy that the United States should adopt in that area, after identifying several options and the probable consequences to the United States of pursuing each option.

23

The Interaction Process

In order to understand how the current international system functions, we must examine the interaction processes among the national and international actors. We will discuss international law, diplomacy, war, intelligence gathering, information distribution, trade, and aid, and try to discern the patterns of interaction that characterize the current international system.

☐ International Law

What is the role of international law in global politics? And what should it be? International law differs from domestic law in several ways. International law is likely to be observed only in technical matters and in cases in which nations do not consider their vital interests to be at stake. However, whenever vital national interests hang in the balance a nation is not likely to delegate the outcome of a conflict to any tribunal, unless it is fairly certain the ruling will be in its favor. International law, then, provides machinery and techniques that nations may use, if they like, to resolve international disputes in a peaceful manner.

International law also plays another important role: it serves as an agent of socialization. Even though international legal norms are not backed by coercive sanctions, they are not useless. The fact that legal norms exist at all, and are quite often observed by nation–states, affects people's perceptions and attitudes; they therefore "contribute to social order by building a consensus on procedural as well as substantive matters."[1] International legal norms, then, are ideal patterns of international behavior; and even though they are not always obeyed they are seldom disparaged. Legal norms, in effect, "teach" national leaders how they *should* behave. Hence international law contains both factual and normative aspects.

Domestic legal systems are centralized: there are specific institutions—legislatures, courts, and police departments—to carry out the legislation, adjudication, and enforcement processes. The international legal system, on the other hand, is highly decentralized. There is no international legislative body. Laws consist primarily of treaties over some limited situation which indicate agreement by the states that ratify them. Even when treaties are drafted by international institutions, they do not take effect until nations ratify them, and even then they only apply to those states that do. Furthermore, even where international laws apply, the absence of a supranational enforcement agency allows each state to evolve its own interpretations. Hence national political considerations often supersede international laws.

Who adjudicates international laws? Three types of judicial institutions perform this function: national courts, the International Court of Justice, and ad hoc international tribunals (**ad hoc** means for a specific case only). Unbelievable as it may seem, national courts handle most international legal questions. This tends to maximize the political nature of international disputes and to minimize the objective nature of legal decisions. These are primarily cases involving citizens or corporations from different countries, and such cases are usually adjudicated by the national courts of one of the parties involved.

The International Court of Justice (World Court)
The fact that legal forms exist at all, although not always observed by nation-states, affects people's attitudes and serves to help socialize them to the standards in question.

The **International Court of Justice** is one of the six organs of the United Nations, and, consequently, all UN members are automatically members of the ICJ. The fifteen judges of the Court are elected by the General Assembly with the recommendation of the Security Council. This creates a highly political situation. The most objective people available are not necessarily the ones chosen. Furthermore the ICJ's advisory decisions are not binding. The greatest weakness of the ICJ is that states must willingly submit cases to it. Can you imagine a criminal standing trial only if he or she is willing to do so? Such is the plight of the world court. In 1984, for example, the United States refused to submit to the ICJ's **adjudication** of Nicaragua's charge that the U.S. was mining the harbor in Managua.

Ad hoc tribunals are sometimes created to deal with specific international disputes. First the states involved must agree to adjudication procedures; then select the judges; and third decide whether some area of international law is to be applied to the case at hand. Sometimes judgments can be made on other than legal grounds. However, these tribunals can function only with the consent of the states involved; consequently political considerations again play a primary role.

Finally, international law enforcement is not used to enforce international law. Indeed, the community of nations is more concerned with peace-breakers than with law-breakers. Keeping the peace is the primary consideration of the UN, not making nations obey international laws. Therefore it is up to the states themselves, individually and sometimes collectively, to enforce the law. In domestic law if someone breaks into your home you may enforce the law by capturing and holding the criminal until the police arrive. But in international relations the police never arrive! Even in the old "Wild West" the sheriff or the marshall eventually showed up and took the "varmint" to jail. In international law the states themselves must act as judge, jury, and executioner; hence political and military considerations generally determine the outcome. At present, that is what international law has to offer us.

Some scholars, such as Grenville Clark and Louis B. Sohn,[2] want more. According to their view, "World law must also be law in the sense of law which is capable of enforcement, as distinguished from a mere set of exhortations or injunctions which it is desirable to observe but for the enforcement of which there is no effective machinery." Furthermore this can be achieved only "by universal and complete disarmament together with the establishment of institutions corresponding in the world field to those which maintain law and order within local communities and nations."[3] In short, world law must be accompanied by world government. This view, whose major spokesmen are Clark and Sohn, implies that anything less cannot truly be called law.

At the other end of the spectrum is Hans Morgenthau, who argues that this legalistic approach is utopian and cannot be substituted for political negotiations.[4] He describes the Clark and Sohn position as "sentimentalist," which in practice leads to "neoisolationism." Morgenthau suggests that world peace can best be attained through skillful diplomacy.

Whatever normative position one may take on this issue, the facts do not fully support either polar position. International law plays a more limited role than Clark and Sohn would like, but a more important one than Morgenthau attributes to it. Although international law is a part of the international interaction process, it is not as significant as other types of interaction. We shall now turn our attention to a more important subject—the most delicate process in international relations—the art of diplomacy.

☐ Diplomacy

War has sometimes been referred to as "a continuation of diplomacy by other means." Perhaps it would be more accurate to say that diplomacy is "war by peaceful means." A game of chess might be similarly described. In international politics each state tries to realize its objectives, often at the expense of other states' objectives. When this interaction process occurs by negotiation, it is called diplomacy. A whole host of diplomatic techniques and practices have evolved, and nations have developed elaborate structures to perform the diplomatic function. **Diplomacy** is generally defined as the practice of conducting relations between states through official representatives. However, nations that do not officially recognize each other's governments sometimes communicate through representatives. For example, before 1972 the United States held informal talks with Communist China through their ambassadors in Warsaw, Poland. Such talks may be deemed "informal" diplomacy.

Formal diplomatic relations begin when countries offer diplomatic recognition to each other. Usually an exchange of ambassadors is preceded by a formal declaration of recognition. This is called **de jure recognition** as opposed to **de facto recognition,** which denotes recognizing a government's existence without entering into formal relations with it.

Diplomats enjoy certain privileges and immunities, such as freedom from arrest, trial, subpoena, civil suit, and legal penalty **(diplomatic immunity).** In short, they are exempt from civil and criminal jurisdictions of the state to which they are accredited (that is, the state in which they officially represent their government). This ancient practice enables diplomats to conduct their business unhampered; however, it implies an intent by diplomatic agents to respect their host country's laws and customs. Even juvenile gangs in New York City observe diplomatic immunities. They usually have meetings between "warlords"

Mediation
P.L.O. leader Yasir
Arafat, U.S. President
Bill Clinton, and Israeli
Prime Minister Itzhak
Rabin clasped hands
on the north lawn of
the White House after
signing the peace
agreement between
the P.L.O. and Israel.

(diplomatic agents) who determine the nature of the conflict and, if necessary, the terms of the "rumble." These diplomatic agents are allowed free passage even in the toughest neighborhoods.

Diplomacy often involves cooperative behavior between states which have similar interests. In such cases most diplomatic activity is routine (for example, processing visas). However, if states have a conflict of interest diplomacy becomes a delicate process—an art. Whenever disputes arise, ways are usually sought to resolve them. Several techniques, which involve participation by third parties, have been devised for the peaceful settlement of disputes.

1. **Good Offices.** In this case a third party acts as a go-between to reestablish bilateral negotiations between parties to an international dispute. The interested parties hopefully will then settle the dispute themselves. The third party does not participate in the negotiations.

2. **Mediation.** This technique involves a third party to a greater degree than does good offices. When using this method, the third party strives to solve the dispute by establishing the facts and by offering substantive suggestions. Great tact and skill is required in order to find a solution that is not offensive to either disputant. Kosygin, the former Russian Prime Minister, played such a role in settling a dispute between India and Pakistan. Former Secretary of State Henry Kissinger and former President Jimmy Carter played this role in the Middle East. In 1993, President Bill Clinton played a role in the agreement between Israel and the PLO. Mediation is an excellent technique if the disputants harbor a

great deal of hostility toward each other. Somehow concessions don't appear to be as humiliating if proposed by a third party rather than by "the enemy." It also makes it easier for each government to gain acceptance by its people for whatever concessions are made. In short, mediation allows national leaders to "save face."

3. **Conciliation.** This technique involves a group of nations whereas mediation involves a single third party. Like the other two methods, conciliation may be established ad hoc. However, unlike mediation and good offices, conciliation is often conducted by permanent structures. Commissions of conciliation are included in the peaceful settlement provisions of many treaties. For example, the Pact of Bogota, which established the Organization of American States (OAS) in 1948, included such provisions.

The simplest form of diplomatic relations is called **conversations** (an exchange of views between governments). Sometimes conversations are merely used to gather information, but often they lead to more detailed negotiations. The main diplomatic processes used to resolve conflicts are *negotiation* and *tacit bargaining.* Fred Charles Iklé defines **negotiation** as "a process in which explicit proposals are put forward ostensibly for the purpose of reaching agreement on an exchange or on the realization of a common interest where conflicting interests are present."[5] Unless each side makes an explicit proposal, according to this definition, negotiation has not taken place. Iklé points out that "two elements must normally be present for negotiation to take place: There must be common interests and issues of conflict. Without common interest there is nothing to negotiate for, without conflict nothing to negotiate about."[6]

Iklé also distinguishes between two kinds of common interests: **identical** and **complementary.**[7] The former describes a mutual interest in a particular object or arrangement; the latter involves an exchange of different objects which each side can obtain only from the other.

Quite often changes in relations between nations are not the result of negotiation but of **tacit bargaining.** This procedure involves reciprocal unilateral actions. No explicit proposals are made; indeed the parties may not even be on speaking terms. A series of tacit bargains kept the Korean War geographically restricted and also limited the level of destruction. This was a case in which explicit negotiations might have been counterproductive because of the general hostility on both sides. Negotiation, however, is necessary if complicated forms of collaboration are involved. It should be noted that negotiations often produce outcomes that may be more significant than any explicit agreement arrived at. A negotiating state may acquire important information, forge new international ties, or score a propaganda victory, any of which may be of greater political significance than a formal agreement.

The great debate in the field of diplomacy is between the advocates of **classical** and **modern diplomacy.** Three issues are involved. The one most hotly debated is whether diplomatic negotiations should be **secret** or **open.** Both sides agree that the results should be made public but disagree on the nature of the negotiating process (open or secret). Realists and idealists often clash on this point. To some people it seems undemocratic for diplomats to meet behind closed doors while conducting public business. If they are honest and have nothing to hide, why can't diplomacy be conducted in public? For example, the release of the *Pentagon Papers,* the Watergate scandal, and the secret exchange of arms for hostages with Iran have increased the number of Americans who are leery of government secrecy.

Whenever negotiations are conducted in public, it is difficult for diplomats to retreat from their initial positions. To do so would make them appear to be "appeasing the enemy" in the eyes of some of their citizens. The ensuing rigidity of positions would make it impossible to reach a compromise; and *compromise is the essence of diplomacy.* At least one side, and usually both, have to make concessions in order to resolve the issue being negotiated. If negotiations take place behind closed doors, it is easier to make mutual concessions on nonvital points. Concessions are very rarely made on vital points. At best the diplomats agree to disagree.

Consider the following scenario: Two countries have been openly hostile toward each other for twenty years—ever since one of them had a revolution which ousted a government that was friendly to the other country. Both governments have publicly denounced each other ever since. Leaders in both capitals now believe it would be mutually beneficial to ease tensions and resume normal diplomatic relations with each other. Something is needed to break the ice with the public in both countries. The governments stop attacking each other publicly. Then one country sends a soccer team to play against the other state's world championship team. Despite a few criticisms about this "soccer diplomacy" the public response is overwhelmingly favorable. Serious negotiations can now begin. All of this was preceded by secret conversations, in which the soccer games were chosen as a trial balloon to test the public's attitude toward such negotiations.

Continuing our hypothetical situation, when their diplomatic agents sit down to negotiate their nations' differences, they select five crucial issues to discuss. They decide very shortly that one side can concede points one and three, the other side can concede points two and four, and they are still far apart on point five. One government decides, however, that its people are still too emotionally hostile to the other government to accept one of the two concessions, so the decision is not publicly announced for six months. When passions have cooled (after the propaganda mills against the other country have been toned down),

Strategic Arms Limitations Talks
Diplomacy has long been described as a continuation of war by peaceful means. Negotiations between nations are a delicate business conducted by specialists suited to the task by training and temperament. Here, former U.S. President George Bush and former Soviet leader Mikhail Gorbachev meet in Malta in 1989.

all decisions are made public. Eighty percent of the conflicting issues have been resolved, and both governments have agreed to coexist peacefully despite remaining differences.

If all this had taken place in the public spotlight, it would have been much more difficult, if not impossible, to reach a compromise. By making nonvital (but emotion-laden) concessions secretly, each side could then play up the other side's concessions to its own public. The result is beneficial to all parties. This is an example of diplomacy at its best. Some may call it devious and deceiving, but the alternative is ineffectiveness. As Sir Harold Nicolson points out, confusion exists on this issue, because the term "diplomacy" is often used to signify both foreign policy and negotiation. He says: "Foreign policy should never be secret, in the sense that the citizen should on no account be committed by his government to treaties or engagements of which he has not been given full previous knowledge. But negotiation must always be confidential."[8]

In addition to secret diplomacy, the classical school advocates *bilateral ministerial negotiations*, while the modern school opts for *multilateral negotiations* and summit meetings (in addition to open diplomacy). **Bilateral negotiations** tend to benefit stronger countries, which can more easily exert pressure on a weaker country because they have greater military, economic, and political resources. Smaller, weaker nations, therefore, prefer **multilateral** conferences. If they're negotiating with stronger powers this process tends to mute the power differential; if they are negotiating with other weak states they can more easily make

Diplomacy
The Paris Peace Talks over Vietnam in January 1973 exemplify ministerial negotiations. The Yalta Conference attended by British Prime Minister Winston Churchill, U.S. President Franklin D. Roosevelt, and Soviet Premier Josef Stalin is an example of summit diplomacy.

concessions and avoid violence, while increasing the possibility of fairness by group decision making.

The argument for **ministerial diplomacy** is compelling. Its proponents argue that **summit diplomacy** (summit conferences between national leaders) often fail; and if ill will results, leaders cannot easily smooth things over. Furthermore, presidents and prime ministers are rarely professional diplomats; hence they are not as capable of recognizing areas of common interest, the intensity which the other side feels about the points at issue, and what realistic solutions may be available.

Career diplomats, as professionals, are more likely to reach agreements, even while protecting their national interests vigorously. And even if they fail, they can be recalled and blamed for any ill will, thereby enabling national leaders to remain on friendly terms with each other. President Eisenhower's catastrophic meeting with Khrushchev in May 1960 is an example of the dangers of summitry.

Before concluding our discussion we should like to say something about conference diplomacy. This type of diplomacy became popular in the eighteenth and nineteenth centuries and was institutionalized in the twentieth. It has often been used by allied powers during wartime to collaborate their efforts, and by the winning side after the war (the inevitable "peace conference" which follows every war, and which seems to set the stage for the next one). **Conference diplomacy** is defined as large-scale multilateral diplomatic negotiations conducted at international meetings. The Congress of Vienna (1815), which followed the Napoleonic Wars, and the Paris Peace Conference (1919) at the conclusion of World War I fall into this category.

The League of Nations and the United Nations are two examples of world diplomatic conferences in permanent session. Many other international organizations may be so described. In addition, ad hoc conferences have been held from time to time, whenever a group of nations had a common interest which required their collective attention. The record is mixed—some failures and a few successes—but this diplomatic technique seems to be popular today and may indeed encourage the solution of problems when national interests are not irreconcilable.

Very often a breakdown of diplomatic relations leads to war. Indeed, to repeat Karl Von Clausewitz' oft-quoted phrase, "War is a continuation of diplomacy by other means." So we shall now examine the role of war in international politics.

☐ War

Few states in the modern world deem war a good thing. Yet war, and the threat of war, form an integral part of the international system. Hostile actions often characterize the interaction process among nation–states. Why is this so? Quincy Wright, in the most exhaustive study of war ever conducted, offers the following reasons:[9]

1. **Reaction to Perceived Threats.** States which feel their self-preservation threatened by others are quite likely to resort to war. The realists' contention that "the ultimate goal of all states is national survival" seems to be true. Whenever states think their national survival is threatened by another state, unless such an act would lead to the physical extinction of its people, states would "rather fight than switch." A state generally will fight to preserve its territory and its way of life.

2. **Enthusiasm for Ideals.** Religious and ideological convictions have motivated states throughout history to fight to preserve their values or to convert others to these values. The religious wars of the sixteenth and seventeenth centuries are prime examples of such behavior. In modern times the ideological component of international hostilities has sometimes led states to fight for or against a particular belief system.

3. **Frustration over Unsatisfactory Conditions.** Leaders sometimes try to divert attention from domestic policy failures by blaming foreign scapegoats for their internal problems. Leaders can sometimes find a substitute object of hostility on which the people can vent their frustrations, lest they blame the leaders or the system itself for their troubles. "The Communist threat," "capitalist encirclement," and "Yankee imperialism" are just a few of the targets used in recent times. Domestic scapegoats are also used to divert the public's attention. American communities at the height of the civil rights movement sometimes preferred to blame their problems on "outside agitators" rather than confronting the real issues.

4. **Belief in the Utility of Threats of War.** To some, war or the threat of war may seem a rational policy to pursue if all else fails to further national interests. But, even when all else has not been tried, some states consider war or the threat of war to be a legitimate instrument in conducting foreign relations. As long as this attitude prevails, and peace is not accorded top priority by nation-states, war will continue to occur.

5. **Belief in the Necessity of Self-help.** Military resistance or attack is sometimes deemed necessary because nations believe there is no other way to defend their national interests.

To these five we add another:

6. **Unstable Territorial Borders.** Border disputes abound because many territorial borders were determined by past wars and are not fully accepted by the losers. Some states still harbor a desire to rectify what they consider to be an injustice inflicted upon them by military force.

In general, the technology of peace has not kept up with the technology of war. It is beyond the scope of this chapter to deal exhaustively with all modes of war. But two modern developments should be mentioned—the development of nuclear weapons and the increased use of **guerrilla warfare** in the twentieth century. Nuclear weapons have radically altered the psychology of war as well as its destructive capacity. Some of the nightmarish debates of the 1950s and 1960s included

countercity vs. **counterforce strategy** and **massive** vs. **measured retaliation.** A countercity strategy involves aiming nuclear weapons at population centers (also called countervalue). Its advocates hope this strategy will deter any aggressor from attacking, because the loss of lives for the attacking country would be unbearable. Counterforce strategists reject this approach to nuclear deterrence because it leaves the opponents' strike force intact to continue wreaking damage upon the country under attack. They claim our missiles should be aimed at the enemy's missiles in order to destroy their ability to continue attacking us. A third group advocates a **mixed strategy** so that we can accomplish both goals.

Those who advocate massive retaliation if we are attacked claim that only such a "total" strategy will deter an aggressor state. The proponents of measured retaliation suggest that we should respond to any attack by inflicting exactly the same amount of damage we receive in a nuclear war. Implicit in the latter strategy are two assumptions: (1) a limited nuclear war can be controlled; that is, everyone will remain perfectly calm as we exchange Los Angeles for Leningrad; and (2) a nuclear war can be "won."

While these debates may seem to be a product of some horror movie, these issues have been seriously discussed in the United States (and, we presume, in the former Soviet Union as well). In our concluding chapter we will discuss the impact of nuclear weapons on international politics in greater detail.

Guerrilla warfare has also been elevated to a rigorous science. Mao Tse-tung[10] and Ernesto "Che" Guevara,[11] among others, have written comprehensive dissertations on the subject. Guerrilla warfare is not a

Guerrilla Warfare
Although not a new phenomenon, guerilla warfare has been given a new tactical dimension by former Communist Chinese leader Mao Tse-tung (left), shown here in 1937. Mao said that every soldier or worker must be thoroughly politicized.

new phenomenon. The American Revolutionary War was largely fought by the colonists using guerrilla warfare tactics, but not until the middle of the twentieth century were these tactics elevated to a military science.

Guerrilla warfare theorists contend that everything is political and that war is merely one form of politics. Mao makes this assertion in all his writings. In one place he writes: "War is a continuation of politics; in this sense war is politics and war itself is a political action, and there has not been a single war since ancient times that does not bear a political character."[12] Further on he states: "War is simply the continuation of politics by other . . . means. When politics has developed to a certain stage beyond which it cannot proceed by the usual means, war breaks out to sweep away the impediments in the way."[13] And again he writes: "Politics are bloodless war while war is the politics of bloodshed."[14]

The main implication of this assertion is that all the components of the guerrilla struggle—soldiers, peasants, workers, and party members—must be thoroughly **politicized.** Indoctrination and political explanations for existing circumstances must go on continuously in order to maintain a high degree of political consciousness among all revolutionary forces. This process is called **political mobilization.**

Mao outlines the following ten principles of guerrilla warfare:

1. Attack dispersed, isolated enemy forces first; attack concentrated, strong enemy forces later.
2. Take small and medium cities and extensive rural areas first; take big cities later.
3. Make wiping out the enemy's effective strength our main objective: Do not make holding or seizing a city or place our main objective. Holding or seizing a city or place is the outcome of wiping out the enemy's effective strength, and often a city or place can be held or seized for good only after it has changed hands a number of times.
4. In every battle concentrate an absolutely superior force (two, three, four, and sometimes even five or six times the enemy's strength), encircle the enemy's forces completely, strive to wipe them out thoroughly and do not let any escape from the net. In special circumstances, use the method of dealing crushing blows to the enemy, that is concentrate all our strength to make a frontal attack and also to attack one or both of his flanks, with the aim of wiping out one part and routing another so that our army can swiftly move its troops to smash other enemy forces. Strive to avoid battles of attrition in which we lose more than we gain or only break even. In this way, although we are inferior as a whole (in terms of numbers), we are absolutely superior in every part and every specific campaign, and this ensures vic-

tory in the campaign. As time goes on, we shall become superior as a whole and eventually wipe out all the enemy.

5. Fight no battle unprepared, fight no battle you are not sure of winning; make every effort to be well prepared for each battle, make every effort to ensure victory in the given set of conditions as between the enemy and ourselves.
6. Give full play to our style of fighting—courage in battle, no fear of sacrifice, no fear of fatigue, and continuous fighting (that is, fighting successive battles in a short time without rest).
7. Strive to wipe out the enemy through mobile warfare. At the same time, pay attention to the tactics of positional attack and capture enemy fortified points and cities.
8. With regard to attacking cities, resolutely seize all enemy fortified points and cities which are weakly defended. Seize at opportune moments all enemy fortified points and cities defended with moderate strength, provided circumstances permit. As for strongly defended enemy fortified points and cities, wait till conditions are ripe and then take them.
9. Replenish our strength with all the arms and most of the personnel captured from the enemy. Our army's main sources of manpower and materiel are at the front.
10. Make good use of the intervals between campaigns to rest, train, and consolidate our troops. Periods of rest, training, and consolidation should in general not be very long, and the enemy should so far as possible be permitted no breathing space.[15]

In regard to guerrilla warfare, both Mao and Che emphasize that this form of struggle is a means toward the objective of seizing state power. Harassment is not its purpose. Unless it leads to seizure of state power it is mere adventurism. Mao and Che also point out that guerrilla warfare develops in three stages:

1. *Strategic defense.* A state in which the guerrilla fighters engage in hit and run activities, and in which they avoid major confrontations with the enemy. During this stage the guerrillas are still weak and small and therefore should avoid casualties. At times they must retreat and avoid confrontations. This is followed by stalemate.
2. *Stalemate.* A stage in which offensive activities are conducted by both the enemy and the guerrillas.
3. *Guerrilla superiority.* In this final stage the guerrillas are on the offensive—capturing big cities and fighting large-scale battles—while the enemy forces collapse in retreat.

Both men also emphasized the need for guerrilla bases to which the men can retreat from hit and run operations. These would eventually become impenetrable sanctuaries which the enemy cannot overrun.

Ernesto "Che" Guevara, Revolutionary Elite
Guevara was the West's most influential guerrilla theorist and a perfect example of Lenin's professional revolutionary. He devoted his life to the revolution, first in Cuba, later in the Bolivian jungles where he was killed.

Guerrilla warfare theorists are not dispassionate scholars. Since their intent is to foster revolutions, they are more interested in inculcating a feeling of revolutionary fervor in their followers than in presenting an objective thesis. Hence their theories are couched in very positive terms, which creates the illusion of invincibility and inevitable triumph. History does not bear them out. Communist guerrillas failed in Malaysia and in the Philippines; and Che lost his life in a futile attempt to mobilize Bolivia's peasant masses.

We have presented a more extensive analysis of guerrilla warfare than of any other kind because it has been so prevalent in recent times. The existence of nuclear weapons pretty much rules out large-scale wars. Therefore guerrilla warfare is a very significant type of interaction between states in our era. The difficulty of combating such tactics, even when they are understood, was made clear to Americans as a result of our involvement in the Indochina War.

Countries, however, still prepare for large-scale conventional wars. The Gulf War in 1991 is an example of traditional conventional warfare, albeit with advanced technology. The collapse of the Soviet empire, and then of the Soviet Union, and the subsequent attempt by Russian leaders to adopt a Democratic capitalist system, has brought about the end of the Cold War. The Warsaw Pact was dissolved in 1991. However, civil wars are raging in some of the former Soviet republics, in the former Yugoslavia, and elsewhere.

☐ **Trade and Aid**

International economic relations are more technical and more complex than any other aspect of international relations. In this section we will focus on trade and aid. The flow of goods, capital investment, and currency across national boundaries has increased enormously in the twentieth century; although as a percentage of all the world's economic activity, it has declined.

Economists generally agree (although there are important exceptions) that **free trade** (no tariffs or other trade restrictions) best serves the interests of all or most nations. It does so because it permits the law of comparative advantage to function unhindered. The **law of absolute advantage** holds that all states can produce some goods or services more efficiently, more cheaply, and of higher quality than can other states. This may be due to natural or human resources, climate, or other factors. This law, first postulated by Adam Smith, was later modified by David Ricardo in his **law of comparative advantage.** The latter recognizes that some countries may not have an absolute advantage in many or any products; hence they should produce those goods which they produce most efficiently (that is, those in which they have a comparative advantage), and then trade for their other needs. If all countries would concentrate on producing only those goods and services in which they have a comparative advantage, the world's production of goods and services would be maximized. If free trade ensues, then all countries will have a higher standard of living than they would otherwise.

Protective **tariffs** (taxes on imports), it is held, merely force the general population to subsidize inefficient businesses within individual countries that cannot compete with more efficient foreign producers. In this view, economic self-sufficiency leads only to a higher cost of living for nations that maintain protective tariffs. Furthermore while tariffs reduce imports and thereby protect some businesses from foreign competitors, other businesses, those that export their products, will be hurt because other nations usually reciprocate by raising their tariff barriers.

The only valid arguments for maintaining tariff barriers, according to free trade advocates, are the national security and infant industry arguments. The national security argument holds that any products needed for national defense should be produced domestically, because in time of war a state may be cut off from its source of supplies.

The infant industry argument is more complex. Some countries, it is held, do not currently produce every item in which they have a comparative advantage, but it would be in their best interests to do so. In the beginning these infant industries cannot possibly compete with older, established firms in other countries, because the latter have more experience and because they enjoy economies of scale that keep their unit costs much lower than new firms will have. Consequently, it is necessary to protect new firms with tariffs that will keep foreign competition out until the infant industry grows up and is able to compete more effectively with the older firms in other countries. This is a plausible argument but unfortunately the tariffs quite often remain after the infant grows up. Consequently, the consumers continue to subsidize certain businesses.

Although the law of comparative advantage, if given free reign, would probably maximize production, it would not necessarily lead to a more equitable distribution of goods and services, because the distribution of natural resources, technological skills, education, and health is uneven throughout the world. The disadvantaged states will continue to be disadvantaged. Unless completely free trade is accompanied by an increase in human and natural resources among poor nations, their relative (and perhaps their actual) standard of living may not improve at all. Indeed some economists have advocated giving underdeveloped countries preferential treatment in trade relations, saying that this is the most effective kind of "foreign aid" they can receive.

Underdeveloped countries generally suffer from unfavorable **terms of trade.** The cost of their imports rises faster than the prices they receive for their exports. They tend to have agrarian economies, so all they can export are raw materials and agricultural goods (if they have a surplus). What do they import? Automobiles, television sets, cameras, and so forth; that is, manufactured products. The prices of cars and TV sets increase more rapidly than the prices of coffee, sugar, or bananas. Indeed prices for food commodities tend to fluctuate widely on the world market and sometimes decline drastically. Unless the industrialized nations either pay underdeveloped countries a high price for their commodities regardless of market conditions or place a ceiling on prices of manufactured goods, every production increase in underdeveloped countries will be wiped out by the terms of trade.

In the current international economic system, then, there is a seemingly inflexible stratification system in which the industrialized non-Communist states occupy the upper stratum and the underdeveloped states occupy the lower stratum.

The greatest division in the world is between rich nations and poor nations, and the gap is growing wider.

The amount of foreign aid rendered by industrialized states to underdeveloped ones is less than 1 percent of the givers' GNP. This is hardly enough to help much. Furthermore most foreign aid is military, not economic; hence underdeveloped countries seem to face a gloomy future. The situation is further complicated by the fact that underdeveloped nations have the highest rate of population growth in the world, so that even countries which experience annual increases in GNP do not enjoy higher per capita incomes, because economic gains are eaten up by population increases.

Problems are also developing in the global ecosystem. Population increases and technological advances are responsible for water, air, and soil pollution and a rapid depletion of our planet's resources. National governments met in Brazil in 1991 and signed an agreement to reduce global pollution, but the agreement was significantly watered down by then-President Bush.

Americans, as the greatest consumers and polluters in the world, are a greater menace to the planet than are, for example, the Indians. Although India's population problems are enormous, the consequences are domestic, not global. Many Indians may die of disease or starvation, but the effects are geographically concentrated. Americans, however, because of their advanced technology and high consumption are polluting spaceship earth and depleting its resources at an alarming rate. Other industrialized countries are also contributing to these problems; and none are doing much to solve them.

To avoid future disaster for the human race, it seems necessary to curb population growth, to control technological developments, and to redistribute the world's wealth more equitably than it is at present. But what developed nation is willing to make such an economic sacrifice? And what underdeveloped nation is willing to forcefully curb its population growth? The longer we postpone dealing with these hard realities, the more difficult it will be to solve these problems of survival. A thinning ozone layer, acid rain, the greenhouse effect, and other life-threatening environmental problems may, if not successfully addressed, render the planet uninhabitable by human beings.

Opening Cacao Pods to Remove the Seeds, Guatemala

Many underdeveloped countries must rely on one agricultural export or mineral resource to supply needed income. The growing harvesting and processing of these products are still unmechanized and require large inputs of hand labor before marketing can take place. When the prices of items such as cocoa, coffee, peanuts, sugar, or copra fluctuate on the world market, virtually every citizen in these one-product economies feels the effects.

☐ Communication

The communication revolution has certainly had a great impact on international affairs. Telecommunications satellites permit everyone in the world with a television set to view simultaneously a landing on the moon, a World Series, or a rerun of a presidential assassination. Speaking about politics, the late Egyptian President Nasser once said, "Radio has changed everything." He was referring to the fact that now even illiterate people could be politicized. However, our purpose here is not to explore all the ramifications of modern communications technology. We intend only to examine political communications as inputs and outputs in foreign policy making. We shall focus first on **intelligence gathering** (inputs) and then on information outputs (both propaganda and objective information).

Foreign policy inputs may be obtained by both overt (open) and covert (secret) means. The most common overt means are direct communications between governments (both friendly and unfriendly) and messages transmitted from a country's diplomatic establishments (embassies and consular offices) and military installations abroad. Foreign visitors and citizens who travel abroad may also provide useful information. In addition, government officials read information published in foreign newspapers, periodicals, and books, and listen to foreign broadcasts.

Covert methods include both "cloak and dagger" type spying and the use of spy satellites which circle the globe and transmit pictures back home. Contrary to what many people believe, overt intelligence gathering is by far the most important. Even the American Central Intelligence Agency obtains much of its information from published material and radio and TV broadcasts abroad.

The major problem confronting modern governments is the processing of the vast number of communications they receive. A great deal

Covert Intelligence Gathering
Sometimes secret information gathering techniques backfire. At the 1960 Paris summit conference Soviet Leader Nikita Khrushchev blasted the U.S. verbally after his country shot down an American U2 spy plane that was photographing the Soviet Union.

of distortion and omission may occur if communication channels become overloaded or blocked. Consider the problems faced by a wealthy country such as the United States which can afford to maintain a vast communications network.

Cables from our embassies abroad reach the State Department where "experts" filter out and analyze these messages. When a message is received, it is sent to all departments and levels with an interest in the matter. If the issue involved can be disposed of at the lower levels, it will be; if not, it must go to the higher-ups.

Quite often, especially if a controversial issue is involved, conflicting advice is given by the desk officers responsible for different countries. Perhaps it is deemed necessary to contact the Department of Defense, the Central Intelligence Agency, and the United States Information Service. Perhaps foreign capitals must be notified. The issue might require UN action, in which case the Office of the Undersecretary for International Organization Affairs must be brought into the matter. The complications are endless. If country *A* is favored, we're in trouble with country *B*, and vice versa. Meanwhile the press has gotten wind of the issue and is asking questions and writing editorials. At the same time the Secretary of State is involved in handling another delicate crisis. Meanwhile a reply must be sent immediately, but only after everyone who has any special interest in the matter (including the Secretary) has been consulted.

The USIS, our embassies abroad, and our allies must be told what we are doing and how to handle the expected response. Some of the information output will consist of straightforward facts; some will be tailored to make us look as good as possible before the world **(propaganda)**. There is no way we can deal with the situation without antagonizing someone. And all this resulted from one original piece of communication. Consider the fact that thousands of such political communiques are received each day, and you can gain a greater appreciation of the complexity of conducting foreign affairs.

☐ Conclusion

We have seen that the interaction process in international relations has many dimensions. All these dimensions are linked when dealing with concrete situations; they operate simultaneously. National actors interact with each other in many ways, at different levels, always with a view toward maximizing national interests. Whenever these interests coincide, international relations run smoothly and peacefully. Whenever they are incompatible, there is conflict. Either way, nations use legal, diplomatic, and economic channels whenever possible. Sometimes, however, they resort to war. Whatever process is employed, whether peaceful or violent, the actions involved represent some type of international communication.

It should be noted that although we have focused in this chapter on the interaction among nation–states, domestic politics are also linked to foreign policies. However, citizens, generally, do not participate to any great extent in foreign-policy decision making, except to establish broad limits beyond which elite decision makers may not commit their nations. This power is important, but by and large it is only exercised whenever the public feels its elected officials have acted unwisely. Otherwise the officials are free to make foreign policy decisions on their own. They usually know how far "the people" will let them go, but once in a while they have to be reminded. For the most part the average citizens in every country are poorly informed about international affairs. They are too busy earning a living and interacting with their families and friends to keep up with global politics, except in a very general sense. Only when they feel personally threatened by the course of events do they exercise their political power. Certain American ethnic groups, however, are foreign policy-oriented, and sometimes exert great pressure on the President and Congress. If you are interested in pursuing this subject further, consult the Selected Reading section for sources.

We have now identified the actors in international affairs and the ways in which they interact. We must now examine the stage upon which the drama is played out—the international system. Just as the size, shape, and other characteristics of a theater determine what can and cannot be done onstage, so does the existing international system place limits on the sociopolitical units we call nation–states, and on the ways in which they may interact. In the following two chapters we examine past, present, and future international systems.

REFERENCES

1. William D. Coplin, "International Law and Assumptions About the State System," in *International Law and Organization*, Richard A. Falk and Wolfram F. Hanrieder, eds. (Philadelphia: J. B. Lippincott, 1968), p. 17.
2. Grenville Clark and Louis B. Sohn, "World Peace Through World Law," in *Contemporary International Politics*, Bruce L. Sanders and Alan C. Durbin, eds. (New York: John Wiley), 1971, p. 352.
3. *Ibid.,* p. 353.
4. He makes this argument in many of his writings. See Hans J. Morgenthau, *Politics Among Nations*, 6th ed. (New York: Knopf, 1978).
5. Fred Charles Iklé, *How Nations Negotiate* (New York: Harper & Row, 1964), p. 2.
6. *Ibid.*
7. *Ibid.*
8. Sir Harold Nicolson, *Diplomacy*, 3rd ed. (Oxford: Clarendon Press, 1963), p. 245.
9. Quincy Wright, *A Study of War*, 2nd ed. (Chicago: University of Chicago Press, 1965).

10. Mao Tse-tung, "On Protracted War," in *World Perspectives on International Politics*, Walter C. Clemens, Jr., ed. (Boston: Little, Brown, 1965), pp. 258–268.
11. Ernesto "Che" Guevara, *Guevara on Guerrilla Warfare*, with an introduction by Major Harries-Clichy Peterson (New York, 1961).
12. Mao Tse-tung, *ibid.*, p. 265.
13. *Ibid.*
14. *Ibid.*, p. 266.
15. Mao Tse-tung, "The Present Situation and Our Tasks," in *World Perspectives*, pp. 268–269.

GLOSSARY

Ad hoc
For a specific case only. A temporary tribunal or a committee that is established to deal with a specific case (as opposed to a permanent tribunal or a standing committee).

Adjudication
A judicial decision made by a permanent court (as opposed to *arbitration*—a decision made by an ad hoc structure).

Bilateral negotiations
Negotiations between two states.

Classical diplomacy
Bilateral, ministerial diplomacy conducted in secret.

Complementary interests
A mutual desire on the part of two states to exchange objects which each side can obtain only from the other. When two states have made such a mutually beneficial exchange it is called a *quid pro quo*.

Conciliation
A diplomatic technique in which a group serves as a third party to help two antagonistic states negotiate their differences. The group helps to ascertain the facts and makes specific suggestions for resolving the conflict. This process is often conducted by permanent structures (commissions of conciliation).

Conference diplomacy
Large-scale multilateral negotiation conducted at international meetings. It may be ad hoc or institutionalized.

Conversations
An exchange of views between governments. Such an exchange often precedes more detailed diplomatic negotiations.

De facto recognition
Recognizing a government's existence without entering into formal relations with it.

De jure recognition
Entering into official diplomatic relations by exchanging ambassadors. It involves a formal declaration of recognition.

Diplomacy
The practice of conducting relations between states through official representatives.

Diplomatic immunity	Freedom from arrest, trial, subpoena, civil suit, and legal penalty for a diplomatic agent in the state to which he or she is accredited.
Good offices	A diplomatic technique in which a third party acts as a go-between to reestablish bilateral negotiations between the parties to an international dispute. However, the parties themselves are responsible for settling the dispute.
Identical interests	A mutual interest by two states in obtaining a particular object or arrangement.
Mediation	A diplomatic technique similar to conciliation. The difference is that mediation involves a *single* third party; conciliation involves a group.
Ministerial diplomacy	Diplomacy carried out by professional diplomats.
Modern diplomacy	Multilateral summit diplomacy conducted in public.
Multilateral negotiations	Negotiations between more than two states.
Negotiation	A process in which explicit proposals are put forward for the purpose of reaching an agreement. It implies a willingness to make mutual concessions (*quid pro quo*).
Open diplomacy	Diplomacy conducted in public.
Secret diplomacy	Diplomacy conducted out of the public spotlight.
Summit diplomacy	Diplomacy between heads of state.
Tacit bargaining	Making unilateral moves which are reciprocated without making any explicit proposals (for example, limitations placed on the Korean War).

Free trade	International trade which takes place in the absence of governmental regulations or control.
Law of absolute advantage (Adam Smith)	Every state can produce some goods more efficiently than every other state and therefore would benefit by producing only those goods.
Law of comparative advantage (David Ricardo)	Each state should concentrate on producing those goods which it can produce most efficiently and trade these for its other needs.
Tariff	A tax levied on imports.
Terms of trade	The relationship between the prices a country receives for its exports and the prices it pays for its imports.

Countercity (Countervalue) strategy	A military strategy in which a state aims its missiles at the enemy's population centers in order to deter a nuclear attack. It presumes that another state is less likely to attack if it is likely to suffer heavy casualties as a consequence.
Counterforce strategy	A military strategy in which a state aims its missiles at the enemy's missile sites and airfields in order to deter a nuclear attack. It presumes that cutting down an attacking state's ability to continue attacking will minimize casualties in the country attacked.
Guerrilla warfare	Irregular warfare fought by small bands against an invading army or in rebellion against an established government.
Massive retaliation	A strategic policy in which an enemy is threatened with nuclear annihilation if he attacks.
Measured retaliation	A strategic policy in which an enemy is threatened with a nuclear response, should he attack, equivalent to the destruction brought about by his attack.
Mixed strategy	A combination of countercity and counterforce nuclear strategy.

International Court of Justice	This "world court" is a permanent organ of the United Nations.
International law	The system of rules on the rights and duties of states in their mutual relations. It is based on the concept of the sovereign equality of states and rests ultimately on agreement among them.
Intelligence gathering	The process engaged in by nation–states for acquiring the information necessary to protect their national interests.
Political mobilization	Engaging in continuous indoctrination and political explanations of existing circumstances in order to maintain a high degree of political consciousness.
Politicize	To make someone or some group aware of and concerned about politics.
Propaganda	Tailoring information to place one's country in a favorable light.

SELECTED READING

Claude, Inis L. Jr., *Swords Into Plowshares: The Problems and Prospects of International Relations,* 4th ed. (New York: Random House, 1972). This is the definitive work on international organizations.

Falk, Richard A., *Revolutionaries and Functionaries: The Dual Face of Terrorism* (New York: Dutton, 1988).
An outstanding analysis of terrorism in modern times.

Finkelstein, Lawrence, S. ed., *Politics in the United Nations System* (Durham, N.C.: Duke University Press, 1988).
This reader has many fine articles on the politicking that goes on behind the scenes at the UN.

Kaplan, Lawrence, *NATO and the United States: The Enduring Alliance* (Boston: G. K. Hall, 1988).
The author deals with America's first "entangling alliance."

Nicolson, Sir Harold George, *Diplomacy*, 3rd. ed. (Oxford: Clarendon Press, 1989).
This is the classic work on diplomacy.

QUESTIONS

1. Which of the following is true about the international legal system?
   a. Legislation, adjudication, and enforcement processes are carried out by centralized institutions.
   b. International political considerations supersede national laws.
   c. International laws are likely to be observed when nation–states consider their vital interests to be at stake.
   d. International laws are ideal patterns of international behavior that, although not always obeyed, are seldom disparaged.

2. The International Court of Justice is one of the institutions responsible for adjudication of international law. Which of the following statements about it is *false?*
   a. The International Court of Justice is a highly political organization.
   b. The decisions of the International Court of Justice are binding.
   c. All United Nations members are automatically members of the International Court of Justice.
   d. The greatest weakness of the International Court of Justice is that states must willingly submit cases to it.

3. In international politics, each state tries to realize its objectives, often at the expense of another state's objectives. When this interaction occurs by negotiation it is called
   a. diplomacy.
   b. adjudication.
   c. political deviousness.
   d. unilateral conflict resolution.

4. Which of the choices below describes the diplomatic technique called mediation?

   If states have a conflict of interest, diplomacy becomes a delicate process. Several techniques involving third parties have been devised for peaceful settlement of disputes.
   a. The third party tries to settle the dispute by establishing the facts and offering substantive suggestions.
   b. The third party does not participate in the negotiations but acts as a sort of referee to reestablish bilateral relations between the interested parties—who will hopefully settle the dispute themselves.
   c. By establishing the facts and offering substantive suggestions, the third party tries to entice the interested parties to settle the dispute themselves.
   d. Rather than a single third party, a group of nations is involved and may be established ad hoc. Such a group is often provided for in the peaceful settlement clauses of treaties.

5. The main diplomatic processes used to resolve conflicts are
   a. negotiation and tacit bargaining.
   b. conversation and negotiation.
   c. tacit bargaining and good offices.
   d. tacit bargaining and conversation.

6. According to Quincy Wright, which of the following are reasons for the hostile actions that often characterize the interaction process among nations?
   (1) enthusiasm for ideals
   (2) striving for the achievement of manifest destiny
   (3) belief in the necessity of self-help
   (4) frustration over unsatisfactory conditions
   (5) natural competitive drive among human beings
   (6) belief in the utility of threats of war
   a. 1, 3, 5, 6
   b. 1, 3, 4, 6
   c. 2, 3, 5
   d. none of the above

7. *(See statements below.)*
   Countercity strategy involves
   a. only (2).
   b. (2) and (4).
   c. (1) and (3).
   d. only (1).

   Nuclear weapons radically altered the psychology of war. Some of the gruesome debates of the 1950s and the 1960s included countercity versus counterforce strategy and massive versus measured retaliation.

(1) aiming the weapons at missile and bomber bases and missile-launching submarines.

(2) aiming the weapons at population centers.

(3) advocating total destruction to deter an aggressor state.

(4) advocating the morality depicted in the biblical saying, "An eye for an eye, a tooth for a tooth."

8. Guerrilla warfare theorists base many of their theories on the idea that
   a. nothing is political, and the people are all-important.
   b. everything is political; war is merely one form of politics.
   c. war is necessary to achieve the goals of the revolution, whether they be political or nonpolitical.
   d. politics is the war of bloodshed.

9. According to the authors, economists generally agree that
   a. tariffs are a necessary evil in the maintenance of international economic balance.
   b. lower tariffs should be imposed on have-not countries, while the imports from wealthier nations should be more heavily taxed.
   c. if free trade ensues, it would inevitably lower the standard of living of all countries involved because enough money could not be generated without a tariff of some sort.
   d. although there are important exceptions, free trade (no tariffs or other trade restrictions) best serves the interests of all or most nations.

10. According to the authors, the most important means of gathering intelligence (inputs) is
    a. covert.
    b. wiretapping.
    c. "cloak-and-dagger" spying.
    d. through published material, radio, and television broadcasts abroad.

QUESTIONS FOR THOUGHT AND DISCUSSION

1. What diplomatic methods did Henry Kissinger and President Carter use while trying to resolve the Israeli–Egyptian conflict?

2. How does international law differ from domestic law?

3. Explain the differences among nuclear, conventional, and guerrilla wars.

24

International Systems: The Past

As noted in a previous chapter the main difference between international politics and any other type of politics is that the former takes place in the absence of a supreme political authority. There is no world government; and the universal and regional organizations that exist do not have *enforceable* rules to control nation-state behavior. It appears, therefore, that what exists is international anarchy and unstable world politics. Yet, despite the many conflicts of interest that do exist, few countries are at war; people in most countries are not in constant fear of foreign invasion; and the world has not been destroyed.

In fact, there *are* certain rules governing international politics, but they do not emanate from governmental laws; and there *is* a degree of stability based upon a number of factors, not the least of which is a universal desire to survive. In short, there is an **international system.** However, according to one theorist, "International systems lack the two prerequisites of domestic political systems—the social basis of a community and the political structure of a government."[1] He goes on to say that within nation-states the whole takes precedence over the parts (it is **system dominant**); but in the international political system the parts take precedence over the whole (it is **subsystem dominant**). In other words, power is decentralized.

Each nation's foreign policy actions are subsystem outputs; the effects are felt in other countries as inputs. The international system consists largely of this interaction process. There are some regularities in this process which permit us to identify the characteristics of the international system. We can discern regular patterns of behavior that can then be analyzed. When nations alter their outputs and cause irregularities in the interaction process, they create dysfunctions in the international system. If these dysfunctions continue they may cause changes within the system itself. If the changes are drastic they may cause the system to collapse and a new one to take its place. The new international system will eventually achieve a homeostatic state as new interaction patterns develop. What we call the international system includes the units (nation-states, international organizations), characteristics (rules of international conduct, decision-making process), and elements that comprise it (distribution of power, level of weapons technology), and is the *result* "of the interacting behavior of all its constituent parts."[2]

All of these factors limit the range of alternative policies available to foreign-policy decision makers. Every national leader is severely restricted by these aspects of the international system in making foreign policy decisions.

Students of international affairs are primarily concerned with the degree of stability inherent in the current system. **Stability** is not merely the ability of the system to perpetuate itself and remain in some sort of equilibrium; stability also means "the tendency to diminish the probability of war."[3] Students of the field are also interested in systemic change (transformation). Change is inherent in all social relations; therefore, in discussing international systems we will not only explain how different systems function but also how they are transformed.

☐ The Balance of Power System

Before discussing the current international system we will examine previous ones to discover how they functioned and why they collapsed. Scholars generally agree that during the eighteenth and the nineteenth centuries a multiple balance of power system prevailed in Europe. It had the following characteristics:

1. It was composed exclusively of autonomous units, nation-states; there were no international organizations.
2. Foreign affairs were conducted by elites (kings, princes, and so forth) who were little influenced by public opinion.
3. These elites shared similar values and foreign policy objectives. In many cases they were blood relatives.
4. The system was limited to a relatively homogeneous Europe.
5. Member states played the game of international politics by the same rules.
6. Wars were limited in terms of objectives and level of destruction. Mercenaries did much of the fighting.
7. Alliances were of short duration, as nations shifted back and forth on specific issues. Ideological differences existed, but they did not polarize these states into rigid blocs.

8. Whenever one nation or one group of nations tried to gain preponderant power within the system, the other states would create countervailing power by uniting against the first group, thereby restoring a balance of power.

Although many wars took place, particularly before 1815, the general public was usually not overly concerned. Volunteer armies, not draftees, were used in the fighting. Destruction was limited because of a low level of weapons technology, because of limited objectives (perhaps retaking a portion of land lost in a previous war), and because **mercenary** armies would usually hit and run or turn tail if faced with the possibility of heavy casualties.

The whole matter was often treated as a chess game; and when one side was checkmated it sued for peace, gave up the objectives it was fighting for, and regrouped for the next fight. As far as the average citizens were concerned, it was King Louis' or King John's war. The people went about their business and even visited relatives in each other's countries, although their leaders were at war with each other.

Morton Kaplan, who is probably the foremost theorist of international systems, says that the following rules characterized nation–state behavior in the multiple balance of power system:[4]

1. Act to increase capabilities but negotiate rather than fight.
2. Fight rather than pass up an opportunity to increase capabilities.
3. Stop fighting rather than eliminate an essential national actor (one who was thought to play a necessary role in the international system; usually a major power).
4. Act to oppose any coalition or single actor that tends to assume a position of predominance with respect to the rest of the system.
5. Act to constrain actors who subscribe to supranational organizing principles.
6. Permit defeated or constrained essential national actors to reenter the system as acceptable role partners, or act to bring some previously inessential actor within the essential actor classification. Treat all essential actors as acceptable role partners.

The last rule is considered necessary, according to most authorities, because at least five **essential actors** are needed to maintain a balance of power system. A smaller number will not permit sufficient flexibility in shifting alliances. Poland (considered an inessential actor by the major powers in the eighteenth century) was divided three times until it no longer existed; but France (an essential actor) was readmitted into the system after the Napoleonic Wars, even though Napoleon had tried to conquer all Europe.

The first two rules underscore the lack of security suffered by each country and are responsible for the frequency of wars. The fourth and

Armies for Hire

Mercenary troops were often hired in the eighteenth and nineteenth centuries. These Hessian mercenaries are surrendering to General Washington after the Battle of Trenton.

fifth rules deal with the most important characteristics of the system, the maintenance of a balance of power. More accurately, it means keeping every member state or bloc in a position subordinate to the rest of the system.

There are a number of interpretations regarding how the system actually functioned. Some scholars claim it operated automatically, like Adam Smith's "invisible hand." In an earlier chapter we pointed out that in his explanation of a market economy Adam Smith assigned a primary role to self-interest. He said that, although businesses are merely trying to make a profit to benefit themselves, they inadvertently benefit society as a whole, because in the process of making money they also provide jobs for people who might otherwise be unemployed, and they produce goods and/or services which consumers could not otherwise enjoy. This may be considered a latent function of self-interest. Likewise some scholars claim that national statesmen were not deliberately trying to maintain a balance of power. They were merely protecting their national interests by increasing their armaments or joining an alliance because they felt threatened by other countries. The result was a balancing process.[5]

A second view suggests that the balance of power functioned in a semiautomatic manner with a strong power playing the role of balancer. The historical justification for this interpretation is the role played by England in the eighteenth and nineteenth centuries. During this period England remained aloof from any entangling alliances. Meanwhile the European continent was often divided into two competing blocs. Regardless of the issues involved England always sided with the weaker bloc to prevent the stronger bloc from dominating the continent. When England gave up this role after the Crimean War, Germany under Bismarck began playing the balancing role.

Britain's role as balancer was possible because it was an island nation, because it was primarily a naval power, and because it had no territorial ambitions in Europe. For the latter reason, other system members did not feel threatened by England's actions.[6]

A third view emphasizes the important role played by statesmen in all the major countries, each carefully analyzing every situation and consciously acting to maintain a stable **equilibrium**.[7] Other interpretations encompass a combination of these three.[8]

The multiple balance of power system began in 1648 with the signing of the Treaty of Westphalia and lasted until the outbreak of World War I in 1914. The boundaries of the system were restricted to Europe. Systemic goals were (1) maintaining the autonomy of the essential actors, (2) keeping wars from becoming too destructive, and (3) maintaining the system. The system survived for over two-and-a-half centuries; however, there were several dysfunctional developments in the latter part of the nineteenth and the early part of the twentieth centuries: several essential actors stopped playing by the system's rules, the balancing mechanism became inflexible, and wars became very destructive.

Balance of Power
British Prime Ministers W. E. Gladstone and Benjamin Disraeli, who ruled during much of the nineteenth century, pursued balance of power politics.

Pax Britannica
The English fleet in the Victorian era was the symbol of Great Britain's role as balancer. Great Britain made few alliances and always sided, in a dispute, with the weaker power bloc.

The European powers became rigidly polarized into two hostile alliances. Extreme animosity existed between France and Germany after Bismarck took Alsace-Lorraine from France following the Franco-Prussian War (1870). This animosity reduced the system's flexibility because now these two countries could not be allied. This rigidity left the system without any structure to perform the balancing function because other countries rallied around these two.

Other dysfunctions developed. World War I caused ten million deaths on the battlefield. Average citizens were now being killed as well as professional soldiers because universal military conscription was introduced. And weapons technology had advanced. Ironically, one of the most important system rules—the use of war as a mechanism to restore a stable equilibrium—became dysfunctional to the system and caused its collapse. The need for a more effective means of preventing war led some world leaders to believe they could ensure peace by creating a collective security system. Woodrow Wilson, the American president, led the fight at the Paris Peace Conference in 1919 to create a collective security system.

☐ The Collective Security System

This new principle, like the balance of power concept, took into account the primacy of power in international relations. But to increase stability the advocates of the collective security system proposed to create a **preponderance of power,** rather than mere countervailing power, to confront any aggressor or potential aggressor. War had become so complete and so terrible that the degree of instability inherent in the balance of power system could no longer be allowed to prevail. Whereas the balance of power used war as an indispensable balancing mechanism, the main function of a collective security system was to prevent war.

The philosophy behind the new system was that peace is indivisible: the eruption of armed conflict anywhere is a threat to the peace everywhere; therefore, all states would find it in their self-interest to unite against any aggressor. An attack on any state is to be regarded as an attack on all states. No state can remain neutral in a collective security system.

Making such a system work entails creating an effective mechanism for confronting an aggressor. This can be accomplished in a variety of ways:

1. Member states can pledge to contribute military units to enforce collective security;
2. They can designate specific units which are then placed at the disposal of the international organization which will coordinate the collective force; or,
3. An international police or military force can be created, under the exclusive control of the international agency, to administer the collective security system.

The collective security system is based upon the following assumptions:

1. *National leaders are rational and prudent.* They are rational enough to recognize their country's inability to cope with the collective might of the rest of the world; and they are prudent enough to avoid such a confrontation.
2. *Every state is vulnerable to collective sanctions.* This is absolutely necessary if every state is to be deterred. (This, however, is not the case today. Given the nuclear capabilities of the two superpowers, a collective force against either one would not be a credible deterrent but could precipitate a horrendous war.)
3. *Aggression is clear-cut and aggressors can be readily identified.* Unfortunately no international body has ever been able to define aggression before the fact. In today's world aggression takes many forms. It is often difficult if not impossible to identify the aggressor in a conflict. If country *A* recruits, trains, and arms insurgents in country *B*, is the ensuing conflict a civil war in country *B* or an act of aggression by country *A?*
4. *There is no such thing as a just war.* Any country that resorts to war, no matter what the provocation or the perceived national

The End of the Balance of Power in Europe
The extreme animosity between France and Germany after 1870 eventually led to the end of the multiple balance of power system in Europe. World War I was the bloody and disillusioning result as 10 million men died on the battlefield.

interests, is in the wrong and must be stopped by collective force. War must be given up forever as an instrument of foreign policy.

Unfortunately this international system, which appears to have been compatible with the distribution of power that emerged after World War I, has never been effectively put into operation. The **League of Nations,** created in 1920, was a weak attempt to institutionalize a collective security system. It failed because of certain dysfunctional factors: First, it was not seriously regarded by many statesmen; second, participation was not universal (the United States never joined and the Soviet Union did not become a member until 1934); and third, sanctions against an aggressor were weak and voluntary.

The crucial years for the League were 1931–1937. Earlier the League had achieved a measure of success. But it was unable to cope with the imperialism of the Axis Powers. Japan marched into Manchuria, Mussolini attacked Ethiopia, and Hitler and Mussolini successfully supported Franco in the Spanish Civil War; later Hitler's aggression extended into Poland and Czechoslovakia. Although, in such cases, the League was supposed to exert several kinds of pressure—moral, economic, and military—it failed to do so. Because the League of Nations failed to function as a collective security system, the world plunged once more into a world war. This time the death toll was over forty million.

Collective Security
The League of Nations attempted to deal with Italy's invasion of Ethiopia in 1935.

For a collective security system to function properly, the following conditions should be met:

1. *Sanctions against an aggressor should be strong and automatic.* There must be no question in the mind of any national leader contemplating an act of aggression. He must believe that such an act will touch off a trip-wire mechanism that will bring into being the collective military might of the rest of the world against his country. The effect should be **deterrence.** If that fails the aggressor should be quickly defeated.

2. *Participation should be universal.* All countries should take part if world peace is to become a reality.

3. *No state should be so powerful that it can ignore the power of the collective security force.* Otherwise that state could commit aggression with impunity. Under no circumstances can there be a superpower. Ideally, there should be a relatively equal distribution of power, at least among the major powers.

4. *There should be a willingness on the part of every nation to make war upon any aggressor* no matter how friendly their previous relations may have been, and no matter how remote to its interests the aggression appears to be.

5. *The system should contain a structure (an international organization) that can identify an aggressor and then direct the collective force against that state.*

6. *Territorial changes are forbidden except by mutual consent.* Since nations rarely are willing to give up territory, the status quo will probably continue.

7. *No military alliances should be permitted* except for the universal one to which every nation belongs.

8. *Only nonmilitary means can be used to settle international disputes.* Each country forsakes war as an instrument of foreign policy.

If all these conditions are met, all states will have equal status. Weaker states will no longer occupy a subordinate position in world affairs resulting from military inferiority. The concept of **external sovereignty** (the legal equality of nation-states under international law) may come closer to describing reality than it ever has before.

During World War II the allies decided to create a more effective collective security system than the League of Nations had been. It was assumed that the United Nations would succeed where the League had failed. This turned out to be a vain hope. Undoubtedly, the UN serves many useful purposes and performs many important functions, but it is not a collective security system. In fact, the veto power of the five permanent members of the Security Council indicates that it was never intended to act in that capacity unless the big five agreed unanimously. The need for the veto is based on the assumption that it is better to have a stalemate in the Security Council than a world war against a major power.

The wartime collaboration of the allies was based on a convergence of national interests. Their common interest in survival, which was being threatened by a common enemy, Hitler, far outweighed their differences. However, once the enemy was defeated the reason for collaboration disappeared and the incompatibility of other national interests became manifest. Thus, collective security gave way to a system of alliances. The latter is called **collective defense** and is distinguished by the fact that the alliance is aimed exclusively at outside threats. NATO, SEATO, CENTO, and the Warsaw Pact were not examples of collective security because internal aggression by one member against another is not covered by the terms of these agreements.

Only the Charter of the Organization of American States (OAS) establishes collective security as well as collective defense in a regional organization. The primary dysfunctional aspect of this system is the preponderant power of the United States. The United States has more military might than all the other OAS members combined. Within this system collective security cannot be used against the United States if it is the aggressor, nor can it be used against anyone else without the consent of the United States.

As a result of the unsuccessful attempts to establish a collective security system, the period from 1920 until the early 1950s should properly be called "collective insecurity." The balance of power system did not function during this period either. To better understand what happened, we will conduct a brief functional analysis of the balance of power and collective security systems. This analysis may shed more light on the transformation to the current international system which we will examine in the next chapter.

□ Functional Analysis

National leaders must be socialized to accept the rules of the international system. They must learn to play their roles properly if the system is to function as it should. To the extent that they understand the system's operation, the part their respective countries play in it, and follow the rules, they contribute to systemic stability. In other words, they perform the *maintenance* and *adaptation* functions. In the balance of power system the leaders stopped playing by the rules; and in the collective security system they never began.

Problems arise whenever national leaders permit their cultural differences to interfere with their observance of the international system rules. If they do, their behavior becomes dysfunctional. It also creates problems with the *integration* function. A system in which the parts are not well coordinated with each other is poorly integrated. The ideal integrating situation is one in which national decision makers share a common set of values and beliefs regarding international behavior and behave accordingly.

System transformation occurs when the rules are no longer observed by the main actors in the system, or when the rules are no longer appropriate. In either case, a transition period occurs in which there is great conflict because national leaders don't really know how

"Grand Illusion" (Jean Cocteau, 1931)
In this classic film of captured French fliers in World War I Germany, the central characters discover that their assumptions about war, international affairs, and honor are outdated and that a group of new leaders, who no longer play by the old rules, are now in control. Economically, socially, politically, artistically, World War I put an end to old ideas and released new forces which seemed impossible to control. (Courtesy of the Museum of Modern Art/ Film Stills Archive)

they are supposed to behave. The old rules do not apply and new ones have not yet been devised. So countries no longer play the game by the same set of rules.

This transition period is marked by a high degree of instability. When a system is stable national leaders know which goals are attainable and which are not; they also know which means can be properly used and which cannot. Consequently, this consensus allows the *goal-attainment* function to be properly performed. However, when the international system is in a transition stage national leaders are confused about ends and means. This confusion throughout the first half of the twentieth century led to two devastating world wars, as several aggressive states tried to impose their own systemic rules. An attempt at world domination by the Axis Powers met great resistance by the allies.

There are two other important functions in the international system—**security** and **conflict resolution.** The primary goal of each country's foreign policy is national security. The degree of security enjoyed (or suffered) by each country varies within and between international systems. Poland might be very secure in an effective collective security system, but it was very insecure in the balance of power system, because it was not considered an essential national actor. On the other hand, England was very secure in the balance of power system. In the transition period no one was secure. Security, then, depends on the existing international system, and on a nation's place in that system.

The techniques which may be rationally used to resolve conflicts vary among alternative international systems. In the balance of power system war is considered an acceptable technique; in a collective security system it is not. In the current system the situation is much more complicated. The conflict resolution function is crucial because it affects stability, security, and all the other previously mentioned functions. In fact, methods devised to resolve conflicts determine whether or not the existing system will survive. In the nuclear age this could conceivably mean the methods will determine whether or not the human race will survive. Now let us turn to a consideration of the current international system.

REFERENCES

1. Joseph Frankel, *International Relations* (London: Oxford University Press, 1969), p. 117.
2. Charles A. McClelland, *Theory and the International System* (New York: Macmillan, 1966), p. 91.
3. Inis L. Claude, Jr., *Power and International Relations* (New York: Random House, 1962), p. 6.

4. Morton A. Kaplan, "Variants of the Six Models of the International System," in James N. Rosenau, ed., rev. ed., *International Politics and Foreign Policy* (New York: The Free Press, 1969), p. 292.

5. Jean-Jacques Rousseau, "Mechanism," in Fredrick H. Gareau, ed., *The Balance of Power and Nuclear Deterrence* (Boston: Houghton Mifflin, 1962), pp. 20–25. See also the article by Lord Henry Brougham, "Idealism," pp. 59–81, in which he compares the workings of the balance of power to those of the solar system.

6. Many historians and political scientists take this position. Even Gareau, in the book mentioned above, appears to take this interpretation for granted (see page 50).

7. This position is presented in Gareau's book by Leonce Donnadieu, "Optimism," pp. 82–88.

8. William D. Coplin, *Introduction to International Politics: A Theoretical Overview* (Chicago: Markham, 1971), p. 302.

GLOSSARY

Balance of power system	The international system that existed from 1648 to 1914. It was comprised of nation-states that were often divided into competing blocs which were fairly equally balanced in terms of power. Alliances were flexible, with members often shifting sides.
Collective defense	An alliance system designed to protect its members from aggression by nonmember states.
Collective security system	An international system in which member states are militarily allied to protect themselves from each other as well as from nonmember states.
Equilibrium	Balance.
International system	A political system that contains all the nation-states that interact with each other. It lacks a formal government or any other supreme political authority. Its constituent parts are nation–states, international organizations (private and public), regional groupings, military blocs, and so forth. It has certain characteristics, elements, rules, and interaction processes. It tends to be subsystem dominant. In this book we analyze international systems in terms of their stability, how they perform various functions (security, conflict resolution, integration, goal attainment, maintenance, and adaptation), and in a number of other ways.
League of Nations	An international organization created in 1920 primarily for the purpose of maintaining peace. It was the first attempt to institutionalize a collective security system. Its failure to cope with aggression in the 1930s led to its demise.

Subsystem dominant	A system in which the parts have more power than the whole. In this case, an international system in which power is decentralized (possessed by nation-states rather than by the international system).
System dominant	A system in which power is centralized (for example, most nation-states).
System transformation	What occurs when a system changes from one type to another. For example, an economic system changing from capitalism to socialism, or an authoritarian political system changing into a democratic one. In this chapter we discussed how world leaders tried to change from a balance of power international system to a collective security system.

Conflict resolution	The process by which individuals or groups (in this case nations) resolve their differences.
Deterrence	Preventing someone from doing something, usually through fear or doubt. One nation deters another from attacking it through fear of retaliation.
Essential national actor	A state whose physical survival and sovereignty was deemed necessary in the balance of power system.
External sovereignty	In international law it means that all states are legally equal (although in terms of power and influence they obviously are not).
Mercenaries	Professional soldiers whose services are for hire. Since they are not fighting for a cause they believe in, or to protect their homeland, bravery is not their most notable characteristic; prudence is.
Preponderance of power	Overwhelming military superiority designed to deter aggression.
Security	A state of being sought by nation-states in which they are free from external and internal threats to their sovereignty and well-being.
Stability	Regarding international systems, a state of being in which established patterns of international politics are observed, in which the existing system functions smoothly, and in which there are few wars (and those that do occur are not very destructive).
Supranational	An authority above the nation-state level (for example, a world government).

SELECTED READING

Claude, Inis L. Jr., *Power and International Relations* (New York: Random House, 1962).

An excellent analysis of the balance of power system, the collective security system, and world government.

Domke, William K., *War and the Changing Global System* (New Haven: Yale University Press, 1988).

An interesting analysis of the evolution of the international system in the mid-eighties.

Finkelstein, Marina and Lawrence, ed., *Collective Security* (San Francisco: Chandler, 1966).

A very good collection of readings on collective security.

Garreau, Fredrick H., *The Balance of Power and Nuclear Deterrence* (Boston: Houghton Mifflin, 1962).

A compilation of important literature on the subject.

Kaplan, Morton, "Variants of the Six Models of International System," James N. Rosenau, ed., *International Policy and Foreign Policy*, rev. ed. (New York: The Free Press, 1969).

A rigorous treatment of international systems theory.

Thompson, William R., ed., *Contending Approaches to World System Analysis* (Beverly Hills: Sage, 1983).

The world system concept has been a field of study in sociology, as well as other social sciences. This reader examines alternative approaches.

QUESTIONS

1. An important characteristic of the international system is that
   a. a supreme authority rules by the existence of a world government.
   b. the whole (system) takes precedence over the parts.
   c. (subsystems) conflicts of interest that exist are held to a minimum.
   d. a degree of stability is based in part on the universal desire to survive.

2. Which of the following was *not* characteristic of European politics in the eighteenth century?
   a. Nation-states observed the same rules of international behavior.
   b. Objectives and levels of destruction were limited.
   c. No one nation or one group of nations was allowed to predominate within the system.

  d. States were grouped into rigid blocs based on ideological differences.
  e. War was used as a balancing mechanism.

3. Wars during the nineteenth century in Europe
  a. disrupted the lives of most citizens.
  b. were characterized as "total" war.
  c. enlisted the efforts of mercenary armies noted for their courage and humanitarianism.
  d. involved mainly leaders who hired mercenaries and who fought limited wars.

4. A collective security system may be defined as
  a. a political system that contains all the nation-states that interact with each other.
  b. an international system in which member states are militarily allied in order to protect themselves from each other.
  c. the international system that was composed of nation-states that were often divided into competing blocs and that were fairly equally balanced in terms of power.
  d. an alliance system designed to protect its members from aggression by nonmember states.
  e. an international system in which peace is maintained by nuclear deterrence.

5. Which of the following is *not* a theory regarding the functioning of the balance-of-power system?
  a. It operated automatically as if guided by an "invisible hand."
  b. Calculated self-interest motivated national leaders to strive to maintain a stable equilibrium.
  c. It operated in a semi-automatic manner, with a strong power playing the role of balancer.
  d. A stable balance was maintained by avoiding war as an instrument of foreign policy.

6. The main function of a collective security system is
  a. the use of war as an indispensable balancing mechanism.
  b. the prevention of war.
  c. the use of war only as a last means of settlement.
  d. the use of limited war but the outlawing of large-scale war.

7. In order for a collective security system to function properly, which of the following conditions must be met?
  a. Sanctions against an aggressor must be strong and automatic.
  b. Participation must be universal.
  c. Individual military alliances must be encouraged.
  d. both (a) and (c) above
  e. both (a) and (b) above

8. Collective defense can best be described as
   a. an international system in which member states are militarily allied in order to protect themselves from each other as well as from nonmember states.
   b. an alliance system designed to protect its members from aggression by nonmember states.
   c. an example of a collective security system on a regional scale.
   d. none of the above.

9. Power is a central concept in
   a. the balance-of-power system.
   b. the collective security system.
   c. international politics generally.
   d. all of the above

10. In the international system power is
   a. decentralized.
   b. centralized.
   c. no longer used.
   d. the exclusive province of a handful of nations.

QUESTIONS FOR THOUGHT AND DISCUSSION

1. Compare the "balance of power" and "collective security" systems.

2. What were the similarities and differences between the League of Nations and the United Nations?

3. Explain the different interpretations of how the "balance of power" system worked.

25

International Systems: The Present and the Future

☐ **The Balance of Terror System**

It is difficult to pinpoint the exact date, but by the 1960s the Soviet Union had developed an invulnerable **second-strike capability,** as had the United States a few years earlier. This meant that either side could absorb a surprise nuclear attack by the other and still inflict devastating damage upon the aggressor. Since either nation would only precipitate a nuclear attack upon itself by attacking the other, both sides were effectively deterred. This phenomenon is sometimes called mutual assured destruction (MAD). The international system is often referred to as a bipolar balance of terror. This system is very different from prior ones and operates on a different set of rules from its predecessors.

Prior technological advances had increased the destructive capacity of weapons, but never before had a qualitative change so radically altered the nature of war and of international relations in general. The bomb tested at Alamogordo, New Mexico, in 1945 had 2,000 times the destructive force of any weapon ever used before, and since then nuclear warheads have been built 3,000 times as powerful as the first atomic blast. Surely weapons have deterred aggression throughout history, but quite often they have failed to do so. Now the awesome destructive capacity of thermonuclear weapons has increased the efficacy of deterrence strategy, but it has correspondingly increased the extent of damage that would occur should nuclear war break out.

Atomic Explosion
The now all-too-familiar mushroom cloud ushered in a new era in international politics. By the 1960's the international system became a "balance of terror."

Weapons Stockpiles

Quite often statistics fail to convey the full meaning intended, but we think the following figures demonstrate clearly why each side has an invulnerable second-strike capability.

The United States had 880 long-range land-based Minuteman missiles and 50 MX missiles with 2,380 warheads in 1993. These **intercontinental ballistic missiles (ICBM's)** travel at speeds in excess of 17,000 miles per hour. This means they can reach any target in the former Soviet Union in about thirty minutes. They carry 1.2 megaton warheads. One **megaton** is equivalent to the destructive capacity of one million tons of TNT. The atomic bombs dropped on Hiroshima and Nagasaki in World War II were only the equivalent of 20,000 tons of TNT (20 **kilotons**).

The Minuteman missiles are placed in deep underground silos and encased in reinforced concrete in order to survive any nuclear attack. The solid fuel permits launching within 32 seconds. Most of them are dispersed throughout the western and midwestern United States, making it very difficult to destroy all of them in a surprise attack. Over 95 percent of U.S. ICBM's are on constant alert. It is possible to launch them from airborne command posts should ground command centers be destroyed.

In addition, the United States has 27 Poseidon and 8 Trident submarines with 16 launching pads each, for a total of 464 missiles with 3,712 warheads. These have one-half to one megaton warheads. The current generation of Poseidon missiles has a range of 3,000 miles and the Trident missiles have a 5,000-mile range. The subs are nuclear powered and can remain submerged for long periods of time (months). Their swiftness, mobility, and concealability make them excellent second-strike forces. They fire their missiles without surfacing, thereby making it very difficult to eliminate them in a surprise attack. They are widely dispersed and follow irregular travel patterns. The primitive state of antisubmarine warfare (ASW) increases their deterrent value. Congress has funded eight more Trident submarines, and the Navy wants four more. The Trident II warheads are being placed on the submarines beginning with the ninth Trident sub. The others are being updated in the 1990s. These warheads will be five times as destructive and more than twice as accurate as the Trident I missiles. Just one Poseidon submarine has enough warheads to destroy every large and medium-sized city in the former Soviet Union. This is less than 2 percent of our strategic nuclear weapons. Each Trident submarine has enough warheads to destroy every Soviet city with a population of 100,000 or more.

Sea-Launched Ballistic Missiles
The nuclear-powered submarine USS George Washington is capable of launching missiles while submerged.

U.S. Intercontinental Ballistic Missiles
Two Minuteman missiles being test-fired represent an important component of America's nuclear deterrence force.

The United States also has 423 long-range bombers that can fly nonstop to the former Soviet Union, drop their nuclear payloads (between 20 and 40 megatons each), and return to their home bases without landing to refuel. About 30 percent of them are kept in a constant state of alert. These include B-52's, FB-111's, and B-1B's. About half are undergoing maintenance or modification. The number of bomber weapons deployed is uncertain, but it is estimated to be 4,500.

Given this quantity, quality, and diversity of weapons and weapons delivery systems, it is highly unlikely that anyone would deliberately launch a nuclear attack against the United States. Even if 90 percent of our strike force were destroyed, the remaining 10 percent is sufficient to inflict horrendous damage on the attacker. The amount of saturation bombing needed to overcome our second-strike force is so great that the attacker would probably be killed by his own fallout.

If you think all this sounds like science fiction, we assure you it is not; and there's more. The new generation of **sea-launched ballistic missiles (SLBM's)** has a longer range and is equipped with **multiple independently targeted reentry vehicles (MIRV's).** As many as fourteen warheads can be placed on each missile, and each warhead can be aimed at a different target. Actually, Minuteman missiles have three warheads and MX missiles have ten. Poseidon missiles carry ten warheads, and Trident missiles have eight, although the newer ones can carry fourteen per missile. The United States has MIRVed all of its nuclear submarines and most of its Minuteman missiles. The Trident submarine has 24 MIRVed missiles of 5,000-mile range. First-generation Trident missiles have been placed on half the Poseidon subs, MIRVed at an 8 to 1 ratio. The Poseidon missiles average 10 warheads each. The U.S. total of strategic sea-launched warheads is 3,712. The supersonic B-1 bomber can fly at twice the speed of sound and can carry two and a half times the bomb load of the B-52 it is supposed to replace (about 100 megatons). The Air Force wants 540 of them, but Congress funded 99, and 84 are in place.

We also have the cruise missile, which can fly at low enough altitudes to evade detection by enemy radar; it is a jet-powered, unmanned aircraft that can travel for thousands of miles and hit a target within ten yards. The cruise missile can be launched by land, sea, or air, and 11,000 are planned. A mobile land-based MX missile was planned that would travel underground by rail for thousands of miles so that an enemy would not know where to attack. However, it was determined that this would be too dangerous, so the Carter administration dropped the MX missile. The Reagan administration received congressional support to build 50 MX missiles and to place them in current Minuteman silos. They want 50 more to put in a rail-mobile basing mode. At this writing, Congress had not given its approval. We have also developed an improved MIRV called MARV (maneuverable reentry vehicle), a warhead whose course can be altered in flight after it has been released from the rocket. The U.S. also has 1,000 nuclear warheads deployed in Europe, and 4,000 stored in the U.S. Thus, its total nuclear arsenal in 1993 was 15,592 warheads.

The former Soviet Union has 1,386 land-based missiles, about 942 sea-based missiles, and 160 long-range bombers. Former Secretary of Defense Robert McNamara estimated in 1967 that a nuclear attack by the USSR in the 1970s would kill 122 million Americans if it were aimed at military targets only, and over 149 million if urban centers were included. A reverse attack would kill 100 million Russians and destroy 80 percent of the USSR's industrial capacity.[1] Those figures are much higher now. This is a "limited" attack. Now you know why the current international system is called "the balance of terror." (See Table 25-1.)

The USSR had more launchers and nuclear megatonnage, while the United States emphasizes accuracy and number of warheads. Qualitatively, the U.S. is ahead by far. Soviet strategic bombers are slower. U.S. bombers are high-speed jet aircraft. U.S. nuclear submarines are faster, quieter, and fire more quickly while submerged. Their missiles are solid fueled. Soviet submarine-launched missiles are almost all (88 percent) liquid fueled, which makes them less reliable, more dangerous, and much slower to fire. About 60 percent of U.S. subs are at sea at any given time. Only 15 percent of Soviet subs operate at sea at any given time. The most vulnerable weapons are land-based missiles because they are stationary. This makes the Soviet Union much more vulnerable to a

Table 25-1
U.S.–former USSR
Strategic Nuclear
Balance, 1992[a]

	Land-Based		Undersea		Airborne		Total	
	U.S.	Former USSR	U.S.	Former USSR	U.S.	Former USSR	U.S.	Former USSR
Launchers	930	1,373	464	942	286	160	1,239	1,857
Warheads	2,380	6,412	3,412	3,378	4,500	680	8,772	9,537

[a] This table does not include intermediate and short-range "theatre" nuclear weapons; the U.S. and its NATO allies have approximately 31,000 nuclear weapons, and the former USSR has about 23,000.

Source: The Defense Monitor, The Center for Defense Information, Vol. XVII, No. 5, 1988 and *Statistical Abstract of the United States, 1992,* p. 342.

surprise attack than the United States. Only 19 percent of U.S. strategic warheads are land-based, but for the Soviets it is 61 percent. The U.S. has developed the stealth bomber, which supposedly cannot be detected by radar.

The strategic arms reductions treaties (START I and START II) are supposed to reduce the U.S. strategic nuclear arsenal to 3,500 warheads, and the former Soviet republics to 3,000 by 2003. However, Ukraine, a former Soviet republic, inherited so many nuclear weapons in the collapse of the Soviet Union that it now ranks third, behind the U.S. and Russia, but ahead of Great Britain, France, and China. It fears for its security against its powerful Russian neighbor (that conquered and incorporated it into the Soviet Union in 1940). Ukraine also lacks the funds needed to dismantle its arsenal. Hence, the treaties are in jeopardy. Even if disarmament occurs as planned, it will leave the two nuclear superpowers with about the same number of nuclear weapons as they had when START I treaty negotiations began in 1969. Ukraine has 176 ICBMs and 40 nuclear-equipped long-range bombers. Two other former Soviet republics have smaller nuclear arsenals.

Dr. Henry Kissinger, who is one of our top experts on military strategy in the nuclear age, believes that "with no advantage to be gained by striking first and no disadvantage to be suffered by striking second, there will be no motive for either surprise or preemptive attack [one launched because word has just been received that the enemy is about to attack]. Mutual invulnerability means mutual deterrence. It is the most stable position from the point of view of preventing all-out war."[2]

Kissinger is referring to the invulnerability of our second-strike force, not of our populations. We hold each other's populations hostage because there is no way to protect them, given the existing level of technology. In the nuclear age offense has greatly outstripped defense. No **antiballistic missile system (ABM)** yet devised can protect populations. Perhaps there will be a technological breakthrough in the future. Ironically if there is, it will have a destabilizing effect on the balance of terror system because the side that has it can destroy the other without fear of being destroyed in return. This is called **first-strike capability.** If either or both sides has such a defense system, the chances of nuclear war are greatly increased.

Kissinger cites four prerequisites for stability in the current international system:

1. *The deterrent threat must be credible.* Each country must believe the other will use nuclear weapons if attacked.
2. *The deterrent threat must be understood.* Each side must be certain the other side actually possesses these weapons. In this case military secrets regarding possession of nuclear weapons are dysfunctional. That is a primary reason why the Soviet Union often displayed its latest weapons in the May Day parade, in case our intelligence reports had been faulty. This is no longer necessary, of course, since we have known for a long time that they have second-strike capability; but it was necessary in the beginning.
3. *The opponent must be rational.* Obviously, if one is dealing with a madman, deterrence strategy will not work.
4. *The penalties of aggression must outweigh its benefits.*[3] This accounts for the enormous quantity and diversity of weapons and weapons delivery systems. If we had only four missiles it is conceivable that an opponent might consider losing four cities an acceptable price to pay in order to conquer the United States. National leaders must not be given the opportunity to conclude that an attack might be worth the risk involved. They must believe that any attack would be tantamount to committing suicide and thus resolve themselves to settling disputes by other means.

Kissinger is claiming that deterrence strategy will be effective only in preventing "all-out war." General Pierre Galois,[4] who was Charles de Gaulle's top nuclear strategist, is more optimistic. Galois believed all wars will be deterred between the superpowers because each fears the possibility of escalation. Rather than accept a single defeat each side could successively increase the level of armaments in a limited war; since there is no longer a great gap between the smallest tactical nuclear weapon* and the largest conventional weapons, the nuclear threshold can be easily crossed. Once that threshold is crossed, a nuclear holocaust will be difficult to avoid. Since both sides are aware of this possibility even limited wars between them are inconceivable. Galois' contention seems to be borne out by the historical facts. Since

---

* The United States has 22,000 tactical nuclear weapons, mostly in Western Europe. These are much smaller weapons with relatively limited destructive capability. They are designed to repel a troop invasion.

U.S. and the former USSR

Wars in the nuclear era have been limited and spheres of influence were respected by both sides. Although we protested vehemently, the U.S. took no action when the Soviet Union sent tanks to Czechoslovakia in 1968. The Soviet Union supported North Vietnam but avoided troop involvement in the Vietnam War.

the end of World War II whenever either the United States or the USSR committed troops anywhere, the other side did not.

Morton Kaplan, who places more emphasis on the bipolarity of this system than he does on the impact of nuclear weapons, attributes the following characteristics to what he calls the loose bipolar international system:

1. Alliances tend to be long-term, to be based on permanent and not shifting interest, and to have ideological components.
2. Wars tend to be limited.

3. Even limited wars are rare.
4. The universal organization (the United Nations) is used primarily for mediation.[5]

These are all significant changes from prior international systems. The last point underscores the fact that the United Nations is not a collective security organization.

There are also other significant developments in the current international system. Since the end of World War II the number of nation–states in the world has more than doubled. The dissolution of colonial empires and the subsequent proliferation of independent African and Asian states has had a great impact on international relations. Since over 160 states now span the globe, the current international system is truly universal. Formerly the colonies were appendages of the European system. One result of decolonization and nuclear stalemate is the shift of conflict primarily to the underdeveloped areas.

Most scholars believe the dramatic advance of weapons technology created a completely new ballgame. Perhaps the most brilliant defense of this view is made by Louis J. Halle in an article entitled "Lessons of the Nuclear Age."[6] The following analysis is based on the six points he makes in his article:

1. *Nuclear weapons are virtually unusable in combat.* The use of force must be related to an objective, and nuclear weapons are too powerful to be used except in very rare instances. One does not use a cannon to kill a mouse; one uses a mousetrap. A response must be commensurate with the action that precipitates it. Furthermore, as long as both sides have a second-strike capability, using nuclear weapons is almost always unfeasible. But even when the United States enjoyed a nuclear monopoly it could not use nuclear weapons to "save" China from a Communist revolution, or even to prevent Russia from acquiring its own nuclear arsenal.

2. *In a nuclear environment wars must be limited.* It took Americans a long time to understand this. In fact, the balance of terror system is still incomprehensible to many. We were accustomed to thinking there are only two states of being in international affairs—war and peace. If a country is at war it uses all the weapons at its disposal in order to achieve a military victory. During peacetime the diplomats do all the work and the military is idle; if diplomacy fails and war occurs the diplomats temporarily step aside and the military men take over until the war ends. Then the military steps aside and the diplomats begin to function once more.

Actually, in the nuclear age diplomats must function all the time. All-out war with all the weapons at one's disposal would lead to mutual annihilation, given the existing stockpile of nuclear weapons.

© 1975 Chicago Daily News

"SURE, WE CAN BLOW UP THE WORLD, BUT IF THE RUSSIANS CAN BLOW UP THE WORLD TWICE, WE'RE GONERS"

Korea was the first trauma we experienced before learning the new rules, and most Americans were unhappy because we did not achieve a total military victory. We were still thinking in terms of the old rules. The fact that we achieved our political objective of denying South Korea to the Communists was actually a political victory for us; and all wars are now political. Coercion can be used only in limited amounts, depending on the importance of objectives, which are themselves limited.

All-out conflicts are permissible with limited weapons, but unlimited weapons require that conflicts be limited. Halle quotes Dr. Irenaus Eibl-Eibesfeldt who points out that fighting among vertebrates of the same species almost never ends in death or serious injury to the combatants. He says, "While species without deadly weapons, such as pigeons with their soft bills and weak feet, may fight each other all-out, those that have the means to do each other mortal injury never fight all-out. Male rattlesnakes, which can kill each other with a single bite, never bit each other in combat."[7] Hence the United States and the USSR never bit each other! Perhaps human beings also have an instinct for survival of the species.

Whether or not this instinct exists, self-preservation requires that in the nuclear age wars be limited. "The only time that nuclear weapons actually have been used in combat was in the context of an essentially unlimited war that had begun in the prenuclear age, when unlimited wars were still practicable."[8]

3. *The usefulness of nuclear armaments in diplomacy is limited to deterrence and defense of the status quo.* Once Russia achieved second-strike

capability both sides thought that this counterbalance to our nuclear power would give the Soviets a diplomatic advantage, because Russia's conventional forces were much greater than ours; hence we thought she could use them to threaten Europe. When Khrushchev began making threats to West Berlin in 1958, we held firm in spite of the apparent logic of giving in. Eventually Russia backed down. Thus Russia's acquisition of nuclear weapons failed to upset the existing situation.

In 1954 the United States threatened massive nuclear retaliation if the Communists took Dien Bien Phu in Indochina. They took it but we did not retaliate. In both cases nuclear threats failed to upset the status quo. The nuclear threats lacked credibility. The Russians were not going to risk nuclear annihilation over West Berlin, and the Americans were not going to do so over Dien Bien Phu. The side that makes the threat is left with the responsibility of starting a nuclear war. In both these cases rationality prevailed.

In Berlin our nuclear weapons sustained the status quo, despite the fact that West Berlin was 110 miles inside East Germany, and the Soviets could have easily overrun our small force stationed there. There is an important lesson to be learned from this experience: *the higher the stakes, the lower the risk that is acceptable.* A two-dollar bet at the race track is acceptable to many people because the stakes are low and a loss is bearable; but even if the chances of our using nuclear weapons to defend West Berlin are one in a hundred, the stakes are so high (the annihilation of Russia) that the Russians could not risk it. Uncertainty is the great deterrent. It appears then that nuclear weapons are not very useful in upsetting the status quo, but very useful in maintaining it.

4. *Nuclear weapons have, consequently, strengthened the status quo.* When World War II ended no one expected the division of Germany and Korea to last more than a few months at most. Korea is still divided and Germany was until 1990. The Communist attempt to take South Korea failed, and America's attempt to conquer North Korea also failed. The war ended when both sides accepted the territorial status quo. America has not been able to oust the Castro regime in Cuba because of the remote possibility that Russia might intervene. However, when the Russians tried to alter the distribution of power in the Western Hemisphere by installing missiles in Cuba, the threat to our security was so great that we deterred them from doing so with nuclear threats. So it appears that the only function of nuclear weapons is deterrence. And since deterrence prevents change, it perpetuates the status quo.

5. *Where the power of both sides is absolute, a bipolar balance is relatively stable.* Nuclear power is absolute because it has the capacity to annihilate an entire society no matter how large. Therefore, nuclear superiority is not important. Past a certain absolute level additional weapons

Chinese Soldier in Korea
Communications between the U.S. and Communist China were poor in the period just before the Korean War. As a consequence, each country's leaders misread the intentions of the other and war resulted.

do not increase security. At this writing the United States and the former Soviet Union have nuclear parity. The situation, however, is no different than it was when the United States had a 3 to 1 or 4 to 1 superiority. As long as both sides have a sufficiently large second-strike capability to inflict unacceptable damage on an attacker, mutual deterrence is achieved. As Halle puts it: "If two men stand with pistols at each other's temples, their fingers on the triggers, the balance between them is perfect even though one pistol is a .45 while the other is only a .22."[9]

6. *In the nuclear age it is even more important to have good communications between antagonists than between allies.* It has often been stated that the Korean War occurred because of poor communications. Secretary of State Dean Acheson and General Douglas MacArthur delivered speeches in which they outlined the areas the United States would defend in case of war. They did not include South Korea. They were speaking in terms of all-out war. The Communists took this to mean we would not defend South Korea under any circumstances, so they attacked. We routed the North Koreans very quickly. We then decided it would be a good idea to "liberate" North Korea from the Communists, but only if the Chinese Army would not intervene. They gave no clear indication that they would, so we marched into North Korea—and the Chinese intervened. Three years and two million lives later the war ended with no significant territorial change. If communications had been clear at the crucial moments, war could have been averted.

In the nuclear age good communication systems are indispensable. During the Cuban Missile Crisis in 1962, when we were on the brink of nuclear war, the leaders of the two superpowers were not communicating instantaneously. Messages required several hours to be transmitted. Shortly thereafter the "hot line" between Moscow and Washington was installed.

Possible Future Dysfunctions

The amount of stability attributed to the balance of terror system by Kissinger, Galois, and Halle is debatable because of possible future dysfunctions.

1. *The possibility of a mechanical or electronic failure exists,* either with warning systems or weapons delivery systems. All such objects are subject to breakdown.
2. *A human error or miscalculation may occur.* The enemy's intentions may be misread; someone may misunderstand an order; or someone may accidentally push the wrong button.
3. *The madman theory may be valid.* An irrational person on either side may deliberately launch a nuclear weapon. Such people have been known to exist in the military.
4. *A limited war might escalate into a nuclear holocaust* because both sides have all types and all sizes of weapons. Pierre Galois may be wrong in assuming this diversity will prevent a conflict between nuclear powers.
5. *The proliferation of nuclear weapons poses the greatest danger to peace.* As the nuclear club grows, the efficacy of deterrence strategy diminishes. The greater the number of nuclear powers, the more difficult it is to identify an attacker.

The proliferation of nuclear weapons, combined with the existence of Polaris-type submarines might create some interesting problems. Consider the following scenario: It is the year 2000, and twenty countries possess submarines equipped with thermonuclear missiles. A nuclear bomb lands in Rio de Janeiro. Does the government in Brasilia retaliate against the Soviet Union or North Korea? Maybe it was China. How would the United States respond? What happens if after learning of the attack communications are disrupted between the Brazilian government and a Brazilian submarine commander with nuclear weapons aboard? Does he release the missiles? If so, will he choose the right target? In order for deterrence strategy to be credible, the submarine commander must be able to retaliate even if communications are disrupted. Would he become so enraged with the perpetrators of such a dastardly deed that he would launch all the nuclear weapons at his disposal, indiscriminately? The thought of seeing his homeland destroyed might provoke just such an irrational reaction. The point is that it is impossible to predict behavior in such a situation. To assume that rationality would survive is the height of folly; and rationality is the major assumption of deterrence strategy.

Another problem created by the proliferation of nuclear weapons is the possibility of a **catalytic war.** A small power might deliberately cause the two major powers to attack each other. One method would be to time the attack to coincide with a period of crisis between the two powers, and to fire nuclear missiles from a submerged submarine in international waters. If such an attack were aimed at the United States, there is a strong possibility that the president would have no recourse other than to attack Russia. The Cuban Missile Crisis of October 1962 might come to mind. In such a highly tense situation almost any incident could act as a tripwire, and a nuclear attack would almost surely trigger an immediate retaliation.

In the balance of power system multipolarity was stable and bipolarity unstable; but in the nuclear age bipolarity is much more stable than multipolarity. A nuclear attack in a bipolar system leaves no doubt in the attacker's mind that he will be identified and counterattacked. In a multipolar situation the attacker might feel he would not be identified and therefore might not be deterred. Thus, after the nuclear club reaches a certain size, nuclear weapons lose their deterrent value.

We have a detection system called the **ballistic missile early warning system (BMEWS),** which cannot be jammed as ordinary radar can. But it gives us only twenty minutes warning time and it cannot distinguish between a missile and a meteorite.

The United States has tried to minimize some of these dangers by taking unilateral measures that do not put us at any disadvantage. Planes that carry nuclear weapons have them disconnected in some manner so the bombs will not detonate if the plane crashes. The incidents at Palomares, Spain, in 1966 and in Greenland in 1968 put this precautionary measure to a test. Several years prior, however, an Air Force bomber crashed in North Carolina with a nuclear bomb aboard, and four of the five safety catches failed; fortunately, the last one held. This near miss led to the safer procedure now employed. However, the expansion of the nuclear club reduces the chances that all members will employ adequate safety measures.

Communications systems have been improved to diminish the possibility of human error or miscalculation of an enemy's intentions. The chances of a madman starting a nuclear war have also been substantially reduced by making it impossible for one person alone to launch a missile or drop a nuclear bomb from a plane; it takes at least two. Finally, we are not likely to escalate a limited war by using nuclear weapons, if our past history is any indication.

Yet a mechanical or human error can still occur; two madmen or one with a gun might still be able to start a nuclear war; there is no guarantee that in the future every leader whose country has nuclear weapons will resist the temptation to escalate a limited war; and the proliferation of nuclear weapons continues, thereby increasing the instability of the "balance of terror."

One of the dangers that Carl Sagan and other scientists warn about is "nuclear winter." Even a limited nuclear exchange could stir up too much dust for the sun's rays to penetrate, causing the whole planet to become a cold desert. Like dinosaurs, humans might become extinct.

The present international system also creates dysfunctions in the subsystems (nation–states). Consider its effects on the United States. It gives great power to certain pressure groups with a large stake in military expenditures. In his farewell address former President Eisenhower warned us of the growing power of the "military-industrial complex." As a result of the Cold War, an immense defense industry was established; and many of our best scientific minds were applied to military problems. This brain-drain used up talent that perhaps could better be used to solve other important problems.

The defense industries hire retired generals and admirals to act as lobbyists with the defense and service branches of our government. These lobbyists inform their former colleagues who are still active in the military about the latest plans for weapons and delivery systems. Each branch of the military supports the development of weapons

"Dr. Strangelove" (Stanley Kubrick, 1963) The film was an exposition of the madman theory of nuclear holocaust, a critique of the balance of terror system for which there is still no final answer.

"...and over on this side, citations from the military-industrial complex!" (*Grin and Bear It* by George Lichty, courtesy of Field Newspaper Syndicate)

systems that permit that branch to play a major role in our national defense. Quite often after the weapons are manufactured, the producer develops a military strategy that requires the use of these weapons and then notifies the particular branch of the military that will play the major role in that strategy, and the rest is easy.

In the process of mediating conflicting demands by the different military branches the Defense Department lets them all have some of the new weapons, in order to offend no one. Members of Congress are usually hesitant to appear "soft" on national defense so they approve the necessary appropriations. The defense industry reaps the profits, the military has new "toys," and the taxpayers foot the bill. Domestic programs are neglected as our leaders must choose between "guns" or "butter."

The current international system also facilitates the creation of a warfare state with the accompanying loss of freedom. Security requires secrecy and loyalty. Unfortunately, some people equate loyalty with complete acquiescence to all governmental policies. This can lead to curtailment of the right to dissent. As Arthur I. Waskow lucidly states: "If during the three short years of the Korean War the United States had to deal with MacArthurism and McCarthyism, what would be the effect of 25 or 50 years of situations like Korea?"[10]

In addition, even though the Cold War is over, defense expenditures now account for the largest single portion of our economic activity; and millions of people are employed in defense and related industries. Even if foreign policy considerations permit us to reduce defense spending we can not do so without creating an economic crisis. This is a terrible dilemma. Even in the new world order, military forces and defense industries are necessary. Another dilemma is that the more the world spends for nuclear armaments, especially if more countries become involved, the less secure everyone is. (See Table 25-2.)

Britain, France, and China do not have second-strike capability. In 1988, the French had 18 long-range land-based missiles, 96 sea-launched missiles, 93 nuclear bombs on aircraft, and 36 on carrier-based aircraft. In 1991, those plans had not changed. The British have a similar number of bombs in their mix of delivery systems, but no land-based missiles. The Chinese have over 300 nuclear weapons. The Russians can easily eliminate the subs and can also destroy most of the land-based missiles if they wanted to, although in the post-Soviet era this is highly unlikely. If the military or the Communists return to power, however, the Cold War could resume. It seems logical to conclude, therefore, that we need a new international system before the

Table 25-2
National Defense Expenditures (constant 1989 dollars)

Country	Per Capita (dollars)			Percent of GNP		
	1980	1984	1989	1980	1984	1989
United States	765	968	1,222	5.3	6.3	5.8
Soviet Union	893	914	1,077	12.8	12.6	11.7
Iraq	1,035	944	—	22.5	42.5	—
Oman	1,460	1,728	1,085	22.1	27.7	20.3
Israel	1,955	1,721	1,323	30.4	27.1	12.8
North Korea	237	256	295	22.6	22.6	20.0
Syria	319	405	186	16.9	22.4	11.6
Saudi Arabia	2,098	1,990	897	14.4	21.3	16.0
Egypt	67	104	67	9.2	13.5	5.0
Nicaragua	67	146	—	5.8	13.4	—
Canada	238	292	656	1.9	2.2	11.9
China	23	23	20	10.5	7.5	3.7
Taiwan	160	196	397	6.6	6.6	5.4
Cuba	143	155	131	6.5	5.9	3.9
East Germany	575	619	848	5.8	6.3	8.8
West Germany	347	360	544	3.3	3.3	2.8
France	375	394	628	4.0	4.1	3.7
Greece	203	260	309	5.5	7.2	5.9
Italy	153	171	360	2.4	2.7	2.4
Japan	84	102	231	0.9	1.2	1.0
South Korea	94	106	213	6.1	5.4	4.3
Norway	370	392	691	3.0	2.9	3.3
Spain	79	91	199	1.9	2.2	2.1
Sweden	329	340	574	3.1	3.1	2.6
Turkey	43	48	56	4.4	4.5	4.1
Great Britain	391	436	605	5.0	5.3	4.2
Czechoslovakia	427	478	534	5.4	5.8	6.8

Source: Statistical Abstract of the United States, 1988; 1992, p. 854.

rules which have created stability until now are either broken or become obsolete. Whatever system is developed, it will almost surely require extensive arms control measures, preferably disarmament. The outlook for disarmament improved when Mikhail Gorbachev became the Soviet leader in 1985. He exemplified a new generation that is tired of a low standard of living, rationing, and wasting scarce resources by projecting Soviet power throughout the world. With his successor Boris Yeltsin in power, the world may still experience a substantial reduction of armaments. The effectiveness of Gorbachev's policies of *glasnost* (openness) and *perestroika* (restructuring) led to his downfall, but Gorbachev was able to negotiate an arms control (IMF) treaty that reduces European intermediate-range missiles in an asymmetrical manner that benefits the West. And he reached the agreement with Ronald Reagan, perhaps the most vocal critic of the former Soviet system, characterizing it as "the evil empire."

The need for disarmament is greater every day. We cannot afford another transition period comparable to the one between the balance of power and the balance of terror systems, because existing weapons are so destructive. If we are aware of the dangers, perhaps we can create a new international system that is stable, and become the architects of a future world order in which peace and security can be achieved.

The bipolar balance of terror actually served us well. As things now stand the near future does not look too menacing, accidents and madmen notwithstanding. But the laws of probability are against everything going smoothly indefinitely. One of the destabilizing contingencies is bound to develop. That is why we must now take a serious look at disarmament. We must be realistic and hardnosed in our analysis, but we must explore possible future international systems that involve extensive disarmament. The disintegration of a stable balance of terror must not catch us without contingency plans.

In order to be realistic we must assume the continuation of conflict; that is, nation–states will periodically have conflicting national interests. We must focus, therefore, on the conflict-resolution function. It must be performed in a manner that will guarantee national security. The security function is vital because nations will not willingly give up long-established international practices unless it is absolutely clear that their security will therefore be enhanced. Nor will they give up their weapons very easily for the same reason. Ukraine is a case in point. As of November 1993, they had not signed the nuclear non-proliferation treaty. Finally, we must place major emphasis on stability.

If the point is reached in which a high level of armaments perpetuates a high degree of insecurity, nations might accept a lower level of weaponry if it leads unmistakably to greater security.

One last word before attacking the problem of disarmament. Peace has been maintained only through deterrence. The new international system cannot be based on any other principle. Every nation on earth must be deterred from making war upon another. National leaders come and go, and some of them will want to make war. They must be deprived of the means.

☐ Arms Control and Disarmament

Arms control includes any measure that limits the quantity or quality of weapons or defense procedures (fallout shelters, warning systems, antiballistic missile systems, and so forth), and also includes disarmament. Some theorists use the term **arms control** to cover anything that tends to limit or prevent conflict (for example, the "hot line" between Washington and Moscow). **Disarmament** refers specifically to a reduction of weapons and weapons delivery systems. Let us now examine the record.

The first disarmament conference in modern times was held at the Hague in 1899; since then there have been many, including a second Hague conference in 1908. What have been the results? The Washington Naval Treaty of 1922 and the London Naval Treaty of 1930 limited the number of certain types of naval vessels. These agreements were in force for just a few years, and their effect was negligible. In fact there was an increase in the production of other types of vessels not covered by the agreements. The only other instance of voluntary arms control until the 1960s was the Rush-Bagot agreement of 1817, limiting naval forces on Lake Champlain and the Great Lakes. That's it!

In the 1960s we managed to negotiate a few minor arms control measures: (1) The United States and the USSR agreed not to deploy weapons or forces in the Antarctic; (2) A limited nuclear test ban treaty was negotiated in 1963. However, some countries, including France and China, did not sign it. This treaty prohibits the testing of nuclear devices in the atmosphere, underwater, and in outer space, but permits underground testing; (3) Many nations also signed an agreement at the United Nations which outlawed nuclear weapons (not just testing) from outer space; and (4) a nuclear nonproliferation treaty was also ratified by a number of nations. The United States, the Soviet Union, and Great Britain agreed not to give nuclear weapons to other countries or to help them develop their own; and the nonnuclear signatories agreed to forsake nuclear weapons.

Of course some nations may develop nuclear weapons without relying on outside assistance; and there are many so-called near-nuclear powers that are capable of doing so. The **strategic arms limitations talks (SALT)** between the United States and the Soviet Union in 1972 merely established arms limitations which were higher than existing arms levels. And there is no guarantee that these limits will not be increased or that they will be enforced. The SALT II agreement was not

Disarmament
Soviet President
Gorbachev and former
U.S. President Reagan
sign a treaty in 1988
reducing intermediate
range missiles in
Europe.

ratified by the U.S. Senate in 1980. Had the U.S. signed, the Soviet Union could not have built up its strategic forces to its current level without violating the treaty. The U.S. had nothing to lose because it maintains strategic levels well below the limit agreed upon. The INF treaty requires the U.S. to dismantle 429 missiles, and the Soviets will dismantle 857 missiles with 1,667 warheads. The INF treaty has extensive verification provisions, but it does not require the destruction of warheads. The U.S. will still have 4,150 nuclear weapons in Europe. The U.S. and the new Russian government signed SALT II in 1992.

If our goal is to stabilize the current international system, we must prevent nuclear proliferation. But if our goal is to create a new system without "terror," we need substantial disarmament. One problem that has always plagued disarmament conferences is the technical problem of categories. Trying to measure the relative weights of troops, tanks, submarines, missiles, and so forth, is difficult indeed. This problem has bogged down many conferences. Another major obstacle to disarmament is the fact that before disarmament can begin it is necessary to compile a reliable inventory of existing stocks of weapons. This requires nations to make public important military secrets.

Intelligence gathering has become so sophisticated that secrets are difficult to conceal. Even a "closed" society such as the former Soviet Union was easily penetrated. Unbelievable as it may seem, our reconnaissance satellites can detect a postage stamp from 50 miles up. They can even quite often help us determine what is inside a building by its size and shape.[11] Other intelligence methods are used as well. The problem of categories can be overcome too, as will be demonstrated in a disarmament proposal discussed below. But first we want to deal with a few fundamental questions.

Basically, there are seven questions that any disarmament negotiators must deal with:

1. *Should disarmament be a one-step or a gradual process?* If disarmament takes place in one uninterrupted operation, it may actually create more international instability. Some countries may complete the process before others do, thereby placing themselves at a great disadvantage. No country can be allowed to maintain arms while others have disarmed. In order to avoid such a situation *it is best to disarm by stages over an extended period of time.* Arbitrarily, let us say we will disarm in ten stages over a five-year period. Each successive stage will not begin until all the participating countries have completed the previous one. If they have, disarmament can continue; if they have not, each country still has 90 percent of its original weapons and has not been placed in a terribly dangerous situation. In fact, the process can be reversed to achieve the original level of armaments. The current START treaties do not accomplish such systematic or comprehensive disarmament.

2. *Should disarmament be unilateral, multilateral, or universal?* That is, should we disarm by ourselves, regardless of what anyone else does? Should we include all the major powers? Or should all nations participate? Advocates of unilateral disarmament claim that our opponents are armed because we are. Therefore, if we disarm we will no longer pose a threat to them, so they too will disarm.

When one points out that other countries may not react in this manner, that they might decide the risk involved in attacking us would be acceptable, unilateralists are not in the least bit dismayed. They advocate a mass education program in passive resistance in conjunction with unilateral disarmament so that any conqueror will be forced to leave. The conquering nation would be expected to leave because without our cooperation it would not be able to occupy our country for very long.[12]

Without arguing the merits of this contention, the possibility that it might be mistaken should lead us to discount it, for if it is wrong, the price we would pay is great indeed. Obviously, if the object of disarming is to increase the stability of the international system we should not tempt other nations to attack us. *Disarmament must be universal.*

3. *Should there be inspection or not?* Anyone who is willing to undertake disarmament without some kind of inspection is an incurable optimist who is probably still saving tsarist war bonds and confederate money! If there is no inspection, disarmament is based on trust; and *if we trusted*

each other there would be no need to disarm. We need to disarm because we *don't* trust each other. Whether or not on-site inspection is necessary is a more reasonable question. However, so much is at stake that even with sophisticated spy satellites *on-site inspection is probably necessary.* Remember, we are trying to increase, not decrease, stability; so why take chances?

4. *Should we begin by reducing the level of armaments, or by settling political questions first?* Some say "the way to disarm is to disarm." Unfortunately, people, not weapons, cause international conflicts. It is necessary to reduce the level of hostilities if we want to avert another arms race. If we don't, as soon as two nations are in conflict they will begin to rearm. At first the level of destruction would be lower than it would have been before disarmament began, but eventually we would be right back where we started. But if we wait until we solve major international problems first, such as the division of Korea or the Middle East and Kashmir problems, disarmament will never take place.

   Both aspects must be dealt with simultaneously. As a stage-by-stage disarmament process begins, conferences must be set up to deal with each of the world's international disputes, major and minor. If progress occurs in either aspect, it will be easier to go forward in the other. The completion of the first stage of disarmament will ease tensions and perhaps make it easier to resolve one or two minor issues. If we resolve some issues it will facilitate a continuation of the disarmament process. Once progress begins the direction of international conflict resolution will be reversed. Once this process picks up momentum it will be difficult to stop, just as its opposite, hostilities and arms races, is hard to reverse.

5. *Should disarmament include nuclear weapons only, conventional weapons only, or both?* To disarm nuclear weapons only would take us back to the transition system we had in the first half of the twentieth century—a period in which the two most destructive wars in history took place; furthermore, a large-scale conventional war today would be worse because today's conventional weapons are much more destructive and we have more of them. But if we disarm only conventional weapons even more devastating wars could occur because small, tactical nuclear weapons have been developed which make nuclear war "feasible." The possibility of escalation to a full-scale nuclear war would be enormous because we already would have crossed the nuclear threshold.

   We might possibly retain just a limited number of ICBM's on each side,[13] but this would lead to a policy of "massive retaliation" and "brinksmanship." When John Foster Dulles was our Secretary of State under President Eisenhower, he advocated going to the brink of nuclear war if necessary to stop "Soviet aggression," by threatening them with

Table 25-3
The U.S.-USSR Strategic
Balance[a] 1989

Weapon Category	Estimates		Maximum Permitted Under SALT Accords		
	U.S.	USSR	U.S.	USSR	
Land-based long-range missiles (ICBM's)	1,000	1,373	1,054	1,618	1,408
Sea-based long-range missiles (SLBM's)	656	950	710	+ or + 740	950
Total offensive long-range missiles	(1,656)	(2,348)	(1,764)		(2,358)
Submarines equipped with nuclear missiles	35	62	44		62
Defensive missiles (ABM's)	under 50	over 60	100		100
Long-range heavy bombers	323	150	Not covered by SALT		
Deliverable warheads[c]	12,683	10,470	Not covered by SALT		

[a] SALT talks, which began in 1969, thus far have only established limits above existing weapons levels. They have not led to a reduction. If the world is to accept a stage-by-stage disarmament process the two superpowers must lead the way, since they are the only ones with huge arsenals of nuclear weapons. SALT I was signed in 1972. SALT II talks were completed, but the U.S. Senate did not ratify the treaty until 1992.
[b] U.S. and Soviet estimates are mid-1988.
[c] United States advantage is due to heavy MIRVing.
Sources: Statistical Abstract of the United States: 1988, p. 322; *1992*, p. 418; The Center for Defense Information, *The Defense Monitor*, Vol. XVII, Number 5, 1988.

massive retaliation. This is a very dangerous policy. If each side retains first-strike capability (the ability to attack without fear of retaliation), there is a great temptation to launch a preventive strike. When each side is faced with the certainty of suffering great devastation without being able to inflict "unacceptable damage" on the aggressor, a preventive nuclear strike becomes very tempting. This is the most unstable system imaginable. *Disarmament must include both nuclear and conventional forces.* Current treaties do not address both.

6. *Is disarmament alone enough, or should other measures be undertaken in conjunction with it?* It should be obvious from the previous discussions that *disarmament alone is not enough. Some method must be devised for policing a world of nations who often come into conflict with each other;* some technique must be developed to settle international disputes peacefully; and some way must be found to maintain a foolproof and permanent inspection system. An organization must be created that can oversee these processes without itself having the power to become a dictatorial force; and an equitable method of taxing nations to finance these operations must be formulated. This is indeed a tall order; but the alternative becomes more dangerous every day.

7. *Should disarmament be total or partial?* By "total" we mean disarming to a minimum level consistent with maintaining internal order. By "partial" we mean reducing the level of armaments significantly below that which is currently maintained by the superpowers and the other major powers. The answer to this question depends upon what international system we want to create to replace the balance of terror. Current disarmament treaties are partial, and they only deal with nuclear weapons.

☐ The Integrated Security System

Assume that the world has experienced a limited nuclear war; it may or may not have been caused accidentally. What is important is that it has had the effect on the nonparticipants (the participants did not survive) of revulsion at the thought that another such war might occur. They decide the only way to ensure the survival of the human race is to achieve total disarmament. They are now faced not only with the task of disarming in a safe, orderly, and realistic manner, but also of creating a new international system that will guarantee security and survival. How can they go about it? The following proposal is not perfect; but it is an example of the kind of thinking that is necessary if we are ever to disarm.

Disarmament

The disarmament process will entail the following steps:

1. Divide each country into 10 regions and assign a number from 1 to 10 to the regions of each country. Obviously, the regions in large countries will be bigger than the ones in smaller countries; however, the important factor at this stage is that there be an equal number of regions in every nation. It is also important to divide each country so that there is a relatively equal distribution of weapons among regions, even if some regions are geographically larger than others.
2. All foreign military bases must be evacuated and the military personnel returned to domestic soil. This includes all land and air forces.
3. Each country's naval forces must also be divided into 10 groups of relatively equal size and assigned numbers from 1 to 10.
4. We must then recruit and train an International Corps of Disarmament Inspectors. It must be composed of people from all nations, representing all political and economic philosophies and systems. Individual governments do not select them. All eligible people from all countries are programmed into a computer and those who are to serve are selected at random.

U.N. Peace-keeping Forces
United Nations peace-keeping forces patrol the streets of Vitez, Bosnia.

Preference is given to those who speak one of the official UN languages; but others can be given language training. All are then trained in arms production and disarmament techniques. After training, they are placed in mixed groups and sent to areas other than their own countries. They are stationed around the periphery of all regions in all countries.

5. A number from 1 to 10 is then chosen by lottery. Whatever number is chosen signifies which region in every country will be simultaneously disarmed. All the inspectors surrounding these regions then converge upon them and oversee the process of disarmament. They have been given maps and information concerning the location of weapons and weapons production centers. They follow a master disarmament plan that has been worked out in advance for each region. After, let us say, region three has been disarmed in all countries a new number is chosen by lottery and the procedure is repeated. This is done until all regions in all countries have been disarmed. Naval forces are disarmed simultaneously at the same rate (10 percent in each stage).

6. The entire process is coordinated by a universal disarmament agency of the United Nations. The UN must have the power to tax every country a certain percentage of its gross national product to finance operations.

7. It is necessary to train the inspectors so that they can dismantle weapons-producing factories as well as the arms themselves. At first many of the weapons will be retained by the UN itself. Some weapons and factories will be permitted, but the exact number of

factories and the amount of production are predetermined. This is one of the stickiest parts of the plan. The Inspector Corps must stay in every country permanently, but the personnel should be rotated to minimize the chance of complicity. You may think a lot of cheating will occur, but bear in mind that the inspectors will be checking on each other; since they are putting in just a four- to six-year hitch, they are still committed to their respective nation–states.

International Police Force

In order to deal with international conflicts, it is necessary to establish a police force to separate the belligerents in case hostilities break out between countries. In all probability only border disputes can erupt in violence because all nations will have been disarmed to a level that will enable them to maintain internal order but deprive them of any additional weapons. Consequently the International Police Force need not be large. Its only job will be to stop any fighting that may develop. Under no circumstances can there be intervention in cases of civil war. Each country has given up only the right to use war as an instrument of foreign policy; no country gives up the right to determine its internal affairs. The current practice of countries fomenting rebellion in neighboring countries will cease because no country will have the armaments to spare for such ventures. To do so would leave a country without the means with which to maintain internal order. We would never again have an ambiguous situation such as Vietnam where some people claim there was a civil war and others claim the war began because of outside interference.

In order to minimize the possibility of the world police force "taking over" the world, we advocate a decentralized force. We propose twelve regional police units instead of one central force. The members are to be recruited universally in the same manner as the Disarmament Corps and are to be mixed thoroughly by economic and political philosophies and systems as well. Officers may serve eight years and enlisted men four years. We do not want to take chances by creating a professional army. We want civilians who consider serving in the police force an interruption of their lives, not their life's goal. The members should also be rotated in staggered two-year tours of duty. The reason for rotating military and inspector units is obvious. It helps prevent the development of close ties with the natives that might lead to corruption.

Twelve military bases, occupied by the world police force, will be strategically located throughout the world. They should be located near the major trouble spots, if possible, but sufficiently dispersed to enable each unit to reach any trouble spot quickly. They must have enough power to deal with any contingency. Actually they would probably have little to do. No country will have enough power to wage either a large-scale war or one far from home. Consequently the world police force would probably just have to separate two neighboring countries until the cause of the conflict is peacefully resolved. This brings us to the third part of the plan.

World Court

Conflicts are inevitable; international conflicts are no exception. There will be times when national interests clash so profoundly that states will be willing to fight for their interests. In order to prevent this from occurring, we need to establish techniques that will ensure the peaceful resolution of international disputes. Whenever two or more states are involved in a dispute, they should be provided with a neutral setting in which to iron out their differences by themselves within a ninety-day period. If they fail, they should be forced to accept one or more disinterested mediators to assist them during an additional ninety-day period. If these six months of negotiations prove fruitless, the matter must then be submitted to the World Court for compulsory adjudication. Fifteen judges, chosen from a list of prominent jurists compiled for such services, should hear the case with advocates on both sides pleading for their client states. The court's decisions should be binding and enforced by the international police force under the aegis of the United Nations. The current World Court has no real power. If world peace is to become a reality, the World Court must be given sufficient power to resolve international conflicts peacefully.

☐ Alternate International Systems

This proposal is not foolproof. It is no more than a point of departure for discussion. There are surely many difficult points that were glossed over. But this plan does create an international system that performs the security and conflict-resolution functions. The rules, if adhered to, would integrate the system, establish goals that are permissible in international affairs, and also the means for achieving them. Once established it would be very difficult to break the rules. Many precautions have been taken to make the system as stable as possible; and if by some chance something goes wrong, it would not lead to a nuclear holocaust.

Of course none of this will take place as long as nation–states believe they can survive with national armed forces, and use war to implement national policies. We are only suggesting one way in which disarmament *might* be accomplished while maintaining a stable international system *if* (and this is a big if) nations ever decide to pursue disarmament seriously.

A second alternative is to establish a world government system. The disarmament process would be similar but the international system would be modeled after national political systems. Unfortunately this would not necessarily be the peaceful utopia some believe it would be. The United States had a government when the Civil War occurred. It was a bloody affair; and a world government would be just as susceptible to civil wars as we were; perhaps more so because there would be even greater differences among the constituent parts.

Another problem involved with world government is deciding what form it would take. Its advocates usually expect it to be a parliamentary democracy. But this is not the form of government most countries have today. A third and related problem is the difficulty of establishing executive, legislative, and judicial branches and determining the power of nation–states vis-à-vis the world government. Actually the proposal we made earlier is simple compared to establishing a world government. The integrated security system has no jurisdiction or control over internal affairs. The only thing the states would no longer be able to do is wage war.

However, if simplicity is what we seek, a collective security system is best. It only requires partial disarmament and nation–states can continue to maintain their own armed forces. For these reasons, though, it is also the easiest to destabilize. We can be sure every state will respond when called upon to wage war against an aggressor only by placing national military units under UN control. This may be the most feasible alternative because it involves fewer drastic departures from current practices; but the dim record of past attempts does not augur well for any future attempt to create a collective security system.

Whatever disarmament process is employed must contain safeguards against cheating; whatever international system is created must guarantee national security; it must establish a mechanism for resolving international conflicts peacefully; and it must provide police power to enforce the rule against making war.

The balance of terror has been modified with the end of the Cold War. But the nuclear weapons that existed in the former Soviet Union are still there, only spread out among the four former Soviet republics that are now independent states: Russia, Ukraine, Belarus and Kazakhstan. The hostility toward the U.S. is no longer present among those in power in these new states, but it is possible that those who do not wish us well will seize power in one or more of these countries in the future. The balance of terror still exists, only it is multipolar.

On November 2, 1993, President Boris Yeltsin approved Russia's first post-Soviet military doctrine. It says that no nation is considered an enemy. There will be no more attempts by the military to export Communism around the world. However, abandoning a longstanding Soviet policy, Russia now is ready to launch nuclear missiles in a first strike if it or its allies are attacked with conventional weapons.

Consequently, it is in the best interests of the United States to

Russian President
Standing in front of an image of Lenin, the founding father of Russian Communism, is Boris Yeltsin, the first elected leader in Russia.

pursue disarmament vigorously. As of January, 1993 the United States had 12,646 nuclear warheads. Under START I, signed in 1991, the U.S. agreed to reduce its warheads to 8,556. Under START II, signed in January, 1993, the number of nuclear warheads is scheduled to be reduced to 3,500 by the year 2003. The Russians are supposed to follow a similar timetable and similar numbers. Ukraine is not complying (as of November, 1993) with its part of the agreement, and if they do not, the Russians are not bound by the agreed reductions. Ukraine has 176 ICBM's and 40 nuclear-armed bombers.

In the meantime, a new tripolar, or trilateral, international system is emerging. However, this competition between the United States, Japan and Western Europe is economic, not nuclear. The North American Free Trade Agreement (NAFTA) was ratified by the U.S., Canada, and Mexico in 1993. The group will have virtually the same amount of economic trade and production as the European Community (EC).

Since World War II, because of the Soviet threat to Europe, Asia and elsewhere, the mutual security concerns of the allied powers were so great that economic conflicts with the United States were of secondary importance. No one challenged U.S. world economic leadership. After the Cold War ended, Japan and Western Europe feel free to challenge the United States on the world economic stage. Regional economic security systems might become more important in the future than a continued U.S.-led global security system. The absence of a common threat to our major allies gives them more confidence to risk policy disputes with the United States.

According to the Berkeley Roundtable on the International Economy (BRIE),[14] there are three possible world scenarios: 1) *managed multilateralism*, which is a continuation of the post-World War II system, but led by the United States, Japan, and Western Europe, instead of just the U.S.; 2) *benign regionalism*, in which the big three become primarily bloc-oriented, while maintaining a lower level of global trade than at present; and 3) *twenty-first-century mercantilism*, which emphasizes regional economic self-sufficiency and intense rivalry among the big three. They believe it will be a combination of the first and third scenarios.

The world, however, is too complex, and any speculation regarding an emerging international system cannot ignore the Middle East, Latin America and SubSaharan Africa. Any new system will be more decentralized. Hence, we now turn to an analysis of regionalism.

☐ Regional Subsystems

We have been dealing with the world as a global social system, with nation-states, international organizations, and multi-national corporations as the units that interact within this framework, while recognizing the primacy of nation-states. It is also analytically useful to examine some of the major regional subsystems within that global system. International subsystems can be military (the North Atlantic Treaty Organization), economic (the European Community), ideological (the communist countries), or regional (based on geographic proximity). We will focus on the latter.

In order for a geographical area to be considered a regional subsystem, it must contain the following characteristics:

1. It must include two or more nation-states. There cannot be a system comprised of just one unit. There must be two or more, interacting with each other.

2. The member states must be geographically close to one another. (Superpowers are exceptions. They can be players in any region of the world.)

3. The members interact with each other more frequently and more intensely than they do with non-member states.

4. Internal and external observers and actors recognize the area as a distinctive regional subsystem (e.g., countries within and outside of the Middle East consider the area to be a regional subsystem).

5. Change in one part of the subsystem affects the other parts and the subsystem as a whole. (Economic problems in the Soviet Union caused Gorbachev to give up the East European empire in 1989, and the collapse of the Soviet Union itself in 1991 further changed the East European subsystem, which had been *hegemonial* since 1947.)

Regional subsystems are both actors and settings in international relations. Therefore, they must be analytically treated separately from both nation-states and international systems. Each subsystem has unique circumstances, and its patterns of interaction can be placed within a classification scheme.

□ Regional Subsystem Typology

Hegemonial

One country dominates the foreign policy of the other countries in the region. At one extreme, that hegemony, or domination, can take the form of troop occupation and total control of the other countries in the region by the dominant power. At the other end of the spectrum, the hegemonial power may simply exercise a veto over its neighbors' foreign policy because they fear to take any action that might antagonize the giant power in their midst. In between, domination may take many forms.

In any event, there are many things the weaker countries cannot or dare not do. They might do some things that antagonize the hegemonial power to a point, if they have the support of another world superpower, but even then, there are many restrictions because they cannot exceed certain limits as the risk is too great.

The Western Hemisphere

The Western hemisphere is a hegemonial regional subsystem, in which the dominant power is the United States. Let us examine the economic, military and political reasons why this is so.

Economic Reasons. The U.S. has the highest GNP (Gross National Product) in the world, although on a per capita basis it ranks behind Japan and several European countries. Nevertheless, it dwarfs the other western hemisphere nations.

Even Canada, with the fifth highest GNP in the world and the ninth highest per capita GNP, is, to some extent, economically dominated by the United States. A significant portion of Canadian industry is American-owned. Many industrial firms in Canada are subsidiaries of large American corporations. When the U.S. suffers from high unemployment or inflation, Canada does also. With the ratification of NAFTA by Canada, Mexico and the United States, the American and Canadian economies will be even more interdependent.

As for Latin America, the economic gap with the United States is even greater. All the countries south of the U.S. are in various stages of underdevelopment. Many of them have monocultures—their economies rely primarily on one agricultural crop, like sugar, coffee, cocoa or bananas or on an extractive industry, like copper, tin or petroleum. They receive much-needed hard currency by exporting these commodities. Between two-thirds and three-fourths of their exports are bought by the United States. They also buy a similar percentage of their imports from the U.S. This exchange gives the United States great leverage when pressuring these countries, especially the poorer ones, to go along with U.S. policies. Trade sanctions, such as not buying a country's sugar quota, or not selling them spare parts for American-made machinery, can have a devastating effect on their economies.

Many of the Latin American countries lack sufficient capital investment to achieve an economic growth rate necessary to lift the people out of poverty. In some cases, the country is so poor that it does not have a sufficient surplus above what is needed to fulfill the basic needs of the majority of the people. In other cases, the countries have the capital, but it is concentrated in the hands of a very few rich families that often invest in safer economies in Europe or North America.

There are three ways these countries can obtain the needed capital: from private investors (usually major corporations), governments (mostly from the U.S.), and international lending agencies (like the World Bank and the Interamerican Development Bank).

Some large U.S. corporations have intervened in the internal affairs of countries in which they have invested. For example, the United Fruit Company was a formidable power in the Central American countries. In Chile, International Telephone and Telegraph played a role in toppling President Salvador Allende in 1973. At the behest of American corporations, the United States sent the Marines into Haiti, the Dominican Republic, Cuba, and several Central and South American countries for three decades after 1898. Thus, some Latin American countries, especially the smaller ones, have compromised their sovereignty by allowing large corporations to invest in their countries. This should not surprise us, because large corporations have a great impact on the U.S. political process as well.

Government-to-government assistance in Latin America comes primarily from the United States. However, U.S. economic aid always has strings attached. For example, if a country wants a loan for an irrigation project, it will have to buy the earth-moving equipment from a U.S. corporation, even if it can buy it for less money from another country.

If they seek a loan from an international lending agency like the World Bank or the Interamerican Development Bank, they find that it is very difficult to acquire the loan if the United States does not approve. In 1970, the IDB approved a multi-million dollar agricultural loan to Chile. Before the aid was received, Chile elected a Marxist president, Salvador Allende. The loan application was re-evaluated, and not re-approved until Allende was overthrown by the Chilean military (with an assist from the CIA and ITT) in 1973.

It is easy to see how the United States can exercise hegemony in Latin America through economic pressure. Now let us examine the military reasons for U.S. dominance.

Military Reasons. Militarily, the United States is the most powerful country in the world. It is also the only nuclear power in the western hemisphere. Canada has the second most powerful military in the west, but it is much weaker than that of the United States. It is a member of NATO, the military alliance headed by the United States; and Canada's military is closely linked to the U.S. military through the North American Command. The only potential enemy that Canada had was the Soviet Union, a country against which it could not defend itself.

Nuclear missiles sent over the North Pole could reach Canada very quickly. An attack from Siberia through the Bering Straits was also possible, however unlikely. Their only defense against Russia was a retaliation by the United States. The U.S. also maintains its ballistic missile early warning system (BMEWS) in Canada. Thus, relying on the protective military umbrella of the United States places Canada in a subordinate position in their bilateral relations.

Looking south of the U.S. border, the military contrast is even more stark. All the Latin American countries are significantly weaker militarily than either Canada or the United States. Through the Monroe Doctrine, articulated by President James Monroe in 1823, the United States warned the rest of the world that the western hemisphere was no longer open to colonization. Backed by Great Britain, the United States was able to prevent any of the great powers of the 19th century from attacking any Latin American country.

With the beginning of American imperialism overseas in 1898, the United States frequently intervened militarily in the internal affairs of

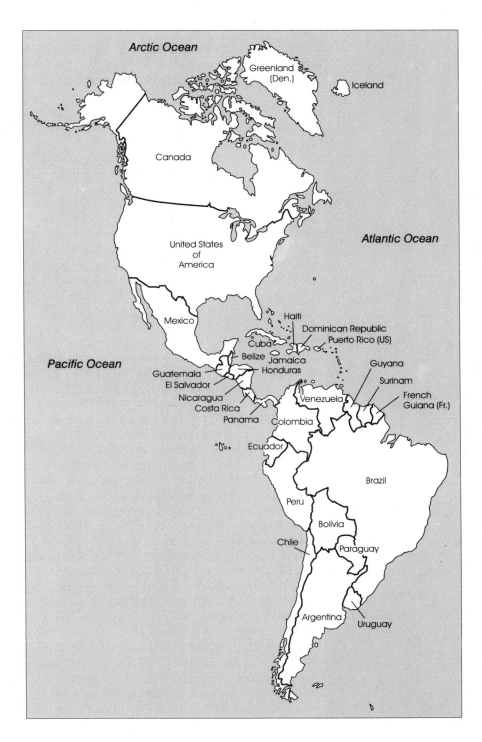

Map 25-1   The Western Hemisphere, 1994

Latin American countries, even in larger countries like Mexico and Venezuela. In 1965 President Lyndon Johnson sent the Marines into the Dominican capital, Santo Domingo, President Reagan invaded Grenada in 1982, and President Bush sent troops into Panama in 1991.

The U.S. provides military assistance to many Latin American countries, and in some cases maintains a military presence to train the native military units in using and maintaining weapons, most of which are manufactured by U.S. corporations. Furthermore, some Latin American military leaders were educated in U.S. military schools; some have even graduated from our military academies. Consequently, many of them maintain close ties to the U.S. military.

Latin American countries rarely fight each other. The role of the military, therefore, has been to preserve the status quo, and to defend the political and economic interests of the ruling elite in their countries. They are used very often to fight against guerrillas, dissidents and others who oppose the government in power. They have very little experience in defending themselves against foreign military forces. Hence, they have relied also on the protective military umbrella of the United States.

Political Reasons. The more politically unstable a country is, the more vulnerable it is to foreign influence and intervention. The U.S. has such a stable political system that it has remained intact despite enormous stresses. The U.S. had a civil war in the 19th century, two world wars and two Asian wars in the 20th century, one of which caused an intense polarization between supporters and opponents of the war.

The U.S. also suffered three major economic depressions in the 19th century, and the worst one in our history in the 1930s. We also had great corruption in the White House that came to light in the administrations of Ulysses Grant, Warren Harding and Richard Nixon. Yet, the democracy remained solid. We have never had an attempted military coup, nor have we ever missed an election, even in the middle of WWII, when Great Britain, the mother of modern democracies, postponed its national elections until after the war. The U.S. has a very stable political system. In Latin America, on the other hand, there has been a great deal of political instability. At least eight countries have had over twenty constitutions, and one country, Bolivia, has had 211 presidents in 175 years, only one of whom was allowed to finish his term of office. Such political instability makes many Latin American countries very vulnerable to foreign penetration.

Given the political, economic, and military factors mentioned above, it is clear that the United States almost could not help being the hegemonial power in the western hemisphere, even if it did not want to be. Anything we do or do not do has serious repercussions throughout the hemisphere. But, in fact, the United States has done a great deal over the years to ensure its dominance in this region. If, as we have stated, the U.S. is the hegemonial power in the western hemisphere, how could Fidel Castro have created a communist totalitarian dictatorship, militarily allied to the Soviet Union, 90 miles from Key West? Does Cuba constitute an exception to U.S. hegemony?

When Fidel Castro began to nationalize American and other corporations, and otherwise radicalize Cuba in 1960, President Dwight Eisenhower began applying economic pressure on the regime by cutting off the sugar quota and not selling spare parts for American automobiles and machinery. However, Nikita Khruschev bailed out Castro by buying Cuba's sugar and providing the country with Czechoslovakian machinery. The United States would not start a war with the Soviet Union, a nuclear power, just because they were trading with Cuba. Thus, Castro embraced Communism as the only means to perpetuate himself in power.

However, this does not mean that Castro is not restricted in his actions. He sent troops to fight in Africa, in Angola and Ethiopia. But, despite the fact that Cuba had the third or fourth most powerful military force in the Western Hemisphere, Castro has not dared to send Cuban troops to fight in any Caribbean or Central or South American country. He has trained guerillas from several Latin American countries and served as a conduit to supply them with Russian weapons, *but he could not send his troops to fight in this hemisphere*. If he did, his actions would have precipitated a strong U.S. military response that would have jeopardized his political power. Hence, there is much that Cuba cannot do because it is in the western hemisphere, a hegemonial regional subsystem dominated by the United States.

Eastern Europe

From 1947 to 1989 Eastern Europe was also a hegemonial regional subsystem. The dominant power was the Soviet Union and the other members were Hungary, Poland, Czechoslovakia, Romania, Bulgaria, and East Germany. World War II significantly weakened the European countries economically and militarily. The Soviets emerged from the war with a vast military supremacy. In fighting against Nazi Germany, Soviet troops passed through many of these countries. When the war ended some troops remained. Communism was then imposed on these countries by Soviet troops and tanks. There was no way for the conquered countries to defend themselves.

After World War II, the victorious powers divided Germany into four sectors, to be occupied by England, France, the United States, and the Soviet Union. The Soviet-occupied sector became East Germany. The three allied democracies eventually left and their combined sectors became West Germany, an independent country. By scavenging East

Germany, sometimes transporting entire factories to the Soviet Union on railroad cars, taking even the pipes in the ground, the Russians rebuilt their own country.

Western Europe was also weakened by the war, and could not prevent the Russians from taking over Eastern Europe. In fact, they were worried about being taken over themselves. That is why they turned to the United States to defend them from a possible Soviet attempt to expand their empire to Western Europe.

For its part, the United States had long been an isolationist country, concerned with its internal affairs, unwilling to get involved in "entangling alliances" (a policy begun by George Washington and Thomas Jefferson). In 1947, President Harry Truman was faced with three alternatives. He could continue the policy of isolationism, thereby leaving Western Europe defenseless. This was not a viable option. He could attack Soviet troops in Eastern Europe and try to "liberate" the area. This could have started World War III, and thus was not an appealing option either.

Instead, he chose to take George Kennan's advice, and put in place a policy of "containment." i.e., to not attack the Soviets, but to not allow them to take another inch of territory in Europe. Thus NATO was created to protect Western Europe (our first entangling alliance in peacetime), the Marshall Plan, the largest and most successful foreign aid plan in history (to rebuild Western Europe's economies), was negotiated, and the Point Four Program (to give military and/or economic aid to underdeveloped countries threatened by communism) was developed. Containment prevented further Soviet expansion in Europe, but it allowed the Eastern European hegemonial system to exist. The alternatives, however, were not acceptable.

Soviet hegemony was much more intensely pursued and institutionalized than was U.S. hegemony. The Warsaw Pact gave the Russians much more control over the East European military than that exercised by the United States in NATO. In the latter, each country has its own independent military. In the Warsaw Pact the Russians had political commissars in charge of political indoctrination in all the East European military units. The same control was exercised in COMECON, the Soviet's economic common market, which, in addition to Eastern Europe, included Cuba, Vietnam and North Korea. The Russians made systemwide production decisions.

The collapse of the Soviet Union in 1991 followed the dismantling of their empire in 1989. The Warsaw Pact and COMECON no longer exist. The East European Regional Subsystem, including the former Soviet Union, is now in a state of transition, as are the individual countries. Some of the countries want to join the West European economic community, but are not likely to be accepted in this century. Internal problems in some of the former Soviet republics and in the former

Soviet-dominated countries make it difficult to predict what type of regional subsystem will emerge in this area.

Integrative

An integrative regional subsystem has five characteristics:

1. The member states are in the process of *voluntarily* integrating economically, militarily and politically.
2. There is no dominant or hegemonial power in the region.
3. The members are not divided into rival blocs or factions.
4. There is no great hostility among the members toward each other, and no extremely divisive issues in the region, although there certainly are differences of opinion on issues, and competing interests.
5. The members have given up war as a method for resolving disputes among themselves.

Western Europe

Western Europe has the only integrative regional subsystem in the world. We are referring here to the twelve members of the European Community (EC). The European Common Market was created in 1958 by Italy, France, Germany, and the Benelux countries: Belgium, The Netherlands and Luxemburg. In 1972 Britain, Denmark and Ireland joined what was then known as the European Economic Community (EEC). Greece became a member in 1982, and Spain and Portugal joined in 1986. The Single European Act of 1987 created the integrated customs union, which was designed to integrate the 12 economies to a much greater extent than had been envisioned in 1958. Finally, in December, 1991 the members signed the Maastricht Treaty, committing to even further integration. The difference between the former hegemony in Eastern European economic integration and the integrative system in Western Europe is that the former was forced upon the others by a superpower, and the latter is a voluntary integration by sovereign states.

There is no hegemonial power in Western Europe. England and France have small stockpiles of nuclear weapons, and Germany has the largest conventional military force in the region. It also has the most potent economy, which is the driving economic force in the region. Although the rivalry between France and Germany led to three wars between them since 1870, including both world wars in the twentieth century, they have buried the hatchet and today have very close relations. Other wars plagued Europe in the eighteenth and nineteenth centuries. In fact, the balance of power system relied upon war to maintain a balance. Now there is no intense rivalry or antagonism among the EC members, and they have certainly given up war as a method for resolving disputes among themselves.

The most interesting turn of events is the high degree of economic integration taking place among the twelve members. They have abolished all tariffs. The entire region has completely free international trade. Citizens of any of the twelve countries can work in any other country. They can travel within the region without a passport. College degrees from any of the member states are recognized in all of the countries. Most importantly, by 1999, the EC-12 is scheduled to have a single currency (the ECU), and a single central banking system located in Frankfurt, Germany.

The member states are also militarily allied, and to some degree, integrated through their common membership in NATO. Each member had to commit certain military units to the alliance. As the only country that could challenge the Soviet Union militarily, and serve as a deterrent to a Soviet takeover of Western Europe during the cold war, the United States has been the undisputed leader of NATO forces. With the disintegration of the Soviet Union, the threat that led to the creation of NATO no longer exists. Its mission is now more political than military, and the leadership will undoubtedly be more widely dispersed. Nonetheless, the members have been reluctant to give up this military relationship. They are in the process of redefining NATO's mission.

Political integration is more difficult to achieve, and there have been some setbacks along the way, but political unification of some sort will probably take place by the year 2000. The United States of Europe is more likely to be a loose confederation, but an integrated polity is probable in the future. There are a number of reasons why political unification is probable:

1. It is difficult to maintain the high degree of economic integration expected by the end of the century, while maintaining twelve separate political entities. The high standard of living of these affluent nations is best secured by a unified free market whose population equals or exceeds that of Japan and the United States combined.

2. The chances of military conflicts in the future are virtually eliminated by political unification. A common foreign policy is planned, based on common national interests.

3. The common European culture, albeit with national variations, is an integrating force. Traveling through Europe, one is struck by the large number of multilingual people, and the similarity of cultural patterns. In every city people are out late at night in the central cities, perhaps sitting at a sidewalk cafe on the Left Bank in Paris, the Piazza Navona in Rome, the Plaza Mayor in Madrid, or the Plaka in Athens; or visiting

London's Trafalgar Square. One sees people taking two to three hour lunches, stopping on the way home from work at a pub/tasca/taverna, etc., drinking uzo/schnappes/sangria/wine, etc. In the month of August the native population dwindles in Athens/Madrid/Rome, and elsewhere as a large percent of the population, even the poor, spends the entire month at the beach.

4. The countries are much smaller than the United States. All of Western Europe fits into the Southern United States, with room left over. It is possible in the U.S. to drive on a superhighway in Florida, Texas, or elsewhere for eight hours and still be in the same state. In some parts of Europe one could drive through portions of three or four countries in the same amount of time. The Europeans go on "holiday" in each other's countries often, since they are all interconnected by excellent railroad systems, airlines, and superhighways. British and German tourists visit the Greek island of Corfu in droves. Scandinavians, as well as Germans and Britons can be found in large numbers also in Majorca and other Spanish islands. Southern France is another mecca for European tourists.

5. They all have similar political systems: parliamentary democracies. They also have similar political parties. In most countries one can find Social Democratic, Christian Democratic, Conservative, and other similar political parties.

6. The European Political Union is designed to forge a common foreign and security policy among the twelve nations. The European Commission is designated to regulate public health, education, agriculture and the environment. Each nation's current veto power will slowly diminish and eventually disappear. The Social Charter is designed to standardize health and workers' safety conditions. Members of the European Parliament are elected separately in each country, not sent by the existing governments. There is a policy to try to equalize the standard of living between the richer countries of Northern Europe and the relatively poorer countries in the South through direct economic aid.

7. For two-and-a-half centuries, Western Europe was the center of world power. After World War II these countries became second-rate military powers as the United States and the Soviet Union became military co-chairs of the world. With the rise of the Japanese economy, the U.S. and Japan became the economic co-chairs. The only way for the Europeans to regain their former pre-eminence, or at least parity with these countries, is to unify. They will do it because it is in each country's best interests.

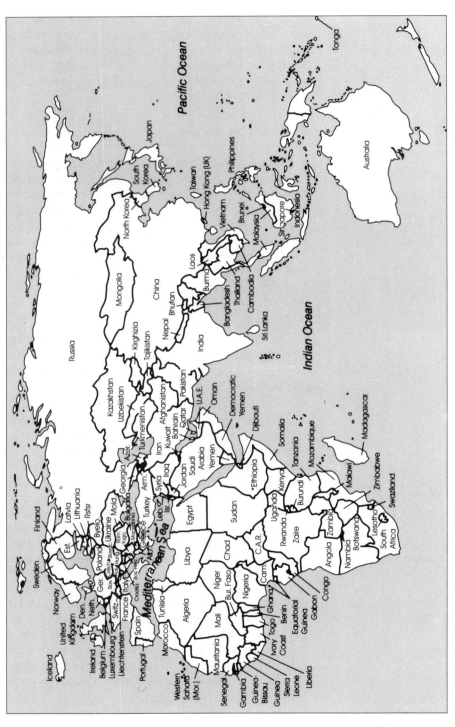

Map 25-2 The Eastern Hemisphere, 1994

8. Many EC members feel that the best way to make sure there will not be a resurgence of militarism and expansionism in Germany is to integrate the Germans completely with the rest of Europe. Thus, it would be counterproductive for any future German governments to engage in hostile acts against other Europeans. The EC also wants to benefit from the German economic engine which is the biggest and most efficient in the region.

On the other hand there have been problems, as periodically one country or another in the EC has failed to ratify the Maastricht Treaty. However, other wealthy European nations, members of the European Free Trade Association (EFTA), have expressed an interest in joining, and some have actually applied. It is possible that by the end of the century the EC will include Switzerland, Austria, Norway, Sweden, Finland, and other high-income countries, not currently members.

By the year 2000 there is a good chance that there will be a United States of Europe. It might not include all twelve current EC members, it might include all, or it might even include some of the EFTA nations. Germany and France will most likely be a part of it. They started the process in 1958, and they have pushed harder than other members for political centralization.

Rigid (Active) Bipolar

This type of regional subsystem has four characteristics:

1. Member states are divided into two rival blocs.
2. The rivalry is characterized by a great deal of hostility.
3. The hostility is caused primarily by one issue that seems impossible to resolve.
4. Warfare breaks out frequently in the region.

The Middle East

The best example of a rigid bipolar system is the Middle East. The two rival blocs have been Israel, on the one hand, and most of the Arab and other Moslem states on the other. As is well-known, this region has been marked by a great deal of hostility and frequent warfare. The issue that seemed impossible to resolve was the Palestinian question.

The area known as Palestine, in which Moslems and Jews lived side-by-side for centuries, was part of the British empire. When the United Nations created the independent state of Israel in 1948, one-and-one-half million Arabs fled because, they said, they did not want to be second-class citizens in their own homeland. Fighting has occurred on a daily basis, and two major wars were fought between Israel and Egypt in 1967 and 1973. Each time Israel was victorious and expanded into occupied territories: the West Bank, the Gaza strip, and the Golan

The Middle East
Israeli soldiers question a Palestinian in East Jerusalem.

Heights. This has been a bone of contention with Jordan, Egypt and Syria.

Both sides have valid positions. On the Israeli side, the contention is that Jews need a national homeland. Judaism began in that very site thousands of years ago. In 70 A.D., Roman soldiers made most of the Jews leave the area. This began the Jewish diaspora—the history of the "wandering Jew." Although they migrated to many countries, the largest number eventually settled in Spain, Germany, Russia and other East European countries. Wherever they concentrated, they faced great discrimination.

The Spanish inquisition burned Jews at the stake, and in 1492 Sephardic (Spanish) Jews were kicked out of the country. In Russia the Romanov tsars were very anti-semitic, especially Alexander III who ruled in the 1880s. That is why two million Russian Jews fled to America between 1880 and 1920. The Holocaust, during the Nazi period in Germany, however, dwarfed all other discrimination faced by the Jews elsewhere, as Hitler murdered six million of the twelve million Jews in the world at the time.

When World War II ended, and the gruesome discovery of the Nazi concentration camps and the gas ovens became known, the remaining Jews said "never again!" Never again would they turn the other cheek. Never again would they face the spectacle of a shipful of Jews who fled Germany being turned away at U.S., Cuban, and European ports. The feeling that Jews needed a homeland that would welcome Jews from anywhere in the world intensified. And where better than in the same region where Judaism began, and where many main religious sites are located.

The Palestinian Arabs have an equally valid claim to that territory. That is where Mohammed created the Islamic religion. That is where their religious sites are located. That is where their people have lived for thousands of years, side-by-side with the Jews, sometimes peacefully and sometimes not so peacefully. This conflict is not like a Hollywood movie with a clearcut division between good guys and bad guys. That is what has made the situation so difficult to resolve.

The United States has tried to be the "honest broker" in the region, remaining friendly with both sides, and trying to maintain the peace. Henry Kissinger started the peace process between Israel and Egypt, a process that was finalized by Jimmy Carter. The president was able to bring Anwar Sadat, the Egyptian president, and Menachem Begin, the Israeli leader, together to sign a peace treaty. In their younger days, both men had fought against the other's country. Begin was the leader of the Likud Party, the most hardline major political Party in Israel. This was a great diplomatic achievement for President Carter.

In 1993, with the Labor Party in power, the Israelis reached an agreement with Yasir Arafat, the leader of the Palestine Liberation Organization (PLO). It remains to be seen if this will lead to a long-lasting peace in the area. The Israelis are willing to return the Gaza strip and the West Bank, but not the Golan Heights.

The Middle East is wracked by other hostilities. The eight-year war between Iraq and Iran left over a million casualties. The Iraqi invasion of Kuwait led to the Gulf War in 1991. Saddam Hussein, the Iraqui leader, was developing a nuclear, chemical, and biological warfare capability. The Gulf War set him back temporarily, but as of this writing he is trying again.

At different times Syria and Libya have fomented terrorist activities in the region. The fact that the major portion of known oil reserves in the world is located in this region and many countries are dependent on that oil contributes to the volatility of the region.

South Asia

South Asia has also been a rigid bipolar subsystem. This area was part of the British Empire as well. When the British gave the people their independence, they separated Hindu India from Moslem Pakistan to minimize conflict. However, East Pakistan was separated from West Pakistan by 900 miles of India. The hostility between the two rival countries is very great, and there have been many wars, although in recent years the fighting has been subdued.

The issue that seems most difficult to resolve is the northern Indian state of Kashmir, where 80 percent of the population is Moslem, but the government is Hindu. Periodically, fighting breaks out between the government and the Moslem population, and many of the latter are killed. Then Pakistan comes to the assistance of their Moslem brothers and sisters, and there is another war in South Asia. This has not happened recently, but this scenario used to occur frequently, and the intense hostility still exists. In the 1970s two events disturbed the power balance. East Pakistan seceded and became the independent state of Bangladesh; and India developed a nuclear bomb. Since then, things have quieted down somewhat, although Pakistan has worked feverishly to develop a nuclear capability of its own.

The United States has been friendly with both sides, but it has given much more military aid to Pakistan, a non-English speaking dictatorship, than it has to India, an English-speaking democracy. India is neutral in world affairs, while Pakistan became a member of the Southeast Asia Treaty Organization (SEATO) in 1954. Its mission was to halt the spread of Asian Communism. The Soviet Union, then a totalitarian Communist dictatorship, began to give massive military aid to India, the English-speaking democracy. As if this were not confusing enough, Pakistan later became friendly with China, against whom SEATO was created, because they both hate India. South Asia is not an easy region to analyze.

Dormant Bipolar

The first three characteristics of a rigid bipolar subsystem apply to a dormant bipolar subsystem as well. Member states are divided into two rival blocs. The rivalry is characterized by a great deal of hostility. The hostility is caused primarily by one issue that seems impossible to resolve. What distinguishes a dormant bipolar regional subsystem is:

4. There is a high degree of verbal hostility, but little or no warfare.

Subsaharan Africa

Subsaharan Africa has been a dormant bipolar subsystem. The two rival sides were the Republic of South Africa on the one hand, and the rest of the African nations on the other. There has been intense hostility, and the issue that seemed impossible to resolve was the racist policies of the white supremacist government of South Africa. The policy of apartheid did not just separate the fifteen percent white population from the 85 percent who are black or colored.

Women and children were forced to live hundreds of miles away, and fathers were only allowed to visit their families one month a year. The men had to live in barracks two or three dozen miles outside the cities where they worked. If a black was caught, for example, in Johannesburg after dark, he was jailed until daylight. In other words, by sundown all blacks had to be out of town. Their jobs were very insecure. Their work permits had to be renewed every two weeks by their employers.

White South Africans enjoyed one of the highest standards of living in the world, while the black population lived in poverty. The black-led African nations could not do much about the situation, other than pass resolutions at the United Nations and condemn the South African government whenever the opportunity arose. They tended to be under-developed economically and much weaker militarily than South Africa. There was also no strong pan-African movement, as each country was caught up in the processes of state-building and nation-building. South Africa's location on the continent's southern cone also made it less vulnerable to a land attack.

Because South Africa is one of the richest countries in the world in natural resources, American, British, German, Italian, French and Dutch companies found it very lucrative to do business in South Africa. It was not until economic pressure was brought to bear by the Western industrialized countries that the white supremacist government began to change.

The less harsh of the two white political parties is in power, and beginning in 1989 the government began a process of transition to majority rule, very slowly, in fits and starts, but a transition process nonetheless. First, black political leaders who had been imprisoned for 25 to 30 years, including Nelson Mandela, were released. Then 29 formerly outlawed political parties were legalized, including the African National Congress (ANC), headed by Mandela.

Prime Minister De Klerk and Mandela recently received the Nobel Peace Prize for their efforts to bring about peaceful change. However, the Zulu leader, Buthelezi, has been challenging the ANC, and both groups have killed each other's members periodically. Buthelezi does not support the agreed-upon arrangement, and he stopped attending the discussions to finalize the agreement. There is also the danger that the white hardline political party that wants to maintain apartheid will return to power.

The trend, however, is positive. A multiracial group to monitor the transition was formed by the government and the ANC. Nelson Mandela was elected president in an all-race election in April 1994.

Fluid Multipolar

Conceptually, this is the least developed subsystem type. A fluid multipolar subsystem has the following characteristics:

Peace?
Nelson Mandela and
F. W. De Klerk receive
the Nobel Prize in
December, 1993.

1. Three or more centers of power.
2. Loose, ambiguous and fluid ties among the members.
3. Large and small states exist side by side.

The Far East

The centers of power in this region are Japan, China, Russia and the United States. Even though we are not there geographically, the United States has had military bases in Japan, Australia, the Philippines (until recently), South Korea and Taiwan. And, of course, the United States fought wars in Korea and Vietnam.

There are several examples of the ambiguous and fluid ties in the region. During the Vietnam War, China was friendly with North Vietnam and allowed Soviet supplies to be transported through its territory. When the Vietnam War ended, China and Vietnam had a number of violent clashes on their mutual border. During the Vietnam War, the North Vietnamese communists helped native communists to gain power in neighboring Laos and Cambodia. After the war, Vietnam took over these countries.

In the West, there have also been changes. The Philippines, a former U.S. colony that was able to repel a communist guerrilla force after World War II with U.S. assistance, and that had allowed the U.S. to maintain the two largest military bases in the world, asked the U.S. to leave those bases, and we have. New Zealand, a member of ANZUS, a military alliance which stands for Australia, New Zealand and the United States, refused to let the U.S. continue to dock its nuclear submarines in their country. President Lyndon Johnson became very upset, and relations cooled between the two countries. The United States fought WWII against Japan, then helped to build the country. Today the two are major economic competitors, but close political and military allies.

Not only are there weak states, like Burma, Laos, Cambodia, Singapore, Malaysia and Indonesia in the region, but there are also mid-level powers like Vietnam, Thailand, the two Koreas, Taiwan, and Australia. Whenever there is a vacuum of power it is filled by a more powerful country. After World War I, and the collapse of the Ottoman and Austro-Hungarian empires, many small states emerged in Eastern Europe. This vacuum of power was filled by Nazi Germany. After WWII, it was filled by Soviet Russia. In the Far East, the weaker countries historically have been taken over by China, Japan, Vietnam, France, Russia and others. This multipolarity, combined with a great power differential, has led to much political instability in the past.

With the collapse of world communism, even large countries like Russia and China (which is still communist) are focusing on internal developments. Their scope of interests are neither global nor regionalist (see chapter 22). Even Vietnam seems to be settling down. However, North Korea is still trying to develop nuclear weapons. Obviously, the Far East is an evolving region that has been impacted primarily by the collapse of the Soviet Union and the rise of Japan as a giant economic power. South Korea, Malaysia and Singapore are also doing very well economically. These Pacific rim countries, and others in the region, might begin a process of economic integration, as has occurred in Western Europe, and will be occurring in the Western Hemisphere in the near future.

Hegemonial and integrative subsystems are much more stable (less likely to be violent) than bipolar and multipolar systems. The emerging world trilateral economic system seems to transcend political and security disputes. A high degree of economic interdependence, without a hegemonial relationship, will provide a strong pillar of the emerging world triad.

The West European pillar is already far along that path, facilitated by the high standard of living that exists among its members. The Pacific rim, led by Japan, would form an equally potent third pillar to complete the foundation of a new international subsystem.

On September 1st, 1993, President Clinton's National Security Advisor, Anthony Lake, announced at The Johns Hopkins University's School of Advanced International Studies, in Washington, D.C., that with the disintegration of the Soviet Union and the end of the Cold War, the policy of containment was no longer necessary. It is to be replaced by a policy of "enlargement" of the world's community of market-oriented democracies. "The four elements of his enlargement strategy: strengthen the core community of market democracies, foster new democracies and market economies, maintain military power to counter aggression of hostile states, and finally, pursue a humanitarian agenda.... We can let this moment slip away. Or we can mobilize our nation in order to enlarge democracy, enlarge markets, and enlarge our future."[15]

REFERENCES

1. *The New York Times*, September 18, 1967, p. 18.
2. Henry A. Kissinger, *The Necessity for Choice* (Garden City, N.Y.: Doubleday, 1962), p. 33.
3. *Ibid.*, p. 41.
4. Pierre Galois, *The Balance of Terror* (Boston: Houghton Mifflin, 1961), p. 23.
5. Morton A. Kaplan, "Variants on the Six Models of the International System," in James N. Rosenau, ed., rev. ed., *International Politics and Foreign Policy* (New York: The Free Press, 1969), pp. 297–298.
6. Louis J. Halle, "Lessons of the Nuclear Age," *Encounter*, Vol. XXX, No. 3 (March 1968), pp. 17–25. Reprinted in Bruce L. Sanders and Alan C. Durbin, eds., *Contemporary International Politics* (New York: Wiley, 1971), pp. 228–244.
7. *Ibid.*, p. 233.
8. *Ibid.*, p. 234.
9. *Ibid.*, p. 240.
10. Arthur I. Waskow, *The Limits of Defense* (Garden City, N.J.: Doubleday, 1962), p. 44.
11. Benjamin M. Becker, "The Myth of Arms Control and Disarmament," *Bulletin of the Atomic Scientists* (April 1971), p. 8.
12. Mulford Q. Sibley, "Unilateral Disarmament," in Robert A. Goldwyn, ed., *America Armed* (Chicago: Rand McNally, 1963).
13. David R. Inglis, "Transition to Disarmament," in Goldwyn.
14. Sandholtz, Wayne, Michael Borrus, John Zysman, Ken Conca, Jay Stowsky, Steven Vogel and Steve Weber, *The Highest Stakes: The Economic Foundations of the Next Security System* (New York: Oxford University Press, 1992).
15. *Sais Calendar*, The Paul H. Nitze School of Advanced International Studies, November 1993, p. 1.

GLOSSARY

Antiballistic Missile System (ABM)	A defense system designed to detect and shoot down incoming missiles. There has been much controversy in this country over the need for such a defense system. Opponents claim our level of technology is too primitive in this field to counteract the offensive power of the former Soviet Union to warrant spending the money necessary to deploy such a system. ABM supporters fall into two categories: one group advocates deployment of a "thin" system to protect our Minuteman sites from Russian SS–9's, which carry 25-megaton warheads capable of destroying these sites. The other group advocates a "thick" ABM system designed to protect populations as well. Opponents reply that any such defensive measure can be easily countered by increasing offensive weapons on the other side; thus nothing is gained, but military expenditures increase.
Arms control	Any measure that limits the quantity or quality of weapons or defense procedures (fallout shelters, warning systems, ABM's, and so on). Disarmament is one type of arms control.
Balance of terror system	An international system in which nations are deterred from attacking each other because they fear nuclear retaliation. All nations are currently unable to protect their populations from a nuclear attack. Thus, only the fear of counterattack ensures that these weapons of mass destruction will not be used.
Ballistic missile early warning system (BMEWS)	A very sophisticated radar system deployed by the United States to give advance warning of an attack. At most it will give us thirty minutes in which to decide whether to counterattack or to wait until the missiles land, thereby making sure we are being attacked. In all probability we would only have about fifteen minutes warning time, and since we have second-strike capability, we would probably wait to make sure we were not mistakenly starting a nuclear exchange.
Catalytic war	A war in which one country causes two other countries to fight each other. Country *A* commits an act of aggression against country *B*, for which country *C* is blamed. As a result, *C* and *B* fight against each other.
Disarmament	A reduction of weapons, or weapons delivery systems, or both.
First-strike capability	The ability of one state to attack another without fear of retaliation. The attacker has the power to destroy the attacked country's retaliatory force in a first strike.
Intercontinental ballistic missile (ICBM)	A weapons delivery system capable of carrying a nuclear-tipped missile to any target in the world.
Kiloton	An explosive force equal to one thousand tons of TNT.

Megaton	An explosive force equal to one million tons of TNT.
Multiple independently targeted reentry vehicle (MIRV)	A device that enables the user to launch a single missile capable of firing anywhere from three to ten warheads, each one destined for a different target. Only the United States and the former Soviet Union currently have these delivery systems. England and France are testing multiple reentry vehicles (MRV) that can fire three warheads per missile but which cannot be targeted for different locations.
Preemptive attack	An attack launched because a nation has just received word that an enemy has just launched, or is about to launch, an attack against it.
Preventive attack	An attack launched in order to destroy an enemy's attack force, because one believes that country is going to attack at some future time. It is designed to deprive the enemy of the means with which to launch a future attack.
SALT talks	Strategic Arms Limitations Talks between the U.S. and USSR which began in 1969 for the purpose of achieving mutually acceptable ceilings on weapons, weapons delivery systems, and defense measures.
Sea-launched ballistic missile (SLBM)	A missile launched from a ship at sea.
Second-strike capability	The ability to absorb a surprise nuclear attack with sufficient retaliatory power to inflict "unacceptable damage" upon an attacker. Second-strike capability is sometimes referred to as mutual assured destruction (MAD).

SELECTED READING

Asmus, Ronald D., Richard L. Kubler and F. Stephen Larrabee, "Building a New NATO," and Owen Harries, "The Collapse of the West," *Foreign Affairs*, September/October 1993, pp. 28–53.

The great debate regarding the future of NATO. Should we build a new NATO to secure Europe's Eastern and Southern flank? or would such a move annoy the Russians, create problems within the alliance, and maybe lead to a useless expenditure of blood and treasure?

Blackwill, Robert D. and Albert Carnesale, ed., *New Nuclear Nations: Consequences for U.S. Policy* (New York: Council on Foreign Relations Press, 1993).

The authors analyze the spread of nuclear weapons, and the possible consequences for the United States.

Bulliet, Richard W., "The Future of the Islamic Movement," *Foreign Affairs*, November/December 1993, pp. 38–44.

The author claims that the militant Islamic movement drove Israel and the PLO into each other's arms. Can they also break the peace?

Bundy, McGeorge, William J. Crowe, Jr., and Sidney D. Drell, *Reducing Nuclear Danger: The Road Away From the Brink* (New York: Council on Foreign Relations Press, 1993).

Three top experts on nuclear affairs offer their prescription for reducing existing nuclear arsenals and preventing further nuclear proliferation.

Donnelly, Jack, "Human Rights in the New World Order," *World Policy Journal*, Spring 1992, pp. 249–278.

A pessimistic analysis of human rights throughout the world.

Garten, Jeffrey E., *A Cold Peace: America, Japan and Germany, and the Struggle for Supremacy* (New York: Times Books, Random House, 1992).

An analysis of the competition among the three political/economic giants.

Goldstein, Walter, "Europe After Maastricht," *Foreign Affairs*, Winter 1992/93, pp. 117–132.

Kristof, Nicholas D., "The Rise of China," *Foreign Affairs*, November/December, pp. 59–74.

China will rise in the next century. Economically, it will ignore environmental concerns; and it will pursue an activist foreign policy, even engaging in military adventures. Those are the author's predictions.

Mandela, Nelson, "South Africa's Future Foreign Policy," *Foreign Affairs*, November/December 1993, pp. 86–97.

The leader of the ANC says his country's foreign policy will emphasize human rights and democracy.

Mearsheimer, John J., "The Case for a Ukrainian Nuclear Deterrent," and Steven E. Miller, "The Case Against a Ukrainian Nuclear Deterrent," *Foreign Affairs*, Summer 1993, pp. 50–80.

An interesting debate regarding Ukraine's nuclear armaments.

Motyl, Alexander J., *Dilemmas of Independence: Ukraine After Totalitarianism* (New York: Council on Foreign Relations Press, 1993).

This is an important introduction to the history, politics and economy of Ukraine.

New World Politics: Power, Ethnicity & Democracy, Essays from the Political Science Quarterly, see especially "A Palestinian State and Israeli Security" by Jerome Slater, and "The Changing Relationship Between Economics and Security" by Aaron L. Frieberg (New York: The Academy of Political Science, 1993).

An outstanding collection of essays on international politics.

O'Flaherty, J. Daniel, "Holding Together South Africa," *Foreign Affairs,* September/October 1993, pp. 126–136.

A discussion of the negotiations currently underway to construct a lasting political center.

Orme, William A. Jr., "NAFTA: Myths versus Facts," and Krugman, Paul, "The Uncomfortable Truth about NAFTA," *Foreign Affairs,* November/December 1993, pp. 2–19.

Orme contends that over time what is good for Mexico will also be good for the United States. Krugman claims that the costs will be small but so will the benefits of NAFTA. He says that essentially we would be helping a friendly neighbor.

Purkitt, Helen, *World Politics 93/94* (Guilford, Conn.: The Dushkin Publishing Group, 1993).

An excellent collection of 57 articles from a variety of sources. This is the 14th annual publication in the series. Previous editions also have very good articles.

Rourke, John T., *Taking Sides:* Clashing Views on Controversial Issues in World Politics, Fifth Edition (Guilford, Conn.: Dushkin Publishing Group, 1994).

This is an excellent reader that presents opposing sides on virtually all the important foreign policy issues of our day.

Ruggie, John Gerard, "The U.N.: Wandering in the Void," *Foreign Affairs,* November/December 1993, pp. 26–31.

The author argues that the U.N. is not well-equipped, militarily or conceptually, to handle the increasing peacekeeping activities it is involved in. Inadequately equipped military forces cannot succeed, and the very infrastructure of the U.N. is being weakened.

Sais Calendar, The Paul H. Nitze School of Advanced International Studies, November, 1993, p. 1.

Contains a synopsis of the U.S. national security advisor, Anthony Lake's speech, outlining the U.S. new post-cold war policy of enlargement, designed to replace containment.

Sandholtz, Wayne, Michael Borrus, John Zysman, Ken Conca, Jay Stowsky, Steven Vogel, and Steve Weber, *The Highest Stakes: The Economic Foundations of the Next Security System* (New York: Oxford University Press, 1992).

The authors offer three alternatives for a new international system.

The Defense Monitor, Center for Defense Information.

Tonelson, Alan, "Superpower Without a Sword," *Foreign Affairs,* Summer 1993, pp. 166–180.

The author claims that President Clinton still wants the United States to play a superpower role to spearhead a democratic world order. However, the author believes the country's proposed defense will not allow the president to do that.

Zubok, Vladislav, "Tyranny of the Weak," *World Policy Journal,* Spring 1992, pp. 192–218.
An examination of Russia's new foreign policy.

QUESTIONS

1. According to the authors, the international system that existed during the cold war was called
   a. A multipolar balance of power.
   b. A collective security system.
   c. A bipolar balance of terror.
   d. An integrated world system.

2. Which of the following statements referring to Kissinger's four prerequisites for stability in the current international system is *false?*
   a. The opponent must be rational.
   b. The penalties for aggression must outweigh the benefits.
   c. Military secrets regarding possession of nuclear weapons must be closely guarded.
   d. The deterrent threat must be credible.
   e. The deterrent threat must be understood.

3. The new American foreign policy announced by the Clinton administration in 1993 is called
   a. Enlargement.
   b. Containment.
   c. Liberation.
   d. Isolation.
   e. Regionalism.

4. According to Louis J. Halle, nuclear weapons are useful in
   a. maintaining and strengthening the status quo.
   b. maintaining military superiority.
   c. absolving conflicts (ending wars).
   d. combat of a limited nature.

5. What type of regional subsystem exists in the western hemisphere?
   a. Hegemonial
   b. Integrative
   c. Rigid bipolar
   d. Dormant bipolar
   e. Fluid multipolar

6. Which of the following most contributes to the *reduction* of stability in the current international system?
   a. bipolarity of the system
   b. economic underdevelopment and political instability of third-world countries
   c. escalation of nuclear armament on the part of the United States and the Soviet Union
   d. the increase in the number of nations that now possess nuclear weapons

7. Disarmament refers specifically to
   a. any measure limiting quantity or quality of weapons or defense procedures.
   b. anything that limits or prevents conflict.
   c. fallout shelters, warning systems, and ABM systems.
   d. the reduction of weapons and weapon delivery systems.

8. The ability of one state to attack another without fear of retaliation is called
   a. first-strike capability.
   b. preventive attack.
   c. second-strike capability.
   d. preemptive attack.

9. What type of regional subsystem exists in Western Europe?
   a. Hegemonial
   b. Integrative
   c. Rigid bipolar
   d. Dormant bipolar
   e. Fluid multipolar

10. Which of the following characteristics does not apply to a rigid bipolar subsystem?
   a. There are two rival blocs or factions.
   b. The rivalry is characterized by a great deal of hostility.
   c. The hostility is caused primarily by one issue that seems impossible to resolve.
   d. Fighting breaks out frequently in the region.
   e. One country dominates the foreign policies of the other members.

11. With the breakup of the Soviet Union, four of the former Soviet Republics kept nuclear weapons. Which one of the following newly independent states does not have nuclear weapons?
    a. Russia
    b. Ukraine
    c. Georgia
    d. Belarus
    e. Kazakhstan

QUESTIONS FOR THOUGHT AND DISCUSSION

1. Explain the balance of terror system.

2. Compare hegemonial, integrative and rigid bipolar regional subsystems, and give examples of each.

3. Analyze the arms control and disarmament treaties negotiated by the United States with Gorbachev and Yeltsin.

4. Explain and analyze the steps that should be taken to achieve global disarmament. Describe the international system that would emerge as a consequence of significant arms reduction.

5. Discuss possible alternative international systems that might develop in the post-Cold War era.

6. Describe and analyze the emerging tripolar/trilateral international system.

Photo Credits

p. 3: PhotoEdit/Kate Denny; p. 4: Stock, Boston/ Anestis Diakopoulos; p. 7: Elsa Dorfman; p. 10: Anthro-Photo/Michael Moseley; p. 15: Harlow Primate Lab, University of Wisconsin; p. 11: Marion Bernstein; p. 30: The Granger Collection; p. 32: Photo Researchers/Ulrike Welsch; p. 34: Animals Animals/Earth Scenes; p. 37: Courtesy of the American Museum of Natural History Neg # 320654; p. 40, left: Baron Hugo van Lawick © National Geographic Society; p. 40, right: Stock, Boston/Vicki Lawrence; p. 41: Reproduced by Courtesy of the Trustees of The British Museum; p. 44: Matrix/Louie Psihoyos; p. 51: Anthro-Photo/ Irven DeVore; p. 52: Peabody Museum, Harvard University; p. 53, top: Peabody Museum, Harvard University; p. 53, bottom left: The Metropolitan Museum of Art, Gift of William H. Riggs, 1913; p. 53, bottom center: Remington Arms Co.; p. 53, bottom right: Chinese Halberd, E. Chou dynasty; Bronze; 8-character inscription. L: .294 m. Special Chinese and Japanese Fund. 12.811. Courtesy of the Museum of Fine Arts, Boston; p. 54: Courtesy of The American Museum of Natural History Neg. # 298390; p. 57: Tony Stone Images/Jim Pickerall; p. 60: Matrix/Bill Luster; p. 61: UPI/ Bettmann; p. 72: Donald Dietz/Dietz-Hamlin; p. 73: Elizabeth Hamlin/Dietz-Hamlin; p. 77: Engraving of French Monk, Courtesy of Photographic Bulloz, Paris; p. 80: Photo Researchers/ Robert A. Isaacs; p. 91, top left: Stock, Boston/ Frederik D. Bodin; p. 91, top right: Woodfin Camp/ Marc and Evelyne Bernhaim; p. 91, bottom left: Photo Researchers/Judy Porter; p. 91, bottom right: AP/Wide World Photos; p. 97: Woodfin Camp/Marc and Evelyne Bernhaim; p. 98: Photo Researchers/Robert A. Isaacs; p. 99: Photo Researchers/Katrina Thomas; p. 103: The Image Works/Jesse Mobley; p. 106: Magnum Photos/ Eugene Richards; p. 107: Stock, Boston/Frank Wing; p. 110: Peter Menzel; p. 123, left: PhotoEdit/ Robert Brenner; p. 123, right: Robert Harding Picture Library/Israel Talby; p. 124: Library of Congress; p. 130: PhotoEdit/John Neubauer; p.

133: Stock, Boston/Cary Wolinsky; p. 135: From D. W. Griffith's *Orphans in the Storm,* Courtesy of The Museum of Modern Art/Film Stills Archive; p. 147: George W. Gardner; p. 152, top: Stock, Boston/Frank Stieman; p. 152, middle: Tony Stone Images/Don Smetzer; p. 152, bottom: Photo Researchers/Bill Bachmann; p. 154: Stock, Boston/Elizabeth Hamlin; p. 155: Woodfin Camp/ Joanne Leonard; p. 160: Tony Stone Images/Don and Pat Valenti; p. 170, left: Shooting Star; p. 170, right: Martha Swope; p. 172: PhotoEdit/Shelley Boyd; p. 173: UPI/The Bettmann Archive, Inc.; p. 177: Anthony Barboza; p. 184: Reuters/The Bettmann Archive, Inc.; p. 185: Charles Gatewood; p. 203: Courtesy of the American Museum of Natural History; p. 208: Image Photos/Clemens Kalisher; p. 209: Stock, Boston/Owen Franken; p. 211: Charles Gatewood; p. 214: Gamma-Liaison/ Jean-Marc Giboux; p. 215: The Image Works/ EBER; p. 222: Photo Researchers/Arvind Garg; p. 223: The Image Works/Harriet Gans; p. 225: Magnum Photos/Sebastiao Salgado; p. 226, left: Stock, Boston/ Frederik Bodin; p. 226, right: Woodfin Camp/M. and E. Bernheim; p. 232: Photo Researchers/Hella Hammid; p. 223: Sipa/Solo Syndication; p. 240: Courtesy, German Information Center, NY; p. 243, left: Shooting Star; p. 243, right: Shooting Star; p. 249: The Metropolitan Museum of Art, The Harris Brisbane Dick Fund; p. 251: A. Vilanni Figli, Bologna; p. 253: Tony Stone Images/Loren Santow; p. 260, top: Photo Researchers/Barbara Rios; p. 260, bottom: Photo Researchers/Robert Smith; p. 264: Stock, Boston/ Peter Southwick; p. 273: The Bettmann Archive, Inc.; p. 274: Courtesy of the Museum of Natural History; p. 276: UPI/The Bettmann Archive, Inc.; p. 277: Image Photos/Clemens Kalisher; p. 279: Reuters/The Bettmann Archive, Inc.; p. 283: Sipa Press/Murray White; p. 290: Elizabeth Crews; p. 295, top: Anthro-Photo/Irven DeVore; p. 295, bottom: Stock, Boston/Owen Franken; p. 296: Elizabeth Crews; p. 300: Alan Mercer; p. 310: Stock, Boston/Owen Franken; p. 311, top: Stock, Boston/

Phyllis Garber Jensen; p. 311, bottom: Stock, Boston/Barbara Alper; p. 312: Stock, Boston/ Peter Vandemark; p. 318: UPI/The Bettmann Archive, Inc.; p. 321: Eric Kroll; p. 324: UPI/The Bettmann Archive, Inc.; p. 325: Magnum/Alex Webb; p. 326: UPI/The Bettmann Archive, Inc.; Los Angeles County Air Pollution Control District; p. 334: Sygma/Michael Philippot; p. 342: The Stock Market/David Pollack; p. 349: The Bettmann Archive, Inc.; p. 352: Courtesy of General Motors; p. 355, left: Culver Pictures; p. 352, right: UPI/The Bettmann Archive, Inc.; p. 357: Culver Pictures; p. 359: Courtesy of the Federal Reserve Bank of New York; p. 363: Magnum/Burk Uzzle; p. 376: FPG International/D. C. Lowe; p. 377: Tony Stone Images/Davil Joel; p. 380: The United Nations Photo Library; p. 389: The Bettmann Archive, Inc.; p. 391: The Bettmann Archive, Inc.; p. 393: Culver Pictures; p. 395: Sovfoto/Eastfoto; p. 398: TASS from Sovfoto; p. 404: Sovfoto/ Eastfoto; p. 409: Sovfoto/Eastfoto; p. 413: Sovfoto/Eastfoto; p. 421: Swedish National Tourist Office; p. 422: Swedish National Tourist Office; p. 423: Swedish National Tourist Office; p. 424: Swedish National Tourist Office; p. 427: Swedish National Tourist Office; p. 428: Swedish National Tourist Office; p. 441: Alan Mercer; p. 442: David Golden; p. 444: FPG International/Mark Reinstein; p. 445: UPI/The Bettmann Archive, Inc.; p. 448: Matrix/Alex Quesada; p. 450: AP/Wide World Photos; p. 451, left: Matrix/Alex Quesada; p. 451, right: Leo de Wys Inc/Nancy Kaye; p. 452: Tony Stone Images/Robert E. Daemmrich; p. 453: Stock, Boston/Bob Daemmrich; p. 455, top: Stock, Boston/Daniel S. Brody; p. 455, middle: Elizabeth Hamlin/Dietz-Hamlin; p. 455, bottom: Photo Researchers/Martin J. Dain; p. 457: UPI/ The Bettmann Archive, Inc.; p. 458: Stock, Boston/Ellis Herwig; p. 467: *The Concord Journal;* p. 468: AP/Wide World Photos; p. 469, left: Matrix/ John Sturrock; p. 469, right: The Image Works/

Topham; p. 471: The White House; p. 474, left: Matrix/Peter Jordan; p. 474, right: AP/Wide World Photos; p. 475: UPI/The Bettmann Archive, Inc.; p. 476: TASS from Sovfoto; p. 477, left: UPI/ The Bettmann Archive, Inc.; p. 477, middle: UPI/ The Bettmann Archive, Inc.; p. 477, right: TASS from Sovfoto; p. 495: Reprinted with special permission of North America Syndicate, Inc.; p. 513: Stanley Forman, *Boston Herald American;* p. 536: AP/Wide World Photos; p. 538: Sygma/Randy Taylor; p. 541: Impact Visuals/Jerome Friar; p. 545: Tony Stone Images/Robert E. Daemmrich; p. 547: Impact Visuals/Ricky Flores; p. 549: Alan Mercer; p. 567: Sygma/Carlos Carrion; p. 571: UPI/The Bettmann Archive, Inc.; p. 578, top: TASS from Sovfoto; p. 578, bottom: TASS from Sovfoto; p. 592: UPI/The Bettmann Archive, Inc.; p. 595: Sovfoto/Eastfoto; p. 597: UPI/The Bettmann Archive, Inc.; p. 601: The United Nations/M. Grant; p. 611: The United Nations; p. 614: Black Star/Dennis Brack; p. 617: Sovfoto/Eastfoto/ Novisti; p. 618, top: AP/Wide World Photos; p. 618, bottom: UPI/The Bettmann Archive, Inc.; p. 621: UPI/The Bettmann Archive, Inc.; p. 624: UPI/The Bettmann Archive, Inc.; p. 627: UPI/The Bettmann Archive, Inc.; p. 628: AP/Wide World Photos; p. 640: The Bettmann Archive, Inc.; p. 641, left: AP/Wide World Photos; p. 641, right: AP/Wide World Photos; p. 643: Culver Pictures; p. 644: UPI/ The Bettmann Archive, Inc.; p. 645: UPI/The Bettmann Archive, Inc.; p. 647: From Jean Cocteau's *Grand Illusion,* Courtesy of The Museum of Modern Art/Film Stills Library; p. 655: USAF Photo; p. 656: U.S. NAVY; p. 657: UPI/The Bettmann Archive, Inc.; p. 661, top: Wide World Photos; p. 661, bottom: UPI/The Bettmann Archive, Inc.; p. 663: Field Newspaper Syndicate; p. 665: Sovfoto/ Eastfoto; p. 668: Culver Pictures; p. 669: p. 673: Sygma/Jacques Langevin; p. 678: Black Star/ Christopher Morris; p. 682: Black Star; p. 696: Wide World Photos; p. 700: Black Star.

Glossary

Accommodation A compromise that prevents or ends conflict. Example: labor and management negotiate a collective bargaining contract that prevents a strike.

Acculturation The process in which individuals or groups adopt aspects of another group's culture.

Achieved status A position that is earned. Example: lawyer. *See also* Ascribed status.

Ad hoc For a specific case only. A temporary tribunal or a committee that is established to deal with a specific case (as opposed to a permanent tribunal or a standing committee).

Adjudication A judicial decision made by a permanent court (as opposed to *arbitration*—a decision made by an ad hoc structure).

Adjustment The psychological state of one who has been successfully socialized and who conforms to the norms of society.

Anglo conformity Uni-directional assimilation in which all other American groups conform to the white Anglo-Saxon Protestant (dominant) culture.

Animism The belief that spirits inhabit and give life to natural objects.

Anomie The psychological state of one who has failed in the process of socialization. The anomic person is not adjusted to societal norms and cannot conform without great personal suffering.

Anthropology The "study of man." Anthropology is divided into two major divisions—physical and cultural—each containing several subdivisions. Physical anthropology is primarily concerned with genetically transmitted characteristics; cultural anthropology is concerned with socially learned traits.

Anthropomorphism The attributing of human qualities to supernatural objects. We might, for example, attribute the qualities of love, kindness, and gentleness to our God.

Antiballistic missile system (ABM) A defense system designed to detect and shoot down incoming missiles. There has been much controversy in this country over the need for such a defense system. Opponents claim our level of technology is too primitive in this field to warrant spending the money necessary to deploy such a system. ABM supporters fall into two categories: one group advocates deployment of a "thin" system to protect our Minuteman sites. The other group advocates a "thick" ABM system designed to protect populations as well. Opponents reply that any such defensive measure can be easily countered by increasing offensive weapons on the other side; thus nothing is gained, but military expenditures increase.

Anticipatory socialization   The "learning-in-advance" of future statuses and roles. Example: parents often prepare young children for school by teaching them some of the behavior that will be expected of them when they go to school.

Anti-intellectualism   A distrust of intellectuals who are thought to be impractical and/or subversive.

Anxiety   Tension caused by fear or apprehension.

Aristocracy (Aristotle)   Government by the few for the good of all.

Arms control   Any measure that limits the quantity or quality of weapons or defense procedures (fallout shelters, warning systems, ABM's, and so on). Disarmament is one type of arms control.

Artifacts   The objects that a society produces and uses, including the tools that are used to produce other objects. The ball-point pen, for instance, is a widely used artifact in contemporary American society.

Ascribed status   A position that is unearned. Example: brother. *See also* Achieved status.

Assimilation   The process of being absorbed by a different culture than one's culture of origin. Some social scientists use *assimilation* interchangeably with *acculturation,* while others treat *assimilation* as *total acculturation.*

Attitude   Learned predisposition of an individual to act in a given way in a given situation. If, for instance, your attitude toward learning is positive, then you will work hard to master the concepts presented in this book.

Authoritarian family   Family in which one parent dominates the decision making. In the traditional Spanish family, for instance, the father makes most of the important decisions.

Authorities   People who occupy positions that enable them to allocate values authoritatively for a political community.

Autocracy   Absolute and arbitrary dictatorship. Dictators are answerable to no one but themselves.

Autonomy   The psychological state of one who is capable of adjusting to societal norms but who refuses to conform when his or her own private judgment dictates otherwise.

Balance of power system   The international system that existed from 1648 to 1914. It was comprised of nation–states that were often divided into competing blocs which were fairly equally balanced in terms of power. Alliances were flexible, with members often shifting sides.

Balance of terror system   An international system in which nations are deterred from attacking each other because they fear nuclear retaliation. All nations are currently unable to protect their populations from a nuclear attack. Thus, only the fear of counterattack ensures that these weapons of mass destruction will not be used.

Ballistic missile early warning system (BMEWS)   A very sophisticated radar system deployed by the United States to give advance warning of an attack. At most it will give us thirty minutes in which to decide whether to counterattack or to wait until the missiles land, thereby making sure we are being attacked. In all probability we would only have about fifteen minutes warning time, and since we have second-strike capability, we would probably wait to make sure we were not mistakenly starting a nuclear exchange.

Behavioral ecology   An approach to the evolution of behaviors that focuses on the relationship of all behaviors to the environment.

Behaviorist   A psychologist who focuses on observable behavior and observable conditions that may cause behavior. Behaviorists often experiment with lower animals such as rats and pigeons to identify behavioral principles that can be applied to human behavior. Sometimes they experiment with humans as well.

Beliefs   A perceived relationship between two things, or between one thing and a characteristic of it. Example: "The sky is blue."

Belief systems   The mental components of culture, the learned and shared ideas that describe, explain, and give meaning and purpose to life. Included within belief systems are religious, magical, and normative or ethical prescriptions for conduct.

Benign regionalism   An international system in which the EC, the U.S., and Japan would focus primarily on their regions, while maintaining a lower level of global trade than they currently have.

Bilateral negotiations   Negotiations between two states.

Bill of Rights   The first ten amendments to the U.S. Constitution.

Blended family   A family unit in which at least one of the spouses has been previously married and in which there are one or more children from the previous marriage or marriages.

Boundary   A border (sometimes fluctuating) that separates two distinguishable classes of things (systems or subsystems) thereby serving as a determinant of inclusion and exclusion.

Bourgeoisie   Marx's name for the capitalist class.

Bureaucracy   The hierarchy of administrative officials in economic, religious, political, and military organizations in complex societies. Impersonality, specialization, reliance on general rules, and considerable distance between upper management personnel and nonsupervisory workers are characteristics of bureaucratic organizations. Example: school administration.

Capability   The military, political, economic, and psychological resources of a nation, which may be employed to influence the behavior of other states in order to further its own national interests.

Capital   Manufactured goods used in the production of more goods and services.

Caste   A kind of class that is based primarily on social inheritance and from which it is relatively difficult to move upward in the stratification system. Example: Americans born into poverty-stricken ghetto situations.

Castration anxiety (Freud)   A young boy's fear that the same-sexed parent will damage his genitals.

Catalytic war   A war in which one country causes two other countries to fight each other. Country *A* commits an act of aggression against country *B*, for which country *C* is blamed. As a result, *C* and *B* fight against each other.

Caudillismo   The Latin American practice of having strong, dictatorial leaders, usually military men.

Checks and balances Each branch of government can limit the power of the others. For example, in the United States, the president can veto legislation; the Supreme Court can rule on the constitutionality of executive or legislative actions; Congress can impeach a president or a Supreme Court justice.

Church A well-established religious organization that consists of a large group of believers. Members are born into churches, and, later they are confirmed. Churches are usually well integrated into the culture. Example: Lutherans.

Class An aggregate of people in a society who share similar amounts of some form of power, privilege, or prestige.

Classical or respondent conditioning The association of one stimulus with another stimulus that originally was not responded to in the same fashion as the first. The association is so strong that if either stimulus is substituted for the other, the same response will be evoked. In the process of learning a language, for example, our association between words and the objects they stand for may cause us to respond as emotionally to words as to the things they stand for. *See also* Operant conditioning.

Classical diplomacy Bilateral, ministerial diplomacy conducted in secret.

Class system A hierarchy of classes ranked according to some particular standard.

Closed system An isolated system that has no significant interaction with an environment.

Collective behavior The spontaneous behavior of numbers of people in unstructured social situations. Crowd behavior, public opinion, and rumor are all examples of collective behavior.

Collective defense An alliance system designed to protect its members from aggression by nonmember states.

Collective security system An international system in which member states are militarily allied to protect themselves from each other as well as from nonmember states.

COMECON The East European Trade Policy Organization created and controlled by the Soviet Union from 1949 to 1991. It included Hungary, Poland, Czechoslovakia, Romania, Bulgaria, East Germany, Mongolia, Vietnam, Cuba, and North Korea.

Communism A totalitarian dictatorship whose ideology stresses equality, internationalism, a classless society, and no government control. This system has developed in pre-democratic and pre-industrial societies with an authoritarian tradition. It is revolutionary, nationalizes the economy, and in some countries is imperialistic. Preexisting elites are eliminated.

Competition The mutually opposed effort of two or more persons or groups of persons to attain the same particular goal. Competition implies a set of rules that governs the conduct of the opposed parties. Example: two football teams compete for the national championship.

Competitiveness An emphasis on winning.

Complementary interests A mutual desire on the part of two states to exchange objects which each side can obtain only from the other. When two states have made such a mutually beneficial exchange it is called a *quid pro quo.*

Composite families Household units that are larger than the nuclear family. Such units may be extended families, joint families, or polygamous families.

Conciliation A diplomatic technique in which a group serves as a third party to help two antagonistic states negotiate their differences. The group helps to ascertain the facts and makes specific suggestions for resolving the conflict. This process is often conducted by permanent structures (commissions of conciliation).

Conditional positive regard (Rogers) The state of receiving only partial support and acceptance from significant people in one's environment. *See also* Unconditional positive regard.

Conditions of worth (Rogers) Standards to judge what is valuable and not valuable about oneself. Conditions of worth initially come from society, and they lead to incongruence.

Conference diplomacy Large-scale multilateral negotiation conducted at international meetings. It may be ad hoc or institutionalized.

Conflict A form of interaction in which two or more opposing persons or groups of persons use whatever means they deem necessary to attain some particular goal. Unlike competition, conflict does not have rules to govern conduct. Example: two nations fight a war.

Conflict model A personality model that assumes that personality is shaped by the interplay of two opposing forces. The psychosocial version holds that one force comes from within the individual; the other comes from groups. The intrapsychic version asserts that both antagonistic forces come from within the individual.

Conflict resolution The process by which individuals or groups resolve their differences.

Conflict theorists Scholars who place great emphasis on class conflict as being responsible for the distribution of scarce values in society.

Congruence (Rogers) The state of having a lack of conflict between one's self-concept and one's potentialities.

Consistency model A personality model that assumes that personality is shaped by the individual's continuous attempt to maintain consistent feedback from the external world. In the cognitive dissonance version, consistency is determined by cognitions. In the activation version, consistency is determined by customary levels of bodily tension.

Conspicuous consumption Spending money for luxury items for the purpose of demonstrating that one has the means to make such purchases rather than for the satisfaction of a normal consumer demand.

Consumer goods and services Any goods or services not used in the production of other goods and services.

Consumer sovereignty The power of the consumer to determine what and how much is produced, through consumer demand.

Containment The policy, also known as the Truman Doctrine, was originated by President Harry Truman in 1947 to halt Soviet expansion after World War II. It included the creation of the NATO military alliance, the Marshall Plan (foreign aid to help rebuild post-WWII Europe), and the Point Four program to give economic and military aid to underdeveloped countries threatened by communism.

Continuismo Self-perpetuation in office.

Continuous reinforcement Reinforcement that occurs each time a particular behavior is emitted.

Contraculture A subculture with customs or belief systems that run directly counter to those of the larger culture. Example: the Mafia.

Convention Standardized folkways that serve to eliminate confusion in human interaction by regulating mutual activities. Example: using a handshake as a standard greeting.

Conversations An exchange of views between governments. Such an exchange often precedes more detailed diplomatic negotiations.

Conversions The process through which inputs are changed to outputs.

Cooperation   The joint effort of two or more persons or groups of persons to attain a common goal.

Corporation   A form of business organization in which ownership of the enterprise is divided into equal shares, any of which may be owned by one or more individuals. Corporations are considered separate entities from their owners, and the shareholders are liable only for the amount of money they have invested in the enterprise.

Correlation   An expression of the degree or strength of the relationship between two or more variables. Correlations may be positive or negative, but a correlation between two variables does not necessarily prove a cause-effect relationship between them.

Countercity strategy   A military strategy in which a state aims its missiles at the enemy's population centers in order to deter a nuclear attack. It presumes that another state is less likely to attack if it is likely to suffer heavy casualties as a consequence.

Counterforce strategy   A military strategy in which a state aims its missiles at the enemy's missile sites and airfields in order to deter a nuclear attack. It presumes that cutting down an attacking state's ability to continue attacking will minimize casualties in the country attacked.

Coup d'etat   A nondemocratic change in leadership, without a corresponding change in the political and other social structures.

Creativity (Rogers)   The talent to produce new and effective behavior and things.

Cultural complex   A number of interrelated traits. A chalkboard and chalk are two of the traits that constitute the traditional classroom learning complex in American society.

Cultural integration   The "fit" or coming together of traits, complexes, and patterns into a meaningful whole. There is great consistency in the values underlying social institutions in cultures that have a high degree of integration.

Cultural lag   The time lapse between the change of everyday behavior of people to accommodate a new device and the change of their beliefs and institutions to include the new device and arrange means to control its effects. Example: the time between the invention of the automobile and the passage of laws to control its speed and direction.

Cultural pattern   Interrelated sets of complexes. Classroom learning and homework are two of the complexes that constitute the traditional pattern of public school education in American society.

Cultural pluralism   The maintenance of a dual identity and dual culture traits, both American and ethnic (subculture) by a large percentage of the U.S. population.

Cultural relativity   An attitude of respect for cultural differences; judging cultures on their own terms. Some social scientists prefer to use the term "cultural relativism" to describe this concept.

Cultural traits   The simplest elements of culture. The determination of whether or not a concrete or abstract unit of meaning is a trait dependent upon how it is treated in a social context, not on some objective quality of the trait itself.

Culture   A learned and shared social heritage that is transmitted from one generation to the next.

Culture conflict   The kind of conflict experienced by second-generation immigrants as their parents teach them one cultural tradition and the dominant society teaches them another.

Culture shock   A gap between expectations and reality with regard to social statuses and roles. Culture shock is experienced by first-generation immigrants.

Customs Group habits; the usual ways of real behavior for the group. For example, it is customary in American society for people to wear clothes in public, while the opposite is true for Karamojans.

Data accumulation The process of gathering information through careful observation.

Data classification The labeling or categorization of accumulated data.

Deductive reasoning The use of logic to infer a specific statement of conditions from a general statement of conditions.

Example: All men are mortal. (general)
        Harry is a man. (specific)
        Therefore,
        Harry is mortal. (specific)
See also Inductive reasoning.

De facto recognition Recognizing a government's existence without entering into formal relations with it.

Defense (Freud) The process in which individuals reduce tension by unconsciously deceiving themselves about their motives and goals.

De jure recognition Entering into official diplomatic relations by exchanging ambassadors. It involves a formal declaration of recognition.

Demand In economics, the desire for a particular good or service, together with the willingness and ability to pay for it. In political terms, a demand is an expression of opinion that an action should or should not be carried out.

Democracy Rule by a majority, with respect for minorities, free elections, limits on the power of leadership, and respect for civil liberties. In a direct democracy adults decide public policies at community meetings. In a representative democracy elected representatives govern on behalf of the people.

Democratic centralism (Lenin) Party policies could be openly debated before the leaders reach a final decision. However, once the party leaders adopt an official position on any issue all debate ceases. There can be no revision of the party line, and no deviation from it.

Dependent variables Variables that are thought to be affected by independent variables. Example: Smoking causes lung cancer (dependent variable).

Depletion allowance A deduction from taxable income derived from an asset, such as an oil well or a coal mine, which cannot be replaced, and the life of which cannot be prolonged by repairs.

Depression A severe decline in economic activity, usually characterized by high unemployment, diminishing profits, and many business failures.

Deterrence Preventing someone from doing something, usually through fear or doubt. One nation deters another from attacking it through fear of retaliation.

Dialectical materialism (Marx) Karl Marx's theory of social change which holds that a class struggle exists between the owners of the means of production (the exploiters) and those who work for them (the exploited). Periodically technological advancements create a new mode of production, thereby rendering the existing social relations of production obsolete. Often a new class rises to power if the owners of the old means of production do not acquire the new means of production. The new group then overthrows the old group and transforms society. The process then repeats itself as the new owners exploit the workers.

Dictatorship Rule by one or a few, with no free elections, no limits on the leaders' power, and no respect for the rights of minorities or for civil liberties. An authoritarian dictator seeks only political control. A totalitarian dictator seeks total control over every aspect of life.

Diffusion The transfer of cultural traits, complexes, and patterns from one society to another. Western society, for example, abandoned its own system of Roman numerals and replaced it with the more useful Eastern system of Arabic numerals.

Diplomacy The practice of conducting relations between states through official representatives.

Diplomatic immunity Freedom from arrest, trial, subpoena, civil suit, and legal penalty for a diplomatic agent in the state to which he or she is accredited.

Direct tax A tax, the burden of which cannot be easily shifted or passed on to someone else by the person required to pay the tax to the government. Example: income taxes.

Disarmament A reduction of weapons, or weapons delivery systems, or both.

Discontinuity The interruption of the continuous process of the social development of the individual. Education systems in complex societies tend to produce discontinuity for the adolescent.

Discovery-invention The process whereby new elements are introduced from within rather than from outside the existing culture. Discovery refers to gaining knowledge of something previously unknown. Invention refers to applying existing knowledge in a new way.

Discount rate The interest rate charged by Federal Reserve banks to commercial banks for loans.

Disposable income National income less direct taxes, plus welfare payments.

Distributive capability The political system's ability to allocate values to individuals and groups in society.

DNA (deoxyribonucleic acid) A chemical substance that supplies coded information to the gene and that controls the heredity of all living organisms.

Dormant bipolar A regional subsystem in which the members are divided into rival factions, that do *not* fight each other frequently.

Duolocal residence Husband and wife living in separate households.

Dysfunction Something disruptive to the smooth operation of a system.

Economic determinism The idea that social evolution is caused by economic forces.

Economic system The social system consisting of structures and roles that function to make decisions regarding the production, distribution, and consumption of goods and services.

Ecosystem A system that contains all the relationships between living organisms and their environment in a given location.

Education Synonymous with socialization, as a rule. More specifically, education is the process by which individuals are systematically exposed to selected knowledge, skills, and attitudes through social structures that have been created specifically for this end. Since much learning takes place incidentally and in unstructured situations, the education system includes both formal and informal learning.

Egalitarian family Family in which both parents, and the children in some cases, share in decision making. Example: a typical middle-class American family.

Ego (Freud) A basic part of personality structure. It has a rational, conscious element that is represented by thinking, perceiving, remembering, and acting in ways that gratify instincts (the pleasure principle functioning). It also has an unconscious element that is represented by the function of defense (the reality principle functioning). *See also* Id, Superego.

Elite The highest ranking segment of any given social category. Elite may be used to describe part of a social class, a status group, a social class, part of a social class system, or part of a whole society. Example: superstars in sports and entertainment. In politics an *elite political culture* refers to the orientations of politically powerful or influential individuals and groups within a society.

Elite political culture The orientations of politically powerful or influential individuals and groups within a society.

Embryonic stage The first two months following conception.

Emerging culture An integrated identity not like either the dominant culture or the subculture.

Endogamy Marriage within a specific group, but outside the nuclear unit. Example: upper class Americans tend to marry other upper class Americans. *See also* Exogamy.

Enlargement A new American foreign policy proclaimed by Bill Clinton's administration in 1993. It is designed to strengthen and enlarge the world's community of market-oriented democracies, pursue a humanitarian agenda, and maintain the military power necessary to counter the aggression of hostile states.

Entrepreneurship A specialized form of labor which functions to initiate a business by combining the proper resources and technology.

Equilibrium Balance.

Essential national actor A state whose physical survival and sovereignty was deemed necessary in the balance of power system.

Estate A kind of class that has legally defined rights and duties. Example: citizens.

Ethnic group A subculture based on a common race, religion, or national origin.

Ethnicity A sense of peoplehood; a feeling of belonging together, of being part of a subculture whose members have a great deal in common with each other.

Ethnocentrism The attitude of valuing one's own culture, while at the same time, devaluing others. The ethnocentric person believes his or her group is "best."

Ethos The characteristic quality of a culture. The ethos of the Zuni, for example, includes moderation, whereas the ethos of Americans includes intense competitiveness.

Etiquette Folkways that prescribe proper manners. Etiquette implies a choice of appropriate behavior for specific circumstances. Example: "You should chew your food with your mouth closed."

European Common Market The forerunner of the EC, created in 1958 by six European countries.

European Community (EC) An economically integrated group of twelve West European democracies. It also includes a variety of political as well as economic institutions.

European Currency Unit (ECU) The monetary unit that all members of the EC are supposed to adopt by 1999.

European Free Trade Association (EFTA) A European free international trade association comprised of seven wealthy democracies. It is not as economically integrated as is the European Community (EC).

European Parliament Its members are elected separately as individuals, or political party members, but not sent as delegates of their countries' governments. Their decisions are supposed to be binding on all members, even those who voted against the decision, but in practice this has not always occurred. Its range of decision-making power is currently very limited, but it is expected to expand.

European Political Union The EC organization designed to create a common security and foreign policy among the twelve members.

Evaluative belief Beliefs based on the relative desirability of something. They are ultimately based on values. Example: "A job promotion is desirable."

Evolution Generally, evolution refers to developmental change of any kind. Perhaps the most commonly thought of type of evolution is biological evolution, which refers to the development of life forms, one from another, over a period of time.

Existential living (Rogers) The traits of adaptability, spontaneity, and flexibility.

Exogamy Marriage outside a specific group. In some simple societies, for instance, people are forbidden to marry anyone from their own village. *See also* Endogamy.

Expectancy (McClelland) An idea as to the content and timing of future events. We learn expectancies by continually experiencing similar events in similar situations.

Experiential freedom (Rogers) The trait of feeling free to choose between alternative courses of action.

Experimental design The performance of controlled experiments with the aim of determining cause-effect relationships.

Expressive symbols Symbols that refer to objects or events that cannot be verified in the external world. Expressive symbols often convey emotional and highly personal meaning. Example: God.

Extended family A composite family in which the married couple and, later, their children live in the same household with the parents of one of the couples. A residence rule determines with which set of parents the couple will live. In a *patrilocal* extended family the couple lives with the groom's parents. In a *matrilocal* extended family the couples lives with the bride's family. *Biolocal* extended families include both sons who have brought their wives into the group and daughters who have brought their husbands.

External sovereignty In international law it means that all states are legally equal (although in terms of power and influence they obviously are not).

Extinction The gradual dying out of a conditioned response. When the conditioned behavior has completely stopped, we say that it has been extinguished.

Extractive capability The political system's ability to utilize the nation's natural and human resources to achieve societal goals.

Fabian socialism A nineteenth-century social philosophical movement whose adherents sought gradual and peaceful reforms within the system. Fabian socialists favored the nationalization of the chief means of production and heavy, progressive taxes on both profits and income. Democratic socialism is the outgrowth of Fabianism.

Family A socially recognized group of persons who are related to one another through the process of reproduction. Most people have two families: the one into which they are born (*family of orientation*) and the one they help create through marriage and the bearing and rearing of children (*family of procreation*). *See also* Extended family, Nuclear family.

Fascism A totalitarian dictatorship whose German variety (Nazism) stressed nationalism, racism, imperialism, inequality, sexism, and the superiority of Aryans (the master race concept). This system in slightly different form developed in Italy as well. Post-democratic and post-industrial societies in crisis seem to be most susceptible to this type of dictatorship. Power was gained constitutionally and there was cooperation with preexisting elites.

Federal Reserve System The central banking system of the United States, consisting of twelve regional banks and run by the Federal Reserve Board which is staffed by members chosen by the government, big banks, and small banks.

Federal system (federalism) Power is divided between the national government and smaller geographical units (states, provinces, cantons). The United States, Canada, and Switzerland are examples.

Feedback The positive or negative message resulting from an output, which then becomes a new input in the conversion process. *See also* Reinforcement.

Fetal stage The third month following conception until birth.

First-order beliefs Primitive beliefs that are inferred from zero-order beliefs. We are usually aware of first-order beliefs, and we can easily imagine alternatives to them. Example: a belief that this book has weight.

First-strike capability The ability of one state to attack another without fear of retaliation. The attacker has the power to destroy the attacked country's retaliatory force in a first strike.

Fiscal policies Approaches to government spending and taxation, designed either to stimulate or depress the economy.

Fixation (Freud) Arrestment in a particular stage of development.

Fluid multipolar A regional subsystem that contains three or more centers of power, and has loose, ambiguous, and fluid ties among some of the members.

Folkways Durable, standardized, and informally enforced norms that are not considered vital to a society's survival.

Foreign policy outputs Decisions and ac-tions of nation–states that affect other states.

Free trade International trade which takes place in the absence of governmental reg-ulations or control.

Fulfillment model A personality model that assumes that personality is shaped by one great force within the person. The actu-alization version sees the force as an in-ternal pressure to realize genetically determined capabilities. The perfection version sees the force as an internal pres-sure which seeks to strive toward ideals of perfection.

Fully functioning person (Rogers) An ideal person who does not have conditions of worth and does not display defensive behavior; has congruence and is continu-ously engaged in the process of actualiza-tion.

Function A purpose served by an individual, group, or institution. A special duty or per-formance required of a person or thing in the course of work or activity (the function of a policeman; the function of the liver). The four functions that must be performed in any system are goal attainment, pattern maintenance, integration, and adaptation. Functions may be either manifest or latent.

Functional Something that enhances the perpetuation of a system.

Functionalism Theory or practice emphasiz-ing the necessity of adapting the structure or design of anything to its function. An analytical approach for studying social systems that stresses the universality and importance of functions.

Functional theorists Scholars who empha-size the need for certain societal functions as being responsible for the distribution of scarce values in society.

Fused powers Executive and legislative branches of government are merged, as in Great Britain.

Gene A distinct unit of inheritance. Our genetic characteristics are produced by the genes we inherit from our parents.

Gene flow The movement of genes from one pool to another. This occurs when an individual from one breeding population mates with an individual from another.

Gene frequencies The rate of occurrence of genes which express themselves within the gene pool. There could be, for instance, a high frequency of blue eyes in a given gene pool.

Gene pool All the genes in a given population at any particular time.

General political culture The core political values accepted by most people and the predominant political behavior patterns of a society.

General proposition A broad statement that explains relationships among data and may further be used as a starting point for speculative thinking. Example: People tend to repeat behavior that has been rewarded.

Genetic drift An individual's genetic potential being lost to the gene pool because mating does not occur.

Genetic recombination A major source of genetic variation that is caused by random combinations of dominant and recessive genes or the combined activity of many genes.

Genetics The scientific study of heredity.

Genotype All of a particular organism's genetic characteristics.

Glasnost Former Soviet leader Gorbachev's policy of openness: the right of the people to express themselves freely, even to criticize the government and its leaders.

Good offices A diplomatic technique in which a third party acts as a go-between to reestablish bilateral negotiations between the parties in an international dispute. However, the parties themselves are responsible for settling the dispute.

Gosplan The central planning agency of the Soviet Union.

Gravedigger theory of capitalism (Marx) Competition among capitalists leads to the introduction of labor-saving machinery. In effect, the capitalist cuts into profit by substituting nonprofitable means of production (machinery) for profitable ones (human labor). At a certain point production becomes unprofitable. Some capitalists are therefore forced out of business. Eventually recovery occurs, but the number of capitalists has been reduced, and there has been a corresponding increase in the number of workers. The cycle then repeats itself, increasing in severity each time. Eventually the large working class becomes disciplined, united, and dissatisfied enough to overthrow capitalism. Thus capitalism digs its own grave.

Gridlock A term used in the United States to describe the inability of the government to bring about changes because the executive and legislative branches are in disagreement.

Gross national product (GNP) The total value of all final goods and services produced by an economy within a specified time period, usually a year.

Group A set of three or more persons who interact with one another and share some joint activities. A single network of relationships connects the interactions of group members. Example: a college sorority.

Growth Biological changes within the individual that take place over time. Specific experience is not necessary for such changes to occur; that is, they occur naturally. At appropriate times, for example, the individual sees, hears, controls voluntary muscles, sits, stands, crawls, and walks.

Guerrilla warfare Irregular warfare fought by small bands against an invading army or in rebellion against an established government.

Head of government Political leader of a country.

Head of state Ceremonial leader of a country.

Hegemonial A regional subsystem in which one nation–state dominates the foreign policies of the other states in the region.

Higher-order beliefs Beliefs in which the credibility of our senses or an external authority is not taken for granted. Example: "We are currently in the midst of a serious environmental crisis."

Historical materialism (Marx) Karl Marx's explanation of the past, present, and future. A series of class struggles based on dialectical materialism eventually leads to pure communism, a future utopia characterized by great material abundance, a classless society, the withering away of government, and a population shorn of selfishness and imbued with generosity. Pure communism is the ultimate historical stage.

Holding company A corporation that holds enough of the stock of another corporation to permit it to direct the latter's affairs.

Homeostasis A dynamic process by which systems maintain internal balances while undergoing changes.

Homogamy Marriage between people of similar social characteristics but outside their respective nuclear units. Example: marriage between people of the same social class.

Horizontal interlocking The linking of systems that occupy the same rank or level in a hierarchical structure. *See also* Vertical interlocking.

Id (Freud) A basic part of personality structure. It is comprised of the instincts, which are nonrational in nature. *See also* Ego, Superego.

Identical interests A mutual interest by two states in obtaining a particular object or arrangement.

Imitation The kind of association that results from repeating the behavior displayed by a model.

Impact-integration A process-oriented theory similar to emerging culture which emphasizes the conflict that accompanies culture contact.

Imperialistic wars, Theory of (Lenin) Capitalist countries had temporarily averted collapse by engaging in imperialism. Through imperialism and colonialism they would create markets for their surplus goods, thus resolving the immediate pressure of overproduction. In this view the underdeveloped countries became the proletariat, and the capitalist imperialist countries became the world bourgeoisie.

Impersonalism A relative lack of concern for others; maintenance of a certain distance in interpersonal relations.

Impersonal market An economy in which the branches and stages of production mesh together without conscious management.

Incest taboo The universal rule forbidding sexual relations within the nuclear family except for those between husband and wife.

Inclusive fitness The genetic representation of the individual through surviving relatives; emphasis is on survival of the gene pool rather than the gene-bearing individual.

Incongruence (Rogers) The state of restricting one's potentialities.

Independent variables Variables that are thought to cause something to happen. Example: Smoking (independent variable) causes lung cancer.

Indirect tax A tax, the burden of which can

easily be shifted or passed on to someone else by the person required to pay the tax to the government. Example: taxes on the sale of gasoline are added to the price and passed on to the consumer.

Individualism   A concern with one's own personal welfare as opposed to a concern with the public welfare. In Latin America this is manifested by reserving the right to decide whether or not to obey a particular law.

Individual proprietorship   A form of business organization in which one individual owns and manages, assumes all the risks of, and derives all the profits from an enterprise.

Inductive reasoning   The use of logic to infer a general conclusion from specific facts.

Example: Harry used to smoke cigarettes. (specific)
Harry died of cancer. (specific)
Therefore, cigarette smoking can cause death.   (general conclusion)

See also Deductive reasoning.

Industrial Revolution   The conditions that existed during the latter part of the eighteenth and the early part of the nineteenth centuries when changes in production techniques caused the factory system to replace the domestic system.

Infancy   About the first two or three years of life.

Inflation   A reduction in the purchasing power of money which usually results when demand increases more rapidly than supply and which is generally reflected by rising prices.

Influence   The ability to help determine decisions made by those who have power.

Informally enforced norms   A classification of norms that includes folkways and mores.

INF treaty   An agreement between the United States and the Soviet Union to eliminate intermediate range nuclear missiles.

Inputs   Factors that enter into a social process, the interplay of which produces an outcome (output).

Insight   Forming a previously unperceived relationship between two aspects of the environment. Insight occurs instantaneously and spontaneously.

Instincts (Freud)   The mental representation of a biologically based urge to act. All instincts have: a source (a bodily process), an energy (tension), an aim (tension reduction), and an object (that which reduces tension). The mental representation of source and object is a wish; the mental representation of energy and aim is uncomfortable emotions. Freud identified three types of instincts—self-preservation, sexual, and death.

Institutions   Distinctive patterns that are centered around major human needs and accompanied by particular modes of social interaction. Example: politics or the political system.

Integrative   A regional subsystem in which the member states are in the process of *voluntarily* integrating economically, militarily, and politically.

Intelligence gathering   The process engaged in by nation–states for acquiring the information necessary to protect their national interests.

Intentions   The desire of a state either to maintain its existing geographical boundaries and its power and influence (*status quo* intentions), or to change one or both factors (*revisionist* intentions).

Interaction   The process by which communicating individuals influence each other's thoughts and actions. Some social scientists now prefer to use the term "transaction" instead of interaction.

Interamerican Development Bank   Created in 1960 by the United States to help the

Latin American countries with their economic development.

Intercontinental ballistic missile (ICBM) A weapon delivery system capable of carrying a nuclear-tipped missile to any target in the world.

Interest aggregation The process of narrowing down and combining the demands made upon authorities to a manageable number of reasonable policy alternatives.

Interest articulation The process of communicating demands to political decision makers.

Intermittent reinforcement Reinforcement that does not occur each time a particular behavior is emitted.

International actors Organizations that contain members from two or more nation–states and that play a role in international relations.

International Court of Justice This "world court" is a permanent organ of the United Nations.

International law The system of rules on the rights and duties of states in their mutual relations. It is based on the concept of the sovereign equality of states and rests ultimately on agreement among them.

International organization A multinational institution whose members (nation–states) retain independent decision-making power.

International politics (We use this term interchangeably with international relations, international affairs, world politics, and global politics.) Relations between people or groups that cut across national boundaries, with special emphasis on the political, military, and economic aspects.

International system A political system that contains all the nation–states that interact with each other. It lacks a formal government or any other supreme political authority. Its constituent parts are nation–states, international organizations

(private and public), regional groupings, military blocs, and so forth. It has certain characteristics, elements, rules, and interaction processes. It tends to be subsystem dominant. In this book we analyze international systems in terms of their stability, how they perform various functions (security, conflict resolution, integration, goal attainment, maintenance, and adaptation), and in a number of other ways.

Intersubjective truth The collective judgment of an overwhelming majority of experts when they agree on something that cannot be empirically proved right or wrong.

Isolationism The foreign policy of the United States towards the eastern hemisphere originated by George Washington in 1796 and pursued until 1947.

Joint family A composite family in which brothers or cousins bring their respective nuclear families together to form a single unit.

Judicial review The power of the Supreme Court to decide if an act of Congress or of the President is constitutional.

Keynesian economics Derived from the theories of the twentieth-century British economist John Maynard Keynes, who held that government could and should maintain equilibrium within the economic system by controlling the level of consumption and investment through its fiscal and monetary policies.

Kiloton An explosive force equal to one thousand tons of TNT.

Kingship (Aristotle) Rule by one for the good of all.

Kin selection The tendency to protect most those individuals with whom one shares the most genes.

Labor theory of value (Marx) The value of a product is the amount of human labor required to produce it, including the labor required to produce any machines involved in production.

Laissez-faire The policy of noninterference in economic matters by the government.

Language A system of symbols that have agreed-upon meanings in a given human population.

Latent An unintended and unrecognized process or result.

Law of absolute advantage (Adam Smith) Every state can produce some goods more efficiently than every other state and therefore would benefit by producing only those goods.

Law of comparative advantage (David Ricardo) Each state should concentrate on producing those goods which it can produce most efficiently and trade these for its other needs.

Law of effect A behavioral principle that states that responses leading to satisfying consequences are strengthened and therefore tend to be repeated, and responses leading to unsatisfying consequences are weakened and therefore tend not to be repeated.

Law of inheritance of acquired characteristics Characteristics gained through use or disuse can be transmitted biologically from one generation to the next. No one has been able to demonstrate that this "law" is correct.

Law of use and disuse Parts of the body that are used will develop and those that are not used will atrophy. This hypothesis seems to be correct.

Laws Deliberately formulated norms that are accompanied by specific, formal sanctions and enforced by some special authority.

League of Nations An international organization created in 1920 primarily for the purpose of maintaining peace. It was the first attempt to institutionalize a collective security system. Its failure to cope with aggression in the 1930's led to its demise.

Learning Modifying behavior as the result of experience. Learning takes place through any of the four kinds of association: classical conditioning, operant conditioning, imitation, and insight.

Legalism Performing within the letter of the law, especially within the framework of a self-written constitution.

Legitimacy The principle that every child should have a sociological father to guide and protect him or her, and to represent the male link between the child and society. Illegitimacy, then, refers to the social condition of not having a father. Also, a characteristic possessed by a political system when the members of the political community believe that the authorities have the right to rule, and that their decisions are binding on the people.

Leninism The social-political-economic philosophy of Vladimir Ilyich Lenin, the architect of the first Communist revolution. Lenin expanded and modified Marx's theories to include the following ideas: a political party (the Communist party), comprised of a small, highly-disciplined, tightly-knit group of professional revolutionaries, would act as the vanguard, or leadership, of the proletariat; democratic centralism; a one-party state; the theory of imperialistic wars; the inevitability of wars between Communist and capitalist nations; the use of tactical retreats; and the weakest-link theory.

Libido (Freud) The energy of the sexual instinct.

Maastricht Treaty The treaty signed in December, 1991 by all EC members, setting a timetable for further integration and unification.

Machismo   A cultural trait of the ideal male in Latin America. It includes extreme masculinity, hard living (in both work and play), bravery, pride, honor, dignity, and sexual prowess.

Magic   The process of attempting to control the supernatural in order to influence events in the real world. The magician, for example, might attempt to use the supernatural to cause unusual behavior in a particular person.

Majority group   The segment of the population within a society that is politically and economically dominant and that may or may not be numerically larger than the subordinate groups it dominates.

Maladjusted person (Rogers)   An individual who has conditions of worth and who displays defensive behavior; is in a state of incongruence.

Managed multilateralism   An international system which would be a continuation of the post WWII system, but led by Western Europe and Japan, as well as the United States.

Management   A specialized form of labor which functions to make decisions regarding the day-to-day operations of a business. *See also* Bureaucracy.

Manifest   An intended and recognized process or result.

Marginal persons   A term used to refer to second-generation immigrants whose culture conflict may leave them feeling uncomfortable with both the dominant society and their own subculture.

Marriage   Two or more individuals sharing a socially recognized mating relationship.

Marxism   The social–political–economic philosophy of Karl Marx. The principal notions contained in Marx's philosophy include: dialectical and historical materialism, the labor theory of value, the sub-sistence theory of wages, the theory of surplus value, and the gravedigger theory of capitalism.

Massive retaliation   A strategic policy in which an enemy is threatened with nuclear annihilation if he attacks.

Materialism   The doctrine that success is measured in terms of the acquisition of money and the objects it can buy.

Matriarchal family   Family in which the mother or grandmother dominates.

Maturation   The unfolding of the person's biological potential. Generally, maturation proceeds through an orderly sequence of stages.

Measured retaliation   A strategic policy in which an enemy is threatened with a nuclear response, should he attack, equivalent to the destruction brought about by his attack.

Mediation   A diplomatic technique similar to conciliation. The difference is that mediation involves a *single* third party; conciliation involves a group.

Megaton   An explosive force equal to one million tons of TNT.

Melting pot   A blending of all the cultures and gene pools in the United States, thus forming an "American" culture different from the original WASP culture.

Mercenaries   Professional soldiers whose services are for hire. Since they are not fighting for a cause they believe in, or to protect their homeland, bravery is not their most notable characteristic; prudence is.

Ministerial diplomacy   Diplomacy carried out by professional diplomats.

Minority group   An ethnic group that is exceptionally disadvantaged, exceptionally discriminated against, or both, and whose members may have physical-characteristics that distinguish them from others. They occupy a subordinate position with respect to the majority group.

Mixed strategy A combination of countercity and counterforce nuclear strategy.

Mode of production (Marx) The technology of production.

Modern diplomacy Multilateral summit diplomacy conducted in public.

Monetary policies Approaches to the control of the money flow within an economic system by means of a central banking system.

Monism There is one center of power in society. Dictatorships are monistic.

Monoculture An economy that relies primarily on one product for export, usually an agricultural crop or an extractive natural resource, such as copper or tin.

Monogamy The marriage of one man to one woman.

Monopoly The condition of having control over the supply of a product, thus permitting the release of the supply at a rate which yields the most profitable price.

Moral anxiety (Freud) Anxiety caused by internal guilt feelings.

Mores Standardized and informally enforced norms that are considered vital to the survival of the society. Mores, always concerned with morality, carry strong sanctions. (Singular: mos.)

Motive (McClelland) A state of mind caused by a stimulus that signals the person that some pleasant or unpleasant change is about to take place. If the anticipated change includes positive affect, the motive is an approach motive; if it includes negative affect, the motive is an avoidance motive.

Muckrakers A group of American writers who exposed unscrupulous and unhealthy business practices in the United States in the late nineteenth and early twentieth centuries.

Multilateral negotiations Negotiations between more than two states.

Multiple independently targeted reentry vehicle (MIRV) A device that enables the user to launch a single missile capable of firing anywhere from three to ten warheads, each one destined for a different target. Only the United States and Russia are currently testing these delivery systems. England and France are testing multiple reentry vehicles (MRV) that can fire three warheads per missile but which cannot be targeted for different locations.

Mutation Abrupt internal change in a gene that occurs spontaneously.

National actors Nation–states that play a role in the international system.

National income Net national product less indirect taxes.

National interests The enduring objectives pursued by nation–states—such as self-preservation (of its people, its territory, and its way of life), control over decision making that affects the above, and economic advantages, international prestige, and so on.

Nation building The development of a feeling of patriotism and nationalism among the people of a state.

Natural monopoly A monopoly due either to natural conditions (for example, a monopoly over the oil in the Middle East and the United States) or to characteristics inherent in a particular business (for example, a monopoly over the electricity in a geographical region).

Natural selection The process by which organisms increase their chance of survival by inheriting characteristics that facilitate their adaptation to the environment. Animals such as polar bears, for example, are able to survive in their harsh natural environment because they have heavy fur.

Naturism The belief in and worship of nature gods.

Need for positive regard (Rogers) One's feeling of satisfaction upon receiving the approval of others and the frustration upon receiving their disapproval.

Need for positive self-regard (Rogers) One's satisfaction or dissatisfaction at the approval or disapproval of oneself.

Negative affect (McClelland) Unpleasant feelings.

Negative reinforcement The removal of something perceived as unpleasant from a situation after a response is emitted.

Negotiation A process in which explicit proposals are put forward for the purpose of reaching an agreement. It implies a willingness to make mutual concessions (*quid pro quo*).

Neolocal residence Residence in which the married couple live together, but separated from both sets of parents.

Neonatal stage Roughly the first four weeks following birth.

Net national product (NNP) Gross national product less depreciation costs.

New Deal A variety of measures initiated by President Franklin D. Roosevelt to promote social security and economic recovery from the Depression in the United States during the 1930's. The various measures dealt with industrial recovery, control of public utility holding companies, farm relief, direct unemployment relief, old-age pensions, and unemployment insurance.

New Economic Policy (NEP), 1921–1928 A tactical retreat by Lenin which was designed to save communism in Russia. Trade and transportation were placed in private hands, and the government abandoned its efforts to collectivize agriculture. Joseph Stalin supported the NEP until 1928, when he began to pursue the collectivization of agriculture and industrialization through strict regimentation and great sacrifice of the population.

Norms Beliefs about what constitutes proper behavior; ideal behavior patterns.

North Atlantic Treaty Organization (NATO) The Western Democratic military alliance created by the United States in 1949 to halt the expansion of the Soviet empire in Europe. It includes the United States, Canada, and fourteen countries on the other side of the Atlantic.

Nuclear family A family unit consisting of a father-husband, a mother-wife, and their children-siblings.

Objective method The process of ranking individuals and classes in a social hierarchy on the basis of selected, fixed criteria. Occupation, education, and income are often the criteria used.

Observational research The systematic observation of the research subject, with no attempt to alter ongoing activities. Observational research can take place in the laboratory, in the field, or in the form of participant observation.

Oedipus conflict (Freud) Conflict in which the child competes with the parent of the same sex for the affection of the parent of the opposite sex.

Oligarchy (Aristotle) Government by the few for their personal interests.

Oligopoly A market situation in which only a handful of companies dominate an industry. These companies compete in terms of packaging and advertising rather than in terms of price.

Open diplomacy Diplomacy conducted in public.

Openness to experience (Rogers) A flexibility to accept and to appreciate new experiences.

Open system A system that interacts with an environment.

Operant conditioning The association of a response to a particular stimulus with a reinforcement. The reinforcement causes the response either to appear or to disappear when the stimulus is sensed. Example: John, who never before had asked a question in class for fear of appearing stupid, finally raised his hand and asked a question. His teacher smiled warmly at him, told the class that the question was an important one, and answered it. The next time John had a question to ask, he raised his hand without hesitation. *See also* Classical conditioning.

Organismic trusting (Rogers) The trait of trusting one's own judgment.

Outputs The end results (decisions and actions) of a social process. Such interaction may alter the system and/or the environment it functions within.

Owen, Robert British utopian socialist who invested heavily in utopian experiments. He is known as the "father of British socialism" because of the important role he played in the cooperative and labor movements.

Palestine Liberation Organization (PLO) The organization headed by Yasir Arafat, that represents the Palestinian population that lives or that did live in what is now Israel. In 1993, this organization, that was very hostile to Israel, signed a peace treaty with Israel that agreed to the creation of a Palestinian state in part of the territories once occupied by Israel.

Parity The condition of being equivalent. The term is often used in regard to the government's policy of guaranteeing prices to farmers for agricultural products by providing farmers with the same buying power they had in whatever year is used as a base.

Partnership A form of business organization created through a contractual arrangement between two or more individuals, each of whom assumes full personal liability for the debts of the joint enterprise.

Paternalism A political relationship between leaders and followers which resembles the relationship between parents and children.

Patriarchal family Family in which the father or grandfather dominates.

Penis envy (Freud) A young girl's feeling of inferiority because she lacks a visible sex organ equal to a boy's.

Per capita income National income divided by the total population.

Perestroika Gorbachev's policy of political and economic restructuring.

Personalism(o) Emphasis on primary relationships. Personal connections prevail in the political process.

Personality An individual's distinctive pattern of thoughts, feelings, and actions.

Personality theorist A social scientist who studies personality.

Phenotype Genetic characteristics that are observable in the organism. Example: the color of your eyes.

Physical development The individual's movement over time from simple to complex levels of organization. In the nine months from conception to birth, for example, the individual develops nervous, circulatory, skeletal, muscular, digestive, and glandular systems that are necessary for survival at birth.

Pluralism There are many centers of power. Democracies are pluralistic.

Political communication The transmission of information (through words or actions) which enable a political system to function.

Political community Any group for which authoritative allocations of values are made.

Political culture A society's beliefs, values, attitudes, habits, and behavior regarding political matters.

Political development The progression through various political stages that are ranked hierarchically according to criteria established by the person(s) doing the ranking; an increase in the capacity of a political system to generate outputs which affect the other social systems. Important aspects of political development are: *state-building* (creating political structures), *nation-building* (developing a sense of nationalism), *participation* (increasing the number of people who are politically involved), and *distribution* (the redistribution of wealth or income by the political system).

Political idealism An approach to the study and practice of international relations which stresses morality and legalism.

Political mobilization Engaging in continuous indoctrination and political explanations of existing circumstances in order to maintain a high degree of political consciousness.

Political realism An approach to the study and practice of international relations which stresses power and interests.

Political recruitment The process of filling political roles.

Political socialization The process through which people learn about and adjust to their political culture.

Political system The social unit comprised of interdependent roles and structures which interact to authoritatively allocate values for a society.

Politicize To make someone or some group aware of and concerned about politics.

Politics The process through which the authoritative allocation of values takes place; the process through which any group selects its leaders, determines its policies, and distributes advantages and disadvantages to its members.

Polygamous family A composite family in which there may be: the marriage of one man to two or more women (*polygyny*); the marriage of one woman to two or more men (*polyandry*); or the marriage of two or more men to two or more women (*cenogamy*).

Positive affect (McClelland) Pleasant feelings.

Positive reinforcement The follow-up of a response with something perceived as pleasant.

Power The probability that an individual or group will be able to do what it wants to do. When power is supported by generally accepted societal norms, we call it *legitimate power,* or *authority.* When power is exercised informally and is based solely on the persuasive ability of one individual or group to manipulate another, we call it *influence.* Power enables an individual or group to make authoritative decisions which allocate values to society.

Preemptive attack An attack launched because a nation has just received word that an enemy has just launched, or is about to launch an attack against it.

Preponderance of power Overwhelming military superiority designed to deter aggression.

Prestige Relative value of a status within a society. Example: accounting is a more prestigious occupation in American society than is bookkeeping.

Preventive attack An attack launched in order to destroy an enemy's attack force, because one believes that country is going to attack at some future time. It is designed to deprive the enemy of the means with which to launch a future attack.

Price leadership The practice in some industries of the largest producer (the price leader) setting prices and the other producers accepting the prices thus set.

Price-pull theory of inflation Higher prices charged by businesses cause workers to demand more pay just to maintain the present level of their purchasing power.

Primary ethnic group An immigrant group that concentrates in a given area and creates a more or less self-contained ethnic community.

Primary groups Small groups in which people have frequent, intimate, and intense face-to-face contacts. Example: the family.

Primates The group of mammals to which humans belong. Primates share several characteristics including: limbs used for grasping, great accuracy of sight, and considerable development of the brain.

Primitive beliefs Beliefs based directly on the credibility of either one's own sensory experience or an external authority. Primitive beliefs are so fundamental that we accept them without question.

Principle of legitimacy The principle that every child should have a sociological father to guide and protect him or her and to represent the male link between the child and society. Illegitimacy, then, refers to the social condition of not having a father.

Private orientation The tendency to stress private affairs as opposed to concern for public issues.

Privilege Possession or control of part of a society's economic surplus.

Problem solving The process whereby we answer questions. Examples of problem-solving methods are: appeal to the supernatural, appeal to human authority, appeal to our own knowledge, intuition, logic, common sense, and scientific method.

Procreative proficiency The ability to produce large numbers of offspring.

Production possibilities Goods and services which may be produced within a society. Production possibilities are limited by the society's natural, human, and capital resources, and by its level of technology.

Economists often refer to natural resources as *land*, and to human resources as *labor*. Land, labor, and capital are often referred to as the *factors of production*.

Projection (Freud) Attributing to another one's own objectionable characteristics and motives.

Proletariat Marx's name for the working class.

Propaganda Tailoring information to place one's country in a favorable light.

Psychosexual stages of development (Freud) Levels of personality development that are identified by distinctive personality characteristics and forms of defense. The psychosexual stages include oral, anal, phallic, latency, and genital.

Punishment The process by which a perceived penalty is associated with an emitted behavior. Punishment decreases the probability that an emitted behavior will be repeated.

Pure command economy An economic system in which the government exercises complete control over the economy.

Pure market economy An economic system in which the government exercises no control over the economy.

Quantitative variables Variables that reflect differences in numerical value. Examples: yearly income; number of years of formal education.

Qualitative variables Variables that reflect differences in category or kind rather than number. Examples: sex, religious affiliation.

Race A subspecies formed as the result of natural selection working on a geographically isolated population.

Racism The belief in the inferiority of one race in relation to another.

Reaction formation (Freud) Replacing one's true wishes and impulses with directly opposite wishes and impulses.

Reality anxiety (Freud) Anxiety caused by external threats.

Recession A minor economic decline.

Referential symbols Symbols that denote or refer to real objects in the external world. Example: chair.

Regime A type of government.

Regional subsystems Areas of the world that contain two or more nation–states, that are geographically contiguous, and that interact with each other frequently and intensely. There are five types of regional subsystems.

Regulated capitalism A modified market system in which the means of production are almost entirely privately owned, but in which there is also a high degree of government regulation and decision making by large corporate enterprises and to a lesser extent by large labor unions. Example: the American economy.

Regulative capability The political system's ability to enforce rules with coercive measures.

Reinforcement The process by which a perceived reward is associated with an emitted behavior. The perceived reward is called a *reinforcer.* B.F. Skinner holds that reinforcement always increases the probability that an emitted behavior will be repeated.

Religion A group of believers who symbolize their conception of the supernatural by sacred objects which they relate to through rituals and beliefs which they value.

Repression (Freud) Forcefully remaining unaware of unpleasant memories or impulses.

Reputational method The process of ranking individuals in a social hierarchy on the basis of the reputation of individuals or groups within their own community.

Reserve requirement The percentage of deposits that a commercial bank must keep on hand to meet the demands of its depositors. The reserve requirement is determined by the Federal Reserve Board.

Responsive capability The political system's ability to produce outputs which reflect demands.

Revolution A radical transformation of the political, economic, and other social structures.

Rigid bipolar A regional subsystem in which the members are divided into two hostile, rival factions that fight each other frequently.

Ritual A series of symbolic acts that are repeated on ceremonial occasions. For example, traditional wedding ritual in American society includes something old, something new, something borrowed, something blue, the bride is dressed in white, throwing rice at the newly married couple, etc.

Role A set of expected behaviors associated with a particular status.

Rule adjudication Determining if a rule has been broken, and, if so, what will be done about it.

Rule application Enforcing and administering societal rules.

Rule making Establishing the rules by which a society will function.

SALT talks Strategic Arms Limitations Talks between the U.S. and USSR which began in 1969 for the purpose of achieving mutually acceptable ceilings on weapons, weapons delivery systems, and defense measures.

Sanctification The process whereby religions make holy certain cultural norms and values. Western religions, for instance, have sanctified the Ten Commandments by treating them as God-given rules.

Sanctions Means by which people are encouraged to obey norms. Positive sanctions are rewards; negative sanctions are punishments.

Scarcity The existence of insufficient means to fulfill relatively unlimited wants.

Schemata (McClelland) Culturally transmitted ideas, values, and social roles that symbolize past experience.

School Structure in the education systems of complex societies that tends to ensure that certain specialized knowledge and skills are mastered by each generation.

Science The systematic attempt to discover and explain relationships among phenomena.

Scientific attitude The open-minded perspective with which scientists approach their investigations. It includes cooperation, openness, skepticism, objectivity, and amorality.

Scientific method The way that scientists solve problems. It includes carefully observing events, accumulating and classifying data, inferring relationships among phenomena, formulating hypotheses and testing them in experiments, and analyzing the results of the experiments.

Scope of interest The size of the geographical area with which a state is concerned in its political activities. It may be *globalist* (encompassing the whole world), *regionalist* (encompassing a limited geographical area—usually including states in close proximity to it), or *isolationist* (concerned only with domestic affairs).

Sea-launched ballistic missile (SLBM) A missile launched from a ship at sea.

Secondary ethnic group People from any country who migrate as individuals or in small groups and who depend entirely on the host society for the satisfaction of basic needs.

Second-strike capability The ability to absorb a surprise nuclear attack with sufficient retaliatory power to inflict "unacceptable damage" upon an attacker. Second-strike capability is sometimes referred to as "assured destruction."

Secret diplomacy Diplomacy conducted out of the public spotlight.

Sect A small religious organization whose members join by voluntary, conscious choice. Sects are not usually well integrated into the culture. Example: Jehovah's Witnesses.

Security A state of being sought by nation–states in which they are free from external and internal threats to their sovereignty and well-being.

Self-actualization (Rogers) The drive to behave in accordance with one's self-concept.

Self-concept One's conscious sense of who and what one is. Interaction within primary groups is particularly important in the development of the self-concept.

Separation of powers The executive, legislative, and judicial branches of government are separate, as in the U.S. system of government.

Shock therapy A rapid, radical transition from a command economy to a market economy instituted by Russia.

Siblingship Relationships between brother–sister, brother–brother, or sister–sister.

Significant others The most influential models imitated by a person.

Smith, Adam An eighteenth-century British economist who is considered the father of modern economics. Smith believed that a free market in which businessmen were motivated by self-interest and in which competition existed throughout the economic process would produce desired goods and services of the best quality, at the most favorable price for the consumer, and in the optimal quantity.

Social contract   The theory holds that there is a reciprocally binding agreement between the people and their governments. Citizens give up certain decision-making rights in exchange for protection, services, and respect for individual rights. John Hobbes, John Locke and Jean-Jacques Rousseau were the major 17th- and 18th-century social contract theorists.

Social Darwinism   A social philosophy prevalent in the latter part of the nineteenth and early part of the twentieth century. Social Darwinists believed that people who were fit to survive would rise to the top of a society and those who were unfit to survive would sink to the bottom. Social Darwinism, then, offered scientific sanction for the exploitation of workers by the "captains of industry."

Social development   The individual's movement over time from simple to complex statuses and roles.

Social distance   The extent to which an individual or group feels relatively close or distant from other individuals or groups.

Social goods and services   Goods and services which are designed to be used jointly rather than individually by the members of a society. Examples: roads, schools, hospitals, welfare services, and facilities.

Social institutions   Distinctive patterns that are centered around major human needs and accompanied by particular modes of social interaction. In this book, we treat social institutions as societal subsystems. Example: education, or the education system.

Socialization   The process whereby individuals learn the roles, rules, relationships, and culture of their society.

Social relations of production (Marx)   The relationship between owners and workers, which varies according to the level and type of production technology.

Social science   The systematic attempt to discover and explain the behavior patterns of people and groups of people. Social science contains several disciplines or subdivisions such as anthropology, psychology, sociology, economics, political science, and international relations. Each discipline concentrates on some aspect of human behavior that is separate and distinct from those which the others concentrate on.

Social stratification   The division of societies into layers or strata, each containing aggregates of people who share similar beliefs, attitudes, values, and life-styles. These strata are ranked according to the relative amounts of power, privilege, and prestige they possess.

Social system   A cluster of interrelated roles and objects that revolve around a certain type of activity.

Society   A self-sufficient and self-perpetuating group which includes persons of both sexes and all ages.

Sociobiology   An approach to the evolution of behaviors that concentrates on social organization and social behavior.

Southeast Asia Treaty Organization (SEATO)   Military treaty created in 1954 by the United States to halt the spread of Asian communism.

Species   Category of plants or animals whose structures are so similar that they can mate and produce fertile offspring. Example: *Homo sapiens* (human beings).

Species-specific brain   A brain whose structure and composition is endemic to a particular species. The human species-specific brain is associated with unique language and intellectual abilities of *Homo sapiens*.

Speculative thinking   The mental exploration of possible relationships among data. It is during the process of speculative thinking that scientists often have flashes of insight into the nature of phenomena.

Stability   A systemic state in which all components remain within defined and recognizable limits no matter what disturbances may occur.

START I treaty   A disarmament agreement between the United States and the Soviet Union in 1991 to reduce nuclear armaments significantly.

START II treaty   A nuclear disarmament treaty between the United States and Russia to reduce armaments to an even greater degree by the year 2003.

State building   The creation of the political structures necessary to govern a country. Examples: political parties, legislatures, courts.

Statistical sample   A selected number of individuals within a given population who together represent the general characteristics of that population. Statistical samples may provide pollsters, for instance, with fairly accurate descriptions of public opinion on any given social issue.

Status   A social position or rank that is accompanied by a role or several roles.

Status group   A kind of class whose members share a common idea of what social honor is. Example: Mexican Americans.

Stereotyping   The process of treating generalizations as though they were universally true. Example: "All women gossip."

Stimulus generalization   The repetition of a response conditioned by one stimulus in the presence of other similar but neutral stimuli.

Stress   Pressure caused by demands which are difficult for the political system.

Structural autonomy   The ability of a structure to perform its function(s) independently.

Structure   An entity (individual, group, or thing) that performs a function.

Subculture   A distinctive culture shared by a particular group within a society. Members of subcultures participate in the way of life of both the larger society and their own subgroup. Example: Orthodox Jews.

Subjective method   The process of ranking individuals in a social hierarchy by means of self-rating.

Sublimation (Freud)   Substituting a socially acceptable activity for an unacceptable one.

Subsistence theory of wages (Marx)   The value of labor in the market is the socially necessary labor it takes to keep the laborer alive. The workers, then, receive only subsistence wages, regardless of the number of hours they work.

Subsystem   A unit (component) of a system that is comprised of other units that interact with each other.

Subsystem dominant   A system in which the parts have more power than the whole. In this case, an international system in which power is decentralized (possessed by nation–states rather than by the international system).

Summit diplomacy   Diplomacy between heads of state.

Superego (Freud)   A basic part of personality structure. It is an internalized set of moral ideas (a conscience). *See also* Ego, Id.

Supernatural   The ultimate—that which transcends or goes beyond everyday experiences. Example: God.

Supply and demand, Theory of   The higher the price for any given good or service, the greater the profit in producing it; therefore, the higher the price, the greater the amount supplied. The higher the price for any given good or service, the less likely is a buyer to buy some of it; therefore, the higher the price, the less the amount demanded. The actual price of a given good or service and the actual quantity produced are determined at the point at which quantity supplied equals quantity demanded.

Supranational   An authority above the nation–state level (for example, a world government).

Supranational organization   An organization that can make decisions which are binding on all members (nation–states), including those that did not vote for that decision.

Surplus value, Theory of (Marx)   Workers are forced to work more hours than their own subsistence demands, but they are paid only enough to subsist. The value of the "extra" labor (the labor not required to subsist) is called surplus value. It is pocketed by the employer as profit.

Survey research   The most often used research method of social scientists. The researcher asks questions of subjects to gain information from them. Questionnaires and interviews are used when doing survey research.

Syllogism   An argument in which two statements or premises are made and a logical conclusion is drawn from them. Example: My senses tell me that this book has weight. My senses tell me true. Therefore, this book has weight.

Symbol   Something that stands for something else. Symbols allow us to think about the thing symbolized.

Symbolic capability   The political system's ability to gain support from the population by manipulating symbols.

Symbolic process   The process of arbitrarily ascribing meanings.

System   A unit comprised of interacting components that performs a function or set of functions. It may be a subsystem of a larger unit. When discussing the internal or comparative aspects of such a unit one refers to it as a system; when discussing it in relation to a larger unit of which it is a part it is called a subsystem.

System dominant   A system in which power is centralized (for example, most nation–states).

System levels   Hierarchical ranks for systems in terms of relationships of authority, range of functions, inclusiveness of membership, or geographical scope.

Systems analysis   An approach to the study of social phenomena that focuses on the interrelatedness of all aspects of social behavior. It also emphasizes the need to examine entire social processes in order to fully understand any aspect of those processes.

System transformation   A change from one system type to another. For example, a change in a family system from monogamy (one spouse) to polygamy (more than one spouse) or an economic system changing from capitalism to socialism.

Taboos   Mores expressed in negative form. Example: "One must not kill."

Tacit bargaining   Making unilateral moves which are reciprocated without making any explicit proposals (for example, limitations placed on the Korean War).

Tariff   A tax levied on imports.

Technicways   Technological folkways; folkways dealing with knowledge and techniques for using machines and tools. Example: knowing how to use a pocket calculator.

Technology   Tools and techniques for adjusting to and changing the environment.

Terms of trade   The relationship between the prices a country receives for its exports and the prices it pays for its imports.

Terror   The arbitrary and unpredictable use of force.

Totemism   The worship of particular species

of plants or animals found within the environment of the worshipers.

Trait (McClelland) The learned tendency of a person to react as he or she has reacted more or less successfully in the past in similar situations when similarly motivated. Traits are initially learned because the individual is consistently rewarded for displaying them. Once learned, however, they continue because they are habits.

Transmission The means by which a continuity between families in successive generations is ensured. The family transmits culture (*socialization*); membership in wider social groups (*descent*); property (*inheritance*); and status (*succession*).

Trilateral international system The emerging world international system, headed by the United States (perhaps, joined by Canada and part of Latin America), the EC (and, perhaps, other European countries), and Japan (perhaps, along with other Asian countries). Its focus will be economic. It will rely increasingly on the United Nations and similar regional organizations to maintain security throughout the world.

Trust A scheme designed to eliminate competition. The voting rights of the majority of the voting stock of two or more corporations are assigned to a number of trustees who then direct the affairs of the corporations to the mutual benefit of all the stockholders. Recently trust has been used to designate any large corporation or combinations of corporations exercising monopolistic control over the production or distribution of a particular good or service.

Turnover tax Tax added to every item sold in the Soviet Union. It varies from 3 percent to 100 percent.

Twenty-first century mercantilism An international system that emphasizes regional self-sufficiency and intense rivalry among the big three economic powers.

Tyranny (Aristotle) Rule by one for personal interest.

Unconditional positive regard (Rogers) The state of receiving total support and acceptance from significant people in one's environment. *See also* Conditional positive regard.

Unitary system All government power resides at the national level. Lower levels of government owe their existence and continuation to the national government. Such systems may be either democratic or dictatorial. Great Britain is an example of a democratic unitary state.

Utopian socialism Nineteenth-century social philosophical movement whose adherents sought to avoid the evils of capitalism by restructuring society according to socialist principles. They sought radical but peaceful changes, emphasizing collective ownership of property and of the means of production, and equal distribution of wealth.

Value An idea of what is intrinsically desirable. Example: freedom.

Variable A factor that can have more than one value. There are several types of variables, including quantitative, qualitative, independent, and dependent.

Vertical interlocking A hierarchical linking of systems ranked at different levels. *See also* Horizontal interlocking.

Wage-push theory of inflation Increased labor costs cause higher prices.

Warsaw Pact The East European military alliance headed by the Soviet Union from 1955 to 1991. The other members were Hungary, Poland, Czechoslovakia, Romania, Bulgaria, and East Germany.

Weakest-link theory (Lenin) The first Communist revolution took place in Russia because the bourgeoisie was weaker there, relative to the proletariat, than in any other country. In the chain of capitalist countries, Russia was the weakest link.

World Bank An international lending agency from which countries can borrow money.

Zero-order beliefs The most basic primitive beliefs. They are learned in childhood and continuously validated by experience throughout life. We are usually unaware not only of our zero-order beliefs, but also of the fact that alternatives to them could exist. Example: a belief that we are alive.

Zero population growth The condition that exists when population size remains constant because the number of births and deaths are equal to one another.

Answer Key

Chapter 1	Chapter 2	Chapter 3	Chapter 4	Chapter 5	Chapter 6	Chapter 7
1. c	1. a	1. a	1. c	1. c	1. c	1. c
2. e	2. b	2. e	2. a	2. d	2. d	2. d
3. a	3. b	3. c	3. a	3. b	3. b	3. b
4. d	4. a	4. c	4. c	4. e	4. e	4. b
5. b	5. c	5. b	5. d	5. c	5. c	5. e
6. d	6. c	6. b	6. b	6. a	6. a	6. e
7. b	7. a	7. a	7. d	7. b	7. b	7. a
8. b	8. e	8. a	8. c	8. e	8. e	8. d
9. d	9. a	9. d	9. d	9. a	9. a	9. c
10. c	10. e	10. d	10. a	10. d	10. d	10. d

Chapter 8	Chapter 9	Chapter 10	Chapter 11	Chapter 12	Chapter 13	Chapter 14
1. d	1. d	1. b	1. d	1. b	1. b	1. d
2. b	2. a	2. d	2. b	2. d	2. e	2. d
3. c	3. b	3. c	3. b	3. c	3. a	3. b
4. e	4. a	4. e	4. e	4. a	4. b	4. a
5. b	5. c	5. c	5. c	5. a	5. a	5. d
6. d	6. e	6. d	6. e	6. b	6. b	6. c
7. a	7. d	7. b	7. a	7. a	7. d	7. a
8. b	8. b	8. c	8. c	8. c	8. e	8. a
9. c	9. c	9. a	9. d	9. b	9. d	9. c
10. c	10. b	10. d	10. c	10. d	10. c	10. c

Chapter 15	Chapter 16	Chapter 17	Chapter 18	Chapter 19	Chapter 20	Chapter 21
1. a	1. b	1. a	1. c	1. d	1. a	1. c
2. b	2. e	2. a	2. a	2. a	2. e	2. a
3. a	3. a	3. d	3. b	3. a	3. e	3. b
4. b	4. c	4. b	4. d	4. a	4. e	4. a
5. a	5. a	5. c	5. c	5. a	5. b	5. c
6. b	6. b	6. d	6. d	6. c	6. c	6. b
7. c	7. c	7. b	7. c	7. d	7. c	7. d
8. a	8. e	8. c	8. e	8. e	8. d	8. b
9. b	9. a	9. d	9. e	9. c	9. c	9. a
10. e	10. a	10. b	10. c	10. e	10. a	10. d

Chapter 22	Chapter 23	Chapter 24	Chapter 25
1. d	1. d	1. d	1. c
2. b	2. b	2. d	2. c
3. b	3. a	3. d	3. a
4. d	4. a	4. b	4. a
5. a	5. a	5. d	5. a
6. d	6. c	6. b	6. d
7. a	7. d	7. e	7. d
8. d	8. b	8. b	8. a
9. a	9. d	9. d	9. b
10. d	10. d	10. a	10. e
			11. c

Index

Italic page numbers indicate text pages on which terms are defined.